ENGLISH
MEDIAEVAL MONASTERIES

Bayham Abbey, Sussex. Arch in the north transept.

Roy Midmer

ENGLISH MEDIAEVAL MONASTERIES

MONASTERIES
(1066–1540)

A Summary

The University of Georgia Press
Athens

International Standard Book Number 0–8203–0488–3
Library of Congress Catalog Card Number 79–53097
The University of Georgia Press
Athens, Georgia 30602

Printed in Great Britain

Contents

Acknowledgements

Over three hundred scholars, authors and writers have contributed to the content of this book, and to each and every one of them I am deeply indebted. It will be seen from the dates of books and articles which have been consulted, that very many of these historians are no longer with us. It would have been a long task to locate the many others in order to obtain permission to quote from their works, and both the authors and the sources are gratefully acknowledged in the gazetteer entries and the bibliography. There is no page in the book which is not indebted to the skills, study and learning of someone.

Countless librarians have provided local and specialised knowledge which has proved invaluable; and particular thanks are due to the staffs of the County Libraries for which no Victoria County Histories exist, namely Cheshire, Devonshire, Herefordshire, Northumberland and Westmorland. Local library staffs have been unstinting in their assistance in the Wilmslow Public Library, the John Rylands Library, Manchester, and especially the Manchester Central Library where Mr H. Horton and his staff have invariably found answers to my numerous queries during many scores of visits to the Social Sciences Section.

The deaths of two particular friends, whose kindness and encouragement are still an inspiration, was a serious loss. Mr Arnold Hyde, a Manchester bibliophile with an encyclopaedic knowledge, never failed to correct or confirm some point at issue. Nothing was too much trouble to look up, however obscure. Secondly, it was the generous and continuing interest of the late Professor David Knowles which, in the early days of my studies, spurred the interest and provided guidance.

Finally, my special thanks are due to my wife for the many hours she has spent working on and checking the manuscript, proving herself to be a veritable paragon of patience.

Preface

Throughout the preparation of this book, three words have dominated the nature of the content: brevity, simplicity and fairness. As a result, there are certain instances where sentences are tantalisingly brief in order to keep the entry in the gazetteer within reasonable bounds. Elsewhere, the notice of a somewhat complex historical circumstance has probably been over simplified. In either case the source is easy to trace if a fuller history is needed.

The last guideline has proved to be the most difficult if one is to avoid a charge of bias against the religious communities, or of recounting only the smoother side of the cloistered life. An endeavour to achieve a balanced assessment of events is explained in the Introduction under the heading Visitations.

Sources of Illustrations

Cambridge University Collection. Copyright reserved:
185, 216, 217.

Crown Copyright — reproduced with permission of the
Controller of Her Majesty's Stationery Office:
61, 87, 102, 112, 113, 116, 123, 135, 189, 195, 199,
202, 225 & 227.

Courtesy of the Runcorn Development Corporation:
238, 239, 240, 241.

Copyright Walter Scott, Bradford:
72, 147, 165, 166, 167, 178.

Reece Winstone:
81.

Courtesy of the City of York Department of Tourism:
342, 343.

Author:
91, 160, 187, 265, 266, 267, 322.

The frontispiece was specially drawn by William Geldart
The drawing on page 15 is by Ferdinand Fizzi

The regional maps on pages 35—44 were specially drawn
by Reginald Piggott from drafts prepared by the author.

Introduction

Never before have monastic ruins throughout the country been more accessible, and the numbers of visitors to the sites have steadily increased during this century. For over 300 years many of the buildings lay desolate, until a slow awakening to the shattered glory of these fragments began when members of the archaeological societies first published details of their excavations and discoveries at the end of the 19th century.

The subsequent increase in interest in the vanished religious houses resulted in a considerably wider appreciation of the enormity of the loss at the Dissolution of much architectural grandeur, historical records, monastic libraries and social and religious benefits which accrued to the nation from their existence.

In consequence there can be few subjects which have been so exhaustively covered over many years than the histories of religious houses. The writings extend from comprehensive studies to simple pamphlets about parish churches which once formed a part of a monastery. Reliable and informative accounts of almost every mediaeval abbey, priory or friary in England can be found in most public libraries or new and secondhand bookshops.

Many of the books devoted to the subject deal mainly with history, architecture, archaeology or activities of the various religious Orders, and the monastic buildings of one or more of the mediaeval monasteries. Alphabetically or regionally arranged books of reference are comparatively few, and none have so far taken the form of a fully comprehensive survey in the style of a complete digest with historical notes.

Any listing of mediaeval monasteries which gives brief details of their histories and remains would, perhaps, be incomplete without some reference to their occupiers and the ultimate closure and destruction of the buildings.

The various Orders are arranged in the following sequence:

INCLUSIONS AND EXCLUSIONS
Inclusions These are essentially the monasteries which existed until the 16th century, together with the sites of those which were either abandoned or exchanged in earlier years for the final location, and belonged to one of the following:

Contemplative Orders

1	AUGUSTINIAN	Canons and Canonesses (or Nuns)
2	BENEDICTINE	Monks and Nuns
3	BONSHOMMES	Brethren
4	BRIDGETTINE	Nuns and Priests
5	CARTHUSIAN	Monks
6	CISTERCIAN	Monks and Nuns
7	CLUNIAC	Monks and Nuns
8	GILBERTINE	Canons and Nuns
9	GRANDMONTINE	Brethren
10	PREMONSTRATENSIAN	Canons and Canonesses
11	TIRONENSIAN	Monks

Mendicant Orders
(a) major:

12	AUGUSTINIAN (Austin)	Friars
13	CARMELITE	Friars
14	DOMINICAN	Friars and Nuns
15	FRANCISCAN	Friars and Nuns

(b) minor:

16	CRUTCHED (Crossed)	Friars
17	PIED	Friars
18	SACK	Friars
19	TRINITARIAN	Friars

Exclusions
1 ALIEN PRIORIES (see also Appendix 1)
2 THE KNIGHTS TEMPLARS
3 THE KNIGHTS HOSPITALLERS
4 HOSPITALS

The Contemplative Orders

1 AUGUSTINIAN Canons and Canonesses (or Nuns)

St Augustine (354–430), bishop of the diocese of Hippo in North Africa, did not found the Augustinian Order of Canons Regular. He was born at Tagaste in Numidia, and at the age of 19 became a convert of the Manicheans and later travelled to Rome. After listening to a sermon by Archbishop Ambrose in Milan he was baptised in 387. Soon afterwards he returned to Africa and entered the priesthood in 390. About 423 he wrote a letter to a congregation of religious women, and from an adaptation of this the canons' Augustinian Rule was modelled, but the early history is undoubtedly obscure and a difficult subject. The Canons Regular lived in monasteries, accepted the monastic life and took priests orders, in contrast with the Canons Secular who served cathedral churches.

The Order was introduced into England between 1093 and 1099 by Archbishop Anselm. The first house was founded by a Benedictine monk named Ainulf and it became the priory of St Julian & St Botolph at Colchester. The number of monasteries increased rapidly during the 12th & 13thCs reaching a peak of 218, and of these 138 were founded before 1175. At the suppression there were about 170. Of the regulations governing the lives of the canons there remains a valuable document: 'The Observances in use at the Augustinian Priory of St Giles & St Andrew at Barnwell, Cambridgeshire' (*v.* Barnwell entry). From their hooded black cloaks and white surplices and black cassocks beneath, they became known as Black Canons. They were not confined to the monastery because many of them ministered in the parish churches which had been appropriated to them. The canons were also responsible for the foundation and care of many of the English hospitals. An abbreviation is 'Austin' canons.

It is not clear when or where the canonesses were introduced into England. There is a reference to their priory of St Mary de Fonte at Clerkenwell, London, *c.* 1144 (Knowles), and vague references to another of their houses at Minster in Sheppey which existed (alternating with Benedictine nuns) perhaps as early as 1130; but there is no doubt that the canonesses were firmly established here by the middle of the 13thC. They had two abbeys in England (Burnham and Lacock) of which substantial remains survive, and at the Dissolution they held 21 priories in addition. It seems that at only two of their houses, Grace Dieu (Leics.) and Brewood (Salop) were they referred to as Nuns.

2 BENEDICTINE Monks and Nuns

St Benedict of Nursia (*c.* 480–543), the Patriarch of Western Monasticism, did not found the Benedictine Order. About 528 he went to Monte Casino where 'he lived with and for his relatively small community of the hill; he left them the memory of a holy life and the codex of the Rule. The influence of that Rule on the religious and cultural life of the West was enormous. It was never imposed as a code'. (*v.* Prof. Knowles: 'Saints & Scholars'). He adds: ' . . . not till 1215 were the autonomous houses of Europe loosely joined in provincial chapters; not till *c.* 1400 were black monks known as Benedictines'. That the primary inspiration of the Rule should have come when chaos lay over the world and social dismemberment, corruption and the abandonment of morals, authority and even religion itself seemed complete, instils the belief that St Benedict must have been the mouthpiece of Divine revelation.

In 597 Augustine[1] came to England and founded the Saxon monastery at Canterbury. Although this may not have been subject to the Rule[2] of St Benedict, it is certain that during the second half of the 7thC English monks had based their lives upon it. Many of these monasteries of Saxon England suffered destruction during the invasions of the Danes. Of these churches very few remain, partly because most of them were probably built of wood but mainly due to the extensive building programme on the same sites in later centuries. A rare example exists at Deerhurst in Gloucestershire (early 9thC), although much of the original building is contained in the 12th and 14th century enlargements. None of the early monastic claustral buildings exist anywhere in Britain.

In the mid-10thC old Benedictine monasteries were revived and new ones founded. Following the Norman Conquest there was a fresh round of new foundations of which many were alien priories (*v.* Appendix 1). But the first was the royal abbey of St Martin at Battle, built in fulfilment of the Conqueror's

---

[1] St Augustine of Canterbury lived over 150 years after St Augustine of Hippo (*v.* Augustinian canons).
[2] The Rule was written during the last 15 years of St Benedict's life and was adopted by both monks and nuns. In 817 the Council of Aachen enforced its universal observance.

vow that should God give him victory over the Saxons he would found a religious house for Benedictines. It survived throughout the reigns of 39 kings, and was second to none in wealth and importance in the 11thC. By the end of this century, great English Benedictine abbeys such as Bury St Edmunds, Canterbury (Cathedral Priory),[1] Chester, Durham, Ely, Gloucester, Norwich, Pershore, Peterborough, Rochester, Romsey, St Albans, Tewkesbury, Winchester and Worcester had been begun, and the number of Benedictine houses had risen to about 130, including the nunneries. At the time of the Dissolution there were about 282 houses of monks and 92 of nuns. The communities wore black habits.

It is to the monks of the Benedictine monasteries that most of the ecclesiastical biographies and chronicles of monastic and national events are due. Amongst the better known, and about whom much has been written, were the Venerable Bede (672–735) of Jarrow and Monkwearmouth; Asser of St David's and later bishop of Sherborne; William of Malmesbury; Jocelin of Bury St Edmunds, and Matthew Paris of St Albans (the greatest of English mediaeval historians . . . and incomparable chronographer and a painter of supreme excellence – Graham).

The nunneries were most numerous in the North and the East Midlands. Prof. Eileen Power in her 'Medieval English Nunneries' writes that of the 138 nunneries which existed in the later Middle Ages (c. 1270–1536), over one half belonged to the Benedictine Order. But the wealthiest were all in the South of England: Shaftesbury, Barking, Wilton, Amesbury and Romsey. The recruits came mostly from the upper classes. Amongst the distinguished abbesses of Barking, for instance, were three queens and two princesses. Many took the veil in order to lead a life of spiritual devotion away from a hostile and unholy world, while others were unwanted daughters who were sent to a nunnery as an alternative to marriage. Others were of illegitimate birth such as the natural daughter of Cardinal Wolsey who became a nun of Shaftesbury Abbey (Cook).

The spiritual lives of nuns differed little from those of the monks, but since many nunneries were much less well endowed with temporal possessions their churches were built on much more modest lines and their buildings often less well maintained. (See also penultimate paragraph of the section on Mitred Abbeys.)

3 BONSHOMMES Brethren

The smallest Order in, and peculiar to, Britain. These priests, who followed the Augustinian Rule and in their way of life were similar to Regular Canons, had

---

[1] As distinct from the other foundation of St Augustine's Abbey in Canterbury.

only two monasteries in England (Ashridge, Herts; and Edington, Wilts.). The first of these was founded by Edmund, earl of Cornwall in 1283. A century passed before William of Edington, bishop of Winchester founded the second house.

4 BRIDGETTINE Nuns and Priests

There was one house in England, founded by Henry V in 1415 at Twickenham. It was moved 16 years later to Syon Abbey near Isleworth. The founder of the Order was St Bridget, a Swedish princess, who built her first monastery at Vadstena shortly after her husband's death. About 70 houses were established, mostly in Scandinavia. Although there were priest-monks in the double houses whose duties were to act as chaplains, confessors and spiritual directors within the abbey, the Order was established primarily for nuns. They kept the Rule of St Bridget.

The Bridgettines are the only English pre-Reformation community to have survived in an unbroken corporate existence, after almost 300 years in exile. They are now established in Devonshire.

5 CARTHUSIAN Monks

Of all the Orders this was the strictest and the most austere. The resulting hardship was the principal reason for its slow growth. The founder was St Bruno who in 1084, with six companions, built the priory of the Grande Chartreuse (near Grenoble) a church with several separate cells. In 1180—1 the first English Charterhouse (the word is an Anglicised 'Chartreuse') was founded at Witham in Somerset, and eight more followed.

The austerity and discipline of their life made them supremely obedient to their beliefs and to the pope. This finally resulted in the martyrdom of many of their members at the time of the general suppression.

The remains of the priory at Mount Grace in Yorkshire display an almost complete layout of the peculiar Carthusian monastery. One cell has been re-built to show the arrangement of a monk's personal home and garden, of which there were originally 21. The church was invariably small and simple since the main devotions of the monks were performed in the solitude of their cells. They kept the Rule of St Benedict. The other priory buildings were equally small and the refectory was used only on Sundays and Feast Days — all other meals being delivered to the cells. There was no infirmary and if a monk became ill he was nursed in his cell. However, it was the Carthusian monks who were responsible for giving the world the Chartreuse liqueur, while they themselves suffered the mortification of a hair shirt next to the skin.

6

6 CISTERCIAN Monks and Nuns

Because of a fall in the standards set by the Rule in the Benedictine monastery at Molesme in Burgundy, the abbot, Robert, and several of his monks left the house in 1098 and settled in a wood at Citeaux (Cistercium) where, under his abbacy, they built a wooden monastery. This foundation of a stricter way of life did not find instant favour, but the reforms of the third abbot, Stephen Harding (an Englishman), established the modified Benedictine-based monasticism which attracted a group of thirty Burgundian nobles, including St Benedict of Clairvaux. It was he who put into practice the reforms of Stephen Harding, including the restoration of manual labour, simplicity in all things and the principles of silence and poverty. In contrast with the autonomous management of the Benedictine houses, Cistercian monasteries were subject to visitations and the appointments of their abbots by the mother house. The monks wore white habits.

Thirty years passed before the first house was founded in England at Waverley in Surrey (1128), followed by Rievaulx in 1131 and Fountains in 1132. It was an ordinance that their abbeys (none were priories) should be built 'in places remote from the habitation of men', and the only exception was the abbey of St Mary Graces, London, which happens to have been the last Cistercian house to be founded in Britain.

The Cistercians employed lay-brothers (conversi), who were not exclusive to the Order, whose purpose was to undertake manual work in the fields and workshops. To the Cistercians, both monks and conversi, this country owes a great deal in respect of the development of farming techniques which established competent sheep-farming and scientific agriculture. The conversi had their own quarters and used the nave of the church west of the pulpitum. They were excluded from any intellectual studies and were not taught to read or write, but they had their own common room in the cloister buildings for their meetings, their own infirmary and separate refectory and dormitory.

The popularity of the White Monks (their habits were white) had grown so much during the 12thC that in 1147 the Cistercians absorbed the 13 Savigniac monasteries then existing in England and Wales. The Order of Savigny had been established in 1112 and Furness Abbey, founded in 1123, was the first English house. Afterwards when it became Cistercian the abbot claimed seniority over Waverley which was founded five years later, but Furness never achieved precedence. At the Dissolution there were about 80 houses in England.

The monasteries of Cistercian nuns, like those of the monks, were usually dedicated to St Mary and all but two were priories. Prof. Knowles states that there seems to be strong evidence that a number of nunneries began as

Benedictine, and later changed to Cistercian to obtain the privileges of that Order. Most of the English houses were in Yorkshire and Lincolnshire, and in common with Benedictine nunneries were often poorly endowed by their founders or patrons. The wealthiest was Tarrant (Kaines) in Dorset of which nothing remains. There was one house in the Isle of Man.

7 CLUNIAC Monks and Nuns

Almost two centuries before the Cistercians sought a stricter life, the duke of Aquitaine founded in 910 a monastery at Cluny in Burgundy for monks to live under the Benedictine Rule. They felt the need of closer communion with God but, in contrast with the simplicity of Cistercian churches, the Cluniacs believed in the right use of wealth and their churches were built with immense visual splendour – in fact the conventual church at Cluny, completed in the 12thC, was 520 feet in length and was said to have been the largest church in Mediaeval Europe. The Cluniacs' wealth was not confined to the development of monasteries, but was also used for the service of man in helping the poor, needy, travellers and pilgrims. The Order differed from the Benedictines inasmuch as priories were subject to the abbot of Cluny, and the government of the Order was based upon this central system.

A Norman noble, William de Warenne, founded the first house in England in 1077 at Lewes in Sussex, and the prior took second rank among all Cluniac priors. Of some 32 houses at the Dissolution all were priories except Bermondsey, which was raised to abbey status after becoming denizen in 1381. A few small houses which were also alien priories at the time, did not relinquish their allegiance to Cluny and finally became extinct during the wars with France (v. Appendix 1). Also, three houses of Cluniac nuns existed in England, one short-lived (v. Appendix 2).

Unfortunately no Cluniac church has survived for parish use, and the most important remains are at Castle Acre (Norfolk) and Wenlock (Shropshire).

8 GILBERTINE Canons and Nuns

In 1131 the only purely English Order was founded by St Gilbert of Sempringham (c. 1089–1189). He was canonised in 1202. Not since the 7thC had monasteries for monks and nuns existed until this institution was revived by St Gilbert. The nuns adopted the Benedictine Rule and the canons took the Augustinian Rule. Lay-brothers and lay-sisters were also members of the double establishments. Of the 24 houses which existed at the time of the Dissolution, 10 were double and the rest for canons only. (Two other houses had become extinct earlier.) All priories of the Order were under the control of the Master of Sempringham (e.g. v. ref. under Clattercote).

Excavations at Watton of one of the double houses show the infinite care with which the buildings for the nuns and canons were designed and built. There was no communication between the two halves of the monastery except for a processional doorway in the presbytery dividing wall, which was used on special occasions. It was ordained that the nuns should have the northern half of the church, the canons the southern, and that the partition wall must be 'high enough so that the canons and nuns cannot see each other, but not so high that the nuns could not hear the celebrations of Masses at the canons' altar'.

The canons wore a black habit with a white cloak and the nuns a black cloak and tunic with a white cowl.

9 GRANDMONTINE Brethren

The Order was founded by St Stephen of Muret in the diocese of Limoges early in the 12thC as an offshoot of the Benedictines. The life was extremely austere. Following the death of Stephen the brethren established their mother house at Grandmont, and although there were many daughter houses throughout France only three were founded in England. Strangely, there are remains of the two alien houses which were suppressed in the 15thC (*v.* Appendix 1), and none of Grosmont (Yorks) which survived until 1536. It had become denizen in 1394.

It seems that St Stephen modified the Rule of St Benedict to promote greater austerity, forbidding the possession of lands beyond the limits of the precinct and not permitting any flesh in the brethren's food, even in sickness. The necessity for solitude within the monastery was enforced to a degree that none, except persons of the highest eminence, passed its threshold.

The churches were generally small and aisleless with an apse at the east, broader than the rest of the building, even when apses in general had died out. (History: English Ecclesiastical Studies, ch. 9, – Graham).

10 PREMONSTRATENSIAN Canons and Canonesses

The founder of the Order was St Norbert, born in N Germany at Xanten, near Kleve, in 1080. His father was Count de Gennep and his mother a cousin of Emperor Henry IV. In 1118 he adopted a life of poverty and in 1121 he and 40 others settled at a place later to be known as Prémontré (foreshown) – some 75 miles NE of Paris near Laon. The Order was centralised under the abbot of the mother house. Also known as Norbertines after their founder, the canons chose the Rule of St Augustine although the constitution tended to follow Cistercian lines. Because their habit, rochet and cap were white they became known as White Canons.

In general their monasteries were built far from towns, and they were usually dedicated to St Mary. In 1143 the first English house was founded at Newsham (sometimes Newhouse), colonised from Liques Abbey, a daughter house of Prémontré. In later years Welbeck Abbey became the head house of the Order in England and some 38 monasteries were founded, of which about 34 survived until the Dissolution. All were abbeys. Each of these was colonised from another English house except for two, Bayham and St Radegund's (Dover), whose colonies came direct from Prémontré.

The influence of the Cistercian way of life is seen in the sending out of colonies to found daughter houses, the remoteness of sites, the inclusion of conversi in their communities, the obligation of manual labour and the insistence on good manners and rigid ceremonial.

Of the canonesses very little appears to be known. Prof. Eileen Power refers to the fact that they were strictly enclosed and that statutes of 1256–7 contained a clause ordering canonesses to remain in their monasteries, whereas canons were not infrequently responsible for the 'care of souls' in parish churches. There were only four houses in England.

11 TIRONENSIAN Monks

The Order, or perhaps more correctly the Congregation, of Tiron was founded *c.* 1105 by St Bernard of Abbeville. He was a professed monk in the abbey of St Cyprian at Poitiers. After some years at a hermitage he was persuaded to return to become abbot. But he left once more with a group of followers and founded an abbey at Nogent before moving to Tiron, which became the mother house and lay between Chartres and Le Mans.

Only four houses of the Order were founded in England and all of them were suppressed as alien priories (*v.* Appendix 1). It is possible that the monks never made much headway in England due to the greater attraction of the Cistercian Order, but the Rule of St Benedict remained their way of life and they preferred to observe a stricter and truer interpretation of the Rule – 'withdrawing from the company of Black Monks, they changed their habit for grey and began to live apart . . .'

The Mendicant Orders

12 AUGUSTINIAN (Austin) Friars, or Hermits
In the early days of the 13thC there were some 15 congregations of Austin
Hermits in Europe, and the idea of uniting these different communities into
a Mendicant Order was projected in 1243. It became established by a papal act
of power in 1256 at the command of Pope Alexander IV, and from an obscure
origin the community finally became known as the Order of Hermit Friars of
St Augustine. The Order was widely spread and in Europe alone in the 16thC
there were said to be 3000 monasteries (Gasquet). In England at the time of
the Dissolution there were 34.

The first English house was founded at Clare (Suffolk) in 1248–9. The
friary in London was established four years later and became the head house
of the Order. Evenso, it appears unlikely that the London friars enjoyed a
reputation for educational works and learning as did their fellow friars at
Oxford. According to an ancient statute every Bachelor of Arts had to join in
debate once a year before the Austin Friars.

The country was divided into four districts called Limits, each under a
prior provincial with administrative centres at Oxford, Cambridge, Lincoln
and York. The London house came under the Limit of Oxford.

The house at Clare was returned to the Austin Friars in 1953 when the
surviving buildings were restored, and a community lives there today.

13 CARMELITE (White) Friars
The origins of this Order are obscure and difficult to trace with any certainty
farther back than the times of the Crusades. But it grew from a community
of hermits who came from Mount Carmel. In the first quarter of the 13thC
the rise of Mohammedan influence in Palestine made it impossible for the
Christian Carmelites to remain in safety, and they spread to Cyprus, Sicily,
Provence and England, where they arrived in 1241. The first houses were
founded at Hulne in the north and Aylesford in the south in the following
year.

The primitive Rule of Carmel had been formulated in Palestine c. 1210.
According to tradition an English hermit was the prior at Carmel c. 1237 and
he returned to England to become the prior-general in 1247. He soon began
to revise the archaic Rule more or less on Dominican lines, relaxing strict
abstinence, reducing the long periods of silence, allowing meals to be taken in
common, and permitting new foundations to be in or near towns (Knowles).

The Order then became Mendicant from being purely Contemplative. In the course of time the Carmelites became the most learned of the religious Orders (VCH. Essex, ii, 182). Their cloaks were white and their houses dedicated to St Mary. At the time of the Dissolution about 36 houses existed.

The country was divided into four districts called Distinctions, with administrative centres in London, Oxford, Norwich and York. The house at Aylesford has in recent years been reoccupied by members of this Order.

14 DOMINICAN (Black) Friars

Dominic de Guzman (1170–1221) was a Spaniard who belonged to the Augustinian Order of Canons Regular at the priory of Osma in Spain. When he founded the Dominican Order (the second major Order of Friars), the principal mission was against the heretics of Southern France and on this account his followers became known as the Friars Preachers. The Rule was founded upon that of St Augustine and was approved in the Council of Lateran in 1215. The founder was canonised in 1234. The first house of the Order was built at Toulouse c. 1216 and from there missions went to Paris, Bologna, Rome, Spain, Hungary and England.

The colony of 13 friars was brought to England by Peter des Roches, bishop of Winchester, under the leadership of Friar Gilbert de Fresnoy. They arrived in Canterbury in 1221 and went on to Oxford where the first house was founded. At the time of the Dissolution there were 49 Dominican monasteries in England.

An important aspect of the Dominican way of life was the accent on study and the establishment of a system of theological training. The purpose was to teach the fraternity to attack ignorance and heretical beliefs by their preaching. Each Province had a studium which could grant degrees. The course lasted 7 years, 3 for philosophy and 4 for theology.

In contrast to the contemplative Orders where the members of the community normally spent their whole lives at one monastery, the Dominican friars were moved from one house to another and life appointments were unknown. The English Province was divided into four districts called Visitations, with administrative centres in London, York, Oxford and Cambridge. The friar's habit consisted of tunic, scapular and hood made of white woollen material, but outside the monastery a long black cloak and a black hood were worn, hence the reference to Black Friars.

There was one house of Dominican nuns at Dartford which was singularly wealthy in comparison with the majority of nunneries in England. St Katherine was the patron saint of the Order (VCH. Hants. ii, p. 189).

15 FRANCISCAN (Grey) Friars

St Francis of Assisi (1182–1226) was an Italian who founded the first major

Mendicant Order, which became established as the Order of Friars Minor. Pope Innocent III gave his verbal sanction to this new form of religious profession in 1209.

Francis, the son of a wealthy merchant, had enjoyed all the delights of the world, but he threw them off for a life of poverty and prayer. His delight in nature resulted in the legend of his preaching to the birds which inspired so many artists. He was canonised in 1228.

In the early days the friars lived in a state of real financial hardship and owned nothing — not even their simple friary. They had no endowments of land and lived largely upon alms and the generosity of the faithful. The Rule of St Francis was based upon the three vows of religion (poverty, chastity and obedience) with special emphasis on poverty. But a troubled history followed due to a less rigid observance of the Rule including a different interpretation of the word poverty. This resulted in fierce controversies between strict and less strict members of the fraternity. Those who adhered to the original ideals of St Francis became known as Observants (a reformed branch instituted c. 1400 by St Bernadine of Sienna); and those who were willing that the Order should own its monasteries were called Conventuals. The result in the 16thC was two separate Orders throughout Europe.

The first English house was established at Canterbury in 1224 and this was followed within a few days by the foundation in London. The country was divided into 7 Custodies to which houses were assigned: Bristol, Cambridge, London, Oxford, Newcastle, Worcester and York. At about the time of the Dissolution there were 64 houses (58 Conventual and 6 Observant).

The nuns, known as Minoresses or Poor Clares, were founded by St Francis and St Clare c. 1212. They followed the Rule of the Friars Minor from which their name was derived. The first house was founded in England in 1293 outside Aldgate, London, a location still called The Minories. Three others were founded elsewhere in the country.

16 CRUTCHED (Crossed) Friars

The origin of the brethren of the Holy Cross is uncertain. The Order existed in Italy in the middle of the 12thC, and in 1169 Pope Alexander III granted the friars a fixed Rule of life and a constitution. Later in that century and early in the 13thC some 16 houses were founded in Ireland and were probably related to the Italian Friars of the Holy Cross. Sometime before 1217 the friars came to England and +1218 established a hospital for the sick and poor at Reigate. Not until sometime before 1269 was a house founded in London, and it is commemorated in Aldgate. In all, about eleven friaries were established of which only five existed at the Dissolution. They all surrendered on

12 November 1538.

The habit was black or brown with a red cross on the breast, and each friar carried a wooden staff surmounted by a cross. Later Pope Pius II ordered the habit to be changed to blue, and substituted a small silver cross for the larger wooden one. No references occur to any nuns belonging to the Order.

17 PIED Friars

This small Order had only a brief existence. The friars were so called from their black and white habits. The Council of Lyons which met in 1274 ordered the communities to join one or other of the four principal Mendicant Orders, or cease recruitment and continue until the community finally became extinct. Thus the Order slowly died out. There were only three houses in England.

18 SACK Friars

So named because their dress was virtually formless and resembled a simple sack, and was made from a coarse cloth not unlike sackcloth. They were also known as Friars of Penance and their origin seems to have been Italian. There were 16 houses in England all of which had been abandoned by 1314. The first foundation appears to have been at Aldgate, London, which later moved a mile or two to Lothbury. This accounts for some references giving 17 houses of the Order in England.

19 TRINITARIAN (Maturin) Friars

The Friars of the Holy Trinity were established about 1197 in Paris near St Maturin's Chapel (hence Maturin) and the Order was confirmed by Pope Innocent III in the following year. They were associated with the Crusades and their purpose was to rescue Christian captives held by the Moslems, and for this reason they were not strictly a Mendicant Order. Their revenues were partly used to bribe or persuade the Moslem captors to part with their prisoners, and they were themselves sometimes forced to act as hostages until the arrival of more funds. It has been estimated that about 90,000 people were ransomed during the three centuries.

The Rule of St Augustine was observed by the friars and their duties were not unlike those of Augustinian canons of the Holy Sepulchre (Knowles). They wore a white habit, similar to the Dominican indoor wear, with a red and blue cross on their breasts, and a cloak with two crosses on the left side (Gasquet).

The first English house was founded at Moatenden (Kent) in 1224 and the Hounslow house later in the same year. The 10 English houses survived until the Dissolution and all were dedicated to the Holy Trinity.

14

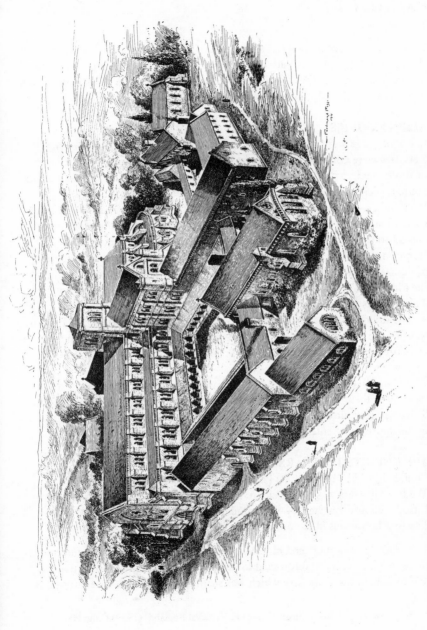

Beaulieu Abbey, Hants. A conjectural reconstruction of the monastic buildings at the time of the Dissolution.

Exclusions

These are almost as numerous (about 1,000) as those included. They consist of alien priories, the two Military Orders and Hospitals. Not much is known about the great majority of these properties and even the sites of many cannot be pinpointed with certainty, especially those of the hospitals.

ALIEN PRIORIES

In effect, these were mainly cells of individual foreign abbeys and priories. Very few were conventual and are better described as granges[1] in which two or three monks would reside, acting as estate agents for the Continental mother houses (Dickinson). Dr Rose Graham observed in her Essay on English Monasteries: 'In the wars between England and France from 1295 until 1413, some monasteries were designated alien priories . . . because they sent money abroad to the mother houses. Owing to their financial difficulties in the Hundred Years War, the more important conventual priories bought charters of denization from the Crown. The majority of alien priories were taken into the king's hands in 1414, and most were subsequently granted away for the endowments of colleges and schools'.

The draining of the resources of the country for the benefit of the French was not the only evil complained of. As most of the monks in the alien priories were Frenchmen, they were liable to act as spies and give information to the enemy.

About 90 houses which had not become denizen were thus dissolved. The remains of these monasteries are not numerous and one of the exceptions is Stogursey (Somerset). Those which changed from alien to English are noted in the appropriate entries. (See Appendix 1 for full list.)

THE KNIGHTS TEMPLARS

Founded in 1118 by Hugh de Payens and nine Knights.
The headquarters was on the site of Solomon's temple, hence the name.
Introduced into England by the founder in 1128.
The first house was in Holborn, London.

The Order was abolished in 1312 by Pope Clement V. It was bound by the three religious vows, and founded in order to protect pilgrims to Jerusalem and to defend the Holy City which was surrounded by Moslem territories. All

[1] Fully covered in 'The Monastic Grange in Medieval England' (1969) Colin Platt.

the preceptories (houses of the Order) in England were subject to the Temple in London. When the Crusades ended so did the purpose of the Knights Templars. During the two centuries of their existence they became both wealthy and arrogant which provoked jealousy. Several factors also added to the decline, not least amongst them was the ceaseless rivalry with the Knights Hospitallers. There were harsh charges brought against the Templars and many of their members suffered imprisonment and worse (in 1310 fifty-four were burned at the stake).

The naves of the churches were circular in imitation of the Holy Sepulchre in Jerusalem. The finest remaining example in England is Temple church in London. At the time of the abolition of the Order there were about 40 preceptories, and most of the possessions of the Templars passed after 1312 to the Hospitallers.

THE KNIGHTS HOSPITALLERS
Founded c. 1113 by Gerard (name and nationality in doubt).
Headquarters in Jerusalem.
Introduced into England c. 1114. Order suppressed 1540.

All members of the Order took the three monastic vows (poverty, chastity and obedience), and their purpose was to care for the sick and the poor — both travellers and Crusaders. Their houses were, as the name implies, hospitals. The English headquarters of the Order was the priory of St John at Clerkenwell, London, the first house to be founded in this country. With the acquisition of the Templars' possessions, the total number of properties rose to about 56, but by 1540 only 15 remained to be suppressed. The prior of Clerkenwell, the Grand Prior of England, ranked as the first baron and took precedence of all the temporal peers of the realm (Cook).

There are no remains in England of the conventual buildings and their arrangement is not known, but part of a church survives. The Norman crypt of St John's Priory church at Clerkenwell is in a fine state of preservation, and the site of the round nave is marked. This house was one of the wealthiest monastic establishments in the whole of Britain, the annual revenue being £2,384 at the time of the Dissolution (roughly £85,000 today).

Hospitals
In the Middle Ages the word hospital had a much wider significance than now because it included almshouses, infirmaries for the aged, hospices for lepers, and hostels for poor pilgrims and travellers. In addition to those established by the Knights Hospitallers, the other monastic houses of monks, nuns and

canons had many hospitals in their care. The loss of many of these was one of the severest social setbacks caused by the closure of the monasteries. Throughout the Middle Ages there were about 960 hospitals in England.

Finance

Following the Norman Conquest, England was in an unsettled state. Vast areas were ravaged and the country was full of dispossessed Saxon thanes. William rewarded his faithful knights by granting them the spoils. He divided the kingdom in such a way that no baron could convert his estates into a province, thereby becoming too powerful. The Conqueror and his followers, accustomed to the vogue of founding religious houses in France, began to found abbeys and priories in England, endowing them with some of their lands. Their faith taught them to believe that their souls, and those of their families and ancestors, could achieve salvation by ensuring that a religious community would pray for them in perpetuity. The enthusiasm of the Normans in using their newly-acquired wealth caused them to look with disdain upon the small Saxon churches — usually built of wood — and to finance the building of large stone monasteries and parish churches, and by the end of the 11thC all the Saxon cathedrals were being replaced on a larger scale.

About 700 new monastic foundations began an era of vast building programmes and only the generous gifts of land, money and goods made escalating activity possible. No accounts have survived to show the actual cost of a complete new monastery, and estimates are almost impossible to compile. Records of the building of Vale Royal Abbey for the first three years after the foundation, 1278–80, give considerable information on payments to various craftsmen and the purchase of materials and tools. And between 1461–79 the cloister, dormitory, chapter house, smithy and part of the church of Syon Abbey cost £6,226; and by 1480 a further £4,138 had been spent on the new church (VCH). Another known example is the cost of building the octagon lantern of Ely, completed in 1342, which amounted to £2,046.6s.11d. This should be multiplied by about 50 for a 1977 equivalent value.

By no means all of the new monastic foundations were adequately endowed to bring revenues capable of sustaining a community. This is particularly true of many nunneries and especially those founded in the 12thC. Poverty is recorded on numerous occasions and there were tax exemptions where the burden became unduly heavy or quite impossible. But Norman benefactors also gave assistance to many houses which suffered from neglect and decay.

The sources of income took several forms. Firstly there were the spiritual and temporal revenues. The former were mainly the receipts from appropriated churches and the associated parochial tithes (the tithe was the setting apart of one-tenth of the annual produce of the land for religious purposes, an ancient English institution). The religious communities were also keenly aware of the financial value of indulgences, and sought after them (Graham). Pilgrims coming to altars dedicated to certain saints could receive relaxations of penances, and such indulgencies would result in a lucrative increase in incomes. Some monasteries obtained substantial funds from shrines and relics at which miracles were reputed to be performed, such as those at Hailes, Gloucester, Boxley, Walsingham, Durham and many others.

The temporal revenues were accounted for by movable and immovable properties which were rents from tenants, and incomes from lands owned and farmed by the community, respectively. Other sources of income under this heading include profits from mills and tanneries, *etc.*, and the sale of such products as wool, grain, timber and fish. In addition there were perquisites from manorial courts.

Other useful takings came from burials within the precincts of the monastic church of laymen and women, especially those who had been benefactors in their lifetimes, and from chantry masses. In later years there were corrodies under which monks and nuns undertook to provide lodging, food, drink, fuel and sometimes clothing, within the monastic buildings, in return for a lump sum. The results were often financially ruinous for the community who had no actuaries to help them estimate the probable total cost.

Very much depended upon the business acumen, or lack of it, of the head of the house and his or her obedientiaries, but in general the successes exceeded the failures by a fair margin. Fortunes varied and whereas Henry III, Edward III and Richard II all turned to Reading Abbey for loans, during the same periods the abbeys of Meaux, Kirkstall and Fountains in Yorkshire were all in debt and borrowing heavily from Jewish or Italian money-lenders and wealthy merchants.

Lawsuits often drained the resources of a monastery faster than income was received due to lengthy delays and the cost of litigation. Encroachments upon rights and property, disputes over cartularies, forgeries, trespass and responsibility for land drainage and highways, for example, are typical causes of legal action. In addition almost every monastery had to find money for the expenses of journeys to Rome, and for subsidies to the Crown and the Papacy.

Not all Orders were able to raise funds for building in the same way, and

Dr Rose Graham observes that whereas the Benedictines made public appeals, the Cistercians were forbidden by the General Chapter from doing so. She adds that but for help through money borrowed from the Jews (Christians were forbidden by the church to engage in money-lending), some of the large scale building developments of Cistercian monasteries could not have been undertaken.

Amongst the problems which faced convents heading towards a financial crisis, was the difficulty experienced by the brethren in finding out where the abbot or abbess was spending the income. In most cases the abbot and chapter would allocate some revenues to the responsible administration of the obedientaries, but if the abbot found himself coming in for criticism it was sometimes met by despatching the critic(s) to one of the abbey's more remote cells. However, in later eras a common treasury in which divided responsibility was allocated proved a more satisfactory form of accountancy.

Since a good deal of the revenue came from the land, the advent of the Black Death (1348–9) ruined the system of farming, which had been so successfully established, due to the lack of labour. Much of the monastic land was subsequently let or sold. Droughts and floods had devastating effects upon income, and ruined crops, cattle disease and a fall in monastic standards resulted in serious food, income and trading losses.

There were few monasteries, even the greatest and best endowed, which did not suffer financial straits at one time or another; and perhaps mergers, partnerships or takeovers on the part of the more resourceful and far-seeing abbots and abbesses in the 15th and 16thCs, might have removed at least one of the causes of the ultimate Dissolution.

Further reading:
English Monastic Finances (1926) R. H. Snape.

Visitations

Nowadays the word inspection would replace visitation. There are many references in the gazetteer to episcopal visits to monasteries, i.e. inspections by the bishop in whose see the abbey or priory was situated.

Not all monasteries were under a bishop's jurisdiction. In general, the houses which were autonomous were subject to visitations, namely Benedictine, Augustinian and Cistercian nuns. The abbeys of Cistercian monks, Premonstratensian canons, the Cluniacs, Gilbertines and Carthusians were exempt, having their own arrangements for periodic inspections of their houses. Monastic cathedrals, i.e. Durham, Norwich and Ely, *etc.*, were invariably independent of the resident bishop.

Whereas the bishops' records were held amongst the diocesan muniments, records of visitations and copies of injunctions issued by them to the convents have, in many cases, survived. But those which were held by the mother-houses within the Orders were mostly destroyed with the destruction of the monastery at the Dissolution. It is therefore understandable that some histories are meagre or totally lacking.

Friaries were not subject to visitations at all.

The object of the inspection was to find out how well the house was managed and the Rule observed. Injunctions issued later had the object of ordering corrections of indiscipline, incontinence, apostasy and contumacy.

There are many entries in the summaries which, it may be thought, concentrate on the less laudable lives of the inmates. What was good and virtuous in the majority of the houses is mainly unrecorded and the injunctions are essentially related to faults and irregularities. It should be remembered that most of the religious were very ordinary men and women who lived an austere and monotonous life, usually of their own choosing, as an alternative to the perilous, hard and uncertain life in the world outside the monastery. There are not infrequent instances of persons who were totally unsuited to the life and whose rebellious nature influenced others. Also, a number of superiors were bad managers and administrators whose examples undoubtedly had a detrimental effect upon the rest of the community. Evenso, the great majority of the men and women observed their vows and lived blameless lives, and this should be borne in mind lest an unfair and unbalanced view be taken of the monastic life.

There are a few instances where the visiting bishop or his agent showed a distinct bias against a house for reasons which history does not record. Whereas the customary period between visits was three years, the interval was often much less when a good deal of indiscipline was revealed. That some superiors ignored the injunctions issued by a bishop is beyond doubt, and some communities must have sorely stretched his patience, but these are exceptions amongst hundreds of monasteries.

The references to apostasy infer an unlicenced absence from the monastery and the abandonment of the regular habit for lay garments, not any denial of faith (Thompson). Incontinence was more serious and meant the breaking of the vow of chastity. Contumacy was frequently subject to special penalties and disciplines because of wilful opposition to authority and disobedience, another serious breach of the three vows.

Finally, there was invariably opposition by the convent to a visitation by anyone other than the bishop of that see or a recognised abbot of the same Order. There are several instances of violent scenes of resistance at monasteries when tyrannical diocesan visitors or their commissaries tried to gain admittance by domination.

Mitred Abbeys

Mitred *Parliamentary* abbots were those summoned by the king to attend Parliament, and therefore they held a rank equivalent to a baron of the realm. They had seats in the Upper House as Spiritual Lords. In 1300 about 80 abbots and priors were summoned to attend Parliament, but after 1341 until the Dissolution the normal number was 27. These were:

Abingdon	Evesham	Selby
Bardney	Glastonbury	Shrewsbury
Battle	Gloucester	Tavistock
Bury St Edmunds	Malmesbury	Tewkesbury
Canterbury	Peterborough	Thorney
(St Augustine's)	Ramsey	Waltham
Cirencester	Reading	Westminster
Colchester	St Alban's	Winchcombe
(St John's)	St Benet of	Winchester (Hyde)
Crowland	Hulme	York (St Mary's)

No Cistercian house had a Parliamentary abbot. The list comprises two Augustinian houses (Cirencester and Waltham) and the remainder were Benedictine.

In addition, two priors wore the mitre and held Parliamentary rank: the Prior of Coventry Cathedral-Priory and the English Prior of the Order of the Knights Hospitallers.

The first abbot to have the right to wear the mitre and sandals conferred upon him was St Aethelsig of St Augustine's, Canterbury, by Pope Nicholas II in 1063. Of the several privileges accorded to one of this status there was exemption from any episcopal visitation or control, he being subject only to the pope.

It was not the right of an abbot who had been honoured with the mitre by the pope to be summoned automatically by the king to attend Parliament, nor was the honour of a seat in Parliament, unlike the honour of a mitre, necessarily coveted by an abbot. Some examples of exclusions were the abbots of Bristol (1398), St Mary Graces, London (1415), Osney (1481) and the prior of Durham (1382). No abbesses attended the Upper House although the abbesses of Barking, Shaftesbury, Wilton and Winchester (St Mary's) all ranked as baronesses.

When the head of a monastic house had been licenced by the pope to wear some or all of the episcopal insignia, the abbey was said to be mitred. The full insignia consisted of the *mitre* (emblematic of Christ, the Head of the Church); the *ring* (signifying that Christ was the spouse of the Church); the *staff* (or crosier, denoting pastoral care); the *gloves* (worn or laid aside to typify the concealment of good works); the *dalmatic* (a seamless coat to signify holy and immaculate piety); the *tunicle* (a shorter or smaller version of the dalmatic); and the *sandals* (the feet being neither covered nor naked, so the gospels should be neither concealed nor rest upon earthly benefits). These were worn within the monastery on solemn days and in State pageants, processions and episcopal synods. (Fosbroke).

Conventual Cathedral Churches

The histories of the great monastic houses which survived destruction at the Dissolution, and became secular cathedrals, have been so thoroughly and frequently publicised that only brief entries have been written here. They are:

Bristol	Oxford
Carlisle	Peterborough
Canterbury	Rochester
(Christchurch)	St Albans
Chester	Southwark
Durham	Winchester
Ely	(St Swithun)
Gloucester	Worcester
Norwich	Westminster (for 10 years)

Also there are a number of abbey churches which have survived in that status, e.g. Milton, Selby, Sherborne and Romsey. These have been given smaller entries because of readily available information from other sources. In many instances all, or part, of a monastic church remains in use today as the parish church, e.g. Binham, Bolton, Dunster, Malmesbury, Nun Monkton, Shrewsbury, Weybourne, *etc.* which have been treated more fully.

The Three Stages of Dissolution

The termination of the Military Order of the Knights Templars can be identified as one of the earliest precedents for the total destruction of monastic life in England in the 16thC; but it is certainly doubtful whether it was in any way the inspiration of those who later brought about the downfall of the religious Orders.

Less doubtful as an early contributory cause was the terrible effect of the Black Death (in which it has been estimated that between one-third and one-half of the total population of England perished) and several subsequent pestilences. From this time onward all of the monastic communities suffered severely, some weakened beyond recovery, and very few regained their former size. Lay brethren no longer existed because the sudden scarcity of labour gave both freedom and wide choice of employment to labourers and peasants.

The economic and social effect of this deep disturbance manifested itself in less well-managed monastic houses in the 15thC with falls in the levels of income, reduced maintenance of the properties, and a lessening of discipline within the monasteries. The signs indicated that there was need for a change.

1 The First Steps
In 1496 Bishop Alcock of Ely acquired the small Benedictine nunnery of St Radegund just outside Cambridge, of which he was patron. There were only two nuns living there, and because of the dilapidated condition of the buildings and his charge of dissolute conduct of the prioress, he obtained a bull from the pope and a licence from the king to take possession of the priory, its land and former properties. On the site he founded Jesus College, of which the nuns' church forms the chapel.

In 1505, Margaret, countess of Richmond and Derby (mother of Henry VII) refounded Christ's College, Cambridge. She bought several small monasteries, including the abbey of North Creake in Norfolk, and in 1507 used these possessions to increase its endowments.

In 1524 Bishop Fisher of Rochester used the properties of two poor nunneries (Broomhall, Berks., and Higham, Kent) to supplement the income of St John's College, Cambridge.

In 1532 the London Augustinian Priory of Holy Trinity, Aldgate — a major house of the Order — had become heavily in debt in the early years of the century. Without any reference to the pope the monastery was surrendered to the king in February of that year, which must have brought considerable concern to all communities.

A few years earlier, in 1519, a move to reform the monasteries had been proposed by Cardinal Wolsey, who had just recently been created Cardinal Legate. He was empowered to do so by a papal bull issued by Pope Leo X. Thomas Wolsey, who was born in Ipswich, had completed a brilliant career at Oxford. He became chaplain to Henry VIII and then Lord Chancellor (the most dictatorial England had known); but his despotism in the church was even worse than on matters of State.

It was in imitation of Bishops Alcock and Fisher that Wolsey began the foundation of colleges at Oxford and Ipswich. A papal bull of 1524 enabled him to dissolve twenty-one religious houses. The 'gracious aid and assistance of the king' was urged in order 'to convert to a far better use the revenues of these monasteries' for a new college at Oxford 'for the increase of good letters and virtue'. It was to be based upon the Augustinian priory of St Frideswide and to be known as Cardinal College, later to become Christ Church College after he was deposed.

These monasteries were:

Bayham (Sussex)
Blackmore (Essex)
Bradwell (Bucks)
Canwell (Staffs)
Daventry (Northants)
Dodnash (Suffolk)
Horkesley (Essex)
Lesnes (Kent)
Littlemore (Oxon)
Oxford (St Frideswide's)
Poughley (Berks)

Pynham (Sussex)
Ravenstone (Bucks)
Sandwell (Staffs)
Snape (Suffolk)
Stansgate (Essex)
Thoby (Essex)
Tickford (Bucks)
Tonbridge (Kent)
Tiptree (Essex)
Wix (Essex)

Wolsey's agents, John Allen and Thomas Cromwell, visited each of them for the sole purpose of seizing their properties, but it does not seem entirely clear why these particular houses were chosen for suppression.

Further papal bulls followed in 1528–9 which permitted the closure of seven more small monasteries, those with less than six religious persons; and others of the same Order (with less than twelve religious) were authorised to be united. Those which Wolsey had selected next for suppression were to provide the finance for his Ipswich college. This was to be based upon the Augustinian priory of St Peter in that town. The plan never matured. Those suppressed were:

Bromehill (Norfolk) Rumburgh (Suffolk)
Felixstowe (Suffolk) St Mary de Pré (Herts)
Flixton (Suffolk) Wallingford (Berks)
Ipswich (St Peter's)

From these events it is clear that the start of the general Dissolution may certainly be attributed to the Cardinal, and it is noteworthy that his principal aide in destroying these religious houses was the unscrupulous Thomas Cromwell. But Wolsey had no time to put the rest of his plans into effect before he was driven from the Chancellorship, and not a voice was raised in protest. In the following year, 1530, Henry summoned him to London to answer a charge of high treason, and while on his way there from Cawood Castle near York, he became ill and died in Leicester Abbey.

2 The Lesser Monasteries

In January 1535 Thomas Cromwell was appointed King's Victor-General, and his position was considerably stronger than Wolsey's had been. He knew that perhaps as much as a quarter of the English lands lay in monastic hands. There is little doubt that the prosperity of the monks and their wealth had been the envy of all classes of laymen for about 100 years, and so it is not surprising that the king should support a project suggested by Cromwell which was, in fact, based upon the very actions of Wolsey himself.

It is essential to appreciate that money, and Henry VIII's need of it, was the central reason for the dissolution of the monasteries. To achieve finance for his administration Henry agreed to any of Cromwell's proposals, and these began with the despatch of several Crown visitors whose job was to report on the condition of the monasteries. These Commissioners have been described by Professor Knowles as 'grasping, worldly and without a trace of spiritual feeling', and by another author as 'notorious self-seekers'. Their report (Comperta) alleged that all the houses were bestial and corrupt, but some were never visited; and where the charges were unsupported by fact the monks or nuns were accused of concealing the truth. Even before the Comperta was finished, Cromwell had decided upon a wide-scale suppression.

26

There followed later in 1535 a valuation of the Church properties, and the findings were published in the Valor Ecclesiasticus. In mid-March 1536 Parliament passed the Act of Suppression, a Bill which had been prepared by Cromwell, and which authorised the closure of monasteries with an annual income of less than 300 marks (£200). In all, more than 300 houses became victims of this Act, of which between 70 and 80 were later exempted from immediate extinction by the payment of fines to the Crown.

So, many of the more defenceless abbeys and priories were lost despite numerous appeals from patrons, benefactors and beneficiaries for them to continue in the service of local communities. The loss of these monasteries brought resentment, resistance and serious economic changes. In Lincolnshire and Yorkshire the king's men were called upon to quell uprisings, and the Pilgrimage of Grace, based upon York, brought cruelty and death to most of the abbots and monks who gave it support.

The next move by Cromwell was to instigate the appointment of a Commission, under the Court of Augmentation, whose purpose was to supervise the closures by suppression of the lesser monasteries and to administer the proceeds. Many of the Deeds are preserved at the Public Record Office in London.

The larger monasteries with net annual incomes in excess of £200 were exempt, and the 'unprincipled knaves, devoid of sympathy or scruple' who were Cromwell's Commissioners, had been instructed not to visit them because they were described as 'great solemn monasteries wherein, thanks be to God, religion is right well kept and observed'. Evidence suggests that for some years Cromwell had thought out long-term proposals for the ultimate destruction of the monasteries; but several historians have been at pains to suggest that the total confiscation of monastic wealth was not originally in Henry VIII's mind.

3 The Final Phase

The Act of Suppression of 1536 was therefore a procedure of reorganisation of monasticism which would permit a large section of the religious Orders to remain in existence. What prompted the decision to reverse this arrangement (Cromwell's devious thinking apart) whereby *all* the abbeys and priories would be swept away is not known. There was in 1537 increasing rumour and hint that a change in government policy was on the way, and that every monastic house was, in fact, doomed. To allay fears Cromwell wrote to the heads of all religious houses in March 1538 giving an assurance that no such proposals were contemplated, adding that what surrenders there had been were 'free and voluntary'.

At this time some 250 monasteries remained and Cromwell, bent upon further closures, had already sent his Visitors on a fresh tour of inspection for the explicit purpose of getting individual houses to hand over their properties to the Crown – for which he had no legal right. (It was not until 1539 that a new Act of Parliament was passed which sanctioned the transfer of further monastic property to the State, and by this time confiscation was almost complete.) Cromwell had initiated the condition of surrender as distinct from suppression of the smaller monasteries. There can be little doubt that the Visitors used threats and made deals in order to obtain the surrenders, but most of the heads of these abbeys and priories were surely well aware that resistance was hopeless in the face of ruthless, determined and untrustworthy government officials. Cardinal Gasquet gives two methods which were employed to gain submissions. There was the skilful selection of men who were appointed as abbots of some abbeys because they were likely to resign their houses when called upon to do so; and secondly, when argument with an abbot was ineffective, terror and severe dealings worked – i.e. there were charges of negligent administration of office or the breaking of the king's injunction resulting in the deprivation of appointment.

Once the religious had been turned from their houses the property was leased or sold to those of whom the Crown approved and those who could afford the price. The pilfering and embezzlement by the men who actually carried out the surrender was considerable, and although the total value of monastic property confiscated was enormous, perhaps little more than one-fifth of the actual value ever reached the royal coffers.

The king's agents removed countless treasures of gold and silver. Lead was stripped from the roofs and melted by fires fuelled with splendid wood carvings which had formed the church screens and stalls. The equally valuable bell-metal was mainly reserved for the king's use in order to make guns. Many hundreds of cartloads of priceless cartularies, books, deeds, manuscripts and ancient documents were burnt or wantonly destroyed.

The dismantling of the conventual church was no doubt made mandatory to ensure there could be no rehabilitation by the former occupants, or any resumption of monastic life – except for such parts that were in use by parishioners. Vast quantities of stone were removed for use in new buildings, road construction and repairs, while some of the monasteries' conventual buildings were frequently converted into private dwellings.

Only a few months after the last monastery had been closed down, the detestable and utterly ruthless Thomas Cromwell was beheaded, without trial and unpitied, on 28 June 1540; while his avaricious collaborator, King Henry VIII, survived him until 28 January 1547.

So ended the most devastating reform England has ever suffered, and for over three centuries the sad wrecks of some of the world's finest architecture were disintegrating, with ivy covering the broken masonry of church and cloister; until an awakening in the 19thC to the achievements of the mediaeval builders caused a slow and purposeful beginning towards the rescue and preservation of the remnants.

Of approximately 820 houses which were closed, roughly one-third of the monasteries existing at the time of the Dissolution have now vanished completely. Rather more than one-third exist as scanty ruins or are partly re-used in later buildings. Slightly less than one-third survive with either substantial ruins or the church is wholly or partly in use today. In many instances fine monastic buildings are incorporated in later private developments.

It has been suggested that the lure of the romantic monastic ruin is an unsolved psychological problem, and that innumerable opportunities are neglected to visit our extant abbeys and cathedrals, still in their full wonder. But a mediaeval abbey or priory ruin was more than a church, it was a whole working complex of buildings, and the fascination lies not only in the broken walls but also in the lost mysticism of an era which has disappeared for ever.

* * * * *

The reader will understand that these notes contribute the bare minimum of introduction to the long and involved story of the Dissolution, and for fuller reading is referred to a number of full-scale works which are available. Notably:

Henry VIII and the English Monasteries (1889) Cardinal Gasquet.
English Monks and the Suppression of the Monasteries (1937) Geoffrey Baskerville.
Letters to Cromwell and others on the Suppression of the Monasteries (1965) G. H. Cook.
The Dissolution of the Monasteries (1966) G. W. O. Woodward.
The Dissolution of the Monasteries (1971) Joyce Youings.

The Black Death

The English people suffered a series of plagues during the Middle Ages and none was more serious or devastating than the Great Pestilence (Black Death) of 1348–9. This terrible scourge, the bubonic plague, began in 1346 possibly when famine and drought resulted in countless unburied Chinese causing disease to spread. The caravans of merchants and the mariners from the Far East brought the infection out of China which later spread from the shores of the Mediterranean to the Baltic.

In the autumn of 1348 the plague arrived in England and a monk of Malmesbury Abbey wrote: 'The cruel pestilence terrible to all future ages came from parts over sea to the south coast of England unto a port called Melcombe (Weymouth) in Dorsetshire' (Hutton). Cardinal Gasquet points out that Weymouth was a great port in the 14thC and Edward III's ships sailed from there in 1348 for the seige of Calais. He thinks it not improbable that the crews of the returning ships brought the plague to England.

The closing months of 1348 were very wet and the conditions no doubt helped the disease to pass rapidly through the southern counties 'killing by midday many who had been fit and well in the morning'. As stated elsewhere, over one-third of England's population of 4 million succumbed. In Bodmin for example, 1500 persons perished including nearly all of the Augustinian canons. At St Albans the abbot and 46 monks died and at Meaux (Yorks.) all but 10 of the 42 monks were carried off. The nunneries suffered no less severely, and no monastic house escaped save one or two Carthusian communities in total seclusion. In London, Sir Walter Manny purchased land for mass burials which afterwards became the site of the London Charterhouse (*v.* gazetteer entry). About 60,000 people perished in Norwich alone.

The Black Death was eventually stayed in September 1349 and its passing laid the country desolate. Land cultivation was impossible and sheep and cattle strayed through fields and corn 'for there was none left who could drive them'. Nothing was to be the same again and the monasteries never recovered from the effects of the calamity. Throughout the country there was an air of revolution and outbreaks of lawless self-indulgence followed everywhere in the wake of the plague, and men searching for work found themselves for the first time masters of the labour market. A redress for these evils took effect by the introduction of the Statute of Labourers in Parliament which ordered every able bodied man or woman under 60 to serve an employer when required at a wage paid to him two years before the plague. Imprisonment was the alternative.

The worst effect for monastic life was the loss of the masters of regular discipline and the seniors of experience, which could not be renewed by the surviving community or the youths who would need years of training to fill the depopulated houses.

There followed further outbreaks of the plague in 1361 and 1368 which made the plight of the religious houses more desperate still.

English Monarchs

When the year of the foundation of a monastery is either unrecorded or has been lost, frequently the only certain fact is the name of the king in whose reign the founder lived. This information is given in some of the entries in the gazetteer.

Monarch	Accession	Died	Age	Reigned
I. – BEFORE THE CONQUEST.				
SAXONS AND DANES				
Egbert	827	839	–	12
Ethelwulf	839	858	–	19
Ethelbald	858	860	–	2
Ethelbert	858	865	–	7
Ethelred	865	871	–	6
Alfred the Great	871	899	50	28
Edward the Elder	899	924	54	25
Athelstan	924	939	45	15
Edmund	939	946	25	7
Eadred	946	955	32	9
Eadwig	955	959	18	3
Edgar	959	975	32	17
Edward the Martyr	975	978	17	3
Ethelred II ("the Unready") .	978	1016	48	37
Edmund Ironside	1016	1016	27	Apr.–Nov.
Canute the Dane	1017	1035	40	18
Harold I	1035	1040	–	5
Hardicanute	1040	1042	24	2
Edward the Confessor . .	1042	1066	62	24
Harold II	1066	1066	44	Jan.–Oct.

Monarch	Accession	Died	Age	Reigned
NORMANS				
William I	1066	1087	60	21
William II	1087	1100	43	13
Henry I	1100	1135	67	35
Stephen, Count of Blois . .	1135	1154	50	19
PLANTAGENETS				
Henry II	1154	1189	56	35
Richard I	1189	1199	42	10
John	1199	1216	50	17
Henry III	1216	1272	65	56
Edward I	1272	1307	68	35
Edward II	1307	dep. 1327	43	20
Edward III	1327	1377	65	50
Richard II	1377	dep. 1399	34	22
Henry IV ⎫	1399	1413	47	13
Henry V ⎬ Lancaster . .	1413	1422	34	9
Henry VI ⎭	1422	dep. 1461	49	39
Edward IV ⎫	1461	1483	41	22
Edward V ⎬ York . . .	1483	1483	13	Apr.–June
Richard III ⎭	1483	1485	32	2
TUDORS				
Henry VII	1485	1509	53	24
Henry VIII	1509	1547	56	38
Edward VI	1547	1553	16	6
Jane	1553	1554	17	9 days
Mary I	1553	1558	43	5
Elizabeth I	1558	1603	69	44

General Information

Abbreviations

−	(minus). Earlier than, e.g. −1154.
+	(plus). Later than, e.g. +1209.
A.M.	Ancient Monument.
B.D.	Black Death (bubonic plague) 1348–9.
B.M.	British Museum.

c.	(circa). About, e.g. *c.* 1094.
ch., chs.	Church, churches. (*Never* chapel, chancel, chantry or charter).
Dec.	Decorated Style.
Ded:	Dedication.
D of E	Department of the Environment.
E.E. or EE	Early English Style.
f., fd. or fdn.	founded. foundation.
F., Fs.	Founder or Foundress. Founders.
L.G.	Little Guide (Methuen's Series).
M.	Mitred (abbey).
N.H. Soc.	Natural History Society.
N.T. or NT.	National Trust.
Perp.	Perpendicular Style.
P.R.O. or R.O.	Public Record Office or Record Office.
v.	(vide). See, e.g. (*v.* Buckland).
VCH	Victoria County History.

(For Journal abbreviations at the end of an entry see Bibliography – 1.)

Access

Remains of monasteries, in many cases incorporated in private buildings, are not necessarily open to the public nor is access in any instance implied. Ruins of buildings in the care of the Department of the Environment and those belonging to local or county councils, together with certain other privately owned monastic premises or remains, are open to visitors at advertised times.

Accuracy

Some entries in the gazetteer are certain to be incomplete or imperfect because of conflicting statements and inaccuracies in the records available. Names and dates in particular are occasionally in dispute between historians. Interpretations, individual opinions and the passage of time also affect historical accuracy. In addition there are many existing sources of information which are not included. Of the innumerable facts assembled, the sources range from books published between 1694 and 1977. To verify some details was often impossible, but the sifted and recorded notes are as accurate as can be reasonably ascertained. Good descriptions of remains of some of the more remote monasteries are especially elusive.

Counties

The names and boundaries of some counties in England were changed by the Local Government Act of 1972. Throughout the gazetteer entries the locations are given according to the old names because almost every bibliographical reference is pre-1972.

Cross references

Many monasteries were known by more than one name: e.g. Creake/North Creake; Bodmin/Petrostock; Newminster/Hyde (Winchester). Even more numerous are the different spellings of names of persons and places, and in respect of the latter — e.g. Gisborough/Guisborough — cross references are included in as many instances as seem reasonable for identification.

Footnotes

These have been reduced to a minimum. The identity of, and authority for, every fact or opinion would have added nothing but distraction and, possibly, irritation.

Definition of Remains

'None' means that nothing of the buildings or their foundations remain above ground. Nevertheless, in many instances remains still exist below ground or existing buildings may have been constructed wholly or partially from materials that once formed or belonged to monastic property. 'None' also includes areas where holes, mounds and ditches mark the sites of monastic buildings, stewponds or other property.

Omissions

Certain statistical details such as the net annual incomes in 1291 (Taxation Roll) and 1535 (Valor Ecclesiasticus), and the size of the community at various times in the history of the monastery, are to be found in 'Medieval Religious Houses in England & Wales' (1971) by David Knowles and R. Neville Hadcock. A duplication of these facts seems unnecessary.

The eight maps indicate where monastic buildings or remains exist, from complete abbey churches to minute structural relics. Although many sites are in private hands and never open to visitors, others are open at advertised times published annually in the ABC Historic Publication. Ruins in the care of the Department of the Environment have the names underlined; all of these are open to the public as advertised. Churches now in use which were wholly or in part monastic have the symbols underlined.

In addition, the gazetteer entries give 105 other locations where minor fragments of former monastic possessions survive, many of them incorporated in later buildings on or near the monastic site (see Appendix 4).

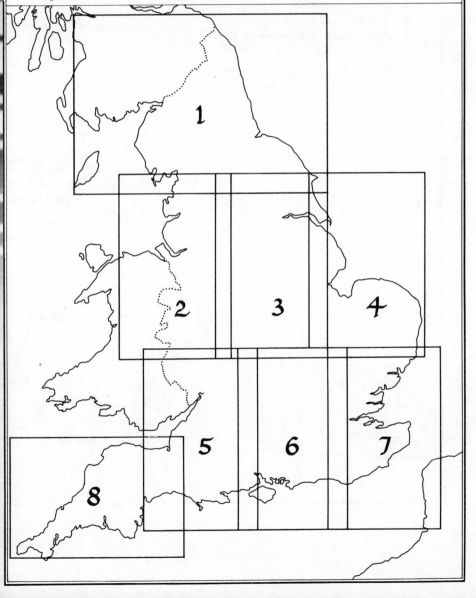

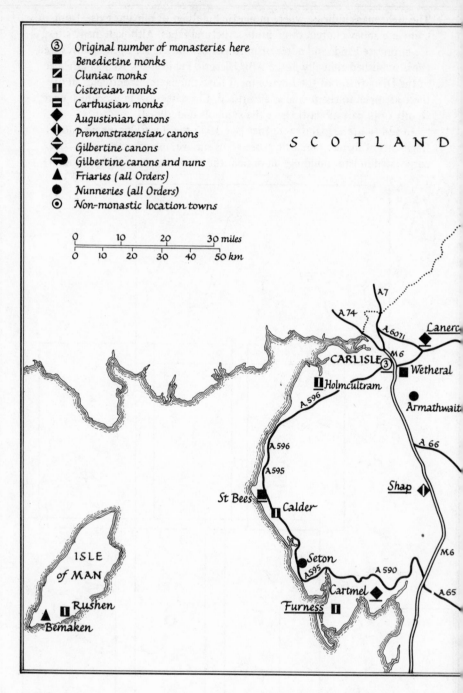

Original number of monasteries here
■ Benedictine monks
◨ Cluniac monks
◫ Cistercian monks
◻ Carthusian monks
◆ Augustinian canons
◈ Premonstratensian canons
⬦ Gilbertine canons
⬱ Gilbertine canons and nuns
▲ Friaries (all Orders)
● Nunneries (all Orders)
⊙ Non-monastic location towns

0   10   20   30 miles
0 10 20 30 40 50 km

SCOTLAND

A7
A74
A6071   Lanerc
M6
CARLISLE ③   ■ Wetheral
◫ Holmcultram
A596   ● Armathwait

A596   A66
A595
Shap ◈
St Bees ◫
◫ Calder
M6
● Seton
A595   A590   M6
Cartmel ◆
Furness ◫   A65

ISLE
of MAN

▲ ◫ Rushen
Bemaken

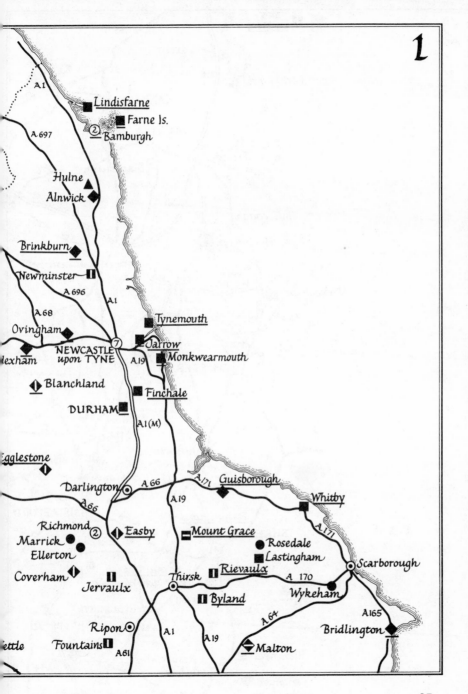

1

A1

Lindisfarne

Farne Is.

② Bamburgh

A.697

Hulne

Alnwick

Brinkburn

Newminster

A 696

A1

A 68

Ovingham

NEWCASTLE ⑦
upon TYNE   A19

Tynemouth

Jarrow

Monkwearmouth

Hexham

Blanchland

Finchale

DURHAM

A1(M)

Egglestone

Darlington ⊙   A 66

A171   Guisborough

A66

A19

Whitby

Richmond ②   Easby

Mount Grace

A171

Marrick
Ellerton

Rosedale

Lastingham

Scarborough

Coverham

Jervaulx

Thirsk   Rievaulx   A 170

Wykeham

Byland

A165

Ripon ⊙   A1

Fountains   A19   A 64

Bridlington

Settle

A61   Malton

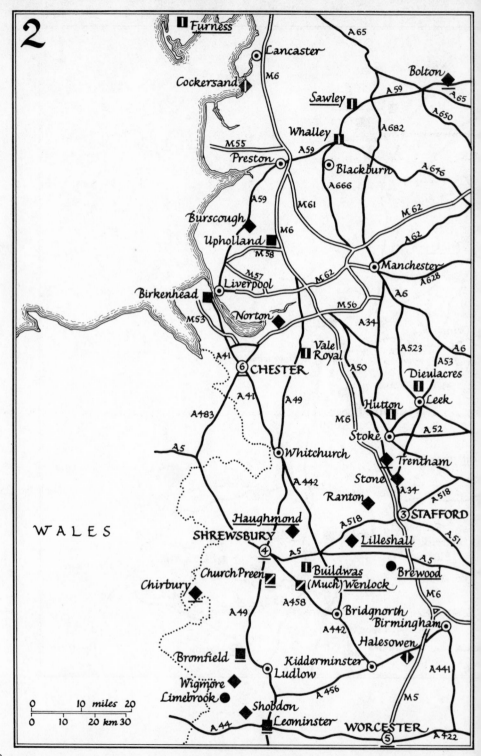

2

Furness

Lancaster

A 65

Bolton

Cockersand

Sawley

A 59

A 65

M 6

A 682

A 650

Whalley

M 55

A 59

Preston

Blackburn

A 646

A 59

A 666

M 61

M 62

Burscough

M 6

Upholland

M 58

A 62

M 57

Manchester

Liverpool

M 62

A 628

Birkenhead

M 56

A 6

M 53

Norton

A 34

Vale Royal

A 523

A 6

CHESTER

A 50

A 53

Dieulacres

A 41

Hutton

Leek

A 41

A 49

A 483

M 6

Stoke

A 52

A 5

Whitchurch

Trentham

A 442

Stone

A 34

A 518

Ranton

WALES

Haughmond

A 518

STAFFORD

SHREWSBURY

Lilleshall

A 51

A 5

Church Preen

Buildwas

Brewood

Chirbury

(Much) Wenlock

M 6

A 49

A 458

Bridgnorth

Birmingham

A 442

Halesowen

Bromfield

Kidderminster

A 441

Wigmore

Ludlow

Limebrook

A 456

M 5

Shobdon

0   10 miles 20

Leominster

WORCESTER

0   10   20 km 30

A 44

A 422

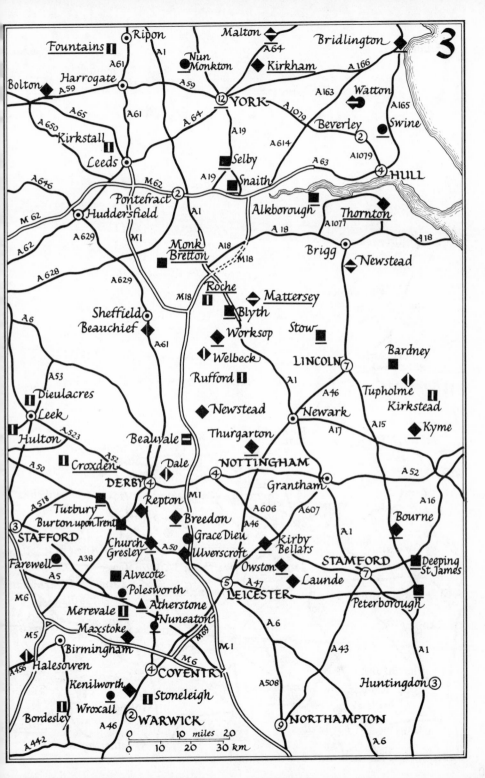

3

Ripon
Fountains ▮
A61
A1
Malton ◆
A64
Bridlington ◆

Bolton ◆
Harrogate ⊙
A59
Nun ● Monkton
Kirkham ◆
A166

A650
A65
A59
A61
A64
A163
Watton ◆
A165

Kirkstall ▮
A61
A19
York ⑫
A1079
Beverley ●
Swine ●

Leeds ⊙
M62
A19
Selby ◆
②
A1079
HULL ④

A646
Pontefract ②
A1
Snaith ◆
A63
Alkborough ◆
Thornton ◆

M62
Huddersfield ⊙
A1
A18
A1077
A18

A62
A629
M1
Monk ◆ Bretton
A18
M18
Brigg ⊙
Newstead ◆

A628
A629
M18
Roche ▮
Mattersey ◆

Sheffield ⊙
Beauchief ◆
A61
Blyth ◆
Worksop ◆
Stow ●

A6
A53
Welbeck ◆
LINCOLN ⑦
Bardney ●

Dieulacres ▮
Leek ●
Rufford ▮
A1
A46
Tupholme ◆ Kirkstead ▮

Hulton ▮
A523
Newstead ◆
Newark ⊙
A15
Kyme ◆

A50
A52
Croxden ▮
Bealvale ▬
Thurgarton ◆
A17

Dale ◆
NOTTINGHAM ④
Grantham ⊙
A52

DERBY ④
Repton ◆
M1
A16

A518
Tutbury ◆
Burton upon Trent
A606
A607
Bourne ◆

STAFFORD ③
Breedon ◆
A46
Kirby ◆ Bellars
A1

Farewell ●
Church Gresley
A50
Grace Dieu ●
Ulverscroft ◆
STAMFORD ⑦
Deeping ◆ St James

A5
A38
Owston ◆
Laune ◆
Peterborough ◆

M6
Alvecote ◆
Polesworth ●
⑤
A47
LEICESTER

Merevale ▮
Atherstone ▲
Nuneaton ●
A6
A43
A1

M5
Maxstoke ◆
M69
M1
Huntingdon ③

Birmingham ⊙
COVENTRY ④
A508

A456
Halesowen ◆
M6
Kenilworth ◆
Stoneleigh ▮

Bordesley ▮
Wroxall ●
A46
WARWICK ②
NORTHAMPTON ⑨

A442
A6

0   10 miles 20
0   10   20   30 km

39

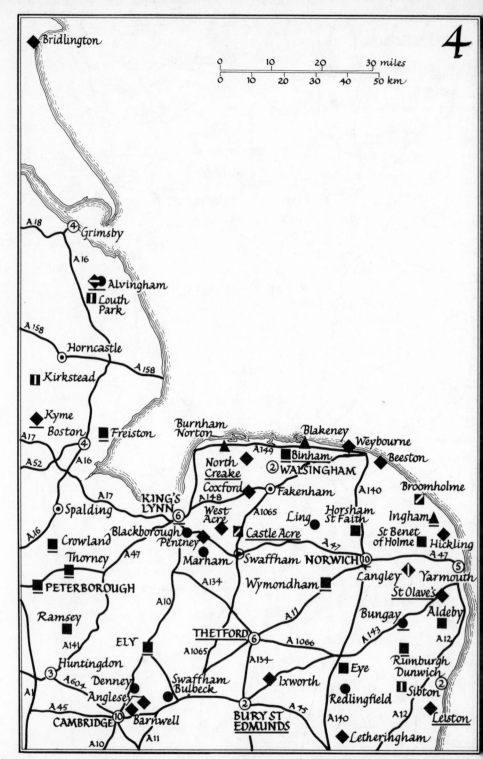

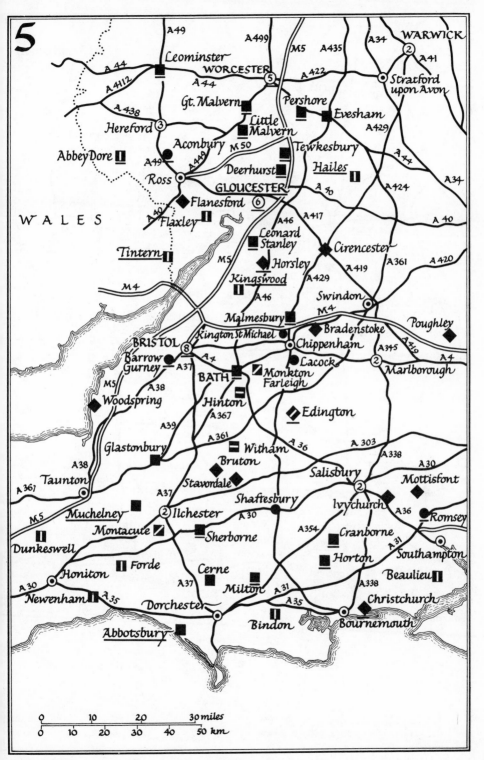

5

A49 A499 M5 A435 A34 WARWICK
Leominster ②
WORCESTER A422 Stratford
A44 ⑤ upon Avon
A4112 A41
Gt. Malvern Pershore Evesham
A438 Little A429
Hereford ③ Malvern A44
Aconbury Tewkesbury Hailes
Abbey Dore M50 Deerhurst A34
A49 Ross A449 GLOUCESTER A424
Flanesford ⑥ A40 A40
Flaxley A417
WALES A46 Leonard Cirencester
Tintern Stanley A361 A420
Horsley A419
M5 Kingswood A429
M4 A46 Swindon
Malmesbury M4 Poughley
Kington St Michael Bradenstoke A419
BRISTOL ⑧ Chippenham A345 A4
Barrow A4 Lacock ②
Gurney A37 Marlborough
M5 BATH Monkton
A38 Farleigh
Woodspring Hinton Edington
A39 A367
A361 Witham A36 A303
Glastonbury Bruton A338
A38 Stavordale Salisbury A30
Taunton A37 Mottisfont
A361 Shaftesbury ②
M5 Ivychurch A36 Romsey
Muchelney ② Ilchester A30
Montacute Sherborne A354 Cranborne A31 Southampton
Dunkeswell Horton Beaulieu
Forde Cerne A338
Honiton A37 A31
A30 Milton A35 Christchurch
Newenham A35 Dorchester Bindon Bournemouth
Abbotsbury

0 10 20 30 miles
0 10 20 30 40 50 km

41

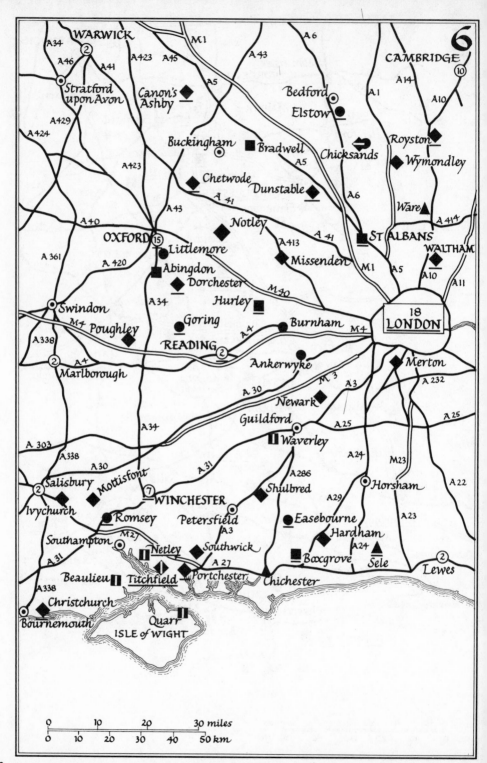

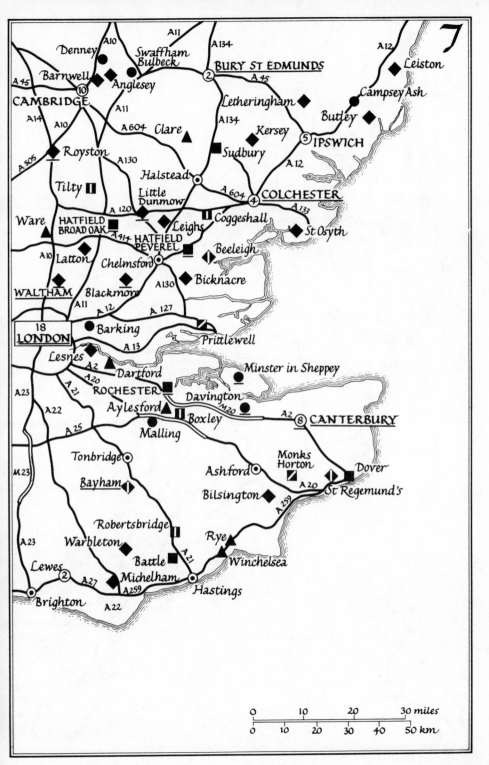

7

Denney
A10
Swaffham
Bulbeck
A11
A134
A12
Leiston
Barnwell
A45
Anglesey
BURY ST EDMUNDS
2
Campsey Ash
CAMBRIDGE
10
A45
Letheringham
Butley
A14
A10
A11
A604
Clare
A134
Kersey
5
IPSWICH
Royston
A505
A130
Sudbury
A12
Tilty
Halstead
A604
4
COLCHESTER
Ware
Little
Dunmow
A120
A133
St Osyth
HATFIELD
BROAD OAK
A414
Leighs
Coggeshall
Latton
A10
HATFIELD
PEVEREL
Beeleigh
WALTHAM
Chelmsford
Bicknacre
Blackmore
A130
A11
A12
A127
Barking
LONDON
18
A13
Prittlewell
Lesnes
A2
Minster in Sheppey
A23
A20
Dartford
ROCHESTER
Davington
A21
Aylesford
A2
8
CANTERBURY
A22
Boxley
A25
Malling
Tonbridge
Monks
Horton
Dover
Bayham
Ashford
A20
St Regemund's
M23
Bilsington
A259
Robertsbridge
A23
Rye
Warbleton
A21
Battle
Winchelsea
Lewes
2
Michelham
A27
A259
Hastings
Brighton
A22

0   10   20   30 miles
0   10   20   30   40   50 km

43

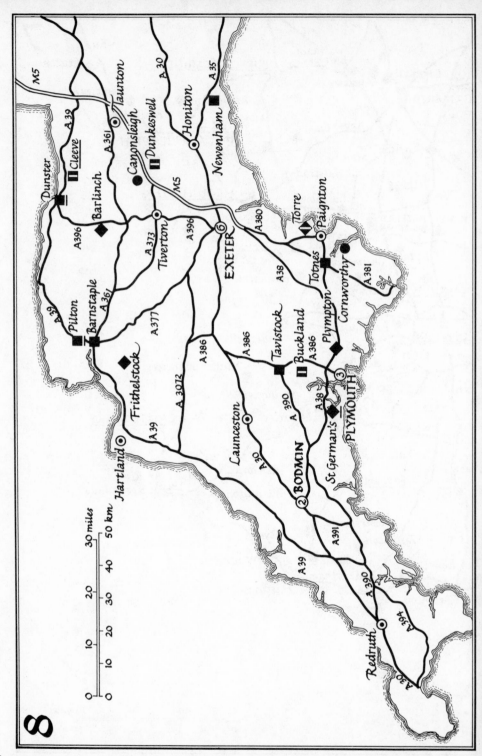

8

44

Gazetteer of Monasteries

Abbey Dore* *Abbey. Herefs. Map 5.*
12m SW of Hereford. (1147–1536).
Cistercian monks. F: Robert de
Ewyas. Ded: St Mary.
Colonised from Morimond. Hardly
anything known of 12thC history. In
13thC colonies were sent to Grace
Dieu (Mon.) 1226, and Darnhall
(*v.* below) 1273. In the latter half of
this century there were several lawsuits. The first 200 years of history
reached its climax and ended with
the death (1346) of the remarkable
Abbot Straddell whose fame long
survived the Dissolution (D. H.
Williams). During its lifetime the
house was often troubled by wars in
the Border country, and in 1371 the
abbey received injuries and violence
from an unnamed source. Abbot
Grisby's rule in the 15thC is one of
the more settled periods, but the rest
of the century was troubled. At the
close of its life the house was 'greatly
in ruin and decay', and little is heard
of the monastery in the 16thC. There
were 2 main sources of income: wool
and timber, and the former was the
highest priced production in England.
There was a valuable library, part of
which still exists including the important Annals of Dore up to 1362.
Remains: Transepts and vaulted aisled
presbytery of 3 bays terminating in
ambulatory – the only Cist. one in
use in England. Nave and all other
bldgs. gone except fragments of one
of the nave's 10 bays. Site excavated
c. 1894. Claustral bldgs. lay N of the
ch. and contained a 12-sided chapter
house. (Tower added in 17thC). Acct.
& plan: Trans. Bristol & Glos. Arch.
Soc. Vol. 27; Hist: The Monmouthshire Antiquary, Vol. 2, pt. 2 (1966)
D. H. Williams. Also Arch. J. Vols. 32
& 34; Br. Arch. Assoc. J. Vol. 27.
* Named after River Dwr.

Abbotsbury *Abbey, Dorset. Map 5.*
10m SE of Bridport. (1044–1539).
Benedictine monks. Fs: Orcus
(steward of K. Canute) and Thola his
wife. Ded: St Peter.
1st. f. *c.* 1026 for secular canons who
were replaced by monks in 1044.
Cartulary lost when a house built on
the abbey site was destroyed in the
Civil War in 1644. In 1268 an inquisition confirmed the numerous rights
and privileges of the abbey. During
the Scottish wars financial aid was
provided, and at the close of the
13thC the monastery provided
hospital facilities for the returning
disabled soldiers. The house later
became burdened with the maintenance of retired royal servants, and in
addition to invaders from the sea and
bad management by several abbots,
the outcome was real poverty in the
14thC. The history of 15thC life here
is extremely scarce. *Remains:* Fdns.

of N wall of ch. (in parish ch'yard); to the S a ruined gable-end of a bldg. probably on the S side of the cloister (care: D of E); remains of outer and inner gatehouses; traces of stewponds; dovecote and magnificent tithe barn (part ruined). Chapel, perhaps a chantry, of St.Catherine $\frac{1}{2}$ m S of village, with fine stone vaultings (care: D of E). Abbey site part excavated 1871 & 1970. Desc: Br. Arch. Assoc. J. Vol. 28. Notes: The Antiquary, Vol. 3. Article: Proc. Dorset N.H. & A.F.C., Vol. 8. Also Med. Arch. Vol. 16 (1971).

Abingdon *Abbey. Berks. Map 6. 7m S of Oxford. (c. 964–1538). Benedictine monks. F: Athelwold, bp. of Winchester. Ded: St Mary.*
1st. f. 675 by Heanus and destroyed by Danes c. 790. Much new bldg. early-12thC by Abbot Faricius. Henry I educated here. Violent thunderstorm in 1265 resulted in bldgs. damaged by fire. Due to financial difficulties in 1318 the king took the abbey under his charge, and in 1327 rioters caused looting and damage estimated at the then enormous sum of £10,000 (VCH). Trials of rioters still in progress 3 years later. Mitred. Very little 15th & 16thC history of interest, but the Chronicle of Abingdon reveals the house as a veritable centre of civilisation upon which the town grew. Controlled 6 hospitals. 6th highest income of Bene. houses at Dissolution. *Remains:* Ch. and claustral bldgs. gone. Site occupied by municipal gardens and offices. Part of gatehouse spans a road (one of the last built by any monastery); the Checker Hall (business office) has the only monastic 13thC chimney stack in England, and the vaulted undercroft contains a 13thC fireplace; 15thC Long Gallery over a stone

undercroft, originally divided into rooms, was probably a guesthouse. A tithe barn at Northcourt now used as a ch. Site excavated 1922. Hist: Antiquity, Vol. 4. Other refs: Archaeologia Vols. 18, 25, 34, 35 & 49. Notes & plan: Med. Arch. Vol. 12 (1968). Book: Monastery of Abingdon (1858) Ed: J. Stevenson.

Aconbury* *Priory. Herefs. Map 5. 4m S of Hereford. (c. 1207–1539). F: Lady Margery, wife of Walter de Lacy. Ded: Holy Cross & St Catherine (now St John, Baptist).*
1st. f. for Sisters of St John with a hospital and changed to Aug. canonesses c. 1235. Ch. built c. 1230–40. Many original deeds and documents exist especially in the B.M. & R.O. which give extensive details of gifts and properties, e.g. the possession of 10 houses in Tetbury (Glos.) and land in Corsham (Wilts.). At the end of the 13thC the prioress made several visits to Goodrich Castle as the guest of the Countess of Pembroke to celebrate religious festivals. In 1354 there occurred a rare instance of an illegitimate nun becoming prioress following a bp's. dispensation. Shortly before suppression Bp. Lee, no lover of monasteries, paid a handsome tribute to the little house when he said: 'where . . . women and children were brought up in virtue and learning' (Baskerville). *Remains:* Priory ch. nave and chancel which are of equal height and width with no chancel arch, aisles or transepts. 15thC wooden porch at W end. Cloister lay on S side of which nothing remains except traces of the W range against ch. wall. The cloister extended beyond present E end of ch. for an unknown distance; E end of ch. may have been longer also. Traces of fishponds in valley. Hist: Woolhope

Naturalist Field Soc. (1885) Trans. also Herefs. Literary, Philosophical & Antiquarian Inst. (1850).
* Originally Acornbury.

Alcester *Abbey/Priory. Warks. 10m W of Stratford-on-Avon. (1140–1536). Benedictine monks. F: Ralph Pincerna. Ded: BVM., St Ann, St Joseph, St John, Baptist & St John, Evangelist*
Also known as 'The Church of Our Lady of the Isle' since it was wholly surrounded by a river and a moat. Small and poor despite fair endowments at the fdn., and subsequent gifts. At a visitation in 1283 some townsmen attacked the archbp. and his servants, pursuing them to the abbey gates. The offenders were excommunicated. In 1335 the abbot was summoned to appear before the king at York on an unknown charge; and in 1366 an injunction ordered better food, no brawlings or wandering beyond the precinct. Only an abbot remained in 1465. In the following year the house became a priory cell dependent upon Evesham, who sent 3 monks to reside at Alcester. *Remains:* None. The area is marked only by earthworks. A mid-17thC record states: 'the very ruins are all digged up and corn sowed where it sometime stood'. Excavations begun in 1938 were abandoned at the outbreak of war. All notes and records were destroyed by bombing.

Aldeby *Priory. Norfolk. Map 4. 7m W of Lowestoft. (c. 1103–1538). Benedictine monks. F: Agnes de Rye. Ded: St Mary.*
Dependent upon Norwich Cath. Priory. The 3 or 4 monks did not have their own ch. but used and maintained the chancel of the parish ch. 12th to 14thC history negligible with only a few refs. to property and burials.

From the 15thC there survives a series of account rolls preserved at Norwich. In 1514 a prior gave a poor account of himself and his house which was then in debt, and 'the gates of the priory and the brewery bldgs. were in a ruinous state'. *Remains:* Some small portions of the conventual bldgs. at one time existed in parts of Priory Farm adjoining the churchyard. Notes: Norfolk Arch. vols 12, 16, 17 & 19.

Alkborough *Priory. Lincs. Map 3. 11m W of Barton-upon-Humber. (1052–1220). Benedictine monks. F: Thorold of Buckenhale. Ded: St John, Baptist.*
The ch. was given to Spalding Priory as a cell for 3 monks. No independent history. Became secular in 1220. *Remains:* The ch. survives with an Anglo Saxon W tower and interior of EE & Dec. styles.

Alnesbourn *(Nacton) Priory/Cell. Suffolk. 5m SE of Ipswich. (c. 1200 to –1514). Augustinian canons. F: Albert de Neville as a priory. Ded: St Mary.*
One of the smallest Aug. houses in the county. Because of impoverishment in the 14thC several chs. were appropriated to the community. In 1424 the canons sold the manor of Hethill to raise funds, but still failing to make ends meet their independence ceased c. 1466, and the house became united with Woodbridge (v. below) as its cell. By 1514 the bldgs. were in complete ruin. *Remains:* None. Priory Farm stands on the site and contains re-used materials.

Alnwick *Abbey. N'land. Map 1. 1m NW of the town. (1147–1539). Premonstratensian canons. F: Eustace Fitz John. Ded: St Mary.*
Colonised from Newsham. Richly endowed. Something of the inner life of

49

the house is reflected in surviving records, especially in respect of its lavish hospitality (Tate). Following the battle of Evesham (1265) it is said that the foot of Simon de Montfort was brought to the abbey by John de Vesci, and became a highly valued relic. In the early-14thC the abbot was summoned to Parliaments on 4 occasions. The refs. to revenues are unfortunately scarce, but it seems that failure of crops and pestilence to livestock brought impoverishment on several occasions. By payment of the large fine of £200 the abbey was permitted to continue beyond 1536. *Remains:* Only the 14thC gatehouse. Site excavated 1884 and the complete ground plan revealed. Main outlines marked in turf including unusual shape of chapter house, almost circular at E end. Accts: Archaeologia Aeliana, NS, Vol. 13 (1889); and Archaeological J. Vols. 41 & 44 with plan (1887).

Alnwick *Carmelite Friary. N'land. See* Hulne.

Alton *Cistercian Abbey. Staffs. See* Cotton.

Alvecote *Priory Warks. Map 3. 2m NW of Polesworth. (1159–1536). Benedictine monks. F: Wm. Burdet. Ded: St Mary.*
Dependent upon Gt Malvern Priory on condition that 2 monks served the ch., and more 'as the capacity of the convent enlarged'. There were few benefactors and the principal temporalities appear to have been a meadow, mill, dovecote and fishing rights. After 2 centuries the ch. and bldgs. were dilapidated. Protection was granted in 1334 and the alms from local chs. given to aid restoration. Remaining history almost a blank. *Remains:* In-

corporated in a farmhouse is a large *c.* 1300 doorway with plain moulding. Fragments of walling exist in a garden, and a 13thC dovecote (Pevsner). A chapel, once the property of the priory but not part of it, is now the small parish ch. of St Matthew.

Alvingham *Priory. Lincs. Map 4. 4m NE of Louth. (c. 1148–1538). Gilbertine canons & nuns. F: unknown (3 possible names – William de Friston; Hugh de Scotene; or Hamelin the Dean). Ded: St Mary.*
Interesting history; cartulary lists over 100 charters and the roll of benefactors is considerable, especially the de Mensa family (Graham). The house had a pact with Louth Abbey in 1174 concerning the use of land. In 1448 the prior claimed the community could not maintain its standard of hospitality because of floods, sterile land, pestilence among livestock and 'other sinister events of the past'. In 1465 the prior was given benefits to offset his heavy losses. Two chs. existed within the priory's precinct, i.e. the parish ch. of St Adelwold (a unique dedication) and the priory ch., both of which still exist in the same churchyard. *Remains:* St Mary's is now the parish ch. of N. Cockerington comprising a nave of 2 bays and a chancel. The tower is 18thC. No other bldgs. exist but extensive earthworks mark the fdns. of the 2 cloisters of this double monastery, and the depressions of the stewponds. (A mansion which once occupied part of the site has now gone).

Amesbury *Abbey/Alien Priory/Priory. Wilts. 8m N of Salisbury. (980–1539). Benedictine nuns. F: Alfrida (Q. Dowager of K. Edgar) as an abbey. Ded: St Mary & St Melor*.*

No cartulary but considerable history exists. Due to complaints about the abbess and nuns in 1177, all were dispersed and the convent reconstituted by Henry II as an alien priory cell of Fontevrault (Anjou) with 24 nuns from there. By the 14thC the numbers had increased to 117 plus staff. Henry III made 4 visits to the house and the royal link was strengthened in 1233 when his cousin Alpesia became a nun. His widow, Q. Eleanor, mother of Edward I, also became a nun and was buried here in 1291. In the 13thC numerous gifts enabled 100 nuns to be supported in the early-14thC. Became denizen *c.* 1486. Of domestic life little is known during the last 140 years, and nothing suggests that the spiritual and moral character of the house was anything but satisfactory. In 1527 the nuns lost the patronage of Poughley Priory. Considerable history in VCH. *Remains:* None. A mansion (mainly 19thC) occupies the site and the exact location of the ch. is still unknown. Building operations in 1840 exposed a few tiles. (There is a theory that the present parish ch., monastic in character, was used by chaplains and lay-brothers attached to the nunnery – Knowles).
* Cornish saint.

Anglesey *Priory. Cambs. Map 4. 6m NE of Cambridge at Lode. (c. 1212–1536). Augustinian canons. F: perhaps Richard de Clare, Earl of Gloucester. Ded: St Mary & St Nicholas.*
1st f. as a hospital. No cartulary traced. Bldgs. erected 1218–36 and the conversion to an Aug. priory achieved by Master Laurence, a papal chaplain of the ch. of St Nicholas. He gave the community land, money, 600 sheep and virtually all the monastic bldgs. (VCH). Considerable information in VCH about grants, gifts and leases. Benefactors were numerous. In 1281 the prior was charged with extravagance and resigned. The house had a valuable library. In 1335 the patron, Lady Elizabeth de Clare, fd. a chantry at the priory and in 1338 re-f. University Hall as Clare Hall (renamed Clare Coll., 1856) in Cambridge. Mid-15thC patron was Richard, Duke of York, and in 16thC Q. Catherine of Aragon. Exact date of surrender unknown. *Remains:* Chapter house and dormitory converted into a house early 17thC. In front, beneath the lawn, aerial photography has revealed the plan of the ch. Fishponds and drainage ditches survive. Note: Med. Arch., Vol. 8 (1964). (N.T.)

Ankerwyke *Priory. Bucks. Map 6. 2½m NW of Staines (at Wraysbury). (c. 1160–1536). Benedictine nuns. F: Gilbert de Mountfitchet. Ded: St Mary Magdalene.*
Nothing known of external life but no doubt the house provided aid for the neighbourhood. Internal history reveals lapses in standards. In 1197 a runaway nun, who had wearied of the cloistered life, gave endless trouble. Apostasy was recorded in 1382 and in 1442 the nuns had numerous complaints, though many were undoubtedly of a trivial nature. The prioress was ordered to consult the sisters about disposal of property. Finally in 1519 two nuns were guilty of apostasy. At the closure the revenues were given to the new fdn. at Bisham (*v.* below). *Remains:* In the grounds of Ankerwyke House (1805) are 3 lengths of priory walling in one of which are 3 windows (one 13thC). Hist: Berks., Bucks. & Oxon

51

Arch. Soc. Vol. 29, (1925). Note: Archaeologia, Vol. 38.

Appleby *Friary. Westmorland. 13m SE of Penrith. (1281–1539). Carmelite. Fs: Lords Vesey, Clifford & Percy. Ded: BVM.*
Edward I occasionally stayed here and acknowledged his hospitality with alms and food. According to wardrobe accounts of the first three Edwards they gave many gifts and offerings to the friary (VCH). The community also benefited from wills. Very few names of friars who lived here have survived. The bldgs. were modest and following the Dissolution they fell into ruin and were quickly robbed of stone. *Remains:* None. The name and site have disappeared. In Battle Barrow is a house named The Friary; and part of a 14thC window head in a barn is perhaps from the monastery.

Arbury *Priory. Warks. 4m SW of Nuneaton. (+1154 to 1536). Augustinian canons. F: Ralph de Sudley. Ded: BVM.*
At first the community pretended to be of the Order of Arrouaise (Picardy), and in 1235 the 5 canons were leading a dissolute life. The pope, through the bp., ordered the establishment of an Aug. house. The original endowments were extensive with further gifts in the 14thC. In 1413 the canons made considerable land purchases in the Nuneaton area. At one visitation the bp. ordered proper accounts to be kept; better food to be provided in the infirmary; and the common seal to be kept under lock and key. *Remains:* None. An Elizabethan mansion occupies the site.

Arden *Priory. Yorks. NR. 5m N of Thirsk. (c. 1147–1536). Benedictine*

nuns. *F: Peter de Hutton. Ded: St Andrew.*
Apart from a dispute with the monks of Byland which was settled in 1189, nothing more is heard of the nuns between the fdn. and 1302. In that year the affairs of the house were put in the care of a canon of Newburgh owing to a sick and enfeebled prioress. Several records of visitations exist and one of 1396 refers to much criticism of a prioress, who was probably deposed. This small and poor house suffered from inadequate endowments, mismanagement and overrecruitment. There was an image of St Bride which, it was claimed, could 'heal sick cows and recover lost ones' (Power). *Remains:* Arden Hall (at Hawnby, 1m NW of the nunnery site) probably contains stone from the priory including a wide chimney breast.

Armathwaite *Priory. C'land (Cumbria). Map 1. 13m N of Penrith. (c. 1200–1537). Benedictine nuns. F: unknown. Ded: St Mary.*
On the strength of a forged charter the house claimed the right of sanctuary; and in 1089 a forged fdn. document attributed K. Rufus as F. The small and poor house suffered deprivation and ruin at the hands of the Scots in 1318, 1331 & 1474. The nuns lost most of their bldgs., books and all the charters and 'evidences'. The house received a number of useful bequests in the 14thC. *Remains:* The approx. site is occupied by a house known as The Nunnery built in 1715 when much of the priory was demolished. A mid-13thC doorway was discovered in the early 1970s in a back wall of the house. Fragments of precinct wall survive.

Arthington *Priory. Yorks. WR. 4m E*

52

*of Otley. (c. 1154–1539). Cluniac
nuns. F: Peter de Arthington. Ded:
St Mary.*
Always small and poor. In 1286
Archbp. Romanus lamented that the
house could not adequately support
the nuns due to a depleted income.
Visitations in 1315 and 1318 resulted
in numerous injunctions including
orders to tend the sick properly;
exhortations to nurture unity, concord and true religion; and that the
prioress should consult the convent
about wool sales, rather than secular
persons who had access to the cloister.
The house, though subordinate to
Cluny, was never treated as alien.
There is a series of unfortunate incidents of wayward members of the
community in the 14th & 15thCs
reported in VCH — almost certainly
instances of young women forced
into, and no doubt entirely unsuited
for, the enclosed life. *Remains:* None.
A house 1m E of the village dated
1585 is called The Nunnery.

Arundel *Priory. Sussex. See* Pynham.

Arundel *Friary. Sussex. (c. 1253–
1538). Dominican. F: unknown. Ded:
unknown.*
Visitation of London. Very little
history known. Earliest mention
1253 when the bp. of Chichester left
the friars 20s. When the bp. of Dover
came to suppress the house in 1538
the 3 friars were too poor to pay even
part of his expenses (Knowles).
Remains: None. The precise location
of the site is uncertain. It is thought
to have been on the N side of Mal-
travers Street.

Ashridge *Priory/College. Herts. 4m N
of Berkhamsted. (1283–1539). Bonshommes. F: Edmund Crouchback,
earl of Cornwall. Ded: Coll. of the*

*Precious Blood (on account of a phial
given by the F. See also* Hailes Abbey.
Edmund's palace was adjacent to his
fdn. (there is no mention of it being
called a monastery — unlike Edington
Priory). The Black Prince was among
the benefactors. After suppression
the property was converted into a
residence for Henry VIII's children. A
priest of Ashridge wrote with bitterness and anger in 1540: '. . . in this
year was beheaded that great heretic
and traitor Thomas Cromwell, who
was the cause of the destruction of all
the religious houses in England.'
Remains: A Gothic-style mansion
built early in the 19thC occupies the
site. The only remnant would seem
to be a 13thC crypt.

Athelney *Abbey. Som. 4m SW of
Bridgwater. (c. 960–1539). Benedictine monks. F: unknown. Ded: St
Peter, St Paul & St Athelwin.*
1st. f. c. 888 by K. Alfred on a site
which had given him refuge from the
Danes, perhaps by enlarging an existing community (Knowles). Early
history obscure and the cartulary is
untraced, but a charter of Alfred
exists. At the time of the Conquest
the house was allied to Glastonbury,
as was Muchelney, in order to resist
direct episcopal visitation. In the
13thC the monks were burdened by
a series of royal pensioners. In 1321
the bldgs. were ruinous; and in 1349
the community was much devastated
by the B.D. By the close of the 15thC
there had been extensive repairs, perhaps even rebuilding. Gasquet quotes*
a documented conversation of 1538
between the abbot and a king's agent
concerning the former's suspicion of
impending suppression. *Remains:*
None. A stone pillar marks the site.
* Henry VIII & the English Monasteries, ii, 301–4.

Atherstone *Friary. Warks. Map 3. 6m NW of Nuneaton. (1375–1538). Austin. F: Ralph, Lord Basset. Ded: St Scholastica (now St Mary).*
The chancel was an independent chapel acquired by the friars in 1375 who added a nave +1383. Virtually no history known about this small house until 1535 when the extent of its poverty is revealed. For almost 300 years after the Dissolution the ch. was used as a grammar school. *Remains:* The chancel of the present parish ch. of St Mary is the original chapel with octagonal tower. New nave and aisles added in 1849.

Axholme *(Epworth) Priory. Lincs. 13m E of Doncaster. (c. 1397–1538). Carthusian monks. F: Thomas Mowbray (later duke of Norfolk). Ded: St Mary.*
Called 'The Priory in the Wood'. Endowments included Monks Kirby Priory. When the F. was banished to Italy in 1398 Monks Kirby was restored to St Nicholas's Abbey, Angers – a serious blow as it formed the major source of income. Finally in 1414 M. K. was restored to Axholme (*v* Alien Priories Appendix). The convent operated a highly successful and profitable agricultural system in the 15thC. Discipline was strictly maintained and the spiritual and moral conditions cannot have been anything but satisfactory to the end. In 1535 the prior was executed for refusing to take the Oath of Supremacy. *Remains:* None. A farmhouse occupies the site. The last fragments survived until the end of the 19thC.

Aylesbury *Friary. Bucks. (1387–1538). Franciscan (Conventual). F: James Butler, earl of Ormond.*
Custody of Oxford. *c.* 1400 a friar was hanged for treason. He had claimed that Richard II was still alive and was confronted by Henry IV on the charge. A mediaeval chronicle records the conversation. Scarcely anything else known. At the Dissolution the house was described as a poor place and in debt, but the ch. was 'well covered with lead over new timber' (Hutton). *Remains:* None. A house named The Friarage occupies the site. Along Friarage Passage are some remnants of the friary's walls.

Aylesford *Friary. Kent. Map 7. 3m N of Maidstone. (1242–1538). Carmelite. F: Richard de Grey. Ded: The Assumption of the Virgin.*
Distinction of London. 2nd house of the Order fd. in England (*v.* Hulne). Early endowments proved inadequate to complete the ch. When the first prior resigned, St Simon Stock was elected who later became prior general of the Order. Bequests and grants of land resulted in a new ch. being ded. in 1417. Numerous small sums of money and bequests given to the friars in the 14th & 15thCs. (VCH). Shortly before the Dissolution two bogus 'commissioners' induced the friars to sell their possessions, most of which had gone when the king's agents arrived to take surrender of the house. *Remains:* The S & W ranges of the claustral bldgs. became a country house. The large outer gatehouse, an inner gatehouse and a guesthouse also survive. In 1949 the whole site was purchased by the Carmelite Friars who have re-established the ancient bldgs. and added others, including the ch. It is the mother house of the Order throughout the world. Desc. & plan: Archaeologia Cantiana, Vol. 80 (1965).

B

Babwell *Franciscan Friary. Suffolk.*
See Bury St Edmunds.

Bamburgh *Priory Cell. N'land. Map 1.*
On coast 15m SE of Berwick.
(c. 1121–c. 1537). Augustinian
canons. F: Henry I gave the ch. to
Nostell Priory. Ded: St Aidan.
There is no evidence of direct personal connection between Nostell
and Bamburgh ch. before 1175.
After the death of a secular rector
the canons built a choir with a crypt
on to the ch. which is still the loveliest part of the bldg. The nave
remained parochial. The estates were
numerous and wealthy in the 13thC
and it is clear that Nostell relied
heavily on the revenues of its cell;
so much so that when the property
suffered severely from Scottish raids
in 1297, the servants at Nostell could
not be paid and tumult resulted.
Nostell remained in low water for
15 years having received no profits
from Bamburgh. The priory had a
powerful neighbour in the castle,
which had both advantages and
drawbacks, because it lay deep in
the inner ward. *Remains:* Chancel
and remarkable crypt of the canons'
ch. Nothing survives of the claustral
bldgs. which lay to the NE. In the
castle is a chapel, no doubt linked
with the early Aug. canons.

Bamburgh *Friary. N'land. Location*
as above. (c. 1265–1539). Domini-
can. F: unknown. Ded: unknown.
Visitation of York. Land and licence
granted by Henry III. The importance
of the town at this time is shown
by the choice of settlement by the
friars. They are mentioned in various
documents and wills in the 13th &

14thCs. Friar John hid certain ecclesiastical possessions when a Scottish
invasion was expected in 1330, and
was loath to part with them when the
danger had passed. In 1450 a monk
of Durham became a Black Friar at
Berwick after failing to be received at
Bamburgh. He did not heed the warning of the prior of Bamburgh and,
finding he could not stand the discipline, returned to Durham. Very
little else is known as the house did
not hold landed estates and few documents existed. At the Dissolution the
property became a farm. *Remains:*
Site occupied by Friary Farm and
there are some sections of walls probably of the NW corner of the chancel
of the ch.

Bardney *Alien Priory/Abbey. Lincs.*
Map 3. 8½m E of Lincoln. (1087–
1538). Benedictine monks. F: Gilbert
of Ghent. Ded: St Peter, St Paul & St
Oswald.
1st f. *c.* 697 by K. Ethelred of Mercia.
After the murder of his queen the k.
joined the abbey as a monk and later
became abbot. Destroyed by Danes
in 870 and for 200 years the history
is obscure. Gilbert's fdn. as an alien
priory was a cell of Charroux Abbey.
Became an abbey in 1116 and never
obtained independence, but never
achieved first rank due to a series of
poor administrators, lawsuits and
quarrels with the king in the 12th &
13thCs. Mitred. No chronicle has
survived but a transcript of a 13thC
cartulary is in the Lincs. Archives
Office. Visitation records of 1383 &
1435 reveal a slackening of monastic
principles and dissension. Later in the
15thC the standards of observance
improved. Little is known of the
16thC until the outbreak of the Lincolnshire rebellion when 6 monks
were executed in 1537. There is no

proof of their instigation, as alleged, but they apparently joined under compulsion. *Remains:* Except for a few fragments of masonry, only grassy mounds show where the fdns. lie. In 1909–12 the site was fully excavated and many interesting discoveries made and described, with plan, in the Arch. J. Vol. 79 (1922). Also the Lincs. Reports of Assoc. Arch. Soc. Vol. 32.

Barham *(Linton) Friary. Cambs. 12m SE of Cambridge. (c. 1293–1538). Crutched (Holy Cross Friars). F: uncertain, perhaps a member of the de Bures family. Ded: St Margaret.*
In 1293 one of the de Bures fd. a house at Welnetham (*v.* below) and at the same time a chapel at Barham was transferred to the Welnetham friars. It seems they sent a few friars to Barham and established an offshoot. From 1339, the year in which the original deeds were lost, little more is heard of the house. In 1531 there is mention of re-thatching the ch. roof, but nothing about the monastic quarters. *Remains:* None.
Barhan Hall stands on the site 1m SE of Linton. Up to the 18thC the friary retained much of its original form (VCH).

Barking *Abbey. Essex. Map 7. 8m NE of London. (c. 975–1539). Benedictine nuns. F: K. Edgar & St Dunstan. Ded: St Mary & St Ethelburga.*
1st f. *c.* 666 by St Erkenwald (later bp. of London) whose sister St Ethelburga became first abbess. Destroyed by Danes in 870 and remained derelict until *c.* 975, when a nun from Wilton became abbess. In 1377 there was serious loss and devastation when the abbey was inundated by the Thames. The abbess had precedence over other abbesses (there were 3) and as a baroness, was required to provide men-at-arms for Henry III and Edward I. Abbey was third wealthiest nunnery and the abbey ch. (bigger than Rochester Cath.-Priory) was the largest and most splendid of any nunnery in mediaeval England. Cloister lay to the N. Amongst abbesses were 3 queens and 2 princesses. The abbey charter laid down in much detail the duties of some obedientaries. The present parish ch. of St Margaret stood within the abbey precinct, and the nuns permitted the parishioners use of the Curfew Gatehouse bell. *Remains:* Hardly a vestige. Site excavated in 1910 and the fdn. lines are now clearly marked with stone in grass. The one remnant is the Curfew Gatehouse, also known as the Fire Bell Tower. An area just N of the frater was investigated in 1970 which disclosed a few wall fdns. (Med. Arch. Vol. 16, 1971).

Barlinch *Priory. Som. Map 8. 1m NW of Dulverton. (+1174–c. 1537). Augustinian canons. F: Wm. de Say (?). Ded: St Nicholas.*
In the 13thC the canons received grants of manors and advowsons of chs. which later proved inadequate as revealed by 14thC records of poverty. Almost nothing is known of internal history apart from elections of priors. Income was aided in the 15thC by a grant to hold 2 fairs a year — at least a mile from the priory. *Remains:* Scanty. Too small to identify. One length of wall, with buttresses and remains of window surrounds, stands alone. A farm occupies the site and a barn wall contains mediaeval window tracery.

Barlings *(Oxeney) Abbey. Lincs. 6m NE of Lincoln. (1154–1537). Premonstratensian canons. F: Ralph de*

Haya. Ded: St Mary.
Original site at Barlings Grange but
soon moved a short distance to island
of Oxeney. Little known of internal
history until end of 15thC when the
house seems to have been of good
standing. In 1210 benefactors doubled
the size of the possessions and sub-
stantially increased the endowments
(Colvin). In 1343 Edward III and Q.
Philippa aided ch. re-bldg. and relieved
the community of tithes (VCH). The
revenues in 1412 were insufficient to
support the 27 canons, but by the
end of the 15thC prosperity had
returned and the abbot was praised
for his administration. Although there
is no shred of evidence that the abbot
had any connection with the murder
of the chancellor during the Lincolnshire Rebellion, he and 6 of his
canons were hanged in 1537 for providing the rebels with victuals
(Gasquet). *Remains:* Almost total
loss. The sole monument is a part of
the N wall of the nave W of the NW
corner of the crossing; also some
carved remnants in a nearby cottage.
Mounds and depressions in the
ground are abundant. The site has not
been excavated.

Barnard Castle *Friary. Durham. 16m
W of Darlington. (1381–c. 1387).*
Austin Friars. F: unknown. Thos.
Beauchamp, earl of Warwick, gave
land. Ded: unknown. Limit of York.
A licence was issued by Archbp.
Neville of York in 1381 and a ch. was
very probably built, but it could not
have lasted long. *Remains:* None. An
old bldg. on the E side of Thorngate
'which had the appearance of a
religious house' existed until *c.* 1900
(VCH).

Barnoldswick *Abbey. Yorks. WR. 8m
SW of Skipton. (1147–1152). Cister-*

*cian monks. F: Henry de Lacy. Ded:
St Mary.*
Colonised from Fountains. The early
establishment suffered from robbers,
poor land and a bleak site, and in 5
years the monks moved to Kirkstall.
Remains: None. The site is covered
by a modern housing estate. The land
remained a grange of Kirkstall and
evidence of a few mediaeval boundary
banks can still be traced W of the city.

Barnstaple *Alien Priory/Priory.
Devon. Map 8. (c. 1107–1536).
Cluniac monks. F: Joel de Totnes.
Ded: St Mary Magdalen.*
Subordinate to the priory of St
Martin-des-Champs, Paris. In 1332 a
prior resigned following 'a scandalous
neglect of duty'. During the wars with
France the revenues were frequently
seized. Became denizen in 1403 on
payment of a fine of 160 marks and
was saved by its 'independent character'. The prior of St James, Exeter,
visited the house in 1420 & 1428 on
behalf of St Martin-des-Champs, even
though the connection had been
severed earlier. Very little history
seems to have survived. A list of most
of the priors and something of their
lives is recorded by Oliver. *Remains:*
Some parts of the ch. are incorporated
in a residence about ½m from the
parish ch. near Boutport Street. The
conversion is referred to in 1882 by
J. R. Chanter in his History of St
Peter's Ch., Barnstaple.

Barnwell *Priory. Cambs. Map 4. 2m
NE of Cambridge. (1112–1538).
Augustinian canons. F: Pain Peverel.
Ded: St Giles & St Andrew.*
1st. f. *c.* 1092 by Picot, sheriff of
Cambs. and Hugoline his wife, (on the
site of a deserted hermitage – Dickin-
son). After their deaths their son,
Robert, fled the country for conspir-

57

acy against Henry I and the house was reduced to poverty. When the F. rescued the community, he moved them from near the castle in the town to Barnwell. Ch. was 96 years being built, though consecrated 79 years after fdn. Conventual bldgs. completed *c.* 1265. In 1287 lightning set fire to the ch. and spread to nearby houses. Income in the 13th & 14thCs enabled considerable bldg. work to proceed including an almonry which cared for 5 poor men and housed a boys school. Considerable history in VCH. *Remains:* Very little. The chapel-by-the-gate is now St Andrews-the-Less ch. Also a 13thC fragment survives at the NW angle of the cloister. Abbey House in Abbey Road, built 1674, contains priory materials as does Corpus Christi Coll. Excavated 1810—12 & 1886. Desc. & plan: Cambs. Arch. Soc. Collns. Vol. 7, 223—49. Book: The Observances in Use at the Aug. Priory of Barnwell (1897) J. Willis Clark.

Barrow Gurney *(Minchinbarrow) Priory. Som. Map 5. 5m SW of Bristol. (−1212 to 1536). Benedictine nuns. F: a member of the Gurney family. Ded: St Mary & St Edward, K.&Martyr.* Documented history is brief. The nuns came from good families but were not exempt from worldly interests. In 1315 a custodian was appointed to administer the temporalities and order a return to a more disciplined life by the community. In 1410 an aged prioress sought to resign and, assuming her plea would be granted, prematurely relinquished her duties. A somewhat unsympathetic bp. ordered her to return to regular observances 'as neglect would endanger her soul's welfare'. From 1460 to the Dissolution the history is blank. *Remains:* Although the parish

ch. has been rebuilt, the S aisle is probably the original nuns' ch. (L.G.) A manor house occupies the site.

Barton *Priory. I.o.W. 2½m SE of Cowes. (1275—1439). Augustinian canons. Fs: The rectors of Shalfleet & Godshill. Ded: Holy Trinity.* Not a normal priory. It contained a prior, 5 chaplains and a clerk, all of whom followed the Aug. Rule and wore a special habit of either black or blue (Knowles & VCH). The constitution of the community is preserved in the Winchester registers of 1289 which lays down 15 rules to be observed. The history is one of neglect and in 1403 a commission was appointed to enquire into the troubles. The house was covenanted in 1439 to Winchester Coll. *Remains:* None.

Baswich *(St Thomas by Stafford) Priory. Staffs. 2m SE of Stafford. (c. 1173—1538). Augustinian canons. F: Gerard fitz Brian. Ded: St Thomas.* Part colonised from Darley. VCH gives considerable detail of properties and benefactions, which were numerous at the end of the 12thC. The Earl of Derby gave generously in the 13thC and the house became wealthy by Aug. standards. But this led to a breakdown in discipline, needless expense and waste in 1347, for which the prior resigned. Little is known of the history during the last 100 years of the priory's existence. Final visitations in 1518 & 1524 reveal a house well ruled and the prior praised by the canons for his skills. A 15thC custumal (book of rituals for a religious community), once the property of the priory, survives. The house delayed suppression in 1536 by paying the large fine of £133.6.8d. *Remains:* Part of the ch. exists in a 13thC length of walling on the N side of Priory Farm. The farmhouse probably contains rooms which were part of the W claustral range. The S wall of the S range of the cloister also survives. Notes & plan: Trans. N. Staffs. Naturalist Field Club, 1879, Book: The Black Canons of Stafford (1931) Lionel Lambert.

Bath *Abbey/Cathedral Priory. Som. Map 5. (1090–1539). Benedictine monks. F: Bp. John de Villula. Ded: St Peter (& St Paul added later).*
1st. fd. *c.* 676 for nuns. *c.* 758 monks replaced nuns, the abbey probably being destroyed later by Danes. Re-f. *c.* 963 and sacked by Robert de Mowbray 1087. All pre-Conquest history obscure. William I appointed the F. 1088 who then began a new ch. with a fresh community, probably Frenchmen like himself. He chose a monk, also named John, as first prior. Soon afterwards Dunster Priory became a dependency. In 1107 became a Cath-Pr. Badly damaged by fire in 1137. 12thC a period of great influence and in early 13thC the convent acquired 3 Irish dependencies. 14th & 15thC historical records name priors who wasted revenues, and one who was unsuccessful in his efforts to secure the use of the mitre. In 1348 more than half of the monks died of the B.D. By 1476 the discipline was lax and the bldgs. dilapidated. In 1499 a new ch. was begun which occupied only the area of the nave of its predecessor. Conventual bldgs. probably never begun. Amongst a number of refs. to priors the last is perhaps the saddest. Wm. Holleway was renowned for his learning and at the Dissolution he is said to have hidden his notes and equipment on alchemy in a wall. Discovering later that they had been stolen he lost his reason, became blind and wandered the country led by a boy (VCH). *Remains:* The fine 16thC ch., completed in the 17thC, is what is seen today but considerably restored 1864–74. Of the Norman ch. only an arch and a column survive at the E end the S chancel aisle. W front noted for the remarkable reproduction of Jacob's Ladder. Nothing else survives. Book: An Account of the Priory of St Peter & St Paul, Bath (1893) Rev. W. Hunt. Illus: Pitkin Pictorial.

Battle *Abbey. Sussex. Map 7. 6m NW of Hastings. (1067–1538). Benedictine monks. F: William I. Ded: St Martin.*
Colonised from Marmoutier, Normandy. 1st. monastery fd. after Conquest. The community was granted exceptional privileges, including that of sanctuary and freedom from episcopal control; and owned widespread estates from Essex to Devon and 2 dependencies in S Wales. There were several exceptional administrators among the abbots, notably Odo (1175–1200) — a man of great piety and learning who had been prior of Canterbury Cath.-Pr. Henry III visited the abbey en route to challenge the barons at the Battle of Lewes in 1264. He and his son were defeated and returned to Battle Abbey 'humiliated and harmless'. Mitred *c.* 1320. The long history shows mainly an even tenor of regular observance of the Rule. Despite Layton's libellous remarks to Cromwell in 1535, the latter attached little value to his words and the house was undisturbed until 1538. *Remains:* Fine Gatehouse of 1338. Ch. gone but fdns. at E end reveal chevet of 5 chapels. Roofless shell of dorter with large gable and vaulted room beneath S end. Low ruins of reredorter. Refectory and chapter house gone. On W side of cloister 13thC abbot's lodging exists

as nucleus of school bldgs. Some 700 ft. of precinct wall to the N. Excavated 1929. Desc. & plan of Abbot's Lodging: Archaeologia, Vol. 83. Books: 1. Chronicle of Battle Abbey (1851) J. R. Smith. 2. Battle Abbey Roll (1889) Duchess of Cleveland. 3. Battle Abbey under 39 Kings (1937) Lilian Boys Behrens. Other refs: Antiquity, Vols. 3 & 9.

Baxterwood *Priory. Durham. 1½m W of Durham. (c. 1180–c. 1196). Augustinian canons. F: Henry Pudsey. Ded: St Mary.*
Because the priory was so near the Benedictine abbey of Durham, the F. granted his endowments to Finchale Priory (*v.* below) and the house was abandoned, probably before any bldgs. were begun. *Remains:* None.

Bayham *Abbey. Sussex. Map 7. 4½m SE of Tunbridge Wells. (c. 1208–1525). Premonstratensian canons. F: Robert de Thornham. Ded: BVM.*
Earlier, *c.* 1180, fdns. at Otham and Brockley (*v.* below) had proved unsuitable and the 2 houses joined at Bayham *c.* 1208. Perhaps to avoid rival claims to paternity the abbey was considered a daughter house of Prémontré (Colvin). Long history of a legal dispute over the advowson of Hailsham ch. between the abbot and the prior of Michelham which lasted 1229–96. Towards the end of the 13thC the ch. was enlarged with an unusually elaborate, and 2 unique, eastern transepts. Few details known of inner history. In 1305 3 canons were arrested for rebellion and in 1315 an abbot was forced to resign. In 1408 the bldgs. were said to be 'in utter ruin'. The good control of temporal affairs was offset by slackness in spiritual matters in 1491, but by 1497 there was nothing but praise

from the visiting bp. for the excellent management of the abbot. Suppressed for Wolsey's Oxford Coll. in 1525. Local men tried to reinstate canons and defend against closure, but to no avail. *Remains:* Full length of the ch. visible with finely-detailed masonry of transepts almost to full height. On S side of nave 3 large window openings. Parts of E & S claustral ranges survive including chapter house. Ruins of gatehouse. Desc. plan & care: D of E. Desc. & plan: The Builder, July 3, 1897. Acct: Br. Arch. Assoc. J. Vol. 30. Also Arch. J. Vol. 62 (1905) and Sussex Arch. Collns. Vol. 9.

Baysdale *Priory. Yorks. NR. 6m SE of Guisborough. (c. 1189–1539). Cistercian nuns. F: Guido de Boving-court. Ded: St Mary.*
1st f. at Hutton (*v.* below) by Ralph de Neville *c.* 1162 who moved the nuns to Nunthorpe *c.* 1167. The F. brought the community to Baysdale and gave them meadows, woodland, pasture and a mountain ridge. In 1304 a custodian was appointed to deal with the temporal affairs. Injunctions following a visitation throw little light upon internal life, but inquiries into irregularities between 1343–5 reveal an unhappy house. From mid-14thC to 1524 little is known, but in that year the nuns were suffering under a singularly bad prioress (VCH), one of a series of unsuitable heads of the nunnery. *Remains:* None. A house occupies the site.

Beadlow *Priory. Beds. 4½m E of Ampthill. (c. 1143–1435). Benedictine monks. F: Henry d'Albini. Ded: St Mary Magdalen.*
This fdn. was soon joined with a small cell at Millbrook (*v.* below), both of which belonged to St Albans Abbey,

Bayham Abbey, Sussex. North transept and north-east pier of the east crossing.

There was a history of poverty which reached a point where the house could no longer support even 2 monks, and it was finally abandoned in 1435. *Remains:* A farm occupies the site. The last vestiges were grass-covered humps & ditches. Some fdn. walls were traced and destroyed: Note: Antiquity, Vol. 10 (1914).

Beauchief* *Abbey. Yorks. WR. (v. Derbys. VCH). Map 3. SW suburb of Sheffield. (c. 1175–1537). Premonstratensian canons. F: Robert Fitz-Ranulph. Ded: BVM & St Thomas, Martyr.*
Dependency of Welbeck. Much of history lost when archives destroyed or secreted at Dissolution, but an early-15thC general cartulary survives which contains copies of numerous private deeds and benefactions. A relatively small house though wealthy, in its heyday, in proportion to its size. Though not subject to diocesan visitations, many records of them survive in the Bodleian. In 1462 the abbots of Shap & Welbeck with the prior of Easby visited the house after hearing of irregularities and promptly deposed Abbot Downham 'for notorious crimes' (VCH). Downham's resistance earned him the greater excommunication. Bp. Redman made a number of visits ending in 1500, and although he made minor orders against the canons, the house was undoubtedly well run. *Remains:* Only the 14thC W tower with E.E. doorway. (Ch. on E side built *c.* 1660). Some walling and reset arches nearby. Many fragments in City Museum and part of the alabaster altarpiece exists at Osberton Manor (Worksop). Excavated 1924–5. Desc. & plans: Trans. Hunter Arch. Soc. Vols. 2 & 3. Paper: Br. Arch. Assoc. J. Vol. 30, 421–30. Books: (1) Hist. of Beauchief Abbey (1801) S. Pegge; (2) Hist. Mem. of Beauchief Abbey (1878) S. O. Addy. * Pronounced Beetchif.

Beaulieu* *(Bellus Locus). Abbey. Hants. Map 6. 7m SE of Lyndhurst. (1204–1538). Cistercian monks. F: K. John. Ded: St Mary.*
1st. f. 1203 at Faringdon (*v.* below). As a royal fdn. the abbey obtained the right of special sanctuary for fugitives. The late fdn. was clearly planned by a Frenchman on the same lines as Clairvaux (Graham). It was colonised from Citeaux. History shows evidence of shrewd administration, numerous acquisitions of property and wool sales to Italian merchants. Despite efforts taken by abbot and monks, the body of the F. was not buried here but at Worcester. B.M. possesses the abbey's account book – the only one of its kind in existence – but only 12 of its 137 pages are complete. *Remains:* Cloister walls on the W side survive with lay-brothers' dorter. On the S side the complete refectory (now parish ch.) with E.E. reader's pulpit approached by an arcaded stair. 13thC gatehouse in use outside while beyond is the Great Gatehouse (Palace House), a private dwelling. Stones from the abbey were taken to Hurst Castle. Fine barn exists at Coxwell (Berks.) once abbey property, with skilfully-engineered timber roof. Excavated 1900–2. Desc. & plan: Arch. J. Vol. 63 (1906). Book: Hist. of Beaulieu Abbey (1911) J. K. Fowler. Illus: Pitkin Pictorial.
* Pronounced Bewli.

Beauvale *Priory. Notts. Map 3. 8m NW of Nottingham. (1343–1539). Carthusian monks. F: Nicholas de Cantilupe. Ded: Holy Trinity, BVM & All Saints.*

Last monastery fd. in the county. Not much internal or external history survives. Late-15thC cartulary contains copies of title deeds, including 10 royal charters, and the privileges enjoyed by the monks are set out in 40 folios. Various manuscripts held in P.R.O. and the Bodleian. c. 1403 the community was granted the small alien grange of Bonby (Lincs). Towards the close of almost 200 years of existence Prior Lawrence suffered an appallingly barbaric death in 1535 for refusing to take the Oath of Supremacy. The community paid a fine of £166.13.4d in 1536 to avoid suppression. When finally dissolved, 2 lay-brothers were still here – unusual at this time. *Remains:* Gatehouse survives as part of farm bldgs. Of the cells surrounding the great cloister, the prior's remains on the S side, now part of the farmhouse. Fragments of ch. walls survive. Excavated 1908. Desc. & plan: Thoroton Soc. Trans. Vol. 12 (1908). Note: Archaeologia, Vol. 13, p. 255.

Bedemans Berg *Priory Cell. Essex. 6m SW of Chelmsford. (−1135 to c. 1536). Benedictine monks. F: Robert, a monk. Ded: unknown.*
Henry II in due course confirmed the possession as a cell of St John's Abbey, Colchester. Very little history known as it had no corporate existence. Its simple privileges included the right to gather nuts in the forest provided 2 monks prayed perpetually for the king's soul. The priors are mentioned in connection with elections of St John's abbots. *Remains:* None.

Bedford *Friary. Beds. (c. 1238−1538). Franciscan. (Conventual). F: Lady Mabel Pateshull. Ded: St Francis.*
Custody of Oxford. Ch. ded. 1295

and Edward I gave oaks for its construction. Site enlarged 1310 with lands given by the nuns of Harrold Priory; and again in 1353 by a gift of 3½ acres. Very little history exists. *Remains:* None. 2 bldgs., the W claustral range and a barn existed until 1899. The site is now covered by a recreation ground, and Grey Friars Walk is the only memory. Desc. & plan: Franciscan Architecture in England (1937) A. R. Martin. Hist. notes: Assoc. Arch. Soc. Vol. 16 (1882).

Bedford *Augustinian canons. See* Newnham.

Bedford *Benedictine nuns. See* Elstow.

Beeding *(Upper) Sussex. See* Sele for 1 Benedictine monks. *See* Sele for 2 Carmelite friars.

Beeleigh *(Maldon) Abbey. Essex. Map 7. 10m E of Chelmsford. (1180−1536). Premonstratensian canons. F: Robert Mantell. Ded: BVM & St Nicholas.*
Colonised from Newsham. 1st. f. −1172 at Great Parndon (*v.* below). In the 13thC there was friction with local friars (*v.* Maldon). It seems an abbot was deposed in 1269 following discord with the canons. 15thC abbots are mentioned in Prémon. records in connection with provincial chapter elections. In 1454 a Prémon. general chapter was held in the Black Friars' ch. at Northampton. Bp. Redman (abbot of Shap) made a number of visitations and found little to reform – 'all things being in good order.' After his last visit in 1500 he reported that 'everything was laudable'. The abbey contained a heart-burial of St Roger, former bp. of London. *Remains:* Mainly the E claustral range

63

incorporating the 13thC chapter house, parlour and warming house with dorter above. Also a small section of the S range with the reredorter site to the S. The whole now a private house. Ch. gone but the plan was possibly similar to Shap Abbey. Desc. & plan: Trans. Essex Arch. Soc. Vol. 16. Book: Beeleigh Abbey (1922) R. C. Fowler & A. W. Clapham.

Beeston *Priory. Norfolk. Map 4. 1m E of Sheringham. (c. 1216–1539). Augustinian canons. F: Isabel de Cressy (?). Margery de Cressy gave endowments. Ded: St Mary.*
Small community which does not seem to have belonged to the main congregation, but to a local Order (Knowles). Early history obscure. In 1317 a canon attacked and wounded a diocesan visitor with a sword, though the reason for the outrage is unknown. In 1494 the visiting bp. found only a prior and one canon living there, while another was absent without leave. Nothing needed correction in 1514 or 1532 but it was still difficult to get the prior to have his accounts presented regularly. Despite low net income (£43) the house survived the suppression of the lesser monasteries, and the canons apparently pretended to be friars in the hope of avoiding closure. *Remains:* The well-preserved flint-built ruins consist mainly of the walls of the ch's. aisleless nave and the chancel; also 2 chapels on the N side of the ch. The garden of a farmhouse occupies the site of the cloister. The range of claustral bldgs. has never been excavated. Hist: Norfolk Arch. vol. 14.

Belvoir* *Priory. Leics. (was Lincs.) 8m W of Grantham. (c. 1076–1539). Benedictine monks. F: Robert de*

Todeni. Ded: St Mary.
A small house belonging to St Albans and with little independent history. Fragments of 13thC cartulary exist. There were many benefactors but evenso there are frequent refs. to poverty and debt. In 1226 a prior was deposed for dissipating ch. goods. At the time of the B.D. Prior Wm. de Belvoir II ruled with exceptional success, and having inherited a large debt against the house, he died leaving it solvent. No records of any serious internal troubles. There is an unusually long list of priors (42) recorded in VCH. *Remains:* None. In 1726 the tomb of the F. was discovered in a part of the ch. then in use as a stable. Site excavated c. 1792. Note: Arch-aeologia, Vol. 17, p. 316.
* Pronounced Beever.

Bemaken *(Arbory) Friary. I.o.M. Map 1. 2½m N of Castletown. (1367–1540). Franciscan (Conventual). F: Wm. Montague, earl of Salisbury. Ded: St Francis (?).*
The community came from Ireland and the ch. was consecrated in 1373 as 'the only place of that Order in the diocese of Sodor'. Very little history known. The fdn. was authorised in 1368 by Pope Urban V at a place known as the 'villa' of St Columba. *Remains:* All has gone except the ch. which stands within a group of farm bldgs. It is mainly 14thC and includes a 'Caernarvon arch' similar to others in Rushen Castle, built by the same F.

Bentley *Priory. M'sex. 2½m NE of Stanmore. (1171–c. 1532). Augustinian canons. F: Ranulf de Glanville. Ded: St Mary Magdalen.*
Little is known of the history of this small house. A prior suffered an accidental death in 1248 when he was suffocated by a sack of corn

which fell on him (VCH). The monastery had been leased to St Gregory's Priory, Canterbury, (*v.* below) in the 14thC, and in 1332 three of its canons went to Bentley to enquire into irregularities which had taken place there. Sometime in the late 15thC it seems that St Gregory's no longer maintained a cell here, and Bentley apparently ceased to exist before 1532. *Remains:* None. An 18thC mansion occupies the site.

Berden *Priory. Essex. 7m N of Bishops Stortford. (c. 1214–1536). Augustinian canons. F: a member of the Rochford family. Ded: St John, Evangelist.*
Began life as a hospital fd. at the end of the 12thC (Dickinson). Very small and poor. Destroyed by a devastating fire in which almost all the bldgs, were destroyed. 21 bps. promised indulgences to all who helped in the rebuilding. Apart from some details of temporalities, singularly little seems to be known about the house. *Remains:* None. An Elizabethan house stands on the site.

Bermondsey *Alien Priory/Priory/ Abbey. Surrey. E London in the Tower Bridge Road area. (1082– 1538). Cluniac monks. F: Alwyn Child (an eminent London citizen). Ded: St Saviour.*
In 1089 4 monks from the abbey of La Charité arrived. Innumerable historical events are recorded: e.g. in 1324 Edward II ordered the arrest of the prior and certain monks for giving sanctuary to some supporters of the ill-fated Thomas, earl of Lancaster – beheaded in 1321. In 1373 Edward III appointed the first English prior. Became denizen in 1381 and elevated to abbey in 1399 – the only Cluniac abbey in the U.K. In the 14thC the

community was afflicted with serious famines and pestilences which heavily taxed the resources. Many illustrious persons entertained here but perhaps none more exalted than Q. Katherine, widow of Henry V, in 1436. She died at the abbey a year later. A second queen ended her days here – Elizabeth Woodville, widow of Edward IV and mother of the princes murdered in the Tower. She became a close prisoner and died in the abbey in 1492. The monastic 'Annals of Bermondsey' (a 71-sheet, mid-14thC manuscript in the BM) commences in 1042 and ends in 1432. Sometime before 1450 the monks were granted the alien priory of Aldermanshaw (*v.* Appendix 1). The house was noted for its miraculous Rood. The last abbot received the unusually large pension of £330.6.8d p.a. (equal to about £16,000 in 1977) at the Dissolution. *Remains:* None. Bermondsey House, now gone, was built on the site. Until 1808 the double-towered gatehouse survived. The only memories are Bermondsey Square and a tithe barn near Yeovil, once its property. Excavations on part of the site 1956, 1963 & 1972. Desc: Br. Arch. Assoc. J. 3rd ser., Vol. 2. Also Med. Arch. Vols. 1 & 8. Book: Bermondsey Historic Memories & Associations (1901) E. T. Clarke.

Beverley *Friary. Yorks. ER. Map 3. 8m N of Hull. (c. 1240–1539). Dominican. F: possibly Stephen Goldsmith. Ded: unknown.*
Visitation of York. The fdn. is also claimed by the town and the Crown (VCH). Little history recorded. A fire destroyed the dormitory and library in 1449. Two 14thC manuscripts formerly belonging to the friary are now at Oxford. *Remains:* A stone and brick buttressed bldg. survives in

Friar Street and two brick archways *c.* 1500 also exist. Mediaeval wall paintings are being restored. Site covered partly by the railway (claustral bldgs) and a factory over the ch. area. Part excavated 1960–63. Desc; Yorks. Arch. Soc. J. Vol. 32 (1935). Excav. notes: Med. Arch. Vols. 5–8.

Beverley *Friary. Yorks. ER. Location as above. (c. 1267–1539). Franciscan (Conventual). F: John de Hightmede (?). Ded: St Francis (?).*
Custody of York. Origin obscure but was fd. within the town walls and later moved to a site outside Keldgate on Westwood Green *c.* 1297. The house lay derelict and uninhabited for many years until Sir John Hotham rebuilt it *c.* 1356 and was reckoned the F. The friary was in the midst of the rebellion of 1536 although the friars had taken the Oath of Supremacy in 1534. An Observant friar from another house was undoubtedly the ring-leader. Baskerville writes: 'A Yorkshire gentleman and his wife stayed here when they wanted a change of air'. *Remains:* None. Desc: Yorks. Arch. J. Vol. 32 (1935).

Bicester *Priory. Oxon. 14m NE of Oxford. (1182–1536). Augustinian canons. F: Gilbert Basset. Ded: St Mary & St Eadburga.*
Not much of the early history is known. Prior Robert must have been a man of wisdom and integrity because he was several times chosen as judge-delegate in 1212. In 1300 a prior was said to be too strict, but it may have been necessary as 2 canons fled in 1306 'having proved themselves irreligious' (VCH). 15thC visitations resulted in only minor corrections, such as stricter observance of silence. The house guarded the relics

of the patron saint in the small ch. (74 ft. long). *Remains:* Nothing above ground. Excavations 1964–6 & 1968 revealed much of the ch. fdns. which lie SE of the parish ch. The present Old Priory House on the site almost certainly contains priory materials. Desc: Oxoniensia, Vols. 33 & 34. Med. Arch. Vol. 13.

Bicknacre *(Woodham Ferrers) Priory. Essex. Map 7. 6m SE of Chelmsford. (1175–1507). Augustinian canons. F: Maurice Fitz Geoffrey. Ded: St Mary & St John, Baptist.*
A hermitage before becoming a small and poor priory and the history contains few interesting notices. The endowments included Woodham Ferrers ch. and in 1285 the canons had licence to enclose 60 acres of forest in the area. Only the first prior is referred to as of Woodham, not Bicknacre. Another charter gives the community licence to hunt hare, fox and cat in the forest. In the early-14thC there was sequestration of possessions due to debt. In the 15thC the house fell gradually into decay and there were too few canons to elect the priors without the bp's. aid. When no canons were left, except the prior who died of the plague in 1507, the property became united with St Mary's Hospital-without-Bishopsgate in 1509 (VCH). *Remains:* One lonely arch which stood on the W side of the crossing. It is mid-13thC (Pevsner). Note: Archaeologia, Vol. 11.

Biddlesden *Abbey, Bucks. 6m NW of Buckingham. (1147–1538). Cistercian monks. F: Ernald de Bosco. Ded: St Mary.*
One of 2 houses colonised from Garendon. 16thC cartulary in BM. Never large or wealthy. Little known of internal history. In 1192 an abbot

was deposed for an unknown reason; and in 1280 an abbot complained of trespass and personal injuries at his London home (VCH). Following some years of poverty there was sufficient prosperity in 1392 to enable the community to take over the alien cell of Weedon Lois (v. Appendix I) from the abbey of St Lucien, Beauvais. Escaped suppression in 1536 by raising the large fine of £133.6.8d. At this time self-accusation included a 'pretenced religion' which consisted mainly of 'dumb ceremonies'; and no one came to correct the discord and abuses which existed. *Remains:* None. Considerable ruins survived until 1712 when Biddlesden Park Manor was built on the site.

Bilsington *Priory. Kent. Map 7. 5m W of Hythe. (1253–1536). Augustinian canons. F: John Mansell. Ded: St Mary.*
The priory was given to St Mary's Abbey, Boulogne, in 1272 though this does not seem to have taken effect (VCH). In the early days the F., a counsellor of Henry III, had entertained generously in his newly-built monastery, but in later years its fortunes declined and it became poor. In 1284 the prior was ordered to cease the waste of woods and other possessions. The canons had licence in 1327 to drain, enclose and cultivate a 60-acre salt marsh at Lydd, but in 1337 the site had been reduced by 20 acres owing to high operational costs. According to the fdn. charter the priory was 2 miles from the sea, but today it is more than double that distance. *Remains:* The ch. has gone and its site is uncertain. Some of the claustral bldgs. were incorporated in a house including the infirmary hall, much altered, with an undercroft and 13thC traceried windows. Book: The

Priory of Bilsington (1928) Ed: N. Neilson.

Bindon *Abbey. Dorset. Map 5. 6m W of Wareham. (1172–1539). Cistercian monks. Fs: Roger Newburgh and Matilda his wife. Ded: St Mary.*
Colonised from Forde. 1st. f. on the E side of Lulworth Cove (Knowles). Better lands were given several years later and the community moved in 1172. The Plantagenets were great supporters of the house. Twice the monks were called upon to assist Edward II with finance for the Scottish wars. The 14thC history is one of debt, disorder, dissension and strife with neighbours. In 1329 a mob raided and looted the abbey property. 15thC history is a blank. Suppression was delayed by payment of £300 to the Crown in 1536. *Remains:* The fdns. of the ch. are still *in situ* and the walls of the NW angle of the nave form the highest part of the ruins. Of the E claustral range the sacristy, chapter house and the subvault of the dorter survive. Of the S & W ranges only low fragments of walls of the refectory, kitchen and laybrothers' quarters can be identified. (Considerable portions of the ch. were still standing in 1733). Desc. & plan: Br. Arch. Assoc. J. Vol. 28 (1872).

Binham *Priory. Norfolk. Map 4. 5m SE of Wells-next-the-Sea. (1091– 1539). Benedictine monks. Fs: Peter de Valoines and Albreda his wife. Ded: St Mary.*
One of St Alban's 13 dependencies. In general, the priors were not good administrators and there are several instances of lawsuits. In 1212 a self-claimed patron, a powerful baron, tried to reinstate a deposed prior but was put to flight by the king's men

67

and died abroad. The priory held property in 21 Norfolk parishes. For some years the community had lived in disobedience and insolence, paying no heed to the censures from St Albans. A deposed prior refused to quit and was supported by all the monks. The feud lasted until 1323 when it seems the disturbances were quelled. In 1454 a quarrelsome monk of St Albans hankered after the priorship of Binham which he achieved by promising to rebuild the dormitory. The fine W facade of the ch. with huge window is believed to have contained the first example of bar-tracery in England. *Remains:* Seven of the original 9 bays of the massive Anglianstyle nave remain as the parish ch. Extensive ruins of the crossing, low walls of the presbytery and of all the claustral bldgs. The 13thC gatehouse once contained a porter's lodge and a jail. Care: D of E. Desc. & plan: Arch. J. Vol. 80 (1923). Notes: Archaeologia, Vols. 17 & 33. Desc. Norfolk Arch. Vol. 17.

Birkenhead *Priory. Cheshire. Map 2. (c. 1150–1536). Benedictine monks. F: Hamon de Masci of Dunham. Ded: St James the Great.*
Probably colonised from Chester Abbey from which the community remained independent. There is a marked absence of records, and the few refs. to the house during its life suggest a well-ordered establishment in which no instances of malpractices are known. In 1201 K. John gave the community protection. Edward I twice came to the priory and on the second occasion, in Aug. 1277, he stayed for 5 days and during the same month laid the fdn. stone of Vale Royal Abbey. Edward II visited the community in 1317 and was told by the prior that the resources of the

house were heavily strained by streams of travellers, and in times of storm the guesthouses were crowded with delayed passengers waiting for the ferry. In 1330 the monks owned the ferry and held the rights of revenue. The name Monks Ferry still survives. Even though the monks had extensive lands in the Wirral and considerable dealings in corn at Liverpool market, taxes were often hard to pay due to high hospitality costs.
Remains: The fine Norman chapter house is well preserved and in use as a chapel. Of the rebuilt 13thC ch. (on the S side of the cloister) there is only a W wall of the N transept and part of the W wall of the N aisle of the nave. Fine crypt on N side of cloister which supported the refectory and a guest chamber. The dormitory, sited E–W off the E cloister walk, has gone. W range is late-13thC with ruined guest hall and parlour with prior's lodging over. Excavated c. 1889. Desc. & plan: Trans. of Hist. Soc. of Lancs. & Ches. Vol. 42 (1890). Book: Birkenhead Priory & the River Mersey (1925) R. Stewart-Brown.

Bisham – 1 *Priory. Berks. 1½m S of Marlow. (1337–1537). Augustinian canons. F: Wm. Montacute, earl of Salisbury. Ded: BVM.*
The late fdn. was due to the takeover of a preceptory formerly owned by the Templars (dissolved 1308–12). The canons built to the NE of the preceptory and it became one of the larger monasteries of the Order. Several illustrious members of the Montacute family, including the F. and 3 succeeding earls, were buried in the conventual ch. At the beginning of the 16thC the Cist. abbey of Medmenham (*v.* below) which had been reduced to a community of an

abbot and one monk, was annexed to Bisham. The last prior, a willing tool of Cromwell, surrendered the house when ordered on 5.7.1537. But the fickle king re-established the house on a more lavish scale and fd.: —

Bisham — 2 *Abbey. Berks. Location as above. (1537–1538). Benedictine monks. F: Henry VIII. Ded: St Mary* The abbot and 15 monks from the suppressed Chertsey Abbey (*v.* below) were installed in December, and the possessions of the small nunnery at Ankerwyke (*v.* above) were given to Bisham. But the abbey lasted for exactly 6 months and the second farcical surrender occurred 19.6.1538. *Remains:* None. Adjacent to, and separate from the abbey, stood the F's. house, largely rebuilt in Elizabethan times; and beneath the lawns to the NE of the mansion lie some of the fdns. of the Aug. priory. A mediaeval barn to the S, owned by the canons, is now a private house. A dovecote also survives. Desc. (mainly of the house): Berks. Arch. Soc. J. Vol. 44 (1940).

Blackborough *Priory. Norfolk. Map 4. 5m SE of King's Lynn. (c. 1200–1537). Benedictine nuns. Fs: Roger de Scales and Muriel his wife. Ded: St Mary & St Katherine.* The original fdn. of *c.* 1150, in the Vale of the Nar, was for monks; and nuns joined the house *c.* 1170. It was established as a nunnery *c.* 1200. Little history known. In 1291 the community held property in 25 Norfolk parishes. History is virtually blank in 14th & 15thCs. In 1347 the nuns were relieved of taxes due to poverty. 16thC records of visitations reveal no matters to be corrected and the convent was 'of good name and fame'. *Remains:* Near Priory

Farm is a length of wall and the gable end of a bldg. In 1834 & 1870 excavations revealed burials and pavements (Messent).

Blackmore *Priory. Essex. Map. 7. 7m SW of Chelmsford. (1152/62–1525). Augustinian canons. Fs: Member(s) of the Sanford family. Ded: St Laurence.* Early history obscure. The first record of a visitation seems to be 1309 when the prior and canons were enjoined to keep better discipline and cease from strife and contention (VCH). Little else known. Dissolved for Wolsey's Oxford Coll., later for Ipswich Coll., and finally granted to Waltham Abbey. *Remains:* The nave of the conventual ch. is now the parish ch. with probably the most impressive timber tower in England, *c.* 1480. The chancel and monastic bldgs. have gone and, from blocked doorways in the ch., the cloister presumably lay to the S. Attractive and rare cresset survives. Desc. of timber tower: Arch. J. Vol. 119 (1962).

Blackwose *Priory. Kent. 2m N of Hythe. (c. 1158–c. 1377). Premonstratensian canons. F: unknown. Ded: St Nicholas.* Originally dependent upon Lavendon (*v.* below). Poverty and debts caused the canons to leave the monastery and search for food, to the scandal of the Order (Knowles). The castle of Saltwood lay only 1m to the S and the priory probably came within its feudal territory. The house was not a success due to lack of effective supervision from Lavendon, and *c.* 1203 it was transferred to St Radegund's Abbey (*v.* below), and the property became its grange. Following devastation during a French invasion in 1216 the abbot of St R's repaired the property at his own expense. Lavendon then tried once more to regain its former cell and the dispute was ended in 1223. Nothing more is heard of its existence until the Dissolution: *Remains:* None.

Blakeney *(Snitterley) Friary. Norfolk. Map 4. 9m W of Sheringham. (1304/ 16—1538). Carmelite. Fs: either Sir Wm. & Lady Roos or 3 of their tenants. Ded: BVM.*
Distinction of Norwich. One ref. gives 1295 as the start of bldg. and 1321 as the completion year. In a brief record of history there is an entry about Friar John de Baconthorpe who became Provincial of the English White Friars. In the 14thC the community clearly progressed and enlarged their site several times. Nothing else known. *Remains:* A few arches in a wall, a buttress and window surrounds are incorporated in a house named The Old Friary, N of the parish ch.

Blanchland *Abbey. N'land. Map 1. 13m SSE of Hexham. (1165—1539). Premonstratensian canons. F: Walter de Bolbec. Ded: St Mary.*
History is known for only the early-14thC and the last 50 years or so. Edward III and his army visited the abbey in 1327. Although no battle with the Scots occurred, the campaign caused enormous damage to crops and abbey bldgs., including the ch., and the king came to the canons' rescue with financial help. Visitations by Bp. Redman between 1478 and 1500 reveal difficulties due to the smallness of the community and inadequate income. So remote was the site that the bp. bade the canons visit him at Newcastle. The bldgs. were in poor shape. He ordered the convent to cease deer hunting and paying prolonged calls upon the abbey's tenants.

Even so, the canons are commended for their faithfulness to their calling. This is the only Premon. ch. still in use, and it is unique in that the site of the abbey and its materials now form the entire village, entered through the original gatehouse. *Remains:* Chancel, N transept and a tower now form the parish ch. (No S transept was ever built). Nave gone except for part of S wall. Abbot's lodging, guest house and monastic kitchen are now part of a hotel and occupy the site of the W claustral range. Cottages occupy the site of the refectory to the S. Desc. & plan: Arch. J. Vol. 59 (1902). Hist: History of Northumberland, Vol. 6 (1902) J. C. Hodgson.

Blithbury *Priory Cell. Staffs. 3½m NE of Rugeley. (+1119 to —1315). Benedictine nuns. F: Hugh de Malveysin (or Midware). Ded: St Giles.*
First colonised by 2 monks from Burton Abbey and some nuns, but from 1158—65 the cell was occupied by nuns only. From the end of the 12thC it seems that a close link existed between the community and the Black Ladies of Brewood (*v.* below), and that by the early 14thC the two became merged. In the 1530s Brewood's largest revenues came from land at Blithbury (VCH). *Remains:* None. Towards the end of the 18thC the last of the bldgs. were demolished. Note: Br. Arch. Assoc. J. Vol. 29.

Blyth *Alien Priory/Priory. Notts. Map 3. 12m S of Doncaster. (1088— 1536). Benedictine monks. F: Roger de Builli. Ded: St Mary.*
First colonised by monks from Holy Trinity Abbey, Rouen. As the house lay close to a busy highway it suffered heavy hospitality costs for wayfarers, and early in the 14thC a visit

by Edward II and his entourage proved so expensive that the house was brought to the brink of ruin. Several unruly French monks were returned to Rouen at different times. After the priory became denizen c. 1409 the king claimed the patronage. Subsequent hist. is mainly a record of the election of priors, some of whom came from St Mary's Abbey, York. *Remains:* The ch. owes its survival to the widening of the S aisle of the nave c. 1290 for parochial use, and is now the parish ch. comprising 5 bays of the original 7-bay nave, and W tower of c. 1400. The crossing, transepts, chancel (which had 3 apses) and the monastic bldgs. have gone. The N & E sides of the ch. lie in private grounds.

Blythburgh *Priory. Suffolk. 4m W of Southwold. (c. 1130–1537). Augustinian canons. F: Abbot and canons of St Osyth's Abbey. Ded: St Mary.* Henry I gave the ch. to the canons. The house achieved only partial independence from the mother house and never obtained the right of self-government. The prior was of some importance in 1217 because he, and the abbots of Sibton & Leiston, went to Lincoln to inquire into the conduct of the archdeacon there. The house was small with rarely more than 4 canons, and although the benefactions were considerable, the revenues were surprisingly small. The B.D. and incursions of the sea caused great hardship. An early-16thC visitation revealed that the chapter house had collapsed and that a chapel in the ch. was in use as a substitute. Wolsey obtained a papal Bull for its suppression for his Ipswich Coll., but this did not take effect. *Remains:* Very little. In a garden of a house NE of the parish ch. are scanty traces. Site excavated c. 1850–60.

Bodmin *Priory. Cornwall. Map 8. (c. 1124–1539). Augustinian canons. Fs: Wm. Warelwast, bp. of Exeter & Algar, dean of Coutances. Ded: St Mary & St Petroc.* Some 180 years earlier a Benedictine monastery had been fd. here by K. Athelstan, later destroyed by the Danes. The great Collegiate ch. which followed was taken over by canons from Merton led by Master Guy who had been recalled from Taunton Priory (*v.* below); and the dean and several secular canons joined the Aug. community. The house was large, well-endowed and wealthy with some of its revenues coming from investments in tin mines. In 1312 an affray in the ch. between a canon and a secular priest resulted in bloodshed. For 2 years services and interments continued in the desecrated house as if nothing had happened. The prior's lax rule was blamed. Between 1435–62 Prior Oliver was a generous benefactor to his house. The priory was famous for its shrine with a casket containing St Petroc's relics. The reliquary still exists. *Remains:* Very little. Near the parish ch. are some fragments of masonry and parts of columns. The site has not apparently been excavated.

Bodmin *Friary. Cornwall. (–1260 to 1538). Franciscan (Conventual). F: John FitzRalph. Ded: St Nicholas.* The origin of the fdn. is obscure. The earls of Cornwall were patrons. Refs. to dedication of the ch. in 1352 suggests rebldg. after the B.D. which was particularly severe in Bodmin. About this time it seems the house was a well-known seat of learning (Martin). The friary stood on the S side of the town. Not much is known of its history. *Remains:* Very little. Some fragments exist in shops in Fore

Bolton Priory, Yorkshire. Nave and north transept from the north-west. The construction of the great tower at the west end was halted by the Dissolution; it would have been three times as high.

Street, the churchyard, and a room in the Assize Courts. The last named occupies the actual site. Until the middle of the last century a notable bldg. (almost certainly the friars' ch.) was standing to the S of Fore Street.

Bolton *Priory* Yorks. WR. Map 2. 6m E of Skipton. (1154–1540). Augustinian canons. Fs: Wm. Meshin & Cecilia de Rumilly his wife. Ded: St Mary & St Cuthbert.*
The original fdn. was at Embsay (*v*. below) and colonised from Huntingdon. The F's. daughter, Alice de Rumilly, translated the canons to Bolton in 1154. They then owned extensive properties from which mining and wool sales enabled the canons to enlarge the priory – a N aisle to the nave in the 13thC and doubling the length of the beautiful presbytery in the 14thC. The nave was always parochial. An interesting entry in an early-14thC Account Roll refers to regular payments to 'the wolf slayers'. Wolves must have been troublesome to the Wharfedale shepherds. Records of injunctions following visitations in the 13th & 14thCs rarely refer to the grosser faults found elsewhere, but slackness and

indiscipline occur in the 1330s. In general the history is uneventful except for plundering by the Scots in the 14thC. *Remains:* Nave in use as the parish ch. with a partially built W tower, halted by the Dissolution. Fine ruins of crossing, transepts and presbytery. Fdns. of claustral bldgs. Part of the infirmary adjacent to the rectory. Gatehouse now the centre-section of Bolton Hall. Desc. & plan: Thoresby Soc. Vol. 30 (1928). Book: Bolton Priory (1924) A. H. Thompson.
* The parish and township is known as Bolton Abbey — not the ruined priory.

Bordesley *Abbey. Worcs. Map 3. ½m NE of Redditch. (1138–1538). Cistercian monks. Fs: Empress Maud and Henry II her son or Waleran de Beaumont, count of Meulan & Worcester, (there is conflict of evidence here – VCH). Ded: St Mary.*
Colonised from Garendon. The abbey received a large number of grants although it was never rich, its possessions were safe. Its income came mainly from wool sales in the 13thC in deals with merchants from Florence. As a royal fdn. the house received numerous privileges from the crown, including freedom from certain tolls, customs and taxes. Although all Cist. monasteries were exempt from any episcopal visitations, Bp. Giffard went to the abbey 5 times, but issued no injunctions. Had there been any cause for complaint it would have been stated, and it would have been certainly no evidence of ill-repute against the house in 1536. After surrender, the house was almost completely dismantled within a fortnight. *Remains:* None. The gatehouse survived until 1807. Since 1968 the University of Birmingham School of History has

excavated the N & S transepts, choir and presbytery of the ch., and the sacristy to the S of the S transept. (*v.* Med. Arch. Vols. 11–21.)

Boston *Friary. Lincs. (1317–1539). Austin. F: unknown (Edward II granted licence). Ded: unknown.*
Limit of Lincoln. There were numerous benefactors in the early days but by the 16thC the house had become 'piteously poor', and readily surrendered to the bp. of Dover. There is no history. *Remains:* None. The site was near St John's Road and the materials probably went into reinforcing the sea walls.

Boston *Friary. Lincs. (1293–1539). Carmelite. F: unknown. Ded: BVM.*
Distinction of York. Bp. Sutton & Master Giffred de Vezano influenced the fdn. of the house. In 1307 the friars moved to the W side of the river to a site given by Wm. de Ros, who has been called the F. During the first half of the 14thC the community received several gifts of land. Three friars attained eminence through their writings. At about the time of the Dissolution Leland noted that the convent owned many books. Not much history known. *Remains:* None. The site lay between West Street and Liquorpond Street.

Boston *Friary. Lincs. Map 4. (–1288 to 1539). Dominican. F: unknown. Ded: unknown.*
Visitation of York. In 1288 a fire swept the town and the friars lost their ch. and refectory (VCH). The history is occasionally stormy. In 1376 at the funeral of the lord of Huntingfield the friars barred the bp. from attendance, and again on the following day when he came to celebrate Mass. In 1376 several rebellious

friars led some 'evil-doers' on an assault of the friary at night. One of the priors, late of Oxford, became head of the Black Friars Schools in London. *Remains:* The shell of the refectory survives having been used as a forge, warehouse, winestore and Baptist meeting house. It is now incorporated in a new theatre. Stonework of other sections of the friary exist in nearby bldgs. (*v.* Med. Arch. Vol. 9, 1965). The site was between Shodfriars Lane and Spain Lane.

Boston *Friary. Lincs. (−1268 to 1539). Franciscan (Conventual). F: unknown. Ded: St Francis.*
Custody of York. In 1268 the friars were charged with theft but the outcome is unknown. *c.* 1354 a sudden inrush of the sea caused the loss of some of the muniments. In 1391 a vagabond friar who had left the community was restored to the house. When an ex-friar of King's Lynn Franciscans was appointed vicar of Boston in 1518, he seems to have steered clear of the Boston Grey Friars. *Remains:* None. A house known as Greyfriars is behind the Grammar School in the SE part of the town. In 1972 the remains of a large stone bldg., aligned N−S, belonging to the friary was discovered. (*v.* Med. Arch. Vol. 18, 1973).

Bourne *Abbey. Lincs. Map 3. 11m NNE of Stamford. (1138−1536). Augustinian canons. F: Baldwin Fitz-Gilbert de Clare. Ded: St Peter & St Paul.*
Colonised from Arrouaise but always an entirely independent house. It was never wealthy nor did it become important although it held abbey status. In the first half of the 14thC a monk, Robert de Brunne, was one of the pioneers in the creation of a standard

English language from the dialects which then existed in the kingdom. In 1401 the small alien cell at Wilsford (Lincs.) which belonged to the great abbey of Bec-Hellouin, Normandy, was granted to Bourne (*v.* Appendix I). Visitations in the 15thC revealed some infringements of the Rule, but compared with other Aug. houses at this time, Bourne was certainly respectable. Nothing is known of 16thC history until the Dissolution. *Remains:* 4 bays of the nave form the parish ch. The crossing, transepts (if any) and the chancel were demolished in 1538. The last named was rebuilt in 1807. The W front was partially rebuilt *c.* 1200 when the SW tower was added − the NW never being completed. No claustral bldgs. survive (which lay to the N) except some blank arcading where the W range joined the ch. (Pevsner).

Boxgrove *Alien Priory/Priory. Sussex. Map 6. 3½m NE of Chichester. (c. 1115−1536). Benedictine monks. F: Robert de Haye. Ded: St Mary & St Blaise*.*
1st. f. pre-Conquest for secular canons and given +1105 by Wm. d'Aubigny to Lessay Abbey, Normandy. When the F. gave land to Lessay, French monks were sent to fd. the priory. 13thC cartulary survives in BM. In 1289 Archbp. Peckham issued a series of injunctions which called upon the canons to observe the Rule more closely. 14thC history negligible. Became denizen 1339. In 1410 the bldgs. were in disrepair but by 1478 the bp. claimed the conditions at the priory were better than at any time during the past 40 years. In the 16thC the house was free of debt. The monks ran a school for 8 children. *Remains:* The perfect 14thC choir survives because at the Dissolution

the parishioners preferred to abandon the nave. It comprises 4 double bays with rare foliage pattern on the vaulting. Transepts unique since each have an upper floor (or ceiling?). One bay remains of the 6 double-bayed nave. The cloister lay to the N and the chapter house entrance survives. To the N is the roofless guest house (A.M.). Desc. & plan: Sussex Arch. Soc. Coll. Vols. 43 & 61.
* Patron saint of woolcombers; martyred in 316.

Boxley *Abbey. Kent. Map 7. 2½m NE of Maidstone. (c. 1146—1538). Cistercian monks. F: William of Ypres. Ded: St Mary.*
Colonised from Clairvaux. Some accounts of the obedientaries survive giving 14th & 15thC household expenses set out in detail. Following a London meeting, the abbots of Boxley, Stratford Langthorne and St Mary Graces made visitations to other Cist. Houses at the pope's request. In 1513 the abbot called for the arrest of '4 rebellious and apostate monks' (VCH). Almost 400 years of history ended dramatically with the exposure of a remotely-controlled image 'miraculously gifted with movement and speech'. The VCH author comments: 'It is probable that the Holy Cross of Grace, for which the abbey was celebrated, did more damage to the case against the monasteries than anything else'. The image was finally burnt in London. *Remains:* Most of the site is occupied by a house. Much of the boundary wall which once enclosed about 17 acres survives. Of the ch. 3 low walls exist which were part of the S transept at the foot of the night stairs. Also an early-14thC tithe barn with 18thC roof. The sites of all 4 cloister walks have been located. Excavated 1952, —59, —66 & —71. Desc. & plan: Arch. Cantiana, Vol. 66 (1953). Notes: Br. Arch. Assoc. J. Vol. 9; and Med. Arch. Vol. 17.

Bradenstoke *Priory. Wilts. Map 5. 9m NE of Chippenham. (c. 1139—1539). Augustinian canons. F: Walter Devereux. Ded: BVM.*
Colonised from Cirencester and obtained its independence between 1184—9. History is sparse and the precise periods of priors' rule can only be dated in 2 cases. The general cartulary, preserved in the BM, is written in a series of 14thC hands. In 1352 Prior Spicer's misdeeds brought misery to the community until he resigned and left England. The subprior who succeeded Spicer was no better, and Bp. Wykeham called him 'that irregular denigrated canon'. But at the time of the Dissolution the spiritual and temporal life is quoted as being well-ordered (VCH). The W claustral range was magnificent and included the prior's lodging on the first floor, which had a fine 15thC fireplace. A drawing of the exterior of the range exists. *Remains:* Part of the undercroft of the W range, very dilapidated, still stands with a square tower at the NW corner. Most of the site is covered by a farm. The guest house, prior's lodging and a large barn were dismantled and taken to St Donat's Castle (S Wales) in the 1930s. Nothing survives of the ch. whose fdns. were dug up in 1666. Desc. & plan: Archaeologia, Vol. 73.

Bradley *Priory. Leics. 4m SSW of Uppingham. (+1220 to 1536). Augustinian canons. F: uncertain, perhaps Robert of Burnebi. Ded: unknown.*
A small and poorly endowed house with perhaps only 4 canons at its

peak. The main benefactor at the end of the 14thC was Lord Scrope of Bolton, which may account for the priory being reported as being in good repair at all times. Very little history known. One prior became abbot of Owston (*v.* below). *Remains:* None.

Bradsole *Abbey. Kent. See* St Radegund's.

Bradwell *Priory. Bucks. Map 6. 1½m S of Wolverton. (−1136/44 to 1524/5), Benedictine monks. F: Meinfelin, lord of Wolverton. Ded: St Mary.*
For most of its existence the house was a cell of Luffield. Little is known of this small and poor monastery except that it appeared to have 'a very high character for the strict observances of the Rule' (VCH). It became independent in the 14thC and later suffered severely at the time of the B.D. A monk of St Albans obtained permission from his abbot to live a more perfect life in holy retirement at this little house. Bp. Gray's visit *c.* 1431 encouraged the 3 monks to recite the office if there were not sufficient voices to sing, and urged that nothing was to hinder the regularity of their life. Their poverty made it impossible for the numbers to be increased. It was one of the houses suppressed for Wolsey's Oxford Coll. *Remains:* A small mid-14thC chapel is an outbldg. of Abbey Farm. Other bldgs. incorporate many fragments of the ch. including doorways, windows and mouldings. Evidence of a moat and fishponds. Partly excavated E of the chapel in 1968 (Med. Arch. Vol. 13).

Breadsall *Priory. Derbys. 3m NE of Derby. (+1200 to 1536). Augustinian*

canons. F: a member of the Curzon family. Ded: Holy Trinity.
Very small and poor. VCH has extensive details of the priors and benefactions. Internal history negligible. In 1488 charters were stolen and the bp. ordered all persons to be informed and the muniments to be returned within 15 days. Whether his threat of widespread excommunication secured the return of the deeds is not known. Only the prior was still here at the Dissolution. *Remains:* None. A Jacobean house, Breadsall Priory, occupies the site, with perhaps an arch from the priory in the basement.

Breamore *Priory. Hants. 3m N of Fordingbridge. (c. 1130−1536). Augustinian canons. Fs: Baldwin de Redvers & Hugh his uncle. Ded: St Michael.*
Although this house was not poor by comparison with many of the lesser Aug. properties, the available history suggests an entirely uneventful 400 years existence. The canons received grants of land, mills and fisheries and were good sheep farmers. *Remains:* None. Excavations in 1898 revealed small traces of burials and the cloister.

Breedon *Priory. Leics. Map 3. 9m SSE of Derby. (−1122 to 1539). Augustinian canons. F: Robert de Ferrers. Ded: St Mary & St Hardulph.*
The F. gave it to Nostell and there may have been a small community here before his time. There was a monastery (sacked by the Danes *c.* 874) at this site from the 7th−9thCs (VCH) of which important and unique traces still exist, especially the remarkable Saxon sculptured stones built into the walls of the late-12thC ch. The house was not well endowed and always remained small, perhaps with never more than 5

canons. In 1244 a prior tried to make the property independent of Nostell but failed and was forced to resign. Debt and dilapidated bldgs. in 1441. At the Dissolution only the prior lived here. *Remains:* The beautiful 13thC choir of the conventual ch. was kept by the parishioners for their use and abandoned the nave. The central tower became the W tower in which the nave arch can still be seen. The S transept survives but the N has gone as well as all the claustral bldgs. Desc. of carved stones: Archaeologia, Vol. 77 (1927).

Bretford *Priory Cell. Warks. 6m E of Coventry. (+1154 to −1167). Benedictine nuns. F: Jeffery de Clinton. Ded: St Mary.*
After about 10 years there were only 2 nuns here and as they disliked the place, the F. transferred the property to Kenilworth Priory. It is not known to which house the nuns were sent. *Remains:* None.

Brewood* *(White Ladies) Priory. Salop. Map 2. 8m NW of Wolverhampton. (late-12thC to 1538). Augustinian nuns. F: unknown. Ded: St Leonard. (Here and at Grace Dieu (v. below) the convent was not referred to as canonesses).*
The nuns had scattered holdings all of which were modest in size and in consequence the community was small. Very little history. The family of la Zouch were benefactors and Elizabeth la Zouch became prioress in 1314. The house normally supported about 6 nuns. Occasionally writers have referred to the community as being Cistercian. In 1338 a prioress was reprimanded for extravagance. Little else is known until 1498 when the pension of a prioress accounted for 20% of the monastery's total

income. *Remains:* Ruins of late-Norman ch. comprise nave and 3-bay square-ended presbytery. Transepts and claustral bldgs., which lay to the N, (and the 16thC house which stood close to the site) have gone. Monograph: Boscobel House & White Ladies Priory (HMSO) R. Gilyard-Beer. Care: D of E. Notes: Br. Arch. Assoc. J. Vol. 17.
* Pronounced Brood.

Brewood *(Black Ladies) Priory. Staffs. 8m NNW of Wolverhampton. (−1150 to 1538). Benedictine nuns. F: Roger de Clinton (?). Ded: St Mary.*
The nuns had a close link with Blithbury (*v.* above) whose lands passed to the Brewood nuns shortly before 1189. The priory was poor, with meagre revenues, and in 1286 the nuns were convicted of the theft of a stag, but were pardoned due to their poverty (VCH). A visitation by Bp. Norbury in 1323 revealed some financial confusion and general laxity of discipline, and he placed several restrictions upon the nuns. A Franciscan friar, perhaps from Stafford, was appointed to hear confessions about this time. It seems the house was always in a state of poverty. *Remains:* None. 16thC Brewood Hall occupies the site and is said to incorporate either remnants of bldgs. or materials. Note: Br. Arch. Assoc. J. Vol. 29.

Bridge End *(Holland Brigge) Priory/ Priory Cell. Lincs. 15m E of Grantham. (−1200 to 1538). Gilbertine canons. F: Godwin, a Lincoln citizen. Ded: St Saviour.*
The F. placed the onus on the canons to keep about 30 bridges in repair along Holland Brigge, after providing for their own support, and the history

77

of the house is largely a record of disputes about the causeway, it being a heavy burden on the income. In 1333 the prior claimed that the revenues from tolls were barely adequate for the canons' maintenance, let alone the causeway. Being so close to Sempringham there is no doubt that benefactors favoured the mother house of the Order before Bridge End. This small priory seems to have been independent until rebuilt following a serious fire in 1445. It then became a cell of Sempringham. *Remains:* None. Some bldgs. stood until 1770 and after demolition the materials were used to build a farmhouse.

Bridgnorth *Friary. Salop. (1244–1538). Franciscan (Conventual). F: unknown. Perhaps John Talbot, earl of Shrewsbury. Ded: St Francis?* Custody of Worcester. Very little history recorded of this small and poor house. Several local families were important benefactors and in the 14thC Robert, Lord Hilton, became a friar and ended his days with the community. At the Dissolution 'there was poverty but not disorder' (VCH) even though the bldgs. were dilapidated and the water supply had broken down. Cromwell's visitor wrote 'it is the poorest house I have ever seen, not worth 10 shillings a year'. *Remains:* None. The entire refectory, converted into an alehouse, survived 'in pristine condition' until 1867. The site is now covered by a carpet factory. Desc. & site drwg.: Salop Arch. & Nat. Hist. Soc. 4th series, Vol. 11 (1927).

Bridgwater *Friary. Somerset. (1245–1538). Franciscan (Conventual). F: William Bruer. Ded: St Francis?* After only a year the site was moved to the W part of the town. The ch.

was rebuilt *c.* 1440. Little is known of the history between the 12th and early-16thCs. *Remains:* None. Excavations at the site before it was covered by a housing estate revealed a line of masonry piers beneath New Road, and may have been part of the infirmary hall. A house known as The Friary and Friarn Street are the only reminders of the existence of a large monastery. Desc. & drwg.: Franciscan Architecture in England (1937) A. R. Martin, 211–18.

Bridlington *Priory. Yorks. ER. Map 1. (c. 1113–1537). Augustinian canons. F: Walter de Gant. Ded: St Mary.* One of the largest and wealthiest houses of the Order, the ch. being bigger than either Beverley Minster or Selby Abbey. Considerable history is known and a 14thC cartulary is in the BM. A number of canons became distinguished for their learning and sanctity, and the good management of Prior John de Tweng (1362–79) resulted in the great influence and prosperity of the house. He became canonised and the shrine of St John of Bridlington was in an elevated chapel behind the High Altar, and attracted many pilgrims. Perhaps because of St John, later priors were granted the right to wear the mitre and other insignia in 1409. *c.* 1407 the alien Cistercian cell at Scarborough was granted to the canons (*v.* Appendix 1). *Remains:* The fine 10-bayed nave is in use as the parish ch. (the purpose it served before the Dissolution). Nothing remains of the claustral bldgs. in which a decagonal chapter house existed. There is the gatehouse (Bayle Gate) lying SW of the ch.

Bridport *Friary. Dorset. (1261 to –1365). Carmelite. F: unknown.*

Ded: BVM. Distinction of London.
In 1365 Sir John Chideock applied
for a licence to re-establish the friary.
The jurors refused to give consent on
the grounds that the interests of the
parish ch. would be injured. From
this date the community appears to
have vacated their premises. Nothing
known of the history for the 100
years of the house's life. *Remains:*
None.

Brightley *Abbey. Devon. 2m N of
Okehampton. (1136–1141). Cistercian monks. F: Richard Fitz Baldwin
de Brioniis, sheriff of Devon. Ded:
St Mary.*
Colonised from Waverley. A more
useful site was given by the F's. sister,
Adelicia, at Forde and the community moved in 1141. *Remains:* None.

Brinkburn *Priory. N'land. Map 1.
11m SSW of Alnwick. (–1135 to
1536). Augustinian canons. F: Wm.
Bertram I of Mitford. Ded: St Peter
& St Paul.*
Colonised from Pentney but became
independent late in the 12thC. Never
wealthy and suffered often from
Scottish raids. The ch. escaped
destruction after the Dissolution because of the canons' pastoral care of
the district and the nave of their ch.
was used by parishioners. Services
lapsed in 1683 and the ch. fell into
ruin until restored in 1858. The site
has exceptionally beautiful surroundings being on a bend of the river
Coquet. *Remains:* The ch. with 6-bay
nave, transepts and presbytery is late-
12thC and in use as the parish ch. S
of the S transept are walls of the
chapter house vestibule. The undercroft of the refectory forms the
cellars of the mansion lying to the S.
A stone-lined watercourse which
served as the intake for the priory

mill exists, and was probably part of
the main drain. Desc. & care: D of E.
Desc. & plan: Northumberland
County History (1844), Vol. 7.
Book: Brinkburn Priory Cartulary
(1893) Wm. Page.

Bristol *Abbey/Cathedral. Glos. Map 5.
(1140–1539). Augustinian canons.
F: Robert Fitzharding. Ded: St
Augustine.*
Order of St Victor. Colonised from
Shobden (*v.* below). 13thC cartulary
exists (Berkeley Muniments). The
first abbot, Richard, wrote to the
abbot of St Victor about the 'tranquillity and the blessings of peace' in
the house. Some 80 years later (1242)
the bp. of Worcester found discipline
woefully relaxed and the abbot
resigned and his prior was deposed.
Again in 1280 censure followed a
visitation and by 1285 the debts were
huge due to financial mismanagement.
By 1340 the community was 'more
worthy of commendation than correction'. Mitred 1398. In 1451 the
convent forced the resignation of an
excellent abbot, appointed an incompetent intruder to replace him and 5
years later, realising their mistake,
restored Abbot Newbury. Considerable history available from many
sources. In 1542 the abbey became a
secular cathedral. *Remains:* Of the
conventual ch., the crossing, transepts
(with ancient nightstairs in the thickness of the E wall of the S transept),
choir and 2 Lady Chapels survive. Rebldg. of the demolished nave abandoned at the Dissolution and not
begun until 1868. Richly ornamented
chapter house; E cloister walk: slype;
Norman arch to lower cloister.
Abbot's lodging and guesthouse now
part of a school. Norman gatehouse
much restored. Desc. & plan:
Archaeologia, Vol. 63 (1911–2).

Book: Hist. & Antiq. of the Abbey & Cathedral of Bristol (1836) J. Britton. Illus: Pitkin Pictorial *Etc.*

Bristol *Priory. Glos. Map 5. (c. 1137– 1540). Benedictine monks. F: Robert, earl of Gloucester. Ded: St James.* Cell of Tewkesbury upon whom it was wholly dependent. F. buried in the ch. in 1147. In 1230 the monks were in conflict with the Dominicans about burial rights, but the bp. of Tewkesbury found in favour of the friars. The history, as with most cells, was uneventful, and it is unlikely that there were ever more than 4 monks here — sent for a time from Tewkesbury. The house had the distinction of being the first monastery to be fd. in the city. The nave was parochial. *Remains:* The W front has Norman interlaced arches and there are 5 bays of the original nave behind it. No other bldgs. survive.

Bristol *Priory. Glos. (c. 1173–1536). Augustinian canonesses. F: Eva, widow of Robert Fitzharding. Ded: St Mary Magdalen.* The F. became prioress. Little history is recorded but it is evident that the community was poor due to slender endowments, and became exempt from taxation from 13thC onwards. At the suppression only an aged prioress and a young novice were living here. *Remains:* None. The site was at the foot of St Michael's Hill on the corner of Maudlin Street and is occupied by the King David Inn. The name survives in Whiteladies Road.

Bristol *Friary. Glos. (1313–1538). Austin. Fs: Simon deMontacute & Wm. de Montacute. Ded: unknown.* Limit of Oxford. This was the only friars house within the city walls. Site enlarged 1344. Very little history

known. In May 1538 the friars refused to surrender their house, but in August an accusation concerning unlawful sale of property forced the closure. The parishioners of Temple received from the friars 'a never-failing flow of pure water' (G. E. Weare). *Remains:* None.

Bristol *Friary. Glos. (1256–1538). Carmelite. F: Edward I (when Prince of Wales). Ded: BVM.* Distinction of Oxford? History obscure. Tanner states that 'the house was the fairest of all the houses of friars in Bristol', and Wm. Worcester wrote that the square tower and steeple reached to some 200 feet. Ingworth (a former Dominican prior of King's Langley) reported that their only source of income was the produce from their extensive gardens. Nothing is known of the plan. *Remains:* None. Some floor tiles are in the city museum. The site is covered by the Colston Hall.

Bristol *Friary. Glos. Map 5. (c. 1230– 1538). Dominican. F: Maurice de Gaunt. Ded: unknown.* Visitation of London. Henry III was a generous benefactor and later kings gave many bounties. Apart from this, the history is almost a blank. In 1534 the prior became head of the English Dominicans; and in that year nearly all the friars fled the country rather than accept the royal supremacy. *Remains:* The masonry of 3 ranges of bldgs. survives round the restored Dec. cloister, which have in past years been used as the Cutlers' Hall, Friends' Meeting House and the Bakers' Hall. Today they form part of the city's Central Register Office. On the S side was a smaller cloister for the infirmary. Desc. & plan:

Dominican Friary, Bristol. Part of 14th century cloister (now altered).

Trans. Bristol & Glos. Arch. Soc.
Vol. 54.

Bristol *Friary. Glos. (−1230 to 1538).*
Franciscan (Conventual). F: unknown.
Ded: St Francis?
Custody of Bristol. The friars moved
to a new site *c.* 1250 in Lewins Mead
near St James's Priory. They had the
right to exact a toll on the fish
brought into the city. A good deal of
history is known due to the survival
of the writings by Wm. Worcester in
1480. The friars' water supply came
via a remarkable conduit which continued in use until early this century.
A part of it exists beneath Upper
Maudlin Street. *Remains:* None
Early this century a small bldg. which
was part of the friary was destroyed,
as were some storage recesses excavated into the face of the nearby cliff.
In 1973 extensive excavations during
building developments revealed much
information about the ch., and some
adjacent stone-walled rooms which
may have been used for teaching or
preaching. Finds include a selection
of utensils and shoes now in the City
Museum. Plan: Med. Arch. Vol. 18
(1974). Notes & plans: Trans. Bristol
& Glos. Arch. Soc. Vol. 54. Book:
The Bristol Friars Minor (1893) G.
E. Weare.

Bristol *Friary. Glos. (−1266 to*
+1286). Friars of the Sack. F:
unknown. Ded: unknown.

Henry III was a benefactor. The friars' ch. is mentioned in 1322 (VCH) but it is very probable that there were no friars at that date. *Remains:* None.

Broadholme *Priory. Notts. 5½m NW of Lincoln. (−1154 to 1536). Premonstratensian canonesses. Fs:* either *Peter de Goxhill and Agnes de Camville his wife* or *the abbot and canons of Newsham. Ded: St Mary.*
The Aubigny family were prominent benefactors. One record suggests the original fdn. was a double-house but by 1319 it contained only canonesses. The recorded history is largely one of disputes with the parent house of Newsham (*v.* below) whose abbots seem to have controlled the convent's interests, hence a comparative obscurity (Colvin). Q. Isabel, patroness in 1327, had a special affection for the nuns and ordinances proclaimed at her request provide a rare glimpse into the meagre history (VCH). The small and remote nunnery suffered two abductions of its sisters in the 14thC, but in neither case is the outcome recorded. In 1534 the net annual income was little more than £16 which could hardly support the community. *Remains:* None. Some carved stones survive in a nearby farmhouse and there are traces of fishponds.

Brockley *Abbey. Kent. 1¼m W of Lewisham, London. (c. 1180– c. 1208). Premonstratensian canons. Fs: Countess Juliana & Michael de Thornham.*
The site proved unsuitable and the canons joined with those of Otham to fd. the abbey at Bayham. *Remains:* None.

Bromehill *(Weeting) Priory. Norfolk.*

7½m NW of Thetford. (−1224 to 1528). Augustinian canons. F: Sir Hugh de Plaiz. Ded: St Mary & St Thomas, Martyr.
History mainly concerned with grants and licences in the 13th & 14thCs. Some discord existed between the canons and the town of Thetford about revenues from Bromehill Fair which was finally resolved in 1331. In 1514 the schoolhouse was in poor repair and since there were no novices under instruction, it must have been for outsiders. At this time the 4 canons complained of poor lighting and food and no barber or servants. The bp. ordered the prior to correct all these matters. In 1520 the canons said all was well but the bp. hardly believed them for he ordered the provision of stocks and chains for their correction. There was a better report in 1525. Suppressed for Wolsey's Ipswich venture but after his downfall the endowments were granted to Christ's Coll., Cambridge (*v.* North Creake). The canons were dispersed to other houses. *Remains:* None. There are some carved stones in a farmhouse at Brandon and the site lies 1½m NE of Brandon Farm.

Bromfield *Priory. Salop. Map 2. 3m NW of Ludlow. (−1105 to 1540). Benedictine monks. F: unknown. Ded: St Mary.*
The house was probably fd. first as a secular coll., *c.* 1061, and became an independent priory sometime before 1105 (Dugdale). In 1155 the monks gave themselves and their lands to St Peter's Abbey, Gloucester, whose cell it became and so remained until the suppression. As a result there is very little independent history. *Remains:* The nave and N aisle of the early-13thC conventual ch. is now the parish ch. with a massive tower at the

NW angle of the nave. The original chancel became part of a private house and the site reverted to ch. property when it was burnt down in the 17thC. No transepts survive. Fine timber and stone gatehouse, part of which is probably 14thC.

Brooke *Priory Cell. Rutland. 2¼m SW of Oakham. (−1153 to 1535). Augustinian canons. F: Hugh de Ferrers. Ded: St Mary.*
The only religious house in the county. Dependent upon Kenilworth. A small cell with perhaps never more than 3 canons. Due to poverty, the priors sent from Kenilworth resigned on any flimsy excuse and dilapidation and decay of the house in the late-13thC due to mismanagement was a local scandal. The history during the 13th & 14thCs is not very edifying (VCH), and from this time onwards practically nothing is known about the house. At the Dissolution the sole inmate was the prior and he told the king's commissioners it was an independent house and he surrendered it as such. This act caused serious difficulty to the abbot of Kenilworth who had entered upon a bond of 1,000 marks as security to a third party in respect of Brooke. How matters were resolved is unknown except that the abbot did not get the priory back. *Remains:* None. Some fdns. lie beneath the turf close to Priory Farm and a house named Brooke Priory may contain some reused materials.

Broomhall *(Bromhale) Priory. Berks. 2m SE of Ascot. (−1200 to 1521). Benedictine nuns. F: unknown. Ded: unknown.*
K. John and Henry de Lacy, earl of Lincoln, were benefactors. In 1231 Henry III granted the nuns free pannage for their 36 pigs, and poverty is again recorded in 1310 & 1327. In 1404 an inquiry looked into a complaint that a nun had led an evil life for 20 years. The reasons are unknown but the offender resigned in 1405. Early charters burnt by mishap in 1462. The disastrous fire left the nuns destitute and alms were collected for them. The annual income in the 16thC is not known but the house was probably very poor. In 1521 it was found that the prioress had resigned and her 2 nuns had abandoned the convent. Dissolution was completed in 1522 when the possessions were granted to St John's Coll., Cambridge (Power). *Remains:* None. Desc: Berks. & Bucks. Arch. Soc. Trans. Vol. 27 (1922).

Bro(o)mholm *(Bacton) Alien Priory/ Priory. Norfolk. Map 4. On the coast 10m SE of Cromer. (1113−1536). Cluniac monks. F: Wm. de Glanville. Ded: St Andrew.*
Colonised from Castle Acre. *c.* 1195 the house became responsible direct to Cluny and *c.* 1390 became denizen. The fortunes of the house declined gradually, affecting the number of monks it could support, despite the possession from 1223 of a cross said to have been made from fragments of the true Cross. It is described in detail by Matthew Paris. Many pilgrims, including Henry III, visited the famous relic. Remaining history is mainly of even tenor until the 15thC when the community complained of their sufferings from incursions of the sea, pestilences and fire. *Remains:* The site is occupied by a farm and is approached through the original gatehouse. Chief remnant of the ch. is the N transept. There is also part of the S aisle wall of the nave. The chapter house walls, undercroft of

the dorter, small pieces of refectory
wall and several scattered pieces of
masonry form the remaining survivals.

Bruern *Abbey. Oxon. 7m N of*
Burford. (1147–1536). Cistercian
monks. F: Nicholas Basset. Ded: St
Mary.
Colonised from Waverley. No cartulary exists but some deeds are preserved in the P.R.O., B.M. and Bodleian.
Originally known as Treton, the name
of a manor held by the convent, but
it disappeared *c.* 1173 (VCH). The
Glos. properties, used for sheep farming, provided most of the monastery's
income. Very little is known about
the abbey itself. In 1252 Abbot
Roger failed to visit Beaulieu when
instructed and was deprived of the
use of his stall for 20 days. It seems
his recalcitrance persisted and he was
finally deposed in 1279. In 1369 the
abbot complained that an imposter
had so wasted the income for 5 years
that only 6 monks could be maintained whereas the community was much
larger. Happier days came in 1382.
Towards the end, 1529–30, the
monks tried to unseat their abbot in
a series of riots (VCH). *Remains:*
None. A house built *c.* 1720 occupies
the site.

Bruisyard *Abbey. Suffolk. 6m NW of*
Saxmundham. (c. 1366–1539). Fran-
ciscan nuns. F: Lionel, duke of Clar-
ence as the Abbey of the Annuncia-
tion.
Daughter house of Denney. Not
under a Custody. 1st. f. 1346 by
Maud, countess of Ulster as a secular
coll., but for several reasons it was
suppressed in Oct. 1366. The Minoresses obtained the property and
entered soon afterwards. Apart from
some records of grants in the 14thC,
little is known of the monastery,

which appears to have been exempt
from episcopal visits. The house
escaped suppression in 1536 on payment of a £60 fine. *Remains:* Very
little. Bruisyard Hall occupies the site
and contains an arch and some walling,
perhaps part of the ch., though the
original positions are uncertain.

Bruton *Priory/Abbey. Somerset.*
Map 5. (c. 1130–1539). Augustinian
canons. F: Wm. de Mohun, later earl
of Somerset. Ded: St Mary.
1st. f. *c.* 1005 by Aethelmar, earl of
Cornwall, for Benedictine monks and
ded. to St Andhelm. It became a
house of Black Canons sometime
between 1127–35. In 1260 Horsley
Priory (*v.* below) became a cell of
Bruton and in the same year the alien
Benedictine cell of Runcton (*v.*
Appendix 1) also became its property.
Practically nothing else is known of
the history of the priory from fdn.
to Dissolution, but it is recorded that
the house attained abbey status in
1511 and, by Aug. standards, was
wealthy. *Remains:* Fdns. of abbey
bldgs. lie beneath a playing field N of
the parish ch. Two possessions survive.
The courthouse, or perhaps the
Steward's house, in the High Street;
and a ruined 3-storeys dovecote on a
hill 1½m E of the parish ch.

Buckenham *Old Priory. Norfolk. 4m*
SE of Attleborough. (c. 1146–1536).
Augustinian canons. F: Wm. de
Albini, earl of Arundel. Ded: St Mary,
St James & All Saints.
The bp. of Norwich ordained that
the canons should follow in all things
the institutes or rules of the ch. of St
Mary of Merton (Dickinson). The F.
gave the canons the materials to build
their priory from his original castle
nearby. No cartulary traced. One
historical note of 1310 recalls the
appreciation of the Crown by ack-

nowledging the prior's willingness to provide Edward II with provisions for his Scottish expedition. The house was never wealthy but seems to have maintained its full number of canons throughout its existence — an unusual achievement. No records of visitations appear before 1492 when a series of complaints against the prior revealed that his canons were rarely consulted, and he did not show tolerance or fairness to the community. Four further visitations in the 16thC reveal minor complaints about some indiscipline, and that 2 canons wore pointed shoes! *Remains:* None. Perhaps some remnants might be traced amongst bldgs. of Castle Farm. Notes: Norfolk Arch. Vol. 17.

Buckfast *Abbey. Devon. 2m S of Ashburton. (1136–1539). Cistercian monks. F: K. Stephen. Ded: St Mary.* 1st. f. 1018 by K. Canute for Benedictine monks and aided by the abbot of Tavistock. Colonised from Winchester or Tavistock, or both. It disappeared from history in 1086. The 2nd. fdn. is recorded in a royal charter of 1136 when lands and property, which had belonged to the previous abbey, were granted to the abbot of Savigny. In 1147 the house became Cistercian. It never achieved first rank even though it was ultimately the richest of the Order in the W of England, and had an uneventful life. A late-14thC abbot, Wm. Slade, was a distinguished writer; and his predecessor established a lucrative fishery in the R. Dart. *Remains:* None. In the early years of the 19thC a small mansion occupied much of the site, and in 1882 the property came into the possession of French Benedictine exiled monks. The present abbey was begun in 1907 1907. Hist: Dom John Stephan (1937).

Buckland *Abbey. Devon. Map 8. 8m N of Plymouth. (1278–1539). Cistercian monks. F: Amicia, countess of Devon. Ded: St Mary & St Benedict.* Colonised from Quarr. The monks were installed without the licence of the bp. of Exeter and were excommunicated for a short time until aided by Q. Eleanor. The house was not far from the larger and much richer abbey of Tavistock and disputes inevitably arose, notably about fisheries (Finberg). The weir of Buckland's salmon trap still exists. It is recorded that the community planted the first orchard in this cider-making county. *Remains:* The ch. was converted into an Elizabethan mansion which came into the possession of Sir Francis Drake in 1581. It comprises the nave, presbytery, central crossing tower and S transept. Now a museum owned by Plymouth Corpn. There also survives a turreted gatehouse among the stables and a fine buttressed tithe barn nearby.

Buckland *(Minchin*Buckland) Priory. Somerset. 5m NE of Taunton. (c. 1180–1539). Augustinian canonesses. F: Henry II. Ded: St John, Baptist.* 1st. f. c. 1166 by Wm. de Erlegh for Aug. canons and they were dispersed sometime before 1180. Henry gave the possessions for a preceptory and house of Sisters of the Order of St John of Jerusalem (i.e. Order of Knights Hospitallers), whose property it remained until it closed c. 1500. From c. 1516 the priory housed Aug. canonesses. In 1383–5 there occurred an incident about an 8-year old girl who had entered the priory 'with the connivance of the prioress' to deprive her of an inheritance in favour of her uncle — a 'jewel of a story from dry-as-dust mediaeval lawbooks' (Power).

Remains: None. At Buckland Farm there are some re-used fragments of stone, some fishponds and, perhaps, the E end of the S wall of a barn which has a single buttress. A 15thC gravestone found on the site in 1836 is in Taunton Museum.
* From the early-English word 'minchery' — a nunnery.

Buildwas *Abbey. Salop. Map 2. 11m SE of Shrewsbury. (1135–1536). Cistercian monks. F: Roger de Clinton, bp. of Lichfield. Ded: St Mary & St Chad.*
Colonised from Savigny. 1147 became Cistercian. As with most Cist. houses, the history was relatively uneventful, but three incidents are noteworthy: in 1342 the abbot was murdered by a monk; in 1350 the abbot was abducted and imprisoned by marauders from Wales; in 1406 the abbey's lands were ruined by followers of Owen Glyndwr (HMSO guidebook). The abbey had a remarkable library and some of its books survive at Trinity Coll., Cambridge, and elsewhere. *Remains:* The shell of the 12thC ch. is almost intact with nave, crossing tower, transepts and crypt below the N transept. Fine chapter house with vaulted ceiling in 9 compartments. Cloister to N of ch. Modern private house to the NW incorporates fragments of the infirmary and the abbot's lodging (1220); other remnants in the outbldgs. Desc., plan & care: D of E. Desc. & plan: Archaeologia Vol. 19.

Bullington *Priory. Lincs. 9m NE of Lincoln (c. 1150–1538). Gilbertine canons and nuns. F: Simon de Kyme. Ded: St Mary.*
Although the number of members of double houses was limited by the statutes of St Gilbert to 100 nuns and 50 canons, there is no evidence that anything like that number was ever supported even though the double house at Tunstall (*v.* below) was transferred here shortly before 1189. Not much history survives. In 1316 Edward II gave a year's protection to the priory's servants for the safe transport of corn and victuals from Leicester (Graham). There was a thriving wool trade in the first half of the 14thC. The community did not recover from the ravages of the B.D. and only about 20 religious were here at the Dissolution. This was one of the 30 monasteries granted to the Duke of Suffolk by Henry VIII. *Remains:* Very small. Perhaps a pillar built from fragments of the priory (Pevsner).

Bungay *Priory. Suffolk. Map 4. 15m SSE of Norwich. (c. 1183*–1536). Benedictine nuns. Fs: Roger de Glanville and Countess Gundreda his wife. Ded: St Mary & the Holy Cross.*
A nun of Bungay suffering from 'madness' was said to have been cured on visiting the tomb of the saintly Robert of Winchelsea, Archbp. of Canterbury (Power). The taxation roll of 1291 contains no ref. to the nunnery and it seems to have had the rare distinction of tax exemption. In 1299 some of the priory's goods were stolen, and in 1301 the prioress and some others stole property in Bungay which belonged to the abbot of Barlings. Visitation records of 2 bps. are entirely to the credit of the convent with nothing to reform, especially in the 16thC. At the suppression the commissioners were unable to enforce eviction 'there not being one nun left therein'. *Remains:* The nave, always parochial, is in use as the parish ch. To the E are the ruins of the nuns' choir (slightly out-of-line with the

Buildwas Abbey, Shropshire. Late 12thC nave of church looking east. The building remained almost unaltered until the Dissolution.

nave) which, along with the claustral bldgs., was destroyed in a disastrous town fire in 1688. In the S aisle of the nave a blocked doorway led to the cloister, now the site of the parish cemetery. A 15thC tower built by the parishioners stands at the W end of the nave's S aisle.
*most refs. give c. 1160

Burnham *Abbey. Bucks. Map 6. 3m NE by E of Maidenhead. (1266– 1539). Augustinian canonesses. F: Richard, K. of the Romans. Ded: St Mary.*
Poverty, so common in nunneries, resulted in tax remissions in the 14thC. The canonesses strongly resisted the order to accept a nomin- ated custodian by John Peckham, Archbp. of Canterbury, to administer the temporalities because of poverty, but the outcome is unknown. In 1339 two nuns were transferred to Goring Priory 'for the peace and quiet of the house' (Power). *Remains:* Extensive. These are now part of an Anglican nunnery. The 13thC ch. (which had been excavated) has gone. The E range of the cloister, which lay to the N, has a 13thC doorway to the chapter house and the 13thC sacristy. The parlour and warming room also survive. The N range included the refectory of which the S wall and part of the N wall remain. The infirmary stands though much repaired. For many years the bldgs. were part of a farm. Desc. & plan: Bucks. Archit. & Archae. Soc. Records, Vols. 8 & 31; also Arch. J. Vol. 60 (1903). Note on threatened ruins: Br. Arch. Assoc. J. Vol. 1, p. 339.

Burnham Norton *Friary. Norfolk. Map 4. 2m NE of Burnham Market. (1253–1538). Carmelite. Fs: Sir Ralph de Hemenhale & Sir Wm. de Calthorp. Ded: BVM.*

1st. f. at a site named Bradmer and moved to B.N. 12 years later. The friary bldgs. were enlarged mid-12thC. Very little history survives. Towards the end of its existence two friars were tried for treason after a threatened insurrection. One was executed and the other imprisoned. A prior, who died in 1503, was the most distinguished Carmelite of the English Province, who studied each year at Oxford and Cambridge. He worked on the annals of the Order (VCH). *Remains:* A fine Dec. gate- house with upper chambers. Next to it the W wall of what was probably an outer chapel. The nearby farm- house to the N contains considerable quantities of re-used materials includ- ing a 14thC doorway and a large buttress.

Burscough *Priory. Lancs. Map 2. 3m NE of Ormskirk. (c. 1190–1536). Augustinian canons. F: Robert Fitz Henry, lord of Lathom. Ded: St Nicholas.*
Perhaps colonised from Norton. Cartulary of c. 1390 survives. At the end of the 12thC the F's relatives dis- puted some of the endowments. In 1339 a curious election of a secular priest to the priorship 'due to negli- gence', resulted in the vicars of Orms- kirk automatically becoming a canon of the house up to the Dissolution. In 1454 a charge of 'black art' was brought against the prior, the vicar of Ormskirk and another canon (VCH). All 3 lost their jobs. Just before the suppression the earl of Derby tried unsuccessfully to save the ch. from destruction as many members of his family lay buried there. It seems the priory had the uncommon feature of two gardens – one for guests, one for the prior. *Remains:* Two late-13thC piers which formed part of the cross-

ing and the N transept, amounting to a broken arch in a field. Excavations in 1886 revealed the plan of the ch. and some claustral bldgs. Desc. & plan: Trans. Hist. Soc. of Lancs. & Cheshire, Vol. 41 (1889). Book: Notes on the History of Burscough Priory (1905) F. H. Cheetham.

Burtle *Priory Cell. Somerset. 8m NW of Glastonbury. (−1270 to 1436). Augustinian canons. F: unknown. Ded: Holy Trinity, BVM & St Stephen.* The house was known by a number of names during its life and occupied the site of a 13thC hermitage (Knowles). The very small cell was a dependency of the Benedictine abbey of Glastonbury (an unusual alliance) and endowed by William de Edington. Probably never more than 2 or 3 canons whose history is unrecorded. A bp. appointed the priors in 1343 & 1349. *Remains:* None.

Burton-upon-trent *Abbey, Staffs. Map 3. (1002−1539). Benedictine monks. F: Wulfric Spott. Ded: St Mary & St Modwen.* Cartulary in BM. Visited during its long life by many kings and a great multitude of travellers which involved the community in heavy expense. The main pursuits were the management of the estates, sheep farming, cloth production and the care of the shrine of St Modwen (an Irish saint). The history is extensive and interesting (*v.* VCH). Financial troubles were a constant problem and 2 abbots were expelled for dissipating property (1094 & 1159). Twice the house came under the king's protection due to debt, and in 1382 mortality of cattle, lawsuits and the cost of corn brought impoverishment. Unhappily during the last 200 years the monastery's spiritual state was as unsound as the

financial, except for the 16thC when no serious troubles are revealed. On the credit side several abbots endowed chantries in the 15thC, and from 1518 until the Dissolution the abbots seem to have been popular and helped the townspeople by providing a market hall, grammar school and an efficient water supply. This was the only house valued twice in 1535 due to the first return being entirely false and under-estimated. *Remains:* Insignificant. Nothing survives of the ch. (which was large having two sets of transepts and two crossing towers). A house known as The Abbey incorporates part of the infirmary. Most of the site, part excavated, now occupied by the parish ch., the Market Place and the Market Hall. Notes: Br. Arch. Assoc. J. Vol. 29. Mid-16thC plan: VCH Staffs. Vol. 2.

Bury St Edmunds *(St Edmundsbury) Abbey. Suffolk. Map 4. (1020−1539). Benedictine monks. F: K. Canute. Ded: St Mary & St Edmund.* 1st. f. *c.* 633 by K. Sigbert. In 903 the remains of St Edmund (martyred at Hoxne in 870 by the Danes) were brought here. Became a secular coll. *c.* 925 and finally a Benedictine community from St Benet of Hulme, sent by K. Canute, replaced the secular priests. The abbey rose to be second only to Glastonbury and had no rivals regarding situation, liberties, ecclesiastical exemptions and spacious bldgs. Wealthy, mitred, large and powerful. Abbot Samson (1182−1211) with strict, efficient and kindly control, freed the abbey from debt. Fire (1150) and riots (1327 & 1381) caused great damage and loss. In 1433 a new royal lodge was built to enable Henry VI to spend Christmas here and he stayed until Easter 1434 at great expense to the monks. Parliaments used the great hall in 1267, 1296 & 1447. Vast quantities of records survive. Of special note is the Chronicle of Jocelin of Brakelond, a monk c. 1156 to +1212. Many volumes from the library now in the BM and University Libraries. *Remains:* Of the ch. meagre ruins of the crossing, transepts, crypt and part of nave (care: D of E). The massive core of the W front of the ch. has private houses built into it. Fairly extensive traces of claustral bldgs. 2 of the 4 gatehouses survive. Abbot's Bridge and considerable lengths of precinct wall. Ruins of Abbot's lodging. Part excavated 1958—63. Desc. plans & care: D of E; also Arch. J. Vol. 108; and Br. Arch. Assoc. J. Vols. 1 & 21.

Bury St Edmunds *(Babwell) Friary. Suffolk. (1263—1538). Franciscan (Conventual). F: unknown (Henry III styled himself as such). Ded: St Francis (?).*
Custody of Cambridge. c. 1233 the friars tried to establish themselves here and at last obtained a Bull in their favour in 1257, but the monks of the abbey remonstrated with them and forced expulsion. But in 1263 the abbot gave the community land at Babwell which was outside the town beyond the N gate where they remained until the Dissolution. Little known history. The site area of 43 acres is the largest recorded for a Franciscan house, much of which was probably under cultivation (Martin). *Remains:* None. Babwell House stands on the site in which some stone from the friary can be seen. The last remnants to disappear were parts of the precinct wall.

Bushmead *Priory. Beds. 9m NNE of Bedford. (c. 1215—1536). Augustin-*

ian canons. F: Hugh de Beauchamp. Ded: St Mary.
An anchorite was the 1st. F. of this house c. 1195 and the chapel of the hermitage later served as the parish ch. when the canons took over the site in the early 13thC. A small house with hardly any history and there is no record of a visitation. In 1283 the prior and 3 canons were accused by a mother of having caused the death of her son, but nothing is known of the circumstances or the outcome. Early in the 14thC a licence was obtained to teach 60 boys 'the science of grammar' (VCH). 11 of the 21 priors who lived here resigned for unknown reasons. It seems probable that the claustral bldgs. may have occupied only two sides of the cloister, thus being L-shaped. *Remains:* The refectory of this insufficiently appreciated priory lay to the S of the cloister and is now attached to an 18thC house. Hist: Bushmead Priory Cartulary (1945) Beds. Hist. Record Soc. Vol. 22.

Butley *Priory. Suffolk. Map 7. 14 m NE by E of Ipswich. (1171—1538). Augustinian canons. F: Sir Ranulph de Glanville (later Lord Chief Justice of England). Ded: St Mary.*
An undistinguished history. It was amongst the wealthier of the Aug. houses and few in the country possessed so much patronage (L.G.). The Chronicle of Butley refers to the constant stream of guests, and that Lord Mounteagle was born while his mother was staying here. History meagre until 1494 when Bp. Goldwell issued injunctions for minor indisciplines. The last visitation in 1532 by Bp. Nykke reveals a less satisfactory house when complaints concerned the lowering of standards of food, drink and hygiene. *Remains:* Of the

Byland Abbey, Yorkshire. West front.

ch., only an arch which led from the S transept into the chancel still stands. Traces of the refectory in farm bldgs. and the fishponds are complete. The finest remnant is the beautiful gatehouse with 35 sculptured heraldic shields on the front wall, and the stone and flintwork makes the bldg. one of the finest of its class in England. Site excavated 1930–3 and a plan of the ch. revealed. Desc: & plan: Arch. J. Vol. 90 (1933). Monograph & plan: Butley Priory (1933) J. N. L. Myers. Desc. Suffolk Inst. of Arch. Vol. 10, pt. 1.

Byland *Abbey. Yorks. NR. (Map 1). 7m SE by E of Thirsk. (1177–1539). Cistercian monks. F: Roger de Mowbray. Ded: St Mary.*
Colonised from Furness (Savigny house) in 1135 to Calder; 1138 moved to Hood; 1143 moved to Old Byland; 1147 moved to Stocking where the site became too small for the growing community, who then drained the swampy land at Byland and made the final move in 1177. The 2nd abbot, Roger (1142–96), was responsible for the growth and grandeur of the huge abbey for 19 years, and also prepared and planned the site beforehand. The history is singularly uneventful. Its most serious days came with the Scottish invasion in 1322 when the Battle of Byland was fought almost against the abbey's walls and Edward II barely escaped capture. Henry II granted the house many privileges. *Remains:* Considerable. Mostly at fdn. level except for the ch. where much of the lower half of the walls still stand. The excavated claustral bldgs. 'provide one of the most interesting of all monastic plans' (Braun). Four features of note: excellent leaf-form decoration on nave capitals in site museum; wealth of

13thC coloured tiles in S transept; ruin of unique wheel-window in W front once 26 ft. dia.; the 'lane' with 35 recesses for seats between lay-brothers range and W claustral walk. Desc., plan & care: D of E.

Bytham *Abbey. Lincs. 9m N of Stamford. (1147 to +1149). Cistercian monks. F: William le Gros, earl of Albermarle. Ded: St Mary.*
Colonised from Fountains. Finding the site unsuitable the monks soon moved to Vaudey (*v.* below).

C

Calceto, *de Sussex. Augustinian canons.*
See Pynham.

Calder I & II *Abbey. C'land (Cumbria). Map 1. 4m SE of Egremont. (I: 1135–1138. II: 1143–1536). Cistercian monks. F: Ranulph Meschin. Ded: St Mary.*
Colonised from Furness. The Scots destroyed the 1st. fdn. and drove out the monks who were refused readmittance to Furness. They went on to fd. Byland. *c.* 1143 Furness sent a 2nd colony to re-establish the abbey which continued until the suppression. Very little known of the history and the abbots do not appear in the public life of the country. Surviving records are mainly devoted to benefactions and properties, though the house was never rich. Lawsuits seem to have concerned the convent's defence of their title to possessions on several occasions. *Remains:* Arches on the N side of the 5-bayed nave; crossing tower, transepts; and chancel of the ruined ch. survive, and a fine W doorway. Also the chapter house with some remnants of vaulting and a

bookroom. Undercroft of the dormitory and part of the refectory are incorporated in a modern house which occupies the S side of the cloister. Nothing remains of the W claustral range. Desc. & plan: Trans. of C'land & W'land Arch. Soc. Vol. 8 (1886).

Caldwell *Priory. Beds. Kempston Road, Bedford. (c. 1154–1536). Augustinian canons. F: unknown, perhaps a member of the Barescote family. Ded: St John, Baptist.*
1st. belonged to the Order of St Sepulchre of Jerusalem and became Aug. *c.* 1275. After the siege and dismantling of Bedford Castle in 1224 the canons received stone to repair their house. In 1248 a prior resigned and fled to Merevale (*v.* below) as he feared a forthcoming visitation. Costly lawsuits with Osney, which were lost, caused the monastery to become 'a very poor place' (VCH). 15th & 16thC visitation records reveal no serious faults, and at the last visit the bp. complained of nothing worse than poverty. Never wealthy and a 13thC ch. owned by the canons was no asset being a constant burden upon their resources. *Remains:* None.

Calke *Priory/Cell. Derbys. 3½m N of Ashby de la Zouch. (c. 1131–1538). Augustinian canons. F: unknown. Ded: St Giles.*
Several gifts of land were made in the 12thC but the house did not prosper. When Repton Priory was built in the 1160s a few canons of Calke went there and the main body transferred in 1172. Calke then became a cell of Repton's and probably only 2 or 3 canons lived here. For at least a century the dignity of the parent house was respected but this acknowledgement lapsed later and it

drifted into independence (VCH). No history seems to be known. *Remains:* None. A house known as Calke Abbey was built on the site and some of its thick walls *may* have been part of the monastic bldgs.

Calwich *Priory. Staffs. 5m SW of Ashbourne. (c. 1130–1532). Augustinian canons. F: unknown. Ded: St Margaret.*
This small house was given later by Nicholas de Gresley to Kenilworth Priory in whose possession it remained for some 200 years, becoming independent again in 1349. From then on the problems probably outweighed the advantages especially as Kenilworth exacted a crippling pension. The remaining history is precarious and in 1385 the 3 canons were 'too feeble to labour for themselves and too poor to hire any' (VCH). By the 16thC the house was clearly in a tottering condition and in 1530 the prior died and the remaining canon was transferred, allowing the Crown to suppress the house illegally in 1532. In 1536 the forlorn cell was granted by Henry VIII to Merton Priory which itself was closed 2 years later. *Remains:* None. Parts of the ch. became a private house in 1540 and in 1849–50 another house was built on the site. This has also gone. Book: History of Calwich (1914) M. T. Fortescue.

Cambridge *Hostel/Priory. Cambs. (c. 1321–c. 1540). Benedictine monks.*
The 1st. fdn. was for student monks of Ely Cathedral-Priory and monks of other Bene. houses studying at Cambridge under a prior. In 1428 Henry VI granted a site to the abbot of Crowland on which a house of regular studies, known as Buckingham Coll., was built. The abbeys of Ely,

Ramsey & Walden united with Crowland in founding the new monastic priory hostel. It was suppressed c. 1540 and in 1542 a charter was granted for the fdn. of St Mary Magdalene Coll. *Remains:* There have been so many changes that it is not possible to identify any component parts. (The monastic plan was not adopted for Buckingham Coll.) The arms of Ely Cath.-Priory still existed in 1777 over a doorway.

Cambridge *Priory. Cambs. Map 4. (c. 1133/8–1496). Benedictine nuns. F: unknown. Ded: St Mary & St Radegund.*
Nigel, bp. of Ely and Malcolm IV, K. of Scotland were early benefactors. In the 13th & 14thCs the house was opulent and well-managed despite damage suffered from fires and storms; but from 1459 the fortunes declined to financial ruin. John Alcock, bp. of Ely, made an effort to bring recovery and reform in 1487 but without success. On a 2nd visitation in 1496 he found decayed bldgs. and only 2 nuns in residence. The bp. obtained dissolution of the nunnery and fd. Jesus Coll. within its walls. *Remains:* The plan is quite different from any other coll. It is essentially monastic, not collegiate. The cloister remains and the conventual bldgs. adapted and altered. Such gems as the entrance to the chapter house are preserved. In the 19thC the original extent of the nuns' ch. (choir) was found and restored. The refectory became the Hall and is raised upon an undercroft – rare in colleges, not unusual in monasteries. The complete plan of the original monastery has been drawn. Hist: The Priory of St Radegund (1898) A. Gray.

Cambridge *Priory. Cambs. (c. 1092– 1112). Augustinian canons. F: Picot, sheriff of Cambs. Ded: St Giles.*
After the F's. death his son was involved in the rebellion of 1095. The priory thus passed into the king's hands and was later reported desolate (Knowles). But the house must have remained in existence because it was not until 1112 that the canons moved to Barnwell (v. above). *Remains:* None.

Cambridge *Priory. Cambs. (1291– 1539). Gilbertine canons. F: unknown. Ded: St Edmunds.*
The chapel of St Edmund, K. & Martyr, was granted to the Gilbertines by 'B' son of Walter for the benefit of students and resident canons studying at Cambridge. Charters and muniments were burnt in 1348 (Graham). At the Dissolution the property went to Peterhouse (the 1st. Coll. fd. in Cambridge). *Remains:* None. The site is now occupied by Old Addenbrooks Hospital, opposite the FitzWilliam Museum.

Cambridge *Friary. Cambs. (–1289 to 1538). Austin. F: unknown. Geoffrey de Picheford moved the friars to a larger site in 1290. Ded: St Augustine (?).*
Limit of Cambridge. This important house of studies was enlarged in 1292 and again a few years later to enable the intake to reach 70 friars. In 1538 they practically dissolved their own house, being the moving spirits in the Reformation here (Knowles). *Remains:* None. In Peas Hill a bank stands on the site of the friars' gatehouse which was demolished in 1720.

Cambridge *Friary. Cambs. (1247–*

1538). Carmelite. F: unknown. Ded: BVM.
The 1st friary was established at Chesterton and 2 years later Michael Malherb gave the friars a house at Newnham where they continued for 42 years. They finally settled in Milne Street *c.* 1292. Friars came from many parts of the country to study here, but at the suppression all but 2 friars had abandoned it. *Remains:* None. The site was immediately N of Queens' Coll. in which, it is said, some stained glass from the friary is reused in the library windows. 5 skeletons and some stone fdns. were revealed during excavations in 1959. (Med. Arch. Vol. 5).

Cambridge *Friary. Cambs. Map 4 (−1238 to 1538). Dominican. Fd: 'by the charity of several devout people' (Tanner). Ded: unknown.*
Visitation of Cambridge. Friars were sent from houses throughout England to study here, and the accommodation was originally intended for 70 students. At the suppression the prior requested authority to remove an image of Our Lady 'from the sight of the many pilgrims who came to the shrine'. *Remains:* The monastic bldgs. were still standing when Sir Walter Mildmay fd. Emmanuel Coll. on the site in 1544. Substantial sections survive on the E, W & S sides of the Second Court − once the friars' cloister. The Hall was built from parts of the ch. and the W range perhaps incorporates some of the dormitory. Preachers' Street, once adjacent to the Coll., is now renamed St Andrew's Street.

Cambridge *Friary. Cambs. (c. 1226−1538). Franciscan. (Conventual). F: unknown. Ded: St Francis (?).*
Custody of Cambridge. 1st premises was a disused synagogue near the town gaol, and annoyance caused by the latter's proximity was solved by incorporating it into the friary bldgs.! Shortly before 1267 the friars moved to a new site. In 1395 jealousy arose with the neighbouring Franciscan house at Ware concerning encroachments upon areas for alms collecting (Martin). The friars had an important library. At the Dissolution the premises were granted to Trinity Coll. who used some of it as a quarry. It was later purchased by Sidney Sussex Coll. who converted the refectory into a chapel which survived almost unaltered until demolished in 1776. *Remains:* None. Excavations in the cloister court of Sidney Sussex Coll. in 1959 revealed part of the conventual ch. and many fragments of late-14thC stained glass. Excav. notes: Med. Arch. Vol. 5. Hist: The Arch. Hist. of the University of Cambridge (1886) J. Willis Clark, Vol. 1, pp. 723−36. Book: The Grey Friars of Cambridge (1952) J. R. H. Moorman.

Cambridge *Friary. Cambs. (1273 to +1319). Pied Friars. F: unknown. Ded: BVM.*
The proctor of the Order purchased a site in 1273 and in 1290 new bldgs. were commenced near the castle. About 20 friars lived here at the peak of its existence, and in 1319 a prior and one friar were still in residence. *Remains:* None. The site had previously been owned by the Carmelites.

Cambridge *Friary. Cambs. (1258−1307). Friars of the Sack. F: unknown. Ded: unknown.*
The Order was obliged to abandon recruitment following a proclamation

by the Second Council of Lyons in 1274. Surviving members of the community were ordered to join one of the four main Mendicant Orders by 1317. *Remains:* None. The property was granted to Peterhouse in 1307. Note: Archaeologia, Vol. 3, p. 130. The site is now occupied by the FitzWilliam Museum. Some details of grants are preserved in Peterhouse Museum.

Campsey Ash *Priory. Suffolk. Map 7. 6m NE of Woodbridge. (c. 1195– 1536). Augustinian canonesses. F: Theobald de Valoines. Ded: BVM.* The F. gave all his estates in this parish to his sisters Joan and Agnes, on condition that they should build a monastery for themselves and other religious women. In 1347 Maud, countess of Ulster (*v.* Bruisyard) took her vows here on the death of her second husband. The house appears to have flourished throughout its life and bore a good reputation. During several visitations the sisters complained that wealthy laymen over taxed their inn-keeping hospitality. The last prioress went to the other extreme and stinted her canonesses, visitors and herself alike. She even appropriated to herself a 14thC laywoman's brass for her tomb (Power). *Remains:* Very little to be found in a farmhouse known as Ash Abbey. Excavations in 1970 on the site of a newly-demolished barn revealed walls, a pier base, floor tiles and at least 7 burials on the presumed S side of the chancel of the nunnery ch. Med. Arch. Vol. 15 (1971). Desc. of tiles: Proc. Suffolk Inst. of Arch. Vol. 32, pt. 2 (1971).

Cannington *Priory. Somerset. 4m NW of Bridgwater. (c. 1138–1536). Benedictine nuns. F: Robert de*

Courcy. Ded: St Mary. This small and poor house supplemented its meagre income with corrodies and boarders. On a number of occasions in the 14thC the nuns received as paying guests ladies of the county when their husbands and brothers were away, and it is certain they brought their worldly ideas with them and influenced detrimentally the good discipline of the house (VCH). The effect of the B.D. was so severe locally that nuns were hard pressed 'to find a confessor at the hour of death'. In 1351 Bp. Ralph had evidence of falling standards due to a weak prioress, and ordered loss of seniority and penances for several nuns, and suspension from duty of the sub-prioress. Little is known of the later history of the priory. After the Dissolution the prioress and about 6 nuns were moved to Shaftesbury. *Remains:* None. A Farm Institute occupies the site. One of the outer walls includes pointed arches over 2 doorways. Note: Arch. J. Vol. 36, pp. 405–6.

Canons Ashby *Priory. N'hants. Map 6. 7m W of Towcester. (c. 1150–1536). Augustinian canons. F: Stephen de Leye. Ded: BVM.* Surviving records mainly concern benefactions and endowments. Amongst the little known history is the enduring poverty in the 13thC caused by heavy demands on the canons' hospitality, because the house was on a highway to Oxford used by many persons studying there. Hardly anything is known of the internal life. Following a visitation in the first half of the 15thC, only the usual perfunctory injunctions were issued. In later years, relatives of the canons who lived locally caused dissent in the monastery. *Remains:* Part of the priory ch. survives, being 2 bays of the nave with its N aisle, and the W doorway with arcading on each side (fine examples of mid-13thC work) all incorporated in the parish ch. – much restored. Large tower NW of the N aisle. The conventual bldgs. were converted into a private house after the Dissolution, but survived for little more than 20 years. Site of claustral bldgs. part excavated 1969 (Med. Arch. Vol. 14).

Canonsleigh *Priory/Abbey. Devon. Map 8. 8m NE of Tiverton. (c. 1161– 1539). Augustinian canons/canonesses. F: Walter de Clavilla. Ded: BVM & St John Evangelist.*
For about 120 years this priory belonged to canons who may have come from Plympton; then, for an unknown reason, during the r. of Edward I (*c.* 1284) Matilda de Clare, countess of Gloucester and Hereford, re-fd. the house as an abbey for canonesses and added St Etheldreda* (Audrey) to the dedication. Because the F. died before she had given adequate endowments for the financial stability of the house, the convent was left in a deplorable situation (Oliver). In 1314 and 1333 the nuns received appropriated chs. to alleviate their distress. 15thC history is negligible. However, at the Dissolution the income was good by nunnery standards, and the community managed to raise a heavy fine of £200 to avoid suppression in 1536.
Remains: Very slight. Fragments of a 15thC gatehouse and 2 small two-light windows; and away to the E a few parts of the abbey mill (Pevsner).
* Abbess of Ely, died 679.

Canterbury *Cathedral-Priory (Christchurch). Kent. Map 7. (1071–1540). Benedictine monks. F: Archbp.*

Lanfranc (rebuilt the whole monastery). Ded: Christ the Saviour. 1st. f. 598 by St Augustine aided by K. Ethelbert. 2nd. fdn. 997, sacked by Danes in 1011 and destroyed by fire 1067. The 3rd. fdn., 1071, consecrated 1130. Here was the cradle of English Christianity, born in Saxon days. On 29.12.1170 Archbp. Thomas Becket was murdered by 4 knights in the ch., and in 1174 Henry II did penance for the crime. The shrine of St Thomas was destroyed in 1538. In 1207 K. John's quarrel with the pope over the appointment of Archbp. Langton resulted in England being laid under an interdict. An outstanding prior was Henry of Eastry who ruled for 46 years and died 1331. In 1376 Edward the 'Black Prince', the first Knight of the Garter, was buried in the Trinity Chapel. In 1413 the alien priory of Panfield, Essex, was granted to the community (*v.* Appendix 1). Of this great monastery, the 3rd wealthiest in Britain, much information is available from many sources. *Remains:* Apart from the magnificent ch. with early-12thC crypt, there is the early-15thC cloister; chapter house *c.* 1400; early-16thC gatehouse; ruins of the infirmary; unique water tower of *c.* 1400 (now a reading room); and the fine Norman staircase which led to the guest hall. Part of the prior's lodging is now the Deanery. Desc. & plans: Archaeologia, Vols. 4, 9, 11, 17 etc. Numerous articles and publications. Books (among many): Canterbury Cathedral Priory (1943) R. A. L. Smith. Architectural History of the Buildings (1869) Prof. Willis. Illus: Pitkin Pictorial.

Canterbury *(St Augustine's) Abbey. Kent. Map 7. (c. 1080–1538).*

Benedictine monks. Fs: Abbots Scotland (1070–87) & Guy (Wido) (1087–99). Ded: St Peter, St Paul & St Augustine.
1st. fd. 598–605 by K. Ethelbert & St Augustine. Then 613–827 the heptarchy. 3 adjacent chs. were built W–E in line on this site: 1. St Peter & St Paul; 2. St Mary; and 3. St Pancras. In 978 St Dunstan enlarged the ch. of St Peter & St Paul which had the earliest known cloister in England. Just before the Conquest Abbot Wulfric II had begun to build a great rotunda to connect chs. 1 & 2. The final 11thC ch. occupied the site of the 3 Saxon chs. in which many kings and abbots were to be buried. Mitred. Famed for compiling national and ecclesiastical histories including a chronicle of abbots up to 1397, and translating classical writers. Trinity Coll., Cambridge, holds the history of the fdn. (Liber Cantuariensis). A mid. 14thC customary of the abbey includes a list of all the bldgs. and their dimension. Serious fire in 1168 almost destroyed the ch., and in 1271 a prodigious storm practically ruined the abbey by flooding. This was the first and chief mother of English monasteries. The abbey, together with Christchurch nearby, probably held the two largest libraries of MSS in England at the Dissolution. *Remains:* Extensive ruins revealing 7thC chs. and the 11thC rotunda beneath the Norman fdns. Cloister lay to the N. Conventual bldgs. and ch. were dismantled to provide materials for one of Henry VIII's palaces. Two fine gateways survive. Part of site now occupied by St Augustine's Coll. Site of infirmary complex lies beneath playing fields. Whole site excavated 1904 and selected areas 1955–6 & 1974. Desc., plan & care: D of E. Desc. & plan:

Archaeologia, Vol. 66 (1915); also Med. Arch. Vols. 1 & 19. Book: A History of St Augustine's Monastery, Canterbury (1901) R. J. E. Boggis.

Canterbury *Priory. Kent. (c. 1123–1536). Augustinian canons. F: Archbp. Corbeil. Ded: St Gregory.*
In 1087 a hospital in the care of 6 priests was fd. by Archbp. Lanfranc and c. 1123 Archbp. Corbeil introduced Aug. canons (v. also Dover Priory). Little history is known and the house was never wealthy. Ch. burnt in 1145 and vandalised in 1241. In 1326 many defects in the monastic life resulted in the suspension of the prior. In the 14thC Bentley Priory (v. above) had been leased to the convent, and 3 canons went there in 1332 to investigate 'irregularities'. The history, in general, is not one of harmony in later years, there being quarrels and injunctions. *Remains:* None. The priory stood outside the North Gate and the site is completely covered by modern bldgs. Excavations for a new Post Office bldg. in 1958 revealed a wall and some tiling, possibly part of the cloister. Med. Arch. Vol. 3.

Canterbury *Priory, Kent. (c. 1100–1536). Benedictine nuns. F: Archbp. Anselm. Ded: St Sepulchre.*
The house was small and the history is all too often associated with neglect, extreme poverty and indiscipline. The year 1284 saw several injunctions from Archbp. Peckham calling for an end to internal disputes and laying stress upon the need for stricter enclosure of the nuns. Other injunctions occur in 1367 and 1511 (Power). The Holy Maid of Kent (Elizabeth Barton) was a nun here for 7 years before her execution at Tyburn in 1534. *Remains:* None. The nunnery

lay about $\frac{1}{4}$-mile outside the old Riding Gate (dismantled 1782).

Canterbury *Friary. Kent. (1318–1538). Austin. F: Archbp. Reynolds. Ded: unknown.* Limit of Oxford. When the friars wished to occupy a new site *c.* 1325 the monks of Christ Church raised objections, but opposition was withdrawn following a financial settlement. The house was rebuilt in 1408 during a prosperous era, but by 1538 there were debts and impoverishment (VCH). Little else known. *Remains:* None.

Canterbury *Friary. Kent. Map 7. (–1237 to 1538). Dominican. F: unknown (perhaps aided by Archbp. Rich). Ded: unknown.* Visitation of London. Henry III granted the community an island site and gave funds for the ch. and kitchen. The house soon thrived and by the end of the 13thC there were 50 friars here. Records give many details of benefactors, burials and acquisitions of property, but little of internal history. In 1535 Archbp. Cranmer complained to the king that the prior had preached against his (Cranmer's) doctrine, but the story ends there and it has been assumed that the prior escaped abroad (VCH). *Remains:* All has gone except the 13thC refectory, supported on a low rib-vaulted undercroft, now in use as a chapel. It incorporates a reader's pulpit projecting from the W wall. The 13thC guest house survives on the opposite bank of the river. Desc. & plan: Arch. J. Vol. 86 (1929). Site excavated 1928 & 1970, the latter work revealing the S wall of the chapter house and part of the N wall of the ch. (Med. Arch. Vols 14 & 15).

Canterbury *Friary. Kent. Map 7. (1224–1538). Franciscan (Conventual/Observant). F: unknown. Ded: St Francis.* Custody of London. The 1st. House of the Order fd. in England in a small room behind a school, given by the monks of Christ Church. *c.* 1268 the community moved to a new site across the river and a new ch. was consecrated in 1325. The house was handed over for the use of the Observants by Henry VII in 1498. In 1534 the warden was executed, 2 friars died and the rest dispersed or were imprisoned. The friary lingered on with a frail existence until finally suppressed in 1538. Considerable history is known and recorded (Martin). *Remains:* One of the loveliest relics of old Canterbury is the little flint and stone 13thC house which spans a branch of the R. Stour. It has been much altered over the years and the original purpose is unknown – perhaps a guesthouse, warden's lodging or school house. Nothing else above ground. Excavations 1972–3 revealed fdns. of a large bldg. on land owned by the friars in 1275. Hist: Arch. Cantiana, Vol. 34 (1920). (Med. Arch. Vols 17 & 18)

Canterbury *Friary. Kent. (–1274 to –1314). Friars of the Sack. F: unknown. Ded: unknown.* History almost a blank. The closure followed a dispute over land (VCH). Only 3 friars lived here at the turn of the century and they probably moved to Cambridge. *Remains:* None. The friary stood in St Peter's Street to the W of the Grey Friars.

Canwell *Priory. Staffs. 5m SW of Tamworth. (c. 1142–1524). Benedictine monks. F: Geva, widow of Justice Geoffrey Ridell. Ded:*

St Mary, St Giles & All Saints.
The internal history of the house is
sketchy and includes several refs. to
disputes with local inhabitants. One
account claims that at least 4 priors
were Cluniacs. Only on rare occasions
did the community exceed 3 monks
and often only one. In 1456 there
were none following the prior's death.
The frequent resignations of priors
in the 15thC suggests the monks
took turns in holding the priorate.
The house was suppressed by Wolsey
to aid endowments for his Cardinal
Coll., Oxford. *Remains:* None.
Canwell House occupies the site and
late-18thC stables were said to utilise
the remaining ruins. Note: Br. Arch.
Assoc. J. Vol. 29, p. 326.

Carham *Cell. N'land. 3m WSW of
Coldstream (on the Border). (+1131
to 1539). Augustinian canons. F:
Walter L'Espec (gave the ch. & lands).
Ded: St Cuthbert.*
The F. gave the property to Kirkham
Priory who sent 2 or 3 Canons to
supervise the new acquisition. There
were frequent sufferings due to the
cell being so near to the Border,
including destruction by the Scots in
1296. Nevertheless, it survived for
over 400 years with hardly any
independent history until suppressed
at the same time as the mother house.
Remains: None.

Carlisle *Priory/Cathedral-Priory.
C'land. Map 1. (1122-1540).
Augustinian canons. F: Henry I.
Ded: St Mary.*
Walter, a Norman noble and wealthy
priest mooted a monastery c. 1102
and gave lands and a ch. Soon after
the F. had begun building, canons
from Nostell were established here,
and Walter became a canon, dying
before the completion of the priory.

In 1133 the house was elevated to
cathedral status and Adelulf, prior
of Nostell, became the 1st. bp. After
his death the bishopric was vacant
for 47 years and the canons associated themselves with Arrouaise.
Later delays in appointing bps. meant
that the community tended to side
with the Scots, as they did in 1218.
The early years were full of troubles.
Fires occurred 1286, 1292 & 1393
of which the 2nd. was by far the most
serious. The prior was apptd. bp. in
1292 and defended the city against
the Scots. By 1304 losses by wars
and fires had severely depleted the
assets and income, and Edward I
gave aid. This was the only Aug.
house to achieve Cath-Pr. dignity.
Considerable history available from
many other sources. *Remains:* The
ch. with 2-bay nave (originally 8),
crossing and 8-bay presbytery with
great 14thC E window. The cloister
and an octagonal chapter house
(except 2 arches of its vestibule) have
gone; but the refectory with 14thC
undercroft (now used as the chapter
house), and the Prior's Lodging
(enlarged) is now the Deanery. Also
the gateway, NW of the nave, built
in 1527. Numerous books refer to
the history of the house. Illus:
Pitkin Pictorial.

Carlisle *Friary. C'land. (1233-1539).
Dominican. F: unknown. Ded:
unknown.*
Visitation of York. The house was
built outside the city walls but the
position chosen was declared a
nuisance. In 1237 the friars appear
to have gained a foothold within the
walls because they obtained leave 'to
make an excavation beneath the
walls to enable a conduit to carry
water to their chambers' (VCH).
From then on only a few notices of

the monastery's existence appear, mainly concerned with endowments. In the great fire of 1292, when much of the city was reduced to ashes, the Dominicans' house survived. *Remains:* None. Blackfriars Street indicates the vicinity of the site.

Carlisle *Friary. C'land. (1233–1539). Franciscan (Conventual). F: unknown. Ded: St Francis.*
Custody of Newcastle. Located within the city walls on the SE side. Totally destroyed by fire in 1292 and rebuilt in the same area. Various fragments of history are recorded including refs. to visits by Edward I (1300) and Edward III (Christmas 1332); and to the 'popularity' of being buried in the precinct of the friars' house, though the requests were invariably opposed by the secular priests in the neighbourhood. *Remains:* None. Friars Court, behind Devonshire Street, marks the site of the friary.

Carrow *Priory. Norfolk.*
See Norwich.

Cartmel *Priory. Lancs. Map 1. 6m E of Ulverston. (c. 1190–1537). Augustinian canons. F: William Marshal (later earl of Pembroke). Ded: St Mary.*
Colonised from Bradenstoke. It was the F's. wish that the house should never become an abbey. Original charter lost but copies survive detailing early endowments. The F. acquired by marriage vast estates in Ireland, and the fraternity of the cathedral ch. in Dublin agreed to entertain any canon from Cartmel as one of themselves. The trips undoubtedly brought disunity to the house and disobedience in 1245. In 1316 & 1322 the priory suffered severely from Scottish raids and at

the end of the century the bldgs. were in ruin, hospitality neglected and the prior reproved for scandal. At this time the cloister was at first on the S side of the nave, but owing to the dilapidated condition at the end of the 14thC it was rebuilt N of the ch. (for reasons not entirely clear) in the early 15thC. History in this century is a blank and there is a large gap in the list of priors. From time immemorial the priory was bound to provide guides for those crossing the Cartmel & Kent Sands on either side of the peninsula. A revised valuation in 1536 should have excluded the house from closure but it was suppressed in 1536. In 1537 the canons returned during the Northern Rising for which some of them were executed. *Remains:* The fine monastic ch., restored 1618, has 3 particular features: Large E window; low square lantern set diagonally on the tower; no W doorway in the nave. Conventual bldgs. gone. Gatehouse of *c.* 1330 (NT) stands in village square. Desc. & drwgs: Arch. J., Vol. 27 (1870). Desc: Trans. of C'land & W'land Arch. Soc. Vol. 45. Book: Cartmel Priory & Sketches of N. Lonsdale (1909) A. M. Wakefield.

Castle Acre *Alien Priory/Priory. Norfolk. Map 4. 4m N of Swaffham. (1089–1537). Cluniac monks. F: William de Warenne II. Ded: St Mary, St Peter & St Paul.*
The priory was 1st fd. within the castle precincts but was moved to the present site about a year later. Daughter house of Lewes and subject to Cluny until the group became denizen in 1373. One record claims that the parties witnessing the first charter 'bit the wax instead of affixing a seal'. What survives of the history is uninteresting. A recalcitrant prior

Castle Acre Priory, Norfolk. Splendid 12thC architecture of the west front of the church. To the right is the prior's lodging with a fine oriel window supported by two oblique arches.

in the late 13thC proved difficult to dislodge when the monastery was heavily in debt. By 1293 the debt had reached 1000 marks and by the following year the number of monks was 'excessively diminished'. In the 14thC several monks wandered as vagabonds in secular habit and a few less serious scandals make up all that is known of the domestic history. At its peak the community owned about 500 acres and 5 mills, while the area enclosed by the priory's precinct wall was about 36 acres. The original Norman ch. was never rebuilt. *Remains:* The most interesting ruins

in Norfolk. The site has been thoroughly excavated and the whole plan revealed. Elaborate 12thC W front of the ch., walls of transepts, remnants of chapter house and conventual bldgs. including dorter and 12-seater reredorter. Complete mediaeval prior's lodging in W range with parlour, solar and chapel (inhabited until 19thC). Late 15thC gatehouse. Desc. plan & care: D of E. Desc. & plan: Br. Arch. Assoc. J. Vol. 14; and Norfolk Archaeology, Vol. 12.

Castle Hedingham *Priory. Essex. 4m NNW of Halstead. (c. 1190–1536).*

Benedictine nuns. Fs: Aubrey de Vere, 1st. earl of Oxford, and Lucy his wife. Ded: BVM, St James & the Holy Cross. The countess became the prioress after her husband died in 1194. Little is known of the priory's possessions or history. In 1279 Archbp. Peckham ordered the convent to admit the daughter of Sir Robert Beauchamp and threatened 'dire punishment' if they refused. The outcome is unrecorded. Remains: Very slight. There are some traces in a farmhouse on the site.

Catesby Priory. Northants. 3½m SW of Daventry. (c. 1175–1536). Cistercian nuns. F: Robert de Esseby (Ashby). Ded: St Mary & St Edmund (and St Thomas?).
There are some refs. to this being a house of Benedictine nuns when 1st. fd. but was certainly Cist. in the 13thC. Until sometime after 1316 several Aug. canons and lay-brothers were attached to the nunnery from Canons Ashby (v. above). At this time it was a well-ordered house in receipt of royal favours, but by the mid-15thC the bad or weak conduct of prioresses had brought the house ill repute, and severe injunctions were served on the convent. At the time of the Dissolution a more devout prioress reigned and offered to buy the priory for the enormous sum of 2000 marks (£1,333) to save it from extinction. Remains: None. A 19thC house stands on the site. A sedilia and piscina from the conventual ch. survive in the parish ch. in the lower village. Evidence of walling and fishponds existed earlier this century.

Catley Priory. Lincs. 7m NNE of Sleaford. (1148–54 to 1538). Gilbertine canons and nuns. F: Peter de

Belingey (Billinghay). Ded: St Mary. One of the poorest houses of the Order and by 1338 it was in serious financial difficulties. The B.D. (1348–9) brought more distress with loss of tenants and sheep. Little history known of this double house. In the 14thC the average annual sales of 7 sacks of wool represented most of the priory's income. Remains: None. The site has not been excavated and no plan or description exists.

Cerne (Abbas) Abbey. Dorset. Map 5. 8m N of Dorchester. (–987 to 1539). Benedictine monks. F: Ailmer, earl of Cornwall. Ded: St Mary, St Peter & St Benedict.
1st. fd. by St Augustine (by tradition). 2nd. fdn. in 9thC perhaps by Egelward, a rich Saxon. Of the great Bene. abbey relatively little history survives and even the layout of the bldgs. or the exact location of the ch. is unknown. Wealthy. The convent held the right of wreck in all their lands by the sea and in 1275 two tuns of wine seized on the shore by the constable of Corfe Castle. The king ordered reparation. In the 14thC the abbey was called upon to provide aid for the Scottish and French wars, and the life boarding for a succession of the king's pensioners. In 1471 Q. Margaret of Anjou stayed here following her landing at Weymouth previous to the 1st battle of Barnet. From the monastery's library two volumes survive: The Book of Cerne, a collection of devotions, in the Univ. Lib. at Cambridge; and some splendid manuscripts are shared between the BM and Trinity Coll., Cambridge. On the eve of the Dissolution the last abbot and the community were charged with serious offences, but although these are no

doubt exaggerated, some blame for laxity of discipline is certain. *Remains:* The abbot's porch leading to his lodging (*not* an abbey gatehouse) with a fine peculiarly monastic oriel window; a guest house probably for the abbot's VIPs; a 15thC cruciform tithe barn; and some relics of the southern gatehouse incorporated in Abbey Farm. Site never excavated. Notes: Br. Arch. Assoc. J. Vol. 28 (1872). Books: 1. Cerne Abbas (1952) Mary D. Jones; 2. Cerne Abbas (1963) A. O. Gibbons.

Chacombe *(Chalcombe) Priory. Northants. 3m NE of Banbury. (t. of Henry II – 1536). Augustinian canons. F: Hugh de Chacombe. Ded: St Peter & St Paul.*
The fdn. charter was witnessed by Walkelin, abbot of St James, Northampton (1180–1206) but no fdn. date or early history is known. Details of possessions and priors are recorded from *c.* 1226. In 1315 a dispute occurred with a local squire following a raid by the canons on his property. The outcome is not clear, but concerning tenancy of lands the canons won their case. Refs. in the 14th–16thCs are without incident or interest being concerned with burials and bequests. *Remains:* None. The exact site is not known. A house, Chacombe Priory, is built with stones from the monastery. A pointed-arch doorway, 3 buttresses and 2 windows are the sole fragments of bldgs. N of the E end of the house is a mediaeval structure known as the Chapel (Pevsner).

Charley *Priory. Leics. 6m E of Ashby-de-la-Zouch. (+1220 to 1465). Augustinian canons. F: Robert, earl of Leicester. Ded: St Mary?*

The original fdn. by Robert Blanchmains occurred *c.* 1160–70 was probably a small hermitage and a solitary place in the forest of Charnwood (Tanner). Not until after 1220 did it become Aug. From its scanty history comes the story of a 15thC unworthy prior whose grievous dissipation of the priory's resources brought about its ruin (Dickinson). Finally, the two patrons petitioned for the house to be united with Ulverscroft (*v.* below) 'because it was empty due to poverty'. This occurred in 1465. *Remains:* None. Note: Br. Arch. Assoc. J. Vol. 19.

Chatteris *Abbey. Cambs. 14m NW of Ely. (c. 1010–1538). Benedictine nuns. F: Ednoth, bp. of Dorchester and formerly abbot of Ramsey. Ded: St Mary.*
Henry I gave the abbey and its lands to Ely, but very little history is known for the first 150 years of its existence. About 1310 the whole monastery was destroyed by fire and the ded. of the new ch. occurred in 1352. Evidence that a part of the ch. was in use earlier than this is confirmed by an order forbidding nuns to bring pets into it during divine service (a not uncommon prohibition). Documents concerning 13thC grants and a 15thC cartulary in the BM. From various records of episcopal visitations in the 14thC there is little of a serious nature. In 1373 the chief complaint was the failure of the abbess to consult the convent on important issues, and in 1379 poverty was a serious problem. 15thC history is a blank. Although the abbey was due for closure in 1536, it received licence to continue unsuppressed and survived until Sept. 1538. *Remains:* None. A manor house stands within the precinct.

Chelmsford *Friary. Essex. (−1277 to 1538). Dominican. F: unknown. Ded: unknown.* Visitation of London. History negligible. In 1341 the friars obtained licence to enlarge the house. *Remains:* None. The sole memory is the existence of Friars Walk near the New London Road. Excavations 1969−71, on site of a new road, revealed most of the ch. fdns., cloister walks and about 100 burials. (Med. Arch. Vols. 14−16).

Chertsey *Abbey. Surrey. 4m S of Staines. (964−1537). Benedictine monks. F: K. Edgar. Ded: St Peter.* 1st. f. 666 by Erkenwald, later bp. of London. 9thC Danish raids ended with murder of abbot and 90 monks. Mid-10thC, Athelwald, bp. of Winchester, sent 13 monks from Abingdon who were replaced by the F. in 964. Thus began a long history of this great abbey (*v.* VCH) which later received both favour and protection from the Conqueror. *c.* 1200 it was one of 6 confederated abbeys (*v.* Winchester Cath-Pr) whose fraternity agreed to foster the religious spirit and pray for each others dead. In 1381 the abbey was attacked and court rolls and muniments destroyed during an insurrection. Much information survives about external history but details of internal life are extremely scanty. In the 13th & 14thCs there were many disputes and expensive litigation greatly taxed the resources. The abbot filled an important part in county affairs and enjoyed the king's favour. There is no mention of bad management at any time. In 1471 the murdered Henry VI was first interred here, then at Windsor. There was debt in 1501 but the extent is not revealed. The surrender of the wealthy abbey in 1537 was made on condition that it should be re-established at Bisham (*v.* above). *Remains:* None. In 1752 a Dr Stukeley wrote: 'Of that noble and splendid pile which took up 4 acres of ground, and looked like a town, nothing remains'. Excavated 1850, 1855 & 1861 but all is again below ground. Most of the materials went into the building of Hampton Court. Tiles in BM. Note re tiles: Archaeologia, Vol. 44; and Br. Arch. Assoc. J. Vol. 29 (1873).

Cheshunt *Priory. Herts. 7m SSE of Hertford. (c. 1183−1536). Benedictine nuns. F: unknown. Ded: St Mary.* This was a poor house, the nuns being reduced to begging in the highways (Power). Two serious fires, 1290 & *c.* 1302, destroyed the ch., goods and charters. The brief history of the house is mainly concerned with financial problems and relief from overdue payments of tithes. Q. Isabella was invariably met by the nuns when she travelled to Hertford. Edward III had great sympathy for the community's distressed state and gave aid on 4 occasions. There seems to have been a close connection between the nunnery and London, and the value of its possessions in the city in 1367 far exceeded that of its property elsewhere. In the 14th & 15thCs the house is often mentioned in wills; evenso, it is not unlikely that poverty probably prompted early surrender of the 4 remaining nuns (VCH), whose bldgs. were almost certainly derelict. *Remains:* None. The house stood N of the main street near the River Lea.

Chester *Abbey. Cheshire. Map 2. (1093−1540). Benedictine monks. F: Hugh Lupus, earl of Chester. Ded: St Werburgh.*

Colonised from Bec. The monastery replaced a ch. of secular canons. The F. entered the abbey as a monk 3 days before his death in 1101. St Werburgh had no special tie with Chester, her remains being brought here *c.* 875 from Hanbury (Staffs.) for safety when the Danes drew near. Fairly prosperous with incomes from manors, properties, tithes and fishing (a ship and 10 nets at Anglesey). Considerable details exist of the abbey's undistinguished history which is readily available from many books. *c.* 1197 Abbot Geoffrey lamented over the 'intolerable ruin by fire of his ch.'. In the second half of the 13thC Abbot Simon carried out an extensive re-bldg. programme incl. Lady Chapel, chapter house and refectory. 14thC visitations reveal an average standard of monastic life 'a decent mediocrity' (Burne). 15thC history is less creditable and a succession of conflicts with the city fathers brought a number of monks before the mayor's court. In 1195 a monk, Lucian, wrote the earliest known guidebook — about Chester. In the mid-14thC another monk, Ranulf Higden, wrote his 7-volume 'Polychronicon', a valuable 'universal history' of England up to his time. *Remains:* The abbey ch. became a cathedral in 1541 and survives complete, though only the N transept and the N wall of the nave aisle are Norman. Shrine of St Werburgh. Very fine 14thC choir stalls. The claustral bldgs. are the most complete in England and include the refectory with pulpit, chapter house with vestibule, Norman undercroft of W range, and cloister walks with lavatorium and carrells. Gatehouse survives at approach to Abbey Square (originally the abbey's court). Short desc. & plan: Arch. J. Vol. 94 (1937). Book: The Monks of Chester

(1962) R. V. H. Burne. Illus: Pitkin Pictorial.

Chester *Priory. Cheshire. Map 2. (c. 1140–1540). Benedictine nuns. F: Ranulf II, earl of Chester. Ded: St Mary.*
The history of the house appears to be the least known of any monastery in the city. There are refs. to many benefactions especially from the F. whose daughter Lucy became the 2nd. prioress. This was never a large or wealthy house and in 1536 it managed to escape suppression on payment of a large fine of £160. It was finally closed on the same day as the abbey — 21.1.1540. *Remains:* Very little. A gateway from the nunnery survives in Grosvenor Park. Part of the site (located NW of the castle walls) known as Nuns' Field excavated in 1964 (Ch. & cloister) when many floor tiles, some pottery and a few burials were found. All fdns. had been robbed earlier. The area is now occupied by the County Police HQ. Notes & plan: Chester & N Wales Arch. Soc. J. Vol. 52 (1965).

Chester *Friary. Cheshire. (–1277 to 1538). Carmelite. F: Thomas Stadham. Ded: BVM.*
More history apparently known than for either of the other 2 Chester friaries, but fewer details of the bldgs., except for the ch's. steeple 'of great height and beauty' erected in 1496. It was a noted sea-mark for direction over the bar to Chester. The friars were both raided (1424) and raiders (1454), both parties no doubt seeking to reduce their poverty. Throughout the life of the house the friars kept their popularity, no doubt due to their compassion. Many citizens chose to be buried within the pre-

cinct and numerous bequests were made to the community. *Remains:* None. The site was in the vicinity of Whitefriars Street and some traces of bldgs. and precinct walls may exist in the walls of property on the S side of Commonhall Street (Bennett). No record of excavations. Hist: Chester & N Wales Arch. Soc. J. Vol. 31 J. H. E. Bennett.

Chester *Friary. Cheshire. (−1236 to 1538). Dominican. F: Henry III. Ded: St Nicholas.*
Visitation of Oxford. A considerable number of chronicles exist giving details of the many benefactions the house received between 1270 & 1505; but for all this the monastery was in a poor way at the time of the Dissolution; with only the choir and one aisle of the nave waterproof. The state was worse than that of either the Grey or White Friars in the city. It is hardly surprising that post-Dissolution owners soon pulled down the remnants. Little is known of the bldgs. or history. *Remains:* None. The exact site is uncertain but it lay at the S end of the parish of St Martin's. A number of skeletons were found in the area in 1977. Hist: Chester & N Wales Arch. Soc. J. Vol. 39 (1952).

Chester *Friary. Cheshire. (1238/40− 1538). Franciscan (Conventual). F: Albert de Pisa. Ded: St Francis.*
Custody of Worcester. From the middle until the end of the 13thC no history is known; and although records survive of bequests and gifts to the friars up to the Dissolution, theirs was an impoverished house in 1538. Their devotion to the sick and dying at the time of the B.D. was certainly unselfish as many friars also perished in the epidemic (they

had been accused of exerting undue influence at deathbeds). In 1528 the friars allowed the merchants and sailors of Chester to use the nave of their ch. for storage of sails and ships-chandlers' stores, on condition they repaired the ch. at their own cost (Martin). It seems that at no time was there a very large community, and only 7 friars in 1538. *Remains:* None. A small section of the precinct wall was the last remnant and many fragments of floor tiles have been found. The site, near the Watergate, was partially excavated in 1920 and a conjectural ground plan produced. Hist. & plans: Chester & N Wales Arch. Soc. J. Vol. 24 (1921). Desc: Franciscan Arch. in England (1937) A. R. Martin.

Chester *Friary. Cheshire. (−1274 to +1284).*
Friars of the Sack. Nothing seems to be known of this short-lived house. Doubt exists whether it was ever established. *Remains:* None.

Chetwode *Priory/Cell. Bucks. Map 6. 5m SW of Buckingham. (1245 to −1535). Augustinian canons. F: Ralph de Norwich. Ded: St Mary & St Nicholas.*
This small and poor house had no more than 3 canons during its life. History is negligible; but up to c. 1350 there are records of disputes over royal deer and laymen's cattle ruining the canons' crops. In 1460 the poverty was so great that the canons could no longer serve local chs., and the house then became a cell of Notley Abbey. In 1480 the priory ch. was given to the parishioners because theirs was in decay. *Remains:* The long chancel of the priory ch. with the parish nave and narrow W tower is still in use. The E end is earlier and

finer than the rest. No other
monastic evidence above ground.

Chichester *Friary. Sussex. (−1280
to 1538). Dominican. F: unknown.
Ded: St Vincent.*
Visitation of London. The limited
history mainly records numerous
bequests and acquisitions of lands.
There were several stages of enlarging
the premises. *Remains:* None. Most
of the bldgs. had been pulled down
by 1550. Site part excavated 1966
& 1972 before new property
occupied the area. Reports by
Chichester Civic Soc. Excavations
Committee (1973).

Chichester *Friary. Sussex. Map 6.
(−1232 to 1538). Franciscan (Conventual). F: unknown. Ded:
St Francis.*
Custody of London. The friars took
over the site of St Mary's Hospital
and soon enlarged it following a gift
of land from their patron Richard,
earl of Cornwall (brother of Henry
III). In 1269 the community moved
to the site of the ruined castle which
lay within the city walls. (The precinct
so formed is now Priory Park recreation ground.) History is scanty since
friars kept few records and details of
the bldgs. and other possessions. It
seems that after the arrival of the
Dominicans in the town the size of
the community dwindled, no doubt
due to the counter attraction (Martin).
Remains: In Priory Park stands the
choir of the friars' ch., completed
1282. Nothing survives of the nave
(if there ever was one) nor of the
conventual bldgs., although 2 blocked
doorways on the N side of the choir
may have led to the cloister. Desc.,
photo & plan: Franciscan Arch. in
England (1937) A. R. Martin.

108

Chicksands *Priory. Beds. Map. 6.
1½m NW of Shefford. (c. 1150−
1538). Gilbertine canons and nuns.
Fs: Pain de Beauchamp and Rose his
wife. Ded: St Mary.*
No cartulary has survived. The
endowments may well have supported
100 religious in the 12thC but in
1257 and again in 1330 the house
was so impoverished that a number
of canons and nuns had to be dispersed, and on 4 occasions remission
of tithes was sought. Of internal
history for 1150−1535 hardly a
trace exists. During the last 100
years of the priory's life the material
prosperity seems to have recovered.
The evil report produced by Cromwell's agents is hardly worth consideration (VCH), and despite the
charges the house survived until
22.10.1538. *Remains:* A house is
ranged round the site of one of the
cloisters. The ch. has gone. The
undercroft of the W range is vaulted
with central piers forming 7 bays and
dates from the first half of the 13thC.
Some of the S, E & W walls are of
considerable thickness. There is also
a 13thC doorway which once led into
the ch. Note: Antiquity, Vol. 11,
p. 214. Early charter notes: Beds.
Hist. Record. Soc. Vol. 1 (1913).

Chipley *Priory. Suffolk. 2m N of
Clare. (−1235 to 1468). Augustinian
canons. F: unknown. Ded: BVM.*
This small house of only 3 or 4 canons
had few possessions and an unrecorded
history. By 1468 it was said that the
bldgs. were in a ruinous state and it
was then annexed to the collegiate
ch. of Stoke by Clare which had
acquired the priory's patronage
(Dickinson). *Remains:* A farmhouse
on the site, Chipley Abbey, incorporates some of the W range of the
claustral bldgs. The ruins of the priory

ch. were dismantled in 1818 (L.G.). There is evidence of fishponds.

Chirbury *Priory. Salop. Map 2. 3m NE of Montgomery. (c. 1195–1536). Augustinian canons. F: Robert de Boullers, lord of Montgomery. Ded: St Michael.* The canons first settled at Snead (some 9m SE of Montgomery) *c.* 1190 and moved to the permanent site about 5 years later. Due to the prior's weakness in 1279 the bp. temporarily entrusted the custody of the house to Wormsley. In 1281 a licence was granted for the canons to return to Snead but it was never used. The reason for the application is unknown because permanent claustral bldgs. were well advanced in 1277. The history is best known from episcopal visitations. There seems to have been plenty to criticise in the 14thC, and even a lay patron endeavoured to bring order. In 1441 warlike Welshmen imposed one of their kinsmen as prior but, despite opposition from the community, the bp. (and later events) proved the man a good choice. In the 15thC there were numerous attacks on the priory by marauders (VCH) and poverty. *Remains:* The nave, aisles and W tower of the conventual ch. survive. Transepts, central tower and chancel have gone, but the last named has been rebuilt. Nothing else. Some fine carved stalls in Montgomery parish ch. are reputed to have come from the priory ch.

Christchurch *Priory. Hants. Map 6. 5m E of Bournemouth. (c. 1150– 1539). Augustinian canons. Fs: Richard de Redvers and his father Baldwin, earl of Devon, at the behest of Bp. Blois of Winchester. Ded: Holy Trinity.*

1st. f. *c.* 1094 by Ralph Flambard for secular canons and known as Twynham Priory. A wealthy house whose resources were often strained through hospitality to expensive and unwelcome guests, including K. John; though renowned for generous alms to the poor. Visitation reports reveal both good and bad conditions. In 1360 the prior complained that the entire household, both sexes, of the earl of Salisbury lodged at the house for months on end. The bp. criticised the earl for abuse of his patronage and ordered removal of the family. An internal rebellion in 1402 forced out the prior and his senior canons, and goods were stolen. The guilty canons were punished with solitary confinement. In 1501 the bp. reported a well-ordered house. The ch. provides a valuable memorial to the age of abbots, the monastic choir being just as it was when the canons left it for the last time (Braun). Beautiful Salisbury chantry. *Remains:* The complete ch. survives (the longest parish ch. in England) probably because of a letter written to Henry VIII by the honest last prior on behalf of some 1600 local people. No claustral bldgs. Two doorways in S aisle of the nave led to the cloister. Traces of night stairs in S transept. Desc. & plan: Arch. J. Vol. 123 (1966); also Vol. 29. Precinct excavations 1968–9 revealed miscellaneous objects near the mill stream (Med. Arch. Vols. 13 & 14).

Christ Church *(St Frideswide's) Priory.* See Oxford.

Church Gresley *Priory. Derbys. Map 3. 4½ SSE of Burton upon Trent. (c. 1135? – 1536). Augustinian*

109

canons. *F: Wm. de Gresley. Ded: St George.*
A small priory of 3 or 4 canons. No cartulary known to survive and only fragments of history which suggest an uneventful existence. Some details are known of possessions and income. In 1493 there were so few canons that they could not elect a prior. A few details of the priory's life can be gleaned from the Gresley family documents in Chetham's Library, Manchester. *Remains:* The nave of the priory ch. exists though much restored in 1896. There are indications of the monastic choir on the E side of the tower, and where there is now a replacement chancel built in 1820. Glass, tiles and burials have been unearthed. Plan in 'The Gresleys of Drakelow' by F. Madan.

Church Preen *Alien Cell/Cell. Salop. Map 2. 6m W of Much Wenlock. (+1150 to +1534). Cluniac monks. F: unknown, probably Richard de Belmeis. Ded: St John, Baptist.*
Very small cell which belonged to Much Wenlock sometime before 1244. It became denizen in 1384 and still remained subject to M. W. Curious ref. to the presence of monks from the Cistercian abbey of Combermere being here (VCH), but the story ends unresolved when the prior of M. W. accused the abbot of Combermere of taking Preen's livestock. Very little recorded history. *Remains:* The ch. dating from the 12th & 13thCs survives. It is long and narrow ($12\frac{3}{4}$ ft.) without aisles or transepts and was for the use of 2 monks and 2 laybrothers. Nothing else exists.

Cirencester *Abbey. Glos. Map 5. (1117–1539). Augustinian canons. F: Henry I. Ded: St Mary.*

A poorly-endowed ch. of secular canons occupied the site before the Aug. fdn. It became the largest community of the Order and the wealthiest house (Aug.) in England at the time of the Dissolution. Colonised from Merton. Mitred 1416. 12th, 13th & 14thC cartularies survive. One of the few Aug. houses fd. as an abbey. It was also one of 4 houses* which entered into an agreement not to finance expensive hospitality to the bps'. representatives (Graham). An early-13thC abbot (Nequam) was one of the most learned men in England. No evidence that the canons kept a chronicle, but they built up a fine library by copying books themselves (Dickinson). There was weak government in 1276 when a prior usurped power under his abbot. In 1342 the prosperous sheep-farmers of Cirencester resented being the abbot's tenants and strife arose in the town. A similar attack on the abbey occurred in 1385 but nothing is known of the outcome. History during the last 100 years is quite obscure. The abbey had, perhaps, one of the finest monastic chs. in England, destroyed upon Henry VIII's express condition that 'the whole of the bldgs. shall be pulled down and carried away'. *Remains:* Every trace has gone except a length of precinct wall and a Norman gateway of *c.* 1180, though much restored. Site part excavated 1959 & 1964–5 revealing the location and plan of the ch., and E claustral range – to the N of the ch. (Med. Arch. Vols. 4, 9 & 10). It is believed that the fan-vaulting in the narrow St Katherine's Chapel in the parish ch. came from the abbey's cloister. Desc: Antiquaries J. Vol. 45 (1965); Br. Arch. Assoc. J. Vol. 25. Notes: Archaeologia Vols. 20 & 26. Book: The Story of Cirencester Abbey (1950) F.W. P.

Hicks. A plaque on a terrace in the Abbey Grounds indicates the site. * The others being Worcester, Gloucester and Lanthony II (Glos).

Clare *Friary. Suffolk. Map 7. 7m NW of Sudbury. (1249–1538). Austin. F: Richard de Clare*, earl of Gloucester & Hertford. Ded: BVM.* Limit of Cambridge. This was the first house of the Order in England, introduced by the F. Not until August 1338 was the ch. dedicated. Little history appears to be known but a Register of Deeds gives details of visitations by bps., and the cost of entertaining their large retinues. It was here that Joan of Acre, 2nd. daughter of Edward I, was buried with great ceremony in 1305. The 'Dialogue of the Grave' between a secular priest and a friar is recorded in the book noted below. In 1953 the property was sold back to the Austin Friars who are there today. *Remains:* Some cloister walls exist and in the E wall is the entrance to the the chapter house and the dormitory staircase. The 14thC infirmary survives beyond the dorter range with its re-redorter. The cellarer's hall in the W range with parlour and buttery are incorporated in the main bldg. Part excavated 1902, 1957 & 1963 resulting in a site plan. (There is a curious change of axis between nave and chancel of the ch.) The central tower was probably octagonal (Med. Arch. Vols. 2 & 8). Book: Clare Priory (1962) Mrs. K. W. Barnardiston. Desc. & plan: Suffolk Inst. of Arch. Vol. 8, Pt. 2. * The de Clare family fd. 15 religious houses in England.

Clattercote *Priory. Oxon. 6m N of Banbury. (c. 1253–1538). Gilbertine canons. F: unknown, perhaps Robert*

de Chesney. Ded: St Leonard. Originally a leper hospital fd. *c.* 1155 and became Gilb. in the time of William, Master of Sempringham (1251–62). In a deed of his the priory had become 'so prosperous in worldly possessions by gifts of the faithful' that the resources could support canons as well as the infirm (VCH). Apart from several refs. to acquisitions of land, nothing is known of the life here. The house was poor at the time of the Dissolution with only a prior and 3 canons. Part of the property went to Christ Church Coll., Oxford. *Remains:* None. In 1614 the ruins were incorporated in a large house. This was replaced early in the 19thC by another property in which 13thC or early-14thC doorway or window mouldings from the priory were incorporated.

Cleeve *(Vallis Florida) Abbey. Som. Map 8. 2m SW of Watchet. (1198–1537). Cistercian monks. F: Wm. de Romara. Ded: St Mary.* Colonised from Revesby. Little known of internal history. Bad harvests and mismanagement in the first quarter of the 14thC caused a decline in fortunes. When the era of lay-brothers ended following the B.D. (1348–9) the convent leased its lands to seculars. The grant of Henry III of right of wreck, as several of the abbey's estates were coastal, brought occasional benefits as well as setbacks. In 1468 there was a dispute with the sheriff of Devon over ownership of a shipwreck. The era 1310–1450 reveals periods of indiscipline and financial instability, but matters improved considerably in the second half of the 15thC (Gilyard-Beer). At this time there were major bldg. developments — the first for over a century — under the skilful rule of

111

Cleeve Abbey, Somerset. Fifteenth century refectory (upper floor) sited east to west; with tiled floor of 13thC refectory in foreground sited north to south.

Cleeve Abbey, Somerset. Interior of 15thC refectory looking west.

Abbot Juyner. In 1535 the abbey was devoting to charity a sum 4 times more than the average monastery of its size. *Remains:* The ch. has gone except for fdns. Here are the most complete Cist. conventual bldgs. in England. The E & S claustral ranges retain their roofs and floors. On the 1st floor of the E range is the perfect dorter, and even the hook upon which the lantern was hung to light the dorter and reredorter at the same time. In the S range the refectory on the 1st floor, sited E & W, replaced a N & S earlier bldg. The W range was rebuilt in the 15thC when no longer needed for lay-brothers. In the N walk of the 13thC cloister wall is a rare example of a recess for the abbot's

seat. Fine gatehouse. Desc., plan & care: D of E. Desc. & plan: Somerset. Arch. Soc. Vol. 35 (1889) & Vol. 77 (1931).

Clerkenwell *Augustinian canonesses* *See* London.

Clifford *Alien Priory/Priory. Herefs. 2m N of Hay-on-Wye. (c. 1129– 1536). Cluniac monks. F: Simon Fitz Richard. Ded: St Mary.* Dependent upon Lewes. Became denizen between 1351–74. Endowed with about 400 acres of land but the revenues were never great. Repairs to bldgs. destroyed or damaged by the Welsh, plus demands upon their hospitality, greatly impoverished the

113

community. A visitation by Bp. Swinfield in 1290, with a train of 36 horses, was a typical strain on resources. However, in times of attack from the Welsh the nearby garrison at the castle gave speedy help, coming down a lane still known as Succour Lane (Duncumb). *Remains:* None. The ch. was destroyed in 1670. A farm house on the site contains stone from the priory bldgs.

Cockerham *Priory/Cell. Lancs. 5m NNW of Garstang. (c. 1207–1477). Augustinian canons. F: William of Lancaster I. Ded: St Michael.*
The ch. of St Michael was given by the F. to Leicester Abbey and it remained a priory ch. until *c.* 1288. About this time the way was paved for the withdrawal of the 2 or 3 canons and only a warden was left in charge of the cell by the middle of the 14thC. (It would seem very probable that the site was never more than a small grange as it was never conventual.) And so it continued until 1477 when the property was leased privately by the abbot of Leicester. *Remains:* None. The ch. of St Michael continues as the parish ch., mainly rebuilt in the early-19thC.

Cockersand *Priory/Abbey. Lancs. Map 2. 5m SSW of Lancaster. (–1190 to 1539). Premonstratensian canons. F: Hugh Garth, a hermit. Ded: St Mary.*
1st. f. *c.* 1184 as a hospital whose principal benefactors were Wm. of Lancaster II and Heloise his wife (Colvin). The extreme isolation of the house 'standing bleakly and object to all winds' (Leland) supports the tradition of fdn. by a hermit. At sometime before 1190 the hospital became a Premon. priory colonised from Croxton, and *c.* 1196 received

abbey status. Leicester Abbey was given lands in the area by the same benefactor which caused disputes, and the canons even considered a new site. Considerable history survives and a 13thC cartulary. The site suffered from inroads of the sea for many years. There was a fine library in 1536. The adjacent hospital continued under the care of the canons until the Dissolution. The commissioners gave the house a good report and permitted its continuance on payment of £400 to the Duchy of Lancaster (Haigh). It was the only Lancs. house exempted from the 1536 Act of Suppression, but at the closure in 1539 only 1 of the 23 canons were ever found employment. *Remains:* The fine 13thC octagonal chapter house, long used as a mausoleum by the Dalton family, is the sole relic apart from fragments of walls of the nave and transept of the ch. In Lancaster's parish ch. are 14 superb 14thC choir stalls from the abbey, described as 'so exquisitely carved that the effect is like the finest lace'. Site part excavated 1923. Desc. & plan: Trans. of Lancs. & Ches. Antiquarian Soc. (new ser.) Vol. 31 (1915) & Vol. 40 (1923). Also: Arch. Review, Vol. 29. Book: The Abbey of St Mary-in-the-Marsh, Cockersand (1925) J. Swarbrick.

Coddenham *Cell. Suffolk. 7½m N of Ipswich. (–1184 to 1537). Augustinian canons. F: Eustace de Merch. Ded: St Mary (?).*
First intended to be a Cistercian nunnery but the ch. here was given to the Aug. canons of Royston Priory who used it as a cell. The history is negligible and there is contradictory evidence in the scanty records concerning whether nuns were ever sent here. It appears certain that no con-

114

ventual ch. ever existed and that any canons (or nuns) would have used the chancel of the parish ch. *Remains:* None.

Coggeshall *Abbey. Essex. Map 7. 9m W of Colchester. (1140–1538). Cistercian monks. F: K. Stephen & Q. Matilda. Ded: St Mary & St John, Baptist.*
Colonised from Savigny; became Cist. 1147. Considerable details in VCH about possessions and benefactions. A raid in 1216 by men of K. John's army stole 22 horses belonging to the bp. of London, and others, staying there. In 1427 Pope Martin licensed the abbot to wear the mitre and other insignia. No other abbots are so mentioned and it was probably a life gift. Poverty in 1370. In 1381 peasants took away goods and charters, suggesting some unpopularity of the abbey. Although the house had adequate possessions to support it, there was considerable debt at the Dissolution. *Remains:* Ch., cloister & conventual bldgs. gone. Some parts of what may have been the infirmary and guesthouse are incorporated in a house, including a complete corridor. The remains show an extensive use of brick as early as *c.* 1220. There is an exceptionally fine 'Chapel-by-the-Gate', restored 1897, dedicated to St Nicholas. Site part excavated 1950. Desc: Essex Arch. Soc. Trans. Vols. 1 (1858) & 15 (1918). Desc. & plan: Br. Arch. Assoc. J. Vol. 18 (1955).

Colchester *(St John's) Abbey. Essex. Map 7. (1096–1539). Benedictine monks. F: Eudo (Seneshal, dapifer or royal chamberlain to William II). Ded: St John, Baptist.*
The monks came from Rochester but as they did not like the place, Eudo

obtained 13 monks from York. One of them became the first abbot in 1102, and he was succeeded by a monk from the abbey of Bec. Mitred. Fine late-13thC cartulary survives setting out details of endowments. There was almost constant strife between the convent and the townsmen concerning liberties within 2 local boroughs. Serious flooding and fires in 1338 due to a severe storm. The rule of Abbot Godfrey at the end of the 14thC was one of constant misfortune, and a dispute with the community caused his arrest in 1392. The house held the privilege of sanctuary which was used on several occasions by felons. The last abbot resisted the suppression of his house and was executed. *Remains:* Nothing but the fine 15thC gateway (care: D of E) with its flint-panelled and pinnacled turrets – a beautiful exercise in the local style (Sitwell). To the S of the town is Bourne Mill, built with stone from the abbey.

Colchester *(St Botolph's) Priory. Essex. Map 7. (c. 1100–1536). Augustinian canons. F: unknown; perhaps Norman, a Kentishman from Bec or one Ainulf. Ded: St Julian & St Botoloph.*
The 1st. house of the Aug. Order in England. *c.* 1095 a ch. served by secular priests existed here with Ainulf heading the community. It seems that he and Norman together brought the first canons to this country. The monastery was given authority over all other Aug. houses in the land, but it did not grow to first rank nor did it exercise the power vested in it. It seems that no incident of importance in the history of the priory has been preserved, but it had the very unusual privilege of exemption from episcopal jurisdiction

115

St Botolph's Priory, Colchester. Twelfth-century west front of the church.

(Dickinson). There are refs. to disputes and jealousies with St John's because the town could hardly contain two such large monasteries. As part of the ch. served the parish much of it survived until the Rebellion in 1648 which brought about its destruction. It remained derelict until 1912.
Remains: Ruins of the late-11th or early-12thC nave built of flint, septaria and Roman brick. Transepts and E end have gone. No claustral bldgs. Desc. plan & care: D of E. Notes: Archaeologia, Vols. 4 & 12.

Colchester *Friary. Essex. (−1235 to 1538). Crutched (Holy Cross). F: unknown, perhaps one of the lords of* the manor of Stanway. Ded: St Mary & the Holy Cross (?).
This may have been the 1st. house of the Order in England. Not being mendicant it was unaffected by the decision of the Council of Lyons in 1274 to prevent further recruitment. Its main function had been a hospital and c. 1392 it continued as such but not under the Order. About 100 years later 4 Crossed friars regained possession and it survived until the general Dissolution. In 1526 a murderer sought sanctuary after leaving the security of St John's Abbey. The friars refused to deliver the felon to the judge claiming their privilege to be as great as St John's. The outcome

116

is unknown. *Remains:* None. Note:
Archaeologia, Vol. 11.

Colchester *Friary. Essex. (−1237 to
1538). Franciscan (Conventual). F:
unknown. Ded: St Francis (?).*
Custody of Cambridge. Relatively
little history survives and nothing
is known of the F. or the fdn. In
1309 & 1338 the possession of
additional land allowed enlargement
of the conventual bldgs. and rebuilding of the ch. *Remains:* None. The
site was in the NE corner of the city
walls which formed two sides of the
precinct boundary, and was next to
the East Gate and almost opposite
St James' ch.

Cold Norton *Priory. Oxon. In
Chipping Norton. (1148/58−1507).
Augustinian canons. F: Avelina de
Norton. Ded: St John, Evangelist.*
The small house was probably for no
more than 5 canons and apparently
had an unhappy history of poverty
due to inadequate endowments,
although there is no record of internal
affairs from any visitation. In 1446
there were only 2 canons, and when
in 1507 the sole survivor, Prior
Wotton, died, the patron conveyed
the rights to the king who gave the
possessions to St Stephen's secular
coll., Westminster. *Remains:* None.
Private property covers the site. After
the Dissolution the bldgs. became a
coaching inn.

Colne *Priory. Essex.*
See Earls Colne.

Colwall *(Brockbury) Priory Cell.
Herefs. 3½m NNE of Ledbury.*
A small Benedictine cell of uncertain
origin, dependent upon Great
Malvern Priory, existed here at the
end of the 12thC. Nothing is known

of its duration. It is unlikely that there
were ever more than 2 monks living
at the site. The name Brockbury is
linked with the cell because it was in
the parish of Colwall. There is further
confusion because of a ref. to a small
Bene. cell at nearby Barton, now
thought to be one and the same as
Brockbury − both, apparently, alternative names for Colwall.

Combe *Abbey. Warks. 4m E of
Coventry. (1150−1539). Cistercian
monks. F: Richard de Camvilla. Ded:
St Mary.*
Colonised from Waverley. 13thC
cartulary in the BM. By far the
wealthiest house in the county which
owned considerable land in it as well
as many houses and rents in Coventry.
By the mid-14thC financial troubles
arose from defective rule. An unusual
bequest was the provision of shoes
for the poor who waited at the gate
daily, to be bought from income
derived from a gift of land (VCH).
Details of internal history are meagre,
but there is a record of the violent
death of Abbot Geoffrey in 1345.
Neither the reason nor the outcome
of the inquest are known. The last
abbot was in office for only one
year − put there by Cromwell to
ensure an easy 'voluntary' surrender.
Remains: A 17thC house standing
on the site is the property of the
City of Coventry and its courtyard
occupies the site of the cloister. The
chapter house entrance exists on the
E side and also a few doorways.
Nothing more. Site excavations in
1965 revealed the almost total
destruction of the abbey in the 16th
& 19thCs (Med. Arch. Vol. 10). Note:
Br. Arch. Assoc. J. Vol. 3.

Combermere *Abbey. Cheshire. 4m
NE of Whitchurch. (1133−1538).*

117

Cistercian monks. F: Hugo de
Malbanc. Ded: St Mary.
Colonised from Savigny. Became
Cist. 1147. History obscure; the
Nantwich historian J. Hall made an
attempt but it has been lost. His notes
survive in the Nantwich P.L. The
abbey's income came from land, fish
and salt interests for which several
notices of rentals exist. The F's
reason for the fdn. are recorded at
great length and include the hope of
redemption for the souls of himself
and his family. The Book of the
Abbots of Combermere, 1289–1538,
described by J. Hall in 1896, is to be
found in the Lancs. & Cheshire Rec.
Soc. J. Vol. 31. *Remains:* None. The
site is occupied by a house begun in
the 16thC. Three Gothic arches on
the ground floor may be part of the
monastery. The intricately carved
choir stalls in St Mary's, Nantwich,
came from the abbey.

Combwell *Abbey/Priory. Kent. 3m
SE of Lamberhurst. (t. Henry II –
1536). Augustinian canons. F:
Robert de Turneham. Ded: St Mary
Magdalen.*
c. 1220 the possessions were too
small to maintain the estates as an
abbey and the house was reduced to
priory status. Bayham's abbot
charged the prior of having deserted
the Premonstratensians, but the
Archbp. of Canterbury ruled it was
an Aug. house. What little history is
recorded during its 350 years does
not suggest a very edifying existence.
Remains: None. Nor is there anything left of the house which took
its place. The present house is
modern (Pevsner).

Conishead *Priory. Lancs. 2m SE of
Ulverston. (–1181 to 1536).
Augustinian canons. F: Gamel de*

Penning and, possibly, Wm. de
Lancaster II. Ded: BVM.
During the reign of Henry II (+ 1154)
the house was fd. as a hospital for
lepers and poor persons, rather than
a priory, presumably to avoid trouble
with Furness which was unwilling to
have another religious house on its
doorstep (Dickinson). Evenso, sometime before 1181 it became Aug.
There is considerable, though uneventful, history (VCH) and details
of the priory's properties and relations with Furness, but little else.
About 1525 Wolsey wished to
suppress the monastery for his Oxford
Coll. venture, but the duke of Suffolk
intervened and the danger temporarily passed. *Remains:* None. The
site of the conventual ch. was located
in 1823 on the S side of the present
19thC house, part of which is
believed to cover the area of the N
transept.

Cook Hill *(Cokehill) Priory. Worcs.
2m W of Alcester. (c. 1180–1538).
Cistercian nuns. F: uncertain. Ded:
St Mary.*
VCH names Isabel, countess of
Warwick as the F. in 1260 but it
seems that she rebuilt the priory at
that time. A poor house due to
under-endowment, and poverty no
doubt was the cause of the several
instances of nuns reported wandering
outside the precincts in the 13th &
15thCs. In 1491 the abbot of the
Cist. abbey of Stratford Langthorne
visited the house which he found in
an unsatisfactory condition, and he
tried in vain to depose the prioress
(Power). For an unknown reason the
house escaped suppression in 1536.
Remains: None.

Coquet Island *Cell. N'land. Off the
coast at Warkworth. (–1125 to 1539).*

*Benedictine monks. F: Robert
Mowbray?. Ded: St Mary.*
A small cell existed here *c.* 684 and is
referred to by Bede as being in use
in St Cuthbert's time (died 587).
Later destroyed by Danes. Robert
Mowbray granted the cell to Tynemouth Priory in the first quarter of
the 12thC and there is little history
of its Benedictine life. The hermit
St Henry, a Dane of noble birth, who
died here in 1127, was accompanied
by only one monk. *Remains:* A
fragment survives in a bldg. converted
in 1840 for the use of Trinity House
(Pevsner).

Cornworthy *Priory. Devon. Map 8.
5m NW of Dartmouth. (−1238 to
1539). Augustinian canonesses. F:
unknown. Perhaps a member of the
Edgecombe family or one of the lords
of Totnes. Ded: St Mary.*
In some refs. the house is styled as
Benedictine. Although not much is
known of the internal history, there
is considerable information about
links with the two other nunneries in
Devon, bequests, possessions, and
the lives of many of the prioresses.
On several occasions poverty is
recorded. In 1470 a certain Laurens
Knight died owing the community
£21.13.4d for 5 years education of his
2 daughters (@ 20d a week for the
two). His widow remarried and
refused to pay her late husband's
debts. Once again the records leave
the story unfinished (Power).
Remains: A ruined early-15thC gatehouse with turrets and ribbed barrel
vaulting survives. Nothing else except
a few indistinct remnants of walls.
Part excavated 1920. Desc. & site
map: Devon & Cornwall Notes and
Queries, Vol. 11, pt. 2 (1921).

Cottingham *Priory. Yorks. ER. 4m*

*NW of Hull. (1322−1325/6).
Augustinian canons. F: Thomas
Wake, lord of Liddell. Ded: St Mary
& the Holy Cross.*
The bldgs. were well in hand by
1325, and canons from Bourne Abbey
had gone there, when it was found
that the F's heirs could have power to
demolish the monastery. A licence to
move resulted in a merging with
Haltemprice Priory in 1327. A canon
of Bourne became the first prior of
Haltemprice. *Remains:* None.

Cotton *Abbey. Staffs. 7½m W of
Ashbourne. (1176−1178). Cistercian
monks. F: Probably Bertram de
Verdun. Ded: St Mary.*
The site of this very short-lived fdn.
has not been verified. Two authorities
suggest for Cotton read Cawton, a
district close to de Verdun's castle
at Alton. However, the monks from
Savigny (the abbey of Aulnay-sur-
Odon) soon moved to the new site at
Croxden. *Remains:* None.

Coventry *Abbey/Cathedral-Priory.
Warks. Map 3. (1043−1539).
Benedictine monks. F: Earl Leofric
and his lady Godiva. Ded: St Mary,
St Peter & St Osburg.*
The abbey stood on the site of a
nunnery of the virgin saint St Osburg
and to retain the memory her name
was added to the dedication. In the
early years the abbey received many
enrichments and in 1102 became a
cathedral-priory. The diocesan bishop
was considered the titular abbot and
the head of the monastery had title
of prior. The prior was entitled to
wear the mitre. In 1143 the monks
were temporarily dispossessed when
the house became a fortress during a
civil strife. Again, *c.* 1191, Bp.
Nonant succeeded in expelling the
monks and replacing them with

119

secular canons. His death in 1198 was followed by a reversal of the decision and the monks returned once more to the priory. This important and wealthy house entertained Henry VI in 1450, Edward IV and his queen during Christmas 1467, Henry VII in 1487 and Henry VIII and his first queen in 1511. *Remains:* W front with pillars and arches, spiral staircase of the SW tower and base of the NW tower in part of the N wall of the former Bluecoat School (Pevsner). Excavations of 1955, 61, 65 & 66 before new developments began revealed much of the monastery plan, the site lying W of the new cathedral. (Med. Arch. Vols. 5, 11 & 12 – incl. plan in Vol. 11).

Coventry *Priory. Warks. Map 3. (1381–1539). Carthusian monks. F: William, Lord Zouche of Harringworth. Ded: St Anne.*
Partly colonised from London and Beauvale. The house was fd. at the request of Q. Anne, wife of Richard II. He laid the fdn. stone and became a great benefactor. Considerable details exist of benefactions and appropriated chs. including the ownership of 5 alien priories closed between 1386 and 1411 (*v.* Appendix 1). Hardly any 14thC history survives. In 1494 Henry VII assigned 2 rectories to the monks in return for daily prayers for himself and family, and a yearly obit afte his death. The monks had trouble in 1537 for sheltering a runaway vicar of Louth who had been implicated in the Lincolnshire Rising. He was arrested on Christmas Eve and declared the monks to be innocent of his identity (VCH). Avoided suppression in 1536 on payment of a £20 fine. *Remains:* The 15thC prior's house survives though much modified, and there

are fragments of wall-paintings. Note: Archaeologia, Vol. 13, p. 255. Site part excavated 1968 when it is believed the fdns. of the ch. were located with a grave beneath the high altar position. Med. Arch. Vol. 13.

Coventry *Friary. Warks. Map 3. (1342–1538). Carmelite. F: St John Poultney. Ded: BVM.*
An unusually late fdn. i.e. 100 years since the 1st. house of the Order was established in England (*v.* Hulne). The average bequests were small and the friary was not extensive until 1384 when a handsome legacy of £300 enabled the ch. to be enlarged. History is fairly brief. The house produced a Provincial Master of the English Carmelites in 1353 and another friar became a distinguished scholar at Oxford. The Guilds of both Carpenters and Smiths of the city held their annual feasts in the friary hall in the 15th & 16thCs. *Remains:* The E claustral range survives with elaborate lierne-vaulted cloister walk. On the ground floor is the chapter house and two vaulted rooms and above was the dormitory – now much altered internally. Ch. fdns. excavated 1960–70 revealed the bldg. to be one of the longest friary chs. in England (303 ft.). Med. Arch. Vols. 5–14, plan Vol. 11 (1966). Site now lies beneath a new road.

Coventry *Friary. Warks. Map 3. (–1234 to 1538). Franciscan (Conventual). F: Ranulph de Blundeville, earl of Chester. Ded: St Francis.*
Custody of Worcester. Exact date of fdn. unknown but in 1234 Henry III gave the friars timber from the Kenilworth Forest. Throughout its existence the house received many bequests and the list of lay-burials in

the ch. is extensive. The friars obtained great celebrity for their Mystery Plays which outlined biblical history. Performances included scenes mounted on carts and drawn through the town and the fame was widespread. Kings and queens came expressly to see the plays. All endeavours by the mayor and aldermen to save the priory from closure in 1538 were of no avail. *Remains:* The octagonal central tower, 96 ft. high, on which stands a steeple; total height 230 ft. (This spire is one of 3 for which Coventry is famous.) On each side are the arches which led into the nave and the choir. Desc. & plan: Franciscan Architecture in England (1937) A. R. Martin.

Coverham *Abbey. Yorks. NR. Map 1. 2m SW of Middleham. (–1202 to 1536). Premonstratensian canons. F: Helewise de Glanville, daughter of the Justiciar of England. Ded: St Mary.*
The original fdn. was at Swainby (*v.* below) *c.* 1187 and when the abbey was moved to Coverham, Ranulf II (Helewise's 3rd son) was careful to transfer the remains of his mother. In 1251 he, too, was buried in the abbey ch. (Colvin). Principal events were the Scottish raids in the 14thC when the abbey was severely damaged and the canons reduced to poverty. By 1475 it appears that rebuilding was complete with a community of 16 canons. Special mention is made, following visitations by the bps., of the 'Excellent condition of the monastery', specially praising Abbot Askogh. *Remains:* A private house incorporates some of the guesthouse. The surviving remnants of the ch. comprise 2 bays of the 14thC S arcade of the nave, parts of the N transept, chancel E wall, part of the

nave's W wall. There is an arch of the gatehouse. Site partly excavated. Notes & plan: VCH. Yorks. NR, Vol. 1 p. 217. Desc: Yorks. Arch. J. Vol. 25 (1918–20).

Cowick *Priory. Devon.*
See Exeter.

Coxford *Priory. Norfolk. Map 4. 5½m W of Fakenham. (c. 1216– 1536). Augustinian canons. F: William Cheney. Ded: St Mary.*
The house was 1st. f. *c.* 1140 at E. Rudham, $\frac{3}{4}$m to the W. Extensive lands were given by the F's nephew to the canons who then moved to Coxford early in the r. of Henry III. Visitations of 1281, 1492 and 1514 reveal a long history of indiscipline and bad management, involving coursing with hounds, irreverently conducted services in the ch. and priory bldgs. in a deplorable state. When the property was granted to Thomas Howard, duke of Norfolk, in 1537 he probably made better use of it. *Remains:* Very little. In a field is a tall arch of the crossing and a chancel arch with a window. Also some fragments of low walling and fdn. mounds in the grass (Pevsner). Desc: Norfolk Arch. Vol. 17 (1908– 10); also Norfolk & Norwich Arch. Soc. Trans. Vol. 10.

Crabhouse *Abbey. Norfolk. 7m S of King's Lynn. (1181–1536). Augustinian canonesses. F: Roger the prior, and the canons of Norman's Barrow (*v.* below) for Lena de Lynne, an anchoress. Ded: BVM & St John, Evangelist.*
The 14thC Register* of Crabhouse Nunnery in the BM contains details of 13th & 14thC bequests. Considerable details in the VCH. Most of the prioresses were good administrators

and many improvements to the monastery are recorded. A serious fire *c.* 1426 did much damage which was caused by 'a careless woman'. An unusual item in 1476 refers to the marriage of a lay-couple in the monastery by special licence from the bp. of Norwich. The house lay in the southern part of the parish of Wiggenhall St Mary Magdalen. *Remains:* None. A house named Crabb's Abbey occupies the site. * see Norfolk & Norwich Arch. Soc. J. Vol. 11 (1892).

Cranborne *Abbey/Priory. Dorset. Map 5. 6m W of Fordingbridge. (c. 980—1540). Benedictine monks. F: Aylward Snew. Ded: St Mary & St Bartholomew.*
In the early days of the new fdn. Tewkesbury Priory was subject to the abbey. Eventually the estates came into the possession of Robert Fitz-Hamon, a generous patron of Tewkesbury, and in 1102 he trans-ferred the abbot of Cranborne and 57 monks to Tewkesbury, which was elevated to an abbey, and Cranborne became a priory subject to Tewkes-bury with only a prior and two monks left behind. The remaining history of the small house is thus meagre and uneventful. *Remains:* The nave of the conventual ch. with a Norman N doorway and a square tower survive. The chancel was rebuilt in 1875. The claustral bldgs. were demolished in 1703 except for the refectory, used as a barn, which lasted until 1870. An interesting mural painting exists on the S wall of the nave.

Creake *Abbey. Norfolk.*
See North Creake.

Crowland *Abbey. Lincs. Map 4. 10m S of Spalding. (c. 716—1539). Bene-dictine monks. F: K. Ethelbald. Ded:*

St Mary, St Bartholomew & St Guthlac.
The monastery was 1st. f. in honour of St Guthlac who lived on the site from 699—714. It was destroyed by the Danes in 870. Rebuilt mid-10thC but suffered fire *c.* 1091, earthquake in 1118 and fire again in 1170. The last edifice was more magnificent than ever before, probably one of the finest Bene. abbey chs. Mitred. The 'Chronicle of Ingulfus' (abbot 1085—1109), a history of the kingdom and the monastery, was eventually established as a forgery, being written some three centuries after his death. Borlase states that in 1213 the relics of St Neot were removed to Crowland by Abbot Henry 'to a fitter shrine than at the priory in Bucks.'. A good deal of history is recorded and a mid-14thC cartulary survives. Until 1539 the abbey was known as Croyland. *Remains:* The N aisle of the nave is in use as the parish ch. Fine W front with carved figures. A carved stone roodscreen survives in the ruined nave beneath the W arch of the crossing. In the town is the strange tripod-shaped bridge of *c.* 1360 which led to the abbey. The sitting figure against a wall is said to have come from the gable of the abbey ch's. W front during partial demolition in 1720. Refs: Archaeo-logia, Vols. 3, 4, 5 & 11.

Croxden *Abbey. Staffs. Map 3. 4m NNW of Uttoxeter. (1178—1538). Cistercian monks. F: Bertram de Verdun. Ded: St Mary.*
1st. fd. at Cotton (*v.* above), a few miles away in 1176, with monks from Aulnay. There is a full chronicle of events (begun *c.* 1296) from 1128—1374, indicating a history which was not prominent in national affairs. A fine library existed, mainly

Croxden Abbey, Staffordshire. East end of church showing foundations of five radiating chapels forming a chevet.

a gift of an abbot in 1303. The 13th and early-14thCs were times of great prosperity, and the house had a flourishing wool trade with Flemish and Florentine customers. The developing war with France severed the foreign trade. Finances were further reduced by poor harvests, floods, the B.D. and heavy taxation, and the house never recovered its former affluence. But there was clearly a later recovery indicated by improvements and extensions to bldgs.; and in 1536 by the ability to pay a fine of £100 to avoid suppression. *Remains:* The ch. is unhappily bisected by a road which leaves the nave and S transept on one side and the N transept, choir and fdns. of a chevet on the other. The W wall of the nave and the S wall of the S transept stand to full height. Lower walls of E claustral range and sections of the S range mainly intact. The chapel-by-the-gate was in use as a parish ch. until demolished in 1886. Ruins survive of the abbot's lodging and the infirmary. Remainder of site occupied by a farm. Excavated *c.* 1908—9. Desc., plan & care: D of E. Book (with plans, photos, etc.): St Mary's Abbey, Croxden (1911). C. Lynam. Notes: Br. Arch. Assoc. J. Vols. 21 & 29.

Croxton* *Abbey. Leics. 8m SW of Grantham. (−1160 to 1538). Premonstratensian canons. F: William, count of Boulogne and Mortain. Ded: St John, Evangelist.* Canons did not arrive until 1162. Colonies were sent out to Blanchland and Cockersand. In 1216 K. John, who was dying in Newark Castle, sent for the Abbot to hear his last confession. The king's heart was buried at Croxton and his body at Worcester. A careless plumber caused a serious fire in 1326 which badly damaged the ch. and some claustral bldgs. Scottish raids on the N of England possessions of the abbey and the heavy toll of the B.D. left the house £2000 in debt. At the end of the 14thC an abbot was deposed for an unknown reason, but visitation reports of the 15thC have nothing but praise for the community and the monastery. *Remains:* None. Site excavated c. 1926. Desc: Archaeologia, Vol. 73 (1923); Plan: Trans. of Leics. Arch. Soc. Vol. 22 (1945). Book: Hist. of Leics. Vol. 1. pt 1. by John Nichols.
* Pronounced Crosson.

D

Dale *(Stanley Park) Priory/Abbey. Derbys. Map 3. 6m NE by E of Derby. (1153−8 to c. 1184) Augustinian canons from Calke. (c. 1185−1538) Premonstratensian canons. F: Serlo de Grandon. Ded: St Mary.*
Four different colonies came here. After some 20 years the Aug. canons became lazy and returned to Calke; next, Premon. canons arrived from Tupholme but returned after 7 years because of poverty; thirdly a community arrived from Welbeck, sent by William, son of Serlo, but they found

the place too poor and left after 4 years, having arrived c. 1196. Finally c. 1200 a colony was sent from Newsham and this settlement was successful. Obtained abbey status c. 1201. From the early-13thC many small endowments enriched the house and by 1345 the community had increased to 25 canons. There is a fine cartulary in the BM comprising 196 leaves. The convent paid £166.13.4d to avoid suppression in 1536.
Remains: The principal remnant is the huge frame of the E window from which the tracery has gone. A timber structure built upon the site of the chapter house contains stone and tile remnants. Some late-15thC stained glass from the abbey is in Morley (Derbys.) parish ch. Site excavated 1878−9. Desc: Derbys. Arch. Soc. J. Vols. 1 & 2 (1879− 80). & internal history Vol. 16 (n.s.) 1942. Plan: Arch. J. Vol. 71; also Arch. Inst. Excursion Programme 1914. Book: Dale and its Abbey (1890) John Ward.

Darley *Abbey. Derbys. 1½m N of Derby. (c. 1146−1538). Augustinian canons. F: Robert Ferrers, 2nd earl of Derby. Ded: St Mary.*
In 1154 the house received most of the canons from St Helen's, Derby (v. below), which then became a cell of Darley. The cartulary is full of interest about county and monastic affairs and includes details of bequests and acquisitions of land which ultimately made it the wealthiest house in the county. A significant part of the prosperity came from wool, of which records survive of sales to Flemish merchants; and lead from the Derbyshire hills for which there was always a great demand. At the end of the 14thC standards of lifestyle had fallen, and in 1384

Richard II took over control of the abbey for 4 years. In the 15thC it seems that the house had regained its former prestige. The full importance of its history is perhaps still unwritten. *Remains:* None. Some mediaeval stonework from the abbey is incorporated in houses at the foot of Old Lane.

Darnhall *Abbey. Cheshire. 2m S of Winsford. (1273–1281). Cistercian monks. F: Prince Edward (later Edward I). Ded: St Mary.*
The fdn. fulfilled a vow made by the F. during a storm at sea. Colonised from Abbey Dore because the prince had received kind treatment from the monks during his imprisonment at Hereford. The manor was given in 1272 and although the monks arrived in 1273, the fdn. date is often given as Jan. 1274. In 1277 the fdn. stone was laid at the new site of Vale Royal (*v.* below) by the F. and Q. Eleanor, and the monks moved there in 1281. The Darnhall site became a grange of Vale Royal. *Remains:* None.

Dartford *Priory. Kent. Map 7. (1356–1539). Dominican nuns. F: Edward III. Ded: St Mary & St Margaret.*
This unique fdn. in England was conceived by Q. Eleanor (wife of Edward I) and projected by her son Edward II. The B.D. delayed developments and the F. (fulfilling the vow of Edward II) commenced building in 1349. The house was occupied in 1356 by 4 nuns from France and completed in 1361. It was subordinate to the Dom. friars of King's Langley (*v.* below) from whom the nuns tried to free themselves in 1415. Strict discipline and plain living were characteristic of

the monastery throughout its existence. The nuns ran a school for the sons and daughters of gentry and became a wealthy community. Suppressed in 1539; re-established by Q. Mary at K.L. in 1557; and finally moved back to Dartford in 1558. Q. Elizabeth suppressed it in 1559. Considerable history in VCH. *Remains:* Minute. A post-Dissolution brick bldg. survives on the site in Hythe Road, and a length of precinct wall exists in Kingsfield Terrace. Excavated 1913. Desc: Arch. J. Vols. 36 (1879), 39 (1883) & 83 (1926) with partial plan. Hist: (chapter in) The Dominican Order in England before the Reformation (1925) by Beryl E. R. Formoy.

Dartford *Priory. Kent. (1356–1539). Dominican Friars.*
Visitation of London. Dependent upon King's Langley. Not a separate house from the nunnery but a part of it. A few friars were attached here from K.L. to hear confessions during the lifetime of the nunnery. *Remains:* None.

Dartmouth *Friary. Devon. (1331– 1347). Austin. F: unknown. Ded: unknown.*
Limit of Oxford. There were struggles with the abbot of Torre Abbey over their oratory, and the friars finally had to admit defeat in 1347 when a verdict ruled that the oratory had been built on land unjustly taken from a widow, and that restitution was to be made. The Court of Rome imposed 'perpetual silence' upon the brethren. *Remains:* None.

Daventry *Alien Priory/Priory. Northants. (c. 1107–1525). Cluniac monks. F: Hugh de Leicester. Ded: St Augustine.*

1st. fd. at Preston Capes (v. below) and moved here c. 1107. The history of the priory's subjection to the abbey of La Charité-sur-Loire is intricate and, although there was no formal separation, from c. 1231 the house was denizen and elected its own priors. In 1284 the patrons, Robert FitzWalter and Petronilla his wife, negotiated an unusual agreement with the prior and convent that religious offices should be held for the family in their private chapel when required. In 1337 the income was supplemented by obtaining the right to grind all malt used for brewing in the town (VCH). In 1451 a notable prior was elected bp. of St Asaph and he held both offices until he resigned Daventry in 1460 and retained the bishopric until his death in 1471. The house was suppressed for Wolsey's Oxford Coll., but the mystery remains why the monks departed beforehand leaving the priory deserted for Wolsey to seize. *Remains:* None. The ruins were pulled down in 1882. Engraving: Br. Arch. Assoc. J. Vol. 1.

Davington *Priory. Kent. Map 7. 1m W of Faversham. (1153–1535). Benedictine nuns. F: Fulk de Newenham. Ded: St Mary Magdalen.*
In common with many nunneries, insufficient endowments were given to support a community of 26 and the numbers fell to 14 by mid-14thC. In 1343 the nuns had most of the demands made upon them by the king for wool and grain, remitted; but poverty finally brought the house to its end. Not much internal history seems to be known. In 1511 one of the nuns claimed that a fall in the house's income was due to 'the guilt of its officers'. When the prioress died in 1535 the last inmate (a novice) left, and the priory and its possessions came into the hands of the king. *Remains:* The nave and N aisle of the conventual ch. is now the parish ch. The lower part of the E wall was the mediaeval stone pulpitum; all 12thC. The W range has been converted into a house with the cloister garth to the rear, i.e. S of the nave. A length of mediaeval wall with a moulded arch survives. Article: Country Life of 9.12.71. Desc: Archaeologia Cantiana, Vol. 22, (1897).

Deeping St James *Priory Cell. Lincs. Map 3. 8m N of Peterborough. (1139–1539). Benedictine monks. F: Baldwin Fitz Gilbert. Ded: St James.*
Dependent upon Thorney. Like all small cells there is very little independent history. There were, perhaps, never more than 3 monks here and it was surrendered with Thorney. *Remains:* Nave of 7 bays, S aisle, chancel and S porch in use as parish ch. Tower is 18thC. The cloister lay to the N.

Deerhurst *Alien Priory/Priory. Glos. Map 5. 3m SW of Tewkesbury. (–1059 to 1540). Benedictine monks. F: Edward the Confessor. Ded: St Mary.*
Said to have been fd. c. 715, though earliest mention 804. The rebuilding by the F. (after Danish destruction c. 975) incorporated part of the Saxon monastery. Only 2 Saxon monastic chs. survived the Conquest. In the 1200 years since the 1st. ch. was built there have been many changes of plan and ownership, fully recorded in the VCH and refs. given below. The house became Crown property during the wars with France and in 1440 its lands were given to Eton Coll. However, in 1443 it became

denizen and was released from the mother house of St Denis. In 1467 it became a cell of Tewkesbury and for the last 100 years of its life very little history is known. *Remains:* An intensely interesting parish ch. comprising 3 periods of change, with nave and N & S aisles, choir and W tower. Intriguing windows in nave's interior W wall. Outside, against S wall of nave are corbels which supported cloister pentice; and a blocked doorway which led from the ch. A number of ancient ornamental bosses survive. The 15thC E claustral range is now a private house. Desc. & plans: Bristol & Glos. Arch. Soc. J. Vols. 61 & 73. Archaeologia, Vol 77.

Delapre *(de Pratis) Priory. Herts. See* St Mary de Pre.

Denney *Priory/Abbey. Cambs. Map 4. 7m NNE of Cambridge. (c. 1159– c. 1170 Benedictine monks); (c. 1170–c. 1312 Knights Templars); (1342–1539 Franciscan nuns). F: (of Minoresses' abbey) Mary de St Paul, Countess of Pembroke. Ded: St James & St Leonard.*
After the K.Ts were suppressed in 1312, Mary was granted the estates and brought some of the nuns from Waterbeach Abbey in 1342. There was some rivalry between the two houses, but Denney became important and influential and Waterbeach finally closed in 1351 (*v.* below) perhaps because several of the more troublesome nuns succumbed to the B.D. There are large gaps in the history of the nunnery and most of what is known is in the last 25 years of its existence, and the venerable abbess Dame Elizabeth Throckmorton (VCH) *Remains:* An 18thC house incorporates part of the ch. including the nave, crossing and transepts. The 4

crossing arches are clear. The refectory N of the cloister is well preserved. Desc. & plan: Br. Soc. of Franciscan Studies, Vol. 18; and Franciscan Architecture in England (1937) both by A. R. Martin.

Derby *Priory/Cell. Derbys. (1137 to +1160). Augustinian canons. F: Towyne, burgess of Derby. Ded: St Helen.*
In less than 20 years after its fdn., a colony was sent in 1154 from St Helen's to the newly-founded Darley Abbey. The priory then became a cell of Darley. The oratory was presided over by a warden for several years until sometime between 1160 and 1190 the house became a hospital. After 1306 there is nothing known and it was probably totally absorbed by Darley. *Remains:* None. The site is occupied by a school.

Derby *Alien Priory/Priory. Derbys. (c. 1140–1536). Cluniac monks. F: Waltheof, son of Sweyn. Ded: St James.*
Dep. upon Bermondsey. Very little history known. A visitation in 1279 recorded insufficient endowments, and debt. *c.* 1335 a serious fire destroyed the priory and its dependent hospital but both were soon rebuilt. At the Dissolution only the prior and 1 monk lived here. *Remains:* None.

Derby *(King's Mead or de Pratis), Priory. Derbys. (c. 1160–1536). Benedictine nuns. F: Aubin, Abbot of Darley. Ded: St Mary.*
Sometime before 1257 the nuns were freed from Darley due to disputes concerning endowments. Poverty in 1327 due to heavy cattle mortality and large numbers of people claiming hospitality. Edward

127

III gave tax relief. Little of note from 1366 onwards. The nuns claimed to have a part of the shirt of St Thomas of Canterbury as a relic. A bogus 'royal visitor' caused alarm in 1534. *Remains:* None.

Derby *Friary. Derbys. (−1239 to 1539). Dominican. F: unknown. Ded: The Annunciation of Our Lady.* Visitation of Oxford. Henry III a great benefactor. Not much history. In 1344 a mob broke into the enclosure, cut down trees and stole goods. 44 men were arrested but the outcome is unknown. For a long time the community averaged 30 friars but on the threat of dissolution many went abroad. *Remains:* None.

Dereham *Abbey. Norfolk. See* West Dereham.

Dieulacres* *Abbey. Staffs. Map 3. 1m N of Leek. (1214−1538). Cistercian monks. F: Ranulph de Blundeville, earl of Chester. Ded: St Mary & St Benedict.* 1st. fd. at Poulton (*v.* below) and the monks moved here in 1214. The name is said to be a distortion of Ranulph's wife's comment on hearing of the fdn: 'Dieu l'encres!' (May God grant it increase). The Dieulacres Chronicle reveals the story of the earl's dream which led to the fdn. The abbey had a flourishing wool trade and the Black Prince was a customer in 1347. There appears to have been a turbulent history of disputes about land ownership with neighbouring abbeys and breaches of the peace, which must have affected the standards of observance. Otherwise there is little evidence of internal life. *Remains:* The bases of two large piers which were probably

part of the crossing. Little else except numerous carved stones visible in the walls of farm bldgs. Site part excavated *c.* 1770 when much of the fdn. stone was removed, and in 1818 the rest was uncovered. Note: Archaeologia, Vol. 43.
* pronounced Der-la-cray.

Dodford *Priory Cell. Worcs. 3m NW of Bromsgrove. (c. 1185−1464). Augustinian canons; (1464−1538) Premonstratensian canons. F: Henry I. Ded: BVM.* In 1332 the Aug. canons were incorporated with the Premon. abbey of Halesowen. In 1464 there was only 1 canon at Dodford and Edward IV then gave the property entirely to Halesowen 'in consideration of the decrease of the fruits and profits of the house which has come so near to dissolution'. From then onwards the abbots of the mother house appointed a prior to keep the bldgs. in repair. *Remains:* One wall with buttresses and a doorway (Pevsner).

Dodlinch *Priory. Somerset.* Unknown location. *c.* 1210 a community of Augustinian canons was established here by William de Courtney at a site not yet identified, and colonised from the abbey of St Victor, Paris. Sometime before 1226 the F. moved the canons to Woodspring Priory (*v.* below).

Dodnash *Priory. Suffolk. 6m SSW of Ipswich at Bentley. (c. 1188−1525). Augustinian canons. Fs: Baldwin de Toeni and his mother Alda. Ded: unknown.* Of this small house with no more than a prior and 3 canons, very little is known. It was clearly poorly endowed (with no chs.) and the 'unimposing house stood on a rustic site'. Care was taken not to infringe the local parochial rights of the distant and powerful Battle Abbey. The house was suppressed for Wolsey's ill-fated Ipswich venture. *Remains:* None. A farm covers the site and some reused materials are incorporated in the bldgs. (L.G.)

Doncaster *Friary. Yorks. WR. (1351–1538). Carmelite. Fs: John Nichbrothene, Maud his wife and Richard Euwere. (John of Gaunt was later considered a F.) Ded: BVM.* Distinction of York. Several members of this house gained eminence as writers. Surviving 14th & 15thC histories are mainly concerned with bequests and burials. In 1536 the friary became the HQ of the Pilgrimage of Grace for a short time, for which the prior was condemned. He was later pardoned but the news arrived too late for he had already been executed at Tyburn. One historical record claims that 'the prior and 6 others were hanged for defending the institution of the monastic life – a crime which now had become as capital as the greatest'. *Remains:* None. Hist: Yorks. Arch. Soc. J. Vol. 32 (1935).

Doncaster *Friary. Yorks. WR. (–1284 to 1538). Franciscan (Conventual). F: unknown. Ded: unknown.* Custody of York. As with most friaries, the history is brief but VCH gives many details of benefactions. One friar was admitted D.D. of Oxford in 1527. Two Observant friars were sent here after their house was suppressed where they soon died, perhaps following severe treatment. *Remains:* None. The name Friars Road is the sole reminder. The house was built on an island between the rivers Cheswold and Don.

Donnington *Friary. Berks. 1m N of Newbury. (c. 1376–1538). Crutched (Holy Cross). F: unknown (Sir Richard Abberbury was a generous donor of lands). Ded: unknown.* Dependent upon London. Not much history known. The greater part of the friary was destroyed during the siege of Donnington Castle in the Civil War. When Donnington hospital was fd. in 1393 the inmates were directed to attend Mass daily in the friars' chapel. *Remains:* Small. The present house on the site, Donnington Priory, incorporates some parts of the original bldgs.

Donnington Wood *Abbey. Salop. 4m NE of Wellington. (c. 1144–c. 1148). Augustinian canons.* An interim stop between the first settlement at Lizard (a few miles away) and the final site at Lilleshall. *Remains:* None.

Dorchester *Friary. Dorset. (–1267 to 1538). Franciscan (Conventual). F: unknown. Perhaps a member of the Chideock family. Ded: St Francis.* Custody of Bristol. The house, on the N side of the town, was built from the ruins of the castle which lay to its W. Records survive of numerous bequests (VCH). There were 3 great alabaster images in the nave of the ch. as well as one of St Francis. In 1485 Sir John Byconil gave the friars a mill and 2 horses to work it, but there were several conditions attached to the gift. Some difficulties arose in obtaining the surrender from the warden, Dr Wm. Jermen, who was in high favour locally. *Remains:* None.

Dorchester *Abbey. Oxon. Map 6. (c. 1140–1536). Augustinian canons.*

129

F: *Alexander. bp. of Lincoln. Ded:
St Peter, St Paul & St Birinus.*
1st. fd. 634 by St Birinus, an Italian,
sent to evangelise areas of England
untouched by St Augustine. In 1072
the bishopric was transferred to
Lincoln and the bp. introduced Aug.
canons *c.* 1140. Early history sparse,
but during the 14thC the house
acquired lands. In 1356 there is an
accusation of neglect of duties in an
appropriated ch.; but in 1441 a
visitation by Bp. Alnwick brought
evidence from older canons that little
was amiss until deeper investigation
disclosed debt, and that all the canons
enjoyed daily hunting, hawking and
fishing. For this the abbot was deposed and two canons fled the house.
4 years later an unruly canon was
sent to another house with stricter
rule. In 1517 the record of a visitation reveals a much better ordered
house with nothing worse than a
dormitory out of repair; but by 1530
the list of accusations for disobedience, negligence and unruly living is
woefully long. Much may have been
due to the inability of an aged abbot
to maintain control. *Remains:* The
monastic ch. incorporating the 14thC
parish ch. the SW aisle. No N aisle to
the nave, but N & S aisles to the
presbytery. The ch. has many unusual
features including the Jesse-tree
window and the shrine of St Birinus.
Cloister lay to the N and the only
other surviving monastic bldg. is the
guesthouse immediately to the W of
the ch. Desc: Arch. J. Vols. 9 & 67.
Book: Dorchester and its Abbey (MS
in Central Library, Manchester).

Dore *Abbey. Herefs.*
See Abbey Dore.

Douglas *Priory. I. o. Man. (−1226 to
1540). Cistercian nuns. F: Reginald,*

*K. of Man; or Auffrica of Connaught,
sister of Reginald. Ded: St Mary (&
St Bridget?).*
Very little history survives. Robert
Bruce stayed at the house in 1313.
In 1422 the prioress ranked as a
baron of Man. *Remains:* Nothing
authenticated. The present mansion,
The Nunnery, is close to the site. A
chapel contains ancient masonry.
19thC sewerage excavations nearby
uncovered many female skeletons.

Dover *Priory. Kent. Map 7. (1131−
1136) Augustinian canons; (1136−
1535) Benedictine monks. F: Archbp.
de Corbeuil brought Aug. canons to
replace secular canons. Ded: St
Martin.*
Corbeuil's action was not favoured
at Canterbury and on his death in
1136 the Aug. canons were forced to
withdraw. The priory then became a
cell of Christchurch Canterbury, and
in later years its Bene. monks had
many disputes with their mother
house concerning grants and appointments. An inoffensive prior was
deposed in 1273 while on a visit to
Rome and imprisoned in his own
priory on return. After 7 weeks he
escaped to Canterbury. The house
was often in debt due to the constant
flow of visitors through the seaport
needing food and shelter. Cartulary
of 1373 survives. In 1476 the monks
were called upon to aid defences by
keeping the town's cannon ready
with powder and stone. *Remains:*
Incorporated in Dover Coll. is the
fine mid-12thC refectory; the guest-
hall (now a chapel); and the attractive
14thC gatehouse. During excavations
in 1974 part of the fdns. of the nave
of the conventual ch. were uncovered.
Med. Arch. Vol. 15.

Drax *Priory. Yorks. WR. 5m SE of*

Selby. (1130/9−1535). Augustinian canons. F: William Paynell. Ded: St Nicholas.
Not a happy history. In 1280 there were a number of injunctions against the prior including the need to ignore unwise counsel from outsiders, and to be more diligent in the spiritual rule. There was no aura of peace. In 1324 inundations from the rivers Ouse and Aire added to the problems. There were Scottish raids and serious cattle losses. These things 'hindered the works of piety and hospitality'. Lastly, 6 canons were publicly punished in the 15thC for being concerned with spiritualism or sorcery. Mid-14thC cartulary survives. *Remains:* None. The site is marked by a few ridges and mounds of grass. 'The fdns. are so broken up, no plan can be taken thereof' (L.G.).

Droitwich *Friary. Worcs. (1331− 1538). Austin. F: either Thomas Beauchamp, earl of Warwick; or Thomas Alleyn of Wyche. Ded: uncertain.*
This was a small and poor establishment. In 1388 an anchorite's cell was attached to the S side of the conventual ch. Very little history survives. The bp. of Dover arrived in 1538 and found great poverty. Evenso, it seems a fair number of people sought to buy the property and it was ultimately sold to 'a wily Mr Pye of Chippenham, Wilts.'. *Remains:* None. The memory survives in Friar Street and Priory House.

Droitwich *Priory.* Augustinian canons. *See* Witton.

Dudley *Alien Priory/Priory. Worcs. 6m SSE of Wolverhampton. (Between 1149−60 to 1539). Cluniac monks. F: Gervase Pagnell. Ded: St James.*

Subject to Wenlock and to the lords of the baronial castle to which it was closely situated. The house was small, normally only 3 monks, with a quiet and uneventful life under the castle's protection. Although the town was within the See of the bp. of Worcester, curiously the castle and priory lay in that of the bp. of Coventry & Lichfield. The priory became denizen in 1395; and perhaps because it was part of the lordship of Dudley it escaped suppression in 1536. *Remains:* Scanty. Adjacent to the castle ruins and the zoo are parts of the ch. walls and some of the conventual bldgs. which lay to the N of the ch. Desc: Br. Arch. Assoc. J. Vol. 29, pp. 361 & 431.

Dunkeswell *Abbey. Devon. Map 5. 7m N of Honiton. (1201−1539). Cistercian monks. F: William de Brewer. Ded: St Mary.*
Colonised from Forde. Of his 4 fdns. the F. chose this house for his burial in 1226. The abbey was well-endowed with many estates throughout Devon, and the extensive farming brought adequate income until the B.D. The loss of the conversi caused crisis and debt for the community. Due to an almost complete loss of documents much of the internal history is unknown, but problems of indiscipline and disputes with lords of adjacent manors are recorded in 1299, c. 1315 and 1384. A complicated incident occurred in 1508 over the wardship of a child, and land left to it by a deceased father, which was challenged by the abbot. Details of the lengthy affair are in the archives of the bp. of Exeter, and it seems that most of the accused and the accusers were pardoned. *Remains:* Of the ch. only a part of the SW corner of the nave and some low

131

walls. Some walls of the W claustral range. Half of the gatehouse, W of the ch. is a dwelling and the rest is in ruins. Part excavated 1841 & 1913.

Dunmow *Priory. Essex.*
See Little Dunmow.

Dunstable *Priory. Beds. Map 6. 5m W of Luton. (−1125 to 1540). Augustinian canons. F: Henry I. Ded: St Peter (now & St Paul).*
Throughout the 400 years of its life the priory has a fine record. There were inevitably minor lapses in discipline plus a local rebellion in 1229 over a tax imposed on the monastery's tenants. Of special note was the outstanding record over 40 years of Prior Richard de Morins, and there are numerous comments to show the tone of the house to be thoroughly praiseworthy. When a man was killed during a wrestling match in Dunstable, the widow unjustly accused the prior and canons. Poverty became serious in the 14thC and funds were too low to advance the education of the canons, now sorely needed because the priory was 'a populous place where a great number of people came together'. Henry VIII chose this monastery for Archbp. Cranmer to announce his divorce from Q. Catherine of Aragon. *Remains:* The nave of the conventual ch. survives, with imposing W front, in use as the parish ch. It was purchased by the townsfolk, but the clerestory was demolished together with the crossing, transepts and chancel. There are ruins of the gatehouse, and a house called The Priory contains a long rib-vaulted room. Desc. & plan: Archaeologia, Vol. 1. Book: Dunstable Priory Digest of Charters (1926) G. H. Fowler.

Dunstable *Friary. Beds. Location as above. (1259−1539). Dominican. F: unknown. Ded: uncertain.*
Visitation of Cambridge. The community came here at the invitation of Henry III and Q. Eleanor. The Aug. canons in the town tried to prevent the establishment but failed; meantime the nuns of Markyate (several miles to the SE) befriended the friars and gave them food. Unhappily their kindness was ill-repaid because the friars insisted upon continuance when the need had passed, and the nuns were poorer than them. One friar joined the canons in 1265 but returned to the friary in 1274. Very little history. *Remains:* None. The site was partially excavated 1921, 1924 & 1966 and is now built upon. Accnt: Br. Arch. Assoc. J. (1927); Arch. J. Vol. 38; and Manshead Arch. Soc. J. No. 17 (1967).

Dunster *Priory. Somerset. Map 8. 2m SE of Minehead. (c. 1090−1539). Benedictine monks. F: William de Mohun. Ded: St George.*
The ch. was given by the F. to the convent of Bath Priory, but it seems that the 1st. conventual ch. was not built until 1150, and it was c. 1332 before the prior and convent of Bath were appointing the priors (Hunt).* In 1498 an Ecclesiastical Court at Glastonbury resolved a dispute by ordering the ch. to be divided for use by monks and parishioners, and the latter had their altar beneath the tower in 1499. In 1500 the unique fan-vaulted Rood Screen was built across the full width of the ch. *Remains:* The Norman nave and aisles, parts of the chancel, the crossing and the S transept are in use as the parish ch. Cloister lay to the N which approximates to the existing

'cloister garden'. Prior's house exists N of the W end of the ch. Dovecote and part of gateway. In the adjacent street a 15thC house known as the 'Nunnery' is no doubt a corruption of the 'almonry'. Book: Dunster Church and Priory (1905) F. Hancock.
* *v.* above: Bath.

Dunwich *Friary. Suffolk. 4m SSW of Southwold. (−1256 to 1538). Dominican. F: Roger de Holish. Ded: unknown.*
Visitation of Cambridge. In 1384 the friars received a licence to build at Blythburgh due to incursions by the sea, but the move never took place. VCH gives a list of distinguished persons buried within the ch., all of whom a writer noted in 1754 'now lie under the insulting waves of the sea'. *Remains:* None. The entire friary was engulfed by the sea.

Dunwich *Friary. Suffolk. Map 4. 4m SSW of Southwold. (−1277 to 1538). Franciscan (Conventual). F: Richard Fitz John and Alice his wife; and later by Henry III. Ded: St Francis.*
Custody of Cambridge. The incursions of the sea forced abandonment of the first site and in 1290 the friars moved inland (Martin). Some of the income was obtained by sea fishing using the king's galley and tackle. Very little history of interest. *Remains:* The precinct wall enclosing about 7 acres is almost intact, and 2 gateways in it survive. The ch. has gone but the S range of the claustral bldgs. includes the cloister walk and the lower walls of the refectory (which was no doubt on the first floor). The ruins are close to the edge of the sea.

Durford *(Dureford) Abbey. Sussex. 5m W of Midhurst at Rogate. (−1161 to 1536). Premonstratensian canons. F: Henry Hussey. Ded: St Mary & St John, Baptist.*
Colonised from Welbeck. Late 13thC cartulary in BM. This small abbey had a history of misfortunes with impoverishment in the 14thC from robberies and vandalism. Early in the 15thC lightning set fire to the ch. In the middle years an abbot was deposed for misrule, and in the latter years a plague carried off all but the abbot and 3 canons. By 1535 the bldgs. were in sad decay. *Remains:* Minute. In 1545 everything was 'ruthlessly destroyed' and now a farm occupies the site with a few fragments of capitals and arches built into a wall. There is evidence of stewponds. Desc: Sussex Arch. Coll. Vol. 8, (1856).

Durham *Cathedral-Priory. Durham. Map 1. (1083−1539). Benedictine monks. F: William of St Carileph. Ded: BVM & St Cuthbert.*
The cathedral ch. was begun in 995 when the remains of St Cuthbert (d. 687) were brought from Chester-le-Street. In 1083 the F. replaced the secular canons with monks, and in 1093 the fdn. stone was laid for a ch. which has become 'one of the grandest bldgs. in the world' (Ditchfield). Of this great monastery so much information is readily available that no history is necessary here. The relics of St Cuthbert lie beneath a massive, but simple, platform of masonry. As the house held a bishop's throne the head of the convent was the lord-prior. Mitred. This was an important centre of book production with a library of some 920 volumes. It was here that the Norman masons solved the problem of roofing with ribbed

133

vaulting in stone. *Remains:* Superb ch. and cloister of which the N walk had 30 carrels. The dorter, *c.* 1400, is on the W side of the cloister and is now the Chapter Library. Fine chapter house; 13thC kitchen; gateway; almonry; and undercroft of frater survive. Famous sanctuary knocker on door of NW portal. Excav. notes & plan: Archaeologia. Vols. 45 & 58. Refs: numerous books. Illus: Pitkin Pictorial.

Durham *Friary. Durham. (c. 1239– c. 1240). Franciscan (Conventual).* Very little known of the house which probably lasted no longer than a year and belonged to the custody of Newcastle. The friars' settlement was opposed and it seems they moved to Hartlepool (Knowles). *Remains:* None.

E

Earl's Colne *Priory. Essex. 10½m NW by W of Colchester. (−1107 to 1536). Benedictine monks. Fs: members of the de Vere family. Ded: St Mary & St John Evangelist (& St Andrew?).* Dependent upon Abingdon. The monks came from the Suffolk cell of Edwardstone (*v.* below). The de Veres became the earls of Oxford, 13 of whom were buried in the priory ch. The town owes its name to the earls. In 1311 the house obtained its independence from Abingdon. *Remains:* None above ground. The site has been excavated revealing the plan of the ch., cloister and chapter house. Desc. & plan: Archaeologia, Vol. 87 (1938). Note: Br. Arch. Assoc. J. Vol. 21.

Easby *(St. Agatha's) Abbey. Yorks. NR. Map 1. ¾m SE of Richmond.*

(1152–1537). Premonstratensian canons. F: Roald, Constable of Richmond Castle. Ded: *St Agatha. The house suffered from many Scottish raids and equally badly in 1346 when an English army, billeted in the abbey, caused great damage. Some internal history derived from diocesan records reveal a well-managed house by good abbots. The abbey probably had the most unusual plan of any monastery (*v.* D of E guidebook). In 1537 the house was named as having resisted suppression in 1536, and was ordered to be attainted and its 'monks' tied up. The abbot, however, was granted a pension. *Remains:* Most of the ch. has gone, but incised circles on the nave's flagged floor mark where the canons stood after the Sunday procession (*v.* Shap). Abbot's lodging and the infirmary, approached through the N transept of the ch. lay to the N. Cloister on the S. Finest ruin of great architectural beauty is the desolate 13thC refectory. Dorter fdns. in the W range. Gatehouse intact. The choir stalls are preserved in St Mary's parish ch., Richmond. Excavated 1886. Desc., plan & care: D of E. Desc. & plan: Yorks. Arch. J. Vol. 10 (1889). VCH Yorks. NR, Vol. 3 (1913).
*A Sicilian saint and martyr. Perhaps relics of her were brought here following a Crusade by the duke of Richmond.

Easebourne *Priory. Sussex. Map 6. 1½m NNE of Midhurst. (−1248 to 1536). Augustinian canonesses. F: Sir Frank de Bohun. Ded: St Mary.* It seems that the house was fd. for Benedictine nuns and at some date in the 14thC or early 15thC became Aug. In 1412 the pitiful condition of the house was blamed upon the sterility of lands, epidemics, deaths

Easby Abbey, Yorkshire. Refectory from the south-west.

of servants and the loss of rents 'kept back by certain sons of iniquity'. In addition, it seems certain that poverty was also the outcome of mismanagement, and the internal history brings little credit to the inmates. An extravagant prioress was deposed in 1441 for making the nuns work long hours with their hands (needlework) and kept the profit from sales herself. Apart from this, life at the priory reveals nothing of special interest. In 1450 an inventory was taken which disclosed an unusually large library for a small house. *Remains:* Of the nuns part of the parish ch. nothing remains, i.e. the choir and presbytery were dismantled in 1536, but the rest

survives. The E end was rebuilt in 1876. To the S lies a house incorporating some of the E and S claustral bldgs., whose entrance corresponds with the E end of the chapter house. Desc: Sussex Arch. Coll. Vol. 9 (1857). Arch. J. Vol. 92 (1935). Book: Cowdray & Easebourne Priory (1919) W. H. St John Hope.

Easton *Royal Friary. Wilts. 5½m SSE of Marlborough. (1251–1536). Trinitarian. F: Stephen of Tisbury. Ded: Holy Trinity.*
1st. f. as a hostel and hospital 1245 but became Trin. in 1251. Some doubt exists about the reason for the remote site in the Vale of Pewsey,

but it probably lay on a vanished highway between Winchester and Cirencester and served to succour wayfarers and pilgrims. It certainly suffered hardship in the 14thC through the effects of poor harvests and costly hospitality. The friary was the burial place of the Hereditary Wardens of Savernake Forest. In 1493 the whole property was destroyed by fire and was still in a ruinous state in 1536. The parishioners used the nave of the ch. *Remains:* None. The site is uncertain but in 1953 masonry and tiles were uncovered in a field during pipe laying. Notes: Wilts. Arch. Mag. Vols. 51 & 56.

Edington *Priory. Wilts. Map 5. 3½m NE of Westbury. (1358–1539). Bonshommes. F: Wm. of Edington, bp. of Winchester. Ded: BVM., St Katherine & All Saints.*
The 1st. fdn. in 1351 was as a secular coll., but in 1358 regular priests of the Order converted the house into a monastery. The name of Edward, Prince of Wales, is often linked with the change and benefactions, but not until Leland's time (16thC) does the name of the Black Prince appear. The house was richly endowed and led a peaceful existence except for the damage in a rebellion in 1450 when the bp. of Salisbury was dragged from the priory ch. and murdered. The house was supervised by a rector. After the Dissolution the last prior was appointed the first bp. of Bristol. *Remains:* The complete and interesting priory ch. is now the parish ch. Of the claustral bldgs., sited some distance away, nothing survives. A house stands on part of the site. Acct: Downside Review, Jan. 1944. Notes: Wilts. Arch. Mag., June 1934.

Edwardstone *Priory Cell. Suffolk.*

11m NW of Colchester. (c. 1114–1160). Benedictine monks. F: Hubert de Monchesney. Ded: St Mary.
Cell of Abingdon. Never more than 3 or 4 monks. Very little recorded history survives. In 1160 the monks were sent to Earls Colne (*v.* above). *Remains:* None. Desc. & plan: Suffolk Inst. of Arch. Vol. 15, pt. 2.

Egglestone *Abbey. Yorks. NR. Map 1. 1½m S of Barnard Castle. (1195–8 to 1540). Premonstratensian canons. F: probably Ralph de Multon. Ded: St Mary & St John, Baptist.*
Colonised from Easby. No fdn. charter exists. The house was beset with poverty throughout its history, aided by serious losses during Scottish raids. The level of religious life was not high and in the 16thC considerable indiscipline prevailed. The abbey's income being only £36 p.a. in 1536, it should have closed, but the king permitted its refdn. in 1537 and it survived until Jan. 1540. The new owner converted the E range into a house in 1548 and dismantled the centre of the ch. *Remains:* The greater part of the nave and chancel of the ch. Crossing gone. Ruins of the E range as converted. Sub-vault of the dorter in the N range contains many worked stones. Desc., plan & care: D of E. Desc. & plan: Yorks. Arch. J. Vol. 18 (1905). VCH, Yorks. NR: plan Vol. 1, desc. Vol. 3.

Ellerton *Priory. Yorks. ER (Spalding Moor). 8m NE of Selby. (−1207 to 1538). Gilbertine canons. F: William FitzPeter. Ded: St Mary & St Laurence.*
Very little history known and almost nothing from early 14thC to Dissolution. One purpose of the fdn. was for the support of 13 poor people, and in 1387 a patron expressed his right to

nominate 8 of them. This was a small and poor house with only 5 or 6 religious in 1538. *Remains:* None. A stained glass window in the parish ch. is said to have come from the priory. Some neglected ruins of the ch. existed until 1847 and were then pulled down to make way for the present ch. *

Ellerton *Priory. Yorks. NR. (Swaledale). Map 1. 8m SW by W of Richmond. (r. of Henry II (?) – 1537). Cistercian nuns. F: uncertain, perhaps Warmer, Steward of the earl of Richmond; or Warmer's son Wymar. Ded: St Mary.*
Date of fdn. extremely vague and the earliest mention of a prioress is 1227. Equally vague is any knowledge of the house or its history except that it was one of the humblest of all monastic fdns. In 1347 the Scots raided the nunnery and stole the charters and writings. *Remains:* Slight. There is a W tower and an arch and a few ruins of the aisleless nave (Pevsner). Site never excavated.

Elsham *Priory. Lincs. 3m NNE of Brigg. (−1166 to 1536). Augustinian canons. F; Beatrice de Amundeville. Ded: St Mary & St Edmund.*
The F's 3 sons greatly increased the endowments of the house which began life as a hospital in the care of 2 canons. At the end of the 12thC the Knights Hospitallers lost a bid to take over the property. Sadly, the standard of life was low, the canons being 'unlearned' and the Rule ill-kept until a new prior brought recovery. Little else known. *Remains:* None. Elsham Hall occupies the site.

Elstow *Abbey. Beds. Map 6. 1m S of Bedford. (c. 1078–1539). Benedictine nuns. F: Judith, niece of William I.*

Ded: St Mary & St Helen.
c. 1337 the chapel of St Helen was built close to the conventual ch. to serve as the parish ch. Little else is known of the external history; but of the internal life a series of injunctions from visiting bps. shows that the nuns' spiritual devotions often took second place to their comfortable living. The house was wealthy by nunnery standards and perhaps the abbesses, who were frequently daughters of baronial families, ensured that the house was well endowed. Not a happy history when one bp. reports that the nuns' way of life was 'more like pensioners living in a boarding house' where they received their friends. *Remains:* The grim nave of the ch. survives and part of the W claustral range, some of which is contained in Hillersdon Hall. Excavations of 1965–71 revealed sites of the choir, transepts and crossing of the ch. Also parts of the claustral ranges and a complex group of bldgs. S of the cloister – Med. Arch. Vols. 10–16 with plans in Vols. 14 & 16. Also Beds. Arch. J. Vols. 3–6. Notes: Archaeologia, Vol. 47. Books: (1) Chronicles of the Abbey of Elstow (1909) S. R. Wigram; (2) The Abbess and Nuns of Elstow (1887); (3) The Nuns of Elstow (1941).

Ely *Abbey/Cathedral-Priory. Cambs. Map 4. 16m NNE of Cambridge. (1083–1539). Benedictine monks. Rebuilt: Simeon, prior of Winchester. Ded: St Peter & St Mary.*
1st. f. by Etheldreda in 673 for nuns and monks for whom she was abbess. Her sister, niece and great-niece were the next 3 abbesses. House destroyed by Danes in 870. Re-fd. as an abbey for monks 970. Simeon began rebldg. 1083. In 1109 it became a cathedral-priory. Of this great and wealthy

monastery considerable information is readily available from other sources. The shrine of St Etheldreda exists. A manual is preserved giving details of gestures to be used by the monks of Ely when at table, because of the rule of silence at meals. Became collegiate after suppression. *Remains:* Splendid ch. with unique 14thC octagon and lantern tower. There are fdns. of an apsidal E end which was never built. Fine choir stalls. Arcades of infirmary hall embedded in post-Dissolution houses to the SE. Much of the prior's splendid and commodious apartments remain, including an exquisite little chapel above an undercroft. Numerous antiquarian refs. Books: (1) The Cathedral Church of Ely (1808) Geo. Miller; (2) Architectural Hist of Ely (1868) D. J. Stewart; (3) Arch. Hist. of the Benedictine Monastery of St Etheldreda at Ely, with plan (1933) T. D. Atkinson. etc. Illus: Pitkin Pictorial.

Embsay *Priory. Yorks. WR. 1½m NNE of Skipton. (1120–1154). Augustinian canons. Fs: Wm. Meschin and Cecilia de Romelli his wife.* No history. The canons moved to Bolton Priory (*v.* above) in 1154 with the consent of the patroness Alice de Romelli, daughter of Cecilia. *Remains:* None.

Esholt *Priory. Yorks. WR. 5m NNE of Bradford. (end of 12thC–1539). Cistercian nuns. F: Geoffrey Haget or Simon Ward. Ded: St Mary & St Leonard.* To supplement the income the convent taught young girls. Debt and poverty were caused by severe flooding and the loss of crops in 1445. Several refs. to nuns' penances for unchaste behaviour. Strangely, an alehouse was set up *within* the mon-

astery's gates in 1535 to sell surplus production. At the suppression of the smaller houses in 1536 the community's income was only a little over £13 p.a. and for an unrecorded reason it was permitted to continue. *Remains:* None. Hist: Yorks. Arch. J. Vols. 9 & 16 (plan Vol. 33).

Evesham *Abbey. Worcs. Map 5. (±996 to 1539). Benedictine monks. 1st. f. c. 701 by St Egwin, 3rd. bp. of Worcester. Ded: St Mary & St Egwin.* Monastic until 941, then collegiate until +996 when monks again introduced. In the mid-12thC Abbot Mannie completely rebuilt the monastery and the number of monks rose to 67 to become an outstanding centre of monastic revival. 5 nuns were attached to the abbey until *c.* 1086, probably serving in the almonry. Mitred. Wealthy. In 1265 Henry III was held prisoner in the abbey after the Battle of Evesham. Simon de Montfort and Hugh le Despenser were buried before the high altar, the king assisting at the ceremony. The house contained a famous library begun by Abbot Marlborough in 13thC. He resisted visitations by bps. (to which the house was *not* subject) but lost the challenge in the courts. Following the settlement the abbey enjoyed a long period of internal peace in the 14th & 15thCs. The ch. had several shrines which attracted numerous pilgrims. External history mainly linked with Welsh, Scottish and the Hundred Years wars. *Remains:* Fine campanile. Almonry now a museum and residence. Gatehouse converted into a dwelling. Entrance arch to chapter house (which was 10-sided and 50 ft. across) survives. Everything else destroyed immediately after the Dissolution. Excavated and plan revealed in 1811–30 and *c.* 1880.

138

Books by E. A. B. Barnard.

Ewyas Harold *Priory. Herefs. 13m NE of Abergavenny. (+1100 to 1359). Benedictine monks. F: Harold de Ewyas. Ded: St James & St Bartholomew.*
1st. f. at Dulas (1m NW) and Robert, the F's. son and a generous benefactor, gave a new site c. 1120 and built the monastery. This cell of St Peter's Abbey, Gloucester, was deserted during the disastrous 20 years of Stephen's reign, and not until Henry II was enthroned were a few monks sent to rehabilitate the house. The history is punctuated by a succession of disputes and frictions. The community flourished sufficiently to enlarge the bldgs. shortly before 1300, but the first half of the 14thC saw growing poverty and a dissolute life of the small colony until in 1358 the abbot of Gloucester withdrew the prior and his 2 monks. In the following year part of the property went to support a vicar of St Michael's ch. *Remains:* None. The location was perhaps just SE of the site of the castle's conical mound and earthworks. The tower of St Michael's parish ch. was transferred from the priory ch.

Exeter *Priory. Devon. Map 8. Fore Street. (1087–1536). Benedictine monks. Ded: St Nicholas.*
The ch. of St Olave and its lands were given to Battle Abbey by William I whose monks built the priory on the estate. It remained a cell of Battle until the Dissolution but was largely independent. The house acquired considerable property and extensive records exist in Exeter. One of the priory's outstanding merits was the distribution of charity. There was a chamber called 'the Poor Men's

Parlour' in which were fed 7 poor men at noon and others later in the day. There was a tough demo. by the women of Exeter when the priory was finally closed. *Remains:* The ch. has gone. Of the claustral bldgs., which lay to the N, the W range and part of the N range survive. S & E ranges gone. W range contained the Prior's Lodging and the guest hall. 13thC walls exist round a crypt adjacent to a 15thC tower in the N range. (Property of Exeter City). Book with plan: St Nicholas Priory (1917) H. L. Parry & H. Brakspear. Hist: Br. Arch. Assoc. J. Vol. 33, pp. 53–69.

Exeter *(Cowick) Alien Priory/Priory. Devon. In SW suburb of the city. (–1144 to 1538). Benedictine monks. F: unknown. Perhaps a member of the Courtney family. Ded: St Andrew.*
The first endowments, which included the ch., came from William Fitz Baldwin who gave them to the abbey of Bec (Normandy). During the wars with France the priory was confiscated, and when it became denizen in 1451 it was granted to Eton Coll. But sometime after 1464 Edward IV gave the priory and its lands to Tavistock Abbey and these acquisitions enabled the abbey to spend its last three-quarters of a century in something like affluence (Finberg). The priory suffered frequent inundation from the River Exe and was badly damaged by fire in 1445. A chequered history. *Remains:* None. The site lay at the end of Flowerpot Lane. Hist: Monasticon Dioecesis Exoniensis (1846) G. Oliver, p. 11–12.

Exeter *(Marsh Barton) Priory Cell. Devon. 1¼m S of city centre. (1142–1539). Augustinian canons. F:*

unknown. *Ded: St Mary (St Mary de Marisco).*
This small cell of Plympton supported only 4 or 5 canons, and fewer still at the end of the 14thC. Very little history. In 1409 a cook attacked the prior with a dagger. The latter, seeing no escape, struck the madman on the head and called a doctor to aid the wound. The cook would accept no help and died 3 days later. The bp. pronounced the prior free from censure (Oliver). The house survived until the closure of Plympton. *Remains:* None. The site is covered by a cattle market.

Exeter *(Polsloe) Priory. Devon. Map 8. 1½m NE of city centre. (c. 1160–1539). Benedictine nuns. F: unknown*. Ded: St Katherine.*
Throughout its history there are continual refs. to poverty, and in 1329 the prioress wrote to Q. Philippa pleading the inability of the house to accept the queen's nominated lay-sister. In 1319 some bldgs. were reported to be ruinous. Even so, the aristocratic ladies managed to have maids to prepare meals for them (Power). In 1319 & 1376 injunctions were issued concerning the nuns' 'wanderings' and freedom. By 1535 the income was way above the poverty line and the nuns paid the huge sum of £400 to the Crown to avoid suppression. *Remains:* Everything has gone except the W claustral range, probably the prioress's rooms and the guest house. On an outer wall there is evidence of a rare two-storied cloister. Excavations planned. Desc. & part site plan: Devon Arch. Exploration Soc. Trans. (1934). Articles: Trans. Devonshire Assoc. 1934, 1935 & 1937.
* Sometimes given as William, Lord Brewer, but this is disproved by

H. M. Colvin.

Exeter *Friary. Devon. (c. 1232–1538). Dominican. F: probably Bp. Wm. Brewer. Ded: unknown.*
Visitation of London. Records give names of some of the illustrious persons buried in the ch., and of the academic achievements of some friars, e.g. one became the first D.D. within the Order; another was 'excellently learned and a curious searcher of antiquities'. In 1441 a general provincial chapter was held here when D.Ds., M.As., B.As. and others of the Order attended from all parts of the country. The house had a fine library. The names of only two priors are known. *Remains:* None. The Post Office bldgs. stand on or very near the site. Hist: The Franciscans & Dominicans of Exeter (1927) A. G. Little & R. C. Easterling.

Exeter *Friary. Devon. (−1240 to 1538). Franciscan. (Conventual). F: unknown. John Gerveys gave the 2nd site. Ded: BVM & St Francis.*
Custody of Bristol. 1st established between the N & W city gates but because of insanitary conditions, which caused the deaths of 9 friars (Oliver), Bp. Bytten of Exeter and others found the friars a new and larger site c. 1300 'a little without the S gate' – after some resistance from the Dominicans and a volte-face by the bp. The community was unusually large and they retained their original site and ch. for almost two centuries. Considerable details exist of bequests and benefactions. Very little history known. In the choir of the ch. were 'fair seats' in addition to stalls, but in the preaching nave the congregations presumably stood (Martin). The friary had a higher school of theology. *Remains:* None.

Hist: The Franciscans & Dominicans of Exeter (1927) A. G. Little & R. C. Easterling.

Eye *Alien Priory/Priory. Suffolk. Map 4. 21m N of Ipswich. (c. 1080–1537). Benedictine monks. F: Robert Malet. Ded: St Peter.*
Colonised from Bernay (Normandy). The house owned chs. at Dunwich where it established a cell (*v.* Appendix 1). Since a substantial part of Eye's income came from Dunwich, the total loss of the cell, swallowed by the sea, was serious. In 1385 the convent paid £60 to the Crown for a charter of denization. Many details of donations and benefactions in VCH. Visitations by bps. in later years reveal much to the inmates' credit, no reforms being needed. In 1536 the inventory included 'the Red Book of Eye with a little silver on one side, worth 20d'. It was the book of St Felix of Dunwich (*c.* 630) and was priceless. *Remains:* Small parts of the S transept and remnants of ch. walls. A separate brick bldg. to the N is early-16thC and may have been the guesthouse. The site, now occupied by a farm, excavated in the 1920s and the plan revealed. Cloister lay to the N.

Eynsham *Abbey. Oxon. 11m NW of Oxford. (–1086 to 1539). Benedictine monks. 1st. F: Aethelmar in 1005. 2nd. F: (restoration) Bp. Remigius before 1086. Ded: St Mary.*
In 1091 the community moved to Stow where they remained for about 3 years before returning to Eynsham. The patron of this ex-Saxon monastery was the bp. and not the king (as was usual). K. Richard claimed patronage but lost the appeal. In 1344 Abbot Nicholas was deposed and returned later with 1,500 men to turn out his

successor and the monks. Nicholas gained control and resigned in 1351 to live in honoured retirement. The history is varied and interesting in the VCH. *Remains:* The last fragments were destroyed in 1843 (L.G.) Site traceable and has been fully investigated. Extent and style of bldgs. unknown. Notes: Archaeologia Vols. 25 & 43. Hist: Eynsham Abbey Cartulary (1907–8) Oxford Historical Soc.

F

Farewell* *Abbey/Priory. Staffs. Map 3. 2½m NW of Lichfield. (c. 1140–1527). Benedictine nuns. F: Bp. Roger de Clinton. Ded: St Mary.*
The house became a priory sometime before 1210 though the reason for the change is in doubt. In 1331 Bp. Norbury's injunctions in respect of various delinquencies were translated into French as the nuns did not understand Latin, and at the same time he commended them for the 'laudable practice' of going for walks in pairs. Principal income came from sheep and arable farming. Little is known of the internal history, but VCH contains considerable information on property and grants. In 1527 Wolsey ordered the closure of the priory and gave it to Lichfield Cathedral. The nuns were dispersed to other houses. *Remains:* Very little. Until 1740 the conventual ch. was the sole survival. It was rebuilt in that year and only the E end is original. Note: Br. Arch. Assoc. J. Vol. 29, p. 326.
* Also Fairwell.

Faringdon *Abbey. Berks. 13m NE of Swindon. (late 1203–early 1204). Cistercian monks. F: K. John. Ded: St Mary.*
After a few months the monks moved

to Beaulieu. The estates remained a grange of Beaulieu Abbey (v. above) and its harvests were stored in the great mediaeval barn surviving at Great Coxwell (N.T.).

Farley *Priory. Wilts. See* Monkton Farleigh.

Farne Island *Cell. N'land. Map 1. Off Bamburgh coast. (c. 1193–c. 1538).*
Following the example of St Cuthbert who established a cell here *c.* 676, a succession of hermits took up their abode at Farne. *c.* 1193 Durham Cath-Pr. gave the island a system of religious life and fd. a cell for 2 or 3 monks, who came to seek seclusion, and which continued until the Dissolution. Very little is known of the 13thC history but starting in 1358 the little community kept a Roll of expenses and receipts up to 1536, which is preserved in the cathedral treasury at Durham. The records reveal an interesting insight into the Benedictine life and many curious and important inferences can be drawn in respect of the monks' domestic economy. *Remains:* A simple ch., *c.* 1370 and ded. to St Cuthbert, possibly occupies the site of St Cuthbert's cell.

Faversham *Abbey. Kent. (c. 1147–1538). Benedictine monks. Fs: K. Stephen & Q. Matilda (Maud). Ded: St Saviour.*
Colonised from Bermondsey (Cluniac) but the house was certainly Bene. by 1288. Q. Maud took great interest in the ch. construction and both she and the K. were buried here. Considerable poverty existed in the 13thC. In 1275 an abbot was deposed because of serious spiritual and temporal failings. The townsmen rebelled at the customs and tolls exacted by the

abbey and the dispute, which began in 1293, lasted 17 years. (One such custom was a charge of ¼d levied on each window where wares were exposed for sale on Saturdays – VCH). In the 16thC the community was lax in providing alms for the poor, but so was the abbot who failed to give his monks adequate food and clothing in winter. Archbp. Warham ordered all matters to be put right. In 1532 the abbot complained that rooks, crows and buzzards were killing doves and destroying fruit in his orchard, and requested licence to use weapons in defence. *Remains:* None. Excavations in 1964 recovered the entire plan of the ch. At the W end were 2 towers, and the choir had three parallel apses. Part of the cloister, which lay to the N, also found. The site lies E of Abbey Street. Excav. acct: Med. Arch., Vol. 9 (1965).

Felixstowe *Priory. Suffolk. (c. 1105–1528). Benedictine monks. F: Roger Bigod, 1st. earl of Norfolk. Ded: St Felix.*
Dependent upon Rochester. Very little recorded history. The surviving accounts for the year 1499 are minutely detailed. Income chiefly came from the sale of corn, farming of pasture and milling; while expenditure was mainly devoted to bldg. repairs and wages to servants. Under a heading of 'rewards' is a payment of 8d to a harp player, and under 'donations' a woman was helped whose house, husband and two children were burnt in a fire. (VCH). The house was dissolved for Wolsey's Ipswich Coll., but on his downfall was granted to the duke of Norfolk. The possessions were stated to be 'very poor'. *Remains:* None. The site was S of the parish ch. and is now partly occupied by a modern house in Priory Road.

Felley *Priory. Notts. 10m NW of Nottingham. (1156–1536). Augustinian canons. F: Ralph Britto. Ded: BVM.*
The house was subject to Worksop until 1260. A 16thC cartulary in the BM contains interesting refs. to charters and grants. VCH has extensive details of properties and bequests and of disputes with Worksop in the early days. A lawsuit between Lord Grey and the prior about the ownership of Attenborough ch. ended in favour of Felley; and at the Dissolution the prior was appointed to the living there. *Remains:* Insignificant. A house occupies the site in which there is some worked masonry, no doubt taken from the monastic bldgs.

Finchale* *Cell/Priory. Durham. Map 1. 4½m N of Durham. (1170–1538). Benedictine monks. F: Henry Pudsey (1196). Ded: St Mary, St John Baptist & St Godric. (St Godric lived on the site 1115–70).*
The property began as a cell of Durham and in 1196 became a priory in its own right though still dependent upon Durham. The F. was forced to abandon his fdn. at Baxterwood (*v.* above) and granted its possessions to Finchale. Evenso, the establishment of regular monastic offices did not commence until *c.* 1237, and during the 14thC the monastery was little more than a rest centre for 4 monks at a time on a 3-weeks rota from Durham, which continued to the suppression. Not much history independent from the mother house. One source of income was from a coal mine with a horse-driven pumping station. *Remains:* Ruins of the ch. with long transepts, presbytery and nave complete to the roof. Refectory almost complete to the eaves. Extensive remains of the prior's lodging and other bldgs. Altogether a fine and memorable ruin. Desc., plan & care: D of E. Desc. & drwgs: Br. Arch. Assoc. J. Vols. 22 & 23. Notes & plan: Arch. J. Vol. 65. Hist: Charters, etc of Finchale Priory (1837) Surtees Soc.
* Pronounced Finkle.

Fineshade *Priory. N'hants. 4m SSW of Stamford. (c. 1200–1536). Augustinian canons. F: Richard Engayne. Ded: St Mary.*
Except for the appointment of priors, little history seems to be known. A disastrous fire occurred *c.* 1422. The house cannot have been prosperous. Only one visitation is recorded and a purely formal injunction followed. *Remains:* None. A house which incorporated some of the priory walls was demolished in 1956.

Flamstead *Priory. Herts. 4m W of Harpenden. (c. 1150–1537). Benedictine nuns. F: Roger de Tony. Ded: St Giles.*
The house was sadly under-endowed and poverty was considerable in 1380–1. The prioress wrote that unless there was relief, the nuns (who had long endured close cloistering) would need to beg from door to door for the necessities of life. In 1382–3 there was a feud with the monks of Redbourn (*v.* below) over land, but the nuns' claim was unsuccessful. Very little known of 15thC history and although Bp. Gray had cause to reprove the nuns in 1431, by 1536 their conduct was reported as irreproachable and the house in good repair. *Remains:* None. Beechwood Park occupies the site. Note: Archaeologia, Vol. 43.

Flanesford *Priory. Herefs. Map 5. 3½m SSW of Ross-on-Wye. (1346–*

1536). *Augustinian canons. F: Sir Richard Talbot. Ded: St John Baptist.* The house was close to Goodrich Castle of which the F. was lord. Although it was no doubt intended to be a large monastery (suggested by the size of the ruined refectory) the late fdn., and the almost immediate B.D., must have prevented adequate endowments or colonisation. Never more than 3 canons. Very little history beyond the names of most of the priors. In 1446 a 40-day indulgence was granted to contributors to the restoration of the ch. and support of the priory, suggesting a serious financial crisis. Extremely poor at the Dissolution. The small ch. (probably never completed) with a simple nave and chancel resembled a friary ch., the fdns. of which lie beneath a barn. The cloister lay to the S. *Remains:* The sole survival is the complete S claustral range. The refectory was above an undercroft but the intervening floor has gone. Dec. windows and, in the N wall, a large fireplace survive. Notes: Woolhope Naturalist Field Club Trans. 1917.

Flaxley *Abbey. Glos. Map 5. 2m NE of Cinderford. (1151–1536/7). Cistercian monks. F: Roger, earl of Hereford. Ded: St Mary.* The F. is said to have built the abbey on the site where his father was killed while hunting in 1143. Never large or wealthy. Uneventful history except for an incident in 1234 when sheriff's men raided the abbey to abduct a refugee. In 1335 misrule and misfortune brought problems and the abbot was suspended; also there were losses and poverty due to the actions of wild beasts in the Forest of Dean. In 1535 the property was in decay and the ch. had been destroyed by fire. *Remains:* W claustral range

exists with virtually unaltered ground floor with guest hall. Fine 12thC rib-vaulting. Above is the restored 14thC abbot's guest hall with chestnut wood arch-braced roof. Only other relic is the lower half of the processional doorway into the ch., which was in the NE corner of the cloister, All the above incorporated in an 18thC mansion. Illus. article: Country Life, 29.3.73.

Flitcham *Priory. Norfolk. 9m NE of King's Lynn. (+1216 to 1538). Augustinian canons. F: Sir Robert Aquillon. Ded: St Mary ad Fontes.* Not much history known of this small and poor house, and the records seem to be confined to an appropriated ch., gifts of land and a series of small grants. In 1514 there were debts due to non-payment to local suppliers for barley and sheep. By 1528 the state of decay was such that Wolsey granted the property to Walsingham who restored it for the use of 4 canons. The report of a visitation in 1530 is illegible due to a damaged Ms. *Remains:* Slight. The site is occupied by a house into which some of the priory's masonry has been built.

Flixton *Priory. Suffolk. 3m SW of Bungay. (1258–1537). Augustinian canonesses. F: Margery, widow of Bartholomew of Creake.* The house suffered severely during the B.D. and never recovered, its income falling by half. VCH refers to compassion shown to an aged and blind ex-prioress who resigned in 1432. There is a good record of religious observance and discipline, but the absence of house accounts by successive prioresses is criticised. In 1520 there were complaints of poor food; and in the same year the prioress was ordered to send all dogs away from the house 'except one she prefers' (Power). Wolsey suppressed the priory in 1528 for his Ipswich Coll., but it escaped downfall until 1537. *Remains:* In the garden of Abbey Farm, built on the site, is part of a wall and an archway. Moat earthworks exist.

Folkestone *Alien Priory/Priory. Kent. (1095–1535). Benedictine monks. Fs: Nigel de Munevilla & Emma his wife. Ded: St Mary & St Eanswith*.* The A.P. was given to Lonlay Abbey, France. In 1137 it was transferred to a new site because of sea encroachments. Became denizen *c.* 1400. Very little recorded history. No prior was present at a visitation in 1511 and an administrator was appointed. Curiously, each of the 3 remaining monks had originally been professed in different Orders – Augustinian, Cluniac & Premonstratensian. In 1535 there was only a prior and one 'sick monk' here and the bldgs. were said to be in 'utter decay'. Another account described the little house as 'well repaired'. The truth is unknown. *Remains:* None.
* Daughter of K. Eadbald of Kent who built the nunnery for her in the 7thC. Priory built on same site. In 1885 St Eanswith's remains were found in the parish ch.

Forde *Abbey. Dorset. Map 5. 4m SE of Chard. (1141–1539). Cistercian monks. Fs: Richard Fitz Baldwin & Adelicia his sister. Ded: St Mary.* 1st. f. 1136 at Brightley (*v.* above). The monks disliked the site and while returning to their mother house of Waverley in 1141, Adelicia took compassion and gave them new land. This fdn. prospered and the most distinguished recruit Baldwin, arch-

deacon of Exeter, was to become archbp. of Canterbury. Most of the history was uneventful. The departure of the lay-brothers after the B.D. became the starting point of the development of the notable abbot's lodging. Here exists one of the finest displays of monastic bldgs. to remain in occupation. Of the long line of abbots the last, Thos. Chard, was probably the wisest and best. *Remains:* The ch. has gone and fdns. not excavated. Chapter house now a private chapel. Other survivals incorporated in a mansion are: 13thC dormitory with undercroft; 15thC refectory; part of early-15th cloister (N walk); graceful 16thC abbot's hall and porch tower; and fishponds. Desc. & part plan: Arch. J. Vol. 70 (1913). Notes: Br. Arch. Assoc. J. Vol. 18.

Fordham *Priory. Cambs. 4½m N of Newmarket. (–1227 to 1538). Gilbertine canons. F: Henry the dean. Ded: St Peter & St Mary Magdalene.* Hugh Malebisse, sometimes named as F., gave endowments. Although the ch. at Fordham was given by Henry III to the nuns of Sempringham, in 1306 it was found necessary to transfer the appropriation to aid Fordham Priory expenses. In 1335 the house, in common with 6 other Gilb. fdns., were all in debt to merchants. The 14th & 15thC histories are blank. When Cromwell's agent visited the priory in 1536 he wrote: 'there is not a poorer house in all England' (Graham). Only a prior and 3 canons were here. *Remains:* None. An 18thC house occupies the site.

Fors *Abbey. Yorks. NR. 1½m SW of Askrigg. (1145–1156). Cistercian monks. F: Akarius Fitz Bardolf. Ded: St Mary.*

145

Three monks from Savigny settled here. Became Cist. 1147. In 1150 nine monks from Byland joined the original three. The land was poor and in 1156 the community transferred to Jervaulx (*v.* below). *Remains:* None.

Fosse *Priory. Lincs. 8m S of Gainsborough. (−1184 to 1539). Cistercian nuns. Fs: the men of Torksey. Ded: St Mary.*
Small and poor. In 1341 the endowments were so slender that the nuns had insufficient to live on without external aid. History is meagre and there are no complaints about conduct; even at the Dissolution when the visitors called it 'a beggarly poor house', the nuns did not complain of their dismal diet and personal discomfort. Perhaps the house survived until 1539 because the commissioners knew that nothing was to be gained by suppressing it. *Remains:* None.

Fotheringhay *Priory. N'hants. 10m SW of Peterborough. (c. 1141−c. 1145). Cluniac nuns. F: Simon St Liz II, earl of Northampton. Ded: St Mary.*
The nuns soon moved to Northampton (Delapré), but retained their original ch. and endowments until the fdn. of a Coll. here c. 1411. *Remains:* None.

Foukeholme *Priory. Yorks. NR. 8m N of Thirsk. (+1199 to +1349). Benedictine nuns. F: unknown. Probably a member of the de Colville family. Ded: St Stephen.*
c. 1240 the prioress and convent left the control of the priory's property to Wm. de Colville. Following the death of the prioress in the B.D., 2 nuns refused to recognise her successor appointed in 1349 but later repented. That is the last record of the house which may have been dissolved before 1500, or the nuns left for another fdn. *Remains:* None. Nunhouse Farm is the sole memory.

Fountains *Abbey. Yorks. WR. Map 3. 7m SW of Ripon. (1132−1539). Cistercian monks. F: Thurston, archbp. of York. Ded: St Mary.*
13 monks left St Mary's Abbey, York, (*v.* below), because of slackening of the Rule, and with the F's. aid settled in the Skell valley. The life became so hard that the community asked permission to leave when Hugh, dean of York, came to retire here and brought his library and great wealth. Between 1138 & 1151 eight colonies were sent out to fd. new abbeys. All known history of the early days comes from the chronicle of Hugo, a monk of Kirkstall, who wrote from verbal accounts given by Serlo, an ex-monk of Fountains. Mitred in 15thC. The abbey owned many granges and the convent developed centralised farming which cut across traditional methods. Wool brought great wealth in the 13thC, and disaster − with huge debts to York Jews. Fortunes changed in the 14th & 15thCs. Considerable history available from many sources. *Remains:* Probably the finest detailed ruins in Europe of a Cist. ch., claustral bldgs. and precincts, much of which is 12thC. Excavated 1887−8. E end of ch. has Chapel of the Nine Altars, later copied by Durham. Desc., plan & care: D of E. Desc. & plan: Yorks. Arch. Soc. J. Vols. 15 & 25. Arch. J. Vol. 15. Book: Fountains Abbey (1910) A. W. Oxford. Hist: Memorials of Fountains Abbey, Surtees Soc. Vols. 42 (1863) & 67 (1878). Illus: Pitkin Pictorial.

Fountains Abbey, Yorkshire. The presbytery leading to the nine altars at the east end of the church.

Freiston *Priory. Lincs. Map 4. 3m E of Boston (+1114 to 1539). Benedictine monks. F: Alan de Creun. Ded: St James.*
The F. gave the ch. to Crowland to whom the priory remained subject until dissolved. In 1431 the convent comprised 7 elderly and infirm monks, and the bp. ordered Crowland to send some young monks to maintain daily offices. Nothing had been done by 1440, but since the house survived until 1539 presumably some action was taken (VCH). *Remains:* The 9-bayed nave of the conventual ch., of which the 3 W bays are E.E. and the

others Norman, is in use as the parish ch. Nothing else.

Frithelstock *Priory. Devon. Map 8. 6m S of Bideford. (c. 1220–1536). Augustinian canons. F: Sir Robert Beauchamp. Ded: St Mary & St Gregory.*
Colonised from Hartland with 5 canons. Each house had a say in the election of the other's priors. The Stapledon family ranked as 2nd Fs. (Oliver). In 1333 the small convent was augmented to 13 canons. It seems that in 1347 Prior Bittendene built a chapel just outside the pre-

147

cinct which was never consecrated. When the bp. heard that divine services were being performed in it he ordered it to be 'utterly demolished'. In 1400, for his 'Imprudence and extravagance', Prior Pynnoke was deposed. His successor proved a most worthy governor. *Remains:* The ruins of the ch. include the N wall of the chancel and the W front with doorway, and 'three towering lancets at the end of its vast empty nave' (Braun). Outline of cloister visible. Cloister Hall Farm developed round the prior's lodging. Hist: Trans. Devon Assoc. for Advancement of Science, Lit. & Art (1929–30) R. P. Chope.

Furness *Abbey. Lancs. Map. 1. 1½m NE of Barrow. (1127–1537). Cistercian monks. F: Stephen, count of Boulogne & Mortain (later K. of England). Ded: St Mary.*
1st. f. 1124 at Tulketh (*v.* below) for Savigny monks who were given the Furness site 3 years later. Became Cist. 1147. Since Furness was fd. before Waverley (1st. Cist. house in England), the abbot claimed precedence over all Cist. abbeys, but the issue was settled in Waverley's favour. This 2nd-wealthiest Cist. house in England derived income from sheepfarming, salmon fisheries and iron smelting, with its own ships for exporting ore. In the early 14thC there was great damage caused by raiding Scots with heavy losses of temporalities. In 1487 Irish invaders landed nearby with the aim of deposing Henry VII, but they were routed and the abbey survived unharmed. In the 16thC there is evidence of generous alms-giving. *Remains:* Of the ch. there are transepts, choir (with fine sedilia) and W tower almost to original height. 13thC chapter house, parlour and

undercroft of dormitory; and much else at fdn. level. Gatehouse now incorporated in a hotel. Desc., plan & care: D of E. Desc. & plan: Trans. C'land & W'land Arch. Soc. Vol. 16 (1900); also Br. Arch. Assoc. J. Vol. 6. Masons' marks: Archaeologia, Vol. 30. Ref. to struggle with Waverley: Br. Arch. Assoc. J. Vol. 26. Book: The Royal Abbey of St Mary, Furness (1774) T. S. J. West.

G

Garendon *Abbey. Leics. 2½m W of Loughborough. (1133–1536). Cistercian monks. F: Robert Bossu, earl of Leicester. Ded: St Mary.*
Probably colonised from Waverley. After an abbot was seriously wounded by a lay-brother in 1196, the General Chapter at Citeaux ordered the dispersal of the conversi. As the command was not at once carried out the abbots of 2 other Cist. houses went there in 1197 to enforce the order. The wild country of Charnwood Forest gave the monks opportunities for agricultural development, and by the end of the 12thC had established 11 granges. Sheep farming was managed on a large scale and in 1225 wool was being exported to Flanders and elsewhere (VCH). Debts had occurred by the end of the 13thC, and an administrator was appointed to control finances. In 1360 reform was needed and the king appointed several laymen as guardians. 15thC history almost a blank. In the 16thC the abbey's Holy Cross was an object for local pilgrimage. Commissioners gave a favourable report on the 14 monks in 1535 stating that divine service was well maintained, though the large old monastery was partly ruinous. *Remains:* A 17thC house

built on part of the site was demolished in 1964 and excavations on the E side of the cloister revealed 14thC fdns. of the chapter house with 5-sided apse; dimensions of the dorter; and part of the main drain. (Med. Arch. Vol. 13, 1969).

Gisborough *Priory. Yorks. NR. See* Guisborough.

Glastonbury *Abbey. Somerset. Map 5. (940–1539). Benedictine monks. Ded: St Mary.*
The most venerated site in England traditionally associated with St Joseph of Arimathea. Vague refs. to a monastery fd. early in 6thC. Re-f. *c.* 705 by K. Ina of Wessex. Became Bene. 940. The most ancient and the most famous monastery of our whole island. St Patrick & St David buried here, also 'King' Arthur and Q. Guinevere. Abbey destroyed by disastrous fire in 1184. Re-bldg. commenced at once, financed by Henry II's generosity. Mitred. Considerable history in VCH, etc., recording a career of unrivalled influence and splendour resulting in the 2nd wealthiest monastery in England at the Dissolution. Long contest in 13thC between the convent and the bp. of Wells when the latter hoped to become the bp. of Glastonbury. On occasions, 500 people were entertained in the great guest hall, and every Wed. & Fri. the poor were charitably provided for. Last abbot was hanged on Tor Hill near his abbey for refusing to surrender the property. *Remains:* Ch. ruins include part of choir walls, 2 piers of the crossing, transeptal chapel and N & S transept walls, chapel of St Mary and galilee porch. Abbot's kitchen and a gatehouse. In Glastonbury: Abbot's tithe barn, court house and Pilgrim Inn. At

Meare: Abbot's House and fish house. Excavated: 1908, 1928–9, 1956 & 1962–4, the latter years devoted to the Lady Chapel. Desc: Archaeologia, Vols. 4, 11, 25, 32 & 50. Also Br. Arch. Assoc. J. Vol. 12. Hist: Glastonbury Abbey Cartulary, Som. Rec. Soc. Vols. 59, 63 & 64 (1947–56). Numerous books incl: Architectural Handbook (1920) Fred B. Bond. Illus: Pitkin Pictorial. Etc.

Gloucester *Abbey. Glos. Map 5. (1058–1540). Benedictine monks. Re-F: Aldred, bp. of Worcester. Ded: St Peter.*
1st. f. as a double house *c.* 681 by Osric whose sister was the first abbess. After desertion −767, re-f. +823 for secular canons who were replaced by Bene. monks *c.* 1022 (Knowles). This house was destroyed by fire and the F. rebuilt it in 1058. Aldred's house did not flourish and in 1072 William I placed his chaplain Serlo there to regenerate the monastery. By 1078 he had increased the convent from 2 to 80 monks. Considerable history available from numerous sources. Mitred. The boy king Henry III crowned here. Poverty in 1272 lasted for over 50 years due in part to fire and extravagant building programmes. After the murdered K. Edward II was interred in 1327, the shrine became a great place of pilgrimage and a vast source of revenue. A new choir was built, the E end of which had the largest window constructed in mediaeval days. Re-f. as a cathedral in 1541. *Remains:* Complete magnificent ch. Cloister most perfect in kingdom with carrels and lavatorium. Fine chapter house. 14thC library. Arches of infirmary hall. Parts of 4 gateways survive of which St Mary's gate is the finest. The original abbot's lodging (later assigned to the prior)

is now the Deanery. History: numerous books. Notes: Arch. J. Vol. 54 by W. H. St John Hope. Illus: Pitkin Pictorial.

Gloucester, *Lanthony*2, Priory. Glos. Map 5. SW outskirts. (1136–1539). Augustinian canons. F: Miles of Gloucester, later earl of Hereford. Ded: St Mary.*
Fd. at the instance of Bp. Robert of Hereford. Because their priory in Monmouthshire (Gwent) was constantly harrassed and pillaged by the Welsh, the canons moved to Gloucester to fd. a refuge. It was also called Lanthony to impress its dependence upon the mother house, but in 1205 due to increased endowments and an enlarged community it became independent. The effect was to produce a reversal of parenthood for in 1481 the Mon. house was subject to Glos., and it was to become one of the Orders wealthiest houses at the Dissolution. There was a library of some 500 volumes, many of which still exist. *Remains:* Slight. Part of a 14thC gatehouse and the ruins of a buttressed tithe barn. The ch. was finally destroyed early in the 19thC to make way for the ship canal. A house on the site embodies some mediaeval work.
* The Welsh mother house being spelled Llanthony, the English site is sometimes written with one 'l' to draw a distinction.

Gloucester *Priory. Glos. Map 5. (c. 1152–1536). Augustinian canons. F: Henry Murdac, archbp. of York (1147–53). Ded: St Oswald.*
1st. f. c. 909 for secular canons to venerate St Oswald whose remains were brought here from Bardney Abbey. Following Archbp. Murdac's introduction of canons regular, the lands and possessions came under the control of York, and there followed 200 years of disputes about the properties between the archbps. of York on the one hand and the bps. of Worcester & the archbps. of Canterbury on the other. In 1300 the bitterness resulted in the bp. of Worcester preventing the townspeople from selling food to the canons. The king caused the ban to be lifted. From the days when kings stayed here, and a close connection existed with the nearby royal palace, the house slowly declined – its greatness forgotten. Following the Dissolution the N aisle of the ch. became the parish ch., which itself was ruined in the Civil War (1643). *Remains:* An arcade of round-headed arches and 2 pointed arches. All the rest used for road-making. Excavations spasmodic 1967–76. Hist. notes: Trans. Bristol & Glos. Arch..Soc. Vol. 43.

Gloucester *Friary. Glos. (c. 1268–1538). Carmelite. Fs: Q. Eleanor of Castille, Sir Thos. Gifford & Sir Thos. Berkeley. Ded: BVM.*
Distinction of Oxford. Very little history known. Flourishing in 1337 with 37 friars but only 3 at the Dissolution. In 1347 the community obtained an aqueduct running through a lead pipe from a spring which lay outside their enclosure near the N gate (VCH). The house was in 'sad decay' in 1536. *Remains:* None.

Gloucester *Friary. Glos. Map. 5. (c. 1239–1538). Dominican. F: unknown. Stephen, lord of Harnhill gave the site. Henry III accounted as F. due to generous gifts. Ded: unknown.*
Visitation of Oxford. Internal history meagre. Numerous refs. to benefactions and grants, including timber

between 1241–65 from the royal forests of Dean. The Edwardian kings also contributed to the development of the friary. In the 13th & 14thCs the number of friars varied from 30 to 40 and there is little doubt that emphasis was placed upon learning. In the S claustral range were carrels for private study (still existing), and the long room is probably the oldest library bldg. in England. Many friars fled to the Continent in the 16thC and the few who remained in 1535 were very poor. Due to penury, most of the goods in the house had been sold by the friars by 1538. *Remains:* 13thC choir and nave of the ch. with 14thC N transept survive, together with part of the E claustral range and much of the S range with unique study-dorter, all of them covered with early roofs. Care: D of E. Excavated 1932–3. Desc., plan & drwgs: *Trans. Bristol & Glos. Arch. Soc.* Vol. 54 (1932). Study of trussed roofs: *Med. Arch.* Vol. 19 (1975). *Hist. Arch. J.* Vol. 39 (1882).

Gloucester *Friary. Glos. Map 5. (–1231 to 1538). Franciscan (Conventual). F: Thomas, Lord Berkeley (Martin). Ded: St Francis (?).*
Custody of Bristol. Earliest ref. to the house is a grant of trees by Henry III in 1231. Enlargements to bldgs. appear to have occurred in 1256 and *c.* 1360. In 1246 the king allowed the friars to set up a school of theology in a tower in the city wall. They had one enemy in the abbot of St Peter's. He refused permission to extend their site in 1285, and quarrelled over burial rights, but Archbp. Peckham found for the friars. Ch. rebuilt early 16thC due to benefactions of the Berkeley family. *Remains:* The nave and N aisle of the friars' ch., of equal width and 7 bays long, roofed in 2

spans; an arrangement without parallel among English mendicant Orders. Care: D of E. Excavations at E end of ch., in advance of new bldg. development, revealed central tower fdns. and dimensions of choir. Burials, tiles, glass & pottery recovered (*Med. Arch.* Vol. 12, 1968). Desc. & plan: *Trans. Bristol & Glos. Arch. Soc.* Vol. 54 (1932).

Godstow *Abbey. Oxon. 2m N of Oxford. (c. 1133–1539). Benedictine nuns. F: Edith, widow of Sir Wm. Launcelene. Ded: St Mary & St John, Baptist. F.*
F. became first abbess. A richly endowed house; evenso a keeper appointed in 1316 to discharge debts due to 'its miserable state'. All through the career of the house the community was constantly warned against the recourse of scholars from Oxford. Fair Rosamund buried here in 1176, but Bp. Hugh ordered the removal of her body outside the ch. in 1196. In 1290 two nuns were abducted from a carriage and 'certain persons' were excommunicated. In the following year the two nuns received the same punishment – as partners in the plot. In 1460 the convent was recorded as being well-learned, and in 1536 Cromwell's agent wrote favourably about the 'great strictness'. *Remains:* Very little. No trace of the ch. A walled enclosure exists which, until 1718, contained part of the cloister arcade. In the SE corner is a small 16thC roofless bldg., possibly the chapel of the abbess's lodging. Excavations N of the existing ruins revealed an area used for the nunnery's outbldgs. Evidence at one point of exceptional flooding, perhaps mid-13thC. (*Med. Arch.* Vol. 5, 1961).

Gokewell *Priory. Lincs. 6m E of Scunthorpe. (−1148 to 1536). Cistercian nuns. F: Wm. Dawtrey. Ded: St Mary.*
Not much known except a story of poverty and the inability to repay creditors from an inadequate income. Endowments poor, and wool sales from their small estate were about 4 sacks p.a. (sack = 364 lbs.). A school for girls up to 10 years of age and boys up to 8 helped the income; evenso in 1440 the nuns could only afford their food and relatives provided clothing. A visitation in that year reported poverty but recorded the house in good order. *Remains:* None. A house occupies the site. Slight evidence of 13thC masonry in farm bldgs.

Goring *Priory. Oxon. Map 6. 10m NW of Reading. (t. Henry I (?) to 1539 (?)). Augustinian canonesses. F: Thomas de Druval. Ded: St Mary.*
Considerable doubt exists about dates of fdn. and closure. (Some refs give t. of Henry II: *c.* 1180 − but in that case Druval was probably not the F.). No cartulary survives. VCH gives a long list of possessions but the income was low. Surprising that £44 p.a. could support 36 nuns in 1301 and it has been presumed that the nuns' relatives gave payments. There are instances of difficulties with elections of prioresses, but no bps.' injunctions exist after 1445. Bldgs. needed repair in latter years. *Remains:* The nave of the conventual ch. is now the parish ch. At the Dissolution the choir, built and used by the nuns, was demolished. In 1885 an apse was built on to the E end. Excavations in 1892 included the nuns' choir (which extended beyond the present apse), N & S transepts and cloister E & S ranges. Only relics: high windows on S wall

of ch. and corbels where cloister pentice abutted.

Gorleston *Friary. Norfolk (was Suffolk). S suburb of Gt. Yarmouth. (−1267 to 1538). Austin. F: Wm. Woderove & Margaret his wife. Ded: St Nicholas.*
Limit of Cambridge. Many distinguished people buried in the handsome ch. The friary had a library of precious books collected by Prior John Brome (d. 1449). In addition to this house the friars owned a cell across the water, commemorated as Austin Row (Corrupted to Ostend Row). *Remains:* None. The square tower collapsed in 1813 in a gale, and a wall and doorway survived until 1836 in the vicinity of Priory Street. Hist: A history of Gorleston (1933) R. H. Teasdale.

Grace Dieu *Priory Leics. Map 3. 4m E of Ashby-de-la-Zouch. (c. 1239− 1538). Augustinian nuns. F: Rose de Verdon. Ded: Holy Trinity & St Mary.*
The nuns thought there was no other house of the Order in England, and described themselves as the White Nuns of St Augustine (*v.* Brewood W. L.). Part of their Rule forbade them ever to leave the precinct. Not much history. A surviving account book covering the period 1414−8 gives a brief glimpse into the nuns' lives. In 1441 the prioress was criticised for concealing accounts from the convent and not keeping the bldgs. in good repair. In 1535 the visiting commissioners earned no thanks from Cromwell for describing the 15 nuns as 'of good and virtuous conversation and living' (Knowles). At this time 9 people were supported by the priory's charity. A licence to continue beyond 1536 was obtained

by the prioress. *Remains:* Shapeless ruins due to a 16thC mansion occupying the site, and since destroyed. Chapter house walls are chief survivals. Site part excavated 1968 in the ch. and chapter house area, and 130 ft. of main drain surveyed (Med. Arch. Vol. 13 1969). Note: Arch. J. Vol. 90; and Archaeologia, Vol. 43.

Grafton Regis *Priory. N'hants. 8m S of Northampton. (between 1180 & 1205 to c. 1483.) Augustinian canons. F: A member of the Wideville family. Ded: St Mary & St Michael.*
Very little known. The small house joined with St James' Abbey, Northampton, at the end of the 14thC. By the end of the 15thC it seems to have been disused after a dispute with the abbey. *Remains:* None.

Grantham *Friary. Lincs. (−1290 to 1539). Franciscan (Conventual). F: Unknown. Ded: St Francis.*
Custody of Oxford. Very little known. VCH records gifts of corn, water supplies and land, also a number of benefactors. In 1339 a murderer took sanctuary here and again in 1419 (VCH), and in 1492 the Premonstratensian Order held a provincial chapter in the friary. *Remains:* None. A house called the Priory contains Dec. & Perp. tracery in some windows, but maybe not from the friary.

Great Malvern *Priory. Worcs. Map 5. (c. 1085−1539/40). Benedictine monks. F: Aldwyn, a monk; aided by St Wulfstan, Bp. of Worcester. Ded: St Mary & St Michael.*
The house was dependent upon Westminster, though with considerable freedom, and from 1217 the monks were empowered to elect their own priors. There was a long struggle

between the abbot of Westminster and the Bp. of Worcester because the latter fought for supremacy here. Scanty history from mid-13thC to 16thCs. By order of Edward II a cook of the royal household was given permanent and free retirement in the monastery. Various efforts to save the priory from suppression, including bribes, failed (as usual). *Remains:* Fine ch., but S transept and all claustral bldgs. have gone. In 1841 a fine wooden guesthouse was pulled down but much of the carved oak work is in the local museum. Part of a much-restored gatehouse survives. Of special note in the ch. are fine mediaeval painted glass windows, misericord seats and over 1000 tiles. Book: Moche Malvern (1885) James Nott.

Great Massingham *Priory/Cell. Norfolk. 13m E of King's Lynn. (−1260 to 1538). Augustinian canons. F: Nicholas de Syre(?). Ded: St Mary & St Nicholas.*
Originally f. as a hospital but as it was soon placed under a prior it was designated a priory. Enlarged in 1302 following several grants. In 1475 the bldgs. were much decayed and the endowments inadequate to restore the property. It was then granted to West Acre and became its cell. Two canons were ordered to remain here to pray for the soul of the F. and others. *Remains:* Slight. Abbey House on the site has a mediaeval doorway, lancet window and a buttress. Traces of fdns. to the W of the house.

Great Parndon *Abbey. Essex. 8m SE of Hertford. (−1172 to 1180). Premonstratensian canons. F: unknown. Ded: St Mary & St Nicholas.*
Nothing known except that in 1180 the canons moved to Beeleigh (*v.*

above) and treated Parndon as an out-
lying manor. *Remains:* None.

Great Paxton *Priory. Hunts. 3m NNE
of St Neots. (+1124 to +1157).
Augustinian canons. F: unknown.
Ded: Holy Trinity.*
A charter of David I of Scotland
refers to Aug. canons serving the ch.
here. It was granted to Holyrood
Abbey, Edinburgh, sometime after
1157. *Remains:* None. Note: Arch.
J. Vol. 118 (1963) pp. 256–7.

Great Yarmouth *Priory & Friaries.
Norfolk. See* Yarmouth.

Greenfield *Priory. Lincs. 10m SE of
Louth. (–1153 to 1536). Cistercian
nuns. Fs: Eudo de Grainsby and
Ralph de Aby his son. Ded: St Mary.*
Very little history. In 1268 it was
claimed that the house was not Cist.
In 1298 a nun from Nun Cotham
(*v.* below) was sent to do penance
here as she was quarrelsome. It seems
that the visiting bp. in 1303 found
the prioress had been absent for 2
years, and the house was in danger of
serious financial loss. It is probable
she resigned. Poverty was serious in
the 14thC and in 1312 the community received a remission of tithes. At
a visitation in 1514 the bp. found no
cause for complaint, but in 1525 two
nuns were found guilty of moral
lapses and were required to lie prone
on the chapter house floor every Wed.
and Fri. for the nuns to walk over
them as they entered, for a 'specified'
period (VCH). *Remains:* None. A
farmhouse occupies the site into
which a few carved stones have been
built.

Greenwich *Friary. E London. (1482–
1534). Franciscan (Observant). F:
K. Edward IV. Ded: St Franics(?).*
Q. Catherine of Aragon greatly
favoured this 1st. fdn. of the Observant friars whose site extended from
the River Thames to Greenwich Park.
This purely royal fdn. was next to
the royal palace. The friary witnessed
the baptisms of Q. Mary and Q. Elizabeth. Because the Observants opposed
Henry VIII's marriage to Anne Boleyn
the house was suppressed in 1534.
For a brief period the Conventual
friars occupied the bldgs. until 1538.
In 1555. Q. Mary brought back the
Observants who were again expelled
by Q. Elizabeth in 1559. *Remains:*
None. Site now occupied by a
hospital. Drwgs. of the monastery's
appearance in 1558 survive (Martin).
Hist. & plan: Arch. J. Vol. 80 (1923).

Grimsby *Abbey. Lincs. See* Wellow.

Grimsby *Priory. Lincs. (–1184 to
1539). Augustinian canonesses. F:
unknown, perhaps Henry II. Ded: St
Leonard.*
Probably one of the most poorly endowed houses in England. The history
is obscure. In 1184 the convent was
shown to be under the protection of
the canons of Wellow. In 1269 the
nuns had to beg for alms, and in 1349
were excused taxes because of
poverty. In 1459, to add to their sad
existence, their bldgs. were burnt and
their lands flooded. In spite of their
minute income in 1536 the house
lingered on until 1539 (*v.* Fosse).
Remains: None.

Grimsby *Friary. Lincs. (1293–1539).
Austin. F: William Fraunk. Ded: unknown.*
Limit of Lincoln. VCH gives details
of gifts of land in 14thC. In the 15thC
an unjust attack on the friary resulted
in the townsfolk being ordered to

desist by the king. In 1536 the warden was involved in the Lincolnshire Rising, and in 1538 Cromwell's agent found the house almost deserted It was very poor and closed in 1539. *Remains:* None.

Grimsby *Friary. Lincs. (−1240 to 1438). Franciscan (Conventual). F: unknown. Ded: unknown.*
Custody of York. Very little history. In 1255 Henry III gave the friars 20 oaks from Sherwood Forest to enlarge their house; and in 1313 they built a subterranean conduit from Holm to their friary (VCH). There are records of bequests and legacies. *Remains:* None.

Grosmont *Alien Priory/Priory. Yorks. NR. 6m SW of Whitby. (c. 1204−1536). Grandmontine brethren. F: Joan Fossard. Ded: St Mary.*
The house was probably colonised from Normandy but it is certain that by 1294 the community was English. The head was known as a 'corrector' which suggests the brethren came from Craswall (*v.* Appendix 1). There is considerable obscurity attached to this Order. In 1394 the link with France ceased. Earlier, in 1360, a serious fire destroyed almost the whole priory but little else appears to be known. *Remains:* None. Desc. & conjectural ground plan: Archaeologia, Vol. 75.

Guildford *Friary. Surrey. (1275−1538). Dominican. F: Q. Eleanor, widow of Henry III. Ded: unknown.*
Visitation of London. In 1318 Edward II proposed to change the house into a Dom. nunnery but his various applications failed. In 1403 Henry IV and family stayed here and gave 40/- on leaving to 'cover damage done to house vessels and gardens in

entertaining royal guests' (VCH). Henry VIII ratified a treaty with Scotland within the friary in 1534. The king expressed 'a great love and affection' for the house and gave the friars a small annuity after staying there in 1537; but it was of little use as the house was suppressed in the following year. *Remains:* None. Demolished *c.* 1620. Commemorated by Friary Street. Excavated 1973−4. Most of the plan revealed. Cloister lay to the N of the ch. Burials and pottery found. Med. Arch. Vols. 18 & 19.

Guisborough *(Gisburn) Priory. Yorks. NR. Map 1. 10m SE by E of Middlesborough. (1119−1540). Augustinian canons. F: Robert de Brus. Ded: St Mary.*
Much of the early history, recorded by a sub-prior, exists. The house was generously endowed when fd. and in subsequent years received numerous gifts from large and small landowners. The canons had a reputation for their strict observance of the Rule in the 12thC. It ultimately became the richest monastery of the Order in Yorks. The great fire of 1289, caused by carelessness, destroyed the ch. with its rare books, fine chalices and relics. This severe loss and the disastrous Scottish raids heavily reduced the financial state in the 14thC. From *c.* 1350 until the Dissolution little history is known. *Remains:* Principal survival is the magnificent late-13thC E end of the ch., a fragment of 'sheer wonder of perfection'. To the SW of the cloister is a vaulted passage; and a 12thC gatehouse survives, shorn of its lodgings, in the NW corner of the precinct. Desc., plan & care: D of E. Hist: Guisborough Priory Cartulary, Surtees Soc. Vols. 86 (1889) & 89 (1894). Note on remains: Archaeo-

155

logia, Vol. 31. Desc. of tiles: Yorks. Arch. J. Vol. 49 (1977).

Guyzance *Priory. N'land. 6m S of Alnwick. (c. 1147–1539). Premonstratensian canonesses/canons. F: Richard Tyson. Ded: St Wilfred.* Small house about which little is known. Controlled by Alnwick Abbey. A prioress is mentioned in 1313 but nothing else. Perhaps became extinct at the Black Death (1348–9). Sometime after 1350 2 canons from Alnwick were sent here until the Dissolution. *Remains:* None. Some featureless walls existed in 1916.

H

Hackness *Cell. Yorks NR. 5m NW of Scarborough. (–1095 to 1539). Benedictine monks. F: William de Percy. Ded: St Peter.* 1st. f. by St Hilda and destroyed by the Danes *c.* 870. Monks of Whitby came here at the end of the 11thC to escape robbers. In due course most returned to Whitby and Hackness was retained as a cell until the Dissolution. Subsequent history is blank as it was not a separate entity. *Remains:* None.

Hagneby *Priory/Abbey. Lincs. 3m SSW of Mablethorpe. (1175–1536). Premonstratensian canons. F: Agnes de Orreby. Ded: St Thomas, Martyr.* In 1250 the house became an abbey. Very little history. Every visitation in the 15thC resulted in a good report on both spiritual and temporal matters. In 1478 there was no debt and money was owed to the canons, and they had 'an abundance of provisions' (VCH). Very high reputation. Nothing known after 1500. At the suppression there was local indigna-

tion at the irreverent manner in which Cromwell's agents tore down the pyx above the altar. *Remains:* None. Fragmentary material built into a farmhouse and lying nearby, including window tracery.

Hailes *Abbey. Glos. Map 5. 9m NE of Cheltenham. (1246–1539). Cistercian monks. F: Richard, earl of Cornwall (brother of Henry III). Ded: St Mary.* Colonised from Beaulieu and one of the last Cist. fdns. In 1270 the F's son Edmund presented the convent with a phial of the Holy Blood, purchased from the Count of Flanders (*v.* Ashridge). This brought many pilgrims and large financial rewards with which the E end of the ch. was rebuilt to contain the shrine, and took the rare form of a chevet. Sheepfarming also an important source of income. A minor disaster occurred in 1337 when the sluice gates of the fishponds failed, and mud flowed through the cloister and E range. Although the house escaped the ravages of the B.D. there was a pestilence in 1361 which carried off many of the monks and lay-brothers. By 1386 the fortunes of the abbey were at a low ebb. The last decades of its life seem to have been the most prosperous. After the Dissolution an analysis of the 'Holy Blood' declared it to have been a fraud. *Remains:* S wall of the nave aisle with processional door. E cloister wall with chapter house arches; and to the S the frater wall with lavatory recess. Small museum. Excavated 1899, 1906 & 9, and intermittently in the 1960s & 70s. Whole plan revealed. Ch. area and features marked in the turf. Owner N. T. Desc., plan & care: D of E. Acct. & plan: Arch. J. Vol.

58 (1901). Also Trans. Bristol & Glos. Arch. Soc. Vol. 24 (1901).

Halesowen *Abbey. Worcs. Map 3. 7m SSW of Birmingham. (1215–1538). Premonstratensian canons. F: Peter des Roches, bp. of Winchester. Ded: BVM. & St John Evangelist.*
K. John granted charter. Colonised from Welbeck in 1218. Never large. Although much enriched in the first half of the 14thC, running expenses were high and in 1343 the abbot complained of the high cost of hospitality to wayfarers. In 1332 Dodford Priory (*v.* above).became its cell, and the abbey took over its lands in 1464. A visitation in 1481 found a lack of observance of the Rule, but in 1488 the bp. wrote that there was 'nothing worthy of correction'. In 1494 the worst complaint was that tonsures were incorrectly cut! (VCH). Though the house was under the jurisdiction of Prémontre until 1512, it was always under the protection of Welbeck. *Remains:* Of the ch. the surviving fragments are: N wall of the presbytery; S & W walls of the S transept, and the S aisle wall of the nave. The latter is now the N wall of a barn. Cloister area occupied by farm bldgs. and part of the S wall of the refectory, with its undercroft of 4 bays, is all that is left of the conventual bldgs. To the SE is a roofed late-13thC bldg., perhaps the abbot's lodging. Excavated 1899, 1938 & the guesthouse site in 1970 (Med. Arch. Vol. 15). Desc. & plan: Arch. J. Vol. 63 (1906). Desc.: Trans. B'ham & Midlands Inst. Vol. 2 (1871).

Haltemprice *Priory. Yorks ER. 4½m NW of Hull. (c. 1326–1536). Augustinian canons. F: Thomas Wake, Lord of Liddell. Ded: St Mary & the Holy Cross.*
1st. f. at Cottingham (1m NE) in 1322 with canons from Bourne. Because of a fault in the charter the F. realised his heirs could demolish the house. It was therefore moved to Newton (renamed Haltemprice). In 1327 a canon of Bourne became first prior. In 1411 a severe storm and a fire damaged the monastery and there was insufficient endowment to ensure solvency. This was the last house to be f. in Yorks. except for 2 Charterhouses. *Remains:* None. Stone walls running 14 ft. and 10 ft. from an angle were located in a garden on the site in 1959. (Med. Arch. Vol. 4).

Halywell *Priory/Chantry. Warks. 3m NNE of Rugby. (mid-13thC to 1325). Augustinian canons. Fs: Robert de Cotes and Richard Fiton. Ded: St Giles.*
Probably only a small chapel for 2 or 3 canons. Dependent upon Rocester. In 1320 the abbot of Rocester had ceased to maintain services here because his canon in charge had been robbed. As the area was lonely and dangerous, the canons were recalled to the parent house in 1325. *Remains:* None. Note: Archaeologia, Vol. 19.

Hampole *Priory. Yorks WR. 6m NNW of Doncaster. (−1156 to 1539). Cistercian nuns. F: Wm. de Clairfai and Avice de Tany, his wife. Ded: St Mary.*
A papal bull of 1156 declares the nuns shall be of the Order of St Benedict, but they were certainly Cist. in the 13thC. In 1267 the number of nuns exceeded the means of the house and dispersion seemed imminent. In 1314 some nuns were reproved for wearing 'new-fashioned, narrow-cut' clothing, 'contrary to the custom of the Order' (VCH). In 1353 bad management brought about a

condition close to financial collapse. At the time of the Dissolution the convent was reported to be 'of good conversation'. *Remains:* Scanty. A few dressed stones in walls, and in a garden a corbel head-stop and a pinnacle (Pevsner). Excavation notes: Yorks. Arch. J. Vol. 34 (1938–9). (Excavated 1937.)

Handale *Priory. Yorks NR. 4½m SE of Saltburn. (1133–1539). Cistercian nuns. F: Wm. fitz Richard de Percy of Dunsley. Ded: St Mary.*
Perhaps the 1st. Cist. nunnery in England. Dugdale's 'Monasticon' refers to Benedictine nuns but no record exists about a change – if it ever was Bene. In 1301 a prioress claimed damages for imprisonment at Yarm, but a jury dismissed her charge. Poverty was rife in this small house, and on 4 occasions between 1268 & 1318 a custodian was ordered to take charge of the accounts, and substitute capable servants for useless ones on the last occasion. The house somehow managed to escape suppression in 1536 after the visiting agents had recorded the nuns as being of good living. *Remains:* None.

Hardham *Priory. Sussex. Map 6. 1m SSW of Pulborough. (+1248 to 1534). Augustinian canons. F: unknown (Sir Wm. Dawtrey?). Ded: St Cross or St George.*
Small with an income to match, the latter being partly derived from operating a ferry at New Shoreham In 1299 the prior was deposed for misrule and sent to Tortington (*v.* below). One ref. claims his influence was such that he became prior of Shulbrede in 1300, but the evidence is shaky. In 1478 the canons were rebuked for frequenting a local tavern Hardly surprising that in 1527 its 4

inmates, with their house in poor repair, were disbanded by the patron before the general suppression. *Remains:* A farmhouse has been built into the refectory walls. Ruins of the chapter house show it must have been a fine bldg. of which the W arched entrance is the best preserved. Desc. & plan: Sussex Arch. Collns. Vol. 18.

Harrold *Priory. Beds. 8m NW of Bedford. (c. 1137–1539). Augustinian canonesses. F: Sampson de Fort. Ded: St Peter.*
The house was small and poor with a convent of probably no more than 4 or 5 nuns who came from France. Very little interesting history. Cartulary in BM. In 1177 the house came under Missenden's control. No accounts of visitations survive other than a prioress's election in 1369. In the early days canons were attached to the house to protect the nuns and guide them in the Rule, but they left in 1181. By 1188 the house had become independent of Arrouaise. *Remains:* None. The exact site is not known but is perhaps beneath Mow Hill School. The last remnant, the refectory used as a barn, was demolished in 1840. Hist: Beds. Hist. & Rec. Soc. Vol. 17 (1935). Beds. Magazine, Vol. 14, No. 107.

Hartland *Abbey. Devon. 3½m SE of Hartland Point. (t. Henry II: c. 1165? to 1539). Augustinian canons. F: Geoffrey de Dinham with the aid of the Bp. of Exeter. Ded: St Mary & St Nectan.*
1st. f. by Gytha (mother of K. Harold) before 1066 as a coll. for secular canons. Became Aug. between 1161–69 by an ancestor of the Lords Dinham. One of the best endowed and largest monastery in the county, but the early bldgs. were probably of a

rude style of architecture (Oliver), the choir of the ch. being dark plus several other defects. St Nectan is described as a martyr buried here. The house had extensive possessions with numerous chapels. At the time of the Dissolution there were probably only 5 canons here. *Remains:* None. A house occupies the site.

Hartlepool *Friary. Durham. (−1240 to 1538). Franciscan, (Conventual). F: probably Robert de Brus VI. Ded: uncertain.*
Custody of Newcastle. Very little known. In 1243 a robber fled to the ch. for sanctuary. In 1344 the friars appealed to the king for a sum given to them by 'the forgotten Brus'. The claim was granted. The garden was said to produce 'the best Ribstone pippins in the country' (Hutton). *Remains:* None. A hospital occupies the site. Friar Terrace lies N of the ch.

Hastings *Priory. Sussex. (Between 1189 & 99 − 1413). Augustinian canons. F: uncertain, probably Walter de Scotney. Ded: Holy Trinity.*
A small priory for some 5 or 6 canons and the little history that has survived does not suggest a trouble-free life. Delapidated bldgs. and a slackening of standards persisted. The end came due to 'encroachments of the sea' (not supported by an archaeological report), and the canons were given new lands at Warbleton (*v.* below) by Sir John Pelham. The cloister lay to the N of the ch. *Remains:* None. Part of the site excavated 1937 and 1971−2. History: Sussex Arch. Collns. Vol. 13. Excavations report: Hastings Area Arch. Papers No. 2 (1973). Also Med. Arch. Vol. 17.

Hatfield Broad Oak *(or Regis) Alien Priory/Priory. Essex. Map 7. 5m SE*

of Bishop's Stortford. (c. 1135−1536). Benedictine monks. F: Aubrey de Vere II. Ded: St Mary & St Melaine*.
Colonised from St Melaine's Abbey, Rennes, Brittany. Became denizen 1254. Many original deeds in BM. Details of grants in VCH. Even after independence, a newly-elected prior had to notify Rennes of his predecessor's death. In 1329 a strange circumstance arose when John Taper spent lavishly on the house and some monks refused to believe in his generosity. He appears to have forgiven the ingratitude because in 1331 he gave the monks a shop in Hatfield (VCH). *Remains:* The 15thC nave with aisles of the conventual ch. in use. All other monastic bldgs. and the rest of the ch. have gone.
* 5thC foundress of a nunnery on the Mount of Olives.

Hatfield Peverel *Priory. Essex. Map 7. 6m NE of Chelmsford. (+1100 to 1536). Benedictine monks. F: William Peverel. Ded: St Mary.*
A house of secular canons was settled here by Ingelrica, mother of the F., during the r. of K. Rufus. When monks were introduced sometime after 1100 the house became a cell of St Albans. In 1231 much of the priory was destroyed by fire but books, vestments and well-stocked barns were saved. VCH records a series of disputes with neighbouring monasteries. The community of 5 was in debt at the Dissolution. *Remains:* The 15thC nave with N aisle of the conventual ch. in use with a 19thC S aisle & chancel. Parts of the central tower and S transept are incorporated. An 18thC house occupies the site of the claustral bldgs.

Hatherop *Priory. Glos. See* **Hinton** (Charterhouse).

Haughmond Abbey, Shropshire. The prior's lodging.

160

Haughmond *Priory/Abbey. Salop.*
Map 2. 4m NE of Shrewsbury. (c.
1135–1539). Augustinian canons
F: William FitzAlan of Clun. Ded:
St John, Evangelist.
One of the few Aug. houses to become an abbey (c. 1155). Perhaps
Arrouaisian. Comparatively wealthy
with an uneventful history. The monastery had the protection of local
lords throughout the Middle Ages and
acquired numerous holdings, of which
there are extensive details in VCH.
Large library housed in its own bldg.
The convent contributed to an establishment which became St Mary's
Coll., Oxford in the 15thC, but owing
to negligence in maintaining a canon
here, was fined 20s. Records contain
more details of temporal administration than that of spiritual life. An unusual feature of the abbey was an
inner court around which the principal
interest now lies. *Remains:* The ch.
has gone but the fdns. are clearly
marked. Of special note is the W front
of the chapter house. The infirmary
hall and the abbot's lodging were converted into a Tudor mansion which
was destroyed in the Civil War. Site
excavated 1906, 1958 & 1975–6.
Entire plan exposed. Desc. & plan:
D of E. Also Arch. J. Vol. 66 (1909);
and Br. Arch. Assoc. J. Vol. 17.
Notes: Archaeologia, Vols. 10, 11 &
25.

Haverholme – *1 Abbey. Lincs. 3½m*
NE of Sleaford. (1137–1139). Cister-
cian monks. F: Alexander, bp. of
Lincoln. Ded: St Mary.
The land was accepted by the abbot
of Fountains and the first bldgs. were
raised. In 1139 a band of monks was
sent to the site under Abbot Gervase,
but they disliked the place and the
bp. then gave them a new site at

Louth Park (*v.* below). *Remains:*
None.

Haverholme – *2 Priory. Lincs. Loca-*
tion as above. (1139–1538). Gilber-
tine canons and nuns. F: Alexander,
bp. of Lincoln. Ded: St Mary.
After the Cistercians had departed, St
Gilbert accepted the F's gift of the
site in 1139, and in the early days the
Gilbertines suffered severe poverty.
In the 13thC there may have been 100
men and women here for there were
valuable benefices given to the house
in the 12thC. By the early 14thC the
convent was selling 15 sacks of wool
p.a. (A sack = 364 lbs.) Hardship in
1327 was caused by burglaries, thefts
from the fisheries and assaults upon
the religious; and in 1330 some
knights broke the banks of the fishery
and flooded 300 acres of meadows,
but there is no evidence of reprisals.
Later history obscure. *Remains:*
None. A house occupies the site. The
last remnant was the base of a
clustered E. E. pier. Site part
excavated 1961–4 when fdns. of
what appeared to be priory outbldgs.
were discovered. The position of the
ch. and cloister has not yet been
located.

Hayles *Abbey. Glos. See* Hailes.

Hazleton *(Hasleden) Abbey. Glos.*
4½m NE of Tetbury. (c. 1150 to
–1154). Cistercian monks. F: Wm.
Berkeley. Ded: St Mary.
The monks of Kingswood bought
land here intending to move and build
on the site, but were soon driven
away. They recovered the land again
but left, due to water shortage, and
settled at Tetbury (*v.* below). The
property became a grange of Kingswood. *Remains:* None. Hazleton
Manor occupies the site.

Heacham *Cell. Norfolk. 2m S of Hunstanton. (−1088 to ?). Cluniac monks. F: William de Warenne. Ded: St Mary.*
Very little is known about the fdn. The F. gave some of his Norfolk lands to Lewes Priory and the site may have been no more than a grange with 1 or 2 monks living here. The parish ch. was owned by Lewes and it is doubtful if any of it was conventual or that monastic bldgs. ever existed. There was nothing in evidence at the time of the Dissolution. *Remains:* None. Rectangular dry depressions in an adjacent wood and raised banks may have been fish stews. Notes: The Archaeology of Heacham and the Adjoining Areas (1967) C. H. Lewton Brain.

Healaugh *(Park) Priory. Yorks. WR. 3m NNE of Tadcaster. (1218−1535). Augustinian canons. Fs: Jordan de Santa Maria and Alice his wife: Ded: St John, Evangelist.*
Between 1160−84 the grandfather of Alice had fd. a hermitage here, and she with her husband established a priory for Aug. canons. The house had considerable possessions though none of much value. In 1307 it was burdened with corrodies and annuities beyond its means and two custodians were appointed to control finances. A small house with little interesting history. In 1324 a canon was given a severe penance for immorality, but the forgiveness of the community was such that they elected him prior in 1333. In 1534 an injunction urged the canons to obey the Rule. *Remains:* Fragments of Perp. windows in 3 post-Dissolution farm bldgs. A barn has 2 large fireplaces near its N end. The ch. is said to have been to the N of the 3 ranges of farm bldgs. (Pevsner). Hist: Heaulaugh Park − Yorks. Arch. Soc. Record Series 42 (1936).

Hempton *Priory. Norfolk. Close to Fakenham. (−1135 to 1536). Augustinian canons. Fs: Roger de St Martin & Richard Ward. Ded: St Stephen.*
1st. f. as a hospital and when it became a small priory, with probably never more than 4 canons, Richard Ward was the 1st. prior *c.* 1140. Troublous times in later years when a prior was accused of taking a neighbouring farmer's cattle and stealing goods being taken to Creake Fair. Some bother with Castle Acre Priory over the rental of a mill, and Hempton got the rent reduced by half. By the 16thC all was well except that the bp. thought the canons should have more to eat. *Remains:* Small. Near Priory Farm a few fdns. and walls survive.

Henwood *Priory. Warks. 9m W of Coventry. (c. 1156−1536). Benedictine nuns. F: Ketelberne de Langdon. Ded: St Margaret.*
First called Estwell but by reason of the tall oaks it became known as Henwood. Although the F. gave considerable lands there was frequent poverty. In 1349 only 3 of the 15 nuns survived the B.D. Although the abbot of Westminster was the patron, he gave the nuns freedom to elect their own prioresses (VCH). At the Dissolution the 6 nuns were 'of good conversation and living' in the charge of an 88-year-old prioress. *Remains:* None. A mansion and farmhouse have successively occupied the site.

Hereford *Priory. Herefs. (1101−1538). Benedictine monks. F: Hugh de Lacy. Ded: St Guthlac*.*
The original fdn. of St Peter's collegiate ch. soon after the Conquest by

Walter de Lacy was richly endowed, and in 1101 his son, Hugh, gave it to Gloucester Abbey whose abbot replaced the secular canons with monks, and formed the priory. There was also a collegiate ch. of St Guthlac within the castle precinct, and in 1143 Bp. Robert de Bethune moved it to a new site outside the walls and combined it with St Peter's Priory, and the real ded. became St Peter, St Paul & St Guthlac. The house is later described as 'opulent'. In 1322 a monk laid claim to the priorship and challenged the prior, and Edward II ordered the priory and all its possessions into the hands of the Crown. Several years later a dispute arose with Llanthony (Mon.) in respect of an annual payment due to St Guthlac's. In 1366 a new consecration of the ch. followed 'pollution by a violent effusion of human blood' (Duncumb). *Remains:* None. A hospital and a bus-station occupy the site.
* A 7thC hermit who died at Crowland (*v.* above).

Hereford *Friary. Herefs. Map 5. (c. 1246—1538). Dominican. F: (1) William Cantilupe?, (2) Sir John Daniel. Ded: unknown.*
Visitation of Oxford. The 1st. site in the Portfield outside St Owen's Gate contained an oratory. A dispute between the friars and the vicars of the cathedral ch. resulted in a move in 1322 to a site in the Widemarsh suburb given by Sir John Daniel. The dedication was attended by Edward III, the Black Prince and 3 archbps. The house was well endowed. The list of distinguished persons buried in the friars' ch. is impressive. There were over 30 friars living here at its peak. *Remains:* Some parts of the W range of the cloister are in Widemarsh

Street. Also the beautiful 14thC preaching cross, the only surviving example of a friars pulpit in England. Part of the ch. and S walk of the cloister were excavated in 1958 in advance of new developments. (Med. Arch. Vol. 3, 1959).

Hereford *Friary. Herefs. (—1228 to 1538). Franciscan (Conventual). F: Sir William Pembrugge. Ded: uncertain.*
Custody of Bristol. Hereford was originally the head of the custody and changed to Bristol *c.* 1236 (Hutton). The bp. of Hereford was one of the fdn. benefactors. Very little history survives. Many distinguished persons buried here including Owen Tudor in 1461 'the handsomest man in England' who was beheaded in Hereford. There was a library of considerable importance from which some 20 books survive. 14 friars at the time of the Dissolution. *Remains:* None. Friars Street is the last reminder. Desc: The Library of the Grey Friars of Hereford (1914) M. R. James in Vol. 1, Brit. Soc. Franc. Studies.

Herringfleet *Priory. Suffolk.* See St Olave's.

Hertford *Priory. Herts. (—1093 to 1538). Benedictine monks. F: Ralph de Limesi. Ded: St Mary.*
A small and poor house, dependent upon St Alban's, with little recorded separate history. Gilbert, Earl Marshal of England, was buried here after an accident in a tournament at Ware (VCH). In the early 14thC the house was in debt and in 1461 a prior helped himself to £50 which the priory could ill afford. Several subsequent priors left the house poorer for their tenure. By 1525—6 the finances

were healthier but it is doubtful if this was due to wise administration. *Remains:* None. The R.C. ch. in St John's Street stands on the site.

Hertford *Friary. Herts. (c. 1261 to –1535). Trinitarian. F: unknown. Ded: Holy Trinity.*
The house was first a leper-hospital f. by Christina, wife of Peter de Maule, sometime before 1199, and ded. to St Mary Magdalene. The Trin. friars ceased to maintain lepers here though VCH suggests the hospital continued to exist under the direction of Easton Royal. In 1448 a community was still here and dependent upon Moatenden. It is not known how the end came, but the house seems to have been abandoned well before the Dissolution (Knowles). Nothing else appears to be known. *Remains:* None.

Hexham *Priory*. N'land. Map 1. (1113–1537). Augustinian canons. F: Thomas II, Archbp. of York. Ded: St Andrew.*
1st. f. 674 by St Wilfred who probably gave the Rule of St Benedict to Hexham. Became a cathedral 678. Destroyed by Danes 875. Secular canons were replaced by Aug. canons in 1113, mainly from Huntingdon. Thence followed a turbulent history with 5 Scottish raids, involvement in the Civil War of the Roses and a rebellion shortly before the Dissolution. 1154 was an important year when the convent took possession of the relics of the Saxon saints; but in 1296 the Scots destroyed them and stole the gems adorning the caskets. The raids caused the canons to disperse in 1311 to priories in Yorks. & Notts. In 1464 the house was caught up in the battle of Hexham. It held the privilege of sanctuary centred round the rare frith stool. By the 16thC

there was a decline in standards. The last prior, a founder member of the Pilgrimage of Grace, was probably hanged on the king's orders by the Duke of Norfolk. 1300th. anniversary service attended by Q. Elizabeth II in 1974. *Remains:* Choir, crossing and transepts are superb mediaeval structures on the site of St Wilfred's monastery. Nave 1908. Fine crypt and night stairs. Monastic bldgs. include slype; chapter house vestibule, ruins of warming house, lavatorium in W walk of cloister and the cellarium; part of the prior's lodging and ruins of the gatehouse. Desc. & plan: Arch. J. Vol. 39. Book: Hexham Abbey by C. C. Hodges (1888). Hist: Memorials of Hexham Priory, Surtees Soc. Vols. 44 & 46 (1864–5).
* Now known as Hexham Abbey.

Heynings *(Knaith) Priory. Lincs. 3½m S of Gainsborough. (+1135 to 1539). Cistercian nuns. F: Rayner de Evermue. Ded: St Mary.*
The fdn. was probably early in K. Stephen's reign with 3 Premonstratensian canons serving as chaplains. The house was small and poor due to meagre endowments and impoverishment following costly repairs, bad harvests and a 'multiplication of corrodies'. An injunction of 1392, aimed at putting the house upon a firm financial basis, is preserved (Power). Other injunctions, during a well-documented history, include correcting lateness at matins, abolition of farm animals or poultry being a nun's own property, no tarrying at Lincoln, and the removal of secular persons from the infirmary. In 1440 there was a complaint that the prioress was not impartial towards all sisters; but in 1519 the house was free from criticism. *Remains:* None. However, Pevsner refers to the parish ch. of St

Hexham Priory (now Abbey), Northumberland. Late 12thC choir of the fine Augustinian church looking west.

Hexham Priory (now Abbey), Northumberland. Remains of the lavatorium on the west side of the cloister.

Mary as 'a curious bldg. of which one does not know at first how it may be orientated'; while J. C. Cox in the 'Little Guide' calls it 'a fragment, perhaps a transept, of the conventual ch.'.

Hickling *Priory. Norfolk. Map 4. 3m SE by E of Stalham. (1185–1536). Augustinian canons. F: Theobald de Valoines. Ded: St Mary, St Augustine & All Saints.*
Considerable details of property, including refs. to possessions in 32 Norfolk parishes, and of gifts, in VCH. Storm water in 1287 rose more than a foot above the high altar and 2 canons saved the horses by leading them up into the dormitory. In 1349 only 2 canons survived the B.D. and a novice became prior. It seems that in 1390 all signs of true religion had disappeared. By 1492 the property was in a sad state and the canons had insufficient food and warmth. In 1532 there was an exceptional order that cudgels be provided for the defence of the priory. *Remains:* At Priory Farm is the undercroft of the W claustral range and a large fragment of masonry probably part of the E range. The cloister area can be recognised in between.

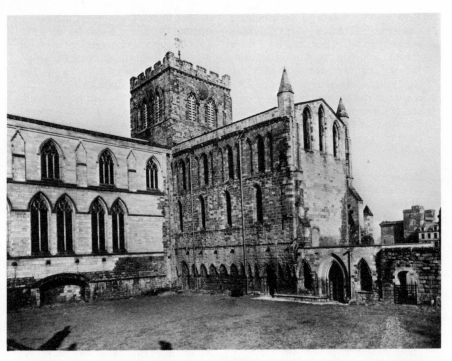

Hexham Priory (now Abbey), Northumberland. Thirteenth-century tower and south transept. The nave, destroyed by the Scots in 1296, was rebuilt in 1908.

Higham *(Lillechurch) Alien Priory/ Priory. Kent. 4½m E of Gravesend. (c. 1148–1522). Benedictine nuns. F: Mary, dau. of K. Stephen. Ded: St Mary.*
1st. fd. at Stratford-by-Bow and moved to Higham when lands were released to Mary while the house was subject to St Sulpice of Rennes, Brittany. Became denizen after 1227. The F. was 1st prioress and later became abbess of Romsey in 1155 (*v.* below). Grants from William (son of K. Stephen), Henry II & Henry III. On 40 feast days throughout the year the nuns received special foods such

as 'crepis' and 'flauns'. The nuns held the valuable asset of the franchise for the Kent to Essex ferry, but Prioress Amfelisia de Dunlege was in trouble for failing to keep the causeway in good repair at the Higham end. She held some kind of record by arranging for 363 religious houses to pray for her soul after her death, which occurred in 1295. The bldgs. were in poor repair in 1521 and the 3 or 4 nuns, whose conduct was far from unblemished, resigned all claims in 1522. By 1524 Bp. Fisher had used the property to supplement the income of St John's Coll., Cambridge. *Remains:* None. 1st. excavated 1959.

Hist. & acct. of excav.: Archaeologia Cantiana, Vol. 80 (1965). Part excavated 1966 when claustral layout was traced including chapter house, calefactory and reredorter in the E range. An 18thC farmhouse covers the SW corner of the cloister and may contain some of the priory's masonry. The fdns. of the ch. lie beneath a farm track — Med. Arch. Vol. 11 (1967).

Hilbre *Island Cell. Cheshire. 2m SW by W of Hoylake. (+1093 to −1539). Benedictine monks. F: unknown. Ded: St Mary.*
1st. a hermitage and later a cell of Chester with never more than 2 monks on this barren island. Their supposed duty was to tend the light given and endowed by John, Earl of Chester (1232–7) (Burne). *Remains:* None. A cave on the W side is said to have been a part of the monks' abode.

Hinchingbrooke *Priory. Hunts.* See Huntingdon.

Hinton *Charterhouse (Locus Dei) Priory. Somerset. Map 5. 5½m SSE of Bath. (1232–1539). Carthusian monks. F: Ela, countess of Salisbury. Ded: St Mary, St John Baptist & All Saints.*
1st. f. 1222 by Earl William Longspee, husband of Ela, at Hatherop (3m N of Fairford, Glos.), but the site proved unsuitable and Ela, now a widow, transferred the monks to Hinton. 2nd. Carth. fdn. in England, following Witham. Even though the convent received many donations, grants and privileges, it did not grow rich and even had insufficient income for its proper support. All Charterhouses were entirely dependent upon a lay labour force and after the B.D. (1349) Edward III gave the monks

licence to employ lay-brothers to operate the priory's tannery. In 1521 a monk, believing himself gifted with prophecy, told the duke of Buckingham that he would become king. The forecast cost the duke his life. *Remains:* 13thC chapter house, with sacristy alongside, in perfect preservation. Refectory with undercroft. Parts of the guesthouse are built into a manor house. Excavations intermittently from 1950. In 1957–8 the fdns. were revealed of the great cloister with 14 cells; little cloister; ch.; site of kitchen and 2 water channels. (Med. Arch. Vols. 2 (with plan) and 3). Desc. & part plan: Som. Arch. & N.H. Soc. Vols. 41 & 96. Book: The Somerset Carthusians (1895) E. Margaret Thompson.

Hirst *(Crowle) Cell. Lincs. 7m W of Scunthorpe. (−1135 to 1540). Augustinian canons. F: Nigel d'Albini. Ded: St Mary.*
Never conventual. Property of Nostell which probably kept only 1 or 2 canons here to manage the estates and collect tithes of corn, malt and fish from the neighbourhood. *Remains:* None. A Georgian house occupies the site.

Hitchin *(Newbiggin) Priory. Herts. 8m NE of Luton (1361/2–1538). Gilbertine canons. F: Sir Edward de Kendale. Ded: St Saviour.*
Very little known of this small house with only 3 or 4 canons. The poor fdn. endowments were augmented in the 14th and 15thCs. No details of the surrender have survived. *Remains:* None. A house called the Biggin stands on the site near the parish ch.

Hitchin *Friary. Herts. 8m NE of Luton. (1317–1538). Carmelite. F:*

Edward II. Ded: BVM.
Distinction of London. Hardly any
history known. VCH refers to bequests in the 14thC and adds that
'nothing is heard of the house in the
15thC'. 5 friars signed the deed of
surrender. *Remains:* Small. A house
named Hitchin Priory (*c.* 1770) incorporates fragments of 14thC bldgs.
and retains its moat.

Holmcultram *(Abbey Town) Abbey.*
C'land (Cumbria). Map 1. 15m SW
by W of Carlisle. (1150–1538).
Cistercian monks. F: Prince Henry,
son of David I, K. of Scotland. Ded:
St Mary.
Colonised from Melrose. The richest
and most influential abbey in
Cumbria. Numerous royal charters
and lavish endowments. Its wealth
came from temporal sources rather
than spiritual. The house suffered
many attacks. In 1216 the Scots stole
everything to hand; in 1319 the
monks took refuge in other monasteries, and in 1322 Robert Bruce
despoiled the abbey ch. in which the
body of his father lay. Grey Abbey,
Ireland, was a daughter house. Although the abbot was not mitred, he
was summoned to Parliament between
1294 and 1312. Whereas the first
abbot ruled for 42 years, there were
4 abbots during the last 7 discredit-
able years of the abbey's life, one of
whom was possibly murdered. Evenso, the house was not in a perpetual
state of siege or trouble and certainly
had periods of repose. *Remains:* 6 of
the 9 bays of the nave survive, shorn
of the aisles. Excavations revealed
crossing, transepts and square-ended
chancel. No claustral bldgs.

Holme *Alien Priory/Priory. Dorset.*
2m SW of Wareham. (mid-12thC to
1539). Cluniac monks. F: Robert de

Lincoln. Ded: unknown.
Cell of Montacute until it became
denizen in 1407 on payment of 300
marks. In 1279 the convent was commended for its observance of the
Rule and religious duties. As a
Cluniac house it was exempt from
episcopal visitations and historical
notes are few. There was difficulty
for one of the priors with a quarrelsome ex-abbot of Bindon. *Remains:*
None (at the site).

Holme Lacy *Premonstratensian*
canons. Herefs.
Projected but never founded.

Holy Island *Northumberland. See*
Lindisfarne.

Holystone *Priory. N'land. 9m W of*
Rothbury. (–1235 to 1539). August-
inian canonesses. F: Robert de Um-
fraville I of Harbottle. Ded: St Mary.
The 1st. f. is given as –1124
(Knowles) when the house may have
been a Benedictine nunnery, and it is
certainly a very early date for Aug.
canonesses. Being right on the Border
the sisters suffered many hostile
attacks and their 'miserable plight'
was exposed in 1313 by the bp. of
Durham (Power). It is probable that
the priory became Aug. soon after
Aug. canons built Brinkburn and
established canonesses here. From 24
inmates in 1291 the number fell to
5 in 1379. Despite its low income it
survived until 1539 no doubt due to
its small value to the Crown and in-
accessible location. *Remains:* None.
Fragments existed in 1812 (L.G.).

Hood *(1) Abbey. Yorks. NR. 1½m E*
of Thirsk. (1138–1143). Cistercian
monks. F: Gundreda, widow of Nigel
d'Albini. Ded: St Mary.
A colony sent from Furness to f.

Calder went on towards York and were given lands at Hood. In 1143 Roger de Mowbray, son of Gundreda, gave the monks a better site at Old Byland to which they moved. They abandoned the site to:

Hood *(2) Priory/Cell. Yorks. NR. Location as above. (1143–1539). Augustinian canons. F: as above. Ded: St Mary.*
A colony of canons sent from Bridlington to f. Newburgh lived here for 2 years until their priory was built. Hood then became a cell, or more probably a grange, of Newburgh until the Dissolution. In 1332 only 1 canon was serving the ch. of St Mary. *Remains:* None. A house, Hood Grange, occupies the site, behind which is a mediaeval barn.

Horkesley *Alien Priory/Priory. Essex. 5½m NNW of Colchester. (–1127 to 1525). Cluniac monks. Fs: Robert fitz Godebold and Beatrice his wife. Ded: St Peter.*
Dependent upon Thetford. Became denizen 1376 but Thetford continued to maintain a tenuous hold. Early charters preserved in the Bodleian. At a visitation in 1379 the community of a prior and 4 monks was said to be leading holy lives. The house was dissolved to provide assets for Wolsey's Oxford Coll. *Remains:* None. A house N of the parish ch. occupies the site.

Hornby *Priory/Cell. Lancs. 7m NE of Lancaster. (+1160? to 1538). Premonstratensian canons. F: A member of the Montgebon family. Ded: St Wilfred.*
Considerable doubts about the fdn. and dates. Dependent upon Croxton and may have been a hospital c. 1160 before becoming a priory some 12 years later. Small, with little history. VCH gives details of disagreement over the ownership of an advowson between the prior and Countess Margaret de Burgh in 1246. The house was surrendered twice; once in 1536 which was presumably cancelled, and again in 1538. *Remains:* None. Site occupied by a farm.

Horsham St Faith* *Alien Priory/Priory. Norfolk. Map 4. 4m N of Norwich. (1107–1536). Benedictine monks. Fs: Robert Fitz-Walter and Sybil his wife. Ded: St Mary.*
1st. f. c. 1105 at Kirkscroft. Dependent upon Conches Abbey, Evreux. Never large or important. In 1307 Robert de Barwe and 26 others raided the priory and held siege for 4 months no doubt in expression of the general attitude towards alien houses at that time. Became denizen 1390. It is not clear why a run-down property with only a prior and 8 monks should have merited the favour of John of Gaunt, but surviving evidence shows that ambitious alterations were made at this time. No further history known until 1534. *Remains:* Site occupied by a farm whose square walled garden represents the cloister area (which lay to the N of the vanished ch.). Chapter house entrance survives in the E wall; and most of the refectory to the N was converted into a house. Remarkable late-13thC wall paintings on E wall of refectory. Notes: The Priory of Horsham St Faith & its Wall Paintings, Norfolk Arch. Vol. 35, pp. 469–73. Desc: Norfolk Arch. (1932).
* A 3rdC martyr of Aquitaine. c. 886 her remains were transferred to Conches Abbey.

Horsley *Alien Priory/Priory. Glos. Map 5. 1½m SSW of Nailsworth.*

*(1262–1380). Augustinian canons.
F: unknown; Roger Montgomery,
earl of Shrewsbury gave manors.
Ded: St Mary (?).* From the reign of William I this was
a Benedictine cell of St Martin's
Abbey, Troarn, Normandy. In 1260
it was granted to Bruton (*v.* above)
whose cell it became with a prior and
1 canon to provide daily dinners for
6 poor persons (Knowles). Two
priors between 1349 and 1376 were
neglectful of their duties, and finally
Bp. Wakefield created Horsley into a
vicarage in 1380. No doubt part of
the bldgs. served as a manse. From
this date history ends. *Remains:* The
Perp. tower of the parish ch. is the
only mediaeval part to survive
(Pevsner). No claustral bldgs.

Horton *Abbey/Priory. Dorset. Map 5.
8m W of Ringwood. (c. 1050–1539).
Benedictine monks. F: uncertain.
Ded: St Wolfrida.*
1st. f. *c.* 970 as an abbey. Destroyed
by Danes 997. Re-f. for Bene. monks
c. 1050 still as an abbey. In 1122
Roger, Bp. of Salisbury, annexed the
house to Sherborne and reduced the
status to a priory. From this date the
history of the small property sinks
into obscurity. *Remains:* The large N
transept attached to the 18thC parish
ch. is all that survives (Braun).

Hounslow *Friary. Middlesex. 6m NE
of Staines. (–1252 to 1538). Trinitarian. F: Richard, King of the Romans
(?). Ded: Holy Trinity.*
1st. f. *c.* 1200 as a hospital. Date of
transfer to Trin. uncertain. VCH gives
extensive details of bequests, grants
and licences. Enjoyed royal patronage
as the house was about midway between Westminster and Windsor. In
the 15thC a friar of this house became
Provincial of the Order in the British

Isles. For a friary it was financially
well-off in 1535 with an income from
rents, a mill and a market amounting
to £80 p.a. *Remains:* None. The ch.
and parts of the friary bldgs. survived
until 1816 when the new parish ch.
was erected on the site.

Hoxne *Priory. Suffolk. 4m NE of
Eye. (1130–1538). Benedictine
monks. Fs: Maurice of Windsor and
Edigia his wife. Ded: St Edmund.*
Dependent upon Norwich Cath.
Priory. 1st. f. *c.* 950 as a religious
house with a chapel supposedly on
the site where K. Edmund was murdered. Some 50 years earlier the
martyr's remains had been taken to
Bury (903). In 1101 Herbert, Bp. of
Norwich, gave the desolate chapel to
Norwich, and by 1130 it had been
rebuilt and was given as a house for
monks by the above Fs. It was not
completed until 1226. The monastery
maintained a school for children of
the parish; and pilgrims came to the
image of St Edmund in the priory's
chapel. *Remains:* None. Abbey Farmhouse occupies the site.

Hull See Kingston-upon-Hull.

Hulne *Friary. N'land. Map 1. 2½m
NW of Alnwick. (1242–1539).
Carmelite. F: Ralph Fresborn. Ded:
BVM.*
The 1st. Carm. house f. in England.
Whether the F. brought a community
from the Holy Land of his own free
will or was persuaded by a member
of the de Vesci family is in doubt,
but in any version the name of Fresborn is the central figure. The de
Vesci family gave lands. Because of
frequent and devastating Scottish
raids, a tower and fortified curtain
wall were built. There survives a catalogue of the friars' library which was

171

larger than that at Farne. Little is known of the history beyond the endowments and grants (Tate). *Remains:* S & W walls of the ch; part of sacristy, chapter house, infirmary, cloister and enclosure walls and the gable of the dormitory. The tower of 1488 is complete (The bldg. to the E of the tower is a late-18thC summer house). Excavated 1888–9. Desc. & plan: Arch. J. Vol. 47 (1890). Also Br. Arch. Assoc. J. Vol. 9 (1903).

Hulton *Abbey. Staffs. Map 3. 2½m NE of Stoke-on-Trent.(1219–1538). Cistercian monks. F: Henry de Audley. Ded: St Mary.*
A small house and prosperous in the golden years of the wool trade. In 1310 the convent gave Edward II's army as much supplies as the far wealthier Burton Abbey (Hibbert). Later its wealth declined with serious poverty in 1351; and a tannery, tile kilns, a pottery and coal mines were its main sources of income. In 1396 the alien priory of Cammeringham was granted to the abbey (*v.* Appendix 1). Very little is known of the spiritual life or its local influence and hardly any history is known for the 15th & 16thCs. In the late 1520s the abbot was accused of controlling the neighbourhood to the exclusion of justice. In reply he referred to the assaults on his smithy at Horton (VCH). The house escaped suppression in 1536 on payment of a fine of £66.13.4d. *Remains:* Excavations between 1961–76 revealed the E end of the ch., including the high altar; the crossing; sacristy walls, and S transept walls, altars and night stairs. There are traces of fishponds. Notes: Med. Arch. Vols. 9–19. Reports: W Midlands Arch. News Sheets, Nos. 16–19 (B'ham Univ.).

Humberston *Abbey. Lincs. 3½m SSE of Grimsby. (c. 1160–1536). Benedictine monks. F: William Fitz Ralph. Ded: St Mary & St Peter.*
Although the house was connected with Hambye Abbey of the Order of Tiron, it was never considered alien. It was not rich and may have supported only 12 monks. The house was destroyed by fire in 1305. VCH records many interesting details but it cannot have been a happy house. 14th and 15thC visitations record 'excesses, insolences and quarrels'. It is clear that indiscipline was occasionally due to the absence of a superior in the chapter house. At the Dissolution the income was only £34 nett p.a. with an abbot, 4 monks and a lay-brother to support. *Remains:* None.

Huntingdon *Priory. Hunts. (−1108 to 1538). Augustinian canons. F: Eustace de Lovetot. Ded: St Mary.*
1st. f. −973 for a small community. The F. sited the priory outside the town to the E c. 1086, and the convent consisted of priests 'under a Rule'. It became Aug. sometime before 1108, perhaps very soon after Colchester. 5 important houses were colonised from here (Barnwell, Hexham, Bolton, Merton and Worksop). The priory was well-endowed. Over the years there were a series of injunctions including emphasis on the duty of reciting the canonical hours and keeping silence. The house escaped suppression in 1536 by paying the large fine of £133.6.8d which preserved its existence for only 2 years. *Remains:* None. Site occupied by a cemetery.

Huntingdon, *Hinchingbrooke Priory. Hunts. Map 3. (−1087 to 1536).*

Benedictine nuns. F: William I. Ded: St James.
1st. f. at Eltisley, Cambs. (Power). Always small and poor. History not easy to trace. When a boarder quarrelled with the prioress she was ejected, but recovered the possession of her room but not the corrody (VCH). In 1425 vandals damaged, and stole from, the priory. Site has been excavated. *Remains:* Hinchingbrooke House occupies the site 1 mile W of the town and is built round the former cloister. During alterations some of the mid-12thC ch. was discovered, also the chapter house entrance was found intact. Mediaeval walling lies to the S, W and E. (Med. Arch. Vols. 10 & 12.)

Huntingdon *Friary. Hunts. (−1258 to 1539). Austin. F: unknown. Ded: St Andrew?*
Earliest mention 1258 when Henry III gave the friars 4 oaks (Knowles). In 1268 the house was burnt down and the rebuilt friary was on a larger scale aided by Edward I and others. Very little history known or information about bequests. In 1354 the friars were in trouble for aiding the escape of a prisoner, already on the gallows, and giving him sanctuary. In 1538 the bp. of Dover found the house very poor. *Remains:* None. A 19thC house on the site may contain stone from the ruins.

Hurley *Priory. Berks. Map 6. 3½m E of Henley. (c. 1086−1536). Benedictine monks. F: Geoffrey de Mandeville. Ded: St Mary.*
Dependent upon Westminster. Extensive details of grants in VCH. Edward III ordered the Wardens of the Hampshire coast in 1347 to cease demanding the aid of a man from Hurley Priory for coastal service, as he had

sent him abroad on royal business. The small priory suffered hardship on numerous occasions when the Thames was in flood, and in 1392 claimed royal assistance on that account 'out of reverence due to Lady Edith, sister of the holy King Edward, the Confessor, buried here' (at Hurley). In the 15thC this flood hazard caused impoverishment and debts which were eased in 1489 by an unexpected gift of £60. *Remains:* Nave of the conventual ch. is in use. Cloister lay to the N. Refectory survives. Part excavated *c.* 1896 when fdns. of the chancel of the ch. and the chapter house were revealed. To the W are a barn and a dovecote. Much of the site is occupied by a manor house. Notes: Berks., Bucks. & Oxon. Arch. Soc. J. Vol. 3.

Hutton *Priory*. Yorks. NR. 1m SW of Guisborough. (c. 1162−c. 1167). Cistercian nuns. F: Ralph de Neville. Ded: St Mary.*
Nothing is known of the house. *c. 1167* a grant of land at Thorp resulted in an early removal of the community to a site which became known as Nunthorpe (*v.* below). *Remains:* None.
* VCH refers to an 'abbey'.

Hyde *Abbey. Hants. See* Winchester.

I

Ickleton *Priory. Cambs. 5m NNW of Saffron Walden. (c. 1154?−1536). Benedictine nuns. F: unknown, perhaps a member of the Valoignes family. Some authorities suggest the 1st. earl of Oxford c. 1190. Ded: St Mary Magdalen.*
The house was neither large nor wealthy although it held extensive

173

estates especially in Essex (VCH). No
serious injunctions, but in 1345 the
nuns were forbidden to keep fowls,
dogs or small birds within the monastery bldgs. – a common custom in
the Middle Ages; and secular persons
were forbidden to continue living
within the precincts. Riots in 1381
resulted in the prioress's court rolls
and other documents being burnt.
Remains: None. Priory Farm occupies
the site. Fragments of worked stone
are often dug up.

Ilchester *Friary. Som. (−1261
to 1538). Dominican. F: uncertain,
Thomas Trevet with Walter and
Matilda Lune gave land. Ded: unknown.*
Visitation of London. A small house
about which nothing seems to be
known except that it existed – for
which there is ample evidence. A
reference to the friars' close connection with the prisoners of Ilchester
gaol may be the reason why they
settled here, as a sphere of their daily
labour (VCH). *Remains:* None.

Ilchester *(White Hall) Priory. Som.
(−1281 to −1463). August-
inian (?) nuns. F: William Dennis.
Ded: Holy Trinity.*
1st. f. *c.* 1220 as a hospital when the
F. gave his house and property for
the benefit of travellers and pilgrims.
It became a priory for sisters or nuns
before 1281 and is described by one
author as 'by far the worst example
of a medieval nunnery'. In 1323 the
nuns were reduced to 'begging
misery'; and in 1335, because of the
'immodesty of the prioress and her
2 nuns in the town', the custody of
the priory was given by the bp. to 2
local rectors. Sometime between
1423 and 1463 the property seems
to have become a free chapel for a

chaplain. *Remains:* None.

Ingham *Friary. Norfolk. Map 4. 1½m
NE of Stalham. (1360−1536). Trinitarian. Fs: Sir Miles Stapleton and
Joan his wife. Ded: Holy Trinity.*
The last house of the Order f. in
England. 1st. f. as a coll. of religious
in 1355 and became Trin. in 1360
with only 3 brethren. It never became large and had high standards as
recorded after visitations in 1492 and
1526. When the commissioners
arrived in 1536 to take stock of the
house all the friars had gone.
Remains: The ch. survives of which
the nave was parochial and the
chancel monastic, rebuilt by the F.
A doorway in the N side led to the
cloister of which there are traces of
some arches. Also some parts of walls
exist of claustral bldgs.

Ipswich *Priory. Suffolk. Map 7.
(−1177 to 1536). Augustinian
canons. F: probably Norman Gast-
rode fitz Eadnoth. Ded: Holy Trinity.*
1st, f. *c.* 1133 for parochial use but
canons were here in 1177. In 1194
the priory was destroyed by fire and
rebuilt by the bp. of Norwich. Never
large or wealthy. In 1393 a royal
pardon was granted to a canon
accused of causing the death of a
cook. No injunctions following visitations in 1493 and 1514 but the bp.
was critical of 'insolent servants'. The
house was to have been dissolved for
Wolsey's local coll. *Remains:* Very
little. Christchurch mansion occupies
the site. In 1674 the fdns. of the ch.
were blown up and cleared away.
Part of precinct walls forms N boundary of St Margaret's churchyard
(L.G.). Fragments in the mansion
(Pevsner).

Ipswich *Priory. Suffolk.*

174

(–1189 to 1528). Augustinian canons. Fs: members of the Lacy family. Ded: St Peter & St Paul. No precise details known of the fdn. and very little of its early history. VCH gives details of grants. Few injunctions against the canons except that they were ordered to rise for matins and be obedient to the prior. Suppressed for Wolsey's secular coll. and grammar school which was to have been on the site of this priory, but it never matured. Remains: None. The site is marked by the Tudor gateway of the coll. Road developments in the early 1970s led to some site investigation. The other reminder is Priory Street.

Ipswich Friary. Suffolk. (c. 1271–1538). Carmelite. Fs: Sir Thomas Londham and others. Ded: BVM.
The house was enlarged in 1297, 1321, 1333 & 1398. In consequence it was often chosen for meetings of provincial chapters of White Friars. In 1452 Henry VI and his entourage were accommodated and entertained. From this friary came a number of learned men including Thomas of Eleigh who wrote 90 volumes, and another who became a University Chancellor in 1445 and was famed for being a historian, philosopher, poet, theologian and orator. Remains: None. All traces gone. It was on the W side of St Stephen's Lane.

Ipswich Friary. Suffolk. Map 7. (1263–1538). Dominican. Fs: probably John Hares and others. Ded: St Mary.
Visitation of Cambridge. VCH gives considerable details of grants. There were some 50 friars at the end of the 13thC. Not much history known. The importance of the friars is

revealed in the list of VIPs who chose to be buried in the friary ch. Remains: In School Street are 7 stone arches which were part of the E wall of the refectory. The rest of the bldg. was demolished c. 1852.

Ipswich Friary. Suffolk. Map 7. (–1236 to 1538). Franciscan (Conventual). F: unknown. Sir Robert Tiptot (d. 1290) and Una his wife were probably benefactors (Knowles). Ded: St Francis.
Custody of Cambridge. Apart from a record that the precincts were enlarged in 1332, very little is known of the history. A single vellum leaf written in the 13thC, used in the rebinding of a 15thC book, gives a glimpse of the friary's early days. An impressive list of 26 VIPs buried in the conventual ch. begins with Sir Robert and his wife (VCH). The house may not have been formally surrendered as Lord Wentworth bought the property on reporting to Cromwell that the Warden had sold the jewels as the only means of subsistence. Remains: A fragment of wall containing 3 arches has been embedded in a central complex of bldgs., and came from the garden of No. 8 Friars Road. Part of site excavated 1974 (Med. Arch. Vo. 19).

Isleworth Abbey. Middlesex. See Twickenham.

Ivinghoe (St Margaret's) Priory. Herts. (was Bucks.) 7½m S of Leighton Buzzard. (–1129 to 1536). Benedictine nuns. F: probably Wm. Giffard, bp. of Winchester (d. 1129). Ded: St. Margaret.
Always small and poor with few

175

benefactors resulting in considerable obscurity of life here. There is evidence of remission of taxes on several occasions. In 1447 a nun of Grace Dieu (*v.* above) requested transfer to Ivinghoe because she sought a 'stricter order of religion'. Letters between the prioress of G.D. and Bp. Alnwick about the proposal, revealed that the nun's sister was prioress of Ivinghoe but, as is so often the case, the outcome is unknown (Power). In the 16thC there were no injunctions from bps. except to order a nun not to visit friends outside the nunnery. *Remains:* None.

Ivychurch *(at Alderbury) Priory. Wilts. Map 6. 3m SE of Salisbury. (−1154 to 1536). Augustinian canons. F: K. Stephen. Ded BVM.*
No fdn. charter survives. Early endowments were small but in the 14thC there were many valuable grants. The B.D. (1348−9) caused the deaths of 13 of the 14 members, including the prior. The survivor became prior, being appointed by the king as there could be no election. Canons sent from other houses to form a new community caused the spiritual and economic life to decline, and by 1394 there were serious hardships. Sometime before 1414 the cell of Upavon, which belonged to St Wandrille's Abbey (W of Rouen), was granted to Ivychurch. In 1433 the priory lands were under Crown protection; and in 1536 the prior and 4 canons were found to be 'of honest conversation'. *Remains:* Some of the ch. exists including a round pier, arches, part of the W front, Norman capitals and fragments built into a farmhouse. On the village green a drinking fountain has been built with colonettes from the cloister of the priory

Ixworth *Priory. Suffolk. Map 4. 6m NE of Bury St Edmunds. (1170−1537). Augustinian canons. F: a member of the Blunt family. Ded: St Mary.*
The fdn. date of 1100 given by Dugdale and in VCH has been discounted as based upon unreliable sources, and perhaps referred to a projected fdn. which failed (Dickinson). Few records of the house survive, apart from some account rolls, to reveal the internal life of the community, and the history of the house is obscure. Early endowments included 7 chs. In 1492 no reforms were necessary and the bp. wrote 'the essentials of religion are laudably observed', but that the bldgs. were in poor condition. A door to the buttery was so placed that 'the brethren had to stand in the rain when they wished to drink' (VCH). None of the later visitations resulted in any serious complaints against the canons, but in 1520 the bp. criticised the building of a new hospice for layfolk when the community had no infirmary for their own sick canons, and ordered one to be speedily provided. It was noted that the clock neither struck nor went (a rare mention of clocks). *Remains:* Ch. has gone but the bases of several piers survive. Site occupied by a 19thC house which incorporates part of the 13thC E claustral range (except the chapter house); the E half of the refectory with very fine undercroft; the slype, now a chapel; and part of the prior's lodging. Interesting historical muniments kept here. Site examination in 1963 disclosed ch. outline and location of central crossing. Also, late-12thC dormitory windows found beneath panelling, (Med. Arch. Vol. 8, 1964). Desc: Proc. Suffolk Inst. of Arch. Vol. 8. Note: Archaeologia, Vol. 10, p. 472.

J

Jarrow *Priory. Durham. Map 1. 5m E of Newcastle-upon-Tyne. (1074–1536). Benedictine monks. Re-f: Aldwin, Prior of Winchcombe with 2 monks from Evesham. Ded: St Paul.*
1st. f. 681 by St Benedict Biscop. The principal history of this ancient fdn. occurs before the Conquest and is inextricably linked with Monk-wearmouth. Although the history has no striking incidents, the two houses had immense influence and formed a basis for civilisation in the country. Bede died here in 735 aged 62. The priory was pillaged by the Danes in 794, *c.* 867 and 973. It was also burnt by William I in 1069. The re-f. as an independent priory in 1074 lasted only a few years and in 1083 it became a cell of Durham. Until the Dissolution the house was inhabited by only a few monks who kept to their horarium, gave shelter to strangers and provided an occasional retreat for the priors of Durham. *Remains:* The 7thC monastic ch. forms the chancel of the present parish ch. There are fragments of 2 walls which were part of the W & S ranges of the 11thC claustral bldgs. Note: Antiquity, Vol. 9.

Jervaulx *Abbey. Yorks. NR. Map 1. 4½m NW of Masham. (1156–1537). Cistercian monks. F: Akarius Fitz Bardolph. Ded: St Mary.*
Originally f. at Fors and the F's son, Hervey, consented to the removal. Colonised from Byland. Began life in very poor circumstances and grew to rank among the greater Yorkshire abbeys. In the 13thC revenue came from iron and coal mines as well as sheep-farming. Early in the 15thC the house was impoverished, but by the 16thC the monks had built up a

reputation for their famous breed of horses which were described as being 'hardy and sound of kind'. Mitred 1409. The last abbot was involved with the Pilgrimage of Grace for which he forfeited his life at Tyburn. *Remains:* Outline of 13thC ch. Ruins of 12thC lay-brothers' range; 13thC chapter house; 14thC abbot's lodging, and 15thC infirmary and kitchen. The whole giving an admirable Cistercian plan. Fine rood screen and abbot's stall in Aysgarth ch. (7m W). Excavated 1807 and 1905. Desc. & plan: Yorks. Arch. J. Vol. 21 (1911).

K

Kalendar *Priory Cell. Northants. 9m NNW of Northampton. (+1155 to –1291). Premonstratensian canons. F: William Buttevillan (gave lands). Ded: St John.*
The house, in the parish of Cottes-brooke, was given by the F. to the abbot and canons of Sulby who made it a cell of the abbey. Very little known. As it is not named in the taxation list of 1291, it had then probably ceased to exist (Knowles). *Remains:* None. The site is re-presented by a moated enclosure at Cottesbrooke. (Colvin).

Keldholme *Priory. Yorks. NR. 1m E of Kirkbymoorside. (–1135 to 1535). Cistercian nuns. F: Robert de Stuteville. Ded: St Mary.*
Very little history known. What survives relates to violent disputes and internal disorders in the 14thC. The period 1308–1321 was one of constant obstruction to the appoint-ment of prioresses and non-observance of the Rule, culminating with harsh penances imposed on

Jervaulx Abbey, Yorkshire. Cloister garth looking south-east. On the left the ruined chapter house with pillars; on the right the dormitory almost to full height.

several nuns, and particularly humiliating ones on a layman (VCH). (Curiously, a nun, severely censured by Archbp. Greenfield, was elected prioress soon after his death in 1315). In 1321 a severe and inhuman penance was served upon a nun by Archbp. Melton (Power). The income was partly derived from a thriving wool trade with Italian merchants to the extent of 12 sacks p.a. From mid-14thC very little is known of the house and nothing of its internal history. Perhaps as well. *Remains:* None. Two incised slabs with foliated crosses are embedded in the wall of

a house and no doubt came from the priory. (Pevsner).

Kenilworth *Priory/Abbey. Warks. Map 3. (c. 1125–1539). Augustinian canons. F: Geoffrey de Clinton. Ded: BVM.*
The nearby renowned castle had the same F. Never wealthy or distinguished even though the F. generously endowed the house with tithes, land and chs. There seems to have been an indeterminate link with Stone Priory (*v.* below) in relation to the advowson of Stone parish ch. Siege of the castle in 1266 caused the

canons much impoverishment. The king's clerk in the 14thC made an exceptionally rare provision for the widow of a man who gave good service to the king in Scotland, by ordering the canons to let her live there as a free servant. In 1361 a prior resigned following an 'unsatisfactory state of the house' and several canons were sent to Brooke (*v.* above) in 1426 for disobedience. Became an abbey +1439. *Remains:* Fdns. of nave and N transept and bases of two crossing piers. Lower walls of slype and apsidal chapter house. 14thC guesthouse and gatehouse survive. The W doorway of the adjacent parish ch. is said to be a former Norman doorway of the conventual ch. Excavated 1890 & 1922–3. Desc. & plan: Birmingham Arch. Soc. Trans. Vol. 52 (1927).

Kersal *Alien Cell/Cell. Lancs. 3m NW of Manchester city centre. (1145/53– 1538). Cluniac monks. F: Ranulf de Gernon, Earl of Chester (d. 1153). Ded: St Leonard.*
The site of this hermitage was given to Lenton whose cell it became. Probably never more than a prior and one monk here. The history is blank beyond a note about a dispute with the rector of Manchester over the burial of parishioners at Kersal. Became denizen in 1392 at the same time as Lenton. *Remains:* None. A house occupies the site. Note: Lancs. & Ches. Antiq. Soc. J. Vol. 1.

Kersey *Priory. Suffolk. Map 7. 11½m W of Ipswich. (c. 1218–1443). Augustinian canons. F: Thomas de Burgh. Ded: BVM. & St Anthony*
Small and poor house which began as a hospital and soon became a priory. F's. widow, Nesta, and her second husband made significant

grants. Evenso it was often impoverished and in 1347 the income could not support the canons who were then excused the king's taxes. The house was suppressed in 1443 and in the following year granted to King's Coll., Cambridge. *Remains:* A major ch. fragment survives being the S chancel chapel with 2 arches and the E wall of the transept. W wall of ch. incorporated in a garden wall. W claustral range, the original hospital bldg., now part of a brick-fronted farmhouse (Pevsner). Excavations of 1958 & 63 recovered the plan of the ch. and revealed the fdns. of 3 of the central tower pillars (Med. Arch. Vols. 3 & 8).

Kerswell *Alien Priory/Priory Cell. Devon. 7m NW of Honiton. (1119/29–1538). Cluniac monks. F: Matilda Peverell (?). Ded: unknown.*
Dependent upon Montacute. Probably for only 2 monks originally though there were 6 c. 1300. Very little recorded. It became denizen in 1407 with Montacute. *Remains:* None. A few fragments are built into a farm including reset parts of a Norman doorway; and a barn.

Keynsham *Abbey. Som. (Avon). 5m SE of Bristol. (1167/72–1539). Augustinian canons. F: William, Earl of Gloucester. Ded: BVM, St Peter & St Paul. Order of St Victor.*
Considerable details in VCH about early licences and charters. In 1242 one of the canons became abbot of Bristol because of the efficiency of the house. There were estates in Ireland and Wales but of little profit to the canons. In the mid-14thC, following the Black Death, neglect of the house and poor discipline crept in. In the 15thC the canons received a number of benefactions,

and in 1495 the Duke if Bedford, uncle to Henry VII, chose to be buried here. Following dissolution, the conventual ch. and bldgs. did not stand for long. *Remains:* Very little. The base of a pier survives in Abbey Park. Many Norman fragments are built into local houses. Series of excavations 1962–75. The A4 Keynsham by-pass cuts through the centre of the abbey site. Desc. & notes: Proc. of Som. Arch. Soc. Vols. 53 and 104. Notes: Med. Arch. Vols. 1, 14 & 15.

Kilburn *Priory. Middlesex. NW of Central London. (1139–1536). Bendictine nuns. F: Herbert, abbot of Westminster. Ded: St Mary & St John, Baptist.*
1st. f. as a hermitage for 3 anchoresses *c.* 1130. Q. Maud was a Bene. nun, and perhaps to obtain her favour the anchorite cell was converted into a nunnery. VCH gives house as Augustinian but other authorities as Benedictine. Certainly the prioresses were appointed by the Bene. abbots of Westminster. Small and poor, and being on a high road out of London was frequently over-burdened with requests for hospitality. The priory received alms from various kings up to 1265 and later royal charities consisted of exemptions from taxes. Considerable details of properties and finances in VCH. *Remains:* None. Part of site excavated in 1850 and 1852. Note: Archaeologia, Vol. 15, p. 267.

Kildale *Friary. Yorks. NR. 5m SE of Guisborough. (1310 to +1313). Crutched (Friars of the Holy Cross). F: Sir Arnold de Percy. Ded: unknown.*
The F. gave land to the friars without royal licence and although Edward II

pardoned the breach, Archbp. Greenfield denounced the community as belonging to an Order not authorised by the pope. It is believed that the community came here from York (*v.* below). Since no more is heard of the fdn., the F. no doubt succumbed to the attack (VCH). *Remains:* None.

Kilpeck *Priory/Cell. Herefs. 8m SSW of Hereford. (1134–1540). Benedictine monks. F: Hugh fitz William the Norman. Ded: St David.*
Very little history. In 1422 the priory was suppressed and the property united with St Peter's Abbey, Gloucester, whose cell it remained until the Dissolution. *Remains:* None. The site was $\frac{1}{4}$-mile from the present parish ch.

King's Langley *Friary. Cambs. 6½m SW of St Albans. (–1308 to 1538). Dominican. F: K. Edward II. Ded: unknown.*
Visitation of Cambridge. The conventual ch. was completed *c.* 1312, meantime the friars lived in a lodge in the royal park. The F. gave the community funds and Edward III gave the friars part of the income from a quarry and in 1358 a local fishery. The F. had planned a nunnery here in 1318 and the fdn. was commenced by his son in 1349 at Dartford, and was considered complementary to K. L. Richard II was brought here before being interred at Westminster. The house was well provided for throughout its history and retained royal connections. After dissolution it was re-f. for nuns by Q. Mary and finally suppressed by Elizabeth I. *Remains:* There survives a long, narrow 14thC two-storeyed bldg. of unknown purpose incorporated in a larger property. It has

original doorways, windows and oak roof. The fdns. of the ch. were exposed in 1831 and cleared away.

King's Lynn *Priory. Norfolk. Map 4. (1101–1539). Benedictine monks: F: Bp. Herbert de Losinga of Norwich. Ded: St Mary Magdalene, St Margaret & all Virgin Saints.* Because the bp. had purchased his bishopric he was instructed to build churches and monasteries in atonement. This was one of them, f. in the year his cathedral-priory in Norwich was ded. It was a parish and conventual ch. Very little history separate from Norwich Cath-Pr. on which it was a dependent. The community consisted of a prior and 3 or 4 monks. VCH gives some details of valuations and annual returns. Invalid monks from Norwich were sent here, and to the Yarmouth dependency, to recuperate. *Remains:* Nothing of the original ch. The monastic chancel survives of the later ch. To the S lies the restored S claustral range converted into a dwelling.

King's Lynn *Friary. Norfolk. Map 4. (–1295 to 1538). Austin. F: unknown. Ded: unknown.* Limit of Cambridge. Margaret de Suthmere gave a house and grounds to the convent in 1295 (earliest mention). In the early-14thC more licences were granted to allow the transfer of land adjoining the original site to the friars, and the premises were enlarged. From the mid-14thC to the Dissolution nothing is known of the friars' lives. *Remains:* In Austin Street there survives the arch of a gateway to the property.

King's Lynn *Friary. Norfolk. Map 4. (c. 1260–1538). Carmelite. F: probably Lord Bardolph. Ded: BVM.*

Distinction of Norwich. Edward I gave the friars 6 oaks in 1277 for use in construction of the ch. The Hastings family were also benefactors. No history survives. The house was not, however, insignificant because there were 42 friars here in 1326. *Remains:* Only a red-brick gateway with 3 empty niches in Bridge Street. Re-used materials from the friary can be seen in nearby bldgs.

King's Lynn *Friary. Norfolk. (–1256 to 1538). Dominican. F: Thomas Gedney. Ded: St Dominic.* Visitation of Cambridge. 40 friars here c. 1276 and 45 in 1328. VCH gives details of gifts to the house and it was large enough for provincial chapters to congregate here on 3 occasions. Suffered fire damage in 1486. Apart from these few notes much of the history is lost. *Remains:* None. The building of the railway engulfed the site. Some prints exist which show some of the bldgs. in 1845 shortly before demolition.

King's Lynn *Friary. Norfolk. Map 4. (c. 1230–1538). Franciscan (Conventual). F: Thomas Feltham. Ded: St Francis.* History exceptionally scanty. Site enlarged 1287 and again in 1364. Details of bequests shed little light on the bldgs; nor does the house seem to have been a favourite for burials, the most important being that of John Stanford, provincial of the Order, who died in 1264. At its peak 38 friars lived here but only 10 at the time of surrender. *Remains:* The sole existing structure is the graceful octagonal steeple of the ch. Some 90 ft. away is a fragment of the E wall of the choir. Desc: Arch. J. Vol. 41. Desc. & plan: Franciscan

181

Architecture in England (1937)
A. R. Martin.

King's Lynn *Friary. Norfolk. (−1272 to +1307). Friars of the Sack. F: unknown. Ded: uncertain.*
Nothing is known of this house during its brief history − the Order being abolished in 1274, i.e. no new members recruited. When the friary closed *c.* 1312 the prior was the head of the whole Order in England. *Remains:* None. Even the site is uncertain. Note: Archaeologia Vol. 3, p. 127.

Kingston-upon-Hull *Priory. Yorks. ER. (1377−1539). Carthusian monks. F: Michael de la Pole. Ded: BVM, St Michael & All Angels and St Thomas, Martyr.*
Franciscan friars were probably on the site before 1377. The F's. father planned a house of Franciscan nuns to replace them but died before achieving it. The F., a wealthy merchant who became Earl of Suffolk and Lord Chancellor of England, changed his father's plans and introduced Carth. monks. It seems that a bldg. called Maison Dieu was given to the monks for their use. Richard II supported the prior and convent in an application to the pope for more endowments due to poverty, and there were disputes over the patronage of a ch. in Lincs. Little other history known. In 1536 the house escaped suppression by paying a large fine of £233.6.8d. Two of the monks, who had spent their latter years in London and went to York in 1536, suffered martyrdom there in May 1537 − charged with refusing to accept the Act of Supremacy. *Remains:* None. Note: Archaeologia, Vol. 13.

Kingston-upon-Hull *Friary. Yorks.*

ER. (−1303 to 1539). Austin. Fs: Geoffrey de Holtham and John de Wetwang. Ded: unknown.
Limit of York. Although the first record is in 1303, it was not until 1317 that the Fs. received royal licence to grant land for the friars' house. *c.* 1380, Friar Hornington, Professor of Theology of Cambridge, chose Hull as his home for life by licence from the prior general. As is so often the case with friaries, historical records are few; but at the Dissolution the size of the estate was unusually small − 49 yds. by 33 yds. (VCH). It was the last Austin friary in England to surrender. *Remains:* None.

Kingston-upon-Hull *Friary. Yorks. ER. (1290−1539). Carmelite. Fs; probably Edward I, Sir Robert Ughtred and Sir Richard de la Pole. Ded: BVM.*
Distinction of York. The earliest mention of the house places it within the town, but in 1307 Edward I gave the friars 3 acres outside the walls in exchange for the first site. Other gifts of land followed and records include several bequests from women to the image of the Virgin in this ch. (VCH). Little else known. *Remains:* None. Site occupied by Trinity House. Whitefriars Gate and Carmelite House commemorate the Order in the town.

Kingston-upon-Hull *Friary. Yorks. ER. (+1307(?) to −1365). Franciscan (Conventual). F: Edward I. Ded: unknown.*
Custody of York. The 1st. fdn. was a coll. for 6 priests who failed to agree among themselves and were turned out. Friars Minor took over but were removed *c.* 1365 when it was intended to fd. a Franciscan nunnery here, but

the house became Carthusian (*v.* above). There appear to be no reliable dates or facts. *Remains:* None.

Kingswood *Abbey. Glos. (was Wilts.). Map 5. 1m SSW of Wotton-under-Edge. (1139–1538). Cistercian monks. F: William de Berkeley. Ded: St Mary.*
Colonised from Tintern. The monks moved to Hazleton and Tetbury (*v.* above & below) after the fdn., and finally resettled at Kingswood *c.* 1170 at a new site. In 1276 the house was prosperous with 8 granges which produced wool sales averaging 40 sacks p.a. during the 2nd half of the 13thC. The B.D. impoverished the monastery and its recovery was greatly helped by the generosity of the Berkeleys. After the murder of Edward II (1327) Kingswood refused to give sepulture and lost a most profitable source of income (*v.* Gloucester Abbey). There was poverty at the end of the 14thC but in the 15thC the house regained some of its prosperity through leasing its granges. The convent's 'painful anxiety' to please Cromwell and avoid suppression was in vain. *Remains:* Only the fine late-14thC vaulted gatehouse (care D of E) and a small section of precinct wall. There is no certainty of location of either of the 2 sites. Desc: Trans. Bristol & Glos. Arch. Soc. Vol. 63 (1954).

Kington St Michael *Priory. Wilts. Map 5. 3m NNW of Chippenham. (–1155 to 1536). Benedictine nuns. F: probably a member of the Wayfer de Brinton family. Ded: St Mary.*
Cartulary and early records of the priory's possessions lost, so how some of the lands were acquired is unknown. Ch. rebuilt in 1225 aided by royal grants and again rebuilt in

15thC. Records of poverty. The bps. of Salisbury were patrons from whom the nuns tried to free themselves, but the efforts failed and a prioress had to resign. In 1326 a nun from Broomhall (*v.* above) was appointed prioress here. A book of obits survives written in 1493, also some detailed accounts of possessions. In 1536 there were only 4 nuns living here. *Remains:* Ch. has gone. Complete 15thC W claustral range and the frater in the S range, of an earlier date, incorporated in a farmhouse, though somewhat altered. Part of the site has been excavated. Desc. & plan: Archaeologia. Vol. 73 (1923).

Kintbury *Priory. Berks. 5m W of Newbury. (+1147 to c. 1155). Benedictine nuns of Fontevrault. F: Richard Bossu, earl of Leicester. Ded: St Mary.*
In the early 1150s Gervase Paynel gave his mill at Inkpen to the nuns which seems to allay the doubts that no nuns ever came here. Not long afterwards he transferred his gift to the priory of Nuneaton, and about this time the F. also transferred his gift of land to his fdn. there. The manor of Kintbury, however, remained the property of Nuneaton Priory until the Dissolution. *Remains:* None.

Kirby Bellars *Priory. Leics. Map 3. 2m SW of Melton Mowbray. (1359–1536). Augustinian canons. F: Sir Robert Beler. Ded: St Peter.*
1st. f. 1316 as a coll. for priests. In 1326 this F. was murdered and in subsequent years difficulties arose about service procedures, until finally Aug. canons were brought here in 1359 – making it almost the last fdn. of the Order in England (*v.* Ovingham). The house was small

183

and history is scarce. At a visitation in 1440 it was found in good spiritual and financial order. Nothing more until 1511 when the bldgs. were in decay due to fire. When suppressed a state of good repair was reported. *Remains:* The ch. survives most of which is from the collegiate fdn. It was later conventual and parochial and is mainly E.E. Of the claustral bldgs., which lay to the N, there is no trace.

Kirkham *Priory. Yorks. ER. Map 3. 12m NE of York. (c. 1122−1539). Augustinian canons. F: Walter L'Espec. Ded: Holy Trinity.*
Most important incident in early history was the pull felt by the canons towards the newly-arrived Cistercian way of life and they all but transferred to the new Order. In 1258 the prior was in dispute with the owner of woodland in which he hunted game with dogs. In the first half of the 13thC the re-bldg. of the great choir and presbytery resulted in heavy debt and 16 corrodies (life pensions to individuals) were sold to raise funds. Late-13thC injunctions ordered restriction of entry of laymen and that 'fools and buffoons' were to be kept out of the refectory. Very little history in 14th & 15thCs (VCH). *Remains:* Of the ch. there is little more than the ground plan Excavation has revealed layout of whole priory. High walls survive of refectory; W side of cloister with fine lavatorium; reredorter and wide-arched late-13th gatehouse with heraldry. Desc., plan & care: D of E.

Kirklees *Priory. Yorks. WR. 2m SE of Brighouse. (−1138(?) to 1539). Cistercian nuns. F: Reiner le Fleming. Ded: St Mary & St James.*
It was here *c.* 1246 that the treacherous prioress is known to romance as having bled Robin Hood to death. In 1317 a custos was appointed to manage the estates (Power). The house was always small and poor which sometimes accounted for irregularities, e.g. 14thC visitations record instances of reproval for apostacy and disobedience. There are few details of internal or external history surviving. Somehow a house with an annual income of less than £20 in 1535 continued to exist until 1539. *Remains:* Part of the gatehouse, added to in the late 16thC, incorporated in farm bldgs., and was probably part of a house succeeding the priory. Excavated 1904−5 and covered again. Hist: Yorks. Arch. Soc. J. Vols. 16 (1902) & 20 (1908).

Kirkstall *Abbey. Yorks. WR. Map 3. 3m NW of Leeds city centre. (1152−1540). Cistercian monks. F: Henry de Lacy. Ded: St Mary.*
Originally fd. at Barnoldswick (*v.* above) and moved by the F. to land at Kirkstall owned by Wm. Peytvin and occupied by a settlement of hermits, some of whom joined the Cist. This large and important house acquired much property. It had a singularly uneventful history between 1200 and the Dissolution. After a century of bad management culminating in the huge debt of £5,248 in 1284, Abbot Hugh Grimstone reduced it to £160 in less than 20 years through his wise and pious rule. This prolonged period of poverty may account for the abbey ruins being mainly of one period, there being very few rebldg. programmes in its history, resulting in a profoundly valuable example of the earliest Cist. architecture. In 1395 the abbey was granted the alien priory of Burstall (*v.* Appendix

Kirkstall Abbey near Leeds, Yorkshire, from the south-west.

185

1). *Remains:* Perhaps the most complete monastic ruins after Fountains — all massive late-Norman. Excavations from 1950—64 revealed most of the complex of walls and drains to the S of the S claustral range. The fdns. of several bldgs. of unknown purpose were also located (Med. Arch. Vols. 1—9). 1st. excavated 1905—6. Desc. & plan: Thoresby Soc. Vol. 16 (1907); Br. Arch. Assoc. J. Vol. 20; Note: Archaeologia, Vol. 16. Hist: Kirkstall Abbey — D. E. Owen.

Kirkstead *Abbey. Lincs. Map 3. 8m SW of Horncastle. (1139—1537). Cistercian monks. F: Hugh Brito. Ded: St Mary.*
Colonised from Fountains. The location given by the F. was 'too small and a place of horror' and his son, Robert, moved the monks to a new site a short distance away in 1187. There was good income in the 13thC but heavy losses in the 14thC. Failure of sheep-farming resulted in the abbot being forced to buy wool from elsewhere to fulfil contracts. In 1303 the alien cell of Covenham was given to the abbey (*v.* Appendix 1). In 1404 an unruly monk opposed an abbot's appointment and even ejected him. The abbot regained control and the monk was condemned to perpetual silence (VCH). Part of the income came from ownership of 4 iron forges. In the Lincolnshire Rising the abbot and 3 monks were executed and the monastery passed to the Crown. *Remains:* One tall fragment of masonry is the SE angle of the S transept. Nearby is the exquisite E.E. chapel-by-the-gate, now the ch. of St Leonard. Several large depressions in a field were probably fishponds. Notes: Arch. J. Vol. 40 (1883); Note: Archaeologia, Vol. 14.

Knaresborough *Friary. Yorks. WR. (c. 1252—1538). Trinitarian. F: probably Richard, Earl of Cornwall. Ded: Holy Trinity & St Robert.*
Robert Flower (d. 1218, canonised sometime before 1252) and a succession of hermits, were probably the forerunners of the friars who were given St Robert's chapel and the parish ch. by Richard. In 1318 the house was destroyed by the Scots and 40 years later the Black Death carried off all but 5 friars. In the 15thC the friars were charged with encroaching upon the rights of others. A fine stone conduit built by them has since been destroyed. The community does not appear to have been distinguished for its learning. *Remains:* None. Abbey Road is near the site.

Kyme *(S Kyme) Priory. Lincs. Map 3. 7½m NE of Sleaford. (—1156 to 1539). Augustinian canons. F: Philip de Kyme. Ded: St Mary.*
Never important. In 1236 the bp. substituted a new prior for an 'unsuitable' one. Amongst later injunctions the bp. ordered more time to be spent in contemplation and study, and in 1440 there was a complaint that too many boys in the choir hindered services. In 1536 the canons paid a heavy fine (£200) to be allowed to continue existence and they faithfully observed the Rule. *Remains:* Present parish ch. is formed by the W end of the S aisle of the conventual ch. together with a S section of the adjacent nave with porch. Nothing else. The whole much altered in 1890.

L

Lacock *Abbey. Wilts. Map 5. 3m S of Chippenham. (1232—1539). August-*

Lacock Abbey, Wiltshire. North cloister walk.

*inian canonesses. F: Ela, Countess of
Salisbury. Ded: BVM & St Bernard.*
Confirmation of fdn. 1230 and the
fdn. stone laid 1232. House in
memory of F's husband. She became
abbess for 17 years. This was a late
fdn. and of the life of the nuns there
is practically no information — not a
single visitation report to rescue
them from obscurity (Power). The
house was a centre of education and
of aid for women bereaved or in sickness. The community was never large,
22 at most. The estates, though not
extensive, yielded sustenance and
revenue enabling some of the produce
to be marketed. In 1476 the community possessed 2,000 sheep and a
coalmine (VCH). In 1536 a fine of
£300 was paid to avoid suppression.
Remains: The ch., without aisles or
transepts, has gone except for the N
wall which became part of a mansion.
Superb claustral bldgs. including
13thC cloister walks, sacristy, chapter
house and parlour together with
altered abbess's hall and lodging.
(N.T.) Ch. excavated 1898–9. Desc.
& plan: Archaeologia, Vol. 57 (1898);
Wilts. Arch. Mag., Dec. 1900:
Articles: Country Life 3, 10 & 17
March 1923.

Lamanna *(St George's Island) Cell.
Cornwall. 1m off the coast of Looe.
(–1114 to +1239). Benedictine
monks. F: unknown. Ded: St George.*
The site was originally a Celtic
monastery and *c.* 1114 it was granted
to Glastonbury as a cell for 2 monks.
After about 100 years Richard, Earl
of Cornwall, gave the abbey freedom
to dispose of the property, and from
the absence in registers after 1257
it seems the abbey disposed of the
asset (Oliver). Mid-14thC there was a
chantry here. *Remains:* None. Some
ruins survived in 1846.

Lambley *(-on-Tyne) Priory. N'land.
6m SW by W of Haltwhistle. (–1190
to 1537). Benedictine nuns. Fs:
probably Adam de Tindale and Helwise
his wife. Ded: St Mary & St Patrick.*
This obscure little nunnery, once in
Scotland, was ravaged by war, famine
and the Scots, and in the case of the
latter 'not by the valour of warriors
but by the dastardly conduct of
thieves' (Chronicle of Lanercost). In
the 13thC the prioress, tired of complaints by the baron of Thirlwall,
challenged him to combat. She hired
a champion to fight for her but
relented at risking his life and paid
£10 compensation. The annals are
thin in the 14th & 15thCs and by the
date of closure the net income was
less than £10 p.a. and the receiver
found no one there. *Remains:* None.
Early in the 17thC Camden recorded
the house as 'undermined by the river
and fallen down'.

Lancaster *Friary. Lancs. (1260–
1539). Dominican. F: Sir Hugh
Harrington. Ded: unknown.*
Visitation of York. Very little history
known. In 1291 the archbp. of York
ordered 3 friars to preach on Holy
Cross Day (14 Sept.), one each in
Lancaster, Kendal and Lonsdale.
House enlarged in 1311. *Remains:*
None. Site near Sulyard St. (Pevsner).

Lanercost *Priory. C'land (Cumbria).
Map 1. 11m NE of Carlisle. (c. 1166–
1537). Augustinian canons. F: Robert
de Vaux. Ded: St Mary Magdalene.*
Probably colonised from Pentney.
Amply endowed by the F. who was
'a valiant soldier, a great judge and a
prudent statesman' (VCH). Edward I
& Q. Eleanor stayed here in 1280
en route to Newcastle. Scottish
armies constantly harrassed the house
particularly in 1296, 1311 (Robert

188

Lanercost Priory, Cumbria, from the north-east. Beyond the ruined south transept and choir of the church the foundations of the chapter house and undercroft of the dormitory can be seen.

Bruce) and 1346 (David II). In 1306 Edward I stayed for 6 months leaving only to go to his death at Burgh (NW of Carlisle). Slender history in 15th & 16thCs. An abstract of a 17th–18thC transcript of the lost cartulary includes the 1296 Lanercost Chronicle (a history plus an unreliable list of religious fdns.). *Remains:* Half-ruined ch. of which nave and N aisle are in use as parish ch., transepts and choir roofless. Subvault of refectory. W claustral range converted to a mansion after 1537 to which was added a massive tower. Part of gate-house to the W. Care: D of E (except

nave). Hist. Acct: Trans. C'land & W'land Arch. Soc. Vol. 1 (1870) and Vol. 26 (1926); Arch. J. Vol. 96, with plan, (1939).

Langdon *(W. Langdon) Abbey. Kent. 3½m N of Dover. (1189–1535). Premonstratensian canons. F: William de Auberville. Ded: St Mary & St Thomas, Martyr.*
Colonised from Leiston. Early-14thC cartulary preserved. House frequently mentioned in Premon. records. 14th & 15thC visitations refer to 'excellent abbots' but exhort canons to rise for matins and pay more

189

attention to tonsures. In 1497 the
ch. was reported in a ruinous state
and still in decay in 1535. It seems
that in the same year the king's commissioner was aware of the abbot's
misconduct and posted servants 'to
keep all starting holes' while he
battered down the door. The 'gentle-
woman' went to prison in Dover and
the abbot to one in Canterbury. No
doubt this caused the premature
surrender. *Remains:* None. House
occupies the site. Excavated 1880.
Desc. & plan: Archaeologia Cantiana,
VoL 15, (1883).

Langley *(at Diseworth) Priory. Leics.*
6m NW of Loughborough. (c. 1150–
1536). Benedictine nuns. Fs: Wm.
Pantulf and Burgia his wife. Ded:
St Mary.
First nuns came from Farewell and
in the early days they claimed to be
Cistercian but were clearly Bene. at
the end of the 13thC. Nothing known
of internal affairs before 14thC, and
visitations of 1354 & 1400 revealed
a well-run house. It was 'miserably
poor' in the 14thC with debts of
£50 p.a. and an income of £20 p.a.,
the nuns on occasions being swindled
by dealers through not making
written contracts. In 1485 the
priory's relics were said to include a
piece of the Holy Cross. The nuns
were highly skilled in embroidery and
in an inventory of 1485 they had 'a
whole sacristy full'. One aristocratic
boarder in the mid-15thC kept 12
dogs in her rooms to the continual
annoyance of the nuns. In 1536 the
house was small and old but in good
repair, and no record survives of the
exact date of its closure. *Remains:*
Slight. A house on the site may make
use of priory materials.

Langley *Abbey. Norfolk. Map 4.*

11m SE by E of Norwich. (1195–
1536). Premonstratensian canons.
F: Robert fitz Roger Helke. Ded:
St Mary.
Colonised from Alnwick. The house
had one of the longest lists of benefactors in the county. In 1343 the
income from market sales were
seriously reduced by flooding from
the sea and river as well as from heavy
hospitality outlay. In 1475 an aged
and sick abbot was the reason for
poor discipline resulting in firm
penances on the canons, and in 1486
they were again in trouble for hunting
and fishing at night. In 1502 poverty
was due to low income, but all the
canons were 'of good name' up to
the closure. *Remains:* Ch. gone. Best
ruin is a 13thC cellarium of the W
claustral range, now a barn. Part of
chapter house, and remnants of the
dormitory and infirmary survive.
Farm occupies the site. Notes &
plan: Norfolk Archaeology, Vol. 21;
Desc: Arch. J. Vol. 28 (new ser.);
Excavated 1906 and again 1921.

Lanthony II *Priory. Glos.*
See Gloucester.

Lastingham *Abbey. Yorks. NR. Map 1.*
3m NE of Kirkbymoorside. (1078–
c. 1230). Benedictine monks. F:
Stephen of Whitby. Ded: St Mary.
1st. f. +654 by St Cedd. Destroyed by
Danes *c.* 870. In 1078 the Conqueror
granted the monastery to monks of
Whitby who were being persecuted
by pirate raids. They built the crypt
(to contain the sacred remains of
St Cedd) and the new abbey except
for a nave. The ch. was never completed. The monks left it and moved
to York to fd. St Olave's and, later,
St Mary's Abbey. It is not entirely
clear why the abbey ch. was abandoned, but the wild area was prob-

ably infested with robbers. For the next 120 years the ecclesiastical duties were carried out by a priest from York and *c.* 1230 it was no longer a cell of St Mary's, but a parish ch. with its own vicar. *Remains:* The crypt of the parish ch., unaltered since 1088, is the only complete apsidal example in England, and is one of the earliest examples of Norman architecture. It is the only part of the monastic ch. to survive. Book: The Monastic Church of Lastingham (1894) J. C. Wall.

Latton *Priory. Essex. Map 7. 3m N of Epping. (−1200 to 1534). Augustinian canons. F: unknown. Ded: St John, Baptist.*
In 1534 the Fs. were named as ancestors of Thomas Shaa. Very little history known of this small house which never exceeded a prior and 2 canons, and was on too small a scale to prosper (Dickinson). A petition of *c.* 1327 concerns the canons' right to retain tithes of bread, beer, flesh, candles and other provisions (VCH). In 1534 an Inquisition found that the house had long been governed by only one canon (the prior) and that many divine services were neglected. However, the sole survivor, John Taillour, had long ago departed voluntarily and the priory had become 'a profane place'. It seems that the house was omitted from the 1535 valuations of monastic properties. *Remains:* The curious survival is a barn formed by the complete crossing of the priory ch. Nothing else.

Launceston *Priory. Cornwall. (1127−1539). Augustinian canons. F: Wm. Warelwast. bp. of Exeter. Ded: St Stephen.*
c. 830 there was a fdn. of secular canons here and in 1127 the F. gave the great college to the canons of Aldgate (London). In due course the community moved to a more suitable site in the town. Although it was to become the wealthiest religious house in the county and famed for its hospitality and charity (Oliver), in 1400 it was said to be on the verge of ruin due to pestilence and, more probably, poor administration. But when in that year the revenues of 3 parishes were taken by the prior, the parishioners complained in parliament that the convent's income was already £1,000 p.a. 15thC cartulary survives and the 'unusually loquacious fdn. charter' (Dickinson). The house had the privilege of sanctuary (Borlase). Furious disturbances in 1532 when a new prior was appointed and 3 canons were imprisoned to ensure the safety of the prior's life. *Remains:* None. Perhaps a Norman arch in the entrance to the White Hart Hotel came from the priory.

Launde *Priory. Leics. Map 3. 13m E of Leicester. (−1125 to 1539). Augustinian canons. Fs: Richard Basset and Maud his wife. Ded: St John, Baptist.*
Small but wealthy by Aug. standards. Full list of fdn. endowments in VCH. A period of internal dissension is suggested by disputed elections in 1289, 1300 & 1350. Later came a series of unsatisfactory priors − 1388, 1398 & 1416. Little is known of the 15thC history. A visitation in 1440 constrained the canons to keep silence and refrain from selling corrodies without the bp's. permission. In 1528 the priory bldgs. were said to be in a ruinous state but there were no serious faults with the canons. The house was taken over by Thomas Cromwell. *Remains:*

Site mainly occupied by a mansion.
Close by is the chancel of the con-
ventual ch. (now a chapel) and a
Norman transept arch.

Lavendon *Abbey. Bucks. 9½m NW by
W of Bedford. (c. 1157–1536). Premonstratensian canons. F: John de
Bidun. Ded: St Mary* & St John,
Baptist.*
VCH gives details of original endowments. During the 1st. C. of its
existence the house was much
troubled by lawsuits and lost nearly
all the chs. with which the F. endowed it. There were also notices of
protection granted to the abbots.
Never rich. A petition to the pope
in 1397 reveals serious financial
difficulties. Being near the highway
there were heavy demands on hospitality. Scant history survives of
internal life in 15th & 16thCs.
Remains: None. A farm occupies the
site.
* Sometimes omitted as referring to
parish ch. only.

Leeds *Priory. Kent. 5m SE by E of
Maidstone. (1119–c. 1540). Augustinian canons. F: Robert de Creve-
coeur. Ded: St Mary & St Nicholas.*
A large house well endowed by the F.
with chs. of his barony, but it was
not intended that all of them should
be served by canons. Other benefactors gave land and money. Part of
the 14thC cartulary survives. In 1318
& 1356 the prior became a visitor to
other Aug. houses in Kent. In 1368
there were no serious injunctions
following a visitation save one which
impugned the cellarer for playing
dice. The house was in debt in 1487,
though comparatively rich, by Aug.
standards, when suppressed. In 1511
the bp. ordered the prior to pay a
teacher to instruct young brethren.

A history of few defects but by 1536
the bldgs. were certainly in a bad
state. The exact date of the closure is
unknown. *Remains:* Nothing above
ground. Excavated 1846 & 1973–4.
The plan of the ch. was revealed
including an apse and crypt at the E
end. Also the main outlines of the
claustral bldgs. Numerous carved
stones, architectural fragments and a
tiled floor were found. Desc: Br.
Arch. Assoc. J. Vol. 2; Med. Arch.
Vols. 18 & 19.

Legbourne *Priory. Lincs. 3½m SE of
Louth. (c. 1150–1536). Cistercian
nuns. F: Robert fitz Gilbert of
Tathwell. Ded: St Mary.*
Originally at Keddington (1m N of
Louth) and sometimes called an abbey.
Moved to Legbourne shortly before
1199. In 1268 it was claimed that
the house was not Cist. In 1395 there
was difficulty in getting labour
following the 'fifth' pestilence
(Power). Not much history, apart
from records of visitations especially
that in 1440 when poverty was rife
and the bldgs. ruinous. There were
complaints about impartial treatment
by the prioress, and that a secular
boarder brought her pet birds into
the dormitory at night whose
'jargoning' broke the silence and
disturbed the nuns. The bp. ordered
her out. In the 14thC a master was
appointed to manage the house's
business affairs. No serious occur-
rences seem to have disrupted the
long history. *Remains:* None. A
house occupies the site.

Leicester *(St Mary de Pratis) Abbey.
Leics. Map 3. (1143–1538). Augustinian canons. F: Robert Bossu, Earl
of Leicester. Ded: St Mary.*
F. endowed the house with possessions
earlier settled upon the collegiate

ch. within Leicester Castle, and there were many subsequent endowments during the 1st. 3½Cs. of its existence. These resulted in the house being the 3rd richest of the Order in England at the suppression (after Cirencester and Merton). Little is known of internal history during these 350 years. Canons from here became abbots and priors of other Aug. houses. After a visitation in 1440 there were a few trivial injunctions. The abbey had a splendid library with adjoining scriptorium, and there was great intellectual improvement in the early 16thC. The closing years of the monastery's life were not flattering for the convent was torn with faction and abuse. The most celebrated event in the abbey's history was the death and burial here of Cardinal Wolsey in 1530. No cartularies survive. *Remains:* None. In Abbey Park is a conjectural layout of the fdns. A few sections of stone and brick precinct wall survive. (The nearby ruins are of a Tudor mansion and the gatehouse is post-Reformation.) Excavations: Br. Arch. Assoc. J. Vols. 1, 6 & 7; Antiquaries J. Vol. 30. Notes: Arch. J. Vol. 27. Book: Abbey of St Mary-in-the-Meadows (1949) A. Hamilton Thompson.

Leicester *Friary. Leics. (1254–1538). Austin. F: unknown. Ded: St Catherine.*
Limit of Lincoln. In 1304 Thomas, earl of Leicester, enlarged the site. Very little history known and the name of only one prior has survived. A friar in the late-14thC, Thomas Ratcliffe, became renowned as a preacher (VCH). *Remains:* None. The friary is remembered by St Augustine Street (or does this record the abbey's existence?). Part excavated 1973–4 when E & W

cloister walks were located with a range of rooms adjacent to the latter. No evidence of the ch., but a massive boundary wall fdn. and part of the main drain in which a large number of shoes were found (Med. Arch. Vols. 18 & 19).

Leicester *Friary. Leics. (–1284 to 1538). Dominican. F: an Earl of Leicester or Simon de Montfort II. Ded: St Clement.*
Visitation of Oxford. Records of alms and bequests bestowed upon the house are far from complete, but are in some measure offset by details of gifts from K. Edwards I, II & III and many knights. Provincial chapters were held here in 1301, 1317 & 1334. The right to fish the R. Soar 3 days a week and never at night, was permitted with nets 'which will not destroy little fishes'. Hardly anything is known of burials in the friars' ch. *Remains:* None. Some bldgs. stood until *c.* 1620. The site was on an island formed by two courses of the river Soar (VCH). The house was also known as 'Black Friars in the Ashes' and is presumed to have been surrounded with ash trees. Notes: Spencer's Illustrated Leicester Almanack, 1897.

Leicester *Friary. Leics. (c. 1230–1538). Franciscan (Conventual). Fs: either Simon de Montfort II or, perhaps, Gilbert Luenor and Ellen his wife. Ded: Holy Trinity.*
Custody of Oxford. In 1402 the warden and 7 friars were convicted of having organised an armed revolt to restore Richard II (deposed 1399, murdered 1400) to the throne, and they were hanged at Tyburn. In 1414 Parliament assembled in the friars' great hall and passed a statute against heretics and Lollards (VCH). In 1485

the body of the ill-fated Richard III, slain at Market Bosworth, the last important battle of the Wars of the Roses, was buried in the conventual ch. The deed of surrender, which still exists, was signed by 7 friars. *Remains:* None. Grey Friars and Friar Lane are on or very near the site. Notes: Spencer's Illustrated Leicester Almanack, 1897.

Leicester *Friary. Leics. (−1274 to −1295). Friars of the Sack. F: unknown. Ded: unknown.*
Nothing is known of the history of this house other than a brief mention in 1283 of a prior. *Remains:* None. Note: Archaeologia, Vol. 3, p. 130.

Leighs *(Little Leighs, or Leez) Priory. Essex. Map 7. 6½m N of Chelmsford. (−1200 to 1536). Augustinian canons. F: Ralph Gernon. Ded: St Mary & St John, Evangelist.*
House acquired wealth rapidly with half the estates located in Suffolk. Not much early history. Following a visitation in 1309 by Bp. Baldock the injunctions included orders that canons and conversi must relinquish personal possessions, and keep strictly to the rule of silence. In 1405 a dispute occurred with the community when a man and his wife complained that their contract for a corrody had not been honoured, especially in respect of agreed food and fuel supplies. A riot in 1432 followed the production of forged charters, and in 1446 the prior was fined £24 (about £1,200 today) for unlawfully expelling a resident from a manor house in Suffolk. The record of the valuation of the priory at the Dissolution is amongst the most complete known. The canons were transferred to Waltham Abbey. *Remains:* There are bases of piers

which supported the crossing tower and miscellaneous shafts, etc. Site has been excavated. (2 Tudor gatehouses in ornate brick survived the general demolition in 1735 of a mansion built on the site). Notes & plan: Essex Arch. Soc. Trans. Vol. 13.

Leiston* *− 1 Abbey/Cell. Suffolk. Map 4. 5m E of Saxmundham. (1183−1365). Premonstratensian canons. F: Ranulph de Glanville, earl of Essex. Ded: St Mary.*
Colonised from Welbeck. Although this was an inconvenient site, the convent increased fast and within 6 years had sent a colony to Langdon. In the first half of the 14thC four royal pensioners, sent at intervals, imposed a heavy burden on the abbey's resources; and the severe effects of the B.D. plus incursions of the sea finally caused the canons to seek a new site 1½ miles inland. They did not abandon this house which became a cell of the new fdn. *Remains:* Slight ruins survive at Minsmere Marshes.
* Pronounced Layston.

Leiston *− 2 Abbey. Suffolk. Map 4. 3½m E of Saxmundham. (1365− 1537). Premonstratensian canons. F: Robert de Ufford, earl of Suffolk. Ded: St Mary.*
The F. erected new and bigger bldgs. for the canons, which were partially destroyed by fire in 1380, the canons probably returning to the old abbey while it was being rebuilt (Knowles). At the visitations in the 15thC few faults were found and the abbot received high praise in 1482 for his administration. When the abbot John Green resigned in 1521, he was consecrated anchorite at the chapel of St Mary in the old house. *Remains:*

Leiston Abbey, Suffolk. Late 14thC south transept and south aisle of the presbytery from the nave.

Ruins of chancel, crossing and transepts. The Lady Chapel has been restored and is in use. All three ranges of claustral bldgs. contain ruined walls, some incorporated in a house. The 16thC gatehouse, added to the W range, has polygonal turrets. Care: D of E. Desc. & plan: Archaeologia, Vol. 73 (1924); and Suckling's 'History of Suffolk' Vol. 2. Also, Proc. Suffolk Inst. of Arch. Vol. 7 (1891).

Lenton *Alien Priory/Priory. Notts. 1½m SW of Nottingham city centre. (–1108 to 1538). Cluniac monks.*

F: William Peverel. Ded: Holy Trinity.
Dependent upon Cluny. Became the most powerful and richest monastery in the county. Held an annual 12-day fair. In 1263 there was the unusual occurrence of a child being born in the priory. The child's mother, a member of the Cantilupe family of local benefactors, was perhaps living here while her mansion was being rebuilt. Became denizen 1392. Considerable history in VCH. No cartulary survives. 4 kings visited the house. The cost of litigation must have been heavy because one

195

dispute, with the Chapter at Lichfield, lasted almost 3 years. Prior Elmham was present with Henry V at Agincourt in 1415, and was supervisor of English Cluniac houses. The last prior and 8 monks were charged with treason in 1536, and 3 of them, the prior included, were executed at Nottingham following trial in 1538 (Gasquet). The remaining 22 monks were turned out without pension or annuity. *Remains:* Site excav. 1936 and the bases of 2 piers found. A font from the priory survives in Lenton parish ch., and masonry from the priory is built into the 19thC Priory Ch. in Gregory Street.

Leominster *Priory. Herefs. Map 2. (c. 1125–1539). Benedictine monks. F: Henry I. Ded: St Peter & St Paul.* 1st. f. c. 660 by Merwald, K of W Mercia. Destroyed by Danes in 9thC. Later re-f. for nuns and suppressed in 1046. F. of the present ch. granted the ruined bldgs. to Reading Abbey to which it belonged until the Dissolution. 13thC cartulary survives in BM. Never large (10 monks in 1379). Early history uncertain, but frequent attacks by the Welsh clearly caused hardship to town and monastery. Throughout its history the abbots of Reading had sole power to appoint and remove priors (Hurry). The house was several times burdened with ex-servants of Reading, as well as the upkeep of monks sent there for discipline by the motherhouse. The unusual ch. had 3 naves: North (Norman), South (E.E. c. 1235), and S Aisle (Dec. c. 1320) – the result of disputes with parishioners over their needs. *Remains:* 3 naves, N aisle and W (Norman) tower in use as parish ch. Site of transepts, chancel and Lady Chapel excavated 1849 & 1950. Priory House, mainly 14thC,

was part of the reredorter. Late 13thC mural, the Wheel of Life, is a remarkable survival in the N aisle. Desc: Arch. J. Vol. 10; Br. Arch. Assoc. J. Vol. 27.

Leonard Stanley *Priory. Glos. Map 5. 3½m SW by W of Stroud. (1146–1538). Benedictine monks. F: Roger de Berkeley III. Ded: St Leonard (now St Swithun).* 1st. f. by Roger de Berkeley II (–1129) for Augustinian canons. Granted to St Peter's Abbey, Gloucester, in 1146. No evidence of number of monks but probably only 3 or 4. VCH gives list of endowments. Never wealthy and in 1317 St Peter's began an annual cash grant to the house. Little else known. *Remains:* Conventual ch. with parishioners' nave, monastic transepts and choir in use as parish ch. The history of adjacent Saxon ch., now a farm bldg., uncertain, but may have been a guesthouse or prior's lodging. Notes: Arch. J. Vol. 6; Archaeologia (plan), Vol. 71.

Lesnes *(Westwood) Abbey. Kent. Map 7. 3m NW of Erith. (1178–1525). Augustinian canons. F: Richard de Lucy, Chief Justice of England. Ded: St Mary & St Thomas Martyr.* Perhaps fd. as a penance for the F's. opposition to Becket (Dickinson) for de Lucy became a canon and died here in 1179. In 1283 the financial control of the house passed from the abbot who had 'injured the property', into the hands of 3 chosen canons; but in all other matters the abbot's word was law. There were injunctions in 1299, 1336, 1340 & 1349 when the aid of the Crown was sought in the latter year to arrest 3 vagabond canons. In 1412 the abbey is referred to as Arrouaisian (VCH). By the early-15thC the house was impoverished and in debt through mismanagement, and the Commons complained in Parliament that the abbot had over-sold corrodies. The abbey was dissolved for Wolsey's Oxford Coll. venture. *Remains:* Only a doorway in the SW corner of the cloister. Layout of fdns. visible. Site excavated 1903–13 and mid-1950s. Book: Lesnes Abbey (1915) A. W. Clapham. Notes: Antiquity, Vol. 3, p. 101. Also Archaeologia, Vol. 1, p. 52.

Letheringham *Priory. Suffolk. Map 4. 2m NW of Wickham Market. (–1200 to 1537). Augustinian canons. F: William de Bovile. Ded: St Mary.* The F. seems to have given his tithes to St Peter's Priory, Ipswich, who then established a small priory here. Never more than 3 or 4 canons. Hardly anything known of the history. *Remains:* 2 Norman bays survive of the nave of the conventual ch. together with the tower as part of the parish ch. Crossing arch, late-15thC brick gatehouse and some boundary wall also. Excavated by D of E in 1961. Desc: Suffolk Inst. of Arch. Vol. 15, pt. 1.

Lewes *Alien Priory/Priory. Sussex. Map 7. (1077–1537). Cluniac monks. Fs: William de Warenne and Gundreda his wife. Ded: St Pancras.* Chief house of the Order in England. Fdn. account survives. 1st. prior (Lanzo) came from Cluny and ruled for 30 years making the house famous for its spiritual excellence. Although later history is very scanty, VCH gives extensive details of the priors. In 1264 Henry III's army greatly defiled the ch. while billeted here. Excellent report following visitation in 1288. In 1301 there was a huge debt of wool and money, and wise administration had reduced it to £2,000 by 1314. Became denizen in 1351 with 5 daughter houses. The ch. had two sets of transepts and a chevet of 5 chapels in the eastern arm in imitation of Cluny. The whole demolished in 1538 and a remarkable account of the destruction survives. *Remains:* Ch. gone. Railway crosses the site through chapter house and SE side of cloister and refectory. Visible ruins include part of refectory vault below lavatorium, undercroft of dorter, gatehouse and fragment of SW ch. tower. Tombs of the Fs. are in Southover ch. (SW suburb). Site excavated 1882 & 1971 in parts. Desc: Sussex Arch. Coll. Vols. 2, 34 & 49. Plan: Arch. J. Vol. 41 (1884); and Br. Arch. Assoc. J. Vols. 1 & 2. Book: The Priory of St Pancras at Lewes (1927) W. H. Godfrey.

Lewes *Friary. Sussex. (–1241 to 1538). Franciscan. (Conventual). F: unknown. Ded: St Mary & St Margaret.* Custody of London. In 1299 Edward I gave 24 shillings for 3 days food and from then on the history is blank until 1533 when VCH relates several local incidents. In 1537 2 friars were punished for spreading a rumour that Henry VIII was dead (Knowles). Probably the last friary to be surrendered. *Remains:* None. Site occupied by a railway goods yard. In Friars' Walk there is an archway, perhaps a relic.

Lichfield *Friary. Staffs. (c. 1237–1538). Franciscan. (Conventual). F: perhaps Bp. Alexander, of Coventry and Lichfield. Ded: St Francis.* Custody of Worcester. When the friary was burnt down in 1291 the destruction brought a wave of sympathy for the Order. Details of bequests and legacies in VCH, but information about bldgs. or personnel is scanty. When a friar preached against tithes, he later apologised to the cathedral chapter. The aggrieved clergy used the occasion to remove seats from the nave of the friars' ch. (a somewhat rare facility, as congregations usually stood). *Remains:* None. Friars Road crosses part of the site, but the area occupied by the ch. and some of the claustral bldgs. is now an open space. Excavated 1934. Desc. & plan: Franciscan Architecture in England (1937) A. R. Martin. Notes: B'ham. & Warks. Arch. Soc. Vol. 58.

Lillechurch *Priory. Kent. See* Higham.

Lilleshall *Abbey. Salop. Map 2. 4m S of Newport. Augustinian canons. (c. 1148–1538). F: Richard de Belmeis. Ded: St Mary.*
Colonised from Dorchester. 1st. fd. at Lizard (2m SE of Lilleshall) *c.* 1143, thence *c.* 1144 to Donnington Wood and finally settling here *c.* 1148. A succession of endowments made the house prosperous. There were a number of lay-brothers until the B.D. in the middle of the 14thC, when the income rapidly declined – including the loss of tolls at Atcham bridge on the Holyhead road. Henry III visited the abbey in 1241 and 1245 on his hunting trips although no other king took any interest in the house. The abbey held the patronage of two leper hospitals in Bridgnorth. One of the canons wrote a manual for the guidance of parish priests *c.* 1400. *Remains:* Amongst the most complete of any Aug. ch.

ruins in England, including W front, crossing and choir. E & S claustral bldgs. with most of chapter house and refectory. Abbey's wooden choir stalls survive in Wolverhampton parish ch. Excavated 1860 & 1962–3. Desc., plan & care: D of E. Desc. & plan: Br. Arch. Assoc. J. Vol. 17 (1861). Notes: Arch. J. Vol. 12; and Med. Arch. Vols. 6 & 7.

Limebrook *Priory. Herefs. Map 2. 4m NE of Prestigne. (c. 1189–1539). Augustinian canonesses. F: Robert de Lingen or a member of the Mortimer family. Ded: St Mary*.*
The house has been inaccurately recorded as alien and Benedictine. In 1227 the prioress was summoned to answer why certain lands were held by the convent, but the outcome is unknown. In 1300 the bp. of Hereford appealed for papal leniency and remission of payments owing to the nuns' poverty. In 1435 an injunction forbade the sisters from attending 'the children's feast of St Nicholas, spectacles and other worldly vanities' outside the nunnery; and in 1437 a further order lays down dress restrictions, e.g. forbidding long trains to mantles. To avoid suppression in 1536 the house paid the large fine of £53.6.8d, nearly 2½ times their net annual income. *Remains:* Very slight. A meagre ruin with roughly recognisable windows and a doorway, perhaps 13thC (Pevsner).
* Some refs. give St Thomas, Martyr.

Lincoln *Priory*. Lincs. Map 3. (c. 1135?–1539). Benedictine monks. F: unknown. Ded: St Mary Magdalene.*
The cell of St Mary's, York, was fd. early in the r. of Henry II. Episcopal registers tell nothing of the history. Never more than a prior and 2 monks

198

Lilleshall Abbey, Shropshire. Choir of the church from the south. In the immediate foreground is the site of the chapter house.

whose function was to supervise the estates. St Mary's had an obligation to celebrate daily services in the chapel for the souls of certain people following a gift of land to the convent, and, in default over 12 months, the plot would become the king's property. Eventually this happened in 1393 after farm stock had been found in the chapel. Later the abbot recovered possession from the king. There were frequent disputes in the 15thC over land usage and ownership. *Remains:* Ruins of 3 walls of the chapel with window tracery; also one wall of a domestic bldg. to the W containing a doorway. * Now known as Monks Abbey.

Lincoln *Priory. Lincs. (c. 1148– 1538). Gilbertine canons. F: Robert de Chesney, bp. of Lincoln. Ded: St Catherine.*
Although fd. for canons, lay-sisters (never nuns) were employed to tend the sick at St Sepulchre's Hospital which was in the convent's care. In 1290 the body of Q. Eleanor rested in the priory ch. on the journey to Westminster, and the first of the 8 Eleanor Crosses was erected outside the gatehouse on Swines Green.

House well endowed. At its peak mid-13thC some 35 sacks of wool were sold p.a., but fortunes changed in the early-14thC due to reckless speculation in respect of wool sales and heavy losses of sheep. Debts to Italian merchants reached £956 in 1332 but the obligations were met. Not much history in 15th or 16thCs. In 1536 the prior was charged with promoting the Lincolnshire Rising and deposed, but he forcibly reinstated himself. *Remains:* None. Excavated 1876. Acct: Arch. J. Vol. 33.

Lincoln *Friary. Lincs. (c. 1269–1539). Austin. F: unknown. Ded: unknown.*
Limit of Lincoln. Very little known. One Gilbert de Stratton named as an early benefactor and a list of bequests is given in VCH. The friars were granted protection by Henry III in 1270. Provincial chapters held here in 1307 and 1332. From 30 members in the 14thC the number was only 4 at the Dissolution, when the bldgs. were in poor condition. *Remains:* None.

Lincoln *Friary. Lincs. (–1260 to 1539). Carmelite. F: Odo of Kilkenny. Ded: BVM.*
Distinction of York. In 1269 Henry III gave beeches for ch. construction. Edward I also a benefactor. At a provincial chapter here in 1287 the Order agreed to adopt the white habit (L.G.) A wealthy merchant, Ranulph de Kyme, no doubt a descendant of the F. of Kyme Priory, was buried here. The house had a valuable library of which one volume survives amongst the Royal MSS in the BM. The house was of little value when surrendered. *Remains:* None. The site is occupied by St Marks

railway station. There was an elaborate water system of which the reconstructed conduit head is in St Mary-le-Wigford churchyard (Martin).

Lincoln *Friary. Lincs. (–1238 to 1539). Dominican. F: unknown. Ded: St Dominic (?).*
Visitation of York. That the first provincial chapter was held here in 1238 suggests it must have been established some years earlier. Other prov. chapters held here in 1244, 1368 and 1388 and at the last of these some statutes were passed regulating the promotion of friars to University degrees. History in the 15thC is a blank. The rebuilt ch. of 1284–90 was perhaps the largest of all the Dominican friaries. *Remains:* None.

Lincoln *Friary. Lincs. (c. 1230–1539). Franciscan. (Conventual). F: probably William of Beningworth. Ded: St Francis.*
Custody of York. From the record of benefactions which were great and small from all sections of the community, the convent was popular but surprisingly it was not a favoured burial place. The site was always small and attempts to enlarge by encroachment on the city walls led to friction with the city authorities (Martin). Most of the historical records are confined to bequests and evidence of building changes. Provincial chapters were held here in 1288, 1293 & 1295, and on 3 occasions in the 15thC provincial chapters of the Premonstratensian canons met in Lincoln Friary (Martin). *Remains:* The ch. survives in Broadgate above an undercroft and is the earliest example of a Franciscan ch. in England. The confined site space

probably accounts for a 1st. floor ch. No domestic bldgs. exist. Cloister lay to the S. Notes: Arch. J. Vols. 92 & 103. Plan & illus: A. R. Martin's 'Franciscan Architecture in England'.

Lincoln *Friary. Lincs. (−1266 to 1307). Friars of the Sack. F: unknown. Ded: unknown.*
The earliest mention is 1266 when Henry III granted the friars a vacant place near their house. The suppression of the Order in 1274 resulted in the community lasting until 1307, when the abbot and convent of Barlings tried unsuccessfully to buy the property for a warehouse. Secular chaplains served the chapel in 1327 and a large chantry was f. here in 1359 (VCH). *Remains:* None. Note: Archaeologia, Vol. 3, p. 130.

Lindisfarne *(Holy Island) Priory. N'land. Map 1. 10m SE of Berwick. (1083−1537). Benedictine monks. F: Bp. Wm. de Carileph. Ded: St Peter.*
Dependent upon Durham. Main history occurs in the pre-mediaeval era. 1st. f. by St Oswald, K. of N'umbria for St Aidan in 635, to become the cradle of Christianity in the north. Destroyed by Danes 793 & 875. St Cuthbert's remains saved from here and finally buried at Durham. The 8thC Lindisfarne Gospels, superb illuminated MSS, in BM. In mediaeval period never more than 9 monks, but they recorded their own story of prosperity and adversity in account rolls submitted to Durham, and now preserved in the Cathedral Treasury. The cell's library seems to have been small. The community does not appear to have had much contact with other cells of Durham. The internal history is uneventful, and the danger of Scottish raids was reduced by the rock outcrop providing a shield. *Remains:* Nothing survives of St Aidan's ch. The Norman ch. has W front, sections of transepts with 2 piers of the crossing, and chancel. Walls of the 14thC claustral bldgs. have some fortification. Desc., plan & care: D of E.

Ling *(Lyng) Priory. Norfolk. Map 4. 12m NW of Norwich. (? to c. 1160). Benedictine nuns.*
An indeterminate fdn. and history. Most of the nuns moved to Thetford c. 1160 but a few were still here in 1249. In 1438 St Edmund's chapel at Ling was in the care of a prior. *Remains:* Ruins of the chapel survive ½-mile to the E of the village.

Little Dunmow *Priory. Essex. Map 7. 6½m W of Braintree. (1106−1536). Augustinian canons. F: Geoffrey Baynard. Ded: St Mary.*
The F's mother, Juga, dedicated a chapel here in 1104 and the priest became the first prior when Aug. canons were introduced 2 years later. A small house and one of very few whose cartulary and chronicle survive (Dickinson). In 1304 inundations of the sea caused serious financial losses. In 1369 a canon was arrested for forging the king's money but he appears to have been cleared. The ancient custom of applying for the bacon flitch brought an applicant before the prior, convent and the whole town. A fascinating book of household expenses for 1528−36 is preserved. *Remains:* The long and narrow parish ch. was the S chancel chapel of the conventual ch. as used by the parishioners. Priory Place nearby may have been the guesthouse (Pevsner). Site has been excavated.

201

Lindisfarne Priory, Northumberland. Nave of church looking west.

Little Malvern *Priory. Worcs. Map 5.*
5m NE of Ledbury. (1171–c. 1537).
Benedictine monks. Fs: Two brothers
– Jocelin and Edred of Worcester
(who became 1st. & 2nd. priors).
Ded: St Giles.
During its life the supremacy of
Worcester was vigorously kept over
this small house. Poverty in early
days was not helped by the effects of
the wars with Wales. There were
also losses among the house's Irish
possessions. In 1323 a series of injunctions was issued by the bp.
calling for greater wisdom and
generosity from the community.
Little else known until 1480 when
some reform was ordered. The 16thC
history was uneventful. Exact date of
suppression not known. *Remains:*
The parish ch. comprises the chancel
and tower of the conventual ch. Ruins
of the N & S transepts and two 2-bay
15thC chapels survive. Nothing of the
claustral bldgs. except, perhaps, the
15thC prior's lodging, now the Court.

Little Marlow *Priory. Bucks. 2m NE*
of Marlow. (–1218 to 1536).
Benedictine nuns. F: unknown. Ded:
St Mary.
Little known of the early history.
No fdn. charters or endowment
lists survive. Considerable poverty in
1300 & 1311 when licences were
granted for the nuns to beg for alms.
The prioress from 1338–50 seems
to have been related to local gentry
and succeeded in getting better
conditions for her nuns. Bp.
Dalderby's injunction tried to com-
pel stricter enclosure in 1300. Immediately before dissolution the
prioress, who kept an orderly house
but had little love for it, tried unsuccessfully to become the prioress
of St Helen's (London). Following
the closure of the nunnery the

prioress was entrusted with the care
of Cromwell's small son Gregory.
Remains: None above ground. Site
excavated 1902. Desc. & plan: Arch.
J. Vol. 59 (1902). Book: C. R. Peers,
'The Benedictine Nunnery of Little
Marlow'.

Littlemore *Priory. Oxon. Map 6.*
3m SSE of Oxford. (–1154 to 1525).
Benedictine nuns. F: Robert de
Sandford. Ded: St Mary &
St Nicholas (and St Edmund).
From a record of poverty in 1245,
when the house received favours
from Henry III and the pope, until
the 16thC the history is almost a
blank. In 1445 the state of the bldgs.
was dangerous and nuns feared to
sleep in the dorter 'lest it should
fall'. There is no doubt that the
priory's proximity to Oxford attracted
some adventurers and this was the
ultimate cause of its early suppression.
Prof. Power says that in the early
16thC the house may justly be
described as 'one of the worst
nunneries of which record has
survived', and the bad moral state was
due to the weakness, and wickedness,
of the prioress. Wolsey's suppression
was justified. *Remains:* E of the
parish ch. is Minchery Farm which
incorporates a bldg. with late 15thC
doorways and windows. It was
probably part of the E claustral
range. The site has not been
excavated.

London *Westminster Abbey. Map 7.*
(c. 959–1540). Benedictine monks.
F: St Dunstan. Ded: St Peter.
1st. fd. in 7thC by Sebert, K. of E.
Saxons. Destroyed by Danes in
9thC. The F's ch. was rebuilt by
Edward the Confessor on an island
in the Thames across fields from the
city, with his palace behind – now

the Houses of Parliament. Of this ch. nothing remains above ground and the present abbey ch. was commenced by Henry III. From 1376 to 1547 the House of Commons normally met in the chapter house or the refectory. Wealthiest Bene. monastery in England. Mitred 1163 (?). In 1389 the alien priory of Steventon was granted to the abbey (*v.* Appendix 1). Since the Confessor's time all English monarchs have been crowned here and it is the burial place of 17 kings and queens. So much history is readily available that no further details are needed here. *Remains:* The great Conventual ch. terminating at the E end with the superb early-16thC Henry VII's chapel of extraordinary beauty. Main cloister and Little (infirmary) cloister linked by the Dark Cloister. Dormitory with undercroft is now the library of the Dean & Chapter and the Great Hall of Westminster School. Fine 13thC chapter house (care: D of E). N wall of refectory. From 1540–50 the ch. was a secular cathedral. Desc: Arch. J. Vols. 33 & 51. Also Royal Comm. of Hist. Monuments, London, Vol. 1 *etc.* Books: 1. Westminster Abbey (1890) W. J. Loftie; 2. Westminster Abbey & its Ancient Art (1926) J. G. Noppen; 3. Westminster Abbey (1909) F. Bond. Illus: Pitkin Pictorial. Numerous refs. in ecclesiastical books.

London *Southwark Priory* (St Mary Overy). Map 7. S end of London Bridge. (1106–1539). Augustinian canons. Fs: Wm. Pont d'Arch and Wm. Dauncey (Norman Knights). Ded:* St Mary.*
1st. fd. as a sisterhood and converted to a coll. of priests *c.* 852. Aug. fdn. aided by Bp. Giffard of Winchester. In 1212 a terrible fire destroyed

most of the monastery, London Bridge with most of its houses, and 1,000 people died. In 1284 Archbp. Peckham issued minor injunctions to the canons and commanded that there were to be no visits to the City of London or Southwark town. Fire again severely damaged the priory in the second half of the 14thC. At a chapter held in Leicester Abbey in 1518 with 36 heads of Aug. houses present, the prior of Southwark made an impassioned appeal for stricter discipline within the Order; and on the concluding day Henry VIII and Q. Catherine of Aragon were received into the Order. *Remains:* Of the ch., the choir, transepts, retro-choir and tower survive though much restored. The nave is modern except for a few Norman fragments. Excavations N & S of the ch. in 1971 revealed evidence of flooding to the N which had occurred *c.* 1294; and to the S indications of a stone bldg. with an external timber structure associated with burials. (Med. Arch. Vol. 17). Illus: Pitkin Pictorial. Numerous refs. in church books.
* Became a cathedral in 1905. Ded: St Saviour since the Dissolution.

London *Aldgate (Christchurch) Priory. Leadenhall Street. (1107–1532). Augustinian canons. F: Q. Maud, aided by Archbp. Anselm. Ded: Holy Trinity.*
Became an immensely important house and with Merton (*v.* below) built up a vast ascendency of the new Order in England (Dickinson). Some very early charters survive. Much of the success of the early years was due to the first 2 priors. House severely damaged by fire in 1132. Henry III aided the community until 1256 when a change of heart may

have been due to the queen's dispute with the canons over custody of a hospital. A prior went to the Tower for contempt of the king, but was released because of the honour paid by the canons to the body of the late queen (Eleanor) which rested in the priory ch. on the way to Westminster. There was impoverishment in the 16thC and the house surrendered to the king in 1532, when the canons are said to have gone to other priories. Thus ended the first of the big London monasteries which had sent colonies to fd. at least 6 daughter houses. *Remains:* None. Desc. & plan: A Dictionary of London (1918) H. A. Harben.

London *Smithfield Priory. Map 7. N of St Bart's Hospital. (+1123 to 1539). Augustinian canons. F: Rahere (a reformed jester of Henry I's court). Ded: St Bartholomew the Great.*
1st. f. as a hospital for poor men but soon developed into a priory with a separate hospital on land granted by the king. Being of royal patronage it was well protected, and Henry II confirmed the privileges. F. became 1st. prior. In 1250 Archbp. Boniface made a visitation and was informed by the prior that only the bp. of London could do this. He flew into a rage, struck the sub-prior and excommunicated the convent obedientiaries. The pope annulled the sentence. A wealthy house throughout its life; but debts due to a falling income in 1409, and weak management in 1423, resulted in the control of revenues being taken out of the community's hands. In the 14thC the ch. was a place of custody for public records. Canonbury, $2\frac{1}{4}$ m N, was a retiring place (bury) for the canons. *Remains:* Fine 12thC choir with 14thC Lady Chapel attached;

crossing; transepts and one bay of the nave of London's oldest ch. Vaulted crypt. Restored E cloister walk. Desc. & plan: Archaeologia, Vol. 64. (1913). Books: 1. Records of St Bartholomew's, Smithfield (2 vols. 1921) E. A. Webb; 2. Book of the foundation of St Bartholomew the Great of Smithfield (1923) from Cotton MSS.

London *Cripplegate (Elsing) Priory. Monkwell Street. (1340–1536). Augustinian canons. F: William Elsing. Ded: St Mary.*
In 1329 there was a house of nuns here in great decay. The F. built a hospital on the site run by 5 secular priests with himself in charge. In 1340 he replaced the priests with Aug. canons (Knowles). The hospital continued under the control of the canons with the blind and sick patients in the care of sisters. At the Dissolution it seems the sisters were assigned a house in which to look after their charges. *Remains:* None. The ch. of St Alphage, demolished in 1917, contained part of the conventual ch.

London *Charterhouse Priory. Map 7. Charterhouse Square. (1371–1537). Carthusian monks. F: Sir Walter Manny encouraged by Bp. Michael Northburgh of London. Ded: The Salutation of the Virgin Mary.*
The original intention of the F. was to build a secular coll. adjacent to a site where 100,000 victims of the B.D. were buried, but Bp. Northburgh recommended Carthusians. Although little is recorded of the lives of the monks before the 16thC, the history of the house is known to an exceptional degree, especially concerning grants, endowments and receipts. In 1430 the monks laid a

pipe from Islington spring to an octagonal conduit in the cloister, and the elaborate plan of water distribution exists. The resistance of some of the community to Henry VIII's Act of Supremacy resulted in the tragic and brutal martyrdom of the saintly Prior Houghton and several of his monks who were charged with treason. *Remains:* Chapter house is a chapel. Some of the bldgs. outside the claustral area survive in modern property. The whole site was excavated after a 1941 air-raid had demolished the area. The tomb of the F. was discovered. Books: 1. The London Charterhouse (1889) Dom L. Hendriks; 2. Charterhouse (1954) M. D. Knowles & W. F. Grimes. Hist: Archaeologia, Vol. 58; and Br. Arch. Assoc. J. Vol. 3.

London *St Mary of Graces (Eastminster) Abbey. E of the Tower on Tower Hill. (1350–1538). Cistercian monks. F: Edward III. Ded: St Mary & St Anne.*
Colonised from Beaulieu. Last Cist. house fd. in England and the only one in London. Like the Charterhouse (above) it was on a site of a B.D. cemetery. Originally for only 6 monks whose early life was hard due to inadequate endowments to support them. At the end of the 14thC the house increased in importance due to royal patronage and papal favour; and detailed accounts, of great interest, survive of expenditure on bldgs. and equipment. Mitred 1415. From 1427 an abbot's bad management resulted in debts amounting to £566 by 1441 (VCH). At the time of the Dissolution it was the 3rd wealthiest Cist. house in England with an income mainly derived from tithes and property rents in London and the suburbs.

Remains: None. Site occupied by the Royal Mint. Desc. & site plan: Archaeologia, Vol. 66, (1914–5).

London *Bishopsgate Priory. Map 7. Between Bishopsgate St. and St Mary Axe. (c. 1212–1538). Benedictine nuns. F: Wm., son of Wm. the goldsmith. Ded: St Helen.*
Nothing known of early endowments. In 1285 Edward I gave the nuns a piece of the Holy Cross. In 1385 a nun with gout got £10 p.a. allowance through the pope, but no sympathy from her sister nuns who suspected intrigue. In the 15thC there was reproof for keeping dogs, hurrying through services, dressing vainly and kissing seculars. In the early-16thC the heavy debts were due to food bills, since a City house was less able to grow and farm its own produce. By 1530 the reports were satisfactory. In 1532 several nuns ran away being alarmed by Henry VIII's proposed religious changes. *Remains:* The whole of the ch. Here was a curious feature of a double nave, for the nuns attached their ch. and claustral bldgs. to the N of an existing parish ch. There is also the S transept. Note: Archaeologia, Vol. 16.

London *Clerkenwell Priory. M'sex. In Clerkenwell Close. (c. 1144–1539). Augustinian canonesses. F: Jordan de Briset (fitz Ralph). Ded: St Mary.*
Sometimes described as Benedictine. There were royal grants in early years and dowries of nuns from landed families during the next 3 centuries (VCH); and in the 13th & 14thCs revenues came from 16 counties outside London. By 1500 the nuns had properties in only 5 of them. Little is known of the size of the community which probably never

exceeded 20, and equally little of the internal history survives, through the absence of records following visitations by the bps. of London. Being close to one of the main roads out of London it cannot have been a quiet house. A wealthy and magnificent monastery, of which the ch. was part parochial, survived as the parish ch. until the 18thC. *Remains:* None. The last remnant of wall disappeared in the 19thC. Note: Archaeologia, Vol. 56.

London *Haliwell Priory. M'sex. Bounded by Shoreditch High Street, Haliwell Lane, Curtain Road and Bateman's Row. (−1150? to 1539). Augustinian canonesses. F: Robert fitz Gelran. Ded: St John, Baptist.* Sometimes described as Benedictine. One of the larger nunneries and ultimately the richest of the Order. Properties extended from Norfolk to Kent. Carelessness of Henry III's bakers caused the nuns' mills to be burnt down in 1244. In 1400 the prioress obtained licence to hear divine service within the oratory of her mansion of Camberwell (Power). Convent distributed money to the poor every Christmas Day. In the r. of Henry VII the Chancellor of the Exchequer, Sir Thomas Lovell, was a great benefactor and was buried in a chapel he built for his wife and himself. Of the lives of the nuns, their numbers or the control of the priory no records survive. *Remains:* None. The railway approaching Liverpool Street Station crosses the site.

London *The Minories Abbey. ¼m N of the Tower of London. (1293−1539). Franciscan nuns. F: Edmund, earl of Lancaster. Ded: BVM & St Francis.*
The F's wife Blanche, Q. of Navarre, brought the nuns from France (or Spain?). 1st. house of the Order (Poor Clares) in England. Probably the abbey was richer in privileges than revenues because in 1338 & 1345 it was excused taxes. VCH gives impressive lists of grants and gifts. The Duke of Gloucester's daughter, among other aristocratic women, became abbess, and as the duke's house adjoined the nuns' ch., he was given free access for his devotions. The alien priory of Appuldurcombe (I. o. W.) was granted to the nuns in 1414 (*v.* Appendix 1). In 1515 27 nuns and some of the lay-servants died of a pestilence. In 1519 the house was seriously damaged by fire and generous aid for rebuilding was freely given. After dissolution part of the bldgs. were used as a town house for the bishopric of Bath & Wells, and part as an armoury by the Tower. *Remains:* None. Hist. notes: Franciscan Architecture in England (1937) A. R. Martin, pp. 265−9. Book: History of the Minories, London (1907) E. M. Tomlinson.

London *Friary. Behind Bank of England at Austin Friars. (1253− 1538). Austin. F: Humphrey Bohun, Earl of Hereford and Essex. Ded: uncertain.*
Limit of Oxford. Bldgs. extended 1334 and ch. rebuilt 1354. In 1381 13 Flemings who had taken refuge in the ch. were dragged out by the mob and killed. The friary had a fine library which received great additions in the 15thC. In 1525 the community was put in the Tower because one of their number had died in the friary prison. In 1534 the friars were said to be undisciplined, but since Cromwell had built a mansion on lands leased from the convent, the rumours were probably due to the prior being a willing tool

207

of Cromwell (VCH). *Remains:* None. Nave used by foreign Protestants until destroyed by a landmine in 1940. A new ch. occupies the site. Hist: W. A. Cater's 'London Austin Friars'. Desc: Trans. London & M'sex Arch. Soc. Ser. 2, Vol. 1.

London *Friary. S of Fleet St. and N of Tudor St. (1247–1538). Carmelite. F: Sir Richard Gray. Ded: BVM.* Distinction of London. Became one of the largest houses of the Order. In 1305, when the house was a repository for treasure, robbers stole £400. One of the friars was convicted as an accomplice and hanged. Between 1344 & 1348 the prior conducted negotiations for the king and pope, and the house received many privileges in return (VCH). Much of the possessions came from the poor men of the City as well as nobility. The house had 'a worthy record of learning'. In 1465 a friar preaching against the beneficed clergy had far reaching effects, but once this had died down the friars lapsed into obscurity. *Remains:* None. Today the offices of 'Punch' and the 'News of the World' occupy the site of the nave. Acct: Br. Arch. Assoc. J. Vol. 16 (1910). Plan: Harben's 'Dictionary of London', p. 624.

London *Ludgate Friary. Between Ludgate Hill and the Thames. (c. 1221–1538). Dominican. F: Hubert de Burgh. Ded: unknown.* Visitation of London. 1st. f. in Holborn, probably the earliest in England, and moved *c.* 1275 to Ludgate although the Holborn site was not sold until 1286. By 1313 the community of 70 needed larger quarters. Edward II sometimes stayed here to transact State business – an

indication of the house's importance. Parliament met here in 1449. Many citizens over 2 centuries chose the ch. or precinct for burials. Rents from shops and houses owned by the community exceeded £100 p.a. Following dissolution the friars had a short revival at Smithfield under Q. Mary. *Remains:* None. Site partly occupied by The Times Newspaper offices and streets. Plan: Bede Jarrett's 'The English Dominicans' (1921). Desc: Archaeologia, Vols. 29 & 63.

London *Friary. N side of Newgate Street. (1224–1538). Franciscan (Conventual). F: John Travers? Ded: St Francis.* Custody of London. 1st. f. at Cornhill where the friars hired a house from John Travers. In 1225 John Iwyn gave them the use of a house and land in Newgate. By 1243 80 friars lived here, and about 100 years later 100 members of the community died in the B.D. A popular community and a remarkable plan of the multitude of Burials in the 300 ft. ch. appears in Vol. 59 of the Arch. J. Q. Margaret, 2nd. wife of Edward I, buried here. The 2nd ch. on the site was completed in 1327 and suffered severe storm damage in 1343. The celebrated Richard Whittington fd. a library at the friary. There was a long connection between the London Grey Friars and the City, and on St Francis' Day (Oct. 4) the mayor and aldermen went in procession to the ch. *Remains:* None. Site occupied by the General Post Office. Notes: Archaeologia, Vols. 35 & 67; and Arch. J. Vol. 59. Books: 1. Chronicle of the Grey Friars of London (1852) J. G. Nichols. 2. The Grey Friars of London (1915) C. L. Kingsford (re-pub. 1965).

London *Friary. Just S of Fenchurch Street Station. (−1269 to 1538). Crutched or Holy Cross. Fs: Ralph Hosier and William Sabernes. Ded: Holy Cross.*
Holy Cross Hospitals existed some years before the establishment of their friaries, which accounts for confused dates; but the earliest mention of a friary in London is 1269 (Knowles). Not much history known. In 1330 Andrew de Bures fd. a chantry here and conveyed the property of the family fdn. at Welnetham (*v.* below) for its support. In the 16thC the community was viewed favourably by the city folk who gave aid to the rebuilding of the friars' ch. in 1520. Shortly before the surrender Prior Dryver was removed from the guardianship for his incautious comments about Henry VIII. *Remains:* Small. St Olave's ch. in Hart Street has a 13thC crypt and some 15thC walling which were perhaps part of the friary bldgs.

London *Friary. Coleman Street, Lothbury, EC2. (1257−1305). Friars of the Sack. F: unknown. Ded: uncertain.*
1st. f. in Aldgate and moved to Coleman St. *c.* 1271 to quarters given by Q. Eleanor, wife of Henry III (Harben). At this site the friars complained of disturbances by the 'howling of Jews' in a nearby synagogue. Henry III gave the friars the synagogue and the Jews built a new one elsewhere. The Order was suppressed in 1274 and the community became extinct early in the 14thC when Edward I granted the property for a chantry of 2 chaplains. *Remains:* None. Note: Archaeologia, Vol. 3.

London *Friary. Somewhere in Westminster. (1267−1317). Pied or Friars of St Mary de Areno. F: William Arnaud, knight of Henry III.*
No mention by Tanner or Dugdale. Friars received alms on Q. Eleanor of Castille's second anniversary and a cash gift from Edward I in 1300. When the last friar, Hugh of York, died, the house became extinct (Knowles). *Remains:* None.

Longleat *Priory. Somerset. 3m SE of Frome. (−1235 to 1529). Augustinian canons. F: perhaps Sir John Vernon. Ded: St Radegund.*
The fdn. is obscure but the F. certainly gave the canons lands in Selwood Forest. The house was small and poor. A record of 1408 declared the priory to be well ordered and no more is heard of it until 1529 when, failing to maintain itself, the property was transferred to the Carthusians at Hinton. *Remains:* None. In 1808 during reconstruction of the house on the site, several coffins containing remains of the canons were discovered.

Lossenham *Friary. Kent. 6m SW of Tenterden (at Newenden). (c. 1242− 1538). Carmelite. F: Sir Thomas Alcher. Ded: BVM.*
Distinction of London. 3rd. house of the Order established in England. Very little history and a poor friary. In 1257 the bldgs. were burnt down by persons unknown. One of the friars, who was buried here in 1390, is said to have written a history of the Order. *Remains:* None.

Louth Park *Abbey. Lincs. Map 4. 1½m E of Louth. (1139−1536). Cistercian monks. F: Alexander, Bp. of Lincoln. Ded: St Mary.*

1st. f. at Haverholme in 1137, colonised from Fountains, but proving unsuitable the community moved to the bp's. own park. A large and important house with 66 monks and 150 lay-brothers in 1230. In his fdn. charter the F. wrote: '. . . it is necessary, considering the wickedness of these days, to provide some deed of justice and purity in this most miserable life'. In 1344 the depressed condition of the abbey's affairs resulted in the house being given the king's protection. In the same year a knight dying in the infirmary made a will giving his property to the convent. His widow contested the validity of the document which an inquisition later found genuine, but awarded her 100 marks p.a. Very soon afterwards the B.D. carried off the abbot and most of the monks. In 1536 one of the disbanded monks, Sir Wm. Moreland, took a prominent part in the Lincolnshire Rising and was executed in 1537. *Remains:* A fragment of the chancel and transept corner. Excavated 1873. Desc: Trans. Lincs. Arch. Soc. Vol. 12.

Loxwell *Abbey. Wilts. 4m SE of Chippenham. (1151−1154). Cistercian monks. Fs: Empress Matilda and her chamberlain Drogo. Ded: St Mary.*
After 3 years the community from Quarr moved 1m N to Stanley but for 50 years they were still known as 'the monks of Chippenham in Locheswella'. *Remains.* None.

Ludlow *Friary. Salop. (1254−1538). Austin. F: perhaps Henry III. Ded: St Augustine.*
The Brampton family were the chief benefactors. Early history obscure. In 1299 Bp. Swinfield of Hereford complained bitterly about the viola-

tion of sanctuary committed by men of Ludlow. In the middle years the house was enriched with gifts and the history is one of seclusion; but in the 16thC the friars were certainly very dependent upon voluntary contributions for their support, and were in a state of great penury. At the Dissolution only 4 signatures appear on the document of surrender. *Remains:* None. The last remnants disappeared beneath a cattle market after a local architect had surveyed the fdns. Desc. & plan: Archaeologia, Vol. 39 (1863). Br. Arch. Assoc. J. Vol. 24.

Ludlow *Friary. Salop. (1350−1538). Carmelite. F: Sir Laurence de Ludlow. Ded: BVM.*
Distinction of Oxford. F. buried in the ch. in 1353. Last but one Carm. house fd. in England (*v.* Doncaster). Early in the 15thC ch. greatly enlarged or rebuilt and a provincial chapter met here in 1416. The house produced a number of learned and distinguished men including 3 bps. In 1459 the Lancastrian soldiers sacked the town and plundered the friary of furniture and other possessions. Their recovery was helped by Edward IV, and another provincial chapter was held here in 1469. To the end the Rule was well kept and the charges of Thomas Vernon, the king's visitor in 1536, cannot be substantiated (VCH). *Remains:* None. The cemetery of St Leonards ch. occupies the site. Perhaps a few carved stones survive in the churchyard wall.

Luffield *Priory. Northants/Bucks. 4½m NE of Brackley, (at Syresham). (+1118 to 1494). Benedictine monks: F: Robert Bossu II, earl of Leicester. Ded: BVM.*
The ch. was in N'hants and the

conventual bldgs. in Bucks. Little known of early history. Sometime before 1155 Bradwell Priory (*v.* above) became its cell. In 1244 Henry III showed much sympathy to the small community after 25 robbers stole its possessions. In 1280 & 1287 the priors resigned under pressure from the bp. At the time of the B.D. the entire community died. From then on there was no prosperity and in 1494, at the request of Henry VII, the priory was annexed to Windsor Coll. In 1504 this was annulled and the property granted to King's Chapel of Westminster Abbey. *Remains:* None.

Lynn *Priory & Friaries. Norfolk.* *See* King's Lynn.

Lytham *Priory Cell/Priory. Lancs. 12m W of Preston, at Ansdell. (1191/4 to +1535). Benedictine monks F: Richard Fitz Roger. Ded: St Mary & St Cuthbert.* A small cell of Durham. A 12thC miracle was claimed when the dying F. was carried into the ch. and made 'a marvellous recovery'. Scottish raids reduced the temporalities and the prior of Durham accused the convent of selling stock in order to maintain themselves — without his permission! In 1428 there was a quarrel with the convent of Vale Royal over tithes (VCH). From 1443 the monks appear to have obtained a greater measure of autonomy and the priors were no longer removable 'at the pleasure of Durham' (Dolan). Between 1535 and 1540 however, the prior of Durham withdrew the monks from Lytham and let the priory's property. *Remains:* None. Notes: Ancient Religious Houses of the County of Lancaster (1893) Dom G. Dolan.

M

Maiden Bradley *Priory. Wilts. 6½m SSE of Frome. (−1201 to 1536). Augustinian canons. F: perhaps Henry Biset. Ded: BVM.* 1st. f. −1164 as a hospital for leprous women by Manasser Biset and whose son increased grants and may have introduced canons *c.* 1190. The fdn. is obscure but it is certain that the hospital was continued. Little useful history available. Grants of property continued in the 12thC but 'the stream of acquisitions dwindled in the next 2 centuries' (VCH). A large number of 14thC farming accounts survive. *Remains:* Nothing of the ch. or claustral bldgs. Never excavated. On the enclosure boundary is an L-shaped bldg. with late mediaeval doorway and window openings. The gateway has a (blocked) 4-centred arch.

Maldon *Friary. Essex. 10m E of Chelmsford. (1293−1538). Carmelite. Fs: Richard Gravesend, bp. of London & Richard Isleham. Ded: BVM.* The fdn. excited the jealousy of the abbot and convent of Beeleigh a mile away, but the matter was settled in 1300 when acceptable limitations were imposed upon the friars. Very little history. One of the poorest religious houses in England at the Dissolution which, in its time, had produced several renowned scholars. *Remains:* None.

Malling, *West Abbey, Kent. Map 7. 6m W of Maidstone. (c. 1090−1538). Benedictine nuns. F: Gundulf, bp. of Rochester. Ded: St Mary.* In 1190 the monastery and most of the town were consumed by fire.

211

The whole history was singularly uneventful, but at intervals between 1300 and the Dissolution a number of injunctions were issued following episcopal visitations, and more than one instance occurred of poor administration. In 1349 the B.D. took two abbesses in quick succession and all but 4 nuns and 4 novices. By 1350 the house was in very reduced circumstances, but recovery was in evidence later that century when considerable repairs and reconstruction took place. Compassion towards one nun in 1400 is revealed by the allocation of a private room because of her infirmities, but she presumably recovered as she died an abbess 39 years later. During the last 100 years the Rule seems to have been well observed. In 1536 an honourable abbess was forced to resign and the prioress of Little Marlow succeeded her — being a personal friend of Cromwell (*v. above*). *Remains:* W front of the Norman ch. incorporates a tower-like structure perhaps of later date. Fine gatehouse and guesthouse, both 15thC. There is a rare and authentic underground passage which was not a main drain. The site became occupied in 1916 by nuns of an Anglican Benedictine Community. Notes & plan: Arch. J. Vol. 88 (1931). Excav. notes & plan: Antiq. J. Vol. 34 (1954): & Med. Arch. Vols. 6 & 7 (1962–3). Monograph: St Mary's Abbey (1953) Alan Maycock.

Malmesbury *Abbey. Wilts. Map 5. 10m N of Chippenham. (c. 965– 1539). Benedictine monks. F: unknown. Ded: BVM & St Aldhelm.* 1st. f. 7thC for nuns. *c.* 637 Maildulph, a monk and hermit, settled here. Then in 676 Aldhelm (one of

Maildulph's pupils whose brilliance is legendary) fd. the abbey, ded. to St Peter & St Paul. Today there is no trace of St Aldhelm's resting place. He died in 709 while bp. of Sherborne and was buried here. The house prospered under K. Athelstan's patronage and he gave land and relics. He died in 940 and was also buried in the abbey ch. Numerous pilgrims were attracted to the famous monastery. *c.* 965 the secular priests were replaced by Bene. monks and the abbey re-ded. to the BVM. Although pillaged by the Danes early in the 11thC and damaged by fire in 1050, Aldhelm's enlarged abbey lasted until 1143 when the new abbey ch. was begun. In 1141 the abbot of Malmesbury, with those of Abingdon and Reading, received the Empress Matilda at Winchester (Knowles). A learned monk, William of Malmesbury (*c.* 1095–1143) left valuable historical records, and made use of the famous library (of which nothing remains) fd. by Abbot Godfrey (obit *c.* 1106). Mitred. In 1010 a monk with scientific knowledge made wings and jumped from the tower. He was injured and blamed his failure on 'the lack of a tail'. *c.* 1200 the abbey drew up an agreement with Evesham covering the sharing of all rights and exchanging of monks. There are no records of a distinguished history, but considerable details of events in the monastery's long life in VCH. *Remains:* Six bays of the nave (12thC with unique and elaborate S porch — recently renovated, 1977). N arch of crossing with piers and wall of S transept. Cloister lay to the N. The hotel to the W probably incorporates part of the guesthouse. A reliquary which belonged to the abbey is in Paris and the ciborium is in New York. Desc.

& plan: Archaeologia, Vol. 64. Notes: Br. Arch. Assoc. J. Vol. 25.

Malton *Priory. Yorks. NR. Map 1. 18m NE of York. (1150–1539). Gilbertine canons. F: Eustace Fitz John. Ded: St Mary.* Supported 3 hospitals (Graham). Accounts of the house exist for the years 1244–1257 and give valuable information about Gilb. finances. Two-thirds of the revenues came from wool sales, much of which was spent purchasing new land. In 1283 2 canons were attacked and their cattle stolen. In 1405 the community joined a rebellion against Henry IV. Many interesting historical details are given in English Ecclesiastical Studies (Graham) *v.* Bibliography 2. In 1535 the prior was charged with involvement in the Pilgrimage of Grace but his fate is unknown. *Remains:* Six bays of the nave of the conventual ch. are now the parish ch. The W front includes the S tower, the N has gone. Both Abbey House and the Cross Keys Inn have vaulted undercrofts which supported the refectory and infirmary respectively. Nothing else.

Malvern *Priories. Worcs.* See Great Malvern and Little Malvern.

Marham *Abbey. Norfolk. Map 4. 8m SE of King's Lynn. (c. 1249– 1536). Cistercian nuns. F: Isabella d'Albini, countess of Arundel. Ded: St Mary, St Barbara & St Edmund.* One of only 2 Cist houses of nuns fd. as an abbey. In 1252 incorporated with Waverley Abbey to whom it remained subordinate. In 1291 the nuns were exempted tithes due to smallness of endowments. 14thC cartulary in Norwich Cathedral library names 16 persons buried in the abbey and gives descriptions of their elaborate mortuary gowns. Subsequent history is dull until 1536 when Cromwell's agents recorded misconduct and claimed that some ch. ornaments were hidden in the dormitory. Evenso, it seems that very few of the nuns wished to quit their religious life (VCH). Bldgs. in 'sore decay' at the Dissolution. *Remains:* Site occupied by a farm. The S wall of the nave survives and parts of the W range including a 14thC room of 2 vaulted bays. Note: Archaeologia, Vol. 23, p. 8.

Markby *Priory. Lincs. 4½m SSW of Mablethorpe. (fdn. date unknown, r. Henry II? to 1536). Augustinian canons. F: Ralph FitzGilbert. Ded: St Peter.* Uninteresting history. *c.* Mid-14thC the prior and cellarer quarrelled over the latter's love of hunting. The Black Death ended the prior's life and it seems that the dismissed canon was reinstated. In 1438 the bp. wrote 'there is not even a shadow of religion kept, and the house is in a worse condition of any in the county'. The prior resigned and one canon, at least, did penance. In 1519 there were no grave faults but the canons were careless about observing silence: *Remains:* None. In the thatched parish ch. is a N doorway and a chancel arch which came from the lost priory.

Markyate *Priory. Herts. (was Beds.). 3½m SW of Luton. (1145–1537). Benedictine nuns. F: Ralf de Langford gave the site and the house was established under the patronage of Geoffrey de Gorron, abbot of St Albans. Ded: Holy Trinity.* The priory seems to have been burnt down soon after completion. A poor house which was frequently in debt and whose reputation was not un-

213

blemished. In 1259 the community sent bread to friars in trouble, but the charity was abused (see Dunstable Dominicans). Apart from bad management, weak prioresses and indiscipline in the 14th & 15thCs, the nunnery was assaulted by 50 robbers at night who stole everything of value (Power). In later years things went from bad to worse and from 1434 to 1443 the house had no prioress. But the origin was very different when an anchoress, Christina (the first prioress) gathered her holy disciples round her and they came under the protection of Abbot Gorron. *Remains:* None. The site was N of the parish ch. and is occupied by a mansion. Note: Br. Arch. Assoc. J. Vol. 26.

Marlborough *Priory. Wilts. (−1189 to 1539). Gilbertine canons. F: uncertain (Henry II or K. John suggested). Ded: St Margaret.* History no more than a series of isolated incidents and nothing is known of the bldgs. Bequests came from Edward III and Q. Philippa in 1334. In 1337 50 men broke into the precinct and burnt trees and timber stocks. Poverty followed the Black Death and heavy losses due to sheep scab. Edward III gave land to alleviate the slender means of the community. *Remains:* None. A derelict cottage near the railway station incorporated a few fragments of the priory.

Marlborough *Friary. Wilts. (c. 1316− 1538). Carmelite. F: unknown. Wm. de Rammeshulle granted an early licence to give the friars land. Ded: BVM.* There is no history apart from some records of charity and poverty. The friars' latrine was a noted landmark.

In 1535 a visiting commissioner was horrified by the dilapidation and poverty of the house. *Remains:* None. The last of the property, which lay to the S of the town, was apparently destroyed by fire in 1820.

Marmont *(Mirmaud) Priory Cell. Cambs. 7m SSE of Wisbech at Upwell. (−1203 to 1538). Gilbertine canons. F: Ralph de Hanville. Ded: BVM.* The whole history of this little house, with only a prior and one canon at the Dissolution, is shrouded in obscurity. The F's son, Thomas, confirmed the fdn. gifts and gave the canons 4 couples of swans and permission to pasture mares and foals (VCH). In 1535 the house was referred to as a cell of Watton. *Remains:* None. The site is occupied by a farm.

Marrick *Priory. Yorks. NR. Map 1. 8m SW by S of Richmond. (c. 1158− 1540). Benedictine nuns. F: Robert de Aske. Ded: St Mary.* Apart from extensive details of the priory's lifestyle which survive from records of visitations in 1252, little is known. Poverty was serious. No guest was permitted to stay more than one night, a cleric was sent to manage the finances and the banning of further recruitment of novices were among the restrictions. In 1536 the rich and beautiful girl, Isabella Beaufort, whom Henry VIII had tried to marry, is said to have obtained sanctuary here for almost 4 years until the house surrendered. The nuns used the nave of the ch. and the parishioners the choir − thus reversing the usual arrangement. *Remains:* Very little. Ch. rebuilt in 1811 and incorporates re-used materials including an acutely-pointed chancel arch and 2 half-arches. No claustral bldgs. survive. Farm bldg. is attached to the N side of the tower.

Marsh Barton *Priory Cell. Devon.*
See Exeter.

Marton *Priory. Yorks. NR. 11m N of York. (c. 1154–1536). Augustinian canons and nuns. F: Bertram de Bulmer. Ded: St Mary.*
Date of fdn. given as during r. of K. Stephen or early Henry II. By 1167 the nuns had left the double house and moved to Moxby under Benedictine Rule. In the 1280s impoverishment and ruin followed wanton behaviour, and canons were sent to other houses 'where religion waxed more strongly' (VCH). In the 14thC poor discipline and devastation of the priory by the Scots continued the depressing history. Little is known of the 15th and 16thC history. *Remains:* None. The site is occupied by a farmhouse.

Mattersey *Priory. Notts. Map 3. 8m N of Retford. (c. 1185–1538). Gilbertine canons. F: Roger de Mattersey. Ded: St Helen.*
A small house of which little history is known. The major historic fact to survive is the serious fire of 1279. It seems that the ch. was probably never entirely rebuilt due to the canons' poverty. At the N end of the E claustral range (where the chapter house would normally be) is the curious positioning of 2 altars, suggesting that this area served for the ch. until rebldg. could begin. The house never recovered from the disaster in which all muniments were destroyed. In later years the community was given the income from Mattersey ch., a weekly fair was granted in 1403, and an indulgence

given by the pope in 1406. *Remains:* Fdns. of ch., cloister and E range. To the S are ruins of the 2-aisled refectory and kitchen with a serving-hatch. A 15thC remnant of a tower overlaps part of the N wall of the nave. Desc., plan & care: D of E. Also desc. & plan: Arch. J. Vol. 87 (1930).

Maxstoke *Priory. Warks. Map 3. 10m E of Birmingham city centre. (1336–1536). Augustinian canons. F: Sir Wm. de Clinton. Ded: Holy Trinity, BVM, St Michael & All Saints.*
1st. f. as a coll. of secular priests and was one of the last Aug. fdns. No cartulary exists but the F's charter survives and gives explicit details of how the house was to be run; but despite clear behaviour rules, one canon attacked another in 1399 and the latter killed his adversary in self defence. The bldgs. were recorded as being grand, stately and in good repair during their 200 years. A valuable register of accounts between 1432 and 1493 is preserved at Trinity Coll. Oxford. *Remains:* Part of crossing, W wall of infirmary and 2 gatehouses – one in ruins the other occupied as a farmhouse. In 1973 a close study was made of the priory's earthworks and water storage & control.

Meaux* *(Melsa) Abbey. Yorks. ER. 7m N of Hull. (1151–1539). Cistercian monks. F: William le Gros, earl of Albermarle. Ded: St Mary.*
A large and important house whose financial straits thrice caused the monks to disperse to other houses: over-manning (1160); lawsuits and poor crops (1180); heavy 'goodwill' fine to K. John (1210). F. buried at

215

Only a few depressions mark the site where the great Cistercian abbey of Meaux, Yorkshire, once stood. To appreciate the savagery of the Dissolution, Gloucester Cathedral (right) was probably rivaled in size by Meaux Abbey church.

Thornton (*v.* below) his other fdn. By 1249 60 monks and 90 lay-brothers lived here. In 1269 debts had reached almost £4,000 (about £200,000 today), reduced to £400 by 1339 mainly by wool sales. Chronicle of Melsa preserved in BM. A hand-carved crucifix made by a lay-brother, using a nude model and designed to attract pilgrims to give alms, resulted merely in arousing their curiosity. In the B.D. (1349) only 10 out of the community of 49 survived. Disputes over elections and lawsuits occurred during the un-distinguished performances of the houses' abbots. The abbey had a splendid library and a remarkable collection of relics. *Remains:* None. Never excavated apart from a tile kiln in the 1950s by the D of E. A cottage on the edge of the site is a museum of architectural fragments. Books: 1. Essays upon the Hist. of Meaux Abbey (1906) A. Earle. 2. Chronicle of the Monastery of Melsa (1886–8) E. A. Bond. *pronounced Mewss.

Medmenham *Abbey. Bucks. 1½m S of Marlow. (1212–1536). Cistercian monks. F: Hugh de Bolbec. Ded:*

216

Gloucester Cathedral from the north. As St Peter's Abbey it survived, while Meaux Abbey (opposite) has wholly vanished.

St Mary.
1st. f. 1201 and colonised from Woburn in 1204, but monks recalled in the same year. Re-f. 1212 by a new colony, but after the death of the F. his daughter, Isabella, Countess of Oxford, reclaimed the land and her brother turned out the monks. By 1230 the dispute was resolved and Isabella gave the monks possession. No other history whatsoever of this small and poor house. In 1524 Wolsey planned to obtain it for his Oxford Coll. but it survived to become annexed to Bisham in the first half of 1536, and only an abbot and one monk were in occupation. *Remains:* One small fragment of an un-identified bldg. The site is occupied by a house.

Melcombe Regis *Friary. Dorset. N suburb of Weymouth. (1418–1538). Dominican. Fs: Sir Hugh Deverell and John Rogers. Ded: St Wilfred.*

Visitation of London. The last Dom. house f. in England. It was opposed by the bp. of Salisbury but obtained a royal licence in 1431. The friars built a tower to aid the town's defences and a jetty 'against the flowing of the sea' (VCH). Very little else known. *Remains:* None. The friary was in Maiden Street. Last remnants pulled down in 1861. Site covered with new housing.

Mendham *Alien Priory/Priory. Suffolk. 1½m SE of Harleston. (c. 1150–1537). Cluniac monks. F: William de Huntingfield. Ded: BVM.*
Cell of Castle Acre. F's. son increased endowments of this small and obscure house. Treated as alien until it became denizen with the mother house between 1351–74; but in 1377 Edward III restored its lands and benefices 'because the prior and monks were Englishmen' (VCH). No

217

record of the net income in 1535 appears in the Valor Ecclesiasticus. *Remains:* None. The site was on the marshes S of the River Waveney.

Merevale *(Mira Vallis) Abbey. Warks. Map 3. 1m W of Atherstone. (1148– 1538). Cistercian monks. F: Robert de Ferrers II, Earl of Derby. Ded: St Mary.*
Colonised from Bordesley. An Augustinian canon of Caldwell fled here in 1248 in fear of the austerity of a bp. at a pending visitation (VCH). By 1291 the finances were straitened and a custodian was appointed in 1297 to manage temporalities. In 1361 a large number of pilgrims visiting the image of the Virgin in the Chapel-by-the-Gate, resulted in 'many being brought near to death by reason of the crush'. The convent held rights in the Peak District Forest. Not much 15th & 16thC history. *Remains:* The large Chapel-by-the-Gate survives as a parish ch. In farm bldgs. is part of the W end of the S aisle of the conventual ch., and the 13thC N and S refectory walls exist with a pulpit and staircase in the S wall. Excavated 1849 (Pevsner).

Merton *Priory. Surrey. Map 6. 1m SW of Wimbledon. (1114–1538). Augustinian canons. F: Gilbert, sheriff of Surrey. Ded: St Mary.*
Moved to a new site 1117. With Aldgate (London) the house built up a vast ascendency of the Order (Dickinson) to become the second richest in England. St Thomas (Martyr) of Canterbury educated here at a time when an Italian, Master Guy, had a great reputation for learning. Q. Maud showed much interest in the fdn. In 1232 Hubert de Burgh, Henry III's justiciar, fled to Merton for sanctuary. Parliament

passed the Statutes of Merton (a new body of laws) in the monastery in 1236. In 1309 poverty was caused by 'the result of ministering to the poor and the exercise of frequent hospitality'. Two alien priories were granted to the canons: Tregoney in 1267 and Patrixbourne in 1409 (*v.* Appendix 1). In 1387 Bp. Wykeham found no serious faults but blamed the canons for neglect of upkeep of the parochial chs. in their care. Entries for the 15th & 16thCs are of small interest apart from the appropriation of Calwich (*v.* above) to the community in 1536. Despite a number of refs. the house was never an abbey. *Remains:* Slight. Length of precinct wall (care N.T.) and a gateway. Much of the materials went into the construction of Nonesuch Palace for Henry VIII. Excavated 1921–2 & 1962–3. Desc. & plan: Archaeologia, Vol. 76 (1926–7); also Surrey Arch. Colls. Vols. 38 (1929) & 64 (1967). Part investigated 1964: Med. Arch. Vol. 9. Book: Records of Merton Priory (1898) A. Heales.

Michelham *Priory. Sussex. Map 7. 2m W of Hailsham. (1229–1536). Augustinian canons. F: Gilbert de Laigle. Ded: Holy Trinity.*
Colonised from Hastings and always independent of it. In 1288 a long dispute with Bayham Abbey was settled over the ownership of Hailsham ch. The convent received many gifts of land and grants in the 14thC, but the spiritualities were never rich. In 1437 Sir Roger Fiennes ejected the prior and seized all the goods of the house. Nothing known of the inner life of the priory until the 15thC, when in 1441 the canons were ordered to keep silence and cease visiting a local tavern. A series of incompetent priors brought

indiscipline within the community and bldgs. into disrepair, and by 1478 the moral tone was at its lowest when a canon returned after 15 years absence 'to poison the convent with evil arguments' (VCH). 3 subsequent visitations record only dilapidated bldgs. *Remains:* Outline of ch. fdns in the turf. Much of refectory though with Tudor alterations, including 13thC lavatorium arches and pulpit stairs. S end of W range with undercroft and guest hall. Fine gateway tower and barn. Desc., plan & care: Sussex Arch. Soc., *v.* Collns. Vols. 6 & 67. Acct: History of Hailsham, L. F. Salzman. Excav. notes: Med. Arch. Vols. 4, 9 & 16.

Middlesbrough *Priory Cell. Yorks. NR. (c. 1120–1537). Benedictine monks. F: Robert de Brus. Ded: St Hilda.*
The F. gave the ch. and lands to Whitby on condition that monks lived here. Guisborough convent, also fd. by de Brus, quarrelled with Whitby over the ownership of the cell. From an unknown cause the house became greatly impoverished and in 1451 only a prior and one monk lived here. Singularly little history. Day and month of the closure is unknown. *Remains:* None.

Millbrook *Priory Cell. Beds. 1m W of Ampthill. (1097–1119 to c. 1143). Benedictine monks. F: Nigel de Waste (gave ch. to St Albans which placed monks here during the time of Abbot Richard). Ded: uncertain.*
c. 1143 the small and poor cell was merged with Beadlow. Fire and the Black Death resulted in the poverty-stricken house hardly supporting 2 monks, and it finally disappeared so completely that even its site was forgotten. *Remains:* None.

Milton Abbas *Abbey. Dorset. Map 5. 6m SW of Blandford. (964–1539). Benedictine monks. Fs: K. Edgar & Archbp. Dunstan. Ded: St Mary, St Michael, St Samson & St Branwalader.*
1st. f. for secular canons c. 938 by K. Athelstan. By 1213 the abbey's affairs were in the hands of custodians. In 1294 the house was given a grant of protection because of money given towards the royal funds. In 1309 the monastery was destroyed by fire following a violent storm. The loss and subsequent ravages of the Black Death reduced the community drastically. By 1378 there was no reference to poverty but some disciplinary injunctions were given. Ch. rebldg. began 1331 and continued until the Suppression, though the nave was never rebuilt. *Remains:* Choir, transepts and crossing of 14th & 15thCs conventual ch. 15thC abbot's hall incorporated in 18thC mansion (now a school). Excavations in 1955 revealed fdns. of the earlier Norman ch. K. Athelstan's chapel of St Catherine, E of the ch., may have been the Chapel-by-the-Gate in pre-Reformation days. Desc: Proc. Dorset Nat. Hist. & Arch. Soc. Vol. 78 (1956).

Minchin Buckland *Priory. Somerset. See* Buckland.

Minster-in-Sheppey *Priory. Kent. Map 7. 2m SE of Sheerness. (–1087 to 1536). Benedictine nuns/ Augustinian canonesses. Ded: St Mary & St Sexburga.*
1st. f. c. 670 by St Sexburga and deserted after Danish raids in 9th or 10thCs. History from thence is confused. Bene. nuns probably lived here at the end of the 11thC and c. 1130 an Aug. archbp. possibly re-f. the

house for Aug. canonesses. By 1186 the priory appears to have been Bene. again and so remained until 1396 when Archbp. William Courtney restored it to the Aug. Order (Knowles). A visitation of 1296 ordered silence to be observed under penalty of solitary confinement. In 1322 the ch. was reconsecrated having been 'polluted by bloodshed' (VCH). In 1511 Archbp. Warham heard there was no infirmary and the prioress never gave the convent any accounts. The nuns employed all the villagers throughout the year in this lonely area. *Remains:* Considerable part of the 7thC ch. survives in the nave with a 14thC chancel and 15thC tower. This ch. contains some of the oldest material existing in any bldgs. standing in the U.K. The nuns' ch. was the northern nave and the 13thC southern nave was parochial. To the W is a 3-storied gatehouse once occupied by the nuns' chaplain and the vicar of the parish ch. Desc: Archaeologia Cantiana, Vol. 22 (1897).

Minster-in-Thanet *Abbey. Kent. 4m W of Ramsgate.*
As the Benedictine monastery flourished and disappeared before the Conquest, it is outside the scope of this list. Today the ch. and bldgs. of a monastic grange once belonging to St Augustine's Abbey, Canterbury, are inhabited by Benedictine nuns.

Mirescog *Abbey. Isle of Man. In Kirk Christ Lezayre parish, later called Sulby Grange (Cowan). (1176– c. 1200). Cistercian monks. F: Godred II, King of Man. Ded: St Mary.*
The site was given to Rievaulx Abbey (Yorks.) and a monastery was commenced. Within a few years the whole property was granted to Rushen Abbey (Cowan). *Remains:* None.

Missenden *Abbey. Bucks. Map 6. 7m NNE of High Wycombe. (1133– 1538). Augustinian canons. F: Wm. of Missenden. Ded: St Mary.*
First Arrouaise house in England from whom it was separated by 1188. One of the larger houses of the Order. There is unusually full information about the internal history in VCH, and from first to last it was singularly unfortunate in its abbots, against whom there were more complaints than any laxity in the canons – until the 16thC. In the 13thC there was great poverty due to crop failures, animal disease and debts. However, in the 16thC there were bad reports, especially in 1530, when it seems that lay persons had undue influence over the house. Not a happy history. *Remains:* Site occupied by a house over the cloister which incorporates 2 of its walls. In the E range the 15thC timber roof of the dormitory survives (Pevsner). Never fully excavated. Notes: Archaeologia, Vol. 47, pp. 50 & 60.

Moatenden *(Mottenden) Friary. Kent. 1½m NNW of Headcorn. (c. 1224–1538). Trinitarian. F: Sir Robert de Rokesley. Ded: Holy Trinity.*
Perhaps the first house of the Order in England (Dugdale). Extensive details of grants in VCH. In 1321 the friars suffered 'great mischief and poverty' owing to the siege of Leeds Castle, poor harvests and cattle disease. In 1372 the minister was appointed provincial of England. The patron of Easton Royal would not accept the nomination, and when his own minister was ordered to attend a general chapter in London

the patron refused him leave. Two volumes from the friary's library survive in Oxford. An archdeacon of Northampton was buried here in 1499. At the Dissolution Cromwell himself took possession of the property. *Remains:* None. A Tudor bldg. on the site incorporates windows and a doorway from the friary (Pevsner).

Mobberley *Priory. Cheshire. 3½m E of Knutsford. (−1204 to ?). Augustinian canons. F: Patrick de Mobberley. Ded: St Mary & St Wilfred.* Surviving charters are almost complete from fdn. to annexing with Rocester (*v.* below). Although there were irregularities in endowments, there is no evidence that the F. had only a life interest in the priory. The link with Rocester came between 1228−40 and it is a mystery why, in the course of the next 50 years, every trace of the arrangement has vanished (Ormerod). It was the abbot of Rocester's responsibility to maintain a few canons here, but in what year or century this service ceased and the priory closed is unknown. *Remains:* None.

Modney *(Hilgay) Priory Cell. Norfolk. 6m S of Downham Market. (−1291 to 1539). Benedictine monks. F: unknown. Ded: unknown.* Nothing is known of this small fdn. which was a cell of Ramsey Abbey, Hunts. The prior acted as bailiff of the estate with possibly one monk with him (Knowles). No history survives. *Remains:* None. (The property may have been no more than a grange, but it is not listed as such).

Monk Bretton *Alien Priory/Priory. Yorks. WR. Map 3. 2m NE of*

Barnsley. (c. 1154−1539). Cluniac/ Benedictine monks. F: Adam Fitz Swane. Ded: St Mary Magdalene. Dependent upon Pontefract. A divergence of grants in the F's. two charters led to frequent disputes between the houses, and in 1279 a visitation of Cluniac priors was refused admission. In 1281 the community swore obedience to the archbp. of York and were henceforth considered Bene. from that day (Jan. 4th), and thus becoming denizen escaped later taxation of alien houses. From then on the fortunes of the priory varied with the business capacity of the priors (Graham) − with alternating prosperity and debt. Some revenue came from ironworks owned by the convent in the area still known as Smithies. Fire destroyed some of the bldgs. in 1286. 15thC history was uneventful. *Remains:* Excavations of 1923−6 have revealed the whole ground plan. Principal ruins in the W range with high walls of the prior's lodging; S wall of the refectory; 14thC gatehouse shell and a detached administrative bldg. Desc. plan & care: D of E. Book: The Priory of Monk Bretton (1926) J. W. Walker

Monks Horton *Alien Priory/Priory. Kent. Map 7. 7m ESE of Ashford. (1142−1536). Cluniac monks. Fs: Robert de Vere and Adelina his wife. Ded: St Mary, St John Evangelist & St Pancras.* Cell of Lewes. The F's. heir, a Constable of England, added to the family's grants of land. A visitation of 1275 resulted in one of the injunctions ordering regular readings in the refectory at dinner, and also the prior and convent were to refrain from eating meat in the presence of seculars (VCH). In 1297 the house was reported to be in an excellent

221

state. During the wars with France the convent had concessions not made to other alien priories because the priors were Englishmen. The house became denizen *c*. 1373. There is little known of 15thC history. *Remains:* Horton Priory, a 20thC house, stands on the site and incorporates a part of the W front of the ch., and the 12thC W range of the cloister forms the W front of the 2-storeyed house with 14thC cusped tracery windows (Pevsner). Note: Archaeologia, Vol. 25. p. 38.

Monkton Farleigh *Alien Priory/ Priory. Wilts. Map 5. 3½m E of Bath. (c. 1123–1536). Cluniac monks. Fs: Maud de Bohun and Humphrey III her son (at the instance of Maud's husband Humphrey II). Ded: St Mary Magdalene.*
The Empress Matilda was a benefactress. Considerable details of endowments in VCH. In 1227 the spiritualities were increased by the bp. of Salisbury due to the poverty of the house and its hospitality to all comers. A visitation of 1276 found the community without reproach except for the prior who was 'disobedient'. As an alien priory in 1294 the lands were taken by the Crown. In 1300 a prior was deposed and re-employed at Lewes as a housekeeper. The priory became denizen in 1373. In 1472 the community was described by a newly-appointed prior as 'destitute of all virtue and good rule'. Surviving accounts indicate mixed farming with little evidence of a large wool trade. The prior's hope of bribing Cromwell to save his house failed. *Remains:* Small fragments are built into the manor house on the site and to the W a lone wall stands with two lancet windows. The 14thC monks' conduit

is in a nearby field. Excavated 1744, 1841, *c.* 1880 & 1911. Desc. & plan: Archaeologia, Vol. 73 (1923).

Monkwearmouth *Abbey/Priory Cell. Durham. Map 1. N suburb of Sunderland. (1075–1536). Benedictine monks. Re-F: Aldwin, Prior of Winchcombe. Ded: St Peter.*
1st. f. 674 by St Benedict Biscop. The pre-Conquest history is inextricably linked with Jarrow and the F. wished the two houses to be joined 'in mutual peace, concord and perpetual affection'. The monastery was several times devastated by Danish raids and in 1070 suffered at the hands of Malcolm, K. of Scotland. In 1075 the house was restored to Bene. monks and in 1083 23 monks from the two houses were sent to Durham to replace secular clergy. The abbey then became a priory cell for only 3 or 4 monks. The history is then obscure. *Remains:* Nothing of the 1st. monastery. The 9th or 10thC W tower over the porch is 'a precious relic . . . in a sordid setting' (Pevsner). 14thC nave and chancel. Note on remains: Archaeologia Aeliana (1947). Site part excavated between 1959–62. Fdns. of E & W claustral ranges located and of other walls. Considerable quantities of pottery and a mass burial (perhaps a Viking massacre) revealed. (Med. Arch. Vols. 4, 6 & 7).

Montacute *Alien Priory/Priory. Somerset. Map 5. 4m W of Yeovil. (c. 1078/90–1539). Cluniac monks. F: Count Robert of Mortain or his son William. Ded: St Peter & St Paul.*
Dependent upon Cluny. Later fdn. dates also occur up to 1102. Uneventful history. In 1261 the prior was

appointed visitor of the Order in England. In 1279 a prior was charged with clipping coins and deposed in 1285 for issuing counterfeit money. In 1407 the house became denizen. The convent owned many chs. and manors and became the third richest house of the Order in England. *Remains:* Nothing except the fine 15thC gatehouse with oriel windows, octagonal turrets and vaulting. Site never excavated. Book: The Story of Montacute (1933), H. Avray Tipping.

Morville *Priory Cell. Salop. 3¼m N of Bridgnorth. (c. 1138–1540). Benedictine monks. F: Robert, bp. of Hereford. Ded: St Gregory.* Dependent upon Shrewsbury to whom the F. granted it *c.* 1086. 1st. fd. as a collegiate ch. in pre-Conquest days, and its decline resulted in the introduction of Bene. monks at the request of the abbot of Shrewsbury *c.* 1138. Very small with a prior and 2 monks at most. History negligible. In 1372, and again in the 16thC, there was only a prior living here. *Remains:* None. Morville Hall occupies the site which has some 12thC stones used in its walls, perhaps from the priory.

Mottisfont *Priory. Hants. Map 6. 4½m NW by N of Romsey. (1201–1536). Augustinian canons. F: William Briwere, or Brewer. Ded: Holy Trinity.*
Q. Eleanor's bequest provided for 7 poor widows to be fed daily in her memory. Twice the prior was ordered to enforce the authority of the pope in England in the 13thC. In 1310 the visiting bp. was 'wholly satisfied' with the house. The B.D. much reduced the size of the community and its income. In 1494 the pope

issued a Bull for the suppression of the house at the request of Henry VII as it could maintain only 3 canons; but in 1500 it was assigned to Westminster Abbey and a community with a household of 29 servants were still there in 1536. *Remains:* A mansion, Mottisfont Abbey, stands on the site. The buttressed N wall of the nave of the ch. and the lower half of the crossing tower form the N front of the house. Other parts of the ch. are in evidence: 13thC blank arcading on the nave's S wall; N transept arch; S transept masonry; and a stone screen from the ch. is now in the kitchen. Also some parts of the claustral bldgs., including the sub-vault of the W range. Desc. & plan: VCH Hants. Vol. 4, p. 504.

Mount Grace *Priory. Yorks. NR. Map 1. 6m NE of Northallerton. (1398–1539). Carthusian monks. F: Thomas de Holland (later duke of Surrey). Ded: St Mary & St Nicholas.* In 1400 the F. was executed at Cirencester for rebelling against Henry IV. 12 years later his body was brought to Mount Grace for burial. Disputes then arose over the ownership of the manor which lasted well into the 15thC. In the 2nd half of this century the house received a number of endowments including grants of lands previously owned by suppressed alien priories, i.e. Hinckley in 1409, Hough *c.* 1414 and Minting 1414 (*v.* Appendix 1). Until its last years the history was uneventful, then in 1534 two monks refused to subscribe to Henry VIII's Act of Succession and were imprisoned. Very little internal history. *Remains:* The most important example of the Order's 9 houses in England. The ruins include the conventual ch., great cloister with one restored cell;

223

gatehouse; barns; and guesthouse –
the latter converted into a private
house. Owners: NT. Guardianship,
desc. & plan: D of E. Excavations
1896 to early-1900s revealed
complete plan. Further intermittent
work 1957–69 extended knowledge
of ch., cells and water system – Med.
Arch. Vols. 2, 3, 5, 6, 7 & 14. Desc.
& plan: Yorks. Arch. J. Vol. 18
(1905). Notes: Archaeologia, Vols. 13,
16 & 20.

Mountjoy *Priory Cell/Priory. Norfolk.*
4m SE of Reepham. (+1189 to 1529).
Benedictine monks/Augustinian
canons. F: William de Gyney. Ded:
St Laurence.
Charters refer to monks and canons
and although the original fdn. was
Bene. as a cell of Wymondham, sometime early in the r. of K. John
(c. 1200) the house became Aug.
The records give far fuller details of
grants, gifts and rents than internal
or external history. In 1515 lands
were let for pastorage and from the
income the prior was to provide a
barrel of tar (to mark sheep?) every
2 years, and a bldg. to store wool
until it was sold (VCH). Although
earmarked by Wolsey for his Ipswich
venture, it finally went to a William
Hales. *Remains:* Scanty. A few fdns.
may be traced to the E of Abbey
Farm 1m SW of Haveringland parish
ch.

Moxby *(Molseby) Priory. Yorks. NR.*
10½m NNW of York at Sheriff
Hutton. (–1167 to 1536). Benedict-
ine nuns/Augustinian canonesses.
F: perhaps Bertram de Bulmer with
land granted by Henry II. Ded:
St John, Evangelist.
The nuns came from Marton, the
double Aug. house, and lived under
the Bene. Rule. In 1314 an injunction

ordered healthy nuns to keep out of
the infirmary, not to wander in the
woods or gossip with seculars. In
1317 the nunnery was burdened by
a curious obligation to supply 14
loaves weekly to the friars of York
(Power). The nuns were dispersed in
1322 because the Scots had devastated
their house, but when they returned
in 1325 they appear to be then
living under the Aug. Rule. In 1327
there were heavy debts and more
Scottish raids came at the end of
the century. Later history appears to
be mainly concerned with elections
of prioresses and a series of now
familiar injunctions. *Remains:* None.
Earthworks mark the site.

Muchelney *Abbey. Somerset. Map 5.*
2m S of Langport. (c. 950–1538).
Benedictine monks. F: K. Athelstan.
Ded: St Peter & St Paul.
1st. f. c. 693 by K. Ina and destroyed
by Danes c. 878. The fdn. by
Athelstan was in 939 and he probably
colonised the house with secular
canons who were replaced by Bene.
monks c. 950. Not a large monastery.
In 1315 the abbot's register tells of a
Knights Templar who was maintained
here for 276 days (VCH). Mitred.
The Crown forced on the abbey
several of its aged servants including
the king's harper in 1328. In 1335
the visiting bp. found the monks
living in luxury and enjoying private
privileges, but his injunctions for
reform met with opposition. At the
same time it seems the ch. was in a
poor state of repair. At the time of
the B.D. (1349) 2 abbots died within
a month. Little known of 15thC
history. An abbot was forced to
resign in 1532 in favour of one more
amenable to acceptance of the forthcoming changes. *Remains:* Outlines
of the 10th & 15thC chs. and the

224

Muchelney Abbey, Somerset. South West angle of the cloister and doorway which led to the refectory.

cloister. Excavated 1948–50. Superb 16thC abbot's lodging; S cloister walk; kitchen and ante-room to refectory. Fine reredorter nearby in farmbldgs. Plan, notes & care: D of E. Hist: Som. Arch. & Nat. Hist. Soc. Vol. 8 (1859).

Much Wenlock *Priory. Salop.* *See* Wenlock.

Mullicourt *(de Bello Loco) Priory/ Priory Cell. Norfolk. 4m W of Downham Market. (–1066? to c. 1539). Benedictine monks. F: unknown. Ded: St Mary.*
Nothing known of the fdn. which may be pre-Conquest. Small house with obscure history. In 1273 the monks regained some land confiscated by an act of trespass of a lay administrator within the priory. The poorly endowed house suffered severely in the 14thC from great storms and flooding. In 1446 there was only one monk here and the house became a cell of Ely. *Remains:* Minimal. Site occupied by a farmhouse.

N

Neasham *Priory. Durham. 3½m SE of Darlington. (–1157 to 1540). Benedictine nuns. F: perhaps a baron of Greystoke. Ded: St Mary.*
The only religious house in the county independent of Durham Cath-Priory. Never wealthy. Uneventful history. Suffered on several occasions through Scottish raids. VCH gives details of land acquisitions and injunctions. In 1429 a poor administrator caused a lapse in manners and morals, and the disobedience of nuns in ignoring injunctions in 1436 resulted in the arrival of commissioners in 1437 to enforce them. In 1503 Princess Margaret, on her bridal journey to Scotland, met the prioress and nuns at the priory gate but it is not known if she entered. *Remains:* None. Site occupied by a house.

Netley *(Laetus Locus) Abbey. Hants. Map 6. 4m SE of Southampton. (1239–1536). Cistercian monks. Fs: Peter des Roches,* Bp. of Winchester & Henry III. Ded: St Mary & St Edward the Confessor.*
When the project was in need of funds in 1251, Henry III took the house under his protection. Relatively little history of this late fdn. By 1328 the abbey was burdened with debt resulting in the sale of its property to regain solvency. In 1341 lambs and wool were stolen by sailors and others appointed to guard the coast of the abbey lands. In 1535 the commissioners found the monks 'of good conversation'. They maintained a light for the guidance of mariners. At the suppression the community went to the mother-house of Beaulieu. *Remains:* The nave of the ch. and E claustral bldgs. became a mansion soon after the closure, but the splendid ch. walls survive when all traces of the house have gone. Other ruins comprise chapter house, warming room, cloister walls, reredorter and abbot's lodging – mostly fine examples of 13thC work. Desc., plan & care: D of E. Notes: Br. Arch. Assoc. J. Vol. 11. Book: Architectural Details of Netley Abbey (1848) Geo. Guillaume.
* Granted land before his death in 1238.

Newark *(Aldbury) Priory. Surrey. Map 6. 2½m E of Woking. (c. 1189– 1538). Augustinian canons. Fs: Ruald de Calva and Beatrice his wife.*

Netley Abbey, Hampshire. View from the south-east.

Ded: St Mary & St Thomas, Martyr.
Evidence suggests the site is much
older and the Fs'. house probably
succeeded a hospital (Dickinson).
Originally named Aldbury, it
gradually changed to Newark or the
New Place of St Thomas by Guildford. In 1281 its temporalities were
considerable. VCH gives extensive
details of an elaborately appointed
chantry and instructions for its
ordinance. In 1387 the bp. during a
visitation found the prior too infirm
to remain in charge, and also a canon
who had succumbed to 'scandalous
excesses'. The latter was placed in
custody at Merton. *Remains:* An
attractive ruin of flint walling, some
to the height of the vaulting, are of

the ch. 'The total architectural effect
must have been remarkable' (Pevsner).
No conventual bldgs. Excavated 1840.
Desc: Surrey Arch. Coll. Vol. 40,
(1934). Note: Archaeologia, Vol. 31,
p. 469.

Newark *Friary. Notts. (1507–1534).*
Franciscan. (Observant). F: Henry
VII. Ded: St Francis?
The province of 6 houses was consti-
tuted in 1499 of which 4 were
originally Conventual and Newark
was the 2nd of 2 new fdns. In 1509
the F. left £200 to aid the convent
'newly begun in the town of
Newark'. The Order was suppressed
in 1534 and the friars imprisoned –
or worse. A scholar, John Rycks, a

227

Fellow of Corpus Christi Coll.,
Cambridge, was warden here at the
time (Little). *Remains:* None.

Newark *Friary. Notts. (1534–1539).
Austin.*
When the Observant Franciscans
were evicted the house was occupied
by this Order. Nothing appears to be
recorded of the brief history.
Remains: None. A house known as
The Friary in Appleton Gate stands
on the site. Perhaps some of the
original masonry is incorporated.

Newbo *Abbey. Lincs. 3m NW by W
of Grantham. (1198–1536). Premonstratensian canons. F: Richard
de Malebisse. Ded: St Mary.*
Colonised from Newsham. The F.
was one of the leaders of the massacre
of the Jews in York c. 1185, to one
of whom he was heavily in debt. No
doubt his fdn. originated from his
fear for his soul rather than his
worldly possessions (Colvin). In 1227
and 1307 a general chapter of the
Order was held here (VCH). In 1402
a pestilence left the house almost
without canons and even seculars
were recruited to restore the community. In 1482 there was heavy
debt which was much reduced by
good administration by 1491. The
abbot's rule was praised in 1500, but
a recalcitrant canon was 'sharply
rebuked for wearing slippers' (VCH).
Remains: None.

Newburgh *Priory. Yorks, NR. ¾m SE
of Coxwold. (1145–1538). Augustinian canons. F: Roger de Mowbray.
Ded: St Mary.*
Colonised from Bridlington. Community 1st. settled at Hood, 1143–5,
(which had been recently vacated by
Cistercians) while their priory was

being built. A prior disgraced his
position in 1252 by impartial treatment of the canons and imputing
crimes to them which they did not
commit. For the next 100 years the
history is sprinkled with varied
injunctions in respect of indiscipline,
such as hurrying through services;
failing to distribute alms to the poor;
having a superfluity of dogs; allowing
strangers in the refectory; and wearing
'novelties in dress'. (VCH). In 1404
a compassionate ruling occurred when
a canon with an impediment in his
tongue was freed for life from saying
Mass in a loud voice and with music.
Little subsequent history of interest
though it seems to have been orderly.
Remains: Very little. An 18thC house
occupies the site and no doubt some
fragments of materials from the
priory survive within the walls.

Newcastle under Lyme *Friary. Staffs.
(–1277 to 1538). Dominican. F:
unknown. Ded: unknown.*
Fdn. date in some doubt but the
friars were in residence in 1277 when
Edward I sent them alms. Very little
known about the history of the
house. In 1291 the friars received
£5 under the will of Q. Eleanor. In
1390 the friary received 'the devout
brethren of the Observants' to the
stimulation of their energies (VCH).
By 1538 the house was very poor –
and in ruins – the roofs ready to fall
down. The inventory reveals few
possessions and everything was 'old,
inferior or in some way defective'.
Remains: None. Some fdns. were
discovered when the cattle market
was laid out in 1870–1. Some of
the bldgs. survived until the early-
18thC. The site, which lay a little E
of the castle, was partly bounded by
Blackfriars Road and Goose Street.
Friarswood Road and Friars Street

also recall the existence of the community.

Newcastle upon Tyne *(Monkchester) Priory. N'land. (c. 1135–1540). Benedictine nuns. F: uncertain – Henry I or K. David of Scotland. Ded: St Bartholomew.* 1st. mentioned 1086. *c.* 1094 Agatha, mother of Q. Margaret of Scotland and Christina her sister, took the veil here after the death at Alnwick of K. Malcolm in 1093. It is doubtful if this nunnery lasted long, and was re-f. *c.* 1135. Considerable details of endowments and gifts (Brand). The monks of Tynemouth gave the nuns an annual quota of wheat from 1223. In 1365 the house was in a miserable state regarding spirituals and temporals and a custodian was appointed to control financial affairs. A nun who had absented herself 'for a just and reasonable cause' was refused readmission by the convent in 1377, but the bp. threatened them with excommunication if they did not change their minds. In the 15thC under-endowments led to debts and misfortunes which were worsened by the effects of fire. In 1428 a nun was appointed prioress of Neasham and was praised for her administrative skills. *Remains:* None. The exact site is in doubt. Some relics survived until 1788. Nun Street is the sole reminder.

Newcastle upon Tyne *Friary. N'land. Map 1. (–1291 to 1539). Austin. F: Wm. Lord Ross. (John de Capella gave land in 1291). Ded: unknown.* Limit of York. Few records survive. Site enlarged in 1306 and again in 1331. *c.* 1389 an Act of Parliament caused Newcastle bailiffs to clear a 'filthy and stinking' road near the friary which was a great annoyance and peril to the community. In 1464 after the Battle of Hexham the bodies of several executed lords were buried in the ch. Princess Margaret was entertained here in 1503 on her way to meet James IV to whom she was betrothed. There were frequent bequests throughout the life of the house. *Remains:* Some parts of the 13thC Wall Tower survive in the SE corner of Carliol Square. Site of ch. lies beneath Holy Jesus Hospital. Part excavated 1970–1, also E range of the cloister – Med. Arch. Vols. 15 & 16.

Newcastle upon Tyne *Friary. N'land. Map 1. (–1262 to 1539). Carmelite. F: John de Byker (gave land). Ded: St Mary.* Distinction of York. 1st. f. at Wall Knoll, but being seriously disturbed by construction of a new town wall they moved in 1307 to a new site vacated by the Sack Friars, on condition that the sole surviving friar there was given subsistence for life. A breach of sanctuary occurred in 1312 when persons were taken from the ch. and beheaded. The culprits were cudgelled. Site enlarged in 1337 and in 1361 the friars gave the Trinitarians their old Wall Knoll property. In 1424 the warden publicly retracted an accusation against the vicar of Newcastle concerning offerings of candles. *Remains:* A blocked arch and some masonry in Forth Street (Pevsner). Site excavated 1965 & 1967. The last remains between Forth Street and Orchard Street stood until the middle of the 18thC (Brand). Excav. notes: Archaeologia Aeliana, Vol. 13 (1889), & Vol. 46 (1968). Desc. & plans: Soc. of Antiq. of N'castle, Vol. 6 (1933–4).

Newcastle upon Tyne *Friary. N'land.*
Map 1. (−1239 to 1539). Dominican.
Fs: Sir Peter Scott and Nicholas his
son. Ded: unknown.
Visitation of York. 3 pious sisters
probably gave the site on which the
friary stood 'whose names have been
ungratefully forgotten' (Brand). An
aqueduct built by the friars also
supplied much of the town with
water. Site enlarged 1318. Mis-
demeanours by several apostate
brethren prohibited them from
receiving their Master Degrees in
1390. A layman requiring water for
his fishpond in 1476 was given
permission to tap a supply from the
friars in a pipe 'large enough to
admit a wheaten straw' (Brand).
Remains: 3 sides of the cloister with
bldgs. of 2 storeys including: late-
13thC chapter house on the E;
refectory on the S and older fragments
on the W; all with modern alterations. Ch. lay to the N and was
destroyed to rebuild North Shields
lighthouse, Site 'cleaned-up' 1957−
8. Desc: Archaeologia Aeliana, Vol.
17 (1920). Site of ch. part excavated
1963−4, and cloister area 1973−4:
Med. Arch. Vols. 8, 9, 18 & 19.

Newcastle upon Tyne *Friary. N'land.*
(−1237 to 1539). Franciscan.
(Conventual/Observant). F: unknown,
probably member(s) of the Carliol
family. Ded: St Francis.
Custody of Newcastle. A famous
Franciscan, Duns Scotus (Dr John
Scot) entered the Order here in
1300; and a learned Carmelite
obtained his D.D. and changed to
this Order where he died in 1336. A
stone conduit supplying water to the
friary and the town was diverted
from the friars one night in 1342,
and 'because of the abuse of the
favour' the king gave the friars sole

use of the water supply (Brand). In
1498 the house was transferred to
the Observants who were later imprisoned when the Order was
suppressed in 1534. From 1536 until
the Dissolution, Conventual friars
were back again. *Remains:* None.
The site lay between Pilgrim Street
and High Friar Street. (Note: An
attempt to establish a house of
Franciscan nuns in the town failed
in 1286).

Newcastle upon Tyne *Friary. N'land.*
(1267−1307). Friars of the Sack.
F: Robert de Bruce (gave land). Ded:
unknown.
No history. In 1300 Edward I gave
money to the friars (as he did to
each of the other Orders of friars at
that time living in the town) during
a visit. In 1307 one friar remained
and the house and property was given
to the Carmelites on the understanding
that he was supplied for life 'in a
manner becoming to his rank'.
Remains: None. Note: Archaeologia.
Vol. 3, p. 130.

Newcastle upon Tyne *Friary. N'land.*
(1361−1539). Trinitarian. F: William
de Acton. Ded: St Michael.
Also known as Holy Trinity Hospital
and occupied the site at Wall Knoll
vacated by the Carmelites in 1307.
The first warden, Wm. Wakefield,
came from Berwick where the Order's
efforts to establish a house were
frustrated by the bp. of Durham. It
was a requirement of the F. that 3
beds were always kept prepared for
'accidental guests'. In 1480 Ralph
Widdrington, knighted for valour in
a campaign against Scotland, and his
wife were given 'the privileges of the
house and the Order' by the master.
Remains: None. Some minor ruins

survived until the end of the 18thC (Brand).

Newhouse *Abbey. Lincs.*
See Newsham.

Newenham *Abbey. Devon. Map 5.*
1m SW of Axminster. (1247–1539).
Cistercian monks. F: Reginald de
Mohun. (Sir Wm. de Mohun, brother
of Reginald, sometimes given as
co-F.). Ded: St Mary.
Colonised from Beaulieu. Both
brothers buried in the ch. In 1265
the abbot went to Beaulieu and
resigned. Curiously a new colony of
monks was despatched to Newenham
who possessed the abbey while the
existing inmates were sent 'on various
errands'. The whole episode was
termed 'a fraudulent device of the
devil'. The Black Death, 1349,
carried off 20 monks and 3 lay-
brothers leaving only the abbot and
2 monks. Henry VII stayed at the
abbey for a week in 1497 but nothing
is known of the circumstances.
Extensive details of property and land
in B.M. and cartulary in Bodleian
Lib., Oxford. *Remains:* Minor
fragments. W end of S wall of the
nave, E part of refectory and some
of its W wall. Book: Hist. of Newenham Abbey (1843), J. Davidson.
Note: Arch. J. Vol. 37.

Newminster *Abbey. N'land. Map 1.*
1m W of Morpeth. (1138–1537).
Cistercian monks. F: Ranulf de
Merlay. Ded: St Mary.
Colonised from Fountains. Destroyed
by the Scots in the year of its completion (probably only wooden bldgs.);
and so frequently were the bldgs.
devastated that repair was impossible.
The monks were reduced to extreme
poverty and no aid was given to the
poor. However, it eventually became

one of the largest Cist. houses in the
N of England. Several visitations in
the 15thC by abbots from other
Cist. houses resulted in severe
penances for lax living (VCH).
Records survive of grants, gifts and
revenues of the abbey together with
details of the abbots' lives and the
lists of obits (Hodgson). The monks
made a temporary return to their
house after suppression in 1536 in
defiance of Cromwell's commissioners. *Remains:* Little other than
exposed fdns. and some masonry of
a chancel chapel. Many fragments
in situ including a reconstructed
section of open arcading on a dwarf
cloister wall. Excavated 1961–5.
Desc. & plan: Archaeologia Aeliana,
Vol. 42 (1964). Also Med. Arch.
Vols. 6–10. (The ch. was said to be
similar in appearance to those at
Kirkstall and Quarr in the 12thC –
Knowles).

New Minster *(Hyde) Abbey. Hants.*
See Winchester.

Newnham *(Newenham) Priory. Beds.*
E suburb of Bedford. (c. 1165–1540).
Augustinian canons. F: Simon de
Beauchamp. Ded: St Paul.
Formerly a collegiate ch. fd. pre-
Conquest in the town but moved by
the canons to the outskirts c. 1180.
Unusually rich in spiritualities with
14 chs. A large house about equal
with Newburgh (i.e. about 26 canons
at its peak). It seems that the F's. son
was no friend of the community and
he opposed the election of a prior.
Little known of internal history.
The records of visitations in 1235,
1249, 1322 & 1431 contain no
charges against the community. In
1387 the bp. ordered peace to be
established with the nearby Aug.
priory of Caldwell, but the cause of

231

dissent is unknown. No details of the surrender survive. *Remains:* Very little. Perhaps a length of wall. Until recent years the precinct survived with rampart and moat on 3 sides (R. Ouse on the 4th) enclosing an area of about 35 acres. Fishponds abound. Notes: Beds. Hist. Soc. J. for 1963–4; also Med. Arch. Vol. 16.

New Romney *(originally Romney) Friary. Kent. (c. 1241–c. 1287). Franciscan (Conventual). F: unknown. Ded: unknown.*
In 1241 Henry III granted the friars £100 to buy clothes out of the revenues of the archbishopric of Canterbury (VCH). Friar Richard of Devon, after many travels, lived here for the last 15 years of his life 'worn out by quartan fevers'. *Remains:* None.

Newsham *(Newhouse) Abbey. Lincs. 10m NW by W of Grimsby. (c. 1143–1536). Premonstratensian canons. F*: Peter de Goxhill. Ded: St Mary & St Martial.*
Colonised from Licques, near Boulogne, and the 1st. house of the Order in England. It seems that the relics of St Martial in the Cluniac abbey of Limoges (with which the F. was associated) were transferred to Newsham c. 1163 because of its claims to have authority over 9 daughter houses at that time (Colvin). The canons were involved in a long lawsuit with the nuns of Elstow over the ownership of a ch. benefice. Finally the nuns were ordered 'to molest the canons no further' after an award in favour of Newsham. In 1385 poverty followed pestilence, barren lands, expensive hospitality and severe storms – which rendered bldgs. ruinous. From 1475–8 an aged and infirm abbot was unable to understand the failing discipline of his house, and 5 of his canons were charged with apostasy. Injunctions in 1482 and 1488 ordered the keeping of silence 'the very key of religious life' (VCH), and in 1491 a canon was excommunicated for the third time. But the last 30 years of the abbey's history reveals high standards of monastic life. *Remains:* None.
* Some refs. give Ralph de Bayeux as co-founder.

Newstead *(by Stamford) Priory. Lincs. 2m E of Stamford, nr. Uffington. (–1247 to 1536). Augustinian canons. F: William d'Albini IV. Ded: St Mary.*
1st. f. –1200 by Wm. d'Albini III as a hospital of 13 beds, and his son seems to have changed the endowment before 1247 into a priory. Small, ill-endowed and insignificant, with very little recorded history. In 1440 there was a prior and three canons listed though one was ill and another lived elsewhere. Shortly before the Dissolution, poverty and the smallness of the community caused the omission of several requiem services from the canons' duties, resulting in the withholding of rent by a tenant for which he was sued (VCH). The bps. who visited the house had no quarrel with it other than to deplore the poverty. *Remains:* None.

Newstead *(on Ancholme) Priory. Lincs. Map 3. 1¾m S of Brigg. (1171–1538). Gilbertine canons. F: Henry II. Ded: Holy Trinity.*
Although 1171 is the first definite record, a fdn. agreement signed by 6 Gilb. priors and 2 other persons in 1164 suggests an earlier date (Knowles). The sale of wool was the

232

principal source of income at 10 sacks p.a. in the 14thC. The Black Death had exceptionally severe effects upon the economy of the house. Some 100 years later Edward IV relieved the canons of part of 'exhorbitant' rents. *Remains:* Site occupied by farm in which one room is vaulted with circular arches and octagonal piers, perhaps part of the refectory. In a W wall of a room upstairs is a 3-light Perp. window (Pevsner).

Newstead *Priory. Notts. Map 3. 9m N of Nottingham. (c. 1170– 1539). Augustinian canons. F: Henry II. Ded: St Mary.* Some refs. give f. date as *c.* 1163 based upon existing undated fdn. charter witnessed by an archbp. (1163–74). 13thC cartulary survives. The convent was found to be 'fervid in religion' in 1252, and 6 years later the prior was advised 'in these evil days' to greet guests with a smile (VCH). The 13thC history reveals debts, lack of discipline, discord and poverty, the last of which may have been furthered by the costly visits of Edward I in 1280 & 1290 and Edward II in 1307 & 1315. Very little known of internal life from *c.* 1330 until the Dissolution. The house escaped suppression in 1536 by paying the large fine of £233.6.8d. *Remains:* Fine late-13thC W front of ch. One of the few examples where the whole claustral complex is preserved in a mansion (Braun); including S transept of ch.; chapter house; warming room; refectory; kitchen and Prior's Lodging. Known as Newstead Abbey. Care: City of Nottingham. Desc. & plan: (1) Br. Arch. Assoc. J. Vol. 9 (1853); (2) Thoroton Soc. Trans. (Notts.), Vol. 23 (1919).

Nocton *Park Priory. Lincs. 7m SE of Lincoln. (t. of K. Stephen to 1536). Augustinian canons. F: Robert Darcy. Ded: St Mary Magdalene.* Seems the patrons kept a tight rein on the canons and protested at the appointment of priors without their consent. Several disputes occurred between Darcys and priors concerning trespass by the patrons. In 1440 a canon who was 'a disadvantage to the priory' was banished to St Osyth's. Little internal history known and only one visitation report survives. Order within the house was good, but some servants were insolent to the canons. *Remains:* None. Rising ground 1m E of the village marks the site. Some carved masonry revealed during ploughing in 1971 (Med. Arch. Vol. 17). Note: Archaeologia, Vol. 40, p. 235.

Norman's Barrow − 1 *(S. Raynham) Priory. Norfolk. 4½m SSW of Fakenham. (c. 1160–c. 1200). Augustinian canons. F: William de Liseurs. Ded: St Mary & St John Evangelist.* Very little known of the brief history. About 1181 the prior and canons, with the consent of the F., fd. the priory of Crabhouse (*v.* above) for Aug. canonesses. Then followed:

Norman's Barrow − 2 *Alien Cell/ Cell. Norfolk. Location as above. (c. 1200–1537). Cluniac monks. F: Godfrey de Liseurs, son of William. Ded: St Mary & St John Evangelist.* About 1200 the property became the cell of Castle Acre on condition that 3 monks lived here. It is not clear whether the canons went elsewhere or joined the Cluniac Order. Became denizen *c.* 1373 at the same time as the mother house. Apart from evidence that the cell had possessions in 5 parishes, its history is blank. *Remains:* None.

Northallerton *Friary. Yorks. NR. (c. 1356–1538). Carmelite. F: Edward III. Ded: BVM.* Other refs. give the Fs. as Thomas Hatfield, bp. of Durham, *and/or* John Yole and Helena his wife, by licence from Edward III. VCH gives details of various bequests, but no other history. *Remains:* None.

Northampton *Abbey. N'hants. (c. 1150–1538). Augustinian canons. F: William Peverel II of Nottingham. Ded: St James.* Some early refs. give fdn. as *c.* 1104 but recent researches reveal it came into existence late in the r. of K. Stephen (Dickinson). 14thC cartulary in BM. Community owned farms in 30 parishes. No entries in diocesan registers throw any light on internal history (VCH). Between 1237 & 1446 at least 20 triennial general chapters of the Order were held here. House held in great esteem by the town especially in the 16thC; and was referred to as 'Stately' and in good repair. Many people of distinction sought interment in the abbey ch. Despite an income in 1536 in excess of £200 p.a. and an exceptionally good report on the canons, the community was forced to pay the huge fine of £333.6.8d. to survive. *Remains:* None. Part of the abbey's precinct wall exists in Weedon Road, and there is the name Abbey Street.

Northampton *Alien Priory/Priory. N'hants. (1093–1538). Cluniac monks. F: Simon St Liz (Leez) I, earl of Northampton. Ded:*

St Andrew. Well endowed with spiritualities including *all* the chs. in Northampton. Even though the house was large and important, it was unpopular with the townsfolk mainly due to some abuses of their established customs by the French priors, and a variety of jealousies. Frequent absence of the prior, poor harvests, royal dues and heavy exactions from Rome brought debts in the 14thC. Surviving records of visitations by other priors reveal valuable insights into Cluniac conditions and discipline. 13thC cartulary in BM. The constant succession of custodians to the priory during the wars with France brought the house to the verge of ruin and the aid of Henry IV in 1405, when the house became denizen, started an era of recovery. Due to the central location of the priory in the country, 39 of the 40 general chapters of the Benedictine Order were held here between 1338 & 1498. *Remains:* None. Much of the site was quickly cleared after the Dissolution. Partial excavations in 1970 revealed no evidence of bldgs., but 12 burials were found. The priory ch. probably stood just NW of the junction of Priory Street and Harding Terrace. Med. Arch. Vol. 15.

Northampton *Delapré Abbey. N'hants. Map 3. (c. 1145–1538). Cluniac nuns. F: Simon St Liz (Leez) II, earl of Northampton. Ded: St Mary.* 1st. fd. at Fotheringhay (*v.* above). House never seems to have been considered alien perhaps due to subjection to diocesan control. 4 Scottish kings gave benefactions to the abbey: Malcolm IV, William I, Baliol & David II. In early 14thC several nuns forsook their religion while others bitterly opposed Bp. Dalderby's restrictions of a freedom they were thoroughly enjoying – 'shamelessly casting aside the modesty of their sex'. Records of 15thC visitations infer a healthier state of affairs. In 1459 the community took charge of the Cistercian nunnery of Sewardsley (*v.* below). The Battle of Northampton (1460) took place next to the nunnery and after the fight Henry VI, the archbp. of Canterbury and the bp. of London rested in the priory, and many of the slain were buried in the churchyard. In 1536 the suppression was postponed on payment of £266.13.4d, and the Crown visitor wrote that 'the house was prettily stored with cattle and corn'. *Remains:* Maybe some remnants of the S wall of the ch. survive in bldgs. of the County Record Office on the site, which surround the original cloister. Book: History of Delapré Abbey (1909) R. M. Sergeantson.

Northampton *Friary. N'hants. (1323–1538). Austin. F: John Longeville. Ded: unknown.* Limit of Oxford. In 1330 George Longeville enlarged the friars' close. Singularly little history. The ch. had an image of considerable repute to which several women willed some of their possessions. At the surrender the friars tried hard to save their small property, which earned the prior the wrath of the commissioners, and they were placed under guard. There seems to have been some unauthorised disposal of plate by the prior who was sent to prison. *Remains:* None. The leaded roof went to the king's lodge at Grafton Regis (VCH). Note: Archaeologia, Vol. 10, p. 67.

Northampton *Friary. N'hants. (–1265 to 1538). Carmelite. Fs: Simon de Montfort I and Thomas Chitwood. Ded: BVM.* Distinction of Oxford. Very little history. In 1275 a package left at the priory was found to contain 2 stolen coats of mail. The robbers escaped leaving their horses behind – also stolen from the same address (VCH). 3 years later the community wished to enclose part of the town wall but was refused because 'the sick often walked on the wall from one gate to another to take the air'. The friars' ch. was large and contained a renowned image of the BVM. One 12thC scholar of this house was celebrated for his 'perpetual almanack to find every year for ever . . . and the aspects of the heavens, the changes of the moon . . . throughout the year'. *Remains:* None. The ch. fdns. were uncovered in 1846 and now lie beneath Kerr Street.

Northampton *Friary. N'hants. (–1233 to 1538). Dominican. F: unknown. Bp. Hugh Wells certainly involved. Ded: unknown.* Visitation of Oxford. Considerable details of grants in VCH. The friary took 67 years to complete and received special benefactions from royalty. In 1239 Henry III gave 10 marks for each friar to cover food costs at a provincial chapter, as well as supplying several casks of wine. A famous Dominican, Robert Holcot, D.D., a professor of Scripture who wrote 26 treaties on theology, died here during the Black Death while ministering to the sick. In 1454 the English Premonstratensian abbots held a general chapter in the friars' hall (*v.* Beeleigh). *Remains:* None. The site was close to the Horsemarket.

235

Northampton *Friary. N'hants.*
(1226–1538). Franciscan (Convent-
ual). F: Sir Richard Gobion. Ded:
St Francis.
Custody of Oxford. The F. gave the
2 friars, who had arrived from
Oxford, a site outside the E gate.
c. 1235 the citizens gave the friars
a new site within the town. The
recorded history is bleak. In 1277
the community regained possession
of a cart and 2 horses, impounded
by the city fathers, because a man
had been killed by the cart. In 1460
the Duke of Buckingham, slain at the
Battle of Northampton, was buried
here. Shortly after the Dissolution
Leland said that 'the Grey Friars had
the best builded and largest house of
all the friars, and it stood a little
beyond the market place'. *Remains:*
None. Excavations in 1971 uncovered part of the ch. and one of
the N–S ranges, perhaps the dorter.
Med. Arch. Vol. 17.

Northampton *Abbey (?) N'hants.*
(–1252 to +1272). Franciscan nuns.
Very little known. 5 sisters
apparently living a conventual life
here in 1252 (Martin). The house,
said to be near the Dominican friary,
was short-lived and the only recorded
fact is that the sheriff was under
instruction to provide the nuns with
5 tunics of russet every 2 years
(VCH). It seems possible that the
little community finally moved to
London. *Remains:* None.

Northampton *Friary. N'hants.*
(–1271 to c. 1300). Sack Friars.
Very little known. In 1271 the friars
received a grant from Henry III for
building their ch. (Knowles). The
house finally disappeared between
1300 & 1303. *Remains:* None.

North Creake *Priory/Abbey. Norfolk.*
Map 4. 8m NW of Fakenham. (1206–
1506). Augustinian canons. F: Lady
Alice de Nerford, widow of Sir
Robert. Ded: St Mary.
1st. f. *c.* 1189 as a hospital by Sir
Robert and Alice de Nerford. In
1230 the F. granted the patronage
to Henry III who elevated the priory
into abbey status in the following
year. The cellarer's Account Roll
for 1331/2 gives exceptional insight
into the economic conditions
(Norfolk Arch. Vol. 6), and denotes
nothing that could be termed
luxurious living (VCH). A disastrous
fire *c.* 1484 (sometimes given as
1378) and perhaps due to arson
resulted in only partial restoration –
the nave and parts of the transepts
were demolished. A worse tragedy
was in store. Early in the 16thC the
community died of a pestilence
leaving only the abbot who, himself,
succumbed in 1506. The house was
purchased by the Countess of
Richmond, and in 1507 she used
the possessions to aid the refounding
of Christ's Coll., Cambridge.
Remains: Parts of transepts, crossing,
choir and chapels. The cloister area
survives with parts of the S & E
ranges and S wall of the ch. nave.
Ch. desc., plan & care: D of E. Hist:
Norfolk Record Soc. Vol. 35.

North Ferriby *Priory. Yorks. ER.*
7m W of Hull. (c. 1140?–1536).
Augustinian canons. F: Eustace Fitz
John (Some refs. give his son, Wm.
de Vescy). Ded: St Mary.
The fdn. was of the Order of St John
of Jerusalem, not the Knights
Templars (Knowles), and even in
1396 the canons were still known as
'the brethren of the Temple'. In
1271 a canon unaccountably claimed
to be the prior and, being disputed

by the convent, an enquiry was ordered by the archbp. The outcome is unknown. 100 years later Archbp. Thoresby gave orders in much detail on how a retired prior was to be treated — covering all eventualities such as blindness. At the close of the history there are frequent changes of priors, perhaps in order to secure as many pensions of a prior's status as possible. In common with many of the smaller Aug. houses details of internal life are far from complete. *Remains:* None.

North Ormsby *Priory. Lincs. 4½m NNW of Louth. (1148–54 to 1538). Gilbertine canons and nuns. F: Gilbert (fitz Robert) of Ormsby. Ded: St Mary.*
Negligible history. The endowments were considerable and the intention was to limit the community to 100 women and 50 men, but these totals were probably never reached. The 7 or 8 granges produced a profitable wool trade — an average of 8 sacks p.a. in early-14thC. Revenues fell greatly after the Black Death. The house had many manuscripts but few books (Graham). It survived suppression in 1536, despite low income, in common with other Gilb. houses. *Remains:* None. A Victorian house, Ormsby Abbey, stands on or near the site.

Norton *Priory/Abbey*. Cheshire. Map 2. 2½m E of Runcorn. (1134– 1536). Augustinian canons. F: Wm. Fitz Nigel, 2nd Baron of Halton.*
1st. f. at Runcorn *c.* 1115 (*v.* below) and perhaps colonised from Bridlington. Considerable land endowments in early years resulted in the priory becoming one of the larger houses of the Order, with massive rebldg. *c.* 1200. In 1236 fire destroyed the

ch. and cloister. The canons were highly skilled in tile making and original kilns survive. Bell-founding occurred on the site, possibly by travelling craftsmen, and a mould survives with replica bell. *c.* 1391 elevated to abbey status. Financial problems occurred in the first half of the 15thC due to flooding of abbey lands and disrepair of bldgs., but by 1529 the bp. reported the house in good order. The last abbot was imprisoned, with others, for refusing to surrender the abbey and a warrant was issued for their execution. The outcome is unknown. *Remains:* Excavations 1970–7 have revealed the whole plan and extensive tile flooring of the ch. which was 300 ft. long. Fine arcaded passage in W range, undercroft and well-preserved Norman doorway *c.* 1180. Excav. reports: Current Arch. Nos. 31 (1972) & 43 (1974); Desc: Arch. J. Vol. 123 (1966); Archaeologia, Vol. 33; and Med. Arch. Vols. 16–21. Museum on site.
* Known as Norton *Priory.*

Norwich *Cathedral-Priory. Norfolk. Map 4. (1096–1539). Benedictine monks. F: Herbert de Losinga (probably a nickname for he was a Norfolk man, not a Norman). Ded: Holy Trinity.*
Norman ground plan is less altered than any other English cathedral. The internal life is recorded from 1271–1539 in over 3,500 rolls and documents. It is a stormy history of the priory's relationship with barons and citizens which began at the end of the 13thC and lasted until the mid-15thC. Also a number of instances of storm and fire damage to the bldgs. As is often the case, the lives and influence of the bps. in a cath-pr. appear to eclipse those of

237

Norton Priory, Cheshire. Arcaded passage between the outer court and the cloister in the west (cellarer's) range.

the priors ruling the monastery. Some bps. were greatly revered by the laity and the professed alike; while another, the hated Bp. Beck, was poisoned by his own servant in 1343. So much interesting information is readily available that no other details are needed here. *Remains:* Splendid Norman ch. 14thC complete cloister. (Chapter house and Lady Chapel pulled down *c.* 1580). Two gateways, 13thC and 15thC, survive. Prior's lodging (now the Deanery) with fine hall *c.* 1280. 3 piers of the infirmary. Long arcaded wall of the refectory. Also the Norman locutory (now a choir school) in the angle

between W cloister wall and S wall of the ch. nave. Desc. & plan: Archaeologia. Vol. 106 (1949). Book: The Glories of Norwich Cathedral (1948) R. H. Mottram. Illus: Pitkin Pictorial.

Norwich *Priory. Norfolk. Map 4. (c. 1094–1538). Benedictine monks. F: Herbert de Losinga, 1st. bp. of Norwich (1091–1119). Ded: St Leonard.*
Built to accommodate several Bene. monks while the cath-pr. (*v.* above) was being built; and on its completion St Leonard's became a dependency for 7 or 8 monks after *c.* 1100.

238

Norton Priory, Cheshire. Thirteenth century kiln in which many of the mosaic tiles, found in situ in the choir of the church, were fired. It is built of clay blocks and waste tiles.

Very little history. The house was noted for images of Henry VI, St Mary, the Holy Cross and St Anthony which attracted many pilgrims; but, curiously, in the elaborate cath-pr. accounts for 1535, the only offerings named for this cell are those made to the image of St Leonard (VCH). *Remains:* In the grounds of an Edwardian house in St Leonard's Road are some fdn. walls a few feet high and a doorway. Nothing else.

Norwich *Cell. Norfolk.*
Adjacent to the chapel of St William* (the boy martyr who died *c.* 1144 and was buried in the cathedral-priory) there existed a small cell of Benedictine monks from the cath-pr.

The chapel was much visited by pilgrims. *Remains:* None. The site was on Mousehold (Monk's hold). * Originally ded. to St Catherine when used as a parish ch. f. *c.* 1068.

Norwich *Carrow Priory. Norfolk. Map 4. (c. 1146–1536). Benedictine nuns. F: unkown. K. Stephen granted lands outside the city. Ded: St Mary.*
A small nunnery existed within the city boundary until the new site was given for a ch. to be built. Priory received numerous benefactions from county families. In 1250 & 1280 the nuns needed the bp's. help to recover lands and rents due to them. The court rolls held by the prioress were burnt in 1327 when

239

Norton Priory, Cheshire. Late 12thC vaulted undercroft in the west (cellarer's) claustral range.

a rebellious peasantry attacked the priory. An anchoress known as St Juliana of Norwich lived here in the 15thC and was probably a nun of Carrow in her youth (VCH). The visitation of 1492 by the bp. was a searching ordeal but nothing was amiss — except an insufficiency of bread. Again in 1526 the house was in good order but the sacrist regretted that the house was without a clock. In 1532 the aged ladies were still in their peaceful cloister and of good report. *Remains:* Part of the W claustral range was converted into a house by the last prioress and is now the smaller, r. hand, part of a

larger property. Part of the ch. wall can be seen with Norman buttresses, and the SE crossing pier is recognisable. S wall of nave survives (Pevsner). Desc: Norfolk & Norwich Arch. Soc. Vol. 9. Book: Carrow Abbey (1889) W. Rye.

Norwich *Friary. Norfolk. Map 4. (−1289 to 1538). Austin. F: Roger Miniot (gave the friars a house). Ded: St Mary & St Augustine.*
Limit of Cambridge. VCH records series of site and house enlargements between 1290 & *c.* 1360, culminating with 'a fine ch. with cloister to the S'. In 1457 a widow left a

*Norton Priory, Cheshire. Fine example of late 12thC Norman doorway –
the best example in the county.*

241

bequest for a library to be built on condition that the names of her husband and herself were inscribed on every book rest. Several Norwich guilds held their services in the nave of the conventual ch. The Lady Chapel bore the name of Scala Celi (Ladder of Heaven) and was a great attraction to the devout in E. Anglia (VCH). *Remains:* Very little. A brewery occupies most of the site. There is a re-sited stone arch in a house in King Street which probably came from the friary. Site excavated *c.* 1820 and plan drawn. Again examined in 1968 when amendments to original plan were made. (Med. Arch. Vol. 13).

Norwich *Friary. Norfolk. (1256–1538). Carmelite. F: Philip de Cowgate. Ded: BVM.*
Distinction of Norwich. (F. assumed the name of the street in which he lived). The friars received several grants in the 14thC and began a large new ch. in the 1340s which was completed in 1382. Because the F. had been a merchant, the friars asked the mayor, sheriffs and citizens in 1486 to become their patrons instead of his descendants. The city gave the White Friars numerous privileges in gratitude. *Remains:* None. The site was E of Cowgate and reused material can be seen locally. In 1958 the footings of several monastic bldgs. were uncovered and numerous burials (perhaps 14thC) located. Med. Arch; Vol. 3.

Norwich *Friary. Norfolk. Map 4. (1226–1538). Dominican. F: Sir Thomas Gelham (gave the old parish ch., called Black Hall, N of the river). Ded: St John, Baptist.*
Visitation of Cambridge. Four sites

in all. *c.* 1307 moved to Sack Friars abandoned site S of the river where a new ch. and accommodation for 60 friars were built. When these bldgs. were destroyed by fire in 1413 the friars returned to Black Hall which they had retained. Finally, the community returned to their restored bldgs. S of the river in 1449. Since Edward II granted the licence to the Dominicans for the Sack Friars' house in 1307 he is named as the 2nd. F. Very little history. In 1534 the prior preached a long sermon in the presence of the city fathers who caused his arrest for alleged political allusion. He was released but was again in trouble in 1535. The outcome is unknown. *Remains:* Only English friars' ch. to survive so complete. Nave is St Andrew's Hall, chancel is Blackfriars Hall. Central tower fell 1712. Part of 14thC cloister walls survive and undercroft of a chapel next to the lost chapter house. W range almost complete. Notes & plan: Norfolk Arch. Soc. J. Vol. 22 (1925); Note: Archaeologia, Vol. 5, p. 26; Arch. J. Vol. 106 (1949); Br. Arch. Assoc. J. Vol. 14 (1858). Plan of N claustral range recovered in 1974 (Med. Arch. Vol. 19).

Norwich *Friary. Norfolk. (1226–1538). Franciscan (Conventual). F: John de Hastingford (gave site). Ded: unknown.*
Custody of Cambridge. Very little known of internal history. VCH gives details of the numerous grants of land and the extension of bldgs. The 14thC ch. was built on a grand scale with cloister to the N. It seems that the entire community perished in the Black Death (Hutton). The convent possessed a fine library which was destroyed at the Dissolution. *Remains:* None. The bldgs. were

mainly demolished in 1564 and business premises now occupy the site. Desc: History of Norfolk, Vol. 4 (1806) Blomefield.

Norwich *Friary. Norfolk. (1253–c. 1307). Pied Friars. F: unknown. Ded: unknown.*
There would appear to be considerable doubt about the fdn. as 3 different fraternities are mentioned. The site was at the NE corner of the churchyard of St Peter Mountergate. It ceased to exist c. 1307 and became a coll. of priests. *Remains:* None.

Norwich *Friary. Norfolk. (c. 1258–c. 1307). Sack Friars. F: unknown. Ded: unknown.*
The house was in the parish of St Peter of Hungate. Only one friar remained in 1306–7 and when the site was given to the Dominicans about that time, they were ordered to provide for his welfare. *Remains:* None. Note: Archaeologia, Vol 3, p. 30.

Nostell *Priory. Yorks. WR. 6m SE of Wakefield. (–1120 to 1539). Augustinian canons. Fs: Ralph Adlave (chaplain to Henry I), Ilbert de Lacy and Robert his son. Ded: St Oswald.*
1st. site (some 3m away) occupied by hermits c. 1114 whose ch. then ded. to St James. Robert introduced Aug. canons when building began on the new site c. 1119. In 1133 Prior Adelulf became 1st. bp. of Carlisle. The house was important and wealthy with 5 cells and over 30 chs. Financial setbacks in 14thC when (a) the community was owed £1,012, (b) the profits on produce from the Bamburgh estates did not mature, and (c) 1,200 sheep and 400 other stock died. Stringent economies were

enforced by the archbp. Within 44 years due to the counsel of 'wiser and older canons' there was a surplus in the treasury. In 1438 costly lawsuits were partly responsible for impoverishment, but in 1535 the house had one of the larger Aug. incomes. VCH gives considerable details of the original and subsequent grants and bequests. *Remains:* None. An 18thC mansion (N.T.) stands to the SE of the site. Some excavated carved stones stored in outbldgs. Note: Archaeologia, Vol. 35, pp. 32 & 41.

Notley *(Nutley) Abbey. Bucks. Map 6. 7m SW of Aylesbury. (c. 1160–1538). Augustinian canons. Fs: Walter Giffard, 2nd earl of Buckingham and Ermengard his wife. Ded: St Mary & St John, Baptist.*
A large house of perhaps 26 canons and the richest monastery in Bucks. Very little history survives for the 12th & 13thCs apart from lawsuits over land ownership. The canons took over responsibility for Chetwode Priory in 1460 (*v.* above). There is no evidence of unfavourable reports during its life of some 378 years, indeed the erring canons of Missenden were sent here for correction. Henry VIII stayed here in 1529. *Remains:* A large house incorporates the main monastic survival – the L-shaped abbot's lodging (hall, parlour & solar) abutting the W side of the cloister, and part of the W range. Also, SE corner of house occupies site of warming room and part of frater and uses some of the remains. A square 14thC dovecote lies to the N of the house. No remains of the ch. except the bases of 2 piers. Excavated 1930–3 & 1937. Desc. & plans: Oxoniensia, Vol. 6, 1941.

243

Nottingham *Priory (?). Notts.*
(c. 1170 to +1188). Augustinian
canons. F: Robert de St Remy.
Ded: St Sepulchre.
This was certainly a hospital in the
care of Aug. canons, but whether a
conventual establishment existed is
unproven. The Order of canons of
St Sepulchre began to lapse in 1188,
but the hospital continued until
c. 1307 — the date of the last record
(Knowles). *Remains:* None.

Nottingham *(Roche) Priory Cell.*
Notts. (? to +1405). Cluniac monks.
F. & Ded. unknown.
Knowledge of this small cell of
Lenton Priory is minimal. In 1405
a prior and only one monk lived here.
There would appear to be nothing
else known of the cell. The 'Archives
de la France Monastique' give the
name as Rockchapel, but records it
as dependent upon Montacute (VCH).
Remains: None.

Nottingham *Friary. Notts. (−1271 to*
1539). Carmelite. Fs: Lord Gray of
Wilton and Sir John Shirley. Ded:
BVM.
Distinction of Oxford (?). History
obscure. The list of donors to the
house given in VCH suggests the
town's affection for the White Friars.
Two friars became renowned writers
and preachers in the 14thC. In 1393
a citizen sought sanctuary in the ch.
after killing his wife. Unable to reach
him the town officials seized his
house and goods. Vandals caused
serious damage in 1482 & 1494. The
general popularity of the friars,
however, is clearly shown by the
continued generous and frequent
bequests. *Remains:* None. The site
lay between Friar Lane and St James'
Lane.

Nottingham *Friary. Notts. (−1230*
to 1539). Franciscan. (Conventual).
F: unknown. Ded: unknown.
Custody of Oxford. This popular
community constructed a quay by
the river 1236—7. In 1291 the warden
was ordered to supply preachers for
Nottingham, Newark and Bingham to
preach on the Crusades. A cross built
by the Grey Friars was referred to
in 1365. The house gave sanctuary to
felons on several occasions. The
friars received many bequests from
citizens. *Remains:* None. The site
was in the SW corner of Broad Marsh
and is commemorated by Grey Friars
Gate (in which stood the Grey Friars
Cross).

Nun Appleton *Priory. Yorks. WR.*
2m NW of Cawood. (c. 1150−1539).
Cistercian nuns. Fs: Eustace de
Merch and Alice de St Quintin his
wife. Ded: St Mary & St John,
Evangelist.
Alice and her son Robert made a
fresh grant to the nuns c. 1165. It
became one of the larger houses with
some 30 nuns. Records of visitations
occur from the second half of the
13thC and from the earliest occasions
lists of injunctions ensued. The admittance of secular women was 'not
conducive to the religious life of the
nuns' (VCH). Heavy expenses and
debt in 1306 resulted in the appointment of a custos to administer
financial affairs. Later that century
the archbp. ordered efficient servants
to replace those who were useless. In
1489 a list of injunctions was issued
in English and appears verbatim in
VCH. Although the net income was
far below £200 p.a. in 1535, the
house survived until 5.12.1539.
Remains: None.

Nunburnholme *Priory. Yorks. ER.*

244

*3m E of Pocklington. (t. Henry II –
1536). Benedictine nuns. F: A
member of the de Merlay family,
either William or Roger I. Ded:
St Mary.*
Very little known either of possessions or the internal and external
affairs. The one outstanding fact is
that Seton Priory in Cumberland
(Cumbria) was a cell, but why is
not known. A nun who had lived
here for 30 years left for 'a more
ascetic life elsewhere', but was soon
accepted back, became prioress, and
died in 1310. An injunction of 1318
ordered the nuns to refrain from
'gossiping with secular persons and
avoiding wearing adorning mantles'.
This was the smallest and poorest
house in the county which survived
until the Dissolution. *Remains:* None.

Nun Cotham *Priory. Lincs. 7m W of
Grimsby. (c. 1150–1539). Cistercian
nuns. F: Alan de Muncells. Ded:
St Mary.*
Bp. Hugh of Lincoln (enthroned
1186; was prior of Witham – *v.*
below) drew up a constitution to
limit the increasing community, and
to urge the nuns to withdraw from
secular affairs. The nuns suffered
severely at the time of the B.D.
Poverty resulted in women boarders
providing a much-needed income
but they brought the world into the
cloister. Several injunctions against
the practice were of no avail. In 1440
the bp. found no breaches of the
Rule nor any signs of luxury, but at
the evening compline a few nuns were
often absent being 'so busy tending
to their flowers'. Poverty persisted
and the poor quality of bread and
beer was a frequent complaint. The
last prioress was admonished for
living as if the house was for her
express use and for keeping her kinsfolk at the convent's expense. A
long list of injunctions was ordered
to be read in chapter once a month.
Remains: None. Note: Archaeologia,
Vol. 47, p. 50 & 55.

Nuneaton *Alien Priory/Priory. Warks.
Map 3. (c. 1155–1539). Benedictine
nuns. F: Robert Bossu, Earl of
Leicester. Ded: St Mary.*
1st. f, +1147 at Kintbury, Berks, on
lands granted by Bossu. The reason
for the move to Eaton (which then
became Nuneaton) is unknown.
Community was of the Order of
Fontevrault. The benefactions were
large and many distinguished ladies
took the veil here. The house had 89
nuns in 1328, reduced to about half
by the Black Death. As the French
wars prevented visitations by the
abbess of Fontevrault the pope
commissioned the bp. of Salisbury
to visit the priory. Sometime after
1412 it became denizen. In the
1460s the misrule of a prioress and
wasteful governance, in collusion
with a brother Simon, caused serious
debts and the house came under
Crown control. But in 1537 one laywoman was moved to write: 'Were it
not for the charity of the prioress I
know not to what straits I would have
been driven (VCH). *Remains:* The
parish ch. in Manor Court Road was
the nuns' ch. Largely rebuilt, there
survives the 12thC crossing piers and
S wall of the S transept. Site has been
excavated.

Nunkeeling *Priory. Yorks. ER. 4m NW
of Hornsea. (1152–1539). Benedictine nuns. F: Agnes de Arches. Ded:
St Mary Magdalene & St Helen.*
Described as Cistercian during its
history. In 1294 the archbp. found
the income hardly sufficient for the
nuns' food and clothes. The visitation

245

of 1314 resulted in a directive to the nuns who had been absent from services 'on account of being occupied by silkwork'. From the early years of the 14thC to the closing years of the 15thC there is a long silence. It is not known why the house escaped suppression in 1536 or why it was re-f. in 1537. *Remains:* None.

Nun Monkton *Priory. Yorks. WR. Map 3. 7m NW of York. (c. 1150– 1536). Benedictine nuns. Fs: Wm. de Arches and Ivetta his wife. Ded: St Mary.*
Fd. for Matilda, daughter of the Fs., who became first prioress. In the 13thC some land left to the nuns was in return for keeping the obits of a local squire, his wife and their daughter. In 1397 the archdeacon of Richmond was displeased to find the prioress wore grey furs and silk veils and indulged in 'festivities' in her chamber with one John Monkton. Her family were wealthy local land-owners and they clearly supplied any of the distaff side who entered the monastery with worldly goods. The house was small but not poor. VCH gives 2 instances of expenses incurred in the 'making' of a nun in the 15thC. *Remains:* The nave of the conventual ch. is the parish ch. with a Norman doorway in the W front. 14thC spiral staircase leads to an exquisite arcaded gallery. All else gone. A 17thC house occupies the site of the domestic bldgs.

Nunnaminster *Abbey. Hants.* *See* Winchester.

Nunthorpe *Priory. Yorks. NR. 3½m SE of Middlesborough. (c. 1167– c. 1189). Cistercian nuns. F: Ralph de Neville. Ded: St Mary.*

1st. f. at Hutton *c.* 1162 where the community cannot have remained for long. There is a ref. to land at 'Torp' – afterwards (and now) known as Nunthorpe. The community went to Baysdale *c.* 1189 but retained their possessions at Nunthorpe until the Dissolution. *Remains:* None.

O

Oldbury *Priory/Cell. Warks. 2m S of Atherstone. (c. 1068–c. 1130). Benedictine nuns. F: perhaps Walter de Hastings. Ded: St Lawrence.*
Soon after the Conquest Sir Robert Marmion expelled the nuns from the priory at Polesworth and they settled at their manor of Oldbury. *c.* 1130 Sir Robert's son, Robert II, and his wife Millicent restored Polesworth to the nuns. Oldbury continued as a cell of Polesworth. *Remains:* None.

Old Byland *Abbey. Yorks. NR. 6m NW by W of Helmsley. (1143–1147). Cistercian monks. F: Roger de Mow-bray. Ded: St Mary.*
1st. f. 1138 at Hood. Because the settlement was too close to Rievaulx the F. granted the monks a new site at Stocking (see below). *Remains:* None.

Orford *(Irford) Priory. Lincs. 7½m NE of Market Rasen (nr. Binbrook). (c. 1158–1539). Premonstratensian canonesses. F: uncertain. Ralph de Aubigny was a principal benefactor (Colvin). Ded: St Mary.*
No fdn. charter survives and very little is known about this small house. Ralph de Aubigny granted land and the ch. to Newsham Abbey between 1155–60. The abbot and canons of this house may have been the true Fs. (Knowles) as at Broadholme

246

(*v.* above). Poverty in 1341. A nun was excommunicated in 1491 for a breach of her chastity vow. No notices of visitations but Bp. Redman ordered that no nuns were to be admitted unless they could read or sing (VCH). *Remains:* None.

Orford *Friary. Suffolk. 10m E of Woodbridge. (c. 1295–1538). Austin. F: Robert Hewell gave land. Ded: Unknown.*
Limit of Cambridge. Building not begun until 1299. Lightning destroyed the house in 1363. Apart from a few records of grants in the 14thC there is no other history. *Remains:* None. Some re-used materials in houses on the site which was bounded by Quay Street and Bridge Street (L.G.).

Osney *(Oseney) Priory/Abbey. Oxon. W suburb of Oxford. (1129–1539). Augustinian canons. F: Robert d'Oilly II at the instance of Editha Forne his wife. Ded: St Mary.*
One of the wealthiest houses in the county with property in 120 localities. *c.* 1154 received abbey status. For 50 years in the 12thC the canons had a dispute with St Frideswide's over the ownership of an Oxford ch. For 50 years in the 13thC the canons operated a large banking business for Oxford residents (VCH). Discipline was high and in the 13thC a number of the canons became the heads of other Aug. monasteries. Mitred 1481. Not a scholarly house. Men came to the abbey to study at Oxford – not the reverse as sometimes claimed. By 1500 the house was in debt and in a poor state of repair. In 1520 a lax canon was excommunicated by the abbot who, in turn, was excommunicated by the bp. The community complained that the bp's. action

brought discredit to the abbey. At its peak perhaps 50 canons; at its close 13. *Remains:* None. Most of the site is occupied by railway property. A small 15thC outbldg. with a 16thC roof, probably of minor purpose, forms part of Osney Mill. (From 1539–46 the abbey ch. became the cathedral of the new diocese of Oxford).

Otham *Abbey. Sussex. 1m NE of Polegate. (–1183 to c. 1208). Premonstratensian canons. F: Ralph of Dene. Ded: St Mary & St Lawrence.*
VCH gives details of early endowments and grants. Bleak and unhealthy situation plus poor endowments made life untenable, and *c.* 1208 the patroness of Bayham Abbey, Ela de Sackville, gave the canons leave to move there. Otham became one of its granges. *Remains:* Some ruins of St Lawrence's chapel survive in a barn. A farm occupies the site.

Otley *Abbey. Oxon. 8½m NE of Oxford. (1137–1140). Cistercian monks. F: Robert Gait. Ded: St Mary.*
On arrival from Waverley the community erected temporary bldgs. The land soon proved unsuitable and the bp. of Lincoln gave the monks a site at Thame (*v.* below), to which they moved in 1140, retaining their property at Otley as a grange. *Remains:* None. Possibly Oddington Grange marks the site.

Ovingham *Priory Cell. N'land. Map 1. 10m W of Newcastle. (1378–1537). Augustinian canons. F: Gilbert de Umfraville III. Ded: St Mary.*
Probably the last house of the Order fd. in England. The F. gave the benefice of the ch. to Hexham so that a master and 2 canons could continue

247

the duties of hospitality there when Scottish raids caused them difficulties. No record exists of the housing arrangements but a vicarage must have been provided for the canons who performed the divine offices for the Umfravilles and Percys (VCH). At the Dissolution a master and 3 canons were still in possession of the cell. *Remains:* A 13thC ch., no doubt served by the canons, survives. The E end of the vicarage, S of the church-yard, is late 14thC and was probably built to house the 3 canons from Hexham and the vicar.

Owston *Abbey. Leics. Map 3. 5m W of Oakham. (−1161 to 1536). Augustinian canons. F: Robert Grimbald, Ch. Justice of England. Ded: St Andrew.*
Fdn. charter stipulates the canons should live under the Aug. Rule of Haughmond (i.e. Arrouaise). Despite its rank as an abbey it remained one of the smaller and poorer Aug. houses. In the 13th & 14thCs there were grants of several manors, but it seems the canons neglected to serve some of the parish chs. in the gift of the abbey (VCH). A visitation of 1440 revealed no serious faults; the bp. recorded his opinion that one of the canons was 'out of his wits'. In 1528 some friction occurred between the canons and the abbot complained that women had visited the abbey. *Remains:* In the parish ch., which has many 19thC additions and alterations, is much of the original chancel and the early-14thC tower at its NW angle are the sole remains of the abbey ch. Two Perp. doorways from the abbey bldgs. are incorporated in the vicarage (Pevsner).

Oxford *(St. Frideswide's) Priory/ (Cathedral). Oxon. Map 6. (1122−*

1524). Augustinian canons. Fs: Roger, bp. of Salisbury and Henry I aided the completion. Ded: Holy Trinity, St Mary & St Frideswide.
1st. f. as a nunnery *c.* 727 by Didan for his daughter Frideswide. Destroyed 1002 and rebuilt by K. Ethelred 1004. Monks and secular canons alternately held possession until it fell into disuse − to be restored by Roger +1122, probably on the Ethelred plan, and completed *c.* 1180. Damaged by fire 1190, though chapter house not rebuilt until mid-13thC. A school was connected with the priory and perhaps the earliest religious teachings occurred at St Frideswide's in the cloister − a tenuous connection with the origins of the University. The canons obtained a curious privilege from the pope by being permitted to wear their caps during devotions 'owing to the cold and damp nature of the site' (Wells). Wolsey suppressed the house in 1524 in order to endow his new fdn. of Cardinal Coll. on that site. His fall from grace in 1529 ended the venture by which time 3 bays of the nave of the conventual ch. and the W claustral range had been removed to make room for the E side of the pre-sent great quadrangle. *Remains:* Conventual ch. became cathedral and Christ Church Coll. chapel in 1546. Shrine of St Frideswide. N, E & part of S cloister walks; slype; 13thC chapter house with Norman doorway; refectory (now coll. rooms), and scanty remnants of dorter in Priory House. Desc: Oxoniensia, Vols. 26 & 27 (1961−2); Notes: Archaeologia, Vol. 2. Numerous books. Illus: Pitkin Pictorial.

Oxford *St Mary's College. Oxon. Map 6. (1435−1540). Augustinian canons. Fs: Thomas Holden and*

248

Elizabeth his wife. Ded: St Mary.
Fd. for Aug. canons studying theology
or canon law (Knowles). Previously
canons of Osney and canons from
other houses lodging there were
under no regular discipline hence the
need for a central coll. The rules
drawn up by the abbot of Osney still
exist (VCH). *Remains:* Lower part of
gatehouse outer gateway with some
traces of vaulting; and a cellar of the
W wing of St Mary's Coll. survives in
Frewen Hall belonging to Brazenose
Coll. A 15thC timber roof removed
from St Mary's Coll. chapel is now
on Brazenose Coll. chapel.

Oxford *Canterbury College. Oxon.*
(c. 1370–c. 1539). Benedictine
monks. F: Archbp. Whittlesea. Ded:
St Peter.
1st est. 1331 by Christchurch,
Canterbury, for 4 monks. Re-f. 1363
by Archbp. Islip for 8 secular clerks
and 4 monks. Finally the F. expelled
the seculars in 1370 and reinstated monks. In later years monks
from other Bene. monasteries e.g
Rochester, Battle, Evesham & Peterborough rented rooms here. In 1462
the head of Gloucester Coll. (see
below) complained that the monks
here did not observe the Bene. Rule
concerning the eating of meat. At
the Dissolution the bldgs. were
acquired by Christ Church. *Remains:*
None. Canterbury Quad occupies the
site immediately to the E of the
Library.

Oxford *Durham College. Oxon. Map*
6. (c. 1381–1540). Benedictine
monks. F: Bp. Thomas de Hatfield.
Ded: St Mary(?).
1st. f. 1286 as a house of studies by
Prior Hugh of Durham and completed
by Prior Richard in 1291.(Knowles).
Prior Richard is cited by VCH as F.

of the coll., but Bp. de Hatfield left
endowments for transferring the cell
into a coll. which his executors put
into effect. New statutes were made
covering the numbers of student
monks and subjects for study. Ceased
to be monastic in 1540 and 9 secular
persons surrendered the house in
1544. *Remains:* Absorbed in Trinity
Coll. which comprises Durham Quad
with a little of the E range (1417–21)
and part of the 14thC W range.

Oxford *Gloucester College. Oxon.*
Map 6. (c. 1283–1538). Benedictine
monks. F: John Giffard, Baron of
Brimsfield. Ded: St John, Evangelist
& St Benedict.
A general house of studies at first
affiliated to Gloucester Abbey but
later many other houses staffed the
coll. including Whitby, Glastonbury,
Malmesbury, St Augustine's Canterbury, Pershore and Abingdon, who
were called upon to support their
own students. The house was presided
over by a prior. In 1321 the coll.
bought the vacated Carmelite property and extended its premises. Building seems to have been slow and the
chapel was still unfinished in 1426.
One of the ordinances of the Bene.
synod who controlled the coll. was
that the monks should be able to
preach when they returned to their
monasteries (VCH). *Remains:* The
site lay at the centre of the present
Worcester Coll. The 15thC, 2-storey
S range which comprised camerae, or
chambers, with what was once the
kitchen at the W end. In the N range
a chapel, hall in the W and library in
the E range. There is one window SE
of the S range which may have survived from the Carmelite house.

Oxford *St Bernard's College. Oxon.*
Map 6. (1437–c. 1542). Cistercian

249

monks. F: Archbp. Chichele. Ded:
St Mary & St Bernard.
The house was in the charge of a
'provisor'. In 1449 the coll. was given
certain rules which survive in a
damaged condition. A Cistercian
decree of 1482 ordered every monastery of 12 monks to send one to
Oxford, and where there were 26,
two should be sent. This should have
resulted in some 60 student monks in
residence on occasions. Possibly the
coll. survived until 1542 as it was
then stated that a rent was due to it.
It became St John's Coll. *Remains:*
The gate-tower and part of the Front
Quad, W range, of 1439; E part of the
Hall of 1501–2 and chapel 1530, N
range; the S range *c.* 1439. The E
range was never completed by the
monks. Below the 15thC buttery in
the N range is a well-preserved vaulted
cellar (Pevsner).

Oxford *Friary. Oxon. (c. 1266–1538).
Austin. Fs: Henry III and Sir John
Handlow. Ded: unknown.*
Limit of Oxford. Community well
established by 1289. In the 14thC
Edward II and Edward III gave land.
A University statute of 1326 ordered
all Faculty of Art students studying
for the B.A. to attend at the friary
twice each year – 'once to dispute
and once to respond'. Many friars of
the Order came here to study, the ch.
serving as a School of Theology and
the refectory and chapter house being
used as classrooms. The library was
located at the end of the dormitory.
The number of students exceeded 50
at the peak in the early 14thC. Financial difficulties caused a decline
later in that century. *Remains:* None.
The site is occupied by Wadham Coll.

Oxford *Friary. Oxon. (1256–1538).
Carmelite. F: Nicholas de Meules*

gave the site. Ded: BVM.
Distinction of Oxford. Perhaps the
largest house of the Order in England.
Many friars noted for their learning
studied here. The 1st. site in Stock-
well St was abandoned in 1318 for a
new site by the N Gate when Edward
II gave the community his manor
known as the Palace of Beaumont. At
the same time the friars at Sheen
moved to this new house. Undesirable
persons in the neighbourhood who
hindered the devotions of the friars
were removed by the mayor and
bailiffs. A longstanding dispute with
Gloucester Coll. flared into combat
in 1534. *Remains:* None. Beaumont
Street covers part of the site.
Materials went to St Frideswide's
Priory and St John's Coll. library
extension.

Oxford *Friary. Oxon. Map 6. (1221–
1538). Dominican. F: 1st. site: unknown. 2nd. site: Isabel de Bolbec,
Countess of Oxford. Ded: St Mary.*
Visitation of Oxford. Considerable
history in VCH, and of 12th–14thC
bequests. When the site in the Jewry
(St Aldgate's) became too small, the
community moved in 1245 to a river-
island in St Ebbe's. The 'Mad Parliament' was held here in 1258 and,
later, general and provincial chapters.
In 1370 some of the students rebelled
against actions of a provincial prior;
but the schools of philosophy and
theology here produced a continuous
flow of learned men. The bps. of
Lincoln had a lodging in the friary for
use when visiting the city. Very little
known about the library. During their
history the friars had several quarrels
with other communities. *Remains:* A
gateway in a rear wall of the Centre
for the Deaf in Norfolk Street is the
sole relic. Site excavated 1961–74
and plan of ch. obtained. Part of W

claustral range located and much of the E range including the chapter house. Med. Arch. Vols. 6, 7, 14, 17, 18 & 19. (The Dominican Order reopened a house in Oxford in 1921.)

Oxford *Friary. Oxon. (1224–1538). Franciscan (Conventual). Fs: uncertain. Robert le Mercer, Richard the Miller and Robert Owen gave the 1st., 2nd. & 3rd. houses.*
The last site was outside the town wall and building commenced in 1245. Richard, earl of Cornwall, was a chief benefactor and his heart was buried here 1272, as was his 3rd. wife. The friary's famous schools owed their origin to Agnellus of Pisa who led the first mission to England. Robert Grosseteste was a theological lecturer here from c. 1230 until he became bp. of Lincoln in 1235. During this time a great reputation for learning began. By 1292 the burden of numerous students was too heavy for the community and foreign friars were sent to London and Cambridge as well. The house had 2 libraries with numerous books bequeathed by Grosseteste in 1253. VCH gives details of many bequests. In 1309 the friars took over the vacated Sack Friars premises. During the last 3 years of the house's existence many friars departed from what had at one time been the greatest of the friaries. *Remains:* None. Excavations 1968–73 revealed the complete plan of the ch. before the redevelopment of the Westgate Centre began. S & W corners of cloister located and the extent of the domestic bldgs. Med. Arch. Vols. 13, 14, 15 & 18. Hist: Oxford Hist. Soc. J. Vol. 20 (1892). Book: The Grey Friars in Oxford (1892) A. G. Little.

Oxford *Friary. Oxon. (1261–c. 1309).*

Sack Friars. F: unknown. Henry III granted licence to build. Ded: unknown.
Many friars from other houses were sent here to study. In 1264 the king gave the convent the ch. of St Budoc* which adjoined their site. Following the suppression of the Order in 1274 the property was finally bought by the Franciscans in 1309 whose house was next door. *Remains:* None.
* 6thC bp. associated with Cornwall and Brittany.

Oxford *Friary. Oxon. (c. 1286–1538). Trinitarian. F: unknown. Edmund, Earl of Cornwall gave land. Ded: Holy Trinity.*
Sometime before 1307 the community obtained land and a shop from St Frideswide's (VCH). In 1312 the friars left their site outside the E Gate for another within the city walls. The Black Death was particularly fatal and only one friar served the E Gate chapel, and he came from Hounslow (VCH). The mayor and burgesses obtained possession of the house in 1486 but it was leased back to the provincial at an agreed rent, when it became known as Trinity Hall. After the suppression the deserted property did not survive long. *Remains:* None.

Oxford *Friary. Oxon. (1342 to +1362) Crutched (i.e. Holy Cross Friars). F: unknown. Simon de Gloucester (of Oxford) gave the site. Ded: Holy Cross.*
Moved to new site near E Gate 1349 to land owned by Merton Coll., whose fellows set down certain regulations which the friars accepted. Building was begun, soon to be halted by the bp. of Lincoln. In 1352 the community held services elsewhere and due to continued opposition and

251

perhaps the ravages of the Black
Death, they seem to have succumbed
in the early 1360s. *Remains:* None.
Even the location is unknown.

Oxford *See also* Osney and Rewley.

Oxney *Cell. N'hants. 2½m NE of
Peterborough. (−1272 to 1538).
Benedictine monks. F: An estate first
acquired by Athelwold, bp. of Winchester, in 972 for Peterborough
Abbey. Ded: St Mary.*
Re-f. −1272 and dependent upon
Peterborough. Although given as a
cell in 'Medieval Religious Houses'
(Knowles & Hadcock), all other refs.
define the property as a *grange* and
its presence in this work may be in-
appropriate. The cell certainly served
as a country retreat for the prior and
monks who needed convalescence or
meditation. At least 2 abbots who
resigned their office ended their days
here. *Remains:* Very little. Several
buttresses to the much-altered grange
and perhaps traces of fdns. in a field
to the S.

P

Partney *Cell/Manor. Lincs. 10m NW
by W of Skegness. (−1318 to c. 1538).
Benedictine monks. F: unknown.
Ded: St Mary Magdalene.*
There was an abbey here in the 7thC
destroyed by Danes *c.* 870. At the
beginning of the 12thC Gilbert of
Ghent gave a chapel to the monks of
Bardney, and a hospital was fd. by
Gilbert's son +1115. In the early
14thC the hospital became a purely
Bene. cell, and its use was mainly for
the benefit of resigned Bardney
abbots (VCH), and no separate
history survives. By 1535 the

property is described as a manor.
Remains: None.

Penrith. *Friary. C'land (Cumbria).
(1291−1539). Austin. F: unknown.
John de Capella gave land. Ded: St
Mary & St Augustine.*
Limit of York. A series of grants
resulted in the estate being enlarged
early in the 14thC. In 1360 & 1365
the inadequacies of voluntary alms
resulted in bps. granting incomes to
the friars from local chs., and a 40-
day indulgence was given to those
who contributed goods to help
maintain a sacred light (VCH). Little
other history. The house was always
poor especially after the B.D.
Remains: None. A house named The
Friary and a street known as Friars'
Gate are the sole remembrances. Trial
excavations in 1970 suggest that the
fdns. of the friary lie beneath the
present house and outbldgs. Med.
Arch. Vol. 15.

Pentney *Priory. Norfolk. Map 4. 8m
SE of King's Lynn. (c. 1130−1537).
Augustinian canons. F: perhaps
Robert de Vaux. Ded: Holy Trinity,
St Mary & St Mary Magdalene.*
A large house well endowed with
lands, advowsons of several chs., a
mill and 2 salt pans. Colonised from
Brinkburn. The F's son entered the
monastery and became its second
prior. The canons succeeded in holding on to their lands in 1167 after the
Earl of Norfolk had unlawfully seized
them. Wormegay Priory's poverty
resulted in it becoming a cell of Pentney in 1486. The few surviving
records of visitations call for no
injunctions against the canons. In
1536 Cromwell's visitors Legh and
Ap Rice were clearly guilty of slander
against the house, for later that year
the county commissioners tried to

halt closure because the canons 'did so much for the poor of the district' (VCH). *Remains:* Only the handsome 14thC gatehouse — a splendid monastic survival. Refs: Norfolk Arch. Vol. 17.

Penwortham *Priory Cell. Lancs. 1m SW of Preston. (−1122 to +1535). Benedictine monks. F: Warine Bussel, Baron of Penwortham. Ded: St Mary.* F. gave a township and incomes from chs. to Evesham Abbey. Throughout its life the house was totally dependent upon Evesham and legally it had no separate property. Owing to the humble status little is known of its history. It had, however, the 'dubious honour' of having the outrageous wastrel Roger Norris, of Canterbury and Evesham, as its prior who, by his oppression, reduced the inmates to penury early in the 13thC (details VCH). From 1340–43 Queen Isabella's steward tried to exact puture, but royal commissioners finally forced him to abandon the claim. It seems that Evesham withdrew its monks between 1535 & 1539. *Remains:* None. A house named Penwortham Priory stands on the site.

Pershore *Abbey. Worcs. Map 5. (c. 972–1540). Benedictine monks. F: K. Edgar and Egelward, duke of Dorset. Ded: St Mary & St Eadburga* (also referred to as Holy Cross). 1st. f. *c.* 689 by K. Oswald for secular canons. After the re-fdn. for Bene. monks *c.* 972 they lost much of their land and Edward the Confessor endowed Westminster Abbey with the abbey and the remainder of its property. This yoke was severed in 1241. Poverty occurred in the 1320s due to dwindling endowments, high hospitality costs and care of the poor. Accounts of visitations in 13th &

14thCs tell nothing of the house management and those of the 15th & 16thCs are of little interest. The abbey suffered several fires, the most serious being in 1287. The last abbot, a learned and blameless man, had difficulty in controlling a monastery in an unhappy and debt-laden condition. The relics of St Eadburga (d. 963), granddaughter of Alfred the Great, were in the S. transept — brought here 'at great expense' from Winchester. At the dissolution the townsfolk elected to keep the choir and the nave was then dismantled. *Remains:* Fine vaulted presbytery, central lantern tower, chancel (with 1847 apse), S transept and cloister archway. N transept fell in 1686. Excavated 1929–30. Notes: Trans. Bristol & Glos. Arch. Soc. Vol. 10 (1885–6).

Peterborough *Abbey. N'hants. Map 3. (c. 966–1539). Benedictine monks. F: Athelwold, bp. of Winchester. Ded: St Peter.* 1st. f. *c.* 655 by Peada, K. of Mercia. Destroyed by Danes 870. Athelwold's fdn. destroyed by fire 1117 and Abbot John de Seez began the present Norman portion of the ch. By 1240 there were 200 inmates but 200 years later only 64. The Chronicon Petroburgense (1122–1294) gives accounts of the reigns of several kings. Considerable history and detail available from numerous sources. Mitred. Abbey had no shrine which seems to be the reason why the Norman choir remained unaltered, but the ch. possessed the relics of 3 saints. Two queens buried here. The library contained about 2,000 books. *Remains:* Splendid conventual ch. Numerous pre-Reformation remnants survive including a fragment of the cloister walls with 5 entrances and book cupboard; slype; infirmary arches; slight ruins of the refectory; Prior's gateway; 14thC Abbot's gatehouse; abbot's prison; vaulted rooms in bp's palace and canonry houses. Hist. & plan: VCH (N'hants) Vol. 2. Illus: Pitkin Pictorial. Numerous accounts in cathedral books and Archaeologia. Book: Hist. & Antiq. of the Abbey & Cathedral Ch. of Peterborough (1828) by John Britton.

Peterstone *Priory/Hospital. Norfolk. 4m W of Wells-next-the-Sea. (−1200 to 1449). Augustinian canons. F: perhaps a member of the Cheney family. Ded: St Peter.*
Fd. as a priory and a hospital. Small, supporting about 6 canons. One author refers to the community as belonging to 'a local Order peculiar to Norfolk'. Disputes with Walsingham canons in 13thC over burial rights. The Black Death (1349), inundations by the sea (1378) and worse flooding in 1387 brought the house to its knees. Annexed to Walsingham in 1449 when it is referred to solely as a hospital. *Remains:* None. A farm occupies the site, the house containing a doorway with hood-mould and a few fragments of masonry from the priory.

Pheleley *Priory. Oxon. 2½m S of Charlbury. (+1100 to c. 1145). Benedictine monks. F: unknown. Ded: St Mary.*
Originally a hermitage. c. 1100 a monk of Tewkesbury retired to a solitary life in Bloxham Wood. The community grew and Henry I assigned the small house to Eynsham as a cell. Finally c. 1145 the monks and the endowments of the priory were transferred to Eynsham at the request of the Count of Meulan. Nothing else is known. *Remains:* None.

Pilton *Priory. Devon. Map 8. ½m N of Barnstaple. (end of 12thC−1539). Benedictine monks. F: unknown. Some refs. give K. Athelstan which cannot be substantiated. Ded: St Mary.*
1st. f. −933. Re-f. as a small cell of Malmesbury for a prior and 3 monks with very little endowed property. Some dispute with a local leper hospital c. 1199 which ended in the prior being ordered to make no demands on the fraternity. One record refers to the ded. of the ch. by Bp. Bronescombe of Exeter in 1259. The 15thC great seal in the BM (with a figure of Athelstan ? on one side). It seems that the cell supplied at least 2 abbots to Malmesbury. *Remains:* One half of the ch. (N aisle) is monastic with evidence on the N side of the cloister roofline. (S aisle late 16thC). Lower section of tower E.E., above rebuilt 1696. In the ch. 'no two lines run true and nothing is straight and nothing is upright' − a 'superstition to confuse the devil'. Book: Some Account of Pilton Priory and Church (1907) W. H. M. Bagley.

Pinley *Priory. Warks. 4m W of Warwick. (−1135 to 1536). Cistercian nuns. F: Robert de Pillarton. Ded: St Mary.*
Some early refs. give the house as Benedictine but it was beyond doubt one of the earliest and smallest of Cist. nunneries. Very little history known. The several 13thC visitations call for no injunctions. In 1350 there was an order to exclude seculars from the precinct because 'by their presence the nuns were defamed' (VCH). At the Dissolution the house was in good repair, though the bldgs. were old. *Remains:* None. A farm covers the site. Some Norman masonry and

254

a 15thC doorway are incorporated in the bldgs.

Pipewell *Abbey. N'hants. 5m NNW of Kettering. (1143–1538). Cistercian monks. F: Wm. de Batevileyn*. Ded: St Mary.*
The wealth of the house lay in the extensive woods and meadows. Causton Grange was the chief possession which was fraudently seized in 1287 by the convent of the alien priory of Monks Kirby, and later restored to Pipewell. Part of mid-13thC cartulary in BM. At the end of the 13thC there was severe impoverishment due to bad management of the abbey's assets, and poverty continued into the 15thC. Fires in 1307 & 1311 caused extensive damage. In the 14thC the community accepted the income from local chs. to relieve the debts. In 1535 the convent was given an excellent character and efforts were made to save the abbey because of the 'great relief and succour to the poor'. At the time of the closure wholesale theft continued night and day 'until nothing was left' (VCH). *Remains:* None. Site excavated 1910. Desc. & plan: Assoc. Archit. Soc. Reports, Vol. 30.
* Other refs. give William Buttevillain.

Plymouth *Friary. Devon. (–1296 to 1538). Carmelite. F: unknown. Ded: BVM.*
Distinction of London? Located at Sutton, E of the town, on land alienated to the Bristol Carmelites *c.* 1296 (Knowles). Some irregularities occurred at the fdn. which infringed the rights and privileges of the parish priest, but Edward II overlooked the incursions and granted a licence to continue the divine services. The ch. was stately with a tall spire – a conspicuous landmark. A prior was excommunicated in 1374 for giving absolution outside his authority but was soon reconciled. Very little history of interest survives. Minor problems relating to funeral rights, etc., are typical. *Remains:* None. A street name, no longer used, was the last reminder.

Plymouth *Friary. Devon. Dominican.*
No monasticon mentions the existence of Dominicans in Plymouth, and no record seems to remain of any community here. However, the Court of Augmentations, set up in 1536, refers to accounts of the late Dominican Priory. Prof. Pevsner (Bldgs. of England – S. Devon) refers to the f. in 1383 (the Franciscan date) and of 'considerable remains in Coate's Distillery in Southside Street'. There is also a Blackfriars Lane. Whatever the truth, Prof. Knowles states: '. . . the evidence is only post-Dissolution'. It seems there was only one Dominican house in Devon and that was in Exeter. Refs: Devon & Cornwall Notes & Queries, Vol. 19. A History of Plymouth (1931) C. W. Bracken.

Plymouth *Friary. Devon. (1383– 1538). Franciscan. (Conventual). F: unknown. Ded: St Francis?*
Custody of Bristol. In 1383–4 4 citizens gave the friars 6 acres of land. The ch. was erected without licence and a bogus bp. 'consecrated' it (Worth). The trouble was eventually reconciled. The house stood in Sutton near the Carmelites. Frequent refs. made to the house in episcopal registers and it was one of the last fdns. in England. No interesting history survives. After suppression part of the conventual ch. became apartments in the long-vanished Mitre

Inn. *Remains:* None. The last remnants were destroyed in 1813.

Plympton *Priory. Devon. Map 8. (1121–1539). Augustinian canons. F. Wm. Warelwast, Bp. of Exeter. Ded: St Peter & St Paul.* 1st. f. *c.* 909 as a rel. coll. whose secular canons were sent, it seems, to Sussex in 1121 to make way for the Aug. canons (Oliver). Became one of the richest houses of the Order in England. F. buried here as were many members of Devon families. Chapel of St Mary built within precinct for parishioners. The canons had extensive properties and powers in Plymouth which were sold in 1440 to the newly-established corporation. Mitred. Archdeacon of Totnes had authority to make visitations and report to the bp. of Exeter, but had no power to order correction. Of internal history details are meagre. The house had property in Exeter and canons were sent to serve at cells of St Mary's de Marisco (*v.* Marsh Barton) and St Anthony in Roseland. The conventual ch. was described by Leland as 'spacious and beautiful'. *Remains:* Very little. A Norman doorway and windows from the undercroft of the refectory survive in a house near the parish ch. Note: Archaeologia, Vol. 18. Site part excavated 1957–9 when fdns. of the S & W walls of the nave of the ch., area of S transept and N claustral walk were discovered. Evidence of rebldg. after early-15thC fire. (Med. Arch. Vols. 2, 3 & 4).

Polesworth *Abbey. Warks. Map 3. 4m NW of Atherstone. (c. 1130–1539). Benedictine nuns. Fs: Robert Marmion II & Milicent his wife. Ded: St Edith.* 1st. f. –839 by K. Egbert for his daughter Edith. Re-f. *c.* 980 for Bene.

nuns by K. Edgar's son, but soon after the Conquest Sir Robert Marmion I expelled the nuns who went to Oldbury. His son restored them to Polesworth *c.* 1130. Numerous details of benefactions given in VCH. In 1362 a nun under the age of 20 became abbess (Power). During 14thC visitations the bps. found little to correct and only a few irregularities occur in the 15thC. The house ran a school for about 30 children. In 1536 a commission of elders thought the town would be ruined if the nunnery closed, and the last abbess, to whom an exceptionally good character was given, bought a reprieve for £50 (Eckenstein). The commissioners reported the children as being 'right virtuously brought up' in 1537. An exceptionally fine history. *Remains:* Nave of the conventual ch. in use. Tower at NE angle. There survives the only effigy of an abbess in England (James). 14thC stone and timber gatehouse. Note: Archaeologia, Vol. 18.

Polsloe *Benedictine nuns. See* Exeter.

Pontefract *Alien Priory/Priory. Yorks. WR. (1090–1539). Cluniac monks. F: Robert de Lacy. Ded: St John Evangelist.* Dep. upon La Charité-sur-Loire. Archbp. Thurston buried here 1140, 11 days after joining the community. Bldgs. destroyed during the Anarchy and the monks went to Broughton (3m W of Skipton) while the ch. was rebuilt *c.* 1153. Ch. consecrated 1159 and as La Charité is not mentioned in the charter of that year, the house was probably then directly dependent upon Cluny (Knowles). Monk Bretton, fd. under Pontefract, resented the control over elections of its priors, and unseemly quarrels with armed interference arose, until in 1281 M.B. became Benedictine and the link was severed. In the 13thC the prior and monks were reported to be leading model lives. The executed earl of Lancaster buried here in 1322 near the high altar (VCH). Many miracles were said to have been wrought at his shrine. Denizen in 1393. Little known of 15th & 16thCs history. The surrender of this well-ordered house was 'very complacent'. *Remains:* None. Thorough site excavations 1957–72 revealed ground plans of 3 consecutive chs.; the outlines of the main claustral bldgs. incl. the 10-sided chapter house; and the infirmary area round a small cloister. Evidence of early 16thC bell-founding (*v.* Norton). Numerous burials located. Desc: Yorks. Arch. Soc. J. Vol. 32, (1935). Med. Arch. Vols. 3–17.

Pontefract *Friary. Yorks. WR. (1256–1538). Dominican. F: Edmund de Lacy, earl of Lincoln. Ded: St Mary, St Dominic & St Richard*.*
Visitation of York. Not much known of the history. When disputes arose between the Cluniac houses of Pontefract and Monk Bretton in 1269 they were settled at this friary. Three preaching stations were established by the community at Pontefract, Rotherham and Wakefield. Provincial chapters held here 1301 & 1321. Long list of burials in the conventual ch. given in VCH. *Remains:* None. Site covered by a hospital. Part excavated 1963 in advance of redevelopment when 8 periods of building or alteration were found – Med. Arch. Vol. 8. Hist: Yorks. Arch. Soc. J. Vol. 32 (1935).
* St Richard (Richard Wych, bp. of Chichester), canonised 1262, was a great friend of the F.

Portchester *Priory. Hants. Map 6. 3m E of Fareham. (1133–c. 1148). Augustinian canons. Fs: Wm. Pont d'Arch and Henry I. Ded: St Mary.*
Located within the outer bailey of the castle, i.e. the Roman enclosure. The site was found to be inconvenient, probably owing to disturbance caused by military movements, and the canons moved to Southwick (*v.* below) between 1145–53. *Remains:* The ch. survives (except for the S transept) with crossing tower. Much repaired 1888. No other monastic evidence other than blocked doorways to the cloister on S side of the nave. Plan of ch.: VCH, Hants. Plan of precinct and position of priory: Current Arch. No. 4, Sept. 1967.

Poughley *Priory. Berks. Map 6. 5½m N of Hungerford. (c. 1160–1525). Augustinian canons. F: Ralph de Chaddleworth. Ded: St Margaret.*
On the site of a hermitage. In 1313 a serious fire destroyed mills, graneries and other bldgs. Little history known for over 100 years. The prior was charged in 1428 with altering the course of a river for a newly-built mill and causing the flooding of meadows. The patronage of the priory was held by the nuns of Amesbury (*v.* above). 16thC history is negligible and finally Wolsey obtained the small house for his Oxford Coll. It seems that the dissolved priory was occupied by scholars while the coll. was being built. In 1529 cartloads of priory property were removed to Oxford. *Remains:* A farmhouse on the site contains part of the W claustral range in its E facade (Pevsner). To the ENE excavations have revealed fdns. of an aisleless ch. To the E, W & S are fishpond hollows. Desc: Newbury District Field Club Trans. Vol. 11 (1872).

257

Poulton *Abbey. Cheshire. 5m S of Chester. (1153–1214). Cistercian monks. F: Robert, butler to Ranulf II, earl of Chester. Ded: St Mary.*
Site first granted to Combermere 1146 which was then Savigniac. 1153 may be the date when building began and in 1158 the colony arrived from Combermere. Numerous gifts were given to the new fdn., but raids by the Welsh made the monks' situation untenable and dangerous (Ormerod). In consequence Ranulph de Blundeville moved the community to Dieulacres (*v.* above) in 1214. *Remains:* None.

Poulton *Priory. Glos. (was Wilts.) 5m E of Cirencester. (1350–1539). Gilbertine canons. F: Sir Thomas Seymour (St.Maur). Ded: St Mary.*
1st. f. 1348 for 5 chaplains but F. introduced canons 2 years later under an agreement with the king. The fdn. charter states that the house would have royal protection. The small community's income was mainly from the sale of wool. Nothing known for the next 130 years. Though the net annual income was very low, in common with all Gilb. houses it was spared suppression in 1536. *Remains:* A manor house occupies the site. The ch. was dismantled in 1873 and the materials reused for a new parish ch. nearby.

Preston *Friary. Lancs. (c. 1260–1539). Franciscan (Conventual). F: a member of the Preston family gave land. Ded: unknown.*
Custody of Worcester. Edmund, Earl of Lancaster was 'the great builder' of the house and also ranks as F. A proposal to remove the house to another Custody in 1330 was quashed. Evidence of active farming interests and the ownership of a windmill, a watermill and a turbary (Martin). The subsequent history is a blank apart from a few notices of small bequests. *Remains:* None. Notes: History of Preston (1900) H. Fishwick.

Preston Capes *Alien Priory. N'hants.*
See Daventry and Appendix 1.

Preston Patrick *Abbey. W'land (Cumbria). 6m S of Kendal. (+1192 to –1201). Premonstratensian canons. F: Thomas Fitz Gospatrick. Ded: St Mary Magdalene.*
Colonised from Cockersand. The short-lived and indeterminate length of stay is unexplained; but the canons moved to Shap (*v.* below) before the F's death (1201), perhaps because he held lands there direct from the Crown, whereas at Preston he was an under-tenant (Colvin). *Remains:* None.

Prittlewell *Alien Priory/Priory. Essex. Map 7. 1½m N of Southend-on-Sea. (c. 1110*–1536). Cluniac monks. F: Robert Fitz-Sweyn. Ded: St Mary.*
Colonised from Lewes. For its size the house was unusually rich in ch. spoils, holding some 18 advowsons, resulting in several legal disputes over ownerships. 13thC records of visitations give valuable insights into Cluniac conditions. In 1314 a difficult prior was deposed despite his apparent fortune in having the king's favour. Subsequent disputes seem to have had an adverse effect on the priory's affairs especially as the deposed prior still had a hold over some of the house's possessions. In 1316 an armed mob under the prior's leadership raided the priory and all were arrested. Not until 1321, after a lamentable series of incidents, did the prior die from head wounds possibly obtained in a scuffle at the

high altar of the ch. Became denizen in 1373. Poverty at the end of the 14thC resulted in help being given to repair the ch. History is then somewhat sparse until the Dissolution. *Remains:* 15thC refectory with fine Norman doorway S of the cloister; on the W side an undercroft with 14thC prior's lodging above. Fdns. of the ch. marked in the turf. Excavated 1953–4. Br. Arch. Assoc. J. Vols. 20 & 21 (1957–8); and Med. Arch. Vols. 11 & 12 (1965–7). No evidence found of a N cloister walk. Care: Borough of Southend-on-Sea. *Most refs. give *c.* 1121.

Pynham (Calceto) Priory. Sussex. 1m S of Arundel. (−1151 to 1525). Augustinian canons. F: Adeliza, Countess of Arundel (widow of Henry I). Ded: St Bartholomew. Small and poor. Fd. to keep the causeway (calceto) in good repair and supervise a small hostel for travellers. Endowments so inadequate that the canons relied upon 'the alms of the faithful' in 1309. A prior was deposed *c.* 1355 for an unknown reason and sent to Shulbrede. Poverty in 1478 and bldgs. in bad repair. The house was finally suppressed by Wolsey for his Oxford Coll. *Remains:* Slight. The base of a 13thC tower is built into an 18thC farmhouse (Pevsner). A railway station occupied some of the site.

Q

Quarr *Abbey. I.o.W. Map 6. 2m W of Ryde. (1132–1536). Cistercian monks. F: Baldwin de Redvers. Ded: St Mary.*
Savigniac until 1147. Never a large or important house but full of interest. Considerable endowments. Many notable persons, including the F.,

buried in the ch. The fdn. charter is an exceedingly rare survival of an original in diploma form (Hockey). Apart from a thriving wool business the house operated a fulling mill for cloth processing, a flourishing tannery and owned ships for importing French claret. The monks maintained a light for the guidance of mariners and at the dissolution the abbey was said to do 'so much to relieve the poor of the district'. *Remains:* A barn represents the W range of the claustral bldgs; walls of the kitchen with serving hatch, and remnants of the infirmary chapel. Numerous low walls. Excavated 1891. Book: Quarr Abbey & its Lands (1970), Dom. S. F. Hockey. New abbey established nearby 1908.

R

Radford *Priory. Notts.*
See Worksop.

Radmore *(Red Moor) Abbey. Staffs. 3m E of Cannock. (1141– 1155). Cistercian monks. F: Empress Matilda. Ded: St Mary.*
1st. f. *c.* 1137 as a hermitage. Matilda persuaded the community to become Cist. and granted a charter. The oppression of foresters, who made frequent depredations, caused the monks to abandon the site and move to Stoneleigh. Within a short time a royal hunting lodge was established on the Radmore site. *Remains:* None.

Ramestede *Priory. Sussex. 1½m SE of Lewes. (−1183 to c. 1202). Benedictine nuns. F: Richard, Archbp. of Canterbury. Ded: St Mary Magdalene.*
Very little known. The scandalous behaviour of some of the nuns resulted in the priory's closure and

259

removal of the nuns by Archbp. Hubert (Knowles). Resettlements unknown. Estates said to be annexed to St Gregory's, Canterbury (Tanner). *Remains:* None.

Ramsey *Abbey. Hunts. Map 4. 10m SE of Peterborough. (969– 1539). Benedictine monks. F: Aylwin, Duke of E. Anglia. Ded: St Mary & St Benedict.*
10th wealthiest house in England. Mitred. In 972 monks arrived from Westbury-on-Trym. Well endowed. Relics, including those of St Ive, enriched the abbey by attracting pilgrims. Problem of rival abbots *c.* 1143 but Walter 'won all hearts by his dovelike simplicity' regained control (VCH). Bp. Grosseteste carried out a searching visitation *c.* 1239 but found no faults. The house had numerous lawsuits including one with Ely which lasted over 200 years. In the mid-15thC when so many houses needed reform, there were no serious complaints against Ramsey – which had a scandal-free history. There was a magnificent library. *Remains:* A mansion occupies the site and incorporates a mid-13thC Lady Chapel and numerous buttresses. Part of the gatehouse survives (N.T.) is uncommonly ornate and the rest of it is at Hinchingbrooke. The 15thC choir stalls are said to be in the parish ch. at Godmanchester. There is a 14thC gilt censer from the abbey in the B.M. Examination of the surviving parts of the abbey incorporated in Bodsey House on the site was made in 1968. (Med. Arch. Vol. 13).

Ranton *(Ronton) Priory. Staffs. Map 2. 6m W of Stafford. (–1166 to c. 1536). Augustinian canons. F: Robert Fitz Noel. Ded: St Mary.*

Cartulary in B.M. Built in a forest clearance and under the rule of Haughmond (*v.* Owston). In 1246–7 the house achieved independence. In the 13thC there was a hospital in the precinct. Turbulent times in 14thC and Bp. Norbury found much to censure including violent opposition to one of his visitations. There were disputes with the Doyle family over lands and 'various injuries' (VCH). In 1372 there was mismanagement of finances. The convent was given the custody of Alberbury Priory in 1386 but 6 years later it had passed into other hands. Although there were low standards of observance in 1518, matters were much improved by 1524. Date of surrender unknown. *Remains:* Nothing but the 15thC W tower and a section of the S wall of the nave. Never excavated. Ruined house on the site.

Ratlinghope *Priory. Salop. 4m NW of Church Stretton. (–1200 to 1538). Augustinian canons. F: perhaps Llewellyn the Great. Ded: St Margaret.*
Few records survive. It seems that an Aug. canon, Walter Corbett, gave the manor of Ratlinghope to Wigmore of which it became a very small cell. Llewellyn enjoined his noblemen to 'be kind to Corbett'. History does not relate whether canons of Wigmore were still here in 1535 but the abbey still owned the property. *Remains:* None.

Ravenstone *Priory. Bucks. 2½m W of Olney. (c. 1255–1525). Augustinian canons. F: Peter Chaceporc (Chaseport). Ded: St Mary.*
House reverted to the Crown after the F.'s death and Henry III was considered the F., because he had given endowments. No records of

260

visitations survive. No known interesting history, nor is it easy to recover any details of internal or external life here (VCH). The small, but not poor, priory had 5 canons when it was dissolved for Wolsey's Oxford Coll. *Remains:* None. Totally demolished *c.* 1526.

Reading *Abbey. Berks. Map 6. (1121–1539). Benedictine monks. F: Henry I. Ded: St Mary & St John, Evangelist.*
Stood on site of Saxon nunnery. The first abbots were Cluniac giving an ill-defined connection with Cluny until mid-12thC. Abbey became famous, powerful and 5th richest in England. Mitred 1289. Many illustrious persons, the F. included, buried in the ch. On frequent occasions Parliament met here, some of great historical significance. Scene of the wedding of John of Gaunt with Blanche, heiress of duke of Lancaster; and in the ch. Edward IV declared Elizabeth Woodville his wife in 1464 (*v.* Bermondsey). The renowned endless canon *Sumer is icumen in*, described as the 'most remarkable ancient musical composition in existence' first set down here *c.* 1225. House had a fine library and a famous school for children. The last abbot was hanged in front of the gatehouse for refusing to acknowledge the king's supremacy in spiritual matters. *Remains:* Mainly flint and rubble, all facing stone gone. S transept arch, walling of E chapels; tunnel-vaulted slype; chapter house; W wall of dormitory and S wall of refectory. Inner gatehouse, much restored, now a museum. Part of abbey mills. Desc: Trans. Berks. Arch. & Architec. Soc. 1880–1. Note: Archaeologia, Vol. 6. E end of ch. excavated 1971–2 during alterations

to H.M. Prison, Med. Arch. Vols. 16 & 17. Plan: VCH, Vol. 3 (1923). Book: Reading Abbey (1901) J. B. Hurry.

Reading *Friary. Berks. Map 6. (1233–1538). Franciscan (Conventual). F: unknown. Abbot de Lathbury granted land. Ded: St Francis (?).*
The site given by the Benedictine Abbot Adam was marshy and became inundated with floodwater in winter. Under pressure a new site was allocated by the monks, and to their niggardly grant was attached a series of unreasonable restrictions. Edward I gave the friars 56 oaks in 1280 and the site was occupied *c.* 1285. Adjoining land was given in 1288. From the end of the 13thC until the suppression little history is known. In 1539, following closure, the warden and one friar were imprisoned in the Tower. *Remains:* After the Dissolution the ch. became partly the new town hall (at a rent of $\frac{1}{2}$d. p.a.) and partly an almshouse, but today it once more serves as a ch., though almost entirely rebuilt. The nave, aisles and fdns. of the S transept are early-14thC. In 1863 the N & S transepts and the E chancel arch (though not the chancel) were rebuilt. Most of the nave piers are original and there is a fine W window. Desc. & plan: Arch. J. Vol. 3 (1846); Franciscan Architecture in England (1937) A. R. Martin; and VCH, Vol. 3 (1923).

Redbourn *(Redburn) Priory. Herts. 4½m NW of St Albans. (+1178 to –1535). Benedictine monks. F: Abbot Simon or Abbot Warin of St Albans. Ded: St Amphibalus.* *
The small cell was used as a rest hostel for the convent of St Albans

261

and was run with a rigid set of rules. A feud with the nuns of Flamstead over land on Redbourn Heath ended in the monks' favour – the nuns losing the support of the earl of Warwick in 1383. History from the end of the 15thC is almost blank. Few monks were there in the 1450s and occasionally none at all. The house seems to have been abandoned by 1535. *Remains:* None.
* The martyr's sepulchre was found at Redbourn in 1178 and the relics taken to St Albans.

Redlingfield *Priory. Suffolk. Map 4. 3m SE of Eye. (1120–1537). Benedictine nuns. Fs: Manasses, Count of Guisnes and Emma de Arras his wife. Ded: St Mary & St Andrew.*
Very little early history. The house must have been exceptionally poor, being omitted from the 1291 Taxation Roll (VCH). In the first half of the 15thC scandals and irregularities were undoubtedly caused by a weak and unprincipled prioress. All the nuns were found to be at fault and in 1427 the deposed prioress was sent to Wix (Power). Although minor evidences of neglect occur in 1514, the visitations from 1520–32 were not followed by a single complaint. There was never a conventual ch., the nuns using the chancel of the parish ch. *Remains:* The ch. survives. In a farm bldg. SSE of the ch. are buttresses and fragments of windows from the nunnery.

Reigate *Priory. Surrey. (+1217 to 1536). Augustinian canons. Fs: Wm. de Warenne and Isabel his wife. Ded: BVM & Holy Cross.*
No fdn. charter survives. The house is termed a hospital in some refs. where the sick and poor were main-

tained. Details of grants and elections of priors given in VCH. Little else. There is a record of an admonition directed against parishioners who hastened to the drinking booths from the parish ch. scarcely before Mass was over (VCH). 'It is significant that the earliest record of Reigate in the chapters of the Aug. canons seems to be in 1509' (Knowles). *Remains:* None. Some reused materials may survive in the parish ch., rebuilt 1779. The priory stood opposite the castle.

Repton *Priory. Derbys. Map 3. 4½m NE of Burton upon Trent. (c. 1153/9–1538). Augustinian canons. F: Matilda, countess of Chester. Ded: St Wystan.*
Probably 1st. fd. early-7thC as a Benedictine nunnery and destroyed by Danes 874. The re-f. had no connection with the earlier fdn., and by her charter the F. stipulated that the canons of Calke should be transferred to Repton. Most of the community arrived from there in 1172. Never a wealthy house. There was illegal interference in the priory's temporal affairs in 1337 by one of Edward III's servants in the interval between the death and new election of priors. The king had licence to elect a new prior but not to seize property. In 1364 a sudden outbreak of violence in the town during an episcopal visitation to the priory almost resulted in the bp's death, and he pronounced greater excommunication upon every person involved. In 1536 the Crown visitors made the usual worthless accusations, but the house was allowed to continue on payment of the huge fine of £266.13.4d. *Remains:* Site occupied by a distinguished school. The 'most beautiful ch. was plucked down in a

single day'. Ruins of the E end of the ch.; nave area occupied by a hall. W claustral range includes the school library and an undercroft is a museum. Prior's hall, c. 1400, has a fine open timber roof. Gatehouse now an arch in a buttressed wall. Excavated 1851, 1869 & 1883. Desc. & plan: Arch. J. Vol. 41; and Br. Arch. Assoc. J. Vol. 7 (1852); also Derbys. Arch. & Nat. Hist. Soc. J. Vols 6 & 7 (1885). Books: (1) Repton Village, Priory & School (1892) F. C. Hipkins; (2) A Short History of Repton (1929) A. MacDonald.

Revesby *Abbey. Lincs. 11m N of Boston. (1142–1538). Cistercian monks. F: Wm. de Romara, earl of Lincoln, with his wife and son. Ded: St Mary & St Laurence.*
The F. ended his days as a monk here and was buried before the high altar. (In 1870 his tomb and those of his 2 sons were found.) Not an eventful history. It became one of the richer houses of the Order. It was several times burdened with having to support unwelcome ex-royal servants, and in 1322 applied for tax relief due to poor harvests, heavy loss of livestock and maintenance of pensioners. In 1340 Edward III bought £115 worth of wool from the community and failed to pay. After much delay and pressure, only £14.14.0d was recovered. Nothing more known until 1527 which relates to some bridge repairs; and in 1538 the abbey bldgs. were said to be in decay and ruin, but no fault was found with the moral standards within the house. *Remains:* None. Partially excavated 1869 when a fine section of tile pavement was uncovered and relaid in the parish ch. Excav. acct: Assoc. Architec. Soc.

Reports & Papers. Vol. 10 (1869).

Rewley *Abbey. Oxon. ¾m NW of Oxford city centre, between the railway and the canal. (1281–1536). Cistercian monks. F: Edmund, Earl of Cornwall. Ded: St Mary.*
Subject to Thame. Never wealthy or important. It soon became a house of study for students sent to Oxford, but how long it so remained is uncertain. It was still a 'studium' up to 1398. The fdn. of St Bernard's Coll. in 1437 (*v.* Oxford) certainly ended studies at Rewley. There are no surviving episcopal registers and the history of the house is practically blank. In 1532 the abbot complained bitterly to Cromwell about oppression from the king's servants quartered at the abbey. *Remains:* Only a length of precinct wall incorporating a blocked 15thC doorway.

Richmond *(Sheen) Friary. Surrey. (1499–1534). Franciscan (Observant). F: Henry VII. Ded: St Francis?*
Did not belong to a Custody. Built adjacent to the F's. royal palace at Sheen. At first Henry VIII gave special aid to the friars, but his favour faded when they opposed his divorce of Q. Catherine. Several friars were among those accused in 1533 of conniving with the Holy Maid of Kent (*v.* Canterbury, St Sepulchre) in denouncing the king's conduct. In 1534 the king's Act of Supremacy was unacceptable to the Observants, and in revenge he ordered them to be speedily suppressed. All were removed in carts to prison where many of them died in chains. *Remains:* None. Some remnants were reported during alterations to a hospital in Richmond in 1915 which was probably on the site (Hutton).

Richmond *(Sheen) Friary. Surrey.*
(1315–1318). Carmelite.
At the command of Edward II twenty-
four friars stayed here until they
joined the Oxford community when
the latter moved to their new site
outside the N gate in 1318.

Richmond *Priory. Yorks. NR. Map 1.*
(c. 1100–1539). Benedictine monks.
F: Wymar, dapifer to the Earl of
Richmond. Ded: St Martin.
The F. gave the chapel and its
possessions to the abbot and convent
of St Mary's, York, whereupon a
community of 9 monks was sent
from York to form the new cell.
Very little history is known and no
records of visitations survive. In 1381
it seems that only a prior and one
monk lived here. *Remains:* Close to
a farm is a small late-15thC embattled
tower, and a Norman doorway in a
piece of wall which may be the W
entrance to the priory ch.

Richmond *Friary. Yorks. NR. Map 1.*
(1258–1539). Franciscan (con-
ventual). F: Ralph Fitz Randall. Ded:
uncertain.
Custody of Newcastle. F's. heart
deposited in recess in the ch. wall.
List of benefactions from local
families and of their burials in the ch.
in VCH. In 1314 the archbp. of York
sent instructions to the warden to
preach against the Scots and arouse
resistance. A dispute with Easby
occurred in 1492 over the disposal of
the possessions of an anchoress who
had died after taking the Franciscan
habit. The curious 15thC ballad 'The
Felon Sow of Rokeby' recalls the
friars' efforts to catch a savage sow
and of the triumphant return to
Richmond. *Remains:* Fine 15thC
square bell-tower with some fragments of walls adjoining the SW

corner, perhaps the E end of the
nave's S aisle. Desc. & plan:
Franciscan Architecture in England,
A. R. Martin, pps. 117–124. Note:
Archaeologia, Vol. 47. Hist: Yorks.
Arch. Soc. J. Vol. 32 (1935).

Rievaulx *Abbey. Yorks. NR. Map 1.*
3m NW of Helmsley. (1132–1538).
Cistercian monks. F: Walter l'Espec.
Ded: St Mary.
Land was given to a colony from
Clairvaux by the F. in 1131, and he
became a monk here for the last 2
years of his life and was buried in the
ch. Growth owed much to the holy
and loving 3rd abbot, Ailred (1147–
67), later canonised and the community was said to number 150
monks and over 500 lay-brothers at
the time of his death. In 1381 there
were only 15 monks and 3 lay-
brothers. Little known of its history
because of exemption from episcopal
visitations, but the abbey rose to be
the premier Cist. house in England.
Considerable sheep-farming income
and a flourishing hide tannery business
brought wealth which was spent in
huge 13thC building programmes
which left the house deep in debt.
The last abbot, Sedburgh, was hanged
at Tyburn for suspected implication
in the Pilgrimage of Grace. (The ch.
was set S–N, but all refs. adopt E–W
orientation as if the layout were
normal.) *Remains:* Superb ruins –
'the majesty of the huge wreck at
Rievaulx' (Braun). The ch.
presbytery and transepts are un-
equalled in Gothic perfection, once
hidden in gloom beneath a roof.
Extensive well-preserved monastic
bldgs. include refectory hall, parts
of dormitory and infirmary; and in
the low-level walls of the chapter
house is the shrine of the 1st. abbot,
St William. Care, desc. & plan: D of

Rievaulx Abbey, Yorkshire. The church looking east with ruins of the nave in the foreground.

E. Numerous refs. and descs. in books. Excavated 1923. Desc: Surtees Soc. Publcns. Vol. 83; VCH, Yorks NR, Vol. 1 pps. 494–502.

Robertsbridge *(Salehurst) Abbey. Sussex. Map 7. 5m N of Battle. (1176–1538). Cistercian monks. F: Alfred de St Martin. Ded: St Mary.* Colonised from Boxley. 1st. f. at Salehurst, about a mile from the present site, from which the community moved *c.* 1250 (Knowles) due to inundations of the sea — the R. Rother was then navigable this far. In the early years the abbot, together with the abbot of Boxley, were sent in 1192 to search for K. Richard

whom they found in Bavaria (VCH). Sea ravages of the abbey's property in Bexhill proved a heavy liability in 1264 & 1309. Little known about internal history, but the reputation of the house appears to have been good. *Remains:* The site is occupied by a farm of which the house, projecting W from the W claustral range, was the abbot's lodging. It has a mid-13thC undercroft with rib-vaulting in 6 bays. Nothing remains of the ch. S precinct area examined 1966 when fdns. of a gatehouse were located (Med. Arch. Vol. 11).

Rocester *Abbey. Staffs. 4½m N of Uttoxeter. (c. 1146–1538). August-*

Rievaulx Abbey. The church from the south-east.

inian canons. *F: Richard Bacon.*
Ded: BVM.
Surprising to find so small a house of
abbey status. Never wealthy. For a
short time in the 13thC a few canons
were attached to the ch. at Mobberley
in Cheshire. The flourishing wool
trade had ended by 1318 when cattle
and sheep plague together with bad
harvests forced the canons to beg
for alms and food. In the mid-14thC
the communal life seems to have
been troubled due to neglect and
disobedience, e.g. in 1337 a canon
went to Bolingbroke castle, imprisoned the Countess of Lincoln and
stole 20 horses. The outcome is

unknown. Nothing enlightening is
preserved about 14th & 15thC
finances. A visitation of 1524 shows
the house was being run efficiently
with satisfactory observances. The
convent prolonged its life by paying
the Crown a £100 fine. *Remains:*
None.

Roche *Abbey. Yorks. WR. Map 3.*
8m SE by E of Rotherham. (1147–
1538). Cistercian monks. Fs: Richard
de Builli and Richard Fitz Turgis.
Ded: St Mary.
The joint Fs. gave land on both sides
of a stream allowing the monks to
build on whichever side they wished

Rievaulx Abbey. Crossing detail.

so long as both men were recognised as Fs. No chronicle survives and little is known of the history but surviving charters give abundant information about further gifts of land. In 1346 the Earl of Surrey on seeing 'the magnificence of the stonework of the abbey' gave spiritualities capable of maintaining a further 13 monks, but the community was considerably reduced by the B.D. 3 years later. One of the rocks near the site bore a resemblance to a cross and became an object of pilgrimage. An account of the destruction of 'this very fair house built entirely of freestone' was given by the son of an eye witness in 1591 and is recorded in VCH. *Remains:* Chancel walls and E walls of both transepts of the ch. Ground floor of gatehouse with vaulting. All else in complete fdn. outline. Splendid example of Cist. layout. Desc., plan & care: D of E. Desc: Br. Arch. Assoc. J. Vols. 10 & 30. Books: (1) History of Roche Abbey from Foundation to Dissolution (1870) J. H. Aveling. (2) History of Roche Abbey (1882) J. C. Atkinson.

Rochester *Cathedral-Priory. Kent. Map 7. (1080–1540). Benedictine monks. F: Gundulf, bp. of Rochester. Ded: St Andrew.*
1st. fd. 604 and later destroyed by Danes. The impoverished ch. was rebuilt by Gundulf who replaced secular canons with 22 Benedictine monks in 1080. Fire wrought havoc in 1138 & 1177, and K. John's army plundered the monastery at the end of the 12thC. But following the murder outside the city of William of Perth (canonised 1251) who was on his way to Jerusalem, he was buried in the ch. in 1201, and miracles said to have occurred at his shrine helped swell the treasury's

funds. Visitations in 1283 & 1299 resulted in many injunctions against the community including orders to attend all services and not to eat with nuns. Considerable information available from many other sources. From 1437, when minor injunctions followed an episcopal visitation, until the Dissolution not much history survives. No account exists of the Crown visitors' report in 1535. *Remains:* Fine parochial/conventual ch. with splendid W front. The cloister was attached to the S side of the *choir*, not the nave. 50 ft. of Bp. Gundulf's tower survives on the N side of the ch. Splendid Dec. doorway to the new chapter house. Wall of dorter undercroft and remains of N wall of frater. Two gateways survive and sections of the precinct wall (a third gateway is a modern replica). Desc. & plans: Arch. Cantiana, Vol. 23 (1898) and Vol. 24. Also Archaeologia, Vol. 49; and Br. Arch. Assoc. J. Vol. 9. Numerous book refs. Illus: Pitkin Pictorial.

Romney *Franciscan Friars. Kent.* See New Romney.

Romsey *Abbey. Hants. Map 6. 8m NW of Southampton. (967–1539). Benedictine nuns. F: K. Edgar. Ded: St Mary & St Elfleda.*
1st. f. c. 907 by K. Edward the Elder whose daughter Elfleda became abbess. Bene. nuns introduced by Edgar 967. Destroyed by Danes c. 993. Abbess Mary, daughter of K. Stephen, left the monastery in 1160 to marry the count of Flanders but later returned in penitence. Q. Margaret of Scotland (canonised 1250) never realised her wish to take the veil here as did her mother and sister; and her 2 daughters lived at the monastery for a while until

Matilda married Henry I (Eckenstein). Records of visitations enable much of internal life to be known from 1284 to 1539. One instance of poverty in 1351 caused the bp. to state that aid given to the nuns was 'a merciful thing in days of increasing illdoing and social deterioration'; and in 1387 an injunction forbade the abbess to keep monkeys in her chamber or the nuns to take birds, rabbits, hounds and 'such frivolous things' into ch. The wicked abbess Elizabeth Broke (1472–1502) caused endless difficulties (Power), and her neglect resulted in neither choir nor dormitory roofs keeping out rain. Master Bryce controlled her life and she was finally forced to resign. The remarkable 'Romsey Psalter' of 1440 is preserved. *Remains:* The finest nuns' ch. to survive – perfection in its antique architecture (Braun). No claustral bldgs., only part of refectory wall. Site of Lady Chapel excavated 1973. Books: 1. Records of Romsey Abbey (1912) H. G. D. Liveing; 2. Pages from the History of Romsey and its Abbey (1948) Sir R. Luce. Notes: Archaeologia, Vols. 1 & 17.

Ronton *Priory. Staffs.*
See Ranton.

Rosedale *Priory. Yorks. NR. Map 1. 6m NNE of Kirkbymoorside. (–1158 to 1535). Cistercian nuns. F: William de Rosedale. Ded: St Mary & St Lawrence.*
Stuteville family confirmed grants and gave land. Considerable 14thC history including successful sheep-farming; ravages from Scottish raids; injunctions following visitations to stop nuns taking puppies into ch., and the wearing of coloured clothing; and the need to cultivate charity. At one time the nuns were disturbed at their devotions by the smoke and noise of a nearby iron forge (Hayes). The house has been referred to as Benedictine and Augustinian, but 3 registers describe it as Cistercian. *Remains:* The base of a tower with W and S buttresses and part of a spiral stair to the NE. Until 1850 the ruins were among the most complete of a small nunnery in the N of England. Masonry from the priory exists in local bldgs.

Rothwell *Priory. N'hants. 4m NW of Kettering. (–1262 to 1537/8). Augustinian canonesses. F: probably Richard, Earl of Gloucester. Ded: St John, Baptist.*
The F. died before completing the endowments and the house was extremely poor – only one ch. supplying the income. Poverty in 1318 & 1392 was particularly severe and the nuns were not only compelled to beg for alms 'like mendicant friars', but were licensed to have a proctor to secure outside aid for them. A penitent nun was confined in chains for 3 years for absconding from the house with a local man. In 1422 a gang of thugs raided the priory and took away a woman boarder (Power). *Remains:* None. A house occupies the site.

Rowney *Priory. Herts. 4m N of Ware. (c. 1162–1457). Benedictine nuns. Fs: Conan, Duke of Brittany and the Earl of Richmond. Ded: St John, Baptist.*
Always small and poor and in 1302 the endowed ch's. benefices were worthless. The scanty history does not reflect credit on the nuns and the suspicion is unavoidable that the house was never well run (VCH). For example, a hand-to-hand scuffle

between the prioress and the chaplain in 1375 resulted in both being fined for drawing blood. Early in the 15thC robbers took ch. valuables and books, and in 1448 there were insufficient funds even to pay for a chaplain. Under hopeless conditions the convent surrendered the property in 1457 to the patron who leased it to the Crown. It then became a chantry with a chaplain and was still in existence in 1548. *Remains:* None.

Royston *Priory. Herts. Map 7. (1173–9 to 1537). Augustinian canons. Fs: Eustace de Merk & Ralph de Rochester. Ded: St John, Baptist & St Thomas, Martyr.*
1st. f. by Eustace for 3 chaplains and his nephew Ralph introduced 7 canons later (Knowles). Early in the 13thC there was discord with other religious houses over liberties and property. Possessions in 1290 included houses in Fleet Street, London. At one period a 'spirit of violence infected the cloister' (VCH) and in 1310 one canon attacked another in the ch. with a sword. It seems that the prior had a 'faculty for surrounding himself with undesirable persons' (VCH). Little is heard of the house from the end of the 14thC until the Dissolution. *Remains:* The nave of the parish ch. is the unaisled chancel of the conventual ch., and the W tower stands on the site of the original nave (Pevsner). Nothing else.

Rudham, *East Priory. Norfolk. 6¼m W of Fakenham. (c. 1140– c. 1216). Augustinian canons. F: William Cheney. Ded: St Mary.*
Began with 4 priests living a common life at the ch. of E. Rudham (Dickinson). The F's. nephew granted the ch. of W Rudham to the

canons who moved $\frac{3}{4}$m to the E and settled at Coxford c. 1216. In 1273 the community claimed tenements and a leat at Rudham. *Remains:* None. Hist: Norfolk Archaeology, Vol. 17 (1908–10).

Rufford *Abbey. Notts. Map 3. 2m S of Ollerton. (1146–1536). Cistercian monks. F: Gilbert de Gant, Earl of Lincoln. Ded: St Mary.*
No interesting history to record, but there exists a full transcript of the cartulary in 188 paper folios. The F. gave generous compensation to those who were dispossessed when the initial clearance of the abbey site began. Being in the centre of Sherwood Forest there are frequent refs. to timber cutting for the use of the monastery and for selling. In 1359 the abbot was charged with over doing the felling and laying waste to an entire wood to the extent of nearly 60 acres. In the absence of any visitation records, because the Cistercians were exempt, little is known of the 15thC life. *Remains:* Beneath a house built on the site is a crypt with 3 central pillars supporting vaulting. Perhaps an undercroft to the refectory? Site excavated 1957 and most of the monastic plan determined. The ch. was a classical 12thC Cist. design. (Med. Arch. Vol. 2). Property of Notts. C.C.

Rumburgh *Priory/Priory Cell. Suffolk. Map 4. 4m NW of Halesworth. (–1064 to 1528). Benedictine monks. Fs: Bp. Ethelmar of Elmham & Abbot Thurston of St Benet of Hulme. Ded: St Michael & St Felix.*
No early history survives. In 1135 the house ceased to be dependent upon St Benet's when Stephen, Earl of Brittany, granted it to St Mary's Abbey, York, and it became a cell of

St Mary's with 3 or 4 monks (Knowles). When an Earl of Richmond claimed to be patron with the right to appoint a prior, a jury ruled that he had no custody of the cell (VCH). Suppressed for Wolsey's Ipswich College in 1528 to which St Mary's objected on the grounds of a 300-year link, but yielded in 1529. There is a ref. to a St Bory to whom there was 'much offering of money and cheese' (VCH). *Remains:* Conventual ch. in use as parish ch., no aisles, no chapels, but with a W tower (Pevsner). Nothing survives of the claustral bldgs. which lay to the N. A 17thC farmhouse occupies the site of the refectory. Excavations in 1963 revealed that no transepts or choir were ever built, and the monks used the E end of the nave. (Med. Arch. Vol. 8).

Runcorn *Priory. Cheshire. (c. 1115– 1134). Augustinian canons. F: Wm. Fitz Nigel, 2nd Baron of Halton. Ded: St Mary.*
It seems that no more than wooden bldgs. were erected at this site before the canons moved to their permanent and more suitable premises at Norton. *Remains:* None. Notes: The Foundation Charter of Runcorn Priory, J. Tait, – Chetham Soc. Vol. 7 (1939).

Rushen *Abbey. Isle of Man. Map 1. (1134–1540). Cistercian monks. F: Olaf I, K. of Man. Ded: St Mary.*
Dependent upon Furness. Community owned considerable land throughout the island. Invasion by the Scots in 1275 and the Irish in 1316 caused extensive damage to the house and wholesale robbery. The considerable powers of the abbot, a baron in his own right, declined from the middle of the 14thC, the power of sanctuary being denied the

monastery in 1422. By 1523 it seems the abbot was no longer allowed to buy choice wines. If the Dissolution is extended to include Manx houses then the I. o. M. monasteries were the last to go – Waltham being the last on the mainland. *Remains:* Ruined ch. crossing tower; W tower; outlines of nave and chancel. E cloister walk; fdns. of sacristy, refectory and guest house. Excavated 1926 and whole plan revealed.

Rusper *Priory. Sussex. 4m N of Horsham. (–1200 to 1537). Benedictine nuns. F: member of the de Braose family. Ded: St Mary Magdalene.*
Small and poor but many of the nuns came from good families. In 1278 a high-handed prioress seized lands of imprisoned tenants, but her bailiff may have been the culprit. The house was in sad decline after the Black Death. In 1442 a visitation by the bp. found only one fault – a lack of business accounts. In 1478 the prioress must have been a splendid manager to have kept the house operating on such slender means; but in 1521 the conditions were poor due to a prioress entertaining her friends at the nunnery's expense. In 1537 the aged prioress and her 1 nun, both of whom had taken their vows together 53 years before, were turned out into the world they had shunned for so long (VCH). *Remains:* None. The last fragments were demolished in 1781 and a house, known as The Nunnery, occupies the site.

Rye *Friary. Sussex. Map 7. 11 m NE of Hastings. (1364–1538). Austin. Fs: William Taillour and 2 others (Knowles). Ded: St Nicholas?*

271

Limit of Oxford. 1st. sited below the E cliff which suffered from incursions of the sea and an attack by the French in 1377. In the following year the friars moved to a new site within the town walls. History is almost a blank. Dwindling membership resulted in the house being almost empty in 1439, but in the 16thC the fortunes increased and the townsfolk helped to get the ruinous bldgs. repaired. *Remains:* Ch. survives on the E side of Conduit Hill. An inserted floor cuts across the blocked windows, but in 4 windows in the S wall some Dec. tracery exists. All else gone.

Rye *Friary. Sussex. Map 7. 11m NE of Hastings. (c. 1263 to −1307). Sack Friars. F: unknown. Ded: unknown.*
No history. The friars were granted permission to live in Rye in 1263 and the house was probably abandoned by 1307. *Remains:* The 'Old Stone House' in Church Square was apparently the NW wing of a larger bldg. of *c.* 1265, and the ch. and other parts of the monastery lay to its S. The stone bldg. farther W called the 'Store House' may have been part of the friary (VCH).

S

St Agatha's *Abbey. Yorks. NR. See* Easby.

St Albans *Abbey. Herts. Map 6. (c. 970−1539). Benedictine monks. Fs: St Oswald & K. Edgar (introduced strict Bene. Rule). Ded: St Alban (1st. English martyr).*
1st. f. 793 by K. Offa II of Mercia on site of ch. where the martyrdom occurred *c.* 209 (Feaver). Ch. rebuilt

c. 1077+ by Abbot Paul of Caen with an immense store of Roman bricks collected by his predecessors. *c.* 1200 stone extensions. Mitred. The premier abbey in which the abbot ranked above all other English abbots. A 13thC monk, Matthew Paris, is one of the best known mediaeval chroniclers. At the Black Death, 1349, the abbot and over 50 monks perished. At the 2nd Battle of St Albans the abbey suffered severe damage (1461) which was followed next day by a thanksgiving service for victory by Q. Margaret and Henry VI. The greatest abbot, Thomas de la Mare, ruled to the highest standard for almost 50 years (obit. 1496). Extensive history and details available from many sources. The abbey was closely associated with Sopwell nunnery. Fine scriptorium saw the production of the beautiful 'Book of the Benefactions of St Albans' now at Cambridge. *Remains:* Splendid conventual ch., much restored, with the longest nave in the U.K. Given cathedral status 1871. Sole remaining relic of vast claustral complex is the massive 14thC gatehouse, now part of a school. Acct: VCH, Herts. Vol. 2; Br. Arch. Assoc. J., Vol. 13. Books: 1. History of the Abbey of St Albans (1917) L. F. R. Williams, 2. The Abbey of St Albans. . . . (1911) V. H. Galbraith, etc. Illus: Pitkin Pictorial (D. R. Feaver).

St Albans *Abbey. Herts. (c. 970− c. 1140). Benedictine nuns. Fs: St Oswald & K. Edgar. Ded: St Alban.*
1st. f. by K. Offa II of Mercia for nuns and monks. Their discipline later became lax. Sometime before 940 and again in 1077 the nuns were confined to the almonry where they tended the poor. Sometime in or before 1140 at the instance of Abbot

Godfrey (1119–46), the community moved to their own house at Sopwell, 1½m to the S (v. below).

St Anthony-in-Roseland *Priory Cell. Cornwall. 2½m E of Falmouth. (–1288 to 1538). Augustinian canons, F: Bp. Robert I of Exeter (granted the ch.) Ded: St Antoninus.* Dependent upon Plympton who kept a prior and one canon here from the fdn. to the Dissolution. The ch. had been given to Plympton by the bp. *c.* 1140 (Knowles). The house was burnt down by the French in 1338 (Oliver). Little else known. *Remains:* Place House occupies the site and incorporates the refectory. Notes: The Parish of St Anthony in Roseland (1852) L. S. Boyne.

St Augustines *Abbey. Kent. See* Canterbury.

St Bees *Priory. C'land (Cumbria). Map 1. 5m S of Whitehaven. (+1120 to 1538). Benedictine monks. F: William Meschin. Ded: St Mary & St Bega.* 1st. f. *c.* 650 by St Bega, a refugee from Ireland, as a nunnery and later destroyed by the Danes. The F. gave the site to St Mary's, York, who established a cell comprising a prior and 6 monks. Many benefactions and details of endowments preserved in fine cartulary. The house had business links with the Isle of Man, through Rushen Abbey; and with Ireland through York. Chief relic was a bracelet said to have belonged to St Bega, which was used to ratify agreements. In the 12thC the priory had an income from iron mining. The last prior was found innocent of any link with the Northern Rising. *Remains:* Conventual ch. including nave, S transept, crossing and W bay of chancel. Cross-

ing tower & E end of chancel 19thC. Splendid W door, finest in the county (Pevsner). Note: Antiquity, Vol. 9.

St Benet of Hulme *(Holme) Abbey. Norfolk. Map 4. 10m NE of Norwich. (1019–1539). Benedictine monks. F: K. Canute. Ded: St Benedict.* 1st. f. *c.* 800 and destroyed by Danes in 870. Never a house of much importance with an undistinguished existence (Knowles). Considerable details of abbots' lives in VCH. In 1287 the sea swamped the abbey's outbldgs. which could only be reached by boats, and horses were sheltered in the nave of the ch. In early 14thC lawless neighbours harassed the monks when they transferred victuals between manors. Mitred. In 1494 the visiting bp. said the community was overburdened with recitals of canticles leaving no time for private study. There were several 16thC complaints including (a) an excess of dogs in 1526 which ate food intended for the poor, (b) lack of service for the sick and (c) the ignorance of some monks who could scarcely read. It was the only religious house in England not dissolved by Henry VIII. *Remains:* Ruins of gatehouse into which an 18thC brick windmill was built. Fragments of fdns., part of a W tower, chapter house and perhaps the infirmary. Notes: Br. Arch. Assoc. J. Vol. 36 (1880).

St Botolph's *Priory. Essex. See* Colchester.

St Carrok *Alien Priory Cell/Priory Cell. Cornwall. 3m NNE of Fowey. (c. 1100–1536). Cluniac monks. Ded: uncertain.* 1st. f. before the Conquest. *c.* 1100 the cell was seized by Robert, count of Mortain, whose son gave it to his fdn. at Montacute (Knowles). Also referred to as the cell of St Cyret & Julette. History obscure with a single ref. 1236 when 2 monks lived here. The house presumably became denizen at the same time as Montacute in 1407. The name of only one prior (the last) is known and at the Dissolution he and one monk surrendered the little cell. *Remains:* Very slight. A house occupies the site at St Veer.

St Denys *Priory. Hants. See* Southampton.

St Frideswide's *Priory. Oxon. See* Oxford.

St Germans *Priory. Cornwall. Map 8. 9m SE of Liskeard. (c. 1180–1539). Augustinian canons. F: Bp. Bartholomew of Exeter (1161–84) introduced Aug. canons towards the end of his pontificate. Ded: St Germanus*.*
K. Athelstan est. a cathedral here *c.* 936 and Bp. Leofric (of Devon & Cornwall) placed secular canons in it who were, in turn, replaced *c.* 1180 as above. The new ch. was ded. in 1261. The community of about 24 canons in the 14thC was more than halved by the B.D. Very little internal history known, or of the canons who fostered its valuable library (Oliver). *Remains:* Much of the conventual ch. survives and is in use as the parish ch. which embodies some of the original Norman bldg. The chancel collapsed in 1592. There was never a crossing tower or transepts. None of the claustral buildings exist.
* *c.* 378–448. Became bp. of Auxerre in 418. Twice visited Britain.

St Ives *Priory Cell. Hunts. 5m E of Huntingdon. (c. 1017–1539). Bene-*

dictine monks. F: Earl Adelmus. Ded: All Saints.
Being a small and poor cell of Ramsey there is scarcely any independent history. The prior appears usually to have been an obedientiary of the mother house. Destroyed by fire in 1207. Several priors became abbots of Ramsey. Only the prior was living here at the Dissolution. *Remains:* Minimal. Some fragments of walling exist near a house now in use as council offices.

St John's *Abbey. Essex. See* Colchester.

St Margaret's *Priory. Herts. See* Ivinghoe.

St Mary De Pre *(de Pratis) Priory. Herts. 2½m NW of St Albans. (1194–1528). Benedictine nuns. F: Warin, abbot of St Albans. Ded: St Mary.*
1st. fd. as a women's leper hospital. As leprosy died out the women became nuns and sisters under the Bene. Rule *c.* 1330; and soon afterwards the sisters became nuns also. From the outset the house was subordinate to St Albans and the nuns were therefore exempt from episcopal visitation (VCH). In the 13thC it seems that the inmates scarcely had the necessities of life and a master was appointed to control the temporal affairs. Something of the internal life is known from a late-14thC ordinance drawn up by the abbot of St Albans, and from detailed accounts which survive for the years 1341–57 and 1461–93 (VCH). In the latter period there is a ref. to the curious custom of eating dried peas on the 5th Sunday in Lent, for which the nuns paid 16d. for 2 bushels. The alien Bene. cell of Wing (Bucks.) was granted to the nuns in 1416 (*v.* Appendix 1). A famous

274

letter from Archbp. Morton in 1490 throws some suspicion on the doubtful relations between the nuns here and the monks of St Albans. This may have some truth in it as a prioress was removed from office. Dissolved for Wolsey's Ipswich Coll. *Remains:* None. The last remnants were demolished in 1849.

St Mary Graces *Abbey. See* London.

St Mary's *Abbey. York. See* York.

St Neots* *Priory/Alien Priory/Priory. Hunts. 9m S of Huntingdon. (c. 974–1539). Benedictine monks. Fs: Earl Aylric and Ethelfleda his wife. Ded: St Neot.*
Dependent upon Ely. Destroyed by Danes 1010. Re-f. by Roisia, wife of Richard Fitz Gilbert de Clare c. 1080. The latter expelled the English monks and gave the house to Bec Abbey who colonised it with Norman monks. As an alien house its fortunes dwindled during the wars with France until it became denizen in 1412. 13thC cartulary survives in BM. In 1439 the property was in poor repair and rain came through the ch. roof 'to fall on the choir books' (VCH). In 1506 the standard of management was low and there was reform on many matters. The relics of the saint are said to have been brought from St Neots in Cornwall and in 1213 were moved once again – to Crowland Abbey (*v.* above). *Remains:* None. Part of site excavated late 1950s. The ch. fdns. lie beneath the yard and outbldgs. of the Cross Keys Hotel.
* Formerly Eynesbury.

St Olave's *(Herringfleet) Priory. Suffolk. Map 4. 6m SW of Great Yarmouth. (c. 1216–1537). Augustinian canons. F: Roger Fitz-Osbert. Ded:*

St Mary & St Olave*.
The F., his wife and son buried in the ch. Very little early history. VCH gives details of patrons and appropriated chs. When Bp. Goldwell visited the house in 1493 he found the canons were scarcely able to live. After a visitation in 1514 the house was praised for the condition of the bldgs. and the observances, but it seems the canons were sometimes lax in rising at midnight for matins. Further visitations in 1520 & 1526 testified to the good conditions which prevailed within the priory. *Remains:* Nave ruins of the single-aisled ch. (the crossing and E end covered by a lane). Part of cloister garth. Frater undercroft of exceptionally early brickwork – late-13th or early-14thC. Barn above. Much of the priory was demolished in 1784. Excavated 1904 and at subsequent periods. Desc., plan & care: D of E.
* Norwegian king and martyr.

St Osyth *(Chich) Priory/Abbey. Essex. Map 7. 10m SE of Colchester. (1121–1539). Augustinian canons. F: Richard de Belmeis, Bp. of London. Ded: St Peter, St Paul & St Osyth*.*
7thC nunnery destroyed by Danes 653. The 12thC fdn. grew rapidly in wealth and fame and gained a reputation for piety and learning (Dickinson). The house given abbey status in or before 1161. The first prior became archbp. of Canterbury. In 1306 a curious incident concerned the removal of a cross from Dunwich hospital by the abbot, who was ordered to restore it to the owners. Mitred 1397. Early in the 15thC the canons obtained valuables from a shipwreck but were prevented from keeping them. Among surviving documents is a balance sheet for 1491

275

and detailed accounts relating to the dissolution of the house. *Remains:* Fine crenellated gatehouse of E Anglian flushwork with flanking wings. Of the claustral bldgs. which lay to the N, 2 13thC W range undercrofts survive; in the E range several undercroft chambers of the dormitory; and the 13thC refectory lobby. Ch. completely gone. Desc. & plan: NE Essex Inventory of the Royal Comm. on Hist. Monuments, Vol. 3, (1922).
* The martyred daughter of K. Frithwald & Q. Wilburga who f. a monastery of which she became first abbess.

St Pancras *Priory. Sussex. See* Lewes.

St Radegund's *(Bradsole) Abbey. Kent. Map 7. 3m W of Dover. (1193–1536). Premonstratensian canons. F: Several. Ded: St Radegund.*
This was a daughter house of Prémontré which sent Hugh*, the 1st abbot, to establish a house. There were many benefactors, none of whom were sufficiently prominent to claim the patronage (Colvin); but several important donors gave land upon which the abbey was built. *c.* 1203 the canons took over the poor and war-torn priory of Blackwose, and Lavendon Abbey received 2d. p.a. in compensation. Prémon. records throw much light on the abbey's history and its possessions, and maintain that the abbot was always the patron. A visitation in 1482 by the abbot of Shap (the senior English abbot) found the need for repairs to bldgs., and ordered some disciplinary measures; but in 1491 there were no complaints. *Remains:* Of the ch. the principal survival is the flint tower in the angle between the nave and N transept. In the S transept is a spiral stair once used for both day and night access between dormitory and ch. Many walls of conventual bldgs. remain, and the refectory (built on a vaulted undercroft) is now a farmhouse. Excavated 1880. Desc. & plan: Archaeologia Cantiana, Vols. 14 (1882) & 43 (1931).
* Hugh is frequently described as the F. but was more likely the moving spirit behind the fdn.

St Radegund's *Priory. Cambs. See* Cambridge.

Salisbury *Friary. Wilts. (1281–1538). Dominican. F: perhaps Archbp. Kilwardby of Canterbury on land given by Edward I. Ded: Holy Trinity.*
Visitation of London. 1st. fd. at Wilton (*v.* below) 36 years earlier. Numerous royal gifts which encouraged local nobility to follow the example. VCH gives details of bequests and gifts which were in kind rather than money in the 13thC, a situation reversed in the 14thC. In 1318 five of the younger friars rescued a man being taken to the gallows because they considered the court's verdict unjust. The man escaped and the friars were pardoned. In 1345 it appears that Mary, Countess of Norfolk, received licence to set up a chantry of 6 chaplains within the friars' house, but it was probably never established. Little is known of the friary in the 14th & 15thCs. At the Dissolution the Crown's agents found the house well cared for but owing £30. *Remains:* None. An inn stood on the site in Fisherton in the 18thC. No evidence of any reused materials locally.

Salisbury *Friary. Wilts. (−1230 to 1538). Franciscan (Conventual). Fs: Bp. Richard le Poer*

(Poore) of Salisbury and Henry III.
Ded: St Francis?
Custody of London. Until *c.* 1331
the house itself was the head of a
Custody. Details of gifts of timber
between 1232 & 1294 for building
and fuel are among the few facts
which throw any light at all upon the
history of the house. Other benefactions are listed in VCH but little else
seems to be known. On two occasions
the English provincial chapter met
here. One 13thC writer recalled that
'the feeling of mutual affection in the
house was the distinguishing note,
and the warden, Stephen, . . . would
not allow anyone to be made sad'.
(VCH). *Remains:* Such parts as
survive are incorporated in Windover
House on the S side of St Anne Street.
Part excavated 1966–8. Excav. notes:
Med. Arch. Vols. 11 & 13.

Salley *Abbey. Yorks. See* Sawley.

Sandleford *Priory. Berks. 1½m S of*
Newbury. (1193/1202–1478).
Augustinian canons. Fs: Geoffrey,
4th Count of Perch and Matilda his
wife. Ded: St John Baptist.
Very small and poor with only 3 or
4 canons. A plan to re-f. the house
for nuns in 1274 never materialised
(Knowles). Information about history
is meagre and fragmentary. In 1317
the canons were called upon to
support a royal pensioner for the rest
of his life; and in 1320 a prior was
forced to resign due to his negligence
in caring for the bldgs. *c.* 1478 it was
said that the religious had wholly
vacated the monastery, but the
reason is unknown. The house was
then appropriated to the collegiate
ch. of Windsor by Bp. Beauchamp of
Salisbury. *Remains:* An 18thC house
occupies the site which incorporates

one roof of the priory bldgs. and part
of a large room.

Sandwell *Priory. Staffs. At W Brom-*
wich, 5m NW of Birmingham (c.
1180–1524). Benedictine monks. F:
William de Offney, Lord of Dudley.
Ded: St Mary Magdalen.
Very small and could probably never
support more than 4 monks. Fortunes
improved in 1230 when W Bromwich
ch. was obtained from the monks of
Worcester. In the 14thC the election
of at least 3 priors was annulled by
the bp., and on 4 occasions only one
monk is recorded as living here. There
were stormy relations with laymen,
also in the 14thC, who invaded priory
lands and stole fish. On the credit side
the priory managed to extend its
property holdings. Hardly any 15th
& 16thC history. The house seems to
have been united with Wenlock
(Cluniac) after 1436, and when suppressed by Wolsey in 1524 the prior
and one monk went to Wenlock, the
former becoming the prior there
(Graham). The dissolution deed survives and comprises 23 vellum pages.
Remains: None. Sandwell Hall covers
the site.

Sandwich *Friary. Kent. (c. 1268–*
1538). Carmelite. F: perhaps Henry
Cowfield. Ded: BVM.
Distinction of London. The first endowments were very small and 20
years later William Lord Clinton was
a much larger benefactor and is often
reputed as sole F. (VCH). In 1370
there is a ref. to 'a fair image of the
blessed virgin and martyr Katherine'
(nowadays presumed mythical).
There was also an image of St Anne,
mother of the BVM. A self-confessed
murderer took sanctuary in the ch.
in 1487. Not much history survives,
but details of bequests, gifts and

277

burials are considerable. *Remains:* None. The site in New Street is occupied by a house. In 1971 part of the ch. fdns. were found and a plan made of the choir walls, cloister walks and rooms in the S range. (Med. Arch. Vol. 17). Desc. & plan: Archaeologia Cantiana, Vol. 80 (1965).

Sawley *(Salley) Abbey. Yorks. WR. Map 2. 3½m NE of Clitheroe. (1147–1536). Cistercian monks. F: William de Percy. Ded: St Mary.* Community arrived from Newminster 1.1.1148. Never wealthy or large with an undistinguished history (Knowles) apart from severe depredation of monastic property at the hands of the Scots. 40 years after the fdn. abandonment was considered, due to a cloudy climate and rain-soaked crops. The Percy family saved the situation by giving ch. endowments. Being on a main N–S highway hospitality costs were high. The establishment of Whalley Abbey in 1296 caused friction, and competition forced up prices of timber, salt, iron and bark (for the tannery) which imperilled Sawley's trading. In 1305 a Cist. general chapter settled the dispute. The expelled community in 1536 were reinstated by insurgents forming part of the Pilgrimage of Grace, for which the abbot was hanged at Lancaster in 1537. *Remains:* Extensive lower course walls of ch. and conventual bldgs. Unusual ch. plan with small nave – shorter in length than width. No window shapes survive. Several unusual features. The two relics of gate-houses by the road are post-suppression. Excavated 1848 & 1907. Care: D of E. Desc. & plan: Yorks. Arch. J. Vol. 20 (1909). Book: Historical Acct. of Cist. Abbey of Salley (1853) J. Harland. Plan: Yorks. Arch. J.

Vol. 30 (1931–2) and ref. to the remarkable Prior Rymyngton.

Sawtry *Abbey. Hunts. 9m NNW of Huntingdon. (1147–1536). Cistercian monks. F: Simon de St Liz, Earl of Northampton. Ded: St Mary.* Colonised from Warden. The convent owned a manor at Swaffham, Norfolk, for the reception of pilgrims making for Walsingham. In the 13thC there were, inevitably, lawsuits over land ownership with Ramsey and Thorney abbeys as all 3 lay so close together. After refs. to poverty and debt in the 14thC the history is blank. At the Dissolution the abbot's efforts to save his house were to no avail, nor were any luxuries found at the monastery; although the abbot's bed had a feather mattress and white curtains (VCH). *Remains:* None. The site has been excavated. Four almost perfect fishponds survive. Notes: Archaeologia, Vols. 43 & 50.

Scalby *Friary. Yorks. NR. 3m NW of Scarborough. (1245–c. 1270). Franciscan (Conventual). F: William de Morpeth. Ded: unknown.* The friars of Scarborough decided to quit their settlement (*v.* below) after conflict with Cistercians who possessed certain property in the town, and moved 3 miles away to land given by the above F. After some 25 years they returned to Scarborough to a permanent establishment even though they were again opposed by the Cistercians. *Remains:* None.

Scarborough *Friary. Yorks. NR. (1319–1539). Carmelite. F: uncertain. Edward II granted 2 houses held in gift of Robert Wauwayn. Ded: BVM.* Distinction of York. As with most friars' houses history is obscure. In the early days the Cistercians gave

278

their consent to the fdn. within their parish of St Mary (Fountains Abbey had land and fishing interests here). Soon after the friars were established, a Thomas de la Rivere and Joan his wife disputed Robert's right to give the property away. Edward II prevented litigation; and in 1341 Joan, now a widow, relinquished her rights to the property in favour of the friars (VCH). Most of the remaining information about the house concerns grants of land and other bequests. *Remains:* None.

Scarborough *Friary. Yorks. NR. (1252–1539). Dominican. F: probably Peter de Brus. Ded: unknown.* Visitation of York. A large house with over 30 friars in the 14thC whose existence in the town was opposed by the Cistercians. One of the greatest benefactors was Isabel de Vescy, kinswoman of Q. Eleanor (wife of Edward I), who built the nave of the ch., cloister and dormitory. She was buried in the choir c. 1335 (VCH). There were many other donors and the site was composed of numerous small plots. 14th & 15thC history is scanty. Many distinguished persons were buried in the ch. and Maud, daughter of the Earl of Westmorland, desired in 1438 to be buried 'at the S end of the high altar where they read the Gospels'. *Remains:* None. Hist: Yorks. Arch. Soc. J. Vol. 32 (1935). Notes: The Reliquary, Vol. 20 (1880).

Scarborough *Friary. Yorks. NR. (1239–1539). Franciscan (Conventual). F: perhaps Reginald Molendinar. Ded: unknown.* Custody of York. The friars, first of the 3 Orders in the town, met with Cistercian opposition and retired in 1245 to Scalby (*v.* above). Some 25 years later they returned to Scarborough to meet further resistance and the struggle continued for another 15 years (Martin). All 3 Orders of friars sent an officer round the town with a handbell on the anniversary of the deaths of their Fs. and benefactors who were buried in their chs. Very little known of internal history. VCH gives details of grants of land and bequests, and of licences to extend property. A lane called 'le Dumple' was enclosed by the friars in 1322, an area also partly occupied by the Dominicans. When the friary was closed the house was said to be so poor that everything had been sold so that 'nothing is left but glass, stone and some good lead'. *Remains:* None. Hist: Yorks. Arch. Soc. J. Vol. 32 (1935).

Scilly *Priory Cell. Cornwall. On the island of Tresco. (1114–c. 1538). Benedictine monks. F: Henry I granted all the chs. and lands in Scilly to Tavistock Abbey. Ded: St Nicholas.* Before the Conquest a confederation of hermits lived here. The abbey kept 2 monks at Tresco who ministered to the islanders and took care of the property; but because the isles were constantly exposed to piratical attacks there was not much value in the possessions (Finberg). c. 1300 the monks received a qualified right of wreck from the Earl of Cornwall, which did not extend to the convent at Tavistock. Nothing is known of the revenues from the property and much of the priory's existence seems to have passed unnoticed. *Remains:* There are 2 arches and some walling which were part of the 13thC ch. A few ornamental fragments exist in the garden (Pevsner).

Selborne *Priory. Hants. 4m SSE of Alton. (1233–1484). Augustinian canons. F: Bp. Peter des Roches of Winchester. Ded: St Mary.*
Here is a rare instance where nearly all the monastic muniments have survived, stored at Magdalen Coll., Oxford. From 1250 there follows a long period of uneventful history until 1376 when a prior was suspended from office for his wasteful and lax administration. In 1387 Bp. Wykeham issued 36 injunctions against the canons most of which are recorded in VCH: but subsequently the bp. held a high opinion of the convent whose prior sent a letter of thanks for 'his great goodness and liberality in giving 100 marks'. Debts, creditors and heavy repair bills forced the prior, the sole occupant in 1484, to close the overburdened house which was given to Magdalen Coll. *Remains:* Extensive excavations near Priory Farm from 1956–69 have revealed fdns. of much of the ch. and some of the claustral bldgs., which lay to the N (Med. Arch. Vols. 1–14; plan Vol. 11). Hist: Selborne Priory, a Calendar of Charters (1891) – Magdalen Coll., Oxford.

Selby *Abbey. Yorks. WR. Map 3. (1069–1539). Benedictine monks. F: William I; inspired by Benedict, a monk of Auxerre. Ded: St Mary & St Germanus*.*
Early history largely obscured by legends, but a manuscript named the *Historia* of 1171, written by a monk, has provided the fdn. story. The 12thC life of the convent was disfigured by (1) a series of personal vendettas in which the spoliation of the abbey's estates was attempted, (2) disputed elections, (3) vacancies in the abbacy and (4) civil war. By the early 13thC the monks had begun

to recover their security and a more regulated future (Dobson). But peace was short lived. A visit by Archbp. Giffard in 1275 revealed the worst reports. The unsavoury reputation was equally bad 5 years later, and in 1334 Archbp. Melton accused 6 monks of spending monastic funds on women (Knowles). The house was seriously damaged by fire in 1346. At the beginning of the 15thC the abbey entered upon decline and revenues fell from £500 to £100 p.a. due to sloth and neglect. Mitred 1486, by which time the house was of comparative insignificance. *Remains:* Splendid ch. Much restored after disastrous fire in 1906. Nothing survives of claustral bldgs. and the last remnant, the great gatehouse, was destroyed 1792. Books: 1. History & Antiquities of Selby (1867) W. W. Morrell. 2. Selby Abbey (1908) C. H. Moody. 3. Selby Abbey and Town (1967) R. B. Dobson. Illus: Pitkin Pictorial. Misc. refs. in Yorks. Arch. J. Vols. 5, 17, 39, 41 & 42.
* *c.* 378–488. Became Bp. of Auxerre in 418.

Sele *– 1 (Upper Beeding) Alien Priory/Priory. Sussex. Map 6. 4m N of Shoreham. (–1096 to 1480). Benedictine monks. F: William de Braose. Ded: St Peter.*
1st. f. 1073 for secular canons. When the last died the F. gave the ch. to the abbey of St Florent-de-Saumer which sent 2 monks. The F's. son confirmed the grants *c.* 1096. The ch. was shared by parishioners and monks for 200 years and at the end of the 13thC the parishioners became liable for their share of ch. repairs. Became denizen in 1396 and the wars with France caused the priory to decline and it was suppressed in 1459 by the bp. of Winchester; but the last prior

was deposed in 1474 for converting the priory for his sole use. One monk was still here in 1480 when the property finally passed to Magdalen Coll., Oxford.

Sele – *2 (upper Beeding) Friary. Sussex. Location as above. (1493–1538). Carmelite. Fs: Fellows of Magdalen Coll., Oxford. Ded: BVM & St Peter.*
Distinction of London. When the friars of Shoreham were driven from their house by river floods, they leased the priory bldgs. and chancel of the ch. from Magdalen Coll. Little is known of their history during the 45 years of tenure, except that they were probably the poorest of all the Sussex friars. The Crown visitor found no one here in 1538 nor had there been for sometime, but the doors were open (VCH). *Remains:* The ch. survives with 19thC extensions. The site of the claustral bldgs. is occupied by a Georgian house. Area N of ch. excavated 1966 revealed wall fdns. (Med. Arch. Vol. 11).

Sempringham – *1 Priory. Lincs. Map 3. 10m N of Bourne. (c. 1131–c. 1139). Gilbertine nuns, primarily. F: St Gilbert. Ded: St Andrew.*
1st. house of the Order. With the help of Bp. Alexander of Lincoln, Gilbert built a dwelling and cloister against the N wall of the parish ch. to enclose 7 maidens who wished to take up a strict religious life. They were given a Rule of holiness which was the humble beginning of the Order of Sempringham (Graham). The community attracted much attention and lay-sisters and lay-brothers, working and living on the lands Gilbert had inherited, soon outgrew the little priory. *Remains:* The parish ch., some of which is Norman, survives.

The N aisle wall was rebuilt in the 19thC so the original siting of the abutment of Gilbert's cloister has gone. According to Pevsner, the dating of some parts of the ch. precludes the possibility of this being St Gilbert's, 'unless building was slow'. No other remains.

Sempringham – *2 Priory. Lincs. ¼m W of the above site. (c. 1139–1538). Gilbertine canons and nuns. F: St Gilbert upon land given by Gilbert of Ghent. Ded: St Mary.*
Having re-established the nuns the F. appointed learned canons early in 1149 to serve the whole community as priests (Graham). F. buried here in 1189. Poverty in early days. Benefactors had compassion upon the community and wool became the chief source of revenue, but the house was never wealthy. Cloth made at the priory was well-known in early-13thC. The priory was in high favour with all three K. Edwards. The Black Death grievously reduced the numbers and lay-brothers, a mainstay of the community, ceased to exist. 15thC history obscure following the abandonment of farming. At the Dissolution all members of the house were reported living blameless lives – neither in poverty nor in wealth. *Remains:* None. Mansion built on site with the materials, though never lived in, has also vanished. Excavated 1938–9. Desc. & plan (of ch.): Br. Arch. Assoc. J. Vol. 5 (1940).

Seton* *(Seaton) Priory. C'land. (Cumbria). Map 1. 8½m NNW of Millom. (–1200 to 1540). Benedictine nuns. F: Henry, son of Arthur, Lord of Millom. Ded: St Mary.*
Cell of Nunburnholme but sometime after 1313 it gained independence. A rough life and continual border war-

fare brought hardship and poverty to the community, and in 1357 the nuns were given patronage of Lancaster hospital because they were so poor. An 8-year-old girl was forced to enter the priory but after several years she escaped and was married in 1383 (Power). The bp. found her story of 'imprisonment' true and she is a rare example of a full release from the observances of the Order. Apart from gifts of land from the monks of Holmcultram in 1459 nothing more is known. *Remains:* Nothing but the E wall of the chancel with 3 lancet windows. Nearby Seaton Hall possibly built with materials from the nunnery. * Anciently known as Lekeley.

Sewardsley *Priory. N'hants. 2m NNE of Towcester. (r. of Henry II – 1536). Cistercian nuns. F: Richard de Lestre. Ded: St Mary.*
Inadequate endowments made the house wretchedly poor and in 1300 a nun found the life unbearable and abandoned her habit. In 1366 & 1378 licences were given to allow the nuns to beg for alms. The poor terms under which much of the property was leased to a layman reveals the desperate plight. By 1432 the morality of the nuns had declined 'to the abandonment of all modesty', and in 1459 the house was appropriated to the Cluniac nuns of DelaPré Abbey in Northampton due to poverty. In 1470 the priory was allegedly associated with witchcraft. A lead image used by the Duchess of Bedford for sorcery had been exhibited at the nunnery. *Remains:* None.

Shaftesbury *Abbey. Dorset. Map 5. (c. 888–1539). Benedictine nuns. F: Alfred the Great. Ded: St Mary & St Edward, king and martyr.*
The F's. daughter became 1st. Abbess.

282

From 1080–1120 the Saxon ch. was replaced by a larger bldg. and ultimately the abbey ch. was as large as Salisbury Cathedral. The house became the largest and richest Bene. nunnery which prompted the saying: 'If the abbot of Glastonbury could marry the abbess of Shaftesbury their heir would hold more land than the king of England'. One of the early causes of troubles was a community too large for the income to support, despite large holdings and the important shrine of K. Edward. In 1380 tempestuous winds, sea innundation of abbey lands, heavy losses of livestock and pestilence caused serious setbacks. The abbess was a baroness of the realm in her own right. Strangely, despite immense influence and historical links the nuns recorded nothing. In 1327 the abbess was granted a rare permission to crenellate the abbey, no doubt for defence reasons. No visitations in the 15thC and few refs. survive during the remainder of the abbey's life except records of elections. Wolsey's daughter, who passed under the name of Dorothy Clansey, was an unprofessed nun here. *Remains:* Fdn. outlines of most of the ch. In 1931 a lead box containing the probable remains of St Edward was discovered hidden in a wall. A modern shrine has been built to enclose the relics. Excavated 1861, 1902–4 & 1931. Book: Shaftesbury Abbey (1959) Laura Sydenham.

Shap *(Hepp) Abbey. W'land (Cumbria). Map 1. 10m S of Penrith. (–1201 to 1540). Premonstratensian canons. F: Thos. Fitz Gospatrick. Ded: St Mary Magdalene.*
1st. fd. at Preston Patrick (v. above). The canons supported a small leper hospital at Appleby. The site of the

abbey was originally known as Hepp (heap) perhaps due to fallen megaliths still nearby. Most of the abbey's records were lost in the 18thC and small fragments of history known today come from 17thC transcripts (Colvin). Community heavily reduced by B.D. Details of grants and ch. appropriations survive. One young and learned canon, Richard Redman, while abbot of Shap became visitor of all houses of the Order in England (1466), bp. of St Asaph (1471), bp. of Exeter (1496) and bp. of Ely (1501) while still retaining the abbacy of Shap, due to his exceptional administrative abilities. The community paid the large fine of £266.13.4d to continue beyond 1536. Incised circles on the nave floor still indicate the exact spot where a canon should stand at the end of a procession (v. Easby). *Remains:* Low walls and fdns. of most of the abbey's 13thC bldgs. on this very cramped site, dominated by the massive W tower of the ch. Excavated 1885–6 and 1956–7. Desc. plan & care: D of E. Acct. & plan: C'land & W'land Arch. Soc. Trans. Vol. 10 (1889); Med. Arch. Vols. 1 & 2.

Sheen *Priory. Surrey. Now Richmond. (1414–1539). Carthusian monks. F: Henry V. Ded: Jesus of Bethlehem.* The last English Charterhouse to be fd. and to surrender. It became the wealthiest of the Order with an income mainly derived from considerable endowments which were confiscations from 6 suppressed alien priories (*v.* Appendix 1) — but not without prolonged protests from the deprived French abbeys. Located close to the royal palace of King's Sheen. In the BM is a 15thC manuscript of the priory's Rule giving precise details of the Carthusian life.

Little known of the internal history apart from the granting of licences, etc. In 1502 a monk murdered the prior of the house in one of the cellars, but the reason and the punishment are unknown. The last prior signed the king's Act of Supremacy in 1534 and regretted that he had not shared 'the crown of martyrdom' with other Carth. monks (*v.* London). *Remains:* None.

Sheen *Carmelite and Franciscan Friars. See* Richmond.

Shelford *Priory. Notts. 6m NE by E of Nottingham. (t. of Henry II – 1536). Augustinian canons. F: Ralph Haunselyn. Ded: St Mary.* Three visitation reports survive. In 1280 the injunctions included banning worthless persons from the refectory; that the canons should refrain from the vice of holding private property, and the prior must end his indulgence in drink (VCH). The house had thriving wool sales in the 13thC. Little other history is recorded apart from details of licences for obtaining gifts of land and receipts from spiritualities. It seems that boys received employment and education during the priory's life (Knowles). *Remains:* None. A manor house stands on the site and no doubt incorporates masonry from the priory.

Sherborne *Cathedral Priory/Priory/ Abbey. Dorset. Map 5. (c. 993– 1539). Benedictine monks. F: Bp. Wolfsige. Ded: St Mary.* 1st. a bishopric in 705. The F. replaced the seculars with monks c. 993. When the see moved to Old Sarum c. 1075 the bp. still remained the titular head of the priory. In 1122 the link was severed and the house became an abbey with the community

283

choosing their own abbots. St Stephen Harding, who later drew up the constitution of the Cistercian Order, was educated in the abbey as a novice. From the 12thC until the mid-15thC the history is uneventful and chiefly composed of disconnected incidents. The famous Sherborne Missal of early-15thC, comprising some 400 leaves with magnificent decoration, is in Alnwick Castle. In 1436 a bitter quarrel between monks and townsfolk ended in a disastrous fire. It took the remainder of the century to restore the bldgs. *Remains:* Fine ch. with the 'aesthetic perfection of Perpendicular stone vaulting' (Braun). Cloister lay to N and there survives in a school part of the dormitory, the guest hall, the abbot's hall with 15thC roof, abbot's lodging and kitchen with large mediaeval chimney. The octagonal conduit/lavatorium from the cloister is now in the town E of the ch. Excavated *c.* 1896 & 1930 and in 1968 work at the W end of the ch. produced evidence of 12thC towers; and in 1974 it was discovered that the E claustral range had been rebuilt late-12thC — Med. Arch. Vols. 13 & 19. Desc. & plan: Archaeologia, Vol. 60 (1907).

Sheringham *Priory Cell. Norfolk. On the N coastline. (−1164 to c. 1345). Augustinian canons. F: Walter Giffard, Earl of Buckingham. Ded: All Saints.* The F. gave the ch. to Notley Abbey which he had fd. at the same time or a little earlier. The canons of Notley established a small cell here composed of 2 or 3 canons, and rents due from abbey lands near King's Lynn were payable at Sheringham (Tanner). By 1345 the ch. appears to have been destitute but Notley retained the rectory until the Dissolution. *Re-*

mains: None. The cell was adjacent to the present churchyard.

Shobden *Priory. Herefs. Map 2. 6m NW by W of Leominster. (c. 1140– c. 1172). Augustinian canons. F: Oliver de Merlimond. Ded: St John, Evangelist.* The F. was steward to the powerful Hugh de Mortimer I who gave Shobden to Oliver. A ch. was begun at the same time as the F. went on a pilgrimage to Spain, and who stayed at the Parisian abbey of St Victor on his way home (Dickinson). Two canons from there were later sent to Shobden. A long series of woes, including Welsh border incidents and the arrogance of Mortimer I, resulted in the canons moving to Eye (6m to the NE), back to Shobden and finally to Wigmore (*v.* below). *Remains:* The priory ch. was demolished but the Norman chancel arch, two Norman doorways with their tympana, all much weather-beaten, were re-erected N of the later ch. to become known as The Shobden Arches.

Shoreham *Friary. Sussex. 6m W of Brighton. (−1317 to 1493). Carmelite. F: Sir John de Mowbray. Ded: BVM.* Distinction of London. In 1326 the friars obtained a house and chapel from the Hospitallers which had formerly belonged to the suppressed Templars. The ch. was enlarged in the 1370s but within 100 years the inroads of the sea threatened its survival. Accordingly the friars abandoned the property and leased a disused priory at Sele (*v.* above) from the fellows of Magdalen Coll., Oxford. *Remains:* None.

Shouldham *Priory. Norfolk. 7m SSE of King's Lynn. (+1193 to 1538). Gilbertine canons and nuns. F: Geof-*

frey fitz Piers (Peters). Ded: BVM & the Holy Cross.
The F. was chief justice of England who later became earl of Essex. The house was well endowed in its early days and came under the patronage of the earls of Warwick in the 13th & 14thCs, several daughters of whom became nuns here. In 1321 a canon was playing football with a lay friend when the latter accidentally ran against the canon's sheathed knife and died 6 days later. The pope exonorated the canon from blame. In 1324 the 3 daughters of Sir Roger de Mortimer of Wigmore (*v.* below) were sent separately to the Gilb. houses of Shouldham, Sempringham and Chicksands. Floods, fires and a great gale overthrew most of the priory bldgs. 'almost to the fdns.' at the end of the 14thC. Little is known of the numbers of canons and nuns during the 340 years of history except at the Dissolution. The almost inevitably untrustworthy reports about the community came from Cromwell's agents in 1536. *Remains:* None. Abbey Farm occupies the site. Re-used Barnack stone from the priory is in many local bldgs.

Shrewsbury *Abbey. Salop. Map 2. (1083–1540). Benedictine monks. F: Earl Roger of Montgomery. Ded: St Peter & St Paul.*
Colonised from St Martin's Abbey, Séez. The F. was encouraged by the eloquence of his chaplain, Odelirius, upon the latter's return from a visit to Rome in 1082. In addition to considerable accessions of property, the greatest possession were the relics of St Winifred obtained in 1138, whose shrine survived for 400 years. Following a visitation by the Archbp. of Canterbury in 1234 the monks were commended for their 'religious and

decorous conduct'. In 1283 the fate of David, Prince of Wales, was sealed in the chapter house by Edward I and Parliament. In 1398 Richard II also assembled his parliament here. Mitred. Abbot Thomas endeavoured to mediate between the armies drawn up at Battlefield in 1403, but the earl of Worcester rejected the offer. In 1495 Henry VII, his mother the countess of Richmond, his queen (Elizabeth of York), and the rest of his family lodged at the abbey. *Remains:* The Norman nave of the ch. is in use as the parish ch., with E end added 1886–8. The choir, transepts and Lady Chapel were destroyed at the Dissolution. Claustral bldgs. demolished in 1836 to make way for a new road on the S side of the ch. Refectory pulpit survives in isolation. Further to the W are ruins of the infirmary. Hist: The Old Churches of Shrewsbury (1922) H. E. Forrest (also covers the 3 friaries which follow).

Shrewsbury *Friary. Salop. (c. 1254–1538). Austin. Fs: unknown. Geoffrey Randolf gave land for the 2nd site c. 1290. Ded: unknown.*
Limit of Lincoln. 1st. site, outside the town, was granted by Henry III. The licence for the better position granted in 1298. This was near the Welsh Bridge on the other side of the town. An important house in the late 14thC at which at least 3 provincial chapters were held. Standards declined in 15thC when life within the friary was disturbed by violence. In 1472 a friar killed a man in self defence and his sanctuary was violated by burgesses, one of whom was also killed in the scuffle. From 1500 to 1536 the general picture is one of poverty and disorder (VCH). At the end, only a prior and 2 Irish friars

occupied the ruinous bldgs. in which was no bedding, food or drink. *Remains:* None. Finally dismantled early 19thC. Excavations when Priory School was built revealed some fdns. of the friary.

Shrewsbury *Friary. Salop. (−1232 to 1539). Dominican. F: perhaps Lady Maud Geneville. Ded: St Mary.*
Visitation of Oxford. Henry III was an early benefactor. Because of river floods the friars built a dam which the monks from the abbey destroyed in 1265. The king upheld the friars' rights. The community continued to acquire land and extend the precinct; and the house maintained good discipline and enjoyed the favours of wealthy and powerful patrons to the last (VCH). Edward IV's second son Richard of Shrewsbury, Duke of York, was born in 1473 to Queen Elizabeth within the friary's guest house. The community received fewer grants from the corporation than the other 2 houses of friars, probably because they were more prosperous. This was the 1st. house of friars to be established in Shropshire and the last to surrender, having opposed the Crown commissioners in 1538. *Remains:* None. Site developed in 1823 when many pieces of moulded masonry were discovered.

Shrewsbury *Friary. Salop. (1245−1538). Franciscan (Conventual). F: Henry III (gave land). Ded: St Francis?*
Richard Price and Laurence Cox gave the ch. and claustral bldgs. respectively. A great benefactor in the 14thC was Hawise Charlton, wife of 1st. Earl of Powis − both of whom were buried in the ch. Small site of only 3 or 4 acres which never seems to have been enlarged. In 1419 the widow of

Henry IV, Q. Joan, and her friar confessor of Shrewsbury were charged with sorcery and sent to the Tower (VCH). A compassionate head of the Order allowed a friar of blameless life and 'broken with age', to enjoy the privacy of his own room and a garden for the rest of his days. The final phase shows the house to be in good order but poor and with few chattels. *Remains:* Close to Greyfriars footbridge are 16thC portions of a friary bldg., of uncertain age, built into some cottages with three 3-light windows and depressed external arches (Martin) at St Julian Friars (Pevsner).

Shulbred(e) *Priory. Sussex. Map 6. 4m SW of Haslemere. (−1200 to 1536). Augustinian canons. F: Sir Ralph de Ardern. Ded: BVM, the Holy Cross & St Eustace*.*
Small with probably never more than 7 canons. History begins in 1263 when the convent was accused of receiving money but not the donor's son as a canon − a condition of the gift. In 1299 there was admonition over the wasteful use of woodland. Several instances of canons from other Aug. houses in Sussex being sent here for correction. Then little of interest until 1414 when a visitation report proclaimed no need of discipline, other than the maintenance of silence. In 1526 Bp. Sherborne of Chichester prematurely suppressed the house presumably because of decadence. He demolished much of the ch., frater and chapter house, together with pavements. He also took 400 sheep and 60 oxen. When Cromwell's agent arrived 10 years later there was little left to suppress, and there may have been (for once) some foundation for his accusations against the 5 canons.

Remains: Bldgs. in the SW corner of the cloister form a house comprising the prior's lodging with vaulted undercroft, and part of the refectory walls with lavatorium on outside of the N wall. Mid-16thC wall paintings, much faded, are amongst best known survivals of the priory. Book: The Priory & Manor of Linchmere and Shulbrede (1920) Arthur Ponsonby.
* Said to be a martyred Roman general, but perhaps a fictional character.

Sibton *Abbey. Suffolk. Map 4. 2½m W of Yoxford. (1150–1536). Cistercian monks. F: William de Cheyney. Ded: St Mary.*
Colonised from Warden. The size of the community increased rapidly in the 13thC and included many lay-brothers. History is singularly bleak, but some rare and valuable records survive concerning running costs from 1362–72. In addition to food and entertaining expenses, costs of repairs in 1363 include tiling, glazing and masonry (VCH). The last abbot, a nominee of the Duke of Norfolk who bought the property, willingly surrendered to Cromwell in 1536, although the net income of the abbey was well above £200 p.a., no doubt to ensure a generous pension. *Remains:* Rather featureless walls. There is the S wall of the nave aisle – *i.e.* the N wall of the cloister. To the S of the cloister are the tall walls of the refectory on an E–W axis, and ruins of the kitchen. Desc. & plan: Suffolk Arch. Proc. Vol. 8, pt. 1.

Sinningthwaite *Priory. Yorks. WR. 6m E of Wetherby, Nr Bilton. (c. 1160–1535). Cistercian nuns. F: Bertram Haget. Ded: St Mary.*
Despite objections by the nuns to an episcopal visitation in 1276, they

seem to have lost the case. Not long afterwards injunctions ordered greater care of the sick, no absence from the precinct without good cause, and a limit on visits from friars to hear confessions. In 1319 the archbp. alludes to the inadequate clothing of the poorer nuns without any relatives to help them, and who were 'afflicted by the cold contrary to the honesty of religion'. He ordered the prioress to clothe them well. A gardener is also ordered to ensure abundance of vegetables. From mid-14thC until the 16thC history is almost blank. Injunctions of 1534 contain no specific accusations, but rather matters to be observed (Power). The severe poverty of the house no doubt caused its early closure. *Remains:* Slight. A farmhouse occupies the site. There are 2 late Norman arches and relics of arcading. In an upper room are Perpendicular windows (Pevsner).

Sittingbourne *Friary. Kent. 9m SE of Rochester. Austin.*
A hospital for poor people existed here for some 40 years until *c.* 1255. In that year the superior joined the Austin Friars, but in 1256 he appears to have refused to accept the newly prescribed life (Knowles). By 1288 the house had been sold and destroyed. *Remains:* None.

Sixhills *Priory. Lincs. 3½m E of Market Rasen. (1148–54 to 1538). Gilbertine canons and nuns. F: probably Robert de Gresley; certainly a member of the de Gresley family. Ded: St Mary.*
The convent owned considerable spiritual and temporal possessions and built up a successful wool trade. Following the execution of David, Prince of Wales, Edward I sent his small daughter, Gladys, to be veiled

287

here. It was her home from 1283 to 1336 (v. Shrewsbury Abbey). Edward I confined Christina Seton, Robert Bruce's sister, here following her husband's execution. The house was much impoverished and the number of inmates greatly diminished by the mid-15thC. Further setbacks occurred shortly before the Dissolution, notably a serious epidemic. *Remains:* None. Four stopheads, 3 of women and one of a man in a cap, are set in the walls of a farmhouse which occupies the site.

Skewkirk *(Tockwith) Priory Cell. Yorks. WR. 9m W of York. (–1114 to 1540). Augustinian canons. F: Geoffrey fitz Pain. Ded: All Saints.*
The F. gave the ch. to the canons of Nostell Priory who established a very small cell here. There is no history recorded and probably the duty of the one or two canons living here was to minister to the parishioners. *Remains:* None.

Sleves Holm *(Methwold). Alien Cell/ Priory Cell. Norfolk. 7m NW of Brandon. (c. 1224–1537). Cluniac monks. F: William de Warenne, Earl of Surrey. Ded: St Mary & St Giles.*
Originally an island granted by the F. to Castle Acre Priory. Became denizen 1373 but was still a dependency of the mother house in 1390. Never more than 1 or 2 monks here. *Remains:* Very little. There were some small remnants of fdns.

Snaith *Priory Cell. Yorks. WR. Map 3. 6m S of Selby. (1310–1539). Benedictine monks. F: Archbp. Gerard. Ded: St Lawrence.*
The F. gave the ch. to Selby c. 1106 and twice a week monks from the abbey ministered to the parishioners. Not until 1310 did 2 monks become continuously resident here, together with a secular priest, and the cell was effectively monastic. Since its earliest days it had been a source of considerable revenue. In 1393 and the early 1400s there were quarrels and complaints over the ownership of the ch., but in 1409 Selby Abbey finally received complete jurisdiction over Snaith. *Remains:* The mainly-14thC parish ch. survives, part of which was certainly served by monks. Book: Snaith Priory (1861) C. B. Robinson.

Snape *Priory. Suffolk. 5m NW by W of Aldeburgh. (1155–1525). Benedictine monks. Fs: William Martel, his wife and son. Ded: St Mary.*
Dependent upon Colchester. On occasions in the 13thC only a prior lived here although the house could support several monks, and in 1400 the Countess of Suffolk obtained independence for the priory. Henry IV disputed the pope's decision and the house remained as a cell of Colchester. A visitation in 1492 revealed nothing in need of reform. In 1508 Henry VII gave the priory to the Augustinian house of Butley who gave it back in 1509. A visitation report of 1520 was not praiseworthy. The monastery was suppressed in favour of Wolsey's Oxford Coll. *Remains:* None. A house occupies the site.

Snead *Priory. Salop. 9m SE of Montgomery. (c. 1190–c. 1195). Augustinian canons. F: Robert de Boullers. Ded: St Michael.*
The F's. endowments included generous pasture rights for 300 mares and 200 cows with offspring (VCH). Sometime before 1198 he had resolved to move the canons to Chirbury (v. above) for which papal assent was received in 1201. *Remains:* None.

Snelshall – *1 Priory. Bucks. 3m W of Bletchley, nr. Tattenhoe. (–1166 to 1203–19). Premonstratensian canons. F: Sybil de Aungervill. Ded: St Leonard.*
The fdn. was a gift to Lavenham Abbey and Henry III's charter of 1227 confirms this (Colvin). But in 1219 there is an agreement between the *monks* of Snelshall and the Augustinian canons of Dunstable. Nothing explains the failure of the Premon. fdn. but maybe inadequate endowments brought the downfall.

Snelshall – *2 Priory. Bucks. Location as above. (1203–19 to 1535). Benedictine monks. F: Ralph Martel, grandson of Sybil de Aungervill. Ded: St Leonard.*
The F. introduced about 6 monks c. 1119 and no record exists for an earlier date. A bp's. visitation of 1321 records the house as so poor that the monks had to beg for the necessities of life. From then on the history is almost a blank. In 1529 there were probably only 3 monks here, and the bp. enjoined the little community to allow no strangers in the priory other than *bona fide* travellers needing hospitality. In 1535 the 3 monks were of good living and without debt though the house was 'wholly in ruin' (VCH). It appears to have closed in the middle of that year. *Remains:* None. Tattenhoe ch. was built in 1540 with materials from the ruined priory (L.G.)

Sopwell *Priory. Herts. 1½m SSE of St Albans. (1140–1537). Benedictine nuns. F: Abbot Geoffrey of St Albans. Ded: St Mary.*
Dependent upon St Albans Abbey and exempt from episcopal visitations. The F. gave 2 holy women living a pious life here spiritual and temporal possessions and doubtless some nuns from St Albans were also sent here. In 1330 the community elected their own prioress which was at once overruled by the abbot of St Albans. In 1338 the abbot's somewhat strict orders to the nuns suggest precautionary measures rather than any lack of discipline. The house received many important visitors including the Duke of Gloucester (1427), Cardinal Beaufort (1428) and the Duchess of Clarence (1429), the last of whom joined the community. It is by no means certain that the accusations made against the house in 1490 by Archbp. Morton, at the instance of the prioress Elizabeth Webbe, are justified (Eckenstein). (*v.* St Mary de Pré). *Remains:* None. Two Tudor houses in succession were built on the site – both demolished. Excavated 1963–66 when parts of the fdns. revealed tiled floors (Med. Arch. Vols. 9, 10 (plan) & 11). Hist: Br. Arch. Assoc. J. Vol. 26.

Sopwick *Priory. Essex. See* Wix.

Southampton *(St Denys) Priory. Hants. At Portswood. (1127–1536). Augustinian canons. F: Henry I. Ded: St Denys.*
Small but adequately endowed. Mainly uneventful history. In 1298 ill-health of a prior resulted in 2 canons being made his attorneys but it seems the internal management was still weak.
In 1329 the election of a new prior was opposed by the bp. due to irregularities of procedure. The burden of corrodies and pensioners resulted in poverty and debt in the 14thC, worsened by the French attack on

Southampton in 1338. 50 years later this destruction was still under repair at great cost and the house received protection through the king's agent. Little is recorded of 15thC history, but in 1509, after an episcopal visitation, there were 24 injunctions calling for minor corrections. *Remains:* None. A housing estate occupies the site. A single fragment survives in Priory Rd.

Southampton *Friary. Hants. (1534–1538). Austin. Limit of Oxford.*
When the Franciscan Observant friars were imprisoned, Austin friars took over their house. There appears to be no certain record of where they came from. *Remains:* Merely a fragment of wall on the right bank of the R. Itchen near St Mary's Ch. Site of ch. located in 1960 (Med. Arch. Vol. 5).

Southampton *Friary. Hants. (c. 1235–1534). Franciscan (Conventual/Observant). F: Isabel de Chekebull, gave the site. Ded: St Francis.*
Custody of London. The burgesses of the town gave the friars a stone cloister but when the English provincial of the Order heard of it, he pulled it down as being contrary to St Francis' Rule. By 1287 a ch. of considerable size had been built. Remaining history obscure until 1498 when Henry VII introduced Observant friars. They were to suffer imprisonment and privations in 1534. An interesting description of the ch. interior survives including refs. to an alabaster altar, doublestalled choir, a good clock with 'a bell to warn the clock' and a library with many chained books. The history of the transfer from Conventuals to Observants, adopted at a London provincial in 1498, is obscure (Martin). *Remains:* See above under Southampton Austin Friars.

Southwark *Priory (St Mary Overy). See* London.

Southwick *Priory. Hants. Map 6. 7m N of Portsmouth. (1145–53 to 1538). Augustinian canons. F: Wm. Pont d'Arch & Henry I. Ded: St Mary.*
1st. f. at Portchester 1133 (*v.* above). Well endowed. A charter of 1204 was challenged in 1280 whereupon the prior produced K. John's seal as proof of manor ownership. In 1383 Bp. Wykeham fd. a chantry here for the souls of his parents. Although the house often had episcopal visitations, the history is singularly free from bp's. injunctions, especially in the 14th & 15thCs. In 1342 taxes were excused the community on their properties in Portsmouth and Southampton following pillage by the French, and *c.* 1494 tenements were destroyed by high winds. The house had many pilgrims to the image of Our Lady of Southwick, being widely famed. *Remains:* Even though successive houses have occupied the site there survives part of the refectory wall, a re-set 14thC doorway and some grassy mounds. The cloister area was located by excavation in 1967. (Med. Arch. Vol. 12).

Spalding *Priory/Alien Priory/Priory. Lincs. (1052–1539). Benedictine monks. F: Thorold of Buckenhale. Ded: St Mary & St Nicholas.*
Dependent upon Crowland. After the Conquest one Ivo Tailbois married a Spalding heiress and because the monks nearby were of Saxon stock he (a Norman) constantly harassed them. *c.* 1071 they left for Crowland and in 1074 Ivo gave the priory to St Nicholas Abbey, Angers. There followed a series of conflicts in the 13thC between Spalding and Crowland over land ownership which was

finally settled in 1332. The house became denizen in 1397. Debt due to mismanagement occurred in the 15thC but at the time of the Dissolution it was amongst the richest houses in Lincs. Wolsey's efforts to secure the monastery in 1526 by replacing the prior were foiled. It was clearly a house of good order. *Remains:* Doubtful. It stood E of Sheep Market. Traditionally Abbey Bldgs. in Priory Road were perhaps the dormitory; and a small stone bldg. 'Prior's Oven' assumed to be a mediaeval lock-up.

Spinney *– 1 Priory. Cambs. 5m S of Ely. (–1227 to 1449). Augustinian canons. Fs: Beatrice Malebiche & Hugh her husband. Ded: St Mary & the Holy Cross.*
A small house for 3 canons. In 1301 Mary of Bassingbourn increased the endowments to support 4 additional canons and an almshouse for 7 poor men. She stipulated a thrice yearly distribution of a dole to 1000 poor persons, which proved unworkable (VCH). Following a series of dissensions, a canon of Anglesey became prior in 1390, and he was murdered in the ch. in 1403. The fate of the guilty men is unknown. The number of canons continued to fall until the house was absorbed by the cathedral priory of Ely in 1449.

Spinney *– 2.Priory. Cambs. Location as above. (1449–1539). Benedictine monks. F: John Tiptoft, Earl of Worcester and patron, consented to the transfer to Ely. Ded: as above.*
In 1453 4 monks of Ely were sent to reside here and maintain prayers for the F. and his 2 wives. Little else is heard of the priory which continued to support Mary Bassingbourn's almshouse for some years. Strangely,

it continued to be listed as Aug. in 1460 & 1510 (VCH). *Remains:* None. Bldgs. survived until 1774. House occupies the site which incorporates re-used materials. Numerous fragments survive about the garden.

Stafford *Priory of St Thomas. See Baswich.*

Stafford *Friary. Staffs. (1344–1538). Austin. F: Ralph de Stafford, later Earl of Stafford. Ded: unknown.*
Limit of Lincoln. The history is obscure and the house received no major benefactions. It produced men who preached well and c. 1370 24 members of the community were ordained and 6 became priests, indicating it was one of the larger houses. Henry IV came here in 1403 after his victory at Shrewsbury. Records survive of the trickery used by Bp. Ingworth, the king's visitor, to obtain the surrender of the house (Hibbert). *Remains:* None. The R C. ch. of St Austin stands on part of the site and is named after the priory.

Stafford *Friary. Staffs. (–1274 to 1538). Franciscan (Conventual). F: perhaps a member of the Stafford family of Sandon. Ded: St Francis.*
Custody of Worcester. Baron Stafford chose to be buried here in 1308 instead of in the family vault at Stone. No outstanding events in the history have come to light. Since friars were freely moved from one house to another the numbers who lived here are uncertain, but 20 was probably a maximum and the house could never have been large. There is evidence that part of the recruitment throughout the history came from Wales. *Remains:* None. The main road in the area is still known as Grey Friars.

Stainfield *Priory. Lincs. 8½m E of Lincoln. (c. 1154–1536). Benedictine nuns. F: William or Henry de Percy. Ded: St Mary.*
Neither large nor wealthy and little is known of the history. In the early 13thC the nuns sold 12 sacks of wool p.a.; but by the early 14thC their prosperity had turned to poverty, partly due to having to support one of Edward II's servants for the rest of her life. Episcopal visitations give no evidence of laxity in the house or of poor conditions of bldgs. in the 14th & 15thCs. There is a ref. in 1436 to the construction of an enclosure on the N side of Winterton parish ch. so that one of the nuns, at her own request, might be 'locked in the joy of her Saviour' (Power). In 1519 conditions were reported to be less favourable with inadequate discipline, e.g. nuns dozing in choir during night offices. Matters must have improved for in 1536 the community received licence to continue – if they moved to Stixwould (*v.* below). *Remains:* None. Successive houses have occupied the site.

Stamford *Priory. Lincs. Map 3. (+1083 to 1538). Benedictine monks. Fs: Bp. Carileph of Durham & William I. Ded: St Leonard.*
1st. f. 658 by St Wilfred, later bp. of York, and destroyed by Danes in 9thC. Bene. house built on same site which soon became a cell of Durham with little independent history. Priors changed frequently and the record of a visitation in 1440 shows why. The income could not support a prior and 2 monks so the priors had no wish to stay. Nothing else known. *Remains:* Highly interesting W front of ch. and 5 bays of the N side of the nave with part of clerestory, in use as the parish ch. It is Stamford's most impressive

mediaeval bldg. Excavations 1967 revealed part of E end of ch. and N transept; W. claustral range; site of kitchen and the frater. Work continued in 1970. Notes & plan: Current Arch. No. 10 (Sept. 1968); and Med. Arch. Vols. 12 (plan) & 15.

Stamford *Friary. Lincs. (1343–1538). Austin. F: Robert de Wodehouse. Ded: unknown.*
Limit of Lincoln. The site had previously belonged to the Sack Friars. Very little history recorded. F. buried in the ch. and he gave the friars all his goods. In 1372 the Gilbertines of Sempringham gave them 10 acres of land. One of the brethren was the provincial prior of the Order in 1382. *Remains:* None. Some sculptured stones from the priory were built into a local house.

Stamford *Friary. Lincs. (–1268 to 1538). Carmelite. F: probably Henry de Hanna. Ded: BVM.*
Distinction of Oxford? The F. was the second provincial prior 1254–71. Provincial chapters held here in 1300 & 1319 and it seems that this convent was of special importance early in the 14thC. VCH gives extensive details of land acquisitions by the friars. Although the White Friars were the most learned of the mendicant Orders, VCH states there is very little evidence that the educational eminence of Stamford was due to them, but then gives the names of 3 D.Ds. who lived there. The Council of Stamford met here in 1392. *Remains:* The 14thC White Friars' Gate survives in Deeping Road at the entrance to the Stamford and Rutland Hospital.

Stamford *Friary. Lincs. (–1241 to 1538). Dominican. F: unknown. Ded: unknown.*

Visitation of Cambridge. The house received royal patronage and aid from Henry III, Edwards I, II & III and Q. Isabella. In 1300 the number of friars exceeded 40 and on at least 5 occasions provincial chapters were held here (VCH). A friar imprisoned for a carnal sin was sent to Cologne where he served a penance, and when he was returned to Stamford in 1396 he was restored to all the graces of the Order and the community were forbidden to allude to the offence. The house had many influential benefactors and a Despenser chapel in the ch. *Remains:* None. The last remnant had disappeared by 1727.

Stamford *Friary. Lincs. (−1230 to 1538). Franciscan. (Conventual). F: unknown. Ded: St Francis?*
Custody of Oxford. 1st. mention is a grant of fuel in Jan. 1230. The community formally welcomed the Austin Friars to England at a general chapter here in 1249, and the latter established their first house at Clare (v. above) soon afterwards. In 1337 all friaries of the Oxford custody (9) met here with the possible idea of establishing a university in the town. Among many notable persons buried in the ch. was the Fair Maid of Kent, wife of the Black Prince and mother of Richard II. In 1534 3 Observant friars were sent here as prisoners following the suppression of the Order. *Remains:* None. Some walls still stood by St Paul's Gate in 1727.

Stamford *Friary. Lincs. (−1274 to +1300). Friars of the Sack.*
Nothing is known of the short period of the Sack Friars existence in the town. Four were still living here in 1300 following the suppression of the Order in 1274. In 1343 the

Austin Friars occupied the site. *Remains:* None.

Stamford* *(Baron) Priory. N'hants. 1m S of Stamford, Lincs. (c. 1155−1536). Benedictine nuns. F: William de Waterville, abbot of Peterborough. Ded: St Mary & St Michael.*
In 1230 the nuns sought to sever their link with Peterboro' via Rome but, having failed, the strained relations between the two houses were soon restored. A monk was sent in 1303 to look into the mismanagement of the priory's revenues and to take charge of temporal affairs. A unique set of account rolls spanning 2 centuries give a close study of the convent's life, but unfortunately the cellaress' catering costs are not included. A sad era began in 1309 for nun Agnes who left the priory, was arrested and imprisoned in chains, and spent the next 2 years in solitary confinement at Cornworthy Priory. Another instance of a woman clearly unsuited to the life and from which, it is hoped, she was compassionately released. In 1354 the distressed priory at Wothorpe (v. below), with only one nun living there, was united with St Michael's. The fortunes of the house declined due to an incompetent and aged prioress in the mid-15thC until it became 'one of the worst houses which records have brought to light' (Power). Very few entries for late-15th & 16thCs. *Remains:* None. The ch. existed in 1727 and was said to be of great beauty.
* Also known as St Michael's Stamford.

Stanlaw *(Stanlow) Abbey. Cheshire. 1m E of Ellesmere Port. (1172−1296). Cistercian monks. F: John, Baron of Halton. Ded: St Mary.*
Colonised from Combermere. The

site was described as 'a place of comfortless desolation'. The community was frequently harassed by incursions of the sea which finally swamped the area in 1279, and a violent storm in 1287 brought down the tower. Two years later a major fire destroyed much of the abbey (Ormerod). There followed further high seas in which 'the total destruction of the monastery was threatened from the fury of the tides'. The last abbot was appointed in 1272 and he, with 20 monks, moved to Whalley (*v.* below) in 1296; but 5 monks stayed behind to continue as long as it remained habitable as a cell. *Remains:* None. The site at Stanlow Point lies between the Mersey and the Manchester Ship Canal.

Stanley *Abbey. Wilts. 3m E of Chippenham. (1154–1536). Cistercian monks. Fs: Empress Maud & Drogo her chamberlain. Ded: St Mary.* 1st. f. 1151 at Loxwell about 2m to the S. Colonised from Quarr. There was constant confusion between Stanley and Stoneleigh (*v.* below). Records show numerous disputes with other houses especially Beaulieu. According to a Bodleian MS. an underground stone conduit from Loxwell was a work of great merit. In the 13thC the thriving wool exporting business reached 40 sacks p.a., and there was licence to dig, smelt and remove iron ore from nearby Pewsham Forest. Land was owned in Wilts., Somerset, Glos., Berks. & Sussex up to the early 14thC, but debts probably worsened due to contributions to the king's war expenses and a theft of £1,000 from the abbey's strongroom in 1321. In 1412 the house was given relief from taxes and tithes. Little is heard of its history for the rest of its existence and there is no evidence about the lives of the monks. *Remains:* None.

Excavated 1905–6. Desc. & plan: Archaeologia, Vol. 60; and Wilts. Arch. Mag., Vol. 35, pp. 541–81.

Stansgate *(Stanesgate) Alien Priory/ Priory. Essex. On the coast 5m E of Maldon. (1112–1121 to 1525). Cluniac monks. F; probably Ralph fitz Brien. Ded: St Mary Magdalene.* A small cell of which little is known of its possessions. The house was first granted to Great Bricett, an alien Augustinian Priory, (*v.* Appendix 1) but later given by the F. to Cluny. It was released by Bricett to Lewes Priory *c.* 1163 (VCH). In 1306 it was impoverished and ruinous and, being alien, was frequently taken into the king's hands. In 1373 it became denizen, i.e. freed from Cluny but still subject to Lewes. Hardly anything of interest known of the 15th & 16thC history. In 1525 it was suppressed in favour of Wolsey's Oxford Coll., then to the Ipswich venture. There were a prior and 2 monks at the time of closure. *Remains:* There survives one wall of part of the ch. in a farm bldg. Desc: Archaeologia, Vol. 56 (1899).

Stavordale *Priory. Somerset. Map 5. 3m SE of Bruton. (–1243 to 1539). Augustinian canons. F: probably Henry, Lord Lovel. Ded: St James the Great.* Belonged to the Order of St Victor of Paris. The origins of the house and why it was built so close to Bruton (*v.* above), are far from clear. The first definite ref. occurs in 1243 when Roger Tyrel and his wife are named as benefactors. Notices in the 13th & 14thCs are chiefly concerned with acquisitions of spiritual and temporal possessions (*v.* VCH). In 1322 a prior resigned after being accused of wasting the priory's goods. Although a generous benefactor restored the ch. and cloister in 1439–43, the house was always hampered by poverty, and this led to the uniting with Taunton Priory in 1533, thus avoiding suppression in 1536. In 1526 Lord Zouch, who apparently had private quarters in the priory and built the surviving chantry chapel, was buried in the ch. *Remains:* The simple 'nave and chancel' ch. survives, converted into a private house. To the N of the chancel is a fine fan-vaulted chapel. Cloister lay to the N and a tower was attached to the S side of the nave, all of which have gone. Notes: Arch. J. Vol. 87 (1931) p. 422; and Som. Arch. & Nat. Hist. Soc. Trans. Vol. 50 (1904). Book: The History of Stavordale Priory (1908) G. Sweetman.

Stixwould – *1 Priory. Lincs. 6m SW of Horncastle. (c. 1135–1536). Cistercian nuns. F: Lucy, countess of Chester. Ded: St Mary.*
Never intended to be large and was one of the quasi-double houses, i.e. canons and lay-brothers are mentioned until 1308. In 1268 a Cistercian General Chapter named Stixwould as one of six houses which did not belong to the Order, although the nuns wore the Cistercian habit. In the 13thC the house had an exceptionally high output of wool for a nunnery – exceeding 15 sacks p.a. (*v.* Winchcombe for values). In the 14th & 15thCs a number of lawsuits are recorded. In 1440 there were 18 children being educated here – one of the largest schools of which records exist (Power). In the same year Bp. Alnwick found irregularities of ritual 'bearing a similarity to those at Nun Cotham' (VCH), but by the time the nuns were disbanded no complaints were made against them.

After their departure Henry VIII ordered the bldgs. to be spared for:

Stixwould – *2 Priory. Location as above. (1536–1537). Benedictine nuns.*
Henry VIII gave the priory to the community lately evicted from Stainfield. There was a much-diminished revenue as the possessions had been laid under the massive fine of 900 marks. This had probably resulted in the sale of most of the priory's livestock. In Jan. 1537 the nuns applied for remission of the burden, being greatly impoverished, and within 6 months they were expelled – to be replaced by:

Stixwould – *3 Priory. Location as above. (1537–1539). Premonstratensian canonesses.*
There is no clear reason why Henry VIII placed a Premon. community here in July 1537, but at least he restored to the house all the possessions which the Cistercians once owned. It seems the Prioress was an ex-Bene. nun of Stainfield, and one ref. suggests that the purpose of the third and last community was to pray for the soul of Q. Jane Seymour. Some of the canonesses may have come from Broadholme. *Remains:* None. A farm occupies the site. Some pieces of moulded stone from the priory exist in St Peter's Ch.

Stocking *Abbey. Yorks. NR. 4½m W of Helmsley. (1147–1177). Cistercian monks. F: Roger de Mowbray. Ded: St Mary.*
The monks arrived from Old Byland (*v.* above) and began to clear the woods and drain swamps. (In this year the Order of Savigny was absorbed by the Cistercian Order, which included these monks.) Here

the community built a stone ch. and cloister and it is difficult to account for the move to Byland (*v.* above) in 1177. Perhaps the bldgs. were too small. The same abbot ruled the community for 54 years, i.e. from Hood to Byland. *Remains:* Some minor ruins survive at this remote site.

Stone *Priory. Staffs. Map 2. (c. 1135–1536). Augustinian canons. F: Enisan de Walton. Ded: St Mary & St Wulfad (& St Michael?).* 1st. f. *c.* 670 for secular canons and later occupied by nuns after the Danish wars. The F. gave the ch. to Kenilworth Abbey and the house was a cell until it obtained almost total independence in 1260. The community guarded the relics of St Wulfad. Because the monastery was adopted by the barons of Stafford it did not remain small, though the community never owned much external land. In 1263 the house was plundered by royalist forces who destroyed the muniments. In the mid-14thC there was near bankruptcy due to frequent calls on hospitality from travellers. 15thC history is well documented especially in regard to notices of petty disputes following injunctions designed to raise the standard of observance. In 1458 the ch. was blessed following its pollution by bloodshed (VCH). At the Dissolution the old connection with Kenilworth was still evident. *Remains:* In the cellar of a house named The Priory in Lichfield Street is a rib-vaulted undercroft formerly part of the W claustral range; and to the E a remnant of, perhaps, the chapter house.

Stoneleigh *Abbey. Warks. Map 3. 4m N of Leamington Spa. (1155–1536). Cistercian monks. F: Empress Matilda. Ded: St Mary.*

1st. f. at Radmore (*v.* above). After some 12 years the monks asked their patron, Henry II, for a new site and he gave them his manor of Stoneleigh. Serious loss by fire in 1241 and in 1288 vandals set fire to the gatehouse and stole deer. In an attack by raiders, which included the Earl of Hereford, the strongroom was broken into and £2,000 in cash, charters, bonds, silver and gold articles stolen. Little is known of the monastery's inner life, but in 1380 the abbey's seal was stolen and used to obtain certain manors and granges with forged documents. In 1536 the community was reported to be 'of good conversation' but the bldgs. were in poor repair. *Remains:* 14thC gatehouse is the only surviving structure serving its original purpose. All trace of the ch. has gone except an archway which stood between the S transept and the nave. The site is occupied by an 18thC mansion which incorporates the vaulted undercroft of the monastic dormitory. Notes: Br. Arch. Assoc. J. Vol. 2, p. 156–8.

Stonely *Priory. Hunts. 7m NW of St Neots. (c. 1180–1536). Augustinian canons. F: perhaps William de Mandeville, earl of Essex. Ded: St Mary.* Small with probably never more than 7 canons. It seems very probable that the house began its existence as a hospital, and is referred to as being one *c.* 1220 (Knowles). Little history known and records of visitations are almost non-existent, but a rare ref. in 1442 mentions 6 canons living there. A prior was accused in the 15thC of maintaining his own kinsfolk out of the revenues, but it was not proven and no charges were made (VCH). No fdn. charter exists. *Remains:* None. A house occupies the site. There is a small stone bldg. nearby of *c.* 1500 which may have been part of the priory's possessions, and evidence of a moat.

Stow *Abbey. Lincs. Map 3. 9m NW of Lincoln. (1091–1109*) Benedictine monks. F: Bp. Remigius. Ded: St Mary.*
1st. f. –1016 by Ednoth, bp. of Dorchester, and enriched by Earl Leofric and Godiva, as a collegiate ch. Desolate at the time of the Conquest, the F. began rebldg, and introduced monks from Eynsham (*v.* above). In 1109 Henry I restored the abbey to Eynsham and the carefully laid plans of Bp. Remigius to make Stow a permanent and separate community were of no avail. The estates of Stow were annexed to Lincoln. No date for the final closure is known. *Remains:* The conventual ch. survives as the parish ch. The Norman nave and chancel are separated by an Anglo-Saxon crossing and transepts. Much restored 1853–64. The ch. is of exceptional interest.
* Some refs. give 1095, but a 4-year tenure seems unlikely.

Stratford-at-Bow *Priory. (was M'sex). 5m NE of London Bridge. (–1122 to 1536). Benedictine nuns. F: a bp. of London, perhaps Richard de Belmeis I (1108–1127). Ded: St Leonard.*
Little is known about the house's possessions but it was frequently mentioned in the wills of London citizens. In 1282 Archbp. Peckham wrote for the third time urging the community to accept a young girl, but the prioress declined saying she was deformed. Eleven years later the girl's father left a legacy to his daughter 'a nun of Stratford' (Power). In the 14thC the monastery acquired prestige following a series of royal visits. There was distress in 1359

when the nuns' lands at Bromley were innundated by the sea. In the closing years the nuns twice appealed to the bp. of London against the appointment of a prioress, but their pleas were ignored. *Remains:* None. Remnants survived until 1842. The site is occupied by a ch. and the conventual plan cannot be determined.

Stratford Langthorne *Abbey. Essex. In the E End of London. (1135–1538). Cistercian monks. F: William de Mountfichet. Ded: St Mary & All Saints.*
Colonised from Savigny. A fragment of the abbey's ledger book is preserved in Trinity Coll., Dublin. In the 12thC the abbess of Barking transferred land to the abbot of Stratford which included the upkeep of bridges and a causeway, the latter resulting in many disputes which were at last settled in 1315. The maintenance of sea walls round the marshes also proved a heavy expense, but the house nevertheless became rich due to its proximity with London and was one of the most important of the Order. In 1381 there was a peasants' insurrection when goods were stolen and charters burned. Henry IV made several visits here. There were no dissensions in the house when Cromwell's agents arrived. *Remains:* None. Abbey Road and Abbey Lane recall the existence, and some stone fragments are to be seen in All Saints Ch., West Ham (Pevsner). Notes on the gateway: Br. Arch. Assoc. J. Vol. 1, p. 328.

Studley *Priory. Oxon. 6½m NE of Oxford. (c. 1176–1539). Benedictine nuns. F: Bernard of St Walery. Ded: St Mary.*
The F's. charter suggests he endowed an existing house of women and about

297

20 years later his son, Thomas, changed the site and is sometimes named as F. A community of 50 nuns lived here at the end of the 13thC and the house was popular with Oxford citizens who were liberal with gifts, although poverty is recorded at this time. In the 15thC the nuns were reproved for wearing silken veils and a confessor 'of ripe judgment and age' was significantly appointed 'since no Oxford scholar should have reason to visit the priory'. Although there appears to be no reference to mismanagement, a prioress who ruled for 58 years 'never once rendered an account to the convent' (Power). It appears that the priory was suppressed in 1536 but continued for an unknown reason. *Remains:* Very little. Site occupied by a mansion now a hotel which may contain some masonry from the priory. In the garden are fragments of tracery. The site of the ch. is not known.

Studley *Priory. Warks. 4m N of Alcester. (c. 1151–1536). Augustinian canons. F: Peter Corbezon. Ded: St Mary.*
1st. f. *c.* 1135 at Witton, nr. Droitwich, from where the F. moved the canons to Studley. A small but well endowed house which was at first mismanaged, but under the patronage of William de Cantilupe its fortunes improved. From *c.* 1260 to *c.* 1300 the house sent 2 canons to the island of Steepholme in the Bristol Channel 'to ensure more frequent celebration of divine service there'. Foresters in the area harassed and burdened the canons. Several records of visitations do not refer to injunctions. No reason is given why the canons opposed a visit 'with bows and other weapons' when the prior of Worcester visited the priory in 1364. *Remains:*

Very little. In the farmhouse of Priory Farm are large fragments of 14thC windows beneath a gable. The cloister lay to the N of the ch.

Sudbury *Priory Cell. Suffolk Map 7. (c. 1115–c. 1538). Benedictine monks. F: Wulfric, Master of the Mint to Henry I gave the ch. to Westminster. Ded: St Bartholomew.*
Practically nothing is known of its history. It is believed that the F. became a monk at Westminster at the time of the cell's fdn. It is doubtful if it was ever much more than a grange, and no typical claustral bldgs. seem to have been built. The name of only one prior is known (1323). *Remains:* Prior's lodging destroyed 1779. Ch. remained in use until *c.* 1830 and is now in ruins near St Bartholomew's Lane. Notes: A Short History of Sudbury (1896) C. F. D. Sperling.

Sudbury *Friary. Suffolk. (–1248 to 1538). Dominican. Fs; probably Baldwin de Shipling and Chabil his wife. Ded: St Saviour.*
Visitation of Cambridge. F. buried in the ch. together with many distinguished persons. John Hodgkin, D.D., a friar of the house and provincial of the English Order, took a prominent part in the pre-Reformation plans to disperse the friars. The house was noted for its theological studies. Little else known of the history. *Remains:* Very little. Most of the surviving bldgs. pulled down in 19thC. There is some re-used material in Friars Street and an archway probably from the gatehouse. Part excavation 1969 revealed fdns. of 2 walls running E–W, 15thC floor tile, remains of shoes and a wooden bucket. (Med. Arch. Vol. 14).

Sulby *(Welford) Abbey. N'hants. 7m SW of Market Harborough. (1155–1538). Premonstratensian canons. F: Wm. de Withville (or Wideville). Ded: St Mary.*
No cartulary known. Many charters survive, and both the above names are used to describe the abbey, which show it to have been well-endowed. There was a close link with Prémontré as the abbots played a vital part in disputes between the English province and Prémontré, of which VCH gives a summary. Records of 8 visitations to Sulby survive and on 1 or 2 occasions scandals came to light, though in 1482 there was 'mutual charity and a happy lack of abuses' (VCH). Some injunctions sought to end the playing of games for money, feeding birds, keeping little dogs, and eating in the dormitory, but it was not a house of bad character. There is a ref. in 1535 to the canons' generous distribution of bread and herrings to 500 people on Maundy Thursday and other occasions. *Remains:* None. A farm occupies the site.

Swaffham Bulbeck *Priory. Cambs. Map 4. 6m W of Newmarket. (c. 1150–1536). Benedictine nuns. F: probably a member of the Bolbec family. Ded: St Mary.*
Small and never rich. The community had an active interest in sea-going barges which traded between east coast and continental ports. In 1346 the bp. of Ely found the bldgs. in sore need of repair, but despite the setback of the Black Death the bp. found the nuns had rebuilt much of their property by 1352. In 1368 the gatehouse was destroyed when a candle set fire to a servant's bed. 15th & 16thC history is uninteresting and concerns bequests and financial diffi-

culties. By 1535 it seems that the spiritual side of life was low and the prioress's reputation was probably the reason. After the Dissolution she apparently lived in a nearby cave. *Remains:* In the semi-basement of a house on the site is a vaulted undercroft, 5 bays long, which was perhaps part of the guest-house or prioress's lodging.

Swainby *Abbey. Yorks. NR. 6m SSW of Northallerton. (c. 1187 to −1202). Premonstratensian canons. F: Helewise dau. of Ranulf I de Glanville. Ded: St Mary.*
F. buried in the ch. Her 3rd. son, Ranulf II, had disputes (of which no details are known) with the canons and he moved their abbey to Coverham (*v.* above) 11m to the W. The F's remains were reburied in the chapter house there. *Remains:* None.

Swine *Priory. Yorks. ER. Map 3. 5m NNE of Kingston-upon-Hull. (−1153 to 1539). Cistercian nuns. F: Robert de Verli. Ded: St Mary.*
In its early years a double monastery with canons, lay-brothers, nuns and sisters, somewhat similar to Gilbertine houses, existed. This led to trouble and after a visitation in 1268, of which very full information exists, the nuns were reported to have complained that the canons were 'daintily provided for' while they were given only bread, cheese, ale and water. A local knight so frightened the community by his dissolute behaviour that the canons gave him a barn full of corn which was meant for the support of the house. This may have been the final act which caused the canons' removal. The last ref. to lay-brothers is 1335. The history is not a happy one judging by the injunctions served upon the nuns, and evidence

of an unruly household occurs in the 13th & 14thCs. Being near the area of Scottish invasions, the bldgs. were in a ruinous state in the 14thC. For some reason this small house escaped suppression in 1536 without any payment to the Crown. *Remains:* All has gone except the chancel of the conventual ch. which survives in the present parish ch. The tower at the W end was rebuilt in 1787 on the site of the crossing tower. It is a rare instance in which the nave and transepts were used by the nuns, hence the destruction, and the chancel was parochial.

Swineshead *Abbey. Lincs. 6m SW by W of Boston. (1135–1536). Cistercian monks. F: Robert de Gresley. Ded: St Mary.*
Colonised from Furness (Savigniac). Very little known of the history yet the house must have been large and important in the early days. K. John stayed here 12–17 Oct. 1216 after his disastrous passage across the Wash. He died at Newark a week later (*v.* also Croxton). One of the monks, Gilbert of Hoyland, continued St Bernard's commentary on the Song of Songs but died before completing the 4th chapter. All the evidence points to a high standard of monastic life apart from an incident in 1401 when an abbot was attacked and a monk imprisoned. In a later incident a monk fled the house because the discipline was too severe. He went to St Mary Graces, London (*v.* above) and was professed a second time. An abbot and 10 monks signed the deed of surrender. *Remains:* None. A house on the site utilises much of the abbey's materials.

Syon *Abbey. M'sex. Between Isleworth and Kew. (1431–1539).*

Bridgettine nuns. F: Henry V. Ded: St Saviour, St Mary & St Bridget.
1st. fd. 1415 at Twickenham (*v.* below). Endowed with incomes from numerous sources, many being forfeited lands from alien priories (*v.* Appendix 1). It became the largest and richest nunnery in England but these were not the sole reasons for fame. The indulgence of St Bridget and other pardons obtainable by pilgrims were widely known. On several occasions in the 15thC extensive privileges and aid were given to the nuns. The monastery had a well-stocked library. The social standing of the nuns was exceptionally high and the choir sisters were drawn from the nobility (VCH). No scandal has ever come to light about the abbey. In 1523 Wolsey 'wrongfully and suddenly' visited the house and forced the community to pay £333 using his legatine powers. (This was one of the charges brought against him after his fall from office). Following suppression in 1539 there was a brief revival under Q. Mary from 1557–9. The nuns then went to the Low Countries and on to Portugal where they stayed until a return to England in 1861. This is the only monastic community with an unbroken history since its mediaeval fdn. Richard Reynolds, a theologian at Syon martyred in 1535, was canonised in 1970. *Remains:* Very little. Syon House occupies the site. In the SW part of the house are 2 undercrofts with 15thC vaulting at right angles to the vanished ch. (This Order rarely placed its bldgs. round a cloister – Gilyard-Beer.) The Bridgettine Community now lives in Devon, and a stone pinnacle from the original abbey gatehouse is preserved there. Notes: Archaeologia, Vols. 1 & 13. Books: 1. History and Antiquity of Syon Monastery (1840) G. J. Aungier;

300

2. The Story of the Bridgettines
(1910) Francesca M. Steele.

T

Tandridge *Priory. Surrey. 6m E of Redhill. (c. 1220—1538). Augustinian canons. F: Odo, son of William de Dammartin. Ded: St James.*
1st. fd. —1199 as a hospital under Aug. rule for priests, poor brethren and sisters. Last mention as a hospital *c.* 1220. Small and poor. At a visitation in 1308 the bp. found no laxity though he ordered silence to be kept, the wearing of uniform habits and that the Rule should be read in chapter 4 times a year. The remaining scanty history concerns the appointments of priors *etc. Remains:* None. A house occupies the site. Book: Tandridge Priory (1885) A. Heales.

Tarrant Kaines* *Abbey. Dorset. 3m SE of Blandford Forum. (—1228 to 1539). Cistercian nuns. Fs: Ralph II de Kahaines & Bp. Richard le Poor of Salisbury. Ded: St Mary & All Saints.*
1st. f. *c.* 1186 for 3 anchoresses by Wm. de Kahaines. The 13thC treatise *Ancren Riwle* (Anchoresses Rule) survives in the B.M. The conjecture that Bp. le Poor wrote it is no longer accepted (Power). The benefactions of the Fs. and others in the 13thC enabled the house to enlarge and become Cistercian, and it grew to be the wealthiest nunnery of the Order. Q. Eleanor, wife of Henry III, became patron after Bp. le Poor's death. Q. Joan, dau. of K. John and wife of K. Alexander II of Scotland, buried here in 1238. Apart from records of temporal possessions, the community rarely emerges from the obscurity that veils its history

(VCH). The 15thC is almost bare of records but it seems certain that the ladies remained true to their vows. *Remains:* Nothing of the ch. or conventual bldgs. which lay close to the parish ch. Abbey House is said to contain part of the abbey's guesthouse. A mediaeval barn which belonged to the nuns survives. Desc: Historical Monuments in the County of Dorset, Vol. 4. North.
* Now known as Tarrant Crawford.

Taunton *Priory. Somerset. (c. 1120—1539). Augustinian canons. F: Wm. Giffard. bp. of Winchester. Ded: St Peter & St Paul.*
1st. f. 904 for secular canons. They were replaced by a community of 5 canons from Merton (*v.* above) led by the philosopher Master Guy. When Buckland, Som. (*v.* above) was dissolved *c.* 1180, 2 canons came to Taunton which developed into a large house with 26 canons in 1339. About this time the ch. was polluted by bloodshed (VCH), and in 1353 a rebellious canon was sent to the stricter custody of St Germans. The prior gained the use of certain pontifical insignia in 1449 but not the episcopal mitre. In 1524 a canon became prior of Stavordale Priory which was united with Taunton in 1533. *Remains:* None. A bldg. intended as the prior's barn survives in Priory Avenue. Vivary Park occupies the site of the monastic stewponds (L.G.). Book: History of Taunton Priory (1860) Thomas Hugo.

Tavistock *Abbey. Devon. Map 8. (975—80 to 1539). Benedictine monks. F: Ordgar, Earl of Devon and completed by Ordulf his son. Ded: St Mary & St Rumon.***
Burnt by Danes in 997 and was soon rebuilt. Although there was never

a large community here, nor was it the richest abbey in Devon, it had no rivals in the county in respect of importance or magnificance of bldgs. (Oliver). In 1114 Henry I granted all the chs. of Scilly to the abbey and 2 monks were sent to Tresco. Mitred 1458. Very full information concerning the abbey's commercial interests and revenues given in a study by. Prof. Finberg. Income also came from offerings at the shrine of St Rumon. In 1464 Cowick Priory (*v.* above) was granted to the abbey by Edward IV. The monastery owned the first printing press in Devon and the first book appeared *c.* 1525. *Remains:* Modern bldgs. and roads cover the site. There survives (a) the Court Gatehouse, (b) the misericord is now a Unitarian chapel, minus the stone pulpit, (c) an arch in the churchyard once in the N walk of the cloister, and (d) ruins in the vicarage garden and fragments in the police station walls. Books: (1) Tavistock Abbey (1929) Lady Radford; (2) Tavistock Abbey (1951) H. P. R. Finberg.
* An Irish bishop.

Tetbury *Abbey. Glos. (−1154 to −1170). Cistercian monks. F: Bernard de St Walery gave the site. Ded: St Mary.*
The community came from Hazleton because of insufficient water there, and at Tetbury they complained of the confined area and a shortage of fuel which they were forced to bring from Kingswood (*v.* above). Roger de Berkeley gave the monks a fresh site at Kingswood where the community erected a new abbey *c.* 1170. *Remains:* At a house named The Priory in the Chipping are parts of the 12thC monastic property, perhaps a refectory (Barnett). Remains

also exist at Nos. 5, 13 & 15 the Chipping (Pevsner). Note: Archaeologia, Vol. 31 (1846) by John Barnett.

Tewkesbury *Priory/Abbey. Glos. Map 5. (1102−1540). Benedictine monks. Fs: Robert Fitzhamon & Abbot Gerald of Cranborne. Ded: St Mary.*
1st. monastic fdn. *c.* 715. Twice destroyed by Danes and became so impoverished that it was put under the larger fdn. at Cranborne (*v.* above) *c.* 980. About 1100 the new ch. was begun and with abbey status it was occupied in 1102 by the community from Cranborne, which then became a cell of Tewkesbury with priory status. F. Robert was buried in the abbey and Gerald at Winchester. The ch. received many noble burials during its history including Prince Edward, only son of Henry VI. Considerable information available from numerous other sources. The house was noted for its learning and literature under a 12thC abbot and prosperity under a saintly abbot in the 13thC. From 1263 onwards there is a dearth of history except for a note about pollution following the Battle of Tewkesbury (1471) and of benefactions. Mitred *c.* 1481 (Willis). In the 16thC there were ruinous bldgs. due to inadequate revenues and heavy hospitality costs. *Remains:* Superb ch. with largest Norman tower in existence. Rebuilt Abbot's gatehouse (the great gatehouse has gone). 15thC Abbey House was abbot's lodging. Traces of cloister and part of precinct wall. Bell tower demolished in 1817. Desc: Numerous refs. in Trans. of Bristol & Glos. Arch. Soc.; also Br. Arch.

Assoc. J. Vols. 11 & 15. Illus:
Pitkin Pictorial.

Thame *Abbey. Oxon. (1140–1539).*
Cistercian monks. Fs: Robert Gait &
Bp. Alexander of Lincoln granted
site. Ded: St Mary.
Colonised from Waverley. 1st. f.
1137 at Otley (*v.* above). Apart
from evidence that the community
became successful farmers and had a
thriving wool trade with overseas
markets in the early 13thC, the
internal history is hardly known. In
1317 there was debt due to bad
weather, high hospitality costs and
sheep murrain. In 1525 the visiting
abbot of Waverley complained that
the house was full of idle boys who
had no business there. He rebuked
the monks for their love of archery
and feasting in taverns, and when
the abbot died in 1529 the bp. said
there was no monk in the monastery
fit to succeed him. The abbot of
Bruern was appointed head of the
wayward house. *Remains:* The
house, Thame Park, occupies the site
and incorporates the 16thC abbot's
lodging to the S and 13th & 14thC
bldgs. on the N side. Site surveyed
c. 1840 but no plan appears to exist.
A 16thC report claimed that the
abbeys of Furness and Thame were
about the same size.

Thelsford – 1 *Priory/Hospital. Warks.*
5m S of Warwick. (+1170/1212 to
1224/40). Augustinian canons of the
Holy Sepulchre. Fs: Henry de
Bereford and Isabel his wife. Ded:
St John Baptist & St Radegund.
Practically nothing is known of the
indeterminate lifetime of the community whose possessions, according
to some refs., passed to the Trinitarians *c.* 1214. Since the Trinitarians
did not arrive in England until 1224

and established their first house at
Moatenden (*v.* above), is *c.* 1214 an
ancient transcription error for 1224?
But the canons had almost certainly
withdrawn by 1240 and the property
had then become:-

Thelsford – 2 *Friary. Warks. Location*
as above. (1224/40 to 1538).
Trinitarian. Re-F: unknown.
Sir. Wm. Lucy of Charlecote gave
additional land and Charlecote ch.
c. 1214 (i.e. before Trinitarians
arrived). Further extensive gifts in
the last quarter of the 13thC
enabled a larger ch. to be built, and
the maintenance of a hospital for
the poor and the reception of pilgrims
(Knowles). VCH gives details of gifts,
grants and burials in the 14th &
15thCs. No internal history known.
A community of 4 friars signed the
deed of surrender. *Remains:* None.
Site partly excavated 1966 & 1972
which revealed that the ch. was stone
built but the conventual bldgs. appear
to have been of timber with stone
footings. Numerous carved fragments
found. (Med. Arch. Vols. 11 & 17.)

Thetford *Alien Priory/Priory.*
Norfolk. Map 4. (1103–4 to 1540).
Cluniac monks. F: Roger Bigod. Ded:
St Mary.
Colonised from Lewes. 1st. f. S of
the river but because the site was
too small a new monastery N of the
river was built and occupied in 1114.
Considerable increase in revenues in
the 13thC made the house wealthy. In
1248 an evil prior was killed by a
monk who was angered by abusive
language and he died a prisoner in
Norwich Castle. A large number of
relics and an image of Our Lady,
said to have miraculous properties,
brought many pilgrims. A riot in 1313
was staged by a mob who burst into

the ch. and killed several monks. The house became denizen in 1376 though the link with Cluny continued. The 15thC history is very brief. The dukes of Norfolk were buried here and the 2nd Howard Duke, of Flodden fame, was buried in the priory ch. in 1513 with 'magnificent pomp before the high altar'. *Remains:* Much of the fdns. of the ch., especially at the E end. Fdns. and walls of the claustral ranges survive together with the prior's lodging. The gatehouse stands to its full height less floors and roof. Desc., plan & care: D of E. Excavated by D of E to the E & W in 1956 & 1972 (Med. Arch. Vols. 1 & 18). Note: Arch. J. Vol. 106, by P. K. Baillie Reynolds.

Thetford — 1 *Priory. Norfolk. (+1020 to c. 1160). Benedictine monks. F: Abbot Uvius of Bury St Edmunds. Ded: St George.*
The house was fd. on the S side of the river in the time of K. Canute and was said to commemorate the fallen in the battles with the Danes. *c.* 1160 the two surviving monks of this cell were withdrawn, and Abbot Hugh and the convent of Bury St Edmunds admitted nuns from Ling (*v.* above) and the house thus became:-

Thetford — 2 *Priory. Norfolk. Map 4. (c. 1160—1537). Benedictine nuns. F: Abbot Hugh of Bury St Edmunds. Ded: St George.*
The community came from Ling (*v.* above) and were supplied with food and beer from the abbey of B. St E. (Knowles). On numerous occasions robbers en route caused serious depletions in supplies. In 1492 a visitation resulted in nothing to reform and in 1514 the only complaint was that some books

needed repairing. No complaints in 1520 or 1532 reveal a house of high standards, but it was invariably very poor. *Remains:* The aisleless ch. is now a barn with a fine Transitional Norman arch which led to the S transept. Another arch survives on the E side of the cloister and further S is a bldg. lying N—S. In the 16thC a house was built amidst the ruins.

Thetford *Priory. Norfolk. Map 4. (c. 1139—1536). Augustinian canons. F: Wm. de Warenne, earl of Surrey. Ded: Holy Cross.*
The canons belonged to the Order of the Holy Sepulchre until *c.* 1260 when the house became independent. It was on the Suffolk side of the river. No cartulary survives but VCH gives details of grants and gifts. Singularly little history of interest apart from details of possessions. No injunctions needed after a visitation in 1492. In 1520 the bldgs. were in sad decay and the income inadequate to support the community. Only 1 canon and a household of 16 in 1536. *Remains:* Aisleless nave and tower of ch. survive in farm bldgs. Excavations in 1969 revealed plan of chancel. Cloister stood to the N but no plan recovered. Numerous carved stones found. Book: Martin's History of Thetford (1779) carried a painstaking account of the priory. (*v.* also Med. Arch. Vol. 14).

Thetford *Friary. Norfolk. (1389— 1538). Austin. F: John of Gaunt. Ded: St Augustine?*
Limit of Cambridge. The F. brought friars to the town and built their ch. on land given by Thomas Morley and Simon Barbour. In 1408 the community obtained licence to demolish a house and extend their ch. and cloister. They maintained a

hospital and hermitage granted to them in 1413 by Henry V. Always a small and poor house with often only 6 friars who evidently ran an elementary school for boys who were candidates of the Order (Knowles). At the Dissolution the Crown visitor reported 'there is no earthly thing here at all but trash and baggage'. *Remains:* None. The fdns. of the aisleless ch. were found in 1807 with a tower placed between it and the cloister. The site is now occupied by Ford Place.

Thetford *Friary. Norfolk. Map 4. (1335–1538). Dominican. F: Henry, earl of Lancaster. Ded: Holy Trinity & St Mary.*
Visitation of Cambridge. The F. gave the friars the old cathedral ch. on the S side of the river abandoned 221 years earlier by the Cluniacs (*v.* above). By an exceptional arrangement the priors were nominated by the lords of Thetford (VCH). In 1386 John of Gaunt was not only the Black Friars' patron but a great friend of the Austin Friars, and in order not to interfere with alms for the Dominicans from persons entering the town, he placed the Aug. friars on the N side of the town. In 1410 fire destroyed the F.'s. original deed of grant. A long list of bequests and burials from 1347 to 1553 exists. *Remains:* W wall and N wall of the N aisle of the ch. with tall arches built into the Boys' Grammar School; and a 14thC narrow tall arch belonging to the central tower (Pevsner). Part excavated 1959 & 1964 which revealed the extent of the cloister and W range. (Med. Arch. Vols. 4 & 9).

Thicket *Priory. Yorks. ER. 9m SE of York, nr. Thorganby. (–1180 to*
1539). Benedictine nuns. F: Roger fitz Roger. Ded: St Mary.
Injunctions in the early 14thC refer to the need for bldg. repairs, the exclusion of seculars from the house, and the introduction of strict economies. A penance imposed on a nun in 1343 by Archbp. Zouche for apostasy is commented upon in VCH as 'one of the most severe punishments visited upon any monk or nun in the York Registers'. The punishments are listed. The house suffered on several occasions from the Scottish raids, and in 1434 the nuns were burdened with a heavy loss of cattle due to floods (Power). At the suppression the community is recorded as 'all of good liffying', and they then possessed no spiritualities. *Remains:* None. A 19thC house of the same name occupies the site, and a few carved fragments have been found.

Thoby *Priory. Essex. 4m NE of Brentwood. (c. 1150–1525). Augustinian canons. Fs: Michael de Capra and Rose his wife. Ded: St Mary & St Leonard.*
The Fs. gave land surrounding the ch. to Robert, bp. of London (1141–51) and their son William increased the endowments. Singularly little history exists about this house which was originally known as Ginges, and very few entries occur in registers. Just before suppression only a prior and 2 canons lived here. After the prior died the canons transferred elsewhere and Wolsey obtained the property for his Oxford Coll. venture. *Remains:* Two 14th or 15thC arches of the chancel of the ch. survive; and some scanty remnants within a house on the site. Notes: Essex Review, Vol. 48 (1939), p. 67.

Thorney *Abbey. Cambs. Map 4. 7m NE of Peterborough. (972– 1539). Benedictine monks. F: St Athelwold, bp. of Winchester. Ded: St Mary, Holy Trinity & St Botolph.* 1st. f. c. 657 for anchorites and destroyed by the Danes c. 870. The ch. was rebuilt at the end of the 11thC by Abbot Gunter and the ded. to Holy Trinity then omitted. Mitred c. 1265. The great abbey was on an island surrounded by marshes and Wm. of Malmesbury described the whole as 'the image of Paradise'. The Thorney Gospel Book in the B.M. lists the names of persons admitted to the abbey's confraternity (VCH). The house reached the peak of prosperity c. 1322. In 1346 an injunction ordered a 'scandalous' book to be burnt but it, or a copy, still existed a year later. No hint exists whether it was heretical or obscene, but more probably the latter. The Black Death killed about 113 members of the religious and their large household. The rest of the abbey's history was uneventful but it seems to have been peaceful. *Remains:* All destroyed except 7 bays of the nave of the ch., shorn of aisles, to which transepts were added in the 19thC. It is now the parish ch. Fine W end with Norman turrets, the whole 'a sad relic of the once mighty abbey' (Braun). Excavations have revealed fdns. of most of the claustral bldgs. Several nearby properties, including Abbey House, were built with materials from the monastery.

Thornholme *Priory. Lincs. 6m NNW of Brigg, nr. Appleby. (–1154 to 1536). Augustinian canons. F: probably K. Stephen. Ded: St Mary.* The manor of Appleby soon passed to John Malherbe who was later considered to be the F. Never a large house. Local families several times challenged the canons' rights to property. Early history is negligible and the earliest notices in episcopal registers occur early in the 15thC when the bp. urged the brethren to live in peace. In 1440 the community accused the prior of harshness of correction, but to his credit it does not seem that the punishment complained of was unjust (VCH). Other complaints of inadequate clothing and food and prevention from gardening seem justified. Nothing is recorded to the discredit of the priory in the 16thC. *Remains:* None. Perhaps the parish ch. of St Bartholomew contains some of the materials. The priory's outer court was excavated in 1976 near the site of the brewhouse and late-13thC bakehouse – Med. Arch. Vol. 21, 1977.

Thornton *Priory/Abbey. Lincs. Map 3. 4m S of Kingston-upon-Hull. (1139–1539). Augustinian canons. F: Wm. le Gros. earl of Albermarle (Aumale). Ded: St Mary.* Colonised from Kirkham. Became an abbey 1148. The rich abbey was well endowed with lands and chs., and from the 13thC onwards the house was one of the largest and most important of the Order in the country. In the 14thC the community contributed heavily towards provisions for the Scottish wars. In 1332 serious inundations caused considerable cattle losses. Little is known of events in the 15thC except that it shared in the general decline of learning and discipline (VCH). An abbot elected in 1439 was quite unable to cope with the laxities and disorders but by 1450, and until dissolution, the house seems to have recovered a higher standard. Mitred 1518. Henry VIII and Q. Jane Seymour were lavishly entertained here shortly before its suppression. 16thC chronicle preserved in the Bodleian Library. *Remains:* A ground-trace of the ch. is visible. There survives the S wall of the S transept; 3 sides of the octagonal chapter house, and fdns. of claustral bldgs. − except to the S which is occupied by a farm. The gatehouse, fortified and crenellated, is the finest in the country. 1st. excavated early 1830s. Desc., plan & care: D of E. Desc: Arch. J. Vol. 103 (1946); Plan of gatehouse: Arch. J. Vol. 66 (1909). Book: The Monastery of Thornton (1835) J. Greenwood.

Thremhall *Priory. Essex. 3m E of Bishop's Stortford. (c. 1150−1536). Augustinian canons. F: Gilbert de Mountfitchet or Richard his son. Ded: St James.*
Small with perhaps no more than 6 canons. The advowson of the manor descended to the earls of Oxford by settlement in 1320 and here the history ends. In 1250 there is a mention of a chantry in the ch. for a canon of St Paul's, London. Nothing else. *Remains:* None. A few traces survived 2m S of Stanstead Mountfitchet until recent years.

Thurgarton *Priory. Notts. Map 3. 3½m S of Southwell. (c. 1140− 1538). Augustinian canons. F: Ralph Deincourt II. Ded: St Peter.*
Fd. on the advice of Archbp. Thurstan, and Ralph gave all the chs. of his barony to the monastery (Dickinson). Much of the cartulary is preserved at Southwell. The community had disagreements over tithes with St Catherine's Priory,

Lincoln, and Kyme Priory concerning wool and milk. Injunctions in 1280 called for the observance of silence and a thrice yearly inspection of lockers 'so that the vice of private property might be obliterated' (VCH). No measures of correction were needed in 1293. Several canons lived at a dependency at Fiskerton 2½m away from *c.* 1140 for an unknown period. By an old custom the prior had the right of a choir stall in Southwell Minster and presumably in the chapter house. The 1536 reports by Cromwell's agents were so inaccurate that they included a ref. to the shrine of St Ethelburg whom they described as a man! *Remains:* Of the conventual ch. there survive the 3 western bays of the nave, the N tower of what must have been splendid twin-towers, and a superb W doorway incorporated in the parish ch. A 13thC undercroft supports an adjacent house.

Tickford *Alien Priory/Priory. Bucks. ½m N of Newport Pagnell. (c. 1100*− 1524). Benedictine monks. F: Fulk Paynel. Ded: St Mary.*
Dependent upon the abbey of Marmoutier at Tours, a house re-f. from Cluny. Some ref. therefore give Tickford as Cluniac. Very little known of early years but in the 13thC there is ample evidence of long-standing disagreements between the abbots of Marmoutier and the bps. of Lincoln, over elections of priors and discipline within the house. In 1233 the bp. complained that the Rule should be better kept and from 1275−91 the prior appears as a particularly unfit person to rule a monastery (VCH). About 1311 a fire destroyed the muniments and charters of the priory but surviving documents show how hard it must

have been to maintain regular life during the wars with France. In 1426 the house became denizen and a dependency of Holy Trinity, York, (*v.* below). Surrender came in Feb. 1524 and the revenues were granted to Wolsey for his Oxford Coll. venture. *Remains:* None. Some fragments are built into walls of a house and outbldgs. on the site (Pevsner).
* Perhaps the first monastic house in Bucks. The fdn. date is as uncertain as that of Ivinghoe.

Tickhill *Friary. Yorks. WR. 8m S of Doncaster. (c. 1256–1538). Austin. F: John Clarel, a canon of Southwell. Ded: unknown.*
Limit of York. Fdn. date obscure but certainly during r. Henry II. Very little history known. In 1291 Q. Eleanor gave benefactions and Ks. Edward I, II & III also helped the house. A Thomas fitzWilliam willed that a tomb in the friars' ch. should be built over his father's body, and in the parish ch. today is a magnificent alabaster monument to William Clarel and his wife taken from the friary at the Dissolution. The friars' property outside the monastery comprised a few acres of arable land, a lime kiln and a cottage in Westgate (VCH). *Remains:* None. The site lay to the W of the town near Clarel Grange.

Tilty* *Abbey. Essex. Map 7. 7½m NE of Bishop's Stortford. (1153–1536). Cistercian monks. Fs: Maurice fitz Geoffrey & Robert de Ferrers, earl of Derby.*
Colonised from Warden. The house thrived greatly in the early years becoming 'a beautiful and opulent abbey in which religious observance and prudence rivalled each other'

(VCH). On Christmas Day 1215 K. John's unruly army plundered the abbey. Considerable trade in wool with Italian merchants at the end of the 13thC but poor marketing later led to debt. For 150 years the history was uneventful until the last years which were troubled with first a deposed abbot (1530) and then an inadequate successor. Letters from the marchioness of Dorset survive and in one she thanks Cromwell for 'the reformation of this poor house of Tilty and for the zeal of the new abbot of Tower Hill'. Although the house surrendered in 1536 the abbot and monks were not immediately turned out, and closed in 1538 only a few days before becoming legally forfeit (Knowles). *Remains:* Some fragments of the W cloister wall exist with springers for vaulting. The chancel of St Mary's parish ch. to the S was the abbey's chapel-by-the-gate. Aerial photographs have revealed clear details of the plan (Med. Arch. Vol. 8). Desc. & Plan: Essex Arch. Soc. Trans. Vol. 18 (NS), (1928). Excavated 1901 & 1942.
* Sometimes confused with Titley (*v.* Appendix 1).

Tintern* *Abbey. Mon. (Gwent). Map 5. 5½m N of Chepstow. (1131–1537). Cistercian monks. F: Walter de Clare (fitz Richard). Ded: St Mary.*
Colonised from L'Aumône, Normandy. Never in the front rank of Cist. houses. As the records were stored in Raglan Castle, they perished at its destruction in 1646 and internal history is meagre. Roger Bigod, earl of Norfolk and a descendant of the de Clares, rebuilt the ch. 1269–1320. Precinct occupied 27 acres. The revenues were not large and of the 12 granges the property at Acle (Norfolk) was the

most valuable (Williams). Income came from the sale of wool, timber, corn, fishing rights, iron ore (Forest of Dean), vegetables and honey. The high standing of cellarers amongst obedientiaries is revealed from the fact that at least 6 became abbots. Edward II sought refuge here in 1326 a few months before his murder in Berkeley Castle. 15thC history almost a blank. Tintern's story is mainly the story of its bldgs. *Remains:* One of the most evocative of all ruins. A ch., intact except for roof and tower, is of great dignity. Numerous remains of claustral bldgs. and the water gatehouse. Excavated 1906–7. Desc., plan & care: D of E. Desc: Mon. Antiq. Tintern Abbey (1965) D. H. Williams.
* Too important to omit. Separated from England by only the width of the River Wye.

Tiptree *Priory. Essex. 9m SW of Colchester. (−1200 to 1525). Augustinian canons. Fs: members of the Tregoz family. Ded: St Mary & St Nicholas.*
Very small with perhaps a max. of 4 canons. Poverty in 1281 resulted in a licence for the canons to enclose 60 acres of forest, and in 1302 there was a generous gift of 153 acres of land. At the end of the 14thC the canons claimed unjust depriving of income by the patron who had, on one occasion, ejected the prior 'by the legs' (VCH). In 1525 Wolsey took over this smallest of Essex priories for his Oxford Coll., and in 1528 the property was transferred to the Ipswich venture. *Remains:* None. A brick Elizabethan mansion was built on or near the site and utilised some secondhand windows, perhaps from the priory.

Titchfield *Abbey. Hants. Map 6. 2½m W of Fareham. (1232−1537). Premonstratensian canons. F: Bp. Peter des Roches of Winchester. Ded: BVM.*
Colonised from Halesowen. Last house of the Order fd. in England. Well endowed in the early years with notable increases in the late 13th & early 14thCs. The ravages of the Black Death were followed by heavy debt in 1370. An uneventful history. As the house did not send money to Prémontré, it was not considered alien and escaped taxation throughout the Hundred Years War. Glimpses of internal life are revealed in Prémontré records of visitations 1478−1502. There was a valuable library next to the chapter house containing 224 books of which only one was in English. The canons presumably had an early warning of imminent suppression for they stripped the ch. of its valuables (VCH). *Remains:* The abbey became a Tudor mansion. The nave of the ch. was converted into a gatehouse with 4 huge turrets in the centre, most of which survive. The E end of the ch., slype and chapter house are marked out in the turf. Low walls round the area of the cloister survive. All else has gone. Desc., plan & care: D of E. Plan: Arch. J. Vol. 63 (1906). Notes: Hants. Field Club, Vols. 3 & 17.

Tockwith *Priory. Yorks. WR.*
See Skewkirk.

Tonbridge *Priory. Kent. (−1192 to 1525). Augustinian canons. F: Richard de Clare, earl of Hertford. Ded: St Mary Magdalen.*
The F. gave the canons 120 swine to pasture in Tonbridge Forest. Some early deeds and documents

are preserved in the Bodleian Library. Much of the history is shrouded in obscurity, but the house was both wealthy and important. Prior John incurred the displeasure of his superiors in 1318 for refusing to contribute towards a lawsuit against Twynham Priory (*v.* Christchurch Priory, Hants.); and in 1329 for non-payment of Peter's pence (a tax paid to the pope in England). The prior later made honourable amends. In 1337 most of the bldgs., including the ch., vestments, relics and books were destroyed by fire. There are instructive details about the weekly consumption of food, payments to servants, and the dress and equipment needed by a novice. The property was granted to Wolsey for his Oxford Coll., and the community of 8 was transferred to other houses. Efforts were made to fd. a grammar school at the site or restore the priory, but when Wolsey fell from grace both plans were lost (VCH). *Remains:* None. The site lies beneath the railway station and the last fragment of the priory disappeared in 1840. Hist. & sketches: Arch. Cantiana, Vol. 14 (1882).

Torksey *Priory. Lincs. 6½m S of Gainsborough. (−1216 to 1536). Augustinian canons. F: unknown. Ded: St Leonard.*
Fdn. year very uncertain, some refs. giving r. of Henry II, others r. of K. John − a span of over 60 years. Poorly endowed and with only 6 canons at the most. Poverty is recorded in 1319. In 1323 the prior was accused of burning and robbing private property and by 1342 his priory was 'greatly wasted by misrule'. Apart from these sad acts nothing is known of the history

until 1440 when a bp's. visitation found no moral faults; but in 1444 a prior was deposed for bringing the house to the brink of ruin. In 1519 all was found to be satisfactory with the community but the house was miserably poor and without either cloister or dormitory. (VCH). *Remains:* None.

Torre *(Tor) Abbey. Devon. Map 8. ½m NW of Torquay town centre. (1196−1539). Premonstratensian canons. F: Wm. Briwere, Sr. (Brewer). Ded: Holy Saviour, Holy Trinity & BVM.*
Colonised from Welbeck. Became the wealthiest house of the Order. At the end of the 13thC the possessions were such that the abbot was a feudal lord of some importance in SE Devon. A beautifully written cartulary preserved in the P.R.O. records the properties (Colvin). The F's. son, Wm. Briwere, Jr., was buried here in 1233 and his obit appears in Beauchief Abbey's necrology for 17 March. In 1382 the abbot was maliciously charged with murdering a canon, but in 1390 the bp. reported the said canon to be alive and well and praised the 'irreproachable character of Abbot Norton' (Oliver). The abbots had a prebend in Exeter Cathedral and a house in St Paul's Street nearby. *Remains:* An 18thC mansion on the site of the S & W claustral ranges incorporates the abbot's lodging with tower and guest hall with undercrofts. Gatehouse (originally 3). Parts of the ch. walls, entrance to chapter house, and splendid 13thC tithe barn. Hist. & care: Torquay Corpn. Desc. & plan: Arch. J. Vol. 70 (1913); and Archaeologia, Vol. 73 (1923). Desc: Br. Arch. Assoc. J. Vol. 18.

Tortington *Priory. Sussex. 2m SSW of Arundel. (c. 1180–c. 1536)*. Augustinian canons. F: probably Hadwisa Corbet. Ded: St Mary Magdalen.*
Small, with 9 canons at most. Very little early history known. A bad state of the house and wasted goods was blamed upon a prior in 1376. However, not long afterwards the priory was selected as a place of banishment and correction for disobedient canons, and later still as a place of retreat for the more worthy residents. Apart from a minor complaint in 1402, later visitations throughout the 15thC revealed no faults. In 1527 the condition of the house was poor, there were few books and the servants incompetent (VCH). *Remains:* What was perhaps the N wall of the nave of the ch. is now the S face of a barn of Priory Farm. There are 2 wall shafts, springing of vaulting and traces of E.E. windows – the last remnants of a most elegant bldg. (Pevsner). Hist: Sussex. Arch. Collec., Vol. 11. Notes: Sussex. Arch. Coll., Vol. 52 (1909).
* The exact date of surrender is unknown, perhaps early 1536.

Totnes *Alien Priory/Priory. Devon. Map 8. (c. 1088–1536). Benedictine monks. F: Juhel fitz Alured. Ded: St Mary.*
Dependent upon the abbey of St Serge, Angers. Never more than 10 monks. The Register of 1259 suggests that the choir of the ch. was conventual and the nave parochial. Records of 12th & 13thC history refer mainly to possessions and covenants. In 1317 a prior was admonished by the bp. for neglect of duty. c. 1383 Wm. de la Zouch changed the house to a Carthusian monastery which lasted only 3 years before reverting to Bene. (Hendriks). Apparently became denizen –1416. The last prior came from Tavistock where he had been the monk in charge of the printing press. A shrewd letter from Sir Peter Edgcumbe, quoted in full by Oliver, made a preemptive bid to Cromwell for the suppressed house, but failed. *Remains:* Some remnants are incorporated in the Guildhall and a house named The Priory (Oliver). Book: History of Totnes Priory, 2 Vols. (1914–17) H. R. Watkin.

Totnes *Friary. Devon. (1271–1508). Trinitarian. F: Delabont (De la Bout), Lord of Totnes. Ded: Holy Trinity.*
Very little seems to be recorded about this obscure house, also referred to as Warland. In 1384 the friary was sacreligiously invaded. Thomas Person was then the Custos. Bp. Oldham (1504–19) suppressed the house early in 1508, by licence from Henry VII, and gave the lands to the vicars of Exeter Cathedral (Oliver). At this time it is referred to as a hospital, probably still under the care of Trinitarians, since Wm. Thompson of the same Order at Hounslow, raised violent objections to the change of ownership. *Remains:* None. In Warland is a house with its lower walls of unusual thickness which may have belonged to the friary. Ruins were in evidence until the end of the 18thC. Notes: Trans. of the Devonshire Assocn. Vol. 12 (1880).

Trentham *Priory. Staffs. Map 3. 4m S of Newcastle-under-Lyme. (c. 1154–1537). Augustinian canons. F: Ranulph II (de Gernon),*

311

*Earl of Chester. Ded: St Mary &
All Saints.*
It is possible there was a Benedictine
monastery here f. *c.* 1087–1100
which, having lapsed, was re-f. as
Aug. just before Ranulph II's death
(Knowles). Always intimately connected with earls – at first of
Chester and later of Lancaster; and
a number of disputes occurred at the
end of the 13thC when the
Lancaster earls defied the will of the
canons. Never wealthy nor large
though it was amongst the richest
of the Staffs. houses. The principal
income came from sheep-farming
and tithes. In 1428 the priory was
plundered and the prior kept a
bodyguard following threats to kill
him (Hibbert). 16thC visitations
revealed the house in good order and
one prior was much praised by his
canons. Curiously little is known of
the last days of the priory and the
actual date of suppression is not
recorded (VCH). *Remains:* None.
The parish ch., rebuilt in 1844,
incorporates some parts of the
conventual ch.

Tresco *Priory Cell. Cornwall.
See.* Scilly.

Truro *Friary. Cornwall. (–1259 to
1538). Dominican. F: a member of
the Reskymer family. Ded: unknown.*
Visitation of London. The house had
a reputation of excelling in theological science. No history of the
house seems to have survived and
only 2 names of priors are known
for certain. *Remains:* None. The
house stood between Kenwyn Road
and the river. Much of the ch. and
a holy well existed at the end of the
18thC. Some sculptured stone from
the friary is preserved in the museum

of the Royal Institution of
Cornwall.

Tulketh *Abbey. Lancs. W suburb of
Preston. (1124–1127). Cistercian
monks. F: Stephen, Count of
Boulogne. Ded: St Mary.*
The F. gave the vill of Tulketh to
the abbot of Savigny, but within 3
years the community left for the
more remote vale of Bekanesgill –
later known as Furness (*v.* above).
This was therefore the first Savigny
fdn. in England and was over 4 years
earlier than the arrival of Cistercian
monks in this country. *Remains:*
None.

Tunstall *Priory. Lincs. 5½m S of
Brigg, nr. Redbourne. (–1164 to
–1189). Gilbertine canons & nuns.
F: Reginald de Crevequer. Ded:
St Mary.*
The monastery's short existence was
probably due to insufficient endowments to support a double community. The F's. son, Alexander, united
the house with Bullington (*v.* above)
and there the history ends. The name
of only one prior is known (VCH).
Remains: None. The location is given
as 'the island of Tunstall near
Redburn'.

Tupholme *Abbey. Lincs. Map 3. 7m
SW by W of Horncastle. (c. 1160–
1536). Premonstratensian canons.
Fs; Gilbert and Alan de Neville,
brothers. Ded: St Mary.*
No chronicle or cartulary of the fdn.
seems to exist. The house was never
wealthy although it supported 24
canons in the 15thC. In 1347 there
was debt and the loss of the abbot
by the Black Death in the following
year brought added hardship. In the
15thC there are records of 2 canons
being guilty of apostasy and others
of less serious charges, but at the

312

century's close, and in 1501, the bp. found nothing to correct. The history is uneventful. *Remains:* The S wall of the refectory survives in farm bldgs. and has 5 lancet windows and a graceful reader's pulpit built into the thickness. Stones from rib-vaulting are visible in other walls of farm bldgs. Plan & drwgs: 'Selections from the Edifices of Lincolnshire' by J. S. Padley.

Tutbury *Alien Priory/Priory. Staffs. Map 3. 4½m NW by W of Burton upon Trent. (+1080 to 1538). Benedictine monks. F: Henry de Ferrers. Ded: St Mary.*
Dependent upon St Pierre-sur-Dives Abbey, Normandy. Extensive endowments by the F. (who was buried in the ch.) and Bertha his wife. Little evidence about internal life but there were frequent difficulties on account of the alien status and French control. Rights of patronage resulted in Robert, Earl of Derby (de Ferrers descent) destroying the priory bldgs. in 1260; and when another patron, Thomas, Earl of Lancaster, was executed in 1322 after the battle of Boroughbridge, the priory played a somewhat doubtful part in events. After the resignation of the last French prior in 1433 it seems the house became denizen, but the link with St Pierre-sur-Dives was never formally broken. The priory played an important part in the annual event of bull-running which continued until 1778 — long after the Dissolution. *Remains:* Only the nave and S aisle of the conventual ch. survive. Tower rebuilt early-17thC and the chancel and apse replaced in 1866. Splendid W front to ch. with exceptional Norman doorway. Desc. & plan: Br. Arch. Assoc. J. Vol. 7 (1852).

Twickenham *(Isleworth) Abbey. M'sex. 8½m SW by W of London Bridge. (1415–1431). Bridgettine nuns. F: Henry V. Ded: St Saviour, St Mary & St Bridget.*
When the site proved too small for the rapidly growing community, Henry V gave permission for the move to a new site at Syon (*v.* above) 1½m to the N where more spacious bldgs. had been erected (Knowles). *Remains:* None.

Tynemouth *Priory. N'land. Map 1. (–1089 to 1539). Benedictine monks. F: Robert de Mowbray, Earl of N'land. Ded: St Mary & St Oswyn.*
1st. f. –651 and thrice destroyed by Danes. 2nd. fdn. 1075 by Earl Waltheof and it became dependent upon Jarrow. The transfer to Durham followed *c.* 1083 but due to disputes with Robert he re-f. the priory with monks from St Albans who arrived in 1090. The monastery lay within the walls of a castle, but from the end of the 11thC the castle was the possession of the priory; an instance without parallel. This resulted in frequent military attacks from both Northumbrians and Scots and these heavy expenses, plus perpetual demands for hospitality, caused great impoverishment. The sacred site held shrines of St Oswyn and St Henry of Coquet, and the house held the right of sanctuary from an early date. Many interesting historical details survive. *Remains:* Nothing of the Saxon fdn. Considerable ruins of the Norman ch. with the complete 15thC Percy Chantry at the E end. Whole plan of claustral bldgs. revealed. Massive 4-storey gatehouse with barbican. Desc., plan & care: D of E. Desc: Arch. J. Vol. 67. Desc. of Ruins: Br. Arch. Assoc. J. Vol. 22.

Tywardreath *Alien Priory/Priory.*
Cornwall. 1m E of St Blazey.
(c. 1088—1536). Benedictine monks.
F: Richard fitz Thurold. Ded:
St Andrew.
One of the larger alien houses and
dependent upon the abbey of St
Serge, Angers. Due to financial
troubles, some attributable to
incursions of the sea, the community
diminished to 1 monk in 1381.
During the wars with France the
Crown took possession of the house
but the order was later repealed, and
it became denizen *c.* 1400 (Knowles).
In 1477 the prior commenced 'perpetual prayers in consideration of
the kind services rendered to the
convent by Lady Hungerford and
Botreaux' (Oliver). Poverty again
in the 16thC due to depredations by
pirates and in 1513 the bp. issued a
series of injunctions 'because immorality and irregularity had crept
into the house'. There survives a fine
psalter and an early 15thC Latin
folio in 5 sections which belonged to
the house. *Remains:* None. Site
occupied by Newhouse Farm. It is
said that the last prior shipped
many loads of carved stones to
Angers which may account for the
complete disappearance of the
priory (L.G.).

U

Ulverscroft *Priory. Leics. Map 3.*
7m NW of Leicester. (c. 1174—1539).
Augustinian canons. F: Robert, Earl
of Leicester. Ded: St Mary.
Early history confused but 1st. f.
1134 for 3 hermits to whom land was
later given by Earl Ranulph of
Leicester (d. 1154). Shortly before
1174 the pope ordered the Aug. Rule
to be observed by which time the

priory seems to have been well
endowed. However, only 3 canons
were here in 1220. In 1439 a prior
resigned following the community's
complaints in the previous year of
lax discipline and little maintenance
of the bldgs. The sub-prior was said
to have been absent for 20 years and
then readmitted without the convent's knowledge! (VCH). The small
priory of Charley (*v.* above) also f.
by an earl of Leicester, was united
with Ulverscroft in 1465. Because
the house had a high reputation for
caring for those in need, it continued
beyond 1536 on payment of the large
fine of £166.13.4d. *Remains:* The
ruins comprise the W tower of the ch.,
S wall of nave with some lofty
windows and a sedilia with exquisite
tracery. There were no transepts and
the chancel has gone. Parts of the
refectory with reader's pulpit S of the
cloister; and the prior's lodging and
guesthouse in W range are now part
of farm bldgs. Desc. & plan: Br. Arch.
Assoc. J. Vol. 19 (1863).

Upholland *Priory. Lancs. Map 2.*
4m W of Wigan. (1319—1536). Bene-
dictine monks. F: Sir Robert de
Holland. Ded: St Thomas, Martyr.
1st. f. 1310 for secular canons who,
having displeased the F., were replaced with Bene. monks by Bp.
Langton of Lichfield. The house
has little history and even the
monastery from which the new
community came is unknown. In
1391 the prior had a violent quarrel
with a local farmer over tithes and
the latter was arrested, brought
before Parliament, and fined. The
condition of the house in 1497 was
bad and an enquiry was ordered to
look into the excesses of the monks
and the dissipation of priory goods,
but the outcome is unknown. To

the credit of the convent, charity was not altogether neglected and both aged persons and children were cared for (VCH). *Remains:* The nave of the present parish ch. was the chancel of the monastic ch. To this has been added a 19thC chancel. The priory ch. was never finished in the 14thC, but at the end of the 15thC a smaller tower than originally planned was added. No transepts or nave were ever built. Very little of the claustral bldgs. survive among houses S of the ch.

V

Vale Royal *Abbey. Cheshire. Map 2. 2½m SW of Northwich. (1277–1539). Cistercian monks. F: Edward I. Ded: St Mary & St Nicasius.*
1st. f. at Darnhall (*v.* above). Fdn. stone laid by the F. & Q. Eleanor and community arrived 1281. Considerable information known about the building of the great ch. with the longest Cist. fdns. in England. In 1360 a gale destroyed the entire nave, which was rebuilt on a reduced scale, and the unique chevet of 7 radiating chapels was probably built between 1359–73. The power conferred upon the abbots was abused and oppression of the tenantry resulted in a stormy history of rebellions, lawsuits and fighting. In the 13thC the abbey was involved in glass manufacture in Cheshire. The important Ledger Book (commenced *c.* 1338) contained a history of abbots; an account of court actions, *etc.;* and a collection of papal bulls concerning the Cist. Order. A copy of 60 of the 90 original folios survives. Considerable hospitality in the 14thC seriously

strained resources; and in 1493 the abbey was wasted by misrule and £1,000 was needed to effect repairs. Efforts to save the abbey were personally overruled by Cromwell at Vale Royal. *Remains:* Small. Site occupied by mansion in which undercrofts of S & W claustral ranges exist. In Nantwich ch. are oak stalls said to have been made of Vale Royal wood *c.* 1390. Ch. excavated 1911–12 & 1958. Hist. notes: Lancs. & Ches. Record Soc. Vols. 16 (1898) & 68 (1914), Ledger Book. Plan: Arch. J. Vol. 94 (1937). Desc. of 1958 excavns: Antiquaries J. Vol. 42 (1962). Plan of E end of ch.: Med. Arch. Vol. 3.

Vaudey *Abbey. Lincs. 4m NW by W of Bourne, in Grimsthorpe Park. (+1149 to 1536). Cistercian monks. F: William, Earl of Albermarle. Ded: St Mary.*
1st. f. 1147 at Bytham (*v.* above). The site at Vaudey with pastures and woods was given by Geoffrey de Brachecourt in exchange for corrodies for himself, wife and 2 servants. Wool was principal source of income in 13thC, but by the early-14thC there were declining fortunes and debts. In 1347 the income hardly sufficed to support the monks. From mid-14thC to 16thC the history is a blank. In 1532 3 visiting Cist. abbots charged the abbot with mismanagement and deposed him. The abbot's plea to Cromwell to be reinstated was rejected but he was advised to offer resignation to qualify for a pension (VCH). A far cry from the early days when the abbey had a good standing within the Order. *Remains:* None. Partly excavated 1851 when the 4 crossing piers of the ch. were revealed (Pevsner).

W

Walden *Priory/Abbey. Essex. 1m W of Saffron Walden. (c. 1141*–1538). Benedictine monks. F: Geoffrey de Mandeville, Earl of Essex. Ded: St Mary & St James.*
The house was generously endowed with the advowsons of 19 chs., 120 acres of arable land and 100 acres of woodland. In 1190 was elevated to abbey status. (VCH states that Rose, wife of the F., fd. Chicksands (*v.* above) and wished to divert some of Walden's benefactions. Presumably she had remarried.) Ch. rebuilt mid-13thC and the history of the next 100 years is mainly concerned with the acquisition and administration of manors, *etc.* The widow of a later earl of Essex became a great benefactress in the 2nd. half of the 14thC. The last abbot had secretly married and it seems he either resigned or was deposed no doubt due to scandal. One of the few Essex houses for which a complete valuation at the suppression exists. *Remains:* None. The mansion Audley End occupies the site. The name Abbey Lane is the last reminder.
* Fdn. date is confused. Some refs. give 1136 but de Mandeville was not an earl in that year. He died in 1144.

Wallingford *Priory. Berks. 13m SSE of Oxford. (c. 1088–1525). Benedictine monks. F: Robert D'Oyley. Ded: Holy Trinity.*
The F. gave the ch. of Holy Trinity to Abbot Paul of St Albans who established a priory cell here, and the house seems to have had little independent history. As a result, Ab. Paul is sometimes credited as the real F. The most eminent of the early priors was John de Cella (1191–5) who had a high reputation for grammar, poetry and physics. He became abbot of St Albans 1195–1214. In 1333 the priory's property at Chalford, Oxon, was burned by raiders who stole horses, cows, pigs and farm implements. The house was surrendered for Wolsey's Ipswich Coll. in 1525, but the closure was delayed until 1528 whilst the Coll. was being built (VCH). *Remains:* None. Priory masonry exists in many houses in the town.

Wallingwells *Priory. Notts. 3½m N of Worksop. (c. 1140/4–1539). Benedictine nuns. F: Ralph de Chevrolcourt. Ded: St Mary.*
The fdn. charter included a curse upon anyone who disturbed the benefactions. In 1262 there was poverty and the nuns were given corn and freed from tithes. Four times a year alms were distributed in memory of the F. An unhappy incident occurred in the 13thC when a girl under 9 years old was forced against her will, and her mother's, to enter the nunnery. By no means a unique incident. VCH states that in 1536 'wonderful to relate' the Crown visitors reported no scandal or slander. By raising the large fine of £66.13.4d the house survived until Dec. 1539. *Remains:* None. A house occupies the site.

Walsingham *Priory. Norfolk. Map 4. 5m N of Fakenham. (c. 1153–1538). Augustinian canons. F: Geoffrey de Favarches. Ded: St Mary.*
The F's. mother built a chapel here, but how the priory obtained the famous statue of Our Lady and the Holy Child and the subsequent ascendancy to national fame is unknown, but Henry III's influence was enormous. Edwards' I, II & III and Henrys' VI, VII & VIII private

316

visits made pilgrimages by nobility more fashionable. Offerings from pilgrims to the shrine, which had avowed healing properties, brought great riches and there grew one of the most magnificent monasteries in mediaeval England (Dickinson). As the community grew, so disorder increased in like ratio (VCH). Prior Snoring was deposed in 1387 for dissipating revenues and in 1514 a prior acted brutally to his canons which produced a quarrelsome community. But it is pleasant to find that at a visitation of 1532 nothing needed reform. The shrine obtained undying fame from a visit by Erasmus, and the reputation was enormous in its last years. Finally the image was burnt at Chelsea in 1538. *Remains:* E end of ch. Bases of W tower piers. S wall of 13thC refectory with reader's pulpit. 14thC dormitory undercroft in E range — probably warming room. Gatehouse *c.* 1440 in High Street. Healing wells E of the ch. House occupies site of part of E claustral range. Part excavated 1853 & 1960−1. Desc: Arch. J. Vol. 13 (1856), & Vol. 125 (1968). Also Br. Arch. Assoc. J. Vol. 14. Books: (1) Hist. of Aug. Priory of Walsingham (1934) H. M. Gillett; (2) The Shrine of Our Lady of Walsingham (1953) J. C. Dickinson. Also Med. Arch. Vols. 6 & 7.

Walsingham *Friary. Norfolk. Map 4. Location as above. (1347−1538). Franciscan (Conventual). F: Elizabeth de Burgh, Countess of Clare. Ded: St Mary.*
Custody of Cambridge. The fdn. met with strenuous opposition from the Aug. canons, but their case was soon lost. The history is extremely scanty and the house must always have been eclipsed by its famous

and wealthy neighbour. Surviving records are confined to details of land acquisitions and property enlargements. Early in the 16thC an anchoress lived within the precinct, perhaps near the main gateway. *Remains:* Ch. gone except for lower parts of chancel S & E walls, and SE corner buttress of the nave. Walls of guest-house, kitchen, little cloister and undercroft of dorter. Fdns. of chapter house. A modern house occupies part of the site. Desc. & plan: Norfolk & Norwich Arch. Soc. Vol. 25 (1934); and Franciscan Architecture in England (1937) A. R. Martin.

Waltham *Priory/Abbey. Essex. Map 7. (1177−1540). Augustinian canons. F: Henry II. Ded: Holy Cross.*
1st. f. by Toni, a landowner for 2 secular priests. *c.* 1060 Harold, later K., increased the number of secular canons to 12. In 1066 Harold's body is said to have been buried here. The canons regular replaced the seculars in 1177. In 1184 the house became an abbey. Mitred. Subsequently the monastery became the 5th wealthiest of the Order with 3 particular credits: 1. the oldest Norman ch. in England; 2. due to size and royal patronage the most important Aug. house; 3. the last of all English monasteries to be dissolved. 4 cartularies preserved in the BM. Considerable 14thC history known and numerous privileges were enjoyed by the community. In 1389 the abbot was appointed president of the English Augustinians. Little history of interest in the 15thC. In 1406 the abbot was a member of a committee which produced the Act settling the succession to the Crown (VCH). *Remains:* Fine 7-bay nave of the conventual ch. with early-14thC Lady

Chapel and crypt on S side, all of which is now the parish ch. W tower c. 1557. Cloister lay to the N of the choir, (the area is marked), and in the NE corner is a rib-vaulted slype. Late-14thC gatehouse with one turret remaining. These survivals are but a fragment of former days. Excavated 1938—9 and 1967—77 (Med. Arch. Vols. 12—21, plan Vol. 12). Also Trans. Essex Arch. Soc. Vol. 4 (1972). Notes: Archaeologia, Vols. 1, 43 & 50. Book: The Foundation of Waltham Abbey (1861) Ed: Wm. Stubbs. Illus: Pitkin Pictorial.

Wangford *Alien Priory/Priory. Suffolk. 3m NW of Southwold. (—1159 to 1540). Cluniac monks. F: perhaps 'Ansered of France' or Sir Geraline de Vernuns. Ded: St Mary.* *
Dependent upon Thetford. Fdn. charter gives conflicting details. Early endowments were generous. In 1275 the prior was imprisoned and not freed until he had paid an 'unjust' fine (VCH). Twice the house came into Crown hands during the wars with France and became denizen c. 1393 after paying a fine of 100 marks to Richard II. From then on there seems to be no history independent of Thetford's. By 1537 the house was ruinous and the small community was recalled to Thetford, and the property let for farming. *Remains:* A few traces of fdns. S of the parish ch.
* After 1393 the ded. was to St Peter. The monks used the chancel of the parish ch. which has since been rebuilt and has no monastic connections.

Warbleton *(Rushlake) Priory. Sussex. Map 7. 8m NW by W of Battle.*

(1413—1536). Augustinian canons. F: Sir John Pelham. Ded: Holy Trinity.
Formerly at Hastings (*v.* above) until allegedly endangered by the sea. At this time there were only 4 canons. Very little known of life within the priory, and visitations in 1442, 1478 and 1521 revealed no moral defects — only the need for fabric repairs and the keeping of accounts. It seems that the house was 'wholly in ruins' in 1527. *Remains:* A few architectural relics are incorporated in a farm, and an outbldg. has 14thC doorways. The farmhouse has a mediaeval buttress to the S and 15thC timbering in the N wing.

Warburton *Priory Cell. Cheshire. 6m E of Warrington. (c. 1200—1271). Premonstratensian canons. F: Adam of Dutton. Ded: St Mary & St Werburgh.*
The ch. was given to the canons of Cockersand who established a cell here. The property had successively been a hermitage and a hospital (Ormerod). In due course the abbot of the mother house returned it to the F's. son Geoffrey, except for some useful land, in return for which the abbot undertook to minister for Adam's soul (Colvin). In 1271 the link with Cockersand was severed. *Remains:* None. The ch. of the canons was doubtless the origin of the present parish ch. To the W is Abbey Croft which was probably the site of the canons' conventual bldgs.

Warden *Abbey. Beds. 7m SE of Bedford. (1136—1537). Cistercian monks. F: Walter l'Espec. Ded: St Mary.*
The early growth must have been rapid as 3 abbeys were colonised from here within the first 20 years.

The house depended upon its wool trade in the 13thC and owned about 800 sheep. The abbot was commissioned to undertake several important assignments by the pope in the 13thC including investigations at Shaftesbury and Tewkesbury. A brutal attack upon the community c. 1224 resulted in the death of one monk and 30 others being dragged through the mud to the perpetrator's castle. He later submitted to penance in the chapter house. 15thC history is a blank with nothing known of internal life. The few insights which occur in the 16thC suggest the Rule was well kept until just before dissolution when 'true religion no longer flourished' (VCH). *Remains:* The site was covered by a 16thC mansion now demolished. Part excavated 1960−1 & 1974 which revealed areas of intricate patterns of tile-mosaic floors and some wall fdns. of the abbey ch. Cartulary: Beds. Hist. Record Soc. Vol. 13 (1930). Med. Arch. Vols. 6, 7 & 19.

Ware *Friary. Herts. Map 7. 3m NE of Hertford. (1338−1538). Franciscan (Conventual). F: Thomas, 2nd. Lord Wake of Liddell. Ded: St Francis.* Custody of Cambridge. Delays in developing the site suggest the F. never saw his scheme completed (Martin). His widow, Blanche, endowed the property with more land and Elizabeth de Burgh, foundress of Walsingham Friary, was also a benefactor. The house was always small and poor. In 1395 the community, occasionally in conflict with the Cambridge Franciscans, was accused of encroaching upon the latter's alms-collecting area. There was serious flooding in 1408. Perhaps due to the house's obscurity, the minister provincial of the Order

chose to end his days here in the 1430s. *Remains:* Site owned by the Town Council and the Council's Offices, in public gardens, incorporate much of the S claustral range, 3 bays of the W range and the guest hall projecting to the W of the latter. Desc. & plan: Franciscan Architecture (1937) A. R. Martin; and East Herts. Arch. Soc. Vol. 1 (1901).

Warrington *Friary. Lancs. (−1272 to 1539). Austin. F: probably Sir Wm. FitzAlmeric Botiler, Lord of Warrington. Ded: unknown.* It is recorded that the friars took over an old hospital in the town. Hardly any history known except details of bequests and gifts. F. buried in the ch. The house was probably large because many friars took holy orders here; and in the 14thC several were appointed penitentiaries. At the Dissolution only 9 friars were present. *Remains:* None. Site excavated 1886. Part of tiled floor in local museum. Desc. & part plan: Trans. of Hist. Soc. of Lancs. & Cheshire, Vol. 41 (1889). Hist: The History of Warrington Friary (Chetham Soc.) Vol. 83 (1872) N. Beaumont. Excavations at Friars Gate in 1978.

Warter *Abbey/Priory. Yorks. ER. 18m E of York. (c. 1132−1536). Augustinian canons. F: Geoffrey Trusbut (or Fitz Pain). Ded: St James.* Evidence suggests this was a daughter house of Arrouaise and was well endowed. Sometime before 1162 it gained independence and at the same time is was recorded as being under a prior. Due to poverty in 1277 it was granted custody of a hospital in Beverley. Amongst 13thC grants is one of 30s. p.a. to buy spices 'for improvement in singing the psalms'

(VCH). A particularly worthy prior, who retired in 1291, was given special care and accommodation in his closing years; but a spendthrift successor 170 years later was deposed and given 3 days to leave. An interesting injunction in 1534 forbids the canons to talk to women on pain of being guilty of incontinence. This suggests that in other houses a similar charge was probably technical rather than a breach of moral law. *Remains:* None. Partly excavated 1899. A house bearing the name does not stand on the site of priory. Note on the fdn.: Yorks. Arch. J. Vol. 31 (1932–4).

Warwick *Priory. Warks. Map 3. (c. 1119–1536). Augustinian canons. F: Henry de Newburgh. 1st. Earl of Warwick. Ded: St Sepulchre.*
The fdn. was completed by F's. son, Roger, in 1123. The canons were of the Order of St Sepulchre of Jerusalem until *c.* 1280 when the house was firmly Aug. Early benefactions included the ch. of St Clement Danes, London. In 1284 a prior 'withdrew' without explanation. Not until 1290 was a new prior appointed to take over from the temporary superior. 5 visitations in the first half of the 14thC resulted in no reforms, but in 1516 the prior of Studley (Warks.) was given administrative control of the house for 6 months following some irregularities. *Remains:* None. Early in the 17thC a mansion occupied the site, much of which was transported to America in 1927 (Pevsner). Excavations in 1970 revealed part of the nave, chancel, and walls of a range of bldgs. W of the ch. (Med. Arch. Vol. 16).

Warwick *Friary. Warks. (–1263 to 1538). Dominican. F: Robert*

Boteler. Ded: unknown.
Visitation of Oxford. One of the larger houses, 30–40 friars, which was aided by several kings who gave bldg. materials. In 1267 Henry III granted an unusual favour by permitting the friars to carry herrings from Norwich without toll or hindrance. The favour of the citizens is shown by numerous bequests and desires to be buried in the ch. At the end of the 15thC one of the friars became bp. of Oliva in Morocco (VCH). *Remains:* None. Friary Street is the sole survivor. The exact location is not clear but perhaps the ch. stood on the N side of Friary St.

Waterbeach *Abbey. Cambs. 6m NNE of Cambridge. (1294–1348). Franciscan nuns. F: Denise Munchensey. Ded: Our Lady of Pity & St Clare.*
The F. received a fdn. licence in 1281 but the nuns did not arrive until 13 years later. Further gifts by the F. in 1294–6 included the advowson of the ch. of Ridgewell, Essex. This caused opposition from the canons of Barnwell who claimed ownership. In 1327 the Countess of Pembroke, patron of Denney, gave her life interest to the nuns of Waterbeach, and in 1342 she transferred these nuns to Denney. Some objected and remained at Waterbeach but there is little doubt that the Black Death ended the rebellion (Power). The estates were merged in 1351 and before long the name of Denise was forgotten. 8 years later the site was desolate. *Remains:* None. Some traces of wall fdns. were found during trial excavations in 1963. (Med. Arch. Vol. 8).

Watton *Priory. Yorks. ER. Map 3. 8m N of Beverley. (1150–1539).*

Gilbertine canons & nuns. F: Eustace Fitz John. Ded: St Mary. The double house rose to be the largest and richest of the Order. An unruly nun, one of many in the Middle Ages primarily unsuited to the life, became pregnant by a lay-brother c. 1160. She was imprisoned in chains and her contrition resulted in 'the miraculous relief of her burden'. The incredulous community called the saintly Abbot Ailred of Rievaulx who was convinced of 'divine intervention' (Eckenstein). What became of the girl is unknown. In 1272 one Agnes de Vesci disturbed the community's devotions with many women and dogs. An order from Henry III put a stop to it. Poverty was notorious here and in 1441 Henry VI exempted the nuns from all taxes. The canons were accused of complicity in the Pilgrimage of Grace in 1536 but there was no proof of treason and the house was not forfeited to Henry VIII. Remains: 15thC prior's hall and an adjacent vaulted undercroft of the prior's lodging are now part of a private house. Excavated 1893–8. Desc. & plan: Arch. J. Vol. 58; Desc: Antiquity, Vol. 11.

Waverley *Abbey. Surrey. Map 6. 2m SE of Farnham. (1128–1536). Cistercian monks. F: Wm. Giffard, bp. of Winchester. Ded: St Mary.* 1st. Cist. fdn. in England, colonised from L'Aumône, Burgundy. Slenderly endowed, yet by 1189, after colonising 5 new abbeys, there were 10 monks and 120 lay-brothers here which can only reflect upon the energy and wise administration of the early abbots. 7 of the monks became abbots between the fdn. and 1291. Furness Abbey (*v.* above) disputed Waverley's supremacy, being

an earlier fdn., but did not succeed. In 1201 & 1233 violent storms brought serious flood damage, and in 1204 the community suffered a grievous famine. The ch. was rebuilt in the 13thC. In 1265 Abbot Ralph twice visited the influential patroness, the Countess Eleanora, wife of Simon de Montfort, at Odiham Castle. 14th & 15thC history is bleak but the friendship between the abbots and bps. of Winchester provide a pleasing side to the history (VCH). There is little doubt that the house was under wise government. *Remains:* Only some sad fragments. Small remnants of the ch. transepts. Chapter house walls. Part of undercroft of lay-brothers W range. S wall of monks' dormitory. Site fully excavated 1899–1903 but now covered. Desc. & plan: Surrey Arch. Soc. J. (1905).

Wearmouth *Priory. Durham. See* Monkwearmouth.

Welbeck *Abbey. Notts. Map 3. 4m SSW of Worksop. (1153–1538). Premonstratensian canons. F: Thomas of Cuckney. Ded: St James.* The F. had a warlike record and the fdn. charter expresses the penitence of a lawless baron who gave endowments to the canons in return for prayers for the souls of his family and 'all those I have unjustly plundered' (Colvin). The 14thC cartulary gives details of grants, possessions and rights. An important house which sent out 7 colonies to f. new abbeys. In the early 14thC a long dispute between the abbot of Prémontré and the English abbeys, concerning income, was largely settled in 1316 due to Welbeck's influence. In 1482 the house's fortunes declined through an evil abbot who was deposed and his

321

Waverley Abbey, Surrey. Undercroft of lay-brothers' dorter.

successor was little better; but by
1491 it was well ruled in all matters
and there was unity and concord
(VCH). There were 11 visitations in
the last 40 years of the 15thC with
no serious faults, but one injunction
ordered the canons to cease their
inclinations for sport, while another
authorised an elderly prior to wear
warmer clothes. In 1512 the abbey
was placed at the head of all houses
of White Canons in England & Wales.
Remains: Part of a vaulted undercroft of the W claustral range and an
early 13thC doorway are 'embedded
like fossils' in the vast 17thC mansion
on the site, Book: The Premon. Abbey

of Welbeck (1938), A. Hamilton
Thompson.

Welford *Abbey. N'hants.*
See Sulby.

Wellow *(by Grimsby) Abbey. Lincs.*
S of the Town railway station.
(c. 1132–1536). Augustinian canons.
F: Henry I. Ded: St Augustine &
St Olaf.
Early history obscure. One of the
very few Aug. houses f. as an abbey.
14thC debts were relieved when the
bp. gave the community aid and
appointed a secular clerk to manage
affairs. In 1368 the canons were

rebuked for visiting Grimsby taverns and gossiping, and in 1372 the abbot was suspended for bad management. Although there were complaints about the convent in the 16thC, it was certainly in a considerably better condition than some other houses of the Order. The prior was said to be associated with the Lincolnshire Rebellion but the charge does not seem to have been pursued. *Remains:* None. Abbey Road is the only memory.

Welnetham* *Friary. Suffolk. 3½m SE by E of Bury St Edmunds. (c. 1274–1538). Crutched or Holy Cross. F: a member of the de Bures family. Ded: St Thomas, Martyr.*
In 1274–5 the friars were in disputes over land holdings, and in 1293 a chapel at Barham (Cambs.) was given to the community who soon afterwards established a cell there. Then in 1330 Andrew de Bures fd. a chantry at the London house of the Order (*v.* above) and conveyed the Welnetham property for its support. Records from the mid-14thC until 1535 are negligible and at the suppression the land fetched only 2½d. an acre. *Remains:* One buttress of the ch. Nearby is Chapel Hill Farm which incorporates some of the friars' dwelling (Hervey). There are wall-tiles and bricks, with the de Bures crosslets, built into the farmhouse walls. Book: Great & Little Whelnetham (1910) S. H. A. Hervey.
* Now usually known as Little Whelnetham.

Wendling *Abbey. Norfolk. 4m W of East Dereham. (1265/7–1536/7). Premonstratensian canons. F: William of Wendling. Ded: St Mary.*
Colonised from Langley. A small house with perhaps never more than

12 canons who had possessions in 29 Norfolk parishes in the 13thC. The patroness through marriage, Lady Margery Foliot, was buried before the high altar in 1330. The house possessed certain relics including an alleged fragment of the true Cross and a foot of St Lucy the Virgin (4thC martyr). An unworthy canon was improperly elected abbot in 1339 but he was presumably deposed since a different name appears several months later. Bp. Redman praised the house for the bldg. developments in 1482 and at his last visitation in 1500 found that 'all was delightful' (VCH). Wolsey ear-marked the house for suppression in 1528 but it escaped. *Remains:* None. In the bldgs. of Abbey Farm are some architectural fragments. Excavated early 19thC and 1957. Plan: Norfolk Arch. Vol. 5 (1859). Note: Br. Arch. Assoc. J. (N.S.) Vol. 28 (1922). Also: Med. Arch. Vol. 2.

Wenlock *Alien Priory/Priory. Salop. Map 2. At Much Wenlock, 13m SE of Shrewsbury. (1080/1–1540). Cluniac monks. F: Roger de Montgomery, Earl of Shrewsbury. Ded: St Michael & St Milburga.*
1st. f. c. 680 by K. Merewald of Mercia for his daughter Milburga, and destroyed by Danes c. 874. 2nd. fdn. c. 1050 by Leofric, Earl of Mercia, for secular canons. Earl Roger made St Milburga's ch. into an abbey colonised with monks from the priory of St Mary of La Charité-sur-Loire c. 1080. By mid-12thC the community probably reached 50. In 1180 Dudley Priory was placed under Wenlock's charge. Extensive rebldg. in 13thC with Henry III a generous benefactor. Denizen 1395 but total break with La Charité did not occur until 1494. Prosperity slowly

returned in 16thC but was too late to be effective. In 1522 the powerful but unpopular Prior Roland secured the personal right to use the mitre, and resigned in 1526 for an unknown reason (Graham). *Remains:* Nothing of St Milburga's ch. Of the post-Conquest ch. there survives 1. part of the W front. 2. 3 W bays of nave S aisle, 3. part of N transept, 4. most of S transept. Chapter house walls; nothing more of claustral bldgs. On the N side of the little cloister is the 12thC infirmary hall with chapel at E end; and on the E side the 15thC prior's lodging with stone-panelled facade – a splendid monastic conversion to a private house. Hist., plan & care: D of E (N.T. and part private). Desc. & hist: Shropshire Arch. Soc. Trans., Vols. 5, 9 etc; Hist: Br. Arch. Assoc. J. Vol. 14 (3rd. ser.). St Milburga's monastery with plan: Archaeologia, Vol. 72.

West Acre *Priory. Norfolk. Map 4. 4½m NW of Swaffham. (c. 1135–1538). Augustinian canons. Fs: Ralph de Toni, Isabel his wife and their sons Roger and Ralph. Ded: St Mary & All Saints.*
One of the larger houses of the Order with property in 74 parishes in 1291. In 1286 there was a major disaster when fire destroyed the ch. and conventual bldgs. 14thC and much of the 15thC history is almost blank until visitation reports in 1494, when a sub-prior was stated to be more interested in rabbit farming and rearing swans than his devotions. Preserved at Cambridge is a small 44-page paper book giving an account of the property owned by the priory at the end of the 15thC. Poverty in 1514 which gave rise to 'a good deal of bickering' (VCH) but no grave evils. Things had little improved by

1520 and the sub-prior was deposed for lack of discipline. At the Dissolution the unscrupulous Crown visitors produced their usual absurd so-called 'confessions' from the canons. *Remains:* A modern house occupies the site of the W claustral range. Of the ch. there is the W end of the S aisle adjoining part of the SW tower, and fragments of the presbytery and N transept. Part of SW corner of chapter house. Much of the 14thC gatehouse. Excavated 1927–8. Desc. & plan: Norfolk Arch. Vol. 23 (1929).

Westbury upon Trym *Priory. Glos. 3m N of Bristol. (c. 1093 to –1112). Benedictine monks. F: Bp. Wulfstan of Worcester. Ded: St Mary.*
1st. f. c. 716. 2nd. fdn. c. 962 for monks who were later replaced by secular canons. Bp. Sampson, who succeeded the 3rd. F., removed Wulfstan's Bene. monks sometime before 1112, and his successor (Bp. Simon, 1125–50) restored the ch. to Worcester, but it is doubtful if monks ever returned to Westbury. In 1285 a college of secular canons was established here; and in 1414 the alien priory of Astley was granted to the canons (*v.* Appendix 1). *Remains:* There are surviving structures of the coll. and the site was excavated in 1968 & 1970 (Med. Arch. Vols. 13 & 15).

West Dereham *Abbey. Norfolk. 4m SW of Swaffham. (1188–1539). Premonstratensian canons. F: Hubert Walter, dean of York. Ded: St Mary.*
F. later became archbp. of Canterbury. One of the larger houses of the Order with possessions in 33 Norfolk parishes. Numerous endowments. Most of the recorded history occurs from the mid-14thC. When Abbot Wygenhale died c. 1455 a magnifi-

cent mortuary roll was issued by the convent, much of which survives (53½" long). A roll of this type is very rare. Bp. Redman made 10 visits to the abbey and only once was a penance necessary – for a novice who knocked a canon to the ground in 1491. Otherwise there was a high standard of internal life. This was the only religious house which could celebrate the obit of the Lord Hubert, archbp. of Canterbury (d. 1205) as that of its F. (Colvin). The slanderous charges made against the canons by Cromwell's notorious agents were later discredited. *Remains:* None. Much of the ground plan has been revealed by air-photography (Med. Arch. Vol. 21, 1977). Abbey Farm lies N of the site.

West Langdon *Abbey. Kent.*
See Langdon.

West Malling *Abbey. Kent.*
See Malling.

Westminster *Abbey.*
See London.

Westwood *Abbey. Kent.*
See Lesnes.

Westwood *Alien Priory/Priory. Worcs. 2m W of Droitwich. (+1154 to 1536). Benedictine nuns. Fs: Osbert Fitz-Hugh and Eusticia de Say his mother. Ded: St Mary.*
The house belonged to the Order of Fontevrault, held in high esteeem by Norman and Plantagenet kings. Except for details of grants, information is not extensive; but the inmates were certainly distinguished for their piety. A copy of the 13thC cartulary survives in the BM listing some 64 deeds. Due to poverty in 1301 the prior of Worcester ordered a remission

of tithes (Power). The salt-pits in the area became one of the nuns' sources of income. There is reference to a prior, prioress, canons and nuns in 1352 (Knowles) of which the prioress was head of the community. It seems that sometime after 1412 the priory became independent of the French abbey, and the last mention of a prior occurs in 1433–4. 15thC history is almost a blank with the names of only 2 prioresses recorded. *Remains:* None. The site is covered by a mansion, Westwood Park.

Wetheral *Priory. C'land (Cumbria). Map 1. 4m E of Carlisle. (c. 1106– 1538). Benedictine monks. F: Ranulph de Meschin. Ded: St Constantine.* *
The F. gave his manor to St Mary's Abbey, York, and the abbot established a cell at Wetheral with a community of 12 monks. The priory had numerous benefactors including Henry I. The bps. of Carlisle supervised the affairs of the house, due to its proximity to the cathedral city, and in 1256 claimed custody of the priory, but the dispute with York was amicably settled. Henry I conferred the right of sanctuary on the house which had far-reaching consequences, and on 3 occasions jurors gave verdicts in favour of the right of sanctuary to felons charged with manslaughter who had taken refuge here. Several priors became abbots of St Mary's Abbey and one of Durham Cathedral. The house suffered during border raids on several occasions. It was reputed to have a portion of the Holy Cross as a relic. *Remains:* All has gone except the 15thC gatehouse, and some walling incorporating a 2-light window which was perhaps the

325

E wall of the E claustral range
(Pevsner).
* Later ded: Holy Trinity, St Mary
& St Constantine.

Weybourne *Priory. Norfolk. Map 4.
3m W of Sheringham. (+1199 to
1536). Augustinian canons. F: Sir
Ralph Mainwaring. Ded: St Mary &
All Saints.*
Dependent upon West Acre. Always
small and poor and on a number of
occasions only 2 canons are recorded
here. The early 13thC was the most
prosperous period of the little
community when enlargements to
the bldgs. took place. Poverty
followed almost inevitably especially
in the 15thC. In 1314 the canons
contested the right of West Acre to
nominate a new prior, and were
granted free elections in return for
an annual payment to W.A. Subsequent visitations which occur in the
meagre history appear to have found
nothing worthy of reform. *Remains:*
Ruins attached to the NE angle of
the parish ch. are somewhat confusing
due to several changes in plan. The
remnant of the crossing tower with
a high E arch and a section of the
nave's N wall are the sole portions of
the original ch. Remainder 13th &
14thCs. Some walls survive of the
claustral bldgs. (N of the ch.)
including W wall of the chapter house
in the E range; 'dark entry' with
stone vaulting and refectory walls in
the N range, with 2 brewing vats in
an undercroft. W range occupied by
modern house. Excavated *c.* 1929.
Desc. & plan: Norfolk Archaeology,
Vols. 10 & 24.

Weybridge *(Acle*) Priory. Norfolk.
8½m W of Yarmouth. (1225 to
1536). Augustinian canons. F: Roger
Bigod, earl of Norfolk. Ded: St Mary.*

A small, poor and insignificant house.
The F's. deed is undated. History is
negligible and the few extant refs.
relate to advowsons and ownership
of lands held in 15 Norfolk parishes.
In 1279 a charge of robbery was
brought against the community but
nothing is known of the outcome. A
long blank occurs until the latter
half of the 15thC which concerns
burials within the ch. *Remains:* None.
The site was occupied by a public
house named the Hermitage in recent
years. Acct: Norfolk Arch. Vol. 10
(1888).
* See ref. under Tintern.

Weymouth *Friary, Dorset.*
See Melcombe Regis.

Whalley *Abbey. Lancs. Map 2. 7m
NNE of Blackburn. (1296–1537).
Cistercian monks. F: Henry de Lacy,
3rd earl of Lincoln. Ded: St Mary.*
1st. f. at Stanlaw (*v.* above) and
re-estab. by this F. The history is
fraught with disputes which must
have involved costly litigation: e.g.
with Sawley due to nearness of the
new fdn.; with Bp. Langton, of
Coventry & Lichfield, over the
income from Whalley parish; with
the mother-house of Combermere
over tithes; and in the 15thC with
the rector of Slaidburn over forest
tithes. Twice in the 14thC the monks
considered a move but unrecorded
reasoning dissuaded them – probably
a thriving wool trade at this time was
an influence. The house possessed an
impressive library of which 7 vols.
survive including a 14thC 'Life of
Ailred' (*v.* Rievaulx). In 1530 Abbot
Paslew assumed the mitre without
permission (Haigh); but after 30
years as abbot he was implicated with
others in the Pilgrimage of Grace and
hanged at Lancaster in 1537.

Remains: Ch. outline of fdns. except for part of S wall of the nave. Walls of E claustral range and fdns. of rare (Cist.) polygonal chapter house. W range complete and occupied. Group of ruins to the E include abbot's lodging and infirmary hall. House on site now a Conference Centre. Excavated 1930–4. Canopied stalls from the abbey survive in parish ch. Two gatehouses remain. 13 icons from the abbey in Blackburn's Art Gallery. Desc. & plan: Whalley Abbey (1962) Owen Ashmore. Book: Short Sketch of history & buildings (1937) J. E. W. Wallis.

Whaplode *Friary. Lincs. 6m E of Spalding. (+1238 to 1260). Crutched (Holy Cross). F: Robert d'Oiri. Ded: unknown.*
The F. invited the friars to occupy a chapel and other bldgs. here but there is no evidence that they arrived before 1244 (Knowles). What happened subsequently is unknown except that the house was abandoned in 1260. *Remains:* None.

Wherwell *Abbey. Hants. 4m SSE of Stockbridge. (c. 986–1539). Benedictine nuns. F: Q. Elfrida, widow of K. Edgar. Ded: Holy Cross & St Peter.*
The cartulary in the BM has copies of 463 charters held by the abbey from the fdn. to 1364. In 1186 the Abbess Maud began a 40-year rule 'of sweet memory' to be followed by Euphemia whose wise, kind and skilful rule is acknowledged at length in the cartulary (*v.* VCH Hants. ii, 132–3). Very few injunctions and no serious complaints throughout the 14thC. Little of interest is known of the 15th & 16thC history. When the abbess declined to give one of the king's servants a farm in 1533 she

was subjected to disgraceful charges, of which she was soon acquitted. But in 1535 the wily Legh induced her to resign for a large pension so that 'a more ready tool for Cromwell's dissolution' could be installed. Throughout its life the abbey was one of Hampshire's 3 important nunneries, though Winchester and Romsey were both older. The house was one of the abbeys in confraternity with St Swithun's, Winchester (*v.* below). *Remains:* None. A house named The Priory occupies the site and may incorporate some mediaeval materials in the cellars.

Whistones *Priory. Worcs. ½m N of Worcester city centre. (−1240 to 1536). Cistercian nuns. F: Walter de Cantilupe, bp. of Worcester. Ded: St Mary Magdalene.*
In 1240 Henry III ordered a cask of wine to be sent from Tewkesbury to the nuns, whose poverty throughout the life of the house was proverbial. In 1275 Bp. Giffard got the community's taxes reduced. The endowments were so slim that the nuns were begging for food in 1308 'to the discredit of religion'. Apart from details of the elections of 2 prioresses, hardly anything is known on the internal affairs of the monastery or of its possessions, but surviving records of episcopal visitations reveal no need for corrections. *Remains:* The E wall of the conventual ch. is built into the W wall of an 18thC domestic range of a Grammar School. Nothing else.

Whitby *Priory/Abbey. Yorks. NR. Map 1. (c. 1077–1539). Benedictine monks. F: William de Percy. Ded: St Peter & St Hilda.*
1st. f. 657 by St Hilda and destroyed by Danes 867. The F. gave the

derelict abbey to Reinfrid, a monk of Evesham, who became prior in 1078. The brother of the F. also aided resucitation of monastic life and later became prior. During early persecutions and piratical raids, Prior Stephen and part of the community went to Lastingham (*v.* above) and thence to York to fd. St Mary's Abbey. How and when the house became an abbey is unknown, but William de Percy II is named as abbot in 1109. In the first half of the 13thC the abbey acquired considerable land and wealth and reached the peak of its existence. In 1320 Archbp. Melton made a visitation and left a sizeable list of injunctions but nothing was seriously amiss. The later abbots wore the mitre and other insignia but had no seat in Parliament. *Remains:* Stark ruins of the 13thC ch. on a coastal hilltop comprising N wall of chancel and its aisle; E end; part of chancel S wall – all to full height. N transept and much of N wall of nave. No claustral bldgs. survive above ground. Desc., plan & care: D of E. Desc: Archaeologia, Vol. 10. Book: Ancient Whitby and its Abbey (1868) Rev. J. C. Atkinson.

White Ladies *Priory. Salop.*
See Brewood.

Wickham Skeith *Priory. Suffolk.*
7m NNE of Stowmarket. (+1135 to −c. 1164). Benedictine monks. F: Robert de Sackville. Ded: uncertain.
Early in the r. of K. Stephen the F. gave the ch. and manor of W.S. to St John's Abbey in Colchester where he himself became a monk. 4 monks were to live at the manor to pray for the F's. soul, but his son consented to the transfer of the little community back to St John's. The manor

remained the property of the abbey until the Dissolution. *Remains:* None.

Wigmore *Abbey. Herefs. Map 2.*
7m SW of Ludlow. (c. 1172−1538). Augustinian canons. F: Hugh Mortimer, Baron of Wigmore. Ded: St James.
1st. f. *c.* 1140 at Shobdon (*v.* above). Fdn. stone laid 1172 (ch. ded. 1179) after 30 troubled years at the hands of the F. who died in 1185 and was buried before the high altar. No cartulary exists, but the early history of the French canons from St Victor's Abbey, nr. Paris, is recounted in a rare 14thC monastic record, the Wigmore Chronicle, now in the library of Chicago University. Much of the history relates to the abbey's links with the Mortimer family. In 1221 the Welsh set fire to the monastery and looted it, but the ch. survived. The fdn. stone of a new ch. laid in 1379. The house was certainly ill-disciplined and canons were sent to Bristol and Keynsham Abbeys for penance and correction. Several abbots were allowed to use the mitre and other episcopal ornaments. *Remains:* Of the ch., nave S wall; gable and W wall of S transept. Abbot's lodging projecting from W claustral range incorporated in modern bldgs. At the W end of the latter bldg. is part of a 14thC gateway of timber and stone. Some carved stones exist in a garden at Letton (2m NE), (Pevsner). Notes on Wigmore Chronicle: Woolhope Naturalist Field Soc. (1967−9). Desc. & plan: Arch. J. Vol. 90 (1934).

Wilberfoss *Priory. Yorks. ER. 8½m E of York. (−1153 to 1539). Benedictine nuns. Fs: Alan de Catton gave his hall and lands;*

Jordan fitz Gilbert gave the ch. Ded: St Mary.
Frequent evidence of poverty and no doubt there were inadequate endowments. In 1283 the nuns were forbidden to take secular women and girls as boarders at the instance of great persons, and by 1294 the finances were in the hands of a custodian. The nuns were reproved in 1308 for wearing red dresses 'like secular women'. In 1348 the prioress was commended for her good governance. Little is known of 15thC history and even less of the 16thC. Why this small and poor nunnery survived until 1539 is not clear, but the prioress's brother-in-law was a wealthy goldsmith and Lord Mayor of York. *Remains:* None. The site lay close to the parish ch. The small stone bridge over the village stream is said to have been built with masonry from the nunnery.

Wilton *Abbey. Wilts. 3½ m W of Salisbury. (−1065 to 1539). Benedictine nuns. F: Edith, wife of Edward the Confessor (she rebuilt the ch. in stone; consecrated 1065). Ded: St Mary, St Bartholomew & St Edith.*
1st. f. 830 as a nunnery by K. Egbert. 2nd. fdn. 890 by K. Alfred. The body of K. Edgar's daughter, St Edith, was enshrined here 984. The whole area was burnt in 1003. Many miracles proclaimed at St Edith's shrine. The other Edith (wife of the Confessor) educated here and from the earliest days the nuns were of the highest birth. Serious fire 1299 after which the abbess obtained licence to fell 60 oaks to effect repairs. Wool and timber were important sources of income. Despite numerous gifts of property, financial problems arose in 13th &

14thCs; and in the 15thC the house was overburdened with boarders nominated by kings. There was occasional difficulty in enforcing the enclosure of the nuns. The abbess was a baroness of the realm. This was a house of the first importance with an excellent record of abbesses, although the last seems to have purchased corruptly her appointment, for the nuns had no say in the election (Power). *Remains:* None. Wilton House occupies the site. *c.* 1960 'a knobbly stone wall' was found reaching high into the core of the present house. To the NE is a 14thC bldg. said to have been the abbesses' Court House. A psalter of *c.* 1250 which belonged to the abbey is preserved in the library of the Royal Coll. of Physicians. Note: Archaeologia, Vol. 25, p. 35−6.

Wilton *Friary. Wilts. Location as above. (1245−1281). Dominican. F: unknown. Ded: unknown.*
Visitation of London. With the growing importance of Salisbury and the waning influence of Wilton, the friars realised after 40 years that the site was a mistake, and in 1281 they moved to a Salisbury suburb. The house was supported by rich patrons during its short life, but the opportunities to preach dwindled. The house became a cell of Salisbury about which many unsolved problems remain. Only one friar lived in the remnants of the friary in 1538 which were described as 'wretched'. *Remains:* None. The site was in West Street.

Winchcombe *Abbey. Glos. 7½m NE of Cheltenham. (c. 970−1539). Benedictine monks. F: Bp. Oswald of Worcester. Ded: St Mary & St Kenelm.*

1st. f. 798 by K. Kenulf whose young son Kenelm was murdered and later buried here. Secular clerks took over from Kenulf's monks until they, in turn, were eventually replaced with monks from Ramsey. c. 1073 Prior Aldwyn went north and with the aid of Bp. Walcher of Durham re-f. Jarrow and Monkwearmouth (*v.* above). In 1151 a serious fire destroyed all books and charters. New ch. built in 12th & 13thCs and consecrated 1239. There was a large wool business in the 14thC, selling an average of 40 sacks p.a. (sack = 364 lbs.) implying a flock of at least 8,000 sheep. In 1315 a visiting bp. found nothing to correct, but injunctions following a visitation in 1329 throw a strong light on internal life (extensive details in VCH). Mitred 1398. In 1428 the house was found to be out of debt, very prosperous and peaceful. Abbot Richard (1488–1525), a great scholar and student of history, compiled a 5-volume history of the abbey to replace records destroyed in 1151. His fine register perished in London during the Great Fire of 1666. The 13thC cartulary 'Winchcombe Landboc' held at the Glos. R.O. *Remains:* None. By the end of the 15thC the abbey was said to be 'equal to a university' (Pevsner). Site established to NE of parish ch. in 1893. Trial excavation 1963. Book: History of Winchcombe Abbey (1947) Gordon Haigh.

Winchelsea *Friary. Sussex. 9½m NE of Hastings. (1318–1538). Dominican. F: Edward I gave the 1st. site; Edward III gave the final site. Ded: St Mary.*
Visitation of London. 1st. fdn. so far from the town few people came to worship, so the friars moved. The 2nd. site was worse and due to inun-

dation by the sea they obtained a new site in the town centre in 1358. The house received numerous legacies. Very little else is known of the history. Although the prior was arrested in 1402 for high treason, the outcome of the trial is unknown. *Remains:* None.

Winchelsea *Friary. Sussex. Map 7. Location as above. (−1242 to 1538). Franciscan (Conventual). F: unknown. Ded: St Francis.*
Custody of London. The great storm of 1287 completely destroyed the ch. which brought the Grey Friars widespread sympathy. When the town was re-f. by Edward I, the barons stipulated that no religious house, except the Friars Minor, should be built. From 1294–1538 the history is a blank except for a ref. to the abbot of Westminster paying a fine of 60 marks divided between Winchelsea and Lichfield, for harbouring an apostate Franciscan. *Remains:* The ruined choir of the conventual ch. is a unique example of an apsidal E end to a ch. of *any* Mendicant Order. The choir arch survives with a stair turret to the S. Of the nave, remnants of the S wall extend some 75 ft. to the W from the stair turret. Desc. & plan: Franciscan Architecture in England (1937) A. R. Martin.

Winchester *(Old Minster) Cathedral-Priory. Hants. Map 6. (964–1539). Benedictine monks. F: Bp. Athelwold at the request of K. Edgar. Ded: Holy Trinity, St Peter, St Paul & St Swithun.*
1st. f. c. 643 by Bp. Birinus,* and the fortification by St Swithun (a prior and later bp. of Winchester) withstood Danish attacks in 860 & 879. Re-bldg. began 1070 under Bp. Walkelin to become the largest ch.

330

in England. Considerable income came from pilgrims to St Swithun's shrine and the grazing of 29,000 sheep. A rich community and a home of learning began under Bp. Wykeham in the 14thC. The cath.-priory was the centre of a spiritual confraternity of 6 monasteries (Abingdon, Chertsey, Romsey, Tewkesbury & Wherwell). Considerable information available from many other sources. *Remains:* Splendid Norman ch. with many subsequent alterations; it contains 8 chantries. Massive arcaded entrance to chapter house (the latter being destroyed 1570) and the N doorway to the dorter. The Deanery, once the Prior's Lodging, has a 13thC entrance. Much of the precinct wall survives. Some 1,400 tons of stone and earth removed from the Norman crypts in 1886. Excavations 1962—5 revealed site of Saxon ch. to the N of the cathedral's nave. Books: Bell's Series (1903); Illustrated Guide to the Cathedrals of G.B. (1902) P. H. Ditchfield, *etc.* Illus: Pitkin Pictorial. Numerous articles.
* See Dorchester Abbey.

Winchester *(New Minster) Hyde Abbey. Hants. Map 6. (964—1539). Benedictine monks. F: Bp. Athelwold. Ded: Holy Trinity, St Mary & St Peter.*
1st. f. 901 by K. Edward the Elder for secular canons who were replaced by Bene. monks in 964. The monks were forced to leave the New Minster *c.* 1110 (which was demolished) and move to Hyde Mead because of its proximity to St Swithun's (Old Minster). At this time a great gold cross given by K. Canute, and the illustrious remains of K. Alfred and his family were taken to Hyde. The abbey perished in 1141 when fire swept the city and rebldg. did

not begin until 1182. 14thC visitations resulted in a charge of 'lukewarmness to the Rule', but nothing to suggest any serious faults. The Black Death (1348) reduced the house to penury, but by 1377 prosperity had returned due to good management. Mitred 1390. 16thC abbatial control was sufficiently lax for charges to be made against the monks. The appointment of the last abbot, a nominee of the Crown, was 'a triumph for unscrupulous dealings' (VCH). *Remains:* Only the 14thC gateway at the entrance to a recreation ground. In St Bartholomew's ch. are a few carved fragments. Site partly excavated 1972—4. Rough plan: Archaeologia, Vol. 13 (1800). Notes: Winchester Rescue. Arch. Report, 1973. Med. Arch. Vols. 17—19.

Winchester *Nunminster (Nunnaminster) Abbey. Hants. (c. 900—1539). Benedictine nuns. Fs: K. Alfred & Q. Eahlswith. Ded: St Mary & (later) St Edburga.*
Bldgs. completed by the F's. son Edward the Elder whose daughter, Edburga, died as abbess in 925 (Knowles). In 963 Bp. Athelwold re-f. the abbey under strict Bene. Rule. Q. Eahlswith lived here after Alfred's death, where she died. Never a rich house and the inadequate endowments in the early years brought poverty later. The few chaplains and canons appointed to help manage temporalities seem to have been a drain on the income. During the 14th & 15thCs cash-flow problems resulted from land sterility, loss of woodland, an over-crowded community and royal exactions. Records of visitations give an insight into internal life which, while not blameless, was without scandal. The

abbess was a baroness of the realm. In 1501 all was in good order and again in 1536 the nuns were said to be 'very clean, virtuous, honest and of charitable conversation'. Many local households survived only by the charity of the nunnery. In 1536 the convent paid the heavy fine of £333.6.8d. to be allowed to continue. *Remains:* None. Considerable ruins survived in the early years of the 17thC. The site lay between High Street and Colebrook Street.

Winchester *Friary. Hants. (−1300 to 1538). Austin. F: unknown. Ded: St Mary.*
Limit of Oxford. In 1302, 1313 & 1328 the site, which was outside the city walls, was enlarged. In 1346 the community moved to bldgs. within the city walls but failed to wait for the king's licence. They were then deprived of these holdings in 1352 which were given to the citizens by Edward III. From this time onwards the history is a blank. *Remains:* None. The later site lay between St Cross Road and Kingsgate Street, about opposite St Michael's ch.

Winchester *Friary. Hants. (−1268 to c. 1538). Carmelite. F: Peter, rector of St Helen's, Winchester. Ded: BVM.*
Distinction of London (?). Only a small house of which practically nothing is known. No inventory of possessions exists, and when the Crown visitor arrived to suppress the friary no one was there. *Remains:* None.

Winchester *Friary. Hants. (−1234 to 1538). Dominican. F: Peter des Roches, bp. of Winchester. Ded: St Katherine.*
Visitation of London. Henry III was

a generous benefactor. Several provincial chapters were held here, notably 1259, 1315 & 1339, and a number of friars of this house were elected English Provincials in the 13th & 14thCs. In 1536 the prior was arrested and indicted for preaching against the fundamentals of his religion, being called a 'soul-murderer'; but testimonials in his favour relieved him of punishment and he resigned the guardianship (VCH). *Remains:* None. Winchester Coll. obtained all four friary sites in 1543. The house lay to the W of Eastgate Street within the city walls.

Winchester *Friary. Hants. (1237−1538). Franciscan (Conventual). F: Albert of Pisa. Ded: St Francis.*
Custody of London. The F. met with much opposition, no doubt from the great abbeys. History is negligible. In the early 1320s 18 friars were ordained of which details appear in VCH. In 1330 the pope agreed to a request from the Countess of Kent that her husband's body should be exhumed from the friary ch. and buried at Westminster. *Remains:* None. The site is uncertain but probably lay between Lower Brook Street and Mid Brook Street.

Wintney* *Priory. Hants. 7m NW of Aldershot. (−1200 to 1536). Cistercian nuns. Fs: probably Richard Holte and Christine his wife. Ded: BVM & St Mary Magdalene.*
In 1243 the wooden ch. was rebuilt by Richard de Herriard who is sometimes named as the F. A fine 13thC book which belonged to the nuns survives among the Cotton MSS (BM), which contains Bene. rules for nuns. In 1265 the prioress and some nuns made visits to

Eleanor, Countess of Leicester, at Odiham Castle to embroider a cope for her chaplain (v. also, Waverley). Early 14thC records of visitations reveal no complaints, but in 1315 a bp. sent a commission to study the 'deplorable conditions of the house'; which may have been due to a serious famine and a lack of food for 2 years. Poverty still existed in the 15thC and 'the poor nuns were heavily encumbered'. A very favourable report on the nuns and their house was sent to Cromwell in 1535. *Remains:* None. A diverted stream enables the site to be located.
* Now known as Hartley Wintney.

Witham[†] *Priory.* Somerset. Map 5. 6m SSW of Frome. (1179–1539). Carthusian monks. F: Henry II. Ded: St Mary, St John, Baptist & All Saints.*
1st. Carth. fdn. in England. 3rd. prior, in 1180, was the saintly Hugh of Avalon from La Grande Chartreuse (later bp. of Lincoln) who built the monastery. At the end of the 12thC a noted scholar, Adam the Scot — late abbot of Dryburgh, Scotland, joined the community and was always sought by St Hugh when he took holidays at Witham. Robert fitz Henry, prior of St Swithun's, Winchester, also ended his days here. The annals of the house are very scant and details of gifts and endowments form the principal information. In the 13thC the priors of Maiden-Bradley (Wilts) and Wormesley (Herefs.) both lost their claims over land ownership with Witham. At the B.D. (1348) none of the monks died due, perhaps, to their isolated existence; but all their servants and retainers succumbed to the pestilence. In the 14thC two alien priories, Spettisbury and Warmington, were

granted to Witham. In 1458 the secular community was so large that extra burial ground was consecrated. From 1461 until the Dissolution the history is a blank. *Remains:* Lay-brothers ch. with 19thC W end addition of bell-cote. To the S is a dove-cote converted into a room. Excavations 1966–9 revealed site of the great cloister and the ch. (Med. Arch. Vols. 11–14). Window tracery and many tiles were found about 1m from the surviving ch. Book: Somerset Carthusians (1895) E. Margaret Thompson.
† Early charters name the house as Selwood.
* Known also as a 'friary' from the Carthusian word fratre for a monk.

Witton *(Wicton) Priory. Worcs. A suburb of Droitwich. (c. 1135–c. 1151). Augustinian canons. F: Peter Corbezon. Ded: St Mary.*
The endowment included a ch., lands, woods and a mill, but for a reason not clear the F. moved the community to Studley, Warks. (v. above) early in the 1150s. *Remains:* None.

Wix* *(Sopwick) Priory. Essex. 8m NE by E of Colchester. (–1133 to 1525). Benedictine nuns. Fs: Walter, Alexander & Edith Mascherell, the 3 children of Walter the deacon. Ded: St Mary.*
No chronicle or register survives, and a charter at the end of Henry I's r. is the only clue to the approx. f. date; and little is recorded of the first 300 years of life here. But in 1283 the house was reduced to such penury that certain grants 'drawn up to the harm of the monastery' were declared void by the pope. The nuns kept 6 hounds to help them catch food. In 1427 the house was ordered to

receive the wicked prioress of Redlingfield to do her penance; and in 1509 the outcome of a visitation forbade the nuns to 'permit any public spectacles to seculars, javelin-play, dances or trading in the streets to the injury of their religion'. This was the largest of the 6 small Essex priories suppressed by Wolsey for his Oxford Coll. *Remains:* None. House occupies the site. Excavated but no fdns. remain exposed.
* Spelt Wicks on modern maps.

Woburn *Abbey. Beds. 6m N of Leighton Buzzard. (1145–1538). Cistercian monks. F: Hugh de Bolbec. Ded: St Mary.*
Colonised from Fountains. Early history obscure. In the 12th & 13thCs the abbots were arbiters in local disputes, and in 1202 the abbot went to Worcester to enquire into the authenticity of miracles performed at St Wulfstan's shrine. In 1234 there was serious poverty due to bad management and monks dispersed to other houses, but prosperity followed with aid given by the canons of Dunstable, and it became one of the wealthiest monasteries in the county. Because there were no episcopal visitations to Cist. houses, nothing is known of 14th & 15thC internal affairs. Considerable details of 16thC history especially of events which led to the fall of the house for political reasons. Although the abbot subscribed to the Act of Supremacy in 1534, he was executed for using words implying papal supremacy for he believed that sooner or later the tide would turn (Knowles). He admired the martyrdom of More and Fisher but he could not imitate them (VCH). *Remains:* None. The ducal mansion covers the area of which the courtyard probably marks

the site of the cloister. The last remains of the abbey were demolished in the 18thC. Hist. at Dissolution: Trans. Royal. Hist. Soc. Vol. 16 (1933).

Wombridge *Priory. Salop. 3m E of Wellington. (–1135 to 1536). Augustinian canons. F: Wm. fitz Alan de Hadley. Ded: St Mary & St Leonard.*
The house was neither large nor affluent. More than 200 small deeds dating from the 12thC are preserved in the priory's cartulary in the BM, and the careful presentation is typical of the tenacity of the house over its possessions. Of internal life very little is known, and from the early 14thC onwards there were rarely more than a prior and 4 canons (VCH). There were too few to allow a student to be maintained at the university, and in 1373 2 canons were said to be unable to write. Apart from the spiritual sources of income the canons received revenue from coal pits, iron works and a smithy on their property. *Remains:* None. The site is covered by a housing estate. Excavations in 1930 revealed traces of the priory in farm bldgs.

Woodbridge *Priory. Suffolk. 8m NE of Ipswich. (c. 1193–1537). Augustinian canons. F: Ernald Rufus. Ded: St Mary.*
Small with mediocre resources chiefly from land and rents. In 1466 the little priory of Alnesbourn became a cell of Woodbridge. Little history is known of the 14th & 15thCs and reports of 16thC visitations are the next mention. At one of these (1514) the prior was urged to collect rents to support the house, and at another (1532) he was accused

of allowing discipline to become lax and of spending too much money on a new water-mill. There was undoubtedly penury at the monastery and the bldgs. were dilapidated. *Remains:* None. A house known as The Abbey stands upon the site.

Woodhouse *Friary. Salop. 9m E of Ludlow, nr. Hopton Wafers. (c. 1250– 1538). Austin. F: uncertain. Ded: unknown.*
Limit of Lincoln. Probably the 2nd. house of the Order in England (following Clare). Established in a remote spot by hermits of Tuscany and it was one of the few houses which did not move to a town following the papal act of the union of Austin friaries in 1256. Tradition claims that Wm. Langland, author of 'Piers Plowman' was a member of the community or was educated here. In the early 15thC the house had a good reputation for observance (VCH). History of the small community is scant. *Remains:* None. A 19thC house occupies the site. A large section of the original rectangular mediaeval moat survives.

Woodkirk *Priory Cell. Yorks. WR. 3m NE of Dewsbury. (–1135 to 1539). Augustinian canons. Fs: Wm. de Warenne, Ralph Lisle & his son William. Ded: St Mary.*
The Fs. gave the ch. to the canons of Nostell and it became one of the 5 cells of that house, whose community sent 3 or 4 canons to Woodkirk. Apart from that, nothing is known for certain about this insignificant house. (Wm. de Warenne's principal aide fd. the nearby nunnery of Kirklees). *Remains:* None. Woodkirk parish ch. has been built on the site of the monastic ch. Excavations in 1964

revealed fdns. of the cloister N of the ch., and of bldgs. in the N & E claustral ranges. Finds are lodged in Batley Museum. (Med. Arch. Vol. 9, 1965).

Woodspring *(Worspring*) Priory. Somerset. Map 5. 4m N of Weston-super-Mare. (–1226 to 1536). Augustinian canons. F: Wm. de Courtney. Ded: Holy Trinity, St Mary & St Thomas, Martyr.*
1st. f. c. 1210 at Dodlinch (*v.* above). The house was in some way connected with Bristol but how is not clear, but both were of the Order of St Victor, Paris. The F. was the grandson of one of the 4 murderers of Becket; while Maud, daughter of one of the other murderers, became a great benefactress. There was poverty in the 13thC and in 1277 a legacy from the bp. of Bath & Wells came at a time of great need. No fdn. charter exists but extensive details of gifts and benefactors survive. It was a poor house without any evidence of disorder. A visitation took place in 1333 but nothing of the outcome is known. In 1419 the canons were summoned for obstructing a footpath. *Remains:* The crossing tower and the nave with N aisle of the conventual ch. form a farmhouse. To the SE a refectory *or* infirmary hall. To the NW a fine 7-bay barn. There is a gateway W of the ch. Excavated 1885. Hist. & plan: Som. Arch & Nat. Hist. Soc. Vol. 51 (1905). Book: Hist. of Woodspring Priory (1908) W. G. Watson.
* Spelling used until the last decade of the 18thC.

Worcester *Cathedral-Priory. Worcs. Map 2. (964 or 969 to 1540). Benedictine monks. F: Bp. Oswald* *(later Archbp. of York and canonised). Ded: St Mary, St Peter, St Oswald & St Wulfstan.* 1st. f. 680 for secular canons. In 743 an adjacent house was endowed for monks and nuns. After the F's. ch. was destroyed by Danes in 1041, the present ch. was f. by Bp. Wulfstan. Fire damage in 1113, 1189 and 1201. K. John buried in the ch. 1216 (*v.* Croxton) between the shrines of St Oswald and St Wulfstan. Many miracles are said to have been performed at the shrine of the latter. The Black Death in 1349 followed by riots in the town almost brought monastic life to a halt. Henry VIII's elder brother, Prince Arthur, buried here in 1502. Extensive history of the Cath.-Pr. available from many other sources. *Remains:* Splendid conventual ch. 14thC cloister and refectory, the latter now part of King's School. Fine circular chapter house. Ruins of dormitory on W of cloister with undercroft. 14thC gatehouse. One wall of the guest hall E of the chapter house (N.T.). Hist. & plan: Arch. J. Vol. 20 (1863). Excavation of dormitory: Archaeologia, Vol. 67 (1915–16). Numerous book refs. Illus: Pitkin Pictorial.

Worcester *White Ladies Nunnery.* *See* Whistones.

Worcester *Friary. Worcs. (1347– 1538). Dominican. F: Wm. Beauchamp, lord of Emley. Ded: St Dominic.* Visitation of Oxford. Probably the last house of the Order f. in England. The F., a kinsman of the earl of Warwick, and Margaret his wife were buried in the ch. Very little history, but records of numerous gifts survive. At the Dissolution an anchoress lived within the priory's precincts. By 1538 the bldgs. were in a sad state of decay. *Remains:* None. The site was adjacent to Broad Street. Part of it was excavated in 1966 when several skeletons were revealed. Med. Arch. Vol. 11.

Worcester *Friary. Worcs. (c. 1226– 1538). Franciscan (Conventual). F: unknown. Ded: unknown.* Custody of Worcester. The site lay within the city walls and, being cramped, the community moved 1236–9 to a site outside the city walls. The ch. is not mentioned until 1268 when Wm. Beauchamp was buried there; and in 1298 his son, also Wm. Beauchamp, 1st. earl of Warwick, was buried in the ch. but not without protests from the monks who tried to claim so illustrious a sepulture. Disputes about other burials resulted in some physical injury to the friars by the monks. 14thC history almost a blank except for details of numerous bequests. In 1485 the state of the bldgs. was so poor that a dormitory collapsed on St Laurence's Day (10.Aug.). In 1535 the house is described as 'More like a house of vicious and incontinent living than a religious place'. Such a charge is so rare against a mendicant house that it is worthy of note (Martin). *Remains:* 1st. site unknown 2nd. site was on the E side of Friar Street and some bldgs. survived until the 1780s. Desc. & plan: Assoc. Archit. Soc. Trans. Vol. 31 (1911).

Worcester *Friary. Worcs. (–1272 to +1284). Sack Friars. F: unknown. Ded: unknown.* Apart from the fact that Henry III augmented the site in 1272 (Knowles), nothing is known of the house. The Council of Lyons suppressed the

Order in 1274, i.e. no new recruits allowed, but the small community was still living here in 1284. *Remains:* None. Note: Arch. J. Vol. 3, p. 130.

Worksop *(Radford) Priory. Notts. Map 3. (+1119 to 1538). Augustinian canons. F: William de Lovetot. Ded: St Mary & St Cuthbert.*
A charter of *c.* 1130 does not give a fdn. date, but it was after the consecration of Archbp. Thurston of York, 1114–40 (Dickinson). Various grants from the Lovetot family in the 12thC established the house as a large priory. 13thC records refer mainly to property ownership, and to a visitation in 1280 which was followed by a series of injunctions to tighten discipline (details VCH). Because Henry III's eldest son Edward had taken the canons' timber 'to make engines of war', the king allowed the convent to take 2 cartloads of heather daily from Sherwood Forest in recompense. Members of the Furnival family and 2 earls of Shrewsbury were buried in the ch. The beautifully illustrated Worksop Psalter is in a New York library. Remaining history uneventful which suggests a well-ordered house. *Remains:* The Norman nave of the conventual ch. survives with twin towers in use as the parish ch. 20thC N & S transepts, central tower and choir. The 13thC Lady Chapel is now attached to the S transept. Cloister lay to the N and the 12thC doorway from the nave survives. Fine 14thC gatehouse S of the ch. Desc. & plan: Br. Arch. Assoc. J. Vol. 30 (1874).

Wormegay *Priory. Norfolk. 6m SSE of King's Lynn. (1189/99–1537). Augustinian canons. F: Wm. de*
Warenne *(Nephew of 3rd earl of Warenne). Ded: BVM., the Holy Cross & St John Evangelist.*
Small and poor with sometimes no more than 2 canons. Very little history of this house with meagre endowments, and from the mid-14thC to 1486 it struggled on in the fight against poverty until in that year it was united with Pentney (*v.* above) to become its cell. *Remains:* None. The site is partly covered by a farmhouse.

Wormsley *(Wormesley)* * *Priory. Herefs. 7m NW of Hereford. (+1200 to 1539). Augustinian canons. F: Gilbert Talbot. Ded: St Mary & St Leonard.*
The canons were of the Order of St Victor, Paris. Fdn. very probably *c.* 1207, i.e. about the middle of the r. of K. John. Inadequate endowments brought extreme poverty in 1278 and the house was exempted from tithe payments. The honest administration in 1279 resulted in the house having temporary custody of the weakly-ruled Chirbury (Salop); and in 1319 the deposed abbot of Wigmore was replaced by the prior of Wormsley. Several other instances occur of the monastery's good record. One historian suggests that Walter Map, the author and poet, was one of the Maps of Wormsley who granted land to the community, and to whom we owe the story of the Holy Grail. In 1537 the earl of Shrewsbury, a descendant of the F., appealed against suppression, and on payment of the large fine of £200 received a new charter 'in perpetuity' which turned out to mean for 2 years. *Remains:* None. Wormsley Grange, W of the site, probably incorporates stone from the priory bldgs.
* Also known as St Leonard of Pyon.

337

Wothorpe *Priory. N'hants. 1½m S of Stamford. (c. 1160?–1354). Benedictine nuns. F: unknown. Ded: St Mary.*
Nothing is known of the origin of the little priory. The earls of Kent were early patrons and its only spiritual possession was Wothorpe ch., now gone. The bldgs. were so ruinous in 1292 that indulgences were granted to penitents who aided repairs. An inquiry was ordered in 1323 to look into discord caused by one of the nuns, but in 1349 all but one had died in the B.D. The poverty and distress which followed resulted in the one nun and the priory being united in 1354 with the nearby nunnery of Stamford (Baron), St Michael's (*v.* above). *Remains:* None.

Wroxall *Priory. Warks. Map 3. 6m NW of Warwick. (c. 1135–1536). Benedictine nuns. F: Hugh, Lord of Halton and Wroxall. Ded: St Leonard.*
Two of the F's. daughters became nuns here. The community was instructed in the Bene. Rule by Dame Edith from Wilton. Records survive of several visitations, e.g. 1269, 1284, 1290, 1300, 1323 *etc.* In 1323 Isabel, Lady Clinton of Maxstoke, the worldly widow of the patron, joined the community and found it hard to adjust to the discipline. Dissension occurred. The bp. poured oil on troubled waters and when Agnes the prioress died, Isabel was appointed to succeed her (Power). In 1339 a prioress resigned following receipt of a long list of injunctions. In the 15th & 16thCs only one record out of several visitations finds anything to reform, and in 1536 all the nuns were of good conversation and living. *Remains:* The N aisle of the nave of the conventual ch. is now the parish ch., with a 16thC post-Dissolution brick W tower. Interesting 14thC heraldic glass. 2 fragments of the claustral bldgs. survive. 1. A small room, perhaps the vestibule to the chapter house. 2. Lying S is the E end of the refectory. Wroxall Abbey, a Victorian mansion, occupies the rest of the site.

Wroxton *Priory. Oxon. 4m NW of Banbury. (c. 1217–1536). Augustinian canons. F: Michael Belet. Ded: St Mary.*
The house was well-endowed with a manor, grounds and advowson of the ch., but in 1221 the heirs of the F. disapproved of the charity and 'disturbed' the canons. Of the internal and external history of this small house very little seems to be known and the discipline, judging by the silence of the bps'. registers, was good (VCH). At the time of the Dissolution each of the 9 members of the community confirmed that all was well. It is doubtful if the report by Cromwell's agent that the prior was rude and unlearned can be relied upon. *Remains:* A 17thC mansion, Wroxton Abbey, now part of a university, occupies the site. A blocked 13thC arch and a 14thC doorway survive in a cellar, and the N wall of the present hall is part of a monastic bldg. (Pevsner). Ch. fdns. excavated to the NE of the house in 1964.

Wykeham *Priory. Yorks. NR. Map 1. 6m SW of Scarborough. (c. 1153–1539). Cistercian nuns. F: Pain Fitz Osbert. Ded: St Mary & St Michael.*
Perhaps 20 nuns in the 13thC but by the beginning of the 14thC the bldgs. were in a ruinous state following Scottish raids. In the early years of Edward III's reign the whole priory – ch., chapter house and 24 bldgs.

were burnt, and the king freed the nuns from taxes for 20 years. The nuns were famed for their embroidery and tapestry, but were ordered not to be absent from divine service on that account. A prioress of bad morals was deposed in 1444; and a little later a curious incident of 2 nuns going on a Jubilee trip to Rome. One of them died on the way and the other returned to live with a man in London. The survivor sought re-admission *c.* 1450, but whether the original journey was genuine is doubtful (VCH). *Remains:* The N wall of the aisleless ch. stands and 2 arches which once connected with the transept (Pevsner). A house, Wykeham Abbey, occupies the rest of the site.

Wymondham* *Priory/Abbey. Norfolk. Map 4. 9m SW of Norwich. (1107−c. 1538). Benedictine monks. F: Wm. de Albini, later earl of Arundel. Ded: St Mary & St Alban.* Richly endowed. Dependent upon St Albans. For a short time Mountjoy (*v.* above) was a cell. 13thC cartulary in BM. Much of the early history consists of records of disputes between the priors and the abbey of St Albans, and also with patrons. In 1446 the remarkable Prior Stephen caused a jealous abbot of St Albans to seek his removal. The subsequent petitions failed and in 1449 Stephen became the first abbot. In this year the house not only became an abbey but also independent of St Albans. Stephen removed St Alban from the ded. and replaced that name with St Thomas, Martyr. Disputes occurred with parishioners and when the octagon lantern was built *c.* 1390 over the original crossing, the monks constructed a solid wall to seal off the monastic E end. The defiant

parishioners built the dignified Perp. tower *c.* 1450 on to the W end of the nave. Visitations in 1492 & 1514 resulted in numerous injunctions upon the undisciplined community; but order was restored before visits in 1520 & 1526. The precise date of surrender is unknown. *Remains:* Nave of conventual ch., with 15thC hammer beam roof of great delicacy, and large N aisle between the bell tower and the ruined lantern comprise the present parish ch. Short S aisle is late 16th C. To the SE stands the lone E wall of the chapter house. Desc. & plans: Archaeologia, Vols. 26 & 43.
* Pronounced Winndam.

Wymondley *(Little) Priory. Herts. Map 6. 3m SE of Hitchin. (c. 1225− 1537). Augustinian canons. F: Richard de Argentein. Ded: St Mary.* 1st. f. 1218 as a hospital for up to seven brethren living under St Augustine's Rule, and very soon afterwards became a priory (Dickinson). Nothing known of endowments. 14thC history is mainly concerned with priors' elections (and their problems) and one of them was charged with 'attempting things prejudicial to the king and his crown'. The offence is unknown. Although all was well in 1442, by 1530 the financial situation was serious. The ch. was in disrepair and of 100 sheep owned by the community only 18 had survived the dreaded murrain − the curse of mediaeval farming. *Remains:* The nave of the ch. became a farmhouse. Stripping the bldg. revealed the N & S walls with 2 late-13thC windows and a 13thC W processional doorway, mainly discovered in 1972. A trussed-rafter roof also uncovered. (Med. Arch.

Vol. 18, 1973). Note: Archaeologia, Vol. 43, p. 234.

Wyresdale *Abbey. Lancs. 7m SE of Lancaster. (1196 to -1204). Cistercian monks. F: Theobald Walter. Ded: St Mary.*
The F. appropriated the ch. of St Michael-on-Wyre to the community which came from Furness. But before 1204 he moved them to his Irish estate on the E coast, and in 1205 to the final site at Abington (Co. Limerick). *Remains:* None. The site is unknown, but the name Abbeystead survives at Over Wyresdale.

Y

Yarm *Friary. Yorks. NR. 6m S of Stockton on Tees. (-1266 to 1538). Dominican. F: uncertain. Ded: The Annunciation.*
Visitation of York. At the end of the 13thC the community received several grants of land to enlarge the site. In 1302 & 1308 vandals despoiled the property, stole timber and injured servants. The reason and outcome are unknown. The plundering by the Scots caused the archbp. to order the prior to stir up local resistance in 1315 and denounce the raiders. Numerous bequests in the 14thC and many burials in the ch. of the Hilton family. *Remains:* None. An 18thC house, The Friarage, to the S of the town occupies the site. Notes: Yorks. Arch. Soc. J. Vol. 32 (1935); & Arch. J. Vol. 37, (1880) 184–92.

Yarmouth *Priory. Norfolk. Map 4. (c. 1100–1539). Benedictine monks. F: Herbert de Losinga, bp. of Norwich. Ded: St Nicholas.*
Cell of Norwich Cath.-Pr. upon which it was entirely dependent, so much so that historical knowledge of monastic life is extremely scanty. The income was considerable in 1356 (£212) but its expenditure was greater. The offerings at the shrine of St Nicholas brought close on half the total revenue. Enlargements to the ch. halted by the B.D. The nave was parochial and the choir monastic hence the cloister was on the S side of the *choir*. Occasionally monks were sent here from Norwich for relaxation (Knowles). Probably never more than a prior, about 5 monks and 3 parish chaplains. *Remains:* Unique 13thC ground plan with narrow nave and the widest aisles of any ch. in the world. The nave arches are Norman. To the S is the sole surviving claustral bldg., probably the refectory, now a school hall. Cloister destroyed 1811, but the other monastic quarters were round a courtyard S of the refectory. Illus: Pitkin Pictorial.

Yarmouth *Austin Friars.*
See Gorleston.

Yarmouth *Friary. Norfolk. (1276–1538). Carmelite. F: Edward I. Ded: BVM.*
Distinction of Norwich. Hardly any history in the first 100 years. In 1378 the friars enlarged their house. Prior Tylney, c. 1430–55, had a high reputation as a professor of divinity at Cambridge (VCH). In 1509 the ch. and claustral bldgs. were burnt down and it is doubtful if much was rebuilt. *Remains:* None.

Yarmouth *Friary. Norfolk. (c. 1267–1538). Dominican. Fs: Henry III gave land; Chas. Pilgrim paid for the ch.; & Thos. Fastolf was a special*

benefactor. Ded: St Dominic.
Visitation of Cambridge. In 1287
the house was swamped by the sea
and a wall was built to prevent further
damage. There were many small
bequests especially at the time of
the B.D. Little else known. In 1525
the ch. was burnt down and never
restored. *Remains:* None. The site
was in the vicinity of Blackfriars
Road and the area of the ch. is now
covered by a fire station. A few
architectural fragments and parts of
skeletons found during excavations
in 1970. Notes & plans: Norfolk
Arch. Vol. 35, pt. 4. Med. Arch.
Vol. 15.

Yarmouth *Friary. Norfolk. Map 4.
(+1226 to 1538). Franciscan
(Conventual). F: probably Sir. Wm.
Gerbridge. Ded: St Francis?*
Custody of Cambridge. Site enlarged
1285. In 1302 the friars complained
of townsmens' destruction of their
defences against inroads of the sea
during violent storms. Bequests and
requests for interment in the ch.
were frequent from 13thC onwards.
Strangely, only one name of all the
community throughout the 300
years of history is known. He lived
at the end of the 15thC and weighed
24-stone. *Remains:* There survives
the southern $\frac{2}{3}$ of the W cloister walk
and a chamber of 2 bays which
contain the only Franciscan vaulting
to remain in England. Queen Street
covers the site of the ch. Desc. &
plan: Franciscan Arch. (1937)
A. R. Martin; also Norfolk Arch.
Vol. 13 (1896). Desc: Br. Arch.
Assoc. J. Vol. 31 (1925).

Yedingham *Priory. Yorks. NR*.
7m SE by E of Pickering. (−1163 to
1539). Benedictine nuns. F: Helewise*

de Clare. Ded: St Mary.
Poverty in 1280 resulted in the
archbp. giving custody of the business
affairs to Robert de Brus. Following
a visitation in 1314 the lay-sisters
were forbidden to wear black veils
(only white); the prioress was
ordered to be more even with her
corrections by 'mingling oil with
wine'; and that nuns should not
absent themselves from divine service
on account of silken embroidery. So
serious was the state of bldgs. at the
priory (some had fallen) in 1456 that
a 40-day indulgence was granted to
all penitents who aided repairs.
Many leases and grants are recorded
and preserved in the P.R.O. One of
1352 is of special interest and refers
in detail to generous treatment of a
corrodian who, in return, undertook
to run the dairy. Despite a very low
income the house continued beyond
1536 and obtained free exemption
from suppression. *Remains:* The S
wall of the aisleless ch. is now one
side of a shed at Abbey Farm with
several blocked doorways.
* The priory lay N of the R. Derwent
while the village is S of the river in
the E. Riding.

York *Abbey. Yorks. At Marygate.
(−1086 to 1088). Benedictine monks.
F: Count Alan of Richmond. Ded:
St Olave.*
The community came to this ch.
from Whitby via Lastingham under
Abbot Stephen. When the canons of
York Minster disputed the fdn.,
K. William changed the site, gave
more land and laid the fdn. stone of
St Mary's (*v.* below). The site of
St Olave's had, in any case, proved
too small. *Remains:* No part of the
monastic ch. survives except perhaps
the tower of *c.* 1500. The remainder
18th−20thCs.

341

York. St Mary's Abbey. North-west corner of the nave and remnant of the west door on the extreme left.

York *Abbey. Yorks. Map 3. (1088–1539). Benedictine monks. F: William II (Rufus). Ded: St Mary.* 1st. f. −1086 at St Olave's (*v.* above). Observances of the Rule became slack in 1132 and the prior and 12 monks left, under stormy conditions, to fd. Fountains. Fire damage in 1137, 1270 & 1376. The house enjoyed many privileges including exemption from royal exactions. Mitred 1245. Dissension between citizens and monks resulted in violent quarrels in 1262 probably on account of the community's immunity from customary monastic responsibilities.

The abbots of St Mary's and Meaux had champions to fight for them from sunrise to sunset to settle fishery rights of Hornsea Mere. The outcome is unknown. Large debt of £4,029 in 1319, but the monastery later became the wealthiest of the northern black monks houses and owned 9 cells. Many refs. in VCH to abbatial power and wealth. There were generous daily aids for the poor in 1534, but a bp. ordered the Rule to be better kept. Numerous records, transferred after the Dissolution to St Mary's Tower, were destroyed in the siege of York in 1644. *Remains:*

York. St Mary's Abbey. North wall of the nave and north aisle arch leading to north transept.

Enough to show the spectacular splendour of the late-13thC ch. architecture comprising N wall of the nave; part of the W front; NW pier of the crossing; and fragments of the N transept. (Fdns. carried down 26 ft.) Extensive lengths of precinct wall. Much altered abbot's lodging (King's Manor) and gatehouse in Marygate. Chapter house vestibule is part of a museum containing numerous stone carvings, wall fdns., column bases and the fireplace from the warming house. Excavated 1902 & 1970s. Desc. & plan: Arch. J. Vol. 91 (1934).

York *Alien Priory/Priory. Yorks.*

Map 3. At Micklegate. (1089–1538). *Benedictine monks. F: Ralph Paynell.* *Ded: Holy Trinity.* 1st. fd. for secular canons and damaged by Danes in 1069 when the city was under siege. The house was ruinous when re-f. 1089. Subject to Marmoutier Abbey. There were numerous benefactors and the community owned 14chs., extensive lands and several fisheries. It survived in 1414 when most alien houses were suppressed and it became denizen in 1426. At the same time Tickford (*v.* above) became a dependency. Due to poverty after the wars it was exempted from taxes in 1446. Aid came in 1478 from the duke of

Gloucester (later Richard III) and conditions at the house greatly improved. Although the prior was implicated in the Pilgrimage of Grace, he lived on pension until 1545. *Remains:* The parish ch. comprises the 13thC nave and W front of the conventual ch. with a 15thC NW tower. (The chancel is 19thC). There are also fragments of the NW and SW crossing piers. Transepts and all else have gone.

York *Priory. Yorks. In Fishergate. (+1087 to −1536). Benedictine monks. F: William II (Rufus) gave the ch. to Whitby. Ded: All Saints.* Very small house to which the first prior, Serlo, was elected in 1109. Revenue from local properties was immersed in Whitby's accounts hence very little history survives. Never more than 3 or 4 monks who came from Whitby to recuperate or retire, including Abbot Benedict *c.* 1148. Sometime before 1536 the house was abandoned. *Remains:* None. All trace has gone and the site was covered by a cattle market.

York *Priory. Yorks. In Clementhorpe. (c. 1130−1536). Benedictine nuns. F: Archbp. Thurston. Ded: St Clement.* In 1192 the archbp. of York planned to subject the house to Godstow (*v.* above) but the nuns would not obey this abbess, and they saved their independence by an appeal to Rome (Eckenstein). Several instances of nuns being unsuited to the life, including one in 1301 who was met at the gate by a horseman and went to live with a man in Darlington for 3 years. Serious troubles resulted in a prioress being forced to resign in 1324 but no details are known. About this time a nun, tired of indiscipline,

became an anchoress at Beeston, near Leeds (Power). Never a large community and the ch. was shared with parishioners. It is said that pilgrims came in veneration of the alleged possession of some of the milk of St Mary. In 1525 one of the nuns was appointed prioress of Rosedale Priory. *Remains:* None. Nunnery Lane is the sole memory. Excavations in 1976 revealed the sites of two bldgs. and numerous burials − Med. Arch. Vol. 21. (1977).

York *Priory. Yorks. In Fishergate. (c. 1200−1538). Gilbertine canons. F: Hugh Murdac, archdeacon of Cleveland. Ded: St Andrew.* The house adjoined St Clement's nunnery (*v.* above). There were probably fewer than the planned 12 canons and only a prior and 3 canons are recorded in 1381 & 1536. In 1280 two canons relinquished their habit and 'furtively departed at night to the peril of their souls' (VCH). Little history exists for the 14th & 15thCs except for an incident in 1487 when the sheriffs of York were ordered to appear before the archbp. for seizing persons who had sought sanctuary at the monastery. *Remains:* None. A section of the precinct wall survives in Blue Bridge Lane.

York *Friary. Yorks. In Lendal. (c. 1272−1538). Austin. F: (by tradition) Lord Scrope of Upsall (not yet identified). Ded: St Mary?* Limit of York. The first community is said to have come from Tickhill (*v.* above) and in 1272 Henry III gave the friars protection. In the 14thC there were, on occasions, 40 friars here. A catalogue of the library survives listing 646 volumes, but only a few are known to exist.

The house received numerous bequests and a number of distinguished burials in the ch. are recorded. Certain disputes between the abbot of St Mary's and the mayor of York were settled in the friars' house in 1493. The monastery was poorly sited 'standing very cold by the water of the Ouse without open air' (VCH), and was valued at only 16d when suppressed. The last prior, John Aske, appears to have given some support to the Pilgrimage of Grace, but he was not punished. *Remains:* None.

York *Friary. Yorks. In Bootham and Stonebow. (−1253 to 1538). Carmelite. F: unknown. Ded: BVM.* Distinction of York. Henry III was an early benefactor and the first mention of the community is his gift of 6 oaks for ch. construction. In 1295 a new site was given by Wm. de Vescy in The Stonebow and the friars moved to their permanent abode. The old site became a hospital. VCH gives details of several grants in the 14thC which enabled the site to be enlarged, some of which lay within the boundaries of nearby parishes and caused friction. There were several lawsuits concerning debts and poor workmanship by laymen at the end of the 14thC. Bequests to the house were very numerous including some from the Percys of Northumberland, who were heirs of the Vescys. Several distinguished scholars were friars here, and some provincial priors of the Order were closely connected with the house. *Remains:* None.

York *Friary. Yorks. (+1307 to c. 1310). Crutched (Holy Cross).* Nothing is known of the beginning of the settlement early in the r. of

Edward II. Archbp. Greenfield discouraged their presence and in all possibility the community moved to Kildale (Knowles). *Remains:* None.

York *Friary. Yorks. At Toft Green. (1227−1538). Dominican. F: probably Henry III. Ded: St Mary Magdalen.* Visitation of York. Provincial chapters held here on 7 occasions (VCH). In the 13thC the friars received several grants of land to extend their premises. In 1316 an unusual event occurred when Friar Nicholas left the house to join the Cistercian abbey at Rievaulx. VCH is full of interesting incidents in connection with the house. A riot in 1381 resulted in broken walls at the friary and the offenders were made to repair all damage. At the close of the 14thC the community received a valuable relic − the right hand of St Mary Magdalen which is said to have survived until the Dissolution. The records of the house list 60 names of persons buried in the ch., and a further 20, omitted from the list, are given in VCH. Bequests were numerous from all stratas of society. Fire in the early 1450s destroyed the cloister and adjacent bldgs. The prior was implicated in the Pilgrimage of Grace in 1536 and hanged at Tyburn in May 1537. *Remains:* None. Note: Yorks. Arch. J. Vol. 32 (1935).

York *Friary. Yorks. Between the R. Ouse and the castle. (c. 1230−1538). Franciscan (Conventual). F: unknown. Ded: St Francis?* Custody of York. The first site proved too small and c. 1243 the friars moved to the location given above, and this was further enlarged in 1280. A number of friars distinguished for their learning were sent to other cities. Edward II stayed here in 1320 and it is probable that Parliament assembled in the friars' ch. in 1322. In 1359 some of the city's officers invaded the precincts to seize persons who had taken sanctuary, and in 1380 the friars came under the special protection of Richard II. In the 14th & 15thCs the community received numerous bequests and gifts and the ch. contained the tombs of many local families, some of whom left explicit instructions such as Brian Roecliff, baron of the Exchequer, who, in 1495, desired burial near the Holy Trinity altar 'with honour-able but not pompous exequies'. A 13thC 'Book of Beasts' from the house survives in Westminster Abbey Library. *Remains:* Very little. A length of wall along the Staith by the river was part of the friary. Nothing else. Note: Yorks. Arch. J. Vol. 32 (1935).

York *Friary. Yorks. (c. 1260 to −1312). Sack Friars.*
Nothing is known about the short life of the house. Only 2 friars lived here in 1274 and 1300. Following the deaths of the two men their lands passed into the king's hands, and it was rented to a layman in 1312 for 8s. p.a. (VCH).

Appendixes

APPENDIX 1

Alien Priories (See p. 16)

(Historical information about these monasteries can be obtained from 'Medieval Religious Houses, England and Wales' (1971), by David Knowles & R. Neville Hadcock.)

Abbreviations:

A	= Augustinian canons	Cl	= Cluniac monks
B	= Benedictine monks	G	= Grandmontine brethren
BN	= Benedictine nuns	P	= Premonstratensian canons
C	= Cell	Pr	= Priory
Cis	= Cistercian monks	T	= Tironensian monks

Site	Status	Order		Fd.	closed	Granted to
Alberbury	Pr	G	Salop	c. 1230 :	c. 1441	All Souls Coll. Oxford
Aldermanshaw	C	Cl	Leics	c. 1220 :	–1450	Bermondsey Abbey
Allerton Mauleverer	Pr	B	Yorks. WR	+1100 :	c. 1414	King's Coll. Cambridge
Andover	Pr	B	Hants	–1087 :	c. 1414	Winchester Coll.
Andwell	Pr	T	Hants	–1135 :	1391	Winchester Coll.
Appuldurcombe	Pr	B	I. of W.	c. 1100 :	1414	Aldgate. The Minories
Arundel	Pr	B	Sussex	1102 :	–1379	Became secular coll.
Astley	Pr	B	Worcs	–1086 :	1414	Westbury-upon-Trym Coll.
Avebury	C	B	Wilts	+1114 :	1378	Winchester Coll.

Beckford	Pr	A	Glos	−1135 : c. 1414	Eton Coll.
Burstall	Pr	B	Yorks. ER	+1115 : 1395	Kirkstall Abbey
Burwell	C	B	Lincs	−1110 : 1427	Tattershall secular coll.
Cammeringham	Pr	P	Lincs	c. 1192 : 1396	Hulton Abbey
Carisbrooke	Pr	B	I. of W.	c. 1156 : 1414	Sheen Priory
Charlton	Pr	P	Wilts	c. 1187 : 1380	St Katherine's Hosp. by the Tower (v. below)
Clare	Pr	B	Suffolk	1090 : 1124	To Stoke-by-Clare (v. below)
Clatford	C	B	Wilts	+1104 : c. 1439	Eton Coll.
Cogges	Pr	B	Oxon	1103 : 1414	Eton Coll.
Corsham	C	B	Wilts	−1135 : 1294	Syon Abbey
Covenham	C	B	Lincs	c. 1082 : 1303	Kirkstead Abbey
Craswall	Pr	G	Herefs	c. 1225 : 1462	Christ's Coll. Cambridge
Dunwich	Pr	B	Suffolk	+1080 : c. 1290	Fell in the sea
Ecclesfield	Pr	B	Yorks. WR	−1135 : 1386	Coventry Carthusian Priory
Edith Weston	C	B	Rutland	c. 1114 : 1394	Coventry Carthusian Priory
Ellingham	C	B	Hants	1160 : 1414	Eton Coll.
Exeter (St James)	Pr	Cl	Devon	1141 : +1428	King's Coll. Cambridge
Frampton	Pr	B	Dorset	−1077 : −1414	St Stephen's Coll. Westminster
Great Bricett	Pr	A	Suffolk	−1119 : 1444	King's Coll. Cambridge
Great Witchingham	C	Cl	Norfolk	+1093 : c. 1414	New Coll. Oxford
Grovebury	Pr	BN	Beds	+1189 : c. 1414	Windsor Coll.
Harmondsworth	C	B	M'sex	−1087 : 1391	Winchester Coll.
Hamble	Pr	T	Hants	+1109 : 1391	Winchester Coll.
Haugham	C	B	Lincs	+1080 : 1397	Coventry Carthusian Priory
Hayling	Pr	B	Hants	c. 1067 : 1413	Sheen Priory
Headley	Pr	B	Yorks. WR	−1125 : 1414	York (Holy Trinity) Priory
Hinckley	Pr	B	Leics	c. 1173 : 1409	Mount Grace Priory
Horsley	Pr	B	Glos	−1087 : 1260	Bruton Priory
Hough	Pr	A	Lincs	c. 1164 : c. 1414	Mount Grace Priory
Ipplepen	Pr	A	Devon	c. 1143 : c. 1414	King's Coll. Cambridge
Isleham	Pr	B	Cambs	−1100 : 1254	Moved to Linton (v. below)

Site	Status	Order		Fd.	closed	Granted to
Lancaster	Pr	B	Lancs	c. 1094 :	1428	Syon Abbey
Lapley	Pr	B	Staffs	+1061 :	1415	Tong Coll.
Lewisham	Pr	B	Kent	1044 :	1414	Sheen Priory
Linton	Pr	B	Cambs	1254 : —	1414	Pembroke Coll. Cambridge
Livers Ocle	C	B	Herefs	1100 : c.	1414	Sheen Priory
Loders	Pr	B	Dorset	c. 1107 :	1414	Syon Abbey
Lyminster	Pr	BN	Sussex	c. 1082 : c.	1414	Eton Coll.
Minster	Pr	B	Cornwall	−1190 : −	1407	Became a rectory
Minster Lovell	C	B	Oxon	−1206 :	1415	Eton Coll.
Minting	Pr	B	Lincs	c. 1129 :	1414	Mount Grace Priory
Modbury	Pr	B	Devon	c. 1140 : c.	1414	Eton Coll.
Monkland	C	B	Herefs	−1100 : c.	1414	Windsor Coll.
Monks Kirby	Pr	B	Warks	1077 :	1414	Axholme Priory
Monks Sherborne	Pr	B	Hants	−1130 :	1414	Queen's Coll. Oxford
Newton Longville	Pr	Cl	Bucks	−1102 :	1414	New Coll. Oxford
Newent	Pr	B	Glos	−1086 :	1399	Fotheringhay Coll.
Ogbourne St George	Pr	B	Wilts	−1147 :	1405	Windsor Coll. (and others)
Otterton	Pr	B	Devon	+1199 :	1414	Syon Abbey
Panfield	C	B	Essex	−1077 :	1413	Christ Church Canterbury
Patrixbourne	Pr	A	Kent	c. 1200 :	1409	Merton Priory
Preston Capes	Pr	Cl	N'hants	c. 1090 : c.	1107	Daventry Priory
Ruislip	Pr	B	M'sex	c. 1087 : c.	1250	Windsor Coll.
Runcton	C	B	Sussex	+1100 :	1260	Bruton Priory
St Cross	C	T	I. of W.	+1132 :	1391	Winchester Coll.
St Helens	C	Cl	I. of W.	−1155 :	1414	Eton Coll.
St Michael's Mount	Pr	B	Cornwall	c. 1091 : c.	1414	Syon Abbey
Scarborough	C	Cis	Yorks. NR	−1203 : c.	1407	Bridlington Priory
Sele	Pr	B	Sussex	−1226 :	1480	Magdalen Coll. Oxford

Spettisbury	Pr	B	Dorset	−1100 : c. 1324	Witham Priory
Sporle	C	B	Norfolk	−1123 : c. 1414	Eton Coll.
Standon	Pr	B	Herts	−1178 : c. 1306	Stoke Coll.
Steventon	Pr	B	Berks	−1135 : 1389	Westminster Abbey
Stogursey	Pr	B	Somerset	−1107 : 1442	Eton Coll.
Stoke-by-Clare	Pr	B	Suffolk	1124 : 1415	Became secular coll.
Stratfield Saye	Pr	B	Berks	c. 1170 : 1399	Eton Coll.
Swavesey	Pr	B	Cambs	−1086 : 1411	Coventry Carthusian Priory
Takeley	Pr	B	Essex	−1086 : c. 1391	New Coll. Oxford & Winchester Coll.
Throwley	Pr	B	Kent	c. 1150 : c. 1414	Syon Abbey
Titley	C	T	Herefs	1121 : 1391	Winchester Coll.
Toft Monks	Pr	B	Norfolk	−1100 : c. 1414	King's Coll. Cambridge
Tooting Bec	Pr	B	Surrey	−1086 : 1315?	Eton Coll.
Tregoney	Pr	A	Cornwall	−1125 : 1267	Merton Priory
Upavon	C	B	Wilts	−1086 : −1414	Ivychurch Priory
Ware	Pr	B	Herts	−1081 : 1414	Sheen Priory
Wareham	C	B	Dorset	−1135 : c. 1414	Sheen Priory
Warmington	Pr	B	Warks	−1123 : c. 1387	Witham Priory
Weedon Bec	Pr	B	N'hants	+1126 : +1329	Eton Coll.
Weedon Lois (Pinkeney)	C	B	N'hants	−1123 : 1392	Biddlesden Abbey
Well Hall	C	B	Norfolk	c. 1081 : 1415	St Stephen's Coll. Westminster
West Mersea	Pr	B	Essex	(?) 1046 : 1400	Higham Ferrers Collegiate Church
West Ravendale	Pr	P	Lincs	c. 1202 : −1413	Southwell Collegiate Church
Wilmington	Pr	B	Sussex	−1086: 1414	Chichester Cathedral
Wilsford	C	B	Lincs	−1154 : c. 1401	Bourne Abbey
Wing	C	B	Bucks	−1086 : 1416	St Mary de Pre Priory
Wolston	C	B	Warks	−1094 : 1394	Coventry Carthusian Priory
Wootton Wawen	Pr	B	Warks	+1086 : 1447	King's Coll. Cambridge

APPENDIX 2

Lists of Monasteries by Orders

Augustinian Canons

Alnesbourne
Anglesey
Arbury
Arundel (*v.* Pynham)
Bamburgh
Barlinch
Barnwell
Baswich
Baxterwood
Beeston
Bentley
Berden
Bicester
Bicknacre
Bilsington
Bisham
Blackmore
Blythburgh
Bodmin
Bolton
Bourne
Bradenstoke
Bradley
Breadsall
Breamore
Breedon
Bridlington
Brinkburn
Bristol
Bromehill
Brooke

Bruton
Buckenham
Buckland
Burscough
Burtle
Bushmead
Butley
Caldwell
Calke
Calwich
Cambridge
Canons Ashby
Canonsleigh
Canterbury
Carham
Carlisle
Cartmel
Chacombe
Charley
Chetwode
Chipley
Chirbury
Christchurch (Hants)
Church Gresley
Cirencester
Cockerham
Coddenham
Colchester
Cold Norton
Combwell
Conishead
Cottingham
Coxford

Darley
Derby
Dodford
Dodlinch
Dodnash
Donnington Wood
Dorchester
Dover
Drax
Droitwich (*v.* Witton)
Dunstable
Elsham
Embsay
Exeter
Felley
Fineshade
Flanesford
Flitcham
Frithelstock
Gloucester (2)
   (*v.* Lanthony)
Grafton Regis
Great Massingham
Great Paxton
Grimsby (*v.* Wellow)
Guisborough
Haltemprice
Halywell
Hardham
Hartland
Hastings
Haughmond
Healaugh

Hempton
Hexham
Hickling
Hirst
Hood
Horsley
Huntingdon
Ipswich (2)
Ivychurch
Ixworth
Kenilworth
Kersey
Keynsham
Kirby Bellars
Kirkham
Kyme
Lanercost
Latton
Launceston
Launde
Leeds (Kent)
Leicester
Leighs
Lesnes
Letheringham
Lilleshall
Little Dunmow
Lanthony (Glos)
London (3)
Longleat
Maiden Bradley
Markby
Marsh Barton (*v*. Exeter)
Marton
Maxstoke
Merton
Michelham
Missenden
Mobberley
Mottisfont
Mountjoy
Newark (Surrey)
Newburgh
Newnham
Newstead (Lincs)
Newstead (Notts)
Nocton
Normans Barrow

Northampton
North Creake
North Ferriby
Norton
Nostell
Notley
Nottingham
Osney
Ovingham
Owston
Oxford (2)
Pentney
Peterstone
Plympton
Portchester
Poughley
Pynham
Ranton
Ratlinghope
Ravenstone
Reigate
Repton
Rocester
Royston
Rudham
Runcorn
St Anthony in Roseland
St Denys
 (*v*. Southampton)
St Germans
St Olaves
St Osyths
Sandleford
Selborne
Shelford
Sheringham
Shobdon
Shulbred
Skewkirk
Snead
Southampton
Southwark (*v*. London)
Southwick
Spinney
Stafford (*v*. Baswich)
Stavordale
Stone
Stonely

Studley
Tandridge
Taunton
Thelsford
Thetford
Thoby
Thornholme
Thornton
Thremhall
Thurgarten
Tiptree
Tonbridge
Torksey
Tortington
Trentham
Ulverscroft
Walsingham
Waltham
Warbleton
Warter
Warwick
Wellow
West Acre
Weybourne
Weybridge
Wigmore
Witton
Wombridge
Woodbridge
Woodkirk
Woodspring
Worksop
Wormegay
Wormsley
Wroxton
Wymondley

Benedictine Monks

Abbotsbury
Abingdon
Alcester
Aldeby
Alkborough
Alvecote
Athelney
Bardney

353

Bath
Battle
Beadlow
Bedemans Berg
Belvoir
Binham
Birkenhead
Bisham
Blackborough
Blithbury
Blyth
Boxgrove
Bradwell
Bristol
Bromfield
Burton upon Trent
Bury St Edmunds
Cambridge
Canterbury (2)
Canwell
Cerne
Chertsey
Chester
Colchester
Coquet Island
Coventry
Cowick
Cranborne
Crowland
Deeping St James
Deerhurst
Denney
Dover
Dunster
Durham
Earls Colne
Edwardstone
Ely
Evesham
Ewyas Harold
Exeter
Eye
Eynsham
Farne Island
Faversham
Felixstowe
Finchale
Folkestone

Freiston
Glastonbury
Gloucester
Great Malvern
Hackness
Hatfield Broadoak
Hatfield Peverel
Hereford
Hertford
Hilbre Island
Horsham St Faith
Horton
Hoxne
Humberstone
Hurley
Jarrow
Kilpeck
Kings Lynn
Lamanna
Lastingham
Leominster
Leonard Stanley
Lincoln
Lindisfarne Island
Little Malvern
Luffield
Lytham
Malmesbury
Middlesbrough
Millbrook
Milton
Modney
Monk Bretton
Monkwearmouth
Morville
Mountjoy
Muchelney
Mullicourt
Norwich (2)
Oxford (3)
Oxney
Partney
Penwortham
Pershore
Peterborough
Pheleley
Pilton
Ramsey

Reading
Redbourn
Richmond (Yorks)
Rochester
Rumburgh
St Albans
St Bees
St Benet of Hulme
St Ives (Hunts)
St Neots
Sandwell
Scilly
Selby
Sherborne
Shrewsbury
Snaith
Snape
Snelshall
Spalding
Spinney
Stamford
Stow
Sudbury
Tavistock
Tewkesbury
Thetford
Thorney
Tickford
Totnes
Tutbury
Tynemouth
Tywardreath
Upholland
Walden
Wallingford
Westbury upon Trym
Westminster
Wetherall
Whitby
Wickham Skeith
Winchcombe
Winchester (2)
Worcester
Wymondham
Yarmouth
York (4)

Bonshommes

Ashridge
Edington

Carthusian Monks

Axholme
Beauvale
Coventry
Hatherop
Hinton
Kingston upon Hull
London
Mount Grace
Sheen
Witham

Cistercian Monks

Abbey Dore
Barnoldswick
Beaulieu
Biddlesden
Bindon
Bordesley
Boxley
Brightley
Bruern
Buckfast
Buckland
Buildwas
Byland
Bytham
Calder
Cleeve
Coggeshall
Combe
Combermere
Cotton
Croxden
Darnhall
Dieulacres
Dunkeswell
Faringdon
Flaxley

Forde
Fors
Fountains
Furness
Garendon
Hailes
Haverholme
Hazleton
Holmcultram
Hood
Hulton
Jervaulx
Kingswood
Kirkstall
Kirkstead
London
Louth Park
Loxwell
Meaux
Medmenham
Merevale
Netley
Newenham
Newminster
Old Byland
Otley
Oxford
Pipewell
Poulton
Quarr
Radmore
Revesby
Rewley
Rievaulx
Robertsbridge
Roche
Rufford
Rushen
Sawley
Sawtry
Sibton
Stanlaw
Stanley
Stocking
Stoneleigh
Stratford
Swineshead
Tetbury

Thame
Tilty
Tintern
Tulketh
Vale Royal
Vaudey
Warden
Waverley
Whalley
Woburn
Wyresdale

Cluniac Monks

Barnstaple
Bermondsey
Broomholm
Castle Acre
Church Preen
Clifford
Daventry
Derby
Dudley
Heacham
Holme
Horkesley
Kersal
Kerswell
Lenton
Lewes
Mendham
Monk Bretton
Monks Horton
Monkton Farleigh
Montacute
Much Wenlock
Normans Barrow
Northampton
Pontefract
Preston Capes
Prittlewell
St Carrok
Sleves Holm
Stansgate
Thetford
Wangford

355

Premonstratensian Canons

Alnwick
Barlings
Bayham
Beauchief
Beeleigh
Blackwose
Blanchland
Brockley
Cockersand
Coverham
Croxton
Dale
Durford
Easby
Egglestone
Great Parndon
Hagneby
Halesowen
Hornby
Kalendar
Langdon
Langley
Lavendon
Leiston
Newbo
Newsham
Otham
Preston Patrick
St Radegund (Kent)
Shap
Snelshall
Sulby
Swainby
Titchfield
Torre
Tupholme
Warburton
Welbeck
Wendling
West Dereham

Gilbertine Canons & Nuns

canons . . . . . (1)

canons & nuns (2)

Alvingham 2
Bridgend 1
Bullington 2
Cambridge 1
Catley 2
Chicksands 2
Clattercote 1
Ellerton 1
Fordham 1
Haverholme 2
Hitchin 1
Lincoln 1
Malton 1
Marlborough 1
Marmont 1
Mattersey 1
Newstead 1
North Ormsby 2
Poulton 1
Sempringham 2
Shouldham 2
Sixhills 2
Tunstall 2
Watton 2
York 1

Grandmontine

Grosmont

Friars

A — Austin
C — Carmelite
Cr — Crutched
D — Dominican
F — Franciscan
P — Pied
S — Sack
T — Trinitarian

Appleby C
Arundel D
Atherstone A
Aylesbury F
Aylesford C
Bamburgh D
Barham Cr
Barnard Castle A
Bedford F
Bemaken F
Beverley D F
Blakeney C
Bodmin F
Boston A C D F
Bridgnorth F
Bridgwater F
Bridport C
Bristol A C D F S
Burnham Norton C
Bury St Edmunds F
Cambridge A C D F P S
Canterbury A D F S
Carlisle D F
Chelmsford D
Chester C D F S
Chichester D F
Clare A
Colchester Cr F
Coventry C F
Dartmouth A
Derby D
Doncaster C F
Donnington Cr
Dorchester F
Droitwich A
Dunstable D
Dunwich D F
Durham F
Easton Royal T
Exeter D F
Gloucester C D F
Gorleston A
Grantham F
Greenwich F
Grimsby A F
Guildford D
Hartlepool F
Hereford D F
Hertford T
Hitchin C
Hounslow T
Hulne C

356

Huntingdon A
Ilchester D
Ingham T
Ipswich C D F
Kildale Cr
Kings Langley D
Kings Lynn A C D F S
Kingston upon Hull
  A C F
Knaresborough T
Lancaster D
Leicester A D F S
Lewes F
Lichfield F
Lincoln A C D F S
London A C Cr D F P S
Lossenham C
Ludlow A C
Maldon C
Marlborough C
Melcombe D
Newark A F
Newcastle under Lyme D
Newcastle upon Tyne
  A C D F S T
New Romney F
Northallerton C
Northampton A C D F S
Norwich A C D F P S
Nottingham C F
Orford A
Oxford A C Cr D F S T
Penrith A
Plymouth C D F
Pontefract D
Preston F
Reading F
Richmond F
Rye A S
Salisbury D F
Sandwich C
Scalby F
Scarborough C D F
Sele C
Shoreham C
Shrewsbury A D F
Sittingbourne A
Southampton A F

Stafford A F
Stamford A C D F S
Sudbury D
Thelsford T
Thetford A D
Tickhill A
Totnes T
Truro D
Walsingham F
Ware F
Warrington A
Warwick D
Welnetham Cr
Waplode Cr
Wilton D
Winchelsea D F
Winchester A C D F
Woodhouse A
Worcester D F S
Yarm D
Yarmouth A C D F
York A C Cr D F S

Nunneries

A — Augustinian
B — Benedictine
Br — Bridgettine
C — Cistercian
Cl — Cluniac
D — Dominican
F — Franciscan
P — Premonstratensian

Aconbury A
Amesbury B
Ankerwyke B
Arden B
Armathwaite B
Arthington Cl
Barking B
Barrow Gurney B
Baysdale C
Blackborough B
Blithbury B
Bretford B
Brewood A B

Bristol A
Broadholme P
Broomhall B
Bruisyard F
Buckland A
Bungay B
Burnham A
Cambridge B
Campsey Ash A
Cannington B
Canonsleigh A
Canterbury B
Castle Hedingham B
Catesby C
Chatteris B
Cheshunt B
Chester B
Cook Hill C
Cornworthy A
Crabhouse A
Dartford D
Davington B
Denney F
Derby B
Douglas C
Easebourne A
Ellerton C
Elstow B
Esholt C
Farewell B
Flamstead B
Flixton A
Fosse C
Fotheringhay Cl
Foukeholme B
Godstow B
Gokewell C
Goring A
Grace Dieu A
Greenfield C
Grimsby A
Guyzance P
Hampole C
Handale C
Harrold A
Henwood B
Heynings C
Higham B

Hinchingbrook B
Holystone A
Hutton C
Ickleton B
Ilchester A
Ivinghoe B
Keldholme C
Kilburn B
Kington St Michael B
Kintbury B
Kirklees C
Lacock A
Lambley-on-Tyne B
Langley B
Legbourne C
Limebrook A
Ling B
Little Marlow B
Littlemore B
London A A B F
Malling B
Marham C
Markyate B
Marrick B
Marton A
Minster A B
Moxby A B
Neasham B

Newcastle upon Tyne B
Northampton Cl F
Norwich B
Nun Appleton C
Nunburnholme B
Nun Cotham C
Nuneaton B
Nunkeeling B
Nun Monkton B
Nunthorpe C
Oldbury B
Orford P
Pinley C
Polesworth B
Polsloe B
Ramestede B
Redlingfield B
Romsey B
Rosedale C
Rothwell A
Rowney B
Rusper B
St Albans B
St Mary de Pre B
Seton B
Sewardsley C Cl
Shaftesbury B
Sinningthwaite C

Sopwell B
Stainfield B
Stamford B
Stixwould B C P
Stratford-at-Bow B
Studley B
Swaffham Bulbeck B
Swine C
Syon Br
Tarrant C
Thetford B
Thicket B
Wallingwells B
Waterbeach F
Westwood B
Wherwell B
Whistones C
Wilberfoss B
Wilton B
Winchester B
Wintney C
Wix B
Wothorpe B
Wroxall B
Wykeham C
Yedingham B
York B

APPENDIX 3

Lists of Monasteries by Counties

(The old county names are given because all but very few bibliographical references are from pre-1972 books. It was in that year that the Local Government Act changed the names of some counties and their boundaries.)

Bedfordshire

Beadlow
Bedford
Bushmead
Caldwell
Chicksands
Dunstable
Elstow
Harrold
Millbrook
Newnham
Warden
Woburn

Berkshire

Abingdon
Bisham
Broomhall
Donnington
Faringdon
Hurley
Kintbury
Poughley
Reading
Sandleford
Wallingford

Buckinghamshire

Ankerwyke
Aylesbury
Biddlesden
Bradwell
Burnham
Chetwode
Lavendon
Little Marlow
Medmenham
Missenden
Notley
Ravenstone
Snelshall
Tickford

Cambridgeshire & Isle of Ely

Anglesey
Barham
Barnwell
Cambridge
Chatteris
Denney
Ely
Fordham

Ickleton
King's Langley
Marmont
Spinney
Swaffham Bulbeck
Thorney
Waterbeach

Cheshire

Birkenhead
Chester
Combermere
Darnhall
Hilbre Island
Mobberley
Norton
Poulton
Runcorn
Stanlaw
Vale Royal
Warburton

Cornwall & Scilly Isles

Bodmin
Lamanna

359

Launceston
St Anthony-in-Roseland
St Carrok
St Germans
Scilly
Truro
Tywardreath

Cumberland

Armathwaite
Calder
Carlisle
Holmcultram
Lanercost
Penrith
St Bees
Seton
Wetheral

Derbyshire

Breadsall
Calke
Church Gresley
Dale
Darley
Derby
Repton

Devonshire

Barnstaple
Brightley
Buckfast
Buckland
Canonsleigh
Cornworthy
Cowick
Dartmouth
Dunkeswell
Exeter
Frithelstock
Hartland
Kerswell
Marsh Barton

Newenham
Pilton
Plymouth
Plympton
Polsloe
Tavistock
Torre
Totnes

Dorset

Abbotsbury
Bindon
Bridport
Cerne
Cranborne
Dorchester
Forde
Holme
Horton
Melcombe
Milton
Shaftesbury
Sherborne
Tarrant

Durham

Barnard Castle
Baxterwood
Durham
Finchale
Hartlepool
Jarrow
Monkwearmouth
Neasham

Essex

Barking
Bedemans Berg
Beeleigh
Berden
Bicknacre
Blackmore
Castle Hedingham

Chelmsford
Coggeshall
Colchester
Earls Colne
Great Parndon
Hatfield Broad Oak
Hatfield Peverel
Horkesley
Latton
Leighs
Little Dunmow
Maldon
Prittlewell
St Osyths
Stansgate
Stratford Langthorn
Thoby
Thremhall
Tilty
Tiptree
Walden
Waltham
Wix

Gloucestershire

Bristol
Cirencester
Deerhurst
Flaxley
Gloucester
Hailes
Hazleton
Horsley
Kingswood
Leonard Stanley
Lanthony
Poulton
Tetbury
Tewkesbury
Westbury upon Trym
Winchcombe

Hampshire & Isle of Wight

Barton

Beaulieu
Breamore
Christchurch
Mottisfont
Netley
Portchester
Quarr
Romsey
St Denys
Selborne
Southampton
Southwick
Titchfield
Wherwell
Winchester
Wintney

Herefordshire

Abbey Dore
Aconbury
Clifford
Ewyas Harold
Flanesford
Hereford
Kilpeck
Leominster
Limebrook
Shobdon
Wigmore
Wormsley

Hertfordshire

Ashridge
Cheshunt
Flamstead
Hertford
Hitchin
Ivinghoe
Markyate
Redbourn
Rowney
Royston
St Albans
St Mary de Pre

Sopwell
Ware
Wymondley

Huntingdonshire

Great Paxton
Hinchingbrooke
Huntingdon
Ramsey
St Ives
St Neots
Sawtry
Stonley

Isle of Man

Bemaken
Douglas
Mirescog
Rushen

Kent

Aylesford
Bilsington
Blackwose
Boxley
Brockley
Canterbury
Combwell
Dartford
Davington
Dover
Faversham
Folkestone
Greenwich
Higham
Langdon
Leeds
Lesnes
Lossenham
Malling
Minster
Moatenden
Monks Horton

New Romney
Rochester
St Radegund's
Sandwich
Sittingbourne
Tonbridge

Lancashire

Burscough
Cartmel
Cockerham
Cockersand
Conishead
Furness
Hornby
Kersal
Lancaster
Lytham
Penwortham
Preston
Tulketh
Upholland
Warrington
Whalley
Wyresdale

Leicestershire

Belvoir
Bradley
Breedon
Charley
Croxton
Garendon
Grace Dieu
Kirby Bellars
Langley
Launde
Leicester
Owston
Ulverscroft

Lincolnshire

Alkborough

Alvingham
Axholme
Bardney
Barlings
Boston
Bourne
Bridge End
Bullington
Bytham
Catley
Crowland
Deeping St James
Elsham
Fosse
Freiston
Gokewell
Grantham
Greenfield
Grimsby
Hagneby
Haverholme
Heynings
Hirst
Humberstone
Kirkstead
Kyme
Legbourne
Lincoln
Louth Park
Markby
Newbo
Newsham
Newstead
Nocton
North Ormsby
Nun Cotham
Orford
Partney
Revesby
Sempringham
Sixhills
Spalding
Stainfield
Stamford
Stixwould
Stow
Swineshead
Thornholme

Thornton
Thwaite
Torksey
Tunstall
Tupholme
Vaudey
Wellow
Whaplode

London

Aldgate
Bishopsgate
Charterhouse
Clerkenwell
Cripplegate
Haliwell
London (6 friaries)
St Mary Graces
Shoreditch
Smithfield
Southwark
The Minories
Westminster

Middlesex

Bentley
Hounslow
Kilburn
Stratford at Bow
Syon
Twickenham

Norfolk

Aldeby
Beeston
Binham
Blackborough
Blakeney
Bromehill
Broomholm
Buckenham
Burnham Norton

Castle Acre
Coxford
Crabhouse
Flitcham
Great Massingham
Heacham
Hempton
Hickling
Horsham St Faith
Ingham
Kings Lynn
Langley
Ling
Marham
Modney
Mountjoy
Mullicourt
Normans Barrow
North Creake
Norwich
Pentney
Peterstone
Rudham
St Benet of Hulme
Sheringham
Shouldham
Sleves Holm
Thetford
Walsingham
Wendling
West Acre
West Dereham
Weybourne
Weybridge
Wormegay
Wymondham
Yarmouth

Northamptonshire

Canons Ashby
Catesby
Chacombe
Daventry
Fineshade
Fotheringhay
Grafton Regis

Kalendar
Luffield
Northampton
Oxney
Peterborough
Pipewell
Preston Capes
Rothwell
Sewardsley
Stamford
Sulby
Wothorpe

Northumberland

Alnwick
Bamburgh
Blanchland
Brinkburn
Carham
Coquet Island
Farne Island
Guyzance
Hexham
Holystone
Hulne
Lambley on Tyne
Lindisfarne
Newcastle upon Tyne
Newminster
Ovingham
Tynemouth

Nottinghamshire

Beauvale
Blyth
Broadholme
Felley
Lenton
Mattersey
Newark
Newstead
Nottingham
Rufford
Shelford

Thurgarton
Wallingwells
Welbeck
Worksop

Oxfordshire

Bicester
Bruern
Clattercote
Cold Norton
Dorchester
Eynsham
Godstow
Goring
Littlemore
Osney
Otley
Oxford
Pheleley
Rewley
Studley
Thame
Wroxton

Rutland

Brooke

Shropshire

Brewood
Bridgnorth
Bromfield
Buildwas
Chirbury
Church Preen
Donnington Wood
Haughmond
Lilleshall
Ludlow
Morville
Ratlinghope
Shrewsbury
Snead

Wenlock
Wombridge
Woodhouse

Somerset

Athelney
Barlinch
Barrow Gurney
Bath
Bridgwater
Bruton
Buckland
Burtle
Cannington
Cleeve
Dodlinch
Dunster
Glastonbury
Hinton
Ilchester
Keynsham
Montacute
Muchelney
Stavordale
Taunton
Witham
Woodspring

Staffordshire

Baswich
Blithbury
Brewood
Burton upon Trent
Calwich
Canwell
Cotton
Croxden
Dieulacres
Farewell
Hulton
Lichfield

Newcastle under Lyme
Radmore
Ranton
Rocester
Sandwell
Stafford
Stone
Trentham
Tutbury

Suffolk

Alnesbourn
Blythburgh
Bruisyard
Bungay
Bury St Edmunds
Butley
Campsey Ash
Chipley
Clare
Coddenham
Dodnash
Dunwich
Edwardstone
Eye
Felixstowe
Flixton
Gorleston
Hoxne
Ipswich
Ixworth
Kersey
Leiston
Letheringham
Mendham
Orford
Redlingfield
Rumburgh
St Olaves
Sibton
Snape
Sudbury
Wangford
Welnetham
Wickham Skeyth
Woodbridge

Surrey

Bermondsey
Chertsey
Guildford
Merton
Newark
Reigate
Sheen
Tandridge
Waverley

Sussex

Arundel
Battle
Bayham
Boxgrove
Chichester
Durford
Easebourne
Hardham
Hastings
Lewes
Michelham
Otham
Pynham
Ramestede
Robertsbridge
Rusper
Rye
Sele
Shoreham
Shulbred
Tortington
Warbleton
Winchelsea

Warwickshire

Alcester
Alvecote
Arbury
Atherstone
Bretford
Combe

Coventry
Halywell
Henwood
Kenilworth
Maxstoke
Merevale
Nuneaton
Oldbury
Pinley
Polesworth
Stoneleigh
Studley
Thelsford
Warwick
Wroxall

Westmorland

Appleby
Preston Patrick
Shap

Wiltshire

Amesbury
Bradenstoke
Easton Royal
Edington
Ivychurch
Kington St Michael
Lacock
Longleat
Loxwell
Maiden Bradley
Malmesbury
Marlborough
Monkton Farleigh
Salisbury
Stanley
Wilton

Worcestershire

Bordesley
Cook Hill

Dodford
Droitwich
Dudley
Evesham
Great Malvern
Halesowen
Little Malvern
Pershore
Westwood
Whistones
Witton
Worcester

Yorkshire

Arden
Arthington
Barnoldswick
Baysdale
Beauchief
Beverley
Bolton
Bridlington
Byland
Cottingham
Coverham
Doncaster
Drax
Easby
Egglestone
Ellerton ER
Ellerton NR
Embsay

Esholt
Fors
Foukeholme
Fountains
Grosmont
Guisborough
Hackness
Haltemprice
Hampole
Handale
Healaugh Park
Hood
Hutton
Jervaulx
Keldholm
Kildale
Kingston upon Hull
Kirkham
Kirklees
Kirkstall
Knaresborough
Lastingham
Malton
Marrick
Marton
Meaux
Middlesbrough
Monk Bretton
Mount Grace
Moxby
Newburgh
Northallerton
North Ferriby

Nostell
Nun Appleton
Nunburnholme
Nunkeeling
Nun Monkton
Nunthorpe
Old Byland
Pontefract
Richmond
Rievaulx
Roche
Rosedale
Sawley
Scalby
Scarborough
Selby
Sinningthwaite
Skewkirk
Snaith
Stocking
Swainby
Swine
Thicket
Tickhill
Warter
Watton
Whitby
Wilberfoss
Woodkirk
Wykeham
Yarm
Yedingham
York

APPENDIX 4

Locations of 105 sites where minor fragments exist

(Not shown on maps)

Ashridge
Barlings
Baswich
Bisham
Broadholme
Bromehill
Bruisyard
Buckland (Som.)
Bushmead
Chacombe
Combe
Combermere
Darley
Dodford
Donnington
Dudley
Durford
Earls Colne
Faversham
Felley
Flitcham
Flixton
Godstow
Gokewell
Greenfield
Hagneby
Hampole
Healaugh
Hempton
Keldholme
Kerswell
Keynsham
King's Langley
Kirklees
Leeds

Lenton
Maiden Bradley
Markby
Moatenden
Morville
Nostell
Orford
Osney
Otham
Oxford
Oxney
Peterstone
Pinley
Pontefract
Poulton
Pynham
Revesby
Rewley
St Anthony in Roseland
St Ives
Salisbury
Sandleford
Sandwich
Sawtrey
Scilly
Selborne
Sinningthwaite
Sixhills
Sopwell
Southampton
Spalding
Spinney
Stamford
Stansgate
Stixwould

Stocking
Stonely
Stratford Langthorne
Studley (Oxon)
Studley (Warks)
Sudbury
Swineshead
Syon
Tarrant Kaines
Taunton
Tetbury
Thame
Thelsford
Thicket
Thoby
Thornholme
Tickford
Tortington
Truro
Wallingford
Wangford
Warden
Waterbeach
Welnetham
Wendling
Westbury upon Trym
Whistones
Wilberfoss
Wilton
Woodhouse
Woodkirk
Wormsley
Wroxton
Yedingham
York

Bibliography 1

Multiple Sources

Journal of the British Archaeological Association. (Br. Arch. Assoc. J.)
The Society of Antiquities of London:
a — Archaeologia
b — Archaeologia Aeliana (Northumbria)
c — Archaeologia Cantiana (Kent)
The Royal Archaeological Institute: Archaeological Journal (Arch. J.)
A Quarterly Review of Archaeology: Antiquity (Antiq.)
The Society of Medieval Archaeology: Medieval Archaeology (Med. Arch.)
Transactions of the Royal Historical Society.
The Antiquities Journal (Antiq. J.)
Thoroton Society Transactions.
Monmouth Antiquary. (Mon. Antiq.)
Transactions of the Ancient Monuments Society.
Reports and Papers of the Associated Architectural Societies.
Transactions or Journals of the Archaeological Societies of various English
Counties.
The Victoria County Histories of England (VCH) Religious Houses sections.
Royal Commission on Ancient and Historical Monuments — Various Counties.
'The Buildings of England' Series. Sir Nikolaus Pevsner and others.
Methuen's 'Little Guides' for the English Counties (L.G.)
Bell's Cathedral Series.
'The King's England' Series. Ed. Arthur Mee.
Monastic Britain: North and South sheets of British Monastic maps. HMSO.
HMSO Guidebooks for sites in the care of the D. of E.

*and miscellaneous publications by antiquarian societies and others which are
noted at the end of some gazetteer entries.*

Bibliography 2

General List
Baines, E. Directory & Gazetteer of Yorkshire. 1969 Ed.
Baskerville, G. English monks and the Suppression of the Monasteries. 1937.
Borlase, Wm. Antiquities Historical and Monumental of the County of Cornwall. 1769.
Brand, J. History and Antiquities of Newcastle. 1789.
Braun, H. English Abbeys. 1971.
Braunfels, W. Monasteries of Western Europe. 1972.
Colvin, H. M. The White Canons of England. 1951.
Cook, G. H. English Monasteries. 1961.
Cook, Olive & Smith, E. English Abbeys & Priories. 1960.
Cowan, Ian B. & Easson, D. E. Medieval Religious Houses, Scotland. 1976.
Cram, R. A. The Ruined Abbeys of Great Britain. 1906.
Cranage, D. H. S. The Home of the Monk. 1926.
Crossley, F. H. The English Abbey. 1935.
Davis, G. R. C. Medieval Cartularies of Great Britain. 1958.
Dickinson, J. C. Monastic Life in Medieval England. 1961.
    The origins of the Austin Canons and their introduction into England. 1950.
Ditchfield, P. H. The Cathedrals of Great Britain. 1902.
Dugdale, Wm. Monasticon Anglicanum (abridged). 1718.
Duncumb, J. History of Herefordshire. 1804.
Eckenstein, Lina. Woman Under Monasticism. 1896.
Fletcher, J. S. The Cistercians in Yorkshire. 1919.
Fosbroke, T. D. British Monachism. 1843.
Fox, S. English Monasticism. 1845.
Gasquet, F. A. English Monastic Life. 1919.
    –   Henry VIII & The English Monasteries. 1893.
Gilyard-Beer, R. Abbeys. 1958.
Goulder, L. Church Life in Medieval England – The Monasteries, 1967.
Graham, Rose. English Ecclesiastical Studies, 1929.
    –   An Essay on English Monasteries. 1939.
    –   St Gilbert of Sempringham & The Gilbertines. 1903.
    –   (presented to): Medieval Studies. 1950.

Haigh, C. Lancashire Monasteries & The Pilgrimage of Grace. 1969.
Harben, H. A. A Dictionary of London. 1918.
Harnett, Cynthia. Monasteries and Monks. 1963.
Harvey, J. Cathedrals of England & Wales. 1974.
Hibbert, F. A. The Dissolution of the Monasteries (Staffordshire). 1910.
Hodgson, J. History of Northumberland. 1839.
Hutton, Ed. The Franciscans in England. 1926.
James, M. R. Abbeys. 1925.
Knowles, M. D. The Religious Orders in England (Vol. 1). 1950.
–   Saints & Scholars. 1963.
–   The Monastic Order in England. 1966.
–   Bare Ruined Choirs. 1976.
Knowles, M. D.,Brooke, C. N. L. & London, Vera C. M. The Heads of Religious
           Houses, England & Wales, 940–1216. 1972.
–   & Hadcock R. N. Medieval Religious Houses, England & Wales.
           1971.
–   & St Joseph, J. K. S. Monastic Sites from the Air. 1952.
Lawton, G. The Religious Houses of Yorkshire. 1853.
Little, B. English Cathedrals. 1972.
MacFarlane, C. & Thompson, T. The Comprehensive History of England
           (4 Vols.) 1861.
Malden, R. H. Abbeys: Their Rise and Fall. 1944.
Messent, C. J. W. The Monastic Remains of Norfolk & Suffolk. 1934.
Martin, A. R. Franciscan Architecture in England. 1937.
Moorman, J. R. H. The Franciscans in England. 1974.
Northumberland County History Committee (15 Vols.) 1838–48.
Oliver, G. Monasticon Dioecesis Exoniensis. 1846.
–   Historic Collections of Monasteries in Devon. 1820.
Ormerod, G. History of Cheshire. 1819.
Power, Eileen. Medieval English Nunneries. 1922.
Raine, J. History & Antiquities of North Durham. 1852.
Sitwell, S. Monks, Nuns & Monasteries. 1965.
Stanhope, W. Monastic London. 1887.
Tanner, Thos. Notitia Monastica. 1744.
Tate, G. History of Alnwick. 1846.
Thompson, A. Hamilton. English Monasteries. 1913.
–   A History of the Medieval Church, 590–1500. 1925.
Thompson, E. Margaret. A History of the Somerset Carthusians. 1896.
Wade, B. Yorkshire's Ruined Abbeys. 1938.
Welford, R. History of Newcastle & Gateshead. 1884–7.
Williams, D. H. The Welsh Cistercians. 1970.
Willis, Browne. Mitred Abbeys. 1718.
Woodward, G. W. O. The Dissolution of the Monasteries. 1969.
Worth, R. N. History of Plymouth. 1890.
Youings, Joyce. The Dissolution of the Monasteries. 1971.
Young, E. & W. Old London Churches. 1956.

Index

Augustinian Order of Canons &
  Canonesses, 3
Augustinian (Austin) Order of Friars, 11
Aulnay-sur-Odon Abbey, France, 119, 122
Aungervill, Sybil de, 289
Aungier, G. J. (author), 300
Aveling, J. H. (author), 268
Aylric, Earl, and Ethelfleda, 275
Aylwin, duke of East Anglia, 260
Ayscough, William, bp. of Salisbury
  (1438–50), 136

Bacon, Richard, 266
Baconthorpe, John de, 70
Bagley, W. H. M. (author), 254
Baldock, Ralph, bp. of London (1306–13),
  194
Baldwin of Exeter, 145
Baliol, King of Scotland (1292–6), 234
Barbour, Simon, 304
Bardolf (ph), family, 145, 181
Barescote, family, 93
Barnard, E. A. B. (author), 139
Barnardiston, Mrs K. W. (author), 111
Barnet, battle of, 103
Bartholomew (Iscanus), bp. of Exeter
  (1161–84), 274
Barton, Elizabeth (Holy Maid of Kent),
  98, 263
Barwe, Robert de, 170
Baskerville, G. (author), 48, 66
Basset, family, 54, 66, 84, 191
Bassingbourn, Mary, 291
Batevileyn, William de, 255
Bayeux, Ralph de, 232
Baynard, Geoffrey and Juga, 201
Beauchamp, Richard, bp. of Salisbury
  (1450–81), 277
Beauchamp, family, 57, 90, 103, 108, 131,
  147, 231, 336
Beaufort, Isabella, 214
Beaumont, Walerand de, 73
Bec-Hellouin Abbey, France, 74, 115, 139
Beck, Anthony de, bp. of Norwich
  (1337–43), 238
Becket, Thomas à, archbp. of Canterbury
  (1162-70), 97, 128, 196, 218
Bede, the Venerable, 5
Bedford, Castle, 93
Bedford, family, 180, 282
Behrens, Lilian B. (author), 60
Beler, Sir Robert, 183
Belet, Michael, 338

Belingey, Peter de, 103
Belmeis, Richard de, bp. of London
  (1108–27), 275, 297
Belmeis, Richard de, 110, 198
Belvoir, William de, 64
Benedictine Order of Monks & Nuns, 4
Beningworth, William of, 200
Bennett, J. H. E. (author), 107
Bereford, Henry de, and Isabel, 303
Berkeley, family, 150, 151, 161, 183, 196,
  302
Berkeley Castle, 309
Bernay Abbey, France, 141
Bertram I, William, 79
Bethune, Robert de, bp. of Hereford
  (1131–48), 150, 163, 223
Bidun, John de, 192
Bigod, Roger, earl of Norfolk, 142, 303,
  308, 326
Biscop, St Benedict, 177
Biset, Henry and Manasser, 211
Birinus (St), bp. of Winchester (634–650),
  130, 330
Bittendene, prior of Frithelstock, 147
Black Death, 24, 30
Blanchmains, Robert, 104
Blois, Henry de, bp. of Winchester (1129–
  71), 109
Blundeville, Ranulf de, earl of Chester, 120,
  128, 258
Blunt, family, 176
Bodleian Library, 62, 63, 84, 170, 307,
  310
Boggis, R. J. E. (author), 98
Bohun, family, 134, 207, 222
Bolbec, family, 70, 216, 250, 299, 334
Boleyn, Anne, 154
Bond, E. A. (author), 216
Bond, F. (author), 149, 204
Boniface of Savoy, archbp. of Canterbury
  (1241–70), 205
Bonshommes, Order of, 5
Boroughbridge, battle of, 313
Bosco, Ernald de, 66
Bossu II, Robert, earl of Leicester, 148,
  192, 210, 245
Bossu, Richard, earl of Leicester, 183
Boteler, Robert, 320
Botiler, Sir William FitzAlmeric, 319
Bovile, William de, 197
Boullers, Robert de, lord of Montgomery,
  109, 288
Boulogne, William, count of, 124

375

376

Mary (dau. of K. Stephen), 167
Mascherell, Walter, Alexander and Edith, 333
Masci, Hamon de, 68
Matilda of Scotland (Maud), wife of Henry I, 73, 180, 204, 210, 218, 269, 294
Matilda of Boulogne (Maud), wife of K. Stephen, 115, 142, 222, 259, 296
Matilda, countess of Chester, 262
Mattersey, Roger de, 215
Maud, abbess of Wherwell, 327
Maule, Peter de, and Christina, 164
Maycock, A. (author), 212
Meinfelin, lord of Wolverton, 76
Melton, William de, archbp. of York (1315-40), 178, 280, 328
Mensa, de, family, 50
Mercer, Robert de, 251
Merch/Merk, Eustace de, Alice, and Robert, 114, 244, 270
Merewald, King of Mercia, 196, 323
Merlay, Ranulf de, and family, 231, 245
Merlimond, Oliver de, 284
Meschin, family, 72, 92, 138, 273, 325
Meules, Nicholas de, 250
Milberga (dau. of K. Merewald), 323
Mildmay, Sir Walter, 95
Miller, G. (author), 138
Miniot, Roger, 240
Missenden, William of, 220
Mitred abbeys, 22
Mobberley, Patrick de, 221
Mohun, de, family, 84, 132, 231
Molendinar, Reginald, 279
Monchesney, Hubert de, 136
Monkton, John, 246
Montacute, family, 68, 80
Montague, William, earl of Salisbury, 64
Montfort I, Simon de, 50, 138, 235, 321
Montfort II, Simon de, 193
Montfort de, Countess Eleanora, 321
Montgebon, family, 170
Montgomery, Roger, earl of Shrewsbury (11thC), 285, 323
Montgomery, Roger, earl of Shrewsbury (13thC), 171
Moody, C. H. (author), 280
Moorman, J. R. H. (author), 95
Moreland, Sir William, 210
Morimond Abbey, France, 47
Morins, Richard de, prior of Dunstable, 132
Morley, Thomas, 304

Morpeth, William de, 278
Morrell, W. W. (author), 280
Mortimer, family, 198, 284, 285, 328
Morton, John, archbp. of Canterbury (1486-1500), 275, 289
Mottram, R. H. (author), 238
Mounteagle, Lord, 90
Mountfichet, family, 51, 297, 307
Mowbray, family, 54, 59, 92, 119, 170, 228, 246, 284, 295, 313
Multon, Ralph de, 136
Muncells, Alan de, 245
Munchesney, Denise, 320
Munevilla, Nigel de, and Emma, 145
Murdac, Henry, archbp. of York (1147-53), 150
Murdac, Hugh of Cleveland, 344
Myers, J. N. L. (author), 92

Nequam, abbot of Cirencester, 110
Nerford, Sir Robert and Lady Alice, 236
Neville, Alexander, archbp. of York (1374-88), 57
Neville, family, 49, 60, 173, 246, 312
Newburgh, Roger and Matilda, 67
Newbury, Walter, abbot of Bristol, 79
Newenham, Fulk de, 126
Neilson, N. (author), 67
Nichbrothene, John and Maud, 129
Nicholas, abbot of Eynsham, 141
Nichols, J. G. (author), 208
Nigel, bp. of Ely (1133-69), 94
Nonant, Hugh de, bp. of Coventry (1184-99), 119
Noppen, J. G. (author), 204
Norbury, Roger de, bp. of Lichfield (1322-59), 77, 141, 260
Norris, Roger, prior of Penwortham, 253
Northampton, battle of, 235, 236
Northburgh, Michael, bp. of London (1354-61), 205
Norton, Avelina de, 117
Norwich Castle, 303
Norwich, Ralph de, 107
Nott, J. (author), 153
Nykke, Richard, bp. of Norwich (1501-35), 91

Odo of Kilkenny, 200
Odiham Castle, 321, 333
Offa II, King of Mercia, 272
Offney, William de, 277
Oilly II, Robert de, and Editha, 247

380

Oiri, Robert d', 327
Olaf, King of Man, 271
Oldham, Hugh, bp. of Exeter (1504–19), 311
Oliver, prior of Bodmin, 71
Omissions, 34
Orcas, steward of K. Canute, 47
Ordgar, earl of Devon, and Ordulf, 301
Orreby, Agnes de, 156
Oswald (St), bp. of Worcester (960–971), later archbp. of York (972–992), 272, 329, 335
Oswald, King, 253
Owen, D. E. (author), 186
Owen, Robert, 251
Oxford, A. W. (author), 146
Oxford (Cardinal) College; see Cardinal College
Oxford Colleges; see Colleges
Oxford, Isabella, Countess of, 217
Oxford, Trinity Hall, 215, 249, 251
Oyley II, Robert de, 316

Padley, J. S. (author), 313
Page, W (author), 79
Pagnell, Gervase, 131
Pantulf, William and Bergia, 190
Paris, Matthew, monk of St Albans, 5, 83, 272
Parry, H. L. (author), 139
Paslew, John, abbot of Whalley, 326
Pateshull, Lady Mabel, 63
Paul, abbot of St Albans, 316
Payens, Hugh de, 16
Paynel, family, 131, 183, 307, 343
Peada, King of Mercia, 253
Peckham, John, archbp. of Canterbury (1279–92), 74, 88, 98, 103, 151, 204, 297
Peers, C. R. (author), 203
Pegge, S. (author), 62
Pelham, Sir John, 159, 318
Pembroke, Mary de St Paul, countess of, 48, 127, 320
Pembrugge, Sir William, 163
Penning, Gamel de, 118
Perch, Geoffrey, count of, and Matilda, 277
Percy, family, 156, 158, 180, 278, 292, 327
Peverel, family, 57, 159, 179, 195, 234
Peterhouse, Cambridge, 94, 96
Peytvin, William, 184

Philippa, Queen (wife of Edward III), 57, 140, 214
Picheford, Geoffrey de, 94
Picot, sheriff of Cambridge, 57, 94
Pied Friars, 14
Pilgrim, Charles, 340
Pillarton, Robert de, 254
Pincerna, Ralph, 49
Pisa, Albert de, 107, 332
Plaiz, Sir Hugh de, 82
Pole, Michael de la (later earl of Suffolk), 182
Pole, Sir Richard de la, 182
Ponsonby, Sir Arthur (author), 287
Poor(e), Richard le, bp. of Salisbury (1217–29), later bp. of Durham (1229–37), 276, 301
Poultney, St John, 120
Premonstratensian Order of Canons & Canonesses, 9
Preston, family, 258
Price, Richard, 286
Pudsey, Henry, 60, 143
Pye of Chippenham, 131
Pynnoke, prior of Frithelstock, 148

Raglan Castle, 308
Rahere of Smithfield, 205
Ralph de Salopia (Shrewsbury), bp. of Wells (1329–63), 96
Rammeshulle, William de, 214
Randolf, Geoffrey, 285
Ranulf II, earl of Chester, 106, 311
Ratcliffe, Thomas, friar of Leicester, 193
Redman, Richard, bp. of St Asaph (1471–96); bp. of Exeter (1496–1501); bp. of Ely (1501–05); concurrently abbot of Shap, 62, 63, 70, 247, 283, 323, 325
Redvers, family, 76, 109, 259
Reginald, King of Man, 130
Remains, definition of, 34
Remigius de Fécamp, bp. of Lincoln (1067–92), 141, 297
Reskymer, family, 312
Reynolds, Walter, archbp. of Canterbury (1313–27), 99
Reynolds, Richard, of Syon, 300
Reynolds, P. K. B. (author), 304
Rich, Edmund, archbp. of Canterbury (1234–40), 99
Richard I, King, 265

381

St Stephen's College, Westminster, 117
St Sulpice Abbey, France, 167
St Swithun, bp. of Winchester (852–862) 330
St Walery, Bernard of, 297, 302
St Wandrille's Abbey, France, 176
St Wilfred, bp. of York (664–678), 292
St Wilfred of Hexham, 164
St William (boy martyr of Norwich), 239
St Victor's Abbey, France, 79, 128, 284, 328, 335
Salzman, L. F. (author), 219
Sandford, Robert de, 203
Sanford, family, 69
Santa Maria, Jordan de, and Alice, 162
Sampson, bp. of Worcester (1096–1112), 324
Samson, abbot of Bury St Edmunds, 89
Say, Eusticia de, 325
Say, William de, 56
Scales, Roger de, and Muriel, 69
Scotene, Hugh de, 50
Scotland, abbot of St Augustine's, Canterbury, 98
Scotney, Walter de, 159
Scott, Sir Peter, and Nicholas, 230
Scotus, Duns (Dr John Scott), 230
Scrope, Lord, 76
Sebert, King of E. Saxons, 203
Sedburgh, abbot of Rievaulx, 264
Seez, John de, abbot of Peterborough, 253
Sergeantson, R. M. (author), 235
Seton, Christina, 288
Seymour, Queen Jane, 295, 307
Seymour, Sir Thomas, 258
Shaa, Thomas, 191
Sherborne, Robert, bp. of Chichester (1508–36), 286
Shipling, Baldwin de, and Chabil, 298
Shirley, Sir John, 244
Shrewsbury, Richard of, duke of York, 286
Sidney Sussex College, Cambridge, 95
Sigbert, King (7thC), 89
Simeon, prior of Winchester, 137
Simon, bp. of Worcester (1125–50), 324
Simon, abbot of Chester, 106
Simon, abbot of St Albans, 261
Sitwell, S. (author), 115
Slade, William, abbot of Buckfast, 85
Smith, R. A. L. (author), 97
Smith, J. R. (author), 60
Snew, Aylward, 122
Snoring, John, prior of Walsingham, 317

Sperling, C. F. D. (author), 298
Spicer, Thomas, prior of Bradenstoke, 75
Spott, Wulfric, 89
Stadham, Thomas, 106
Stafford, family, 291, 296
Stamford, Council of, 292
Stanford, John, 181
Stapledon, family, 147
Stapleton, Sir Miles, and Joan, 174
Steele, Francesca M. (author) 301
Stephan, Dom John (author), 85
Stephen, King, 85, 115, 142, 148, 176, 239, 268, 306, 312
Stephen, lord of Harnhill, 150
Stephen, earl of Brittany, 270
Stephen, abbot of Wymondham, 339
Stevenson, J. (author), 48
Stewart, D. J. (author), 138
Stewart-Brown, R. (author), 68
Straddell, abbot of Abbey Dore, 47
Stratton, Gilbert de, 200
Stukeley, Dr (historian), 105
Stuteville, Robert de, and family, 177, 269
Sudley, Ralph de, 52
Suffolk, duke of, 86
Suthmere, Margaret de, 181
Sutton, Oliver, bp. of Lincoln (1280–99), 73
Swarbrick, J. (author), 114
Sweetman, G. (author), 295
Swinfield, Richard, bp. of Hereford (1283–1316), 114, 210
Sydenham, Laura (author), 282
Syre, Nicholas de, 153

Tailbois, Ivo, 290
Taillour, John, 191
Taillour, William, 271
Tait, J. (author), 271
Talbot, John, earl of Shrewsbury, 78
Talbot, Sir Richard, 144
Tanner, Thomas (historian), 80, 95, 104, 260, 284
Tany, Avice de, 157
Taper, John, 159
Tate, G. (author), 50, 172
Teasdale, R. H. (author), 152
Tewkesbury, battle of, 302
Thola, wife of Orcas, 47
Thomas II, archbp. of York (1108–14), 164
Thomas, abbot of Shrewsbury, 285
Thompson, E. Margaret (author), 168, 333

Wendling, William of, 323
West, T. S. J. (author), 148
Wetwang, John de, 182
Whitby, Stephen of, abbot of Lastingham, 190
Whittington, Richard, 208
Whittlesea, William, archbp. of Canterbury (1368–74), 249
Widdrington, Ralph, 230
Wideville, family, 153, 299
Wido (Guy), abbot of St Augustine's, Canterbury, 98
Wigram, S. R. (author), 137
William I, King, 59, 139, 149, 173, 190, 280, 292, 341
William II (Rufus), King, 52, 159, 342, 344
William, son of K. Stephen, 167
Williams, D. H. (author), 47
Williams, L. F. R. (author), 272
Willis, Professor (author), 97
Winchelsea, Robert, archbp. of Canterbury (1292–1313), 86
Winchester College, Winchester, 58, 332, 348–351
Windsor College, 211, 349, 350
Windsor, Maurice of, and Edigia, 171
Wodehouse, Robert de, 292
Woderove, William and Margaret, 152
Wolfsige, bp. of Sherborne (993–1001), 283
Wolsey, Thomas, cardinal, 25, 26, 60, 69, 71, 76, 82, 100, 118, 126, 129, 141, 142, 144, 170, 174, 175, 193, 197, 217, 224, 248, 257, 259, 261, 271, 275, 282, 288, 294, 305, 308, 309, 310, 316, 323, 334
Woodville, Elizabeth (wife of Edward IV), 65, 261
Worcester College, Oxford, 249
Worcester, William of, 80
Wulfric II, abbot of St Augustine's, Canterbury, 98
Wulfric (r. of Henry I), 298
Wulfstan (St), bp. of Worcester (1062–95), 153, 324, 336
Wych, Richard de, bp. of Chichester (1245–53), 257
Wygenhale, abbot of West Dereham, 324
Wykeham, William de, bp. of Winchester (1367–1404), 75, 218, 280, 290, 331
Wymar of Richmond (Yorks.), 264
Wymar, son of Warmer, 137

Yole, John and Helena, 234
York, Richard, duke of, 51
Ypres, William de, 75

Zouch, Elizabeth la, 77
Zouch, Lord John (16thC), 295
Zouche, William la, archbp. of York (1342–52), 305
Zouche, Lord William (14thC), 120